International Acclai

"The story is above all about Polanc
crushed between the two most ruthl
gressive nations of the century. . . . No subject is more messy than the Polish question before, during, and after the war. Davies, today's most distinguished historian—and advocate—of Poland, lets it remain that way."

—Simon Sebag Montefiore, *The New York Review of Books*

"Monumental . . . a powerful and compelling account of . . . 'one of the great tragedies of the twentieth century.'"

—Michael Kenney, *The Boston Globe*

"An enormous book, written with verve."

—John Lukacs, *Los Angeles Times Book Review*

"A heartfelt tribute . . . Davies covers the Uprising in close and enthralling detail."

—David Pryce-Jones, *National Review*

"Davies writes as an impassioned partisan, determined to force the world to remember the betrayal of the Poles."

—Mark Lewis, *The Washington Post*

"Absorbing . . . a fascinating, comprehensive and necessary study of a modern Thermopylae."

—Gordon Haber, *The New York Sun*

"Norman Davies knows more about Poland than any other historian in the West, and possesses a deep romantic love for the Polish people. Both his knowledge and his passion—reflected in rage towards the Allies who betrayed the Rising—are displayed in this notable book. His research among Polish and Soviet sources is exhaustive. . . . A moving elegy for those doomed romantics who fought so nobly, and to such tragic purposes, in Warsaw in the autumn of 1944."

—Max Hastings, *Sunday Telegraph*

"A splendid book, long overdue, and a worthy memorial to its noble subject . . . Norman Davies tells this darkly magnificent story with his customary skill and controlled passion. He peppers his narrative with the evidence of eyewitnesses, and ingeniously contrasts the cold-blooded decisions of the great powers with the consequences for ordinary Poles."

—Daniel Johnson, *Daily Telegraph*

"For those who believe that wars can successfully be fought for 'freedom and democracy,' and talk as if history has some moral compass, Norman Davies' *Rising '44* should be compulsory reading. The story of the Warsaw Uprising of August 1944 rips away at many of our lazy assumptions about the outcome of the Second World War."

—Angus McQueen, *The Guardian*

"This well-argued book is the first in any language to put the Warsaw Uprising in its full historical context. In its range and depth it is a fine contribution not just to Polish history but to the history of Europe."

—Stefan Wagstyl, *Financial Times*

"Davies is at his best when he focuses on issues such as everyday life during the Uprising and the terrible deprivations of life in a city that was slowly being turning to rubble."

—Anne Applebaum, *Evening Standard*

"An extraordinary story . . . fairly and honestly told here. Davies is an intelligent and balanced guide through its intricacies, and he is always entertaining."

—Adam Zamoyski, *The Spectator*

PENGUIN BOOKS

RISING '44

Norman Davies is Britain's bestselling author of *Europe: A History* and *The Isles: A History,* as well as the definitive history of Poland, *God's Playground,* and several books on European history. Davies is a graduate of Magdalen College, Oxford, and the University of Sussex. He is a Supernumerary Fellow at Wolfson College, Oxford, and is a Fellow of the British Academy, Fellow of the Royal Historical Society, and Professor Emeritus of London University.

NORMAN DAVIES

RISING '44

'The Battle for Warsaw'

PENGUIN BOOKS

PENGUIN BOOKS
Published by the Penguin Group
Penguin Group (USA) Inc., 375 Hudson Street, New York, New York 10014, U.S.A.
Penguin Group (Canada), 90 Eglinton Avenue East, Suite 700, Toronto,
Ontario, Canada M4P 2Y3 (a division of Pearson Penguin Canada Inc.)
Penguin Books Ltd, 80 Strand, London WC2R 0RL, England
Penguin Ireland, 25 St Stephen's Green, Dublin 2, Ireland (a division of Penguin Books Ltd)
Penguin Group (Australia), 250 Camberwell Road, Camberwell,
Victoria 3124, Australia (a division of Pearson Australia Group Pty Ltd)
Penguin Books India Pvt Ltd, 11 Community Centre, Panchsheel Park, New Delhi – 110 017, India
Penguin Group (NZ), cnr Airborne and Rosedale Roads, Albany,
Auckland 1310, New Zealand (a division of Pearson New Zealand Ltd)
Penguin Books (South Africa) (Pty) Ltd, 24 Sturdee Avenue,
Rosebank, Johannesburg 2196, South Africa

Penguin Books Ltd, Registered Offices:
80 Strand, London WC2R 0RL, England

First published in the United States of America by Viking Penguin,
a member of Penguin Group (USA) Inc. 2004
Published in Penguin Books 2005

10 9 8 7 6 5 4 3 2 1

Map artwork by Martin Lubikowski

Grateful acknowledgment is made for permission to use the following copyrighted works:

Three cartoons by David Low. Copyright © Atlantic Syndication.

"As I Please, September 1, 1944" from *The Collected Essays, Journalism and Letters of George Orwell*, Volume III: *As I Please 1943–1945*. Copyright © 1968 by Sonia Brownell Orwell and renewed 1996 by Mark Hamilton. Reprinted by permission of Harcourt, Inc.

Excerpt from "Campo di Fiori" from *The Collected Poems, 1931–1987* by Czeslaw Milosz (Viking, London, 1988). Copyright 1943 by Czeslaw Milosz. By permission of The Wylie Agency, Inc.

Cover of *Poland* by W. J. Rose (Penguin Books, London, 1939). By permission of Penguin Books Ltd.

THE LIBRARY OF CONGRESS HAS CATALOGED THE HARDCOVER EDITION AS FOLLOWS:
Davies, Norman, 1939–
Rising '44 : the battle for Warsaw / Norman Davies.
p. cm.
Includes bibliographical references and index.
Originally published: London : Macmillan, 2003.
ISBN 0-670-03284-0 (hc.)
ISBN 0 14 30.3540 1 (pbk.)
1. Warsaw (Poland)—History—Uprising, 1944.
2. Poland—History—Occupation, 1939–1945. I. Title.
D765.2.W3D34 2003
940.53'18'0943841—dc22 2003062199

Printed in the United States of America
Set in Dante MT

To WARSAW

*And to all who
fight tyranny
regardless*

Europe: June 1944

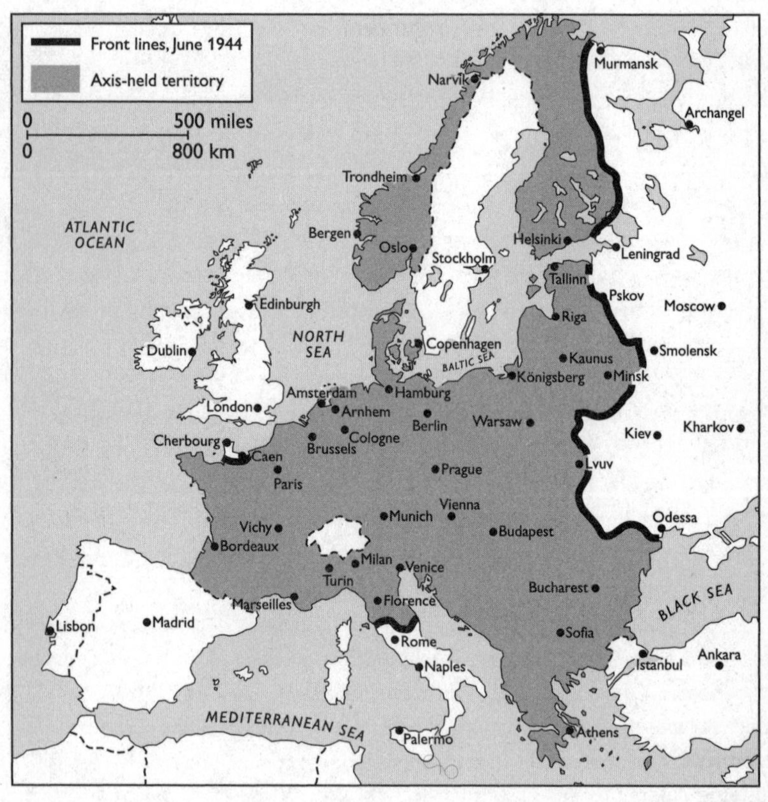

Foreword

My aim in writing *Rising '44* was nothing more complicated than to tell the story of one of the great tragedies of the twentieth century. It is a story that has never been properly told, even though it reveals some fundamental truths about the Second World War and challenges many conventional assumptions. For half a century and more, it was the subject of severe censorship by post-war authorities who did not wish to see the historical realities publicized; and, as a topic of acute embarrassment for the Western Powers, it has not been given prominence in Western interpretations. Although it resulted in the near-total destruction of one of Europe's ancient capitals, and in enormous loss of life, it was never brought for examination before the Nuremberg Tribunal. Equally, since it was not seen as one of the critical 'turning points', on which the fortunes of the war depended, it has rarely attracted the close scrutiny of British or American historians. The historiography of the subject, in consequence, tends to be somewhat parochial.

Of course, many people are likely to have heard of a 'rising' or of an 'uprising' in Warsaw. They may have read books, watched films, or listened to survivors' accounts. And they may well be under the impression that the event has been fully aired and discussed. If so, they will not have to explore very far to realize that much of the existing information in these matters is highly selective and misleading.

It may be of some help to point out that the Underground fighters who launched 'the Warsaw Rising' did not themselves use the term. For reasons connected with developments on the Eastern Front, they called it 'the Battle for Warsaw'. It was only after the city had been destroyed, and especially after the war, that 'the Warsaw Rising' or 'Uprising' came to be widely used, but by different people for different purposes.

Warsaw was, and is, the capital of a country whose most important alliance in 1944 was with Great Britain. Politically, this alliance put the country's exiled government firmly in the camp of liberal democracies led by Britain and USA. In an old-fashioned world, where the 'Great Powers' alone attended the top table and would decide things among themselves on behalf of less powerful clients, it also meant that the Anglo-Americans had assumed a degree of responsibility for their ally. Geographically, however, Warsaw lay plumb in the middle of Europe, immediately adjacent to the two largest combatant powers – that is, to Nazi Germany and the Soviet Union. As a result, the Rising inevitably erupted in the very cockpit of European conflict. Not only did it take place close to the front of the titanic German–Soviet War. It was embroiled at a sensitive interface of the three-sided arena where Western Democracy confronted Fascism on the one hand and Stalinist Communism on the other. It was no local skirmish.

The difficulties of explaining these matters are legion. The particulars of Central European history are not widely studied outside Central Europe; and the valiant contributions of lesser members of the Allied coalition of 1939–45 are largely forgotten. In history-writing, as in contemporary politics, countries which were once in the Allied camp but which later found themselves in different company have been obliged to wage an uphill battle. Their interests have often been eclipsed by publicists working for more vocal or more favoured competitors. For this reason, in constructing a narrative about the Warsaw Rising, it was essential to locate Warsaw firmly within the Allied, German, and Soviet strands of the war, and only to move on to the Rising after the complicated setting had been fully expounded.

Since the Western Powers enjoyed a clear-cut victory over Germany in their part of Europe, Western readers invariably make a clear-cut mental distinction between the wartime and the post-war years. In Russia too, where the victory of 1945 has remained a sacred memory, the time before and after 'Liberation' is presented as the difference between night and day. But in many countries of Central Europe, where one totalitarian occupation was succeeded by another, the significance of VE-Day is greatly reduced. Indeed, the very idea of 'Liberation', and of a clear break with conflict and suffering, was often considered a bad joke. Hence, it would have been unjust to close the story of the Varsovian insurgents at the end of the Rising or at the end of the war in May 1945, and to pretend that the survivors lived happily ever after. Instead, it seemed absolutely vital to trace the fate of the insurgents, and of their vilified reputation, into the post-war world.

*

The sources for a study of the Warsaw Rising are immense. I have encountered a score of general works on the topic; each with its special slant, and each with its special weaknesses. The catalogue of the Bodleian Library lists seventy-five titles. There are negative interpretations, and positive accounts; but few which approach all the participants with equal scepticism.[1] There is also a huge mass of specialized literature that deals with everything from diplomatic and military aspects to the design of barricades, the organization of the underground security services, or the adventures of individual units. And there is a large body of memoirs and diaries, both published and unpublished. Since the collapse of the Communist regime in 1990, veterans have been free to print their own journals, notably the monthly *Biuletyn Informacyjny*; and a great deal of work has been put into compilations of documents, chronicles, and encyclopaedias.[2]

Archival sources are more problematical. For many years, the only systematic publication of relevant documents was undertaken abroad, particularly at the Polish Institute and the Underground Study Trust (SPP) in London. Much could also be found on the diplomatic and military front in the Public Record Office, the Imperial War Museum, the National Archives in Washington, or in the *Bundesarchiv* in Bonn. Yet many key collections have remained closed, or are, at best, half-open. The British intelligence archives, for instance, which will someday reveal numerous insights into the affairs of 1944, were still 95 per cent unavailable at the turn of the century. The records of the post-war Polish security services, which are vital to an understanding of Stalinist repressions, are being released only slowly. Worst of all, after a brief promise of more liberal policies, the ex-Soviet archives in Moscow are still not fully accessible. A small number of selected documents were published in the 1990s. And determined foreign researchers with local assistance can gain limited access to some collections. But by the start of the twenty-first century, the main documents relating to Stalin's decisions in 1944 had still not been placed in the public domain. For this reason alone, I have no doubt that the definitive academic study of the Warsaw Rising still awaits its author.

As I have written on several occasions, historians inevitably form part of their own histories. And the times in which historians write, unavoidably influence what is written. In this regard, the history of an Allied coalition, which failed to live up to its obligations, may not be entirely unconnected to the present time.

*

Most people think of a good history book, as they think of a good novel, in linear terms. The readers start at the beginning, where they are pointed in a certain direction. They then plunge into a journey – through the jungle, up the mountain, along the road, or wherever – admiring the passing landscape, enjoying the adventures and surprises, but always heading unswervingly towards the chosen goal. At some point, better sooner than later, they reach the central drama of the story – the divorce of Henry VIII, the assassination of Abraham Lincoln, the encirclement of the German army before Stalingrad, or whatever – and they then move on to the denouement. It is a very satisfying intellectual experience.

At some point, however, I realized that the linear model is not the only design which may be followed to good effect. Different types of subject matter demand different types of treatment. In *Heart of Europe*, for instance, which was relating the memories of the past to the problems of the present, I decided that the story was best told in reverse chronological order.[3] Sometime later, when faced with the enormous task of writing 'The Oxford History of Europe', I again decided that radical measures had to be taken. *Europe: a history* (1996) was written on three levels simultaneously. The main text consisted, indeed, of a linear narrative. It proceeded in twelve giant strides across Europe's past from prehistory to the late twentieth century. But each of the chapters was enhanced both by 'Snapshots' and by 'Capsules'. The 'Snapshots', which were mini-chapters in themselves, treated a series of key moments, giving the reader a more detailed view of life and issues in a particular age. The three hundred 'Capsules' scattered through the text in discrete boxes touched on an array of highly eccentric and exotic topics, which contrasted sharply with the generalizations of the surrounding chapters and created an illusion of comprehensive coverage.[4]

To my great relief, I found that this relatively complicated structure did not repel the readers. On the contrary, it gave them the opportunity of navigating their individual ways through the huge maze which is European history, of taking a change and a rest at numerous points in the long journey, and of dawdling and dipping whenever they wished to do so.

Faced with *Rising '44*, therefore, I decided yet again that the conventional linear approach was not suitable. The subject matter was unfamiliar to English-language readers; and a series of solid introductory chapters was unavoidable. As a result, the first part, 'Before the Rising', would be bulkier than one might have wished; and the reader's pace would be under threat. The solution was to start with a dramatic Prologue, and then to write four linear chapters in parallel, each presenting a different route towards the outbreak of the Rising on 1 August 1944. The readers may follow each of these routes in turn if they wish, absorbing the narrative and the informational passages as they meet them.

The Rising itself was always going to constitute the main focus of the story. Yet here I had to solve another problem. Having interviewed a large number of participants and survivors, and read numerous personal accounts, I had gained possession of a mass of fascinating memoir material, which was necessarily subjective and anecdotal but which nonetheless threw true and telling light on the human ordeals with which the story abounded. It would have been possible to weave parts of this material into the main text. But remembering the precedent of *Europe: a history*, I decided to keep it separate, and to place it in a series of eyewitness 'capsules', each presenting one person's view of a particular episode. These capsules may be read alongside and in conjunction with my own historian's narrative; or they may be picked from the tree at random as the tastebuds dictate.

The last part of the book, 'After the Rising', contains three chronological chapters, taking the reader from 1944 to the present. I am happy to say that each of them is written in standard linear fashion. They are rounded off by a concluding Interim Report:

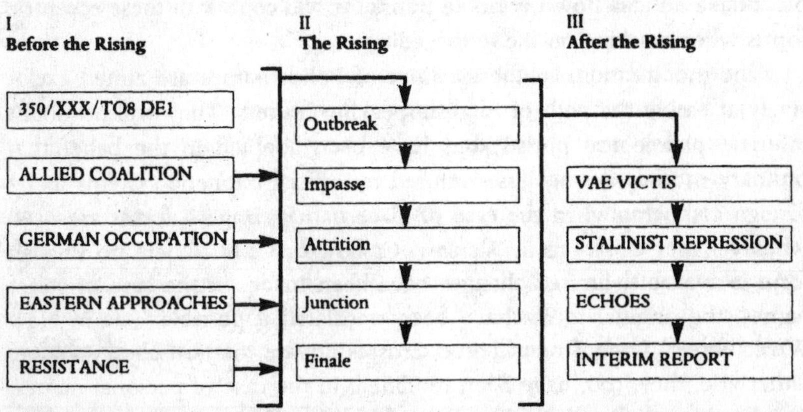

From hard experience, I know that foreign names and places can create havoc in the psyche of English-speaking readers. Indeed, in the case of some languages like Polish, I believe they constitute a near insurmountable barrier to a full understanding of the country's affairs. For it is not just a problem of unfamiliarity. It is unfamiliarity compounded by an incomprehensible system of orthography and by unique, jaw-breaking combinations of consonants and syllables that are uniquely disturbing. Charles Dickens, who met a number of Polish émigrés in London after the Rising of 1863, had a wonderful ear for this problem: 'A gentleman called on me this morning,' he once remarked, 'with two thirds of all the English consonants in his name, and none of the vowels.'[5] The joke is that God created Polish by dropping his Scrabble box. But this is not just a laughing matter. If readers cannot retain the names in a narrative, they cannot follow the plot. And if they cannot follow the plot, they cannot be expected to analyse or to understand it.[6]

At all events, I have decided to conduct an experiment. Wherever possible I have refrained from using foreign names altogether. I have referred to people's positions – saying the 'Premier' instead of Mikołajczyk, or the 'President' instead of Raczkiewicz, and I have been greatly helped by the wartime practice whereby many members of the Underground and Government were known by pseudonyms, nicknames, or *noms de guerre*, which can either be anglicized or translated into short, manageable forms. Hence Gen. Bór-Komorowski becomes 'Boor', Gen. Okulicki becomes 'Bear Cub', Premier Mikołajczyk becomes Premier 'Mick', and Lt. Fleischfarb becomes Lt. 'Light'. I also took the liberty of modifying the spelling of Polish place names, thereby rendering them more readily pronounceable. I have no idea how my noble translator will cope with these eccentric forms when working on the Polish edition.

The modifications in the spellings of Polish names are aimed exclusively at easing the path of English-speaking readers. They will no doubt infuriate philological purists, but have been adopted in the belief that ordinary mortals are no less confused by official phonetic systems as by foreign orthography. In the case of place names, English forms are used wherever they exist – as in Warsaw, Cracow or Lodz. Where no English form is available, limited changes have been made. In the case of street names, the original forms have been translated if possible – as in New World Street, Long Street, Three Crosses Square, or Jerusalem Avenue. Otherwise, they, too, have been modified. In the case of personal names, well-known items such as Sikorski, Wojtyła, or Wałęsa have been left in the original; and anglicized forms such as Casimir, Stanislas, or Thaddeus are used where appropriate. As far as possible, however, the difficulties have been obviated either by reducing surnames to initials – Maria D. for Maria Dąbrowska or Adam M. for Adam Mickiewicz – or by resorting exclusively to the pseudonyms. Detailed explanations of the changes may be found in Appendix 35, or on occasion in relevant endnotes.

I owe many thanks to many institutions and to many individuals. Among the institutions, I would single out the Karta Centre in Warsaw, the Polish Underground Study Trust, the Home Army Veterans Association, the Hoover Institution, the Roosevelt Library, the Public Record Office, the State Archives of the Russian Federation, the Wolfson College Library, and the British Academy. The latter generously awarded me a Small Research Grant.

Among the individuals, I must mention my chief researcher Roger Moorhouse, my special adviser, Mr Andrzej Suchcitz, and a long list of consultants, including Dr Andrzej Krzysztof Kunert, Dr Alison Millett, Mr Zbigniew Stańczyk, Dr Krzysztof Szwagrzyk, Mgr Michaela Todorowa and Mr Zbigniew Siemaszko. Valuable assistance was also rendered by Professor Andrzej Ajnenkiel, Professor W. Bartoszewski, Gill Beeston, Katarzyna Benda, Anthony Beevor, Włodzimierz Bolecki, Krzysztof Bożejewicz, Alexander Boyd, Cathy Brocklehurst, Professor W. Brus, Tadeusz Filipkowski, Max Hastings, Professor Jerzy Holzer, Dr Polly Jones, Professor L. Kołakowski, Dr Maria Korzeniewicz, Glenda Lane, Bolesław Mazur, Jan Nowak-Jeziorański, Professor Krystyna Orzechowska-Juzwenko, Dr Z. Pełczyński, Michael Schmidt, Professor Tomasz Strzembosz, Luba Vinogradova, Ken Wilson, Wanda Wyporska, and Michał Zarzycki.

The number of people who kindly responded to requests for information, completed questionnaires, contributed their reminiscences, or otherwise engaged in correspondence, is almost too large to mention. Several in the meantime have passed on. But all have earned my sincere gratitude. Their contributions, great and small, have given the book a very special, and I would hope, an authentic flavour: Jerzy Adamski, Stanisław Aronson, Stanisław Barański, Wojciech Barański, Maria Bobrzyńska (née Peygert), Zbigniew Borkiewicz, Dr Anna Borkiewicz-Celińska, Stanisław Brzosko, Marek Burdajewicz, Bogdan Celiński, Wiesław Chodorowski, Antoni Chomicki, Z. Drymulski, Jolanta Dzierżawska-Żaczkiewicz, Jacek Fedorowicz, W. Fiedler, Irena Findeisen (née Zieleniewska) now Bellert, Anna Frączek, Czesław Gawłowski, Maria Getka, Wacław Gluth-Nowowiejski, Zbigniew Grabiański, Lech A. Halko, Jan Hoppe, Anna Jakubowska, Father Andrzej Janicki, Ryszard Kapuściński, Stanisław Karolkiewicz, Lucjan Kindlein, Professor Jerzy Kłoczowski, Adam Komorowski, Edward

Kossoj, Bogusław Koziorowski, Czesław Kwaśniewski, Wanda Lesisz-Gutowska, Stanislas Likiernik, Lech Lipiński, Jerzy Lunicz-Adamski, Irena Makowska, Halina Martinowa, Kamila Merwartowa, Wacław Micuta, Krystyna Mierzejewska, Zbigniew Edward Mróz, Sebastian Niewiadomski, Andrzej Nowakowski, Zofia Nowiak, Izabela Nowicka-Kuczyńska, Elżbieta Ostrowska, Feliks Ostrowski, Mieczysław Pawłowski, Wiesław Polkowski, Waldemar Pomaski, Danuta Przyszłasz, Zofia Radecka, Jan Rakowicz (Radajewski), Kazimierz Rakowski, Janina Rendznerowa, Andrzej Rey, Janusz Rosikoń, Bogdan Rostropowicz, Nelli Turzańska-Szymborska, Anna Sadkowska, Father Piotr Sasin, Jan Sidorowicz, Stanisław Sieradzki, Lucjan Sikora, Dr Krzysztof Stoliński, Tadeusz Sumiński, Tadeusz-Marian Szwejczewski, Professor Jerzy Świderski, Anna Świrszczyńska, Bolesław Taborski, Tadeusz Tarmas, Helena Tyrankiewiczowa, Maria Umińska, Professor Wagner, Danuta Wardle-Wiśniowiecka, Andrew Weiss, Kazimierz Wołłk-Karaszewski, J. J. Wyszogrodski, Janusz Zadarnowski, Krzysztof Zanussi, Hanna Zbirohowska-Kościa, and Professor Jerzy Zubrzycki.

As always, the turmoil of an author in the throes of writing and delivery demands enormous forbearance from friends, family and publishers. For their understanding, I offer appropriate apologies and, on completion, a sheepish grin.

I am not quite sure how best to advise the would-be reader on exploring this book. But if a linear narrative may be likened to a chain made up of links, the present construction may be better likened to a more complex building made up of several blocks and of many bricks. I am tempted to liken *Rising '44* to one of the barricades which the insurgents built from paving stones and which featured so prominently in their extraordinary exploits. At all events, the accompanying diagram may help to clarify the literary architecture. As both sides learned to their cost, the best way of surmounting one of these barricades is not necessarily by frontal assault.

Norman Davies
15 April 2003

Contents

List of Illustrations

Part One

Part Two

Propaganda: Coalition: 'We are not alone'. Catholic (Polish Underground Movement (1939–1945) Study Trust, London). 'When the cow bellows, don't stand in the doorway!' (Polish Underground Movement (1939–1945) Study Trust, London)

Greetings: from the Communist Army: 'The Giant and the expectorated dwarf of reaction' (Museum of Warsaw Rising, Warsaw). from the Parasol Battalion, Stalag VIIA, Murnau (Bavaria), Easter 1945 **Western**

Airlift: A Halifax on the tarmac at Brindisi (Imperial War Museum Picture Archive). A Liberator over the Adriatic (Imperial War Museum Picture Archive). USAAF Flying Fortress at Poltava, Ukraine, 'Frantic mission' (Imperial War Museum Picture Archive). A successful drop in the Old Town (Polish Underground Movement (1939–1945) Study Trust, London)

International Politics: 15 August 1944, Premier 'Mick' returns from Moscow – empty-handed (Polish Underground Movement (1939–1945) Study Trust, London). Roosevelt and Churchill: sixty days to save Warsaw (Hulton Getty). J. M. Keynes at Bretton Woods, August 1944: no Poles present (Hulton Getty). Western leaders at Quebec, September 1944: *not* discussing Warsaw (Hulton Getty)

Devastation: Vola in the wake of Dirlewanger (Karta Institute, Warsaw). Grave of a Gestapo agent (Karta Institute, Warsaw). Burying the dead (Karta Institute, Warsaw). Walking home (Polish Underground Movement (1939–1945) Study Trust, London)

The Entry of Berling's Army, September 1944: Welcome in Praga (Karta Institute, Warsaw). 'There'll be a Poland' (Karta Institute, Warsaw). Crossing the Vistula (Museum of Warsaw Rising, Warsaw). Berling's soliders in captivity (Karta Institute, Warsaw)

Terminal Affairs: Countess Tarnovska (Polish Red Cross) in truce talks (AKG London). Blindfolding the negotiators (Hulton Getty). Ozarov, 2 October: signing the capitulation (Polish Underground Movement (1939–1945) Study Trust, London). Von dem Bach receives General 'Boor' in surrender: 5 October 1944 (Polish Underground Movement (1939–1945) Study Trust, London)

Last March of the Home Army: *Stolze Polen!* (Proud Poles!) (Karta Institute, Warsaw). Members of the Women's Auxiliary Service

Part Three

RISING '44

350/XXX/999 TO8 DE1

1944. Summer afternoons in wartime England could be deceptive. In London's leafy suburbs it was easy to believe that the war, and the warfarers, were far, far away. The sun shone. Scattered clouds sailed lazily across the sky. Birds were singing in the fields and gardens. Although V1 rockets occasionally strayed into the vicinity, the mass bombing of the Blitz was already a bad memory. The fierce fighting in Normandy was safely across the Channel, out of earshot. The still grander and fiercer battles on Europe's Eastern Front were taking place well beyond the range of close observation or accurate reporting. The mass atrocities being perpetrated in the East were sketchily reported and poorly understood. They were not troubling the public conscience. After years when Britain's very survival had been at stake, the general mood was lightening. The Allied cause was prospering. Talk on the Continent was of impending Liberation.

From the outside, Barnes Lodge looked much like any other English country house of Edwardian vintage. Brick-built under a low-sloping grey slate roof, and largely covered in white plaster, it was set four-square on a clearing at the top of a steep drive overlooking the valley of the River Gade in Hertfordshire. A dozen main rooms were arranged on two storeys round a central staircase. They were light, airy and elegant, thanks to the high walls and moulded ceilings, and were lit by large octagonal sash windows. They offered views over a wide lawn at the front and over an unspoiled rural setting at the back.

Yet the occupants had been seeking other advantages. The building had no immediate neighbours, though it was located less than a mile from the mainline railway running north from London to Bletchley and the Midlands. Except at the back, it was surrounded either by pine trees or by thickets of hawthorn, alder, and hazel. The winding drive climbed up the hill with no sight of its destination. The iron gates, which stood back from the main road at the bottom, were wreathed in shrubbery, giving no hint of the guardhouse and the steel-net fence lurking beyond. A discreet notice read 'Private'. Motorists driving past the village of King's Langley on the

A41 were unlikely to give a second thought as they negotiated the bend and the railway arch just after the drive. Passengers on the express steam trains which ran alongside the road had other things to watch. On the other side of the line, they could take their fill of the garish placards, cut-out cows, and mock-Tudor barns of the model Ovaltine Egg Farm. Commuters waiting on the platform of King's Langley halt for their twenty-five-minute journey to Euston would have noticed nothing. They would only have seen the Ovaltine factory, the red-tiled roofs of the village, and a wooded hillside in the distance. Villagers drinking in the isolated Eagle pub two hundred yards from the gates, or at Ye Olde Red Lion beside the railway arch, would have known that the Lodge had been given over to 'war work'. But they would have been warned by the local constable to ask no questions. The War Office had been looking for seclusion and convenience. They had known exactly what they were doing when they requisitioned Barnes Lodge soon after the outbreak of war.[1]

By 1944, the progress of the Second World War in Europe had reached its critical point. The fortunes of battle were about to swing irreversibly in favour of the Grand Alliance. For the previous twelve months, Hitler's Wehrmacht had been retreating without respite on the Eastern Front, reeling from crushing defeats at Stalingrad and Kursk. It could still hope to organize an effective line of defence in the rapidly narrowing space between the mountains and the sea, but only on condition that an overwhelming part of its forces were concentrated on that single task. Yet in the weeks since 6 June, the armies of the Western Allies had established a powerful beachhead in Normandy, in addition to their steadily strengthening grip on Italy. The Reich was now facing the ultimate nightmare which German generals had feared throughout the twentieth century – a war of attrition on two fronts against superior numbers and superior resources. Moreover, Germany's ordeal was made considerably worse both by its effective withdrawal from the naval contest, which had long menaced the Allies' lifeline across the Atlantic, and by the unchallengeable supremacy of Western air power, which was steadily reducing all the major cities of Germany to rubble. If the Allied momentum was not quickly contained, two major developments loomed. Firstly, the Nazis were going to be thrown out of the countries immediately adjacent to the Reich. And secondly, the Reich itself was going to be invaded.[2]

Mid-1944 was also the time when the outlines of a post-war world dominated by the USA were coming into view. In the space of three brief years, the USA had created an unprecedented lead in economic production, financial power, technological expertise, and military potential; and it was now translating its might into political muscle. Almost completely unscathed by the fighting which, with the exception of one day at Pearl Harbor, had never reached American shores, the world's new 'superpower' held important levers of influence over its British and Soviet partners; and President Roosevelt was exercising ever greater clout among the 'Big Three'. Whilst Churchill and Stalin were turning their thoughts to post-war recovery, Roosevelt's team was drawing up plans for the perpetuation of American dominance. It was Roosevelt who had invented the Allied policy of 'unconditional surrender'; and between July and October 1944, it was the USA which planned a new, American-led world order.

The men and women working at Barnes Lodge were in closer touch with some of these developments than almost anyone else in Britain. They formed a special unit of long-distance radio-telegraphists, maintaining constant contact with Allied forces on the Continent. To be exact, Barnes Lodge was a listening and receiving station. It was linked by a fifty-six-strand cable to transmitters a couple of miles away at Chipperfield House and Tower Hill, and by a battery of teleprinters and over 50km (thirty miles) of landline to the 6th Bureau of Army Command in London, SW1. Code-named 'Martha', it was station number eight in a chain of ninety-five, including one recently established near Brindisi in southern Italy.[3]

The Headquarters Communications Company based at Barnes Lodge was associated with a much wider radio network. A neighbouring unit in the village of Boxmoor, for example, was engaged in foreign radio-intelligence. Divided into two sections, German and Russian, it reported directly to the top-secret intelligence centre at Bletchley Park. The German Section was headed by two high-powered mathematicians, who had pioneered the pre-war work on the German Enigma codes, and the Russian Section by a former Professor of Sanskrit. A third unit, based in Mill Hill, was dedicated to civilian communications. It belonged officially to the Ministry of Internal Affairs, and was put mainly at the disposal of the Premier. A fourth belonged to the Foreign Ministry and was used to keep contact with embassies, legations, and consulates around the world.

Barnes Lodge had a staff of 127. It was commanded by a military captain, who was also a professional engineer, and was divided into a Correspondence Section and a Technical Services Section. Of the eight officers, two were electronics experts. There were thirty-nine telegraphists, eleven radio mechanics, and five female teleprinter operators. Twenty-eight soldiers serviced the transmitters and kept the register of transmissions. A team of nineteen maintained the antennas. Seventeen more were responsible for various clerical, kitchen, and guard duties. The senior personnel were either accommodated in rooms on the top floor of the Lodge or billeted in the village; junior ranks lived in dormitories converted from garages and stables. Everyone knew everyone else. Two men played a special role liaising with the higher British authorities. One was an affluent businessman who had worked in Belgium and volunteered for military service in 1939, the other a young cadet who had recently completed his schooling at Ampleforth College.

The Allied cause was completely dominated by the 'Big Three', although the routes followed by each of the three had been very different. The British Empire had been engaged almost from the start, having declared war on the Third Reich on 3 September 1939. Under the combative leadership of the Prime Minister, Winston Churchill, it had moved away from the pre-war stance of well-intentioned appeasement to one of principled defiance. The United States of America, in contrast, had steered clear of the war in Europe for over two years. But President Franklin D. Roosevelt had moved in 1941 from undercover support for Britain to open engagement, and, thanks to America's vast resources, to the status of the Free World's leading champion. America's role in Europe was limited only by her simultaneous commitment to the war against Japan. For its part, the Soviet Union had spent the first two wartime years as an active partner of the Third Reich. The secret protocols of the Nazi–Soviet Pact, which had made Hitler's initial aggressions possible, had enabled 'Marshal Stalin' to perpetrate similar depredations. Hitler's surprise attack on the USSR in June 1941, however, had transformed Europe's military alignments overnight. Henceforth, the USSR and the Third Reich were engaged in a fight to the death. Moreover, the crushing Soviet victories, when they came, were all the more impressive because they were so unexpected. Despite the manifestly undemocratic character of the Stalinist regime, they gave Stalin enormous prestige and admiration even among Western democrats. So the 'Big Three' drew ever closer. Their aim was unconditional surrender. They called themselves 'the United Nations'.[4]

In 1944, radio-telegraphy and radio-telephony were still in the early stages of their development. The equipment was cumbersome and heavy; transmissions needed high levels of electrical power. Reception was often poor. Detection was relatively easy. Allied telegraphists, as at Barnes Lodge, relied mainly on hand-operated circuit stoppers or 'sounders' which required the operator to tap out the laborious dots and dashes of the international variant (Q) of the Morse code. They received incoming messages on pre-selected wavelengths through the crackling earphones and they wrote them down letter by letter with pencil and paper. Since the enemy could easily eavesdrop, they were obliged to use ciphers at every stage. This meant that incoming messages were not normally intelligible at Barnes Lodge. Their text could only be rendered recognizable by the headquarters staff and by the banks of cipher clerks who worked in support of them at the other end of the teleprinters. Security demanded that the telegraphists and the cipher clerks be always kept apart. Decipherment was still more laborious than transmitting. The clerks had to conduct all manner of checks and to refer to a series of ever-changing keys, tables, and combinations; and they worked on material according to a strict hierarchy of importance. Messages marked XXX were to be dealt with immediately. Those marked VVV had second priority, whilst those marked VV remained at the bottom of the pile. Processing, therefore, was slow. Delays were frequent. If replies to short notes of the highest priority were ready within a matter of hours, things were going well.[5]

Of course, it was to overcome these problems of delay and decipherment that the German Command had adopted their mechanized 'Enigma' system. Yet, as the Allies had discovered, the advanced Enigma machines proved vulnerable to advanced methods of code-breaking.[6] Barnes Lodge was a technological museum compared to nearby Bletchley Park. But in the long run, it was better to be slow and safe than to be fast and fallible.

The wisdom of this policy had been confirmed prior to the D-Day landings. As a precaution, all foreign organizations in Britain, with the exception of American and Soviet military missions, had been forbidden to transmit enciphered radio messages. One of the Governments-in-Exile defied the order. But it was allowed to continue when the British 'listeners' were unable to break in. If the British experts could not master the cipher, it was correctly assumed that the Germans would not be able to do so either.[7]

The work of these covert communication networks was complemented by that of regular radio stations broadcasting *en clair*. By far the most important was the BBC World Service, which broadcast from Bush House in dozens of languages and which ran a dedicated section for every enemy-occupied country. But there were many lesser outfits as well, organized for special purposes. Radio 'Vaver', for instance, used prearranged code-words buried in open messages to communicate with underground groups that possessed no special equipment. The messages were sent from a transmitter at Fawley Court near Henley. Their reception could be confirmed by ciphered signals received at Barnes Lodge. Radio 'Dawn', in contrast, which belonged to the Ministry of Information, pretended to be broadcasting from the middle of Nazi-occupied Europe. In reality, its programmes were transmitted from a ship moored off the coast of East Anglia.

As the range of BBC World Service broadcasts showed, membership of the Allied camp was considerably more diverse than talk on the top table of the 'Big Three' might have suggested. Britain's war effort was supported by the armed forces of the dominions and colonies – notably by the Canadians, the Australians, the New Zealanders, the South Africans, and the Indians. France had been the principal partner to begin with, and the catastrophic fall of France in 1940 had not severed the French connection. The Free French Movement, formed from 'all Frenchmen who rally to the Allied cause', was a permanent (and troublesome) fixture of wartime London. So, too, were the exiled Governments of Belgium, Czechoslovakia, Greece, Luxembourg, the Netherlands, Norway, Poland, and Yugoslavia. General de Gaulle, Prime Minister Pierlot, President Beneš, King George II, Grand Duchess Charlotte, Queen Wilhelmina, King Haakon VII, General Sikorski, who died in 1943, and King Peter II were all respected figures, featuring regularly in the British and American press. All of them put armed forces and intelligence services at Britain's disposal. The Poles were specially numerous, and, by reputation, the most single-minded. It was Hitler's attack on their country on 1 September 1939 which had started the war. Both individually and cumulatively, therefore, the so-called 'lesser allies' were making an invaluable contribution. Though often sidelined by the 'Big Three', they formed an integral element in the Allied cause. What is more, their political significance was reviving as the Allied armies advanced. It was hard to imagine the process of liberation without them.

Allied liaison with foreign underground movements was problematical. For one thing, messages had often to be translated as well as encoded and decoded. For another, clandestine transmitters in Nazi-occupied Europe were easily located by enemy direction-finders. So, to avoid arrest, they had to be portable, and their operating teams extremely mobile. They could only feel reasonably secure if they kept to remote forests and mountains, where their services were in least demand. They were in great danger when sending from occupied cities that were swarming with the

German military: sending time there was usually limited to ten minutes. The most effective of the European Resistance movements – in Poland, Yugoslavia, and northern Italy – were also the furthest removed from Britain. Hence airdrops of equipment and personnel were hard to arrange. The portable sets were not particularly portable. The standard A1 type transmitter, which was built in a factory in Stanmore and dropped by the hundred into Europe behind enemy lines, was popularly known as the 'Pipstock'. It measured 9 x 25 x 30cm (3.5 x 10 x 12 in), fitted comfortably into a medium-sized suitcase, or, so as not to attract attention, was most conveniently carried in a sack; and it weighed about 10kg (22 lb). It sent out a 10-watt signal on a sky-wave at very high frequencies. To be fully operational, it needed a telegraphist, a cipher clerk, a strong bagman, a look-out, and a messenger; it was dependent on a fixed power supply; and its transformer had a nasty tendency to heat up.

The threat from overheating, however, was no less worrying than that from Gestapo snoopers. Hence, being deliberately designed to emit only a minimal ground-wave, the transmitters could not be used for local communication. This meant that clandestine stations operating on the same network within the same European city could only talk to each other via Barnes Lodge more than a thousand miles away.[8]

For all these reasons, many of the exiled Governments in London continued to entrust their most vital messages to couriers or to prearranged nonsense statements broadcast *en clair* by the BBC. Advance warnings about the imminence of Operation Overlord (the invasion of Normandy) had recently been passed to the French Resistance by BBC presenters making magical announcements like: *Je regrette les neiges d'antan.*[9]

Not surprisingly, the occupants of Barnes Lodge had to employ great ingenuity to keep regular contact with their unseen collaborators. Only eighteen of their thirty-nine receivers were of the most modern type, and only two of the forty-six radio towers at Chipperfield were mounted with the most suitable rhomboid aerials. To cap it all, mid-1944 coincided with the low point of the eleven-year sunspot cycle and incoming signals were frequently interrupted or distorted. Even so, work never stopped. As the surviving Register indicates, Barnes Lodge exchanged 2,522 telegrams in July and 4,341 in August.[10]

The radio telegraphists were trained to the highest standards: Telegraphists 1st Class had to transmit and receive faultlessly at a minimum of 120 letters a minute, and Telegraphists 2nd and 3rd Class at 80 and 40 respectively. In addition, to save time, especially when signing on and off, they used the large number of internationally recognized abbreviations, such as VVV – 'hello', QRK? – 'how are you receiving me?', QTCO – 'I am not sending a message', and R – 'understood'.

Britain's efforts to coordinate Underground activities in the occupied countries of her allies were largely organized by the Special Operations Executive (SOE). Formed in July 1940 by the merger of the sabotage section of MI6, the research branch of the War Office, and one of the propaganda departments of the Foreign Office, it had agents and representatives on all continents. Its headquarters were located at a secret address in Baker Street, a short walk from Euston Station and close to the (non-existent) rooms of the fictional Sherlock Holmes. Directly subordinated to the British Chiefs of Staff, it was headed in its early days by a seconded diplomat, Gladwyn Jebb, and from 1943 by a dashing Highland officer born in Yokohama, Maj.Gen. Colin Gubbins. Some 13,000 courageous men and women, all volunteers, formed the core. But the greater part of its agents were foreigners who were trained by SOE experts for secret service in their own occupied countries. Training camps were set up in the remote Scottish Highlands and at Beaulieu House in Hampshire, and overseas at 'Camp X' at Oshawa in Ontario, at Mount Carmel in Palestine, and at Singapore. Transport was provided, sometimes reluctantly, by RAF units specializing in parachute drops, and occasionally by Royal Navy submarines. Communications were maintained by an autonomous signals section, which through a series of accidents became the chief channel between London and Washington. Churchill loved SOE. MI6 and the Foreign Office loathed it.[11]

Armed insurrections were designed as the culmination of Allied plans to undermine Nazi rule. In the early years of the war, resistance had been limited to sabotage, anti-Nazi propaganda, small-scale guerrilla actions, and occasional assassinations. The spectacular, and spectacularly avenged, SOE-assisted killing of *SS-Ogruf.* Reinhard Heydrich in Prague in June 1942 demonstrated both the possibilities and the dangers.[12] Yet as the war progressed, and the Allied cause gained strength, both civilian and military subversion were planned on an ever-growing scale. Of course, local circumstances varied enormously. Generally speaking, the Nazi Occupation regimes were far milder in Western Europe than in countries in the East which the Nazis had earmarked for their *Lebensraum*. Generally speaking, it was less risky to engage in subversive operations in France or Italy than in Poland or Yugoslavia. Even so, the overall trend was unmistakable. As the German forces of occupation came under attack from the Allied armies, they could also expect to come under pressure from organized groups of local patriots and partisans.

Western air power was a crucial consideration in planning risings. For two years past, Bomber Command had been pounding German cities with impunity, and during Overlord tactical air support was the one branch of the battle in which the British and Americans enjoyed marked superiority. By mid-1944, therefore, all would-be insurgents knew that the Allies possessed the capacity to supply them from the air, to bombard airfields, to disrupt enemy troop concentrations, and to deploy reinforcements by parachute. If, as was generally agreed, the resistance were to assist the Allied armies, by the same token the Allies were expected to assist the resistance.

Both sides paid special attention to capital cities. The Germans planned to dig in and to defend the capitals as symbols of their all-conquering supremacy. The resistance planned to seize them in order to emphasize the restoration of national independence. Timing was crucial. If the ill-armed patriots took to the streets too soon, they could not hope to hold out for long against vastly superior German firepower. If they left their risings too late, the chance of striking a blow at the hated Nazis might be missed. The ideal time was the moment when a panicky German garrison came under attack from the advancing Allied armies. With luck, the Underground fighters would only have to hold their capital for two or three days before the Germans surrendered. Rome showed the way on 5 June 1944 – on the eve of Overlord – when the US Army swept into the Eternal City and Ivano Bonomi's anti-fascist Committee of National Liberation fell on the retreating Germans to seize the reins of Italian Government.[13] After Rome, the line-up for further risings was a long one. It included Paris, Brussels, Amsterdam, Oslo, Copenhagen, Warsaw, Belgrade, Budapest, and Prague. Everything depended on the routes and the rate of the Allied advance. Yet the rest of June and the whole of July passed with no further outbreak.

1 August 1944 was a Tuesday. Anyone reading *The Times* that morning in London – or on the platform at King's Langley – would not have found any war news that was particularly sensational. Indeed, one could not

have found any war news at all before page 4. Page 1, as always, was taken up by everyday notices of births, marriages, and deaths. Page 2 was given over to Home News. It contained an article about 'Children in Care', and a long letter to the editor pointing out that the Balfour Declaration had not promised support for a Jewish state but for a Jewish national home. The weather forecast stated that the hot sunny spell would continue. Page 3 was reserved for 'Imperial and Foreign'. The largest piece discussed 'Renaissance Art in Rome'. It was accompanied by other items about 'Russian Memories of 1914', the 'Red Army Mission to Greece', a 'Hill-top Affray in Normandy', and 'Joy in a Liberated French Village'. The only substantial piece of diplomatic comment concerned the Polish Premier's forthcoming mission to Moscow – about which as yet there was nothing substantial to report.

The war news on page 4 consisted of half a dozen major reports. The first was headed 'Americans Clearing the Normandy Coast'. Its optimism contrasted with the dubious column alongside headed 'More Progress at Caumont'. The third report was headed 'Severe Air Blows'. 'Fighter-bomber activity', it announced, 'was at first handicapped yesterday by what the Americans call "smog" – a mixture of smoke and fog'. The fourth concerned a 'Stiff Fight for Florence'. The fifth, which filled the entire right-hand side of the page, described 'The Red Army's Rapid Drive on East Prussia'. It consisted of two parts – 'Street Fighting in Kaunas' and the 'Ferocious Battle for Warsaw'. The latter was backed up by a 'news snippet' on the following page. 'Russian forces which are in sight of Warsaw', it read, 'are massing on the Vistula, where the line to the south is one of acute danger to the Germans'.

That day *The Times* carried two main leaders. 'The National Medical Service' debated one of the current domestic issues. 'Nearing Warsaw' debated the latest development on the foreign front. 'According to German reports', it repeated, 'Marshal Rokossovsky's men were fighting within six miles of Warsaw. Thus the first of the martyred cities of Europe to suffer the horrors of German air bombardment and of National Socialist rule, is also the first to see deliverance at hand.' The conclusion drawn from this information was confined to military prognosis. 'The approaching fall of Warsaw,' *The Times* concluded, 'taken in conjunction with the capture of Kaunas . . . opens up the way for a convergent attack on East Prussia.'

Passing to page 6, the diligent reader could have skimmed the court circular. Businessmen heading for the City could have been most interested in 'Finance and Commerce' on page 7. Photographs were reserved for the top half of page 8. The largest showed troops of Montgomery's Second Army in the shell-shattered town of Caumont. The others showed scenes from 'The King in Italy'; one was subtitled 'The King is seen decorating Sepoy Kamal Ram, 8th Punjab Regiment, with the Victoria Cross ribbon'.

Below the photographs were the daily listings. 'Broadcasting' started with 'Home Service; 7 a.m. News, 7.15 a.m. Physical Exercises': 'Opera and Ballet' was taken up with performances by the two companies at Sadler's Wells. London's theatres were showing Noël Coward's *Blithe Spirit* at the Duchess, *Macbeth* at the Lyric, and *Arsenic and Old Lace* at the Strand. Under 'Non-stop Review', the Windmill invited reviewers to the saucy *Revudeville* with its proud slogan 'We Never Closed'.

No one from Barnes Lodge travelled up to London or to anywhere else on 1 August. The listeners were on duty round the clock. As one of the operators remembered, 'A feverish atmosphere reigned'.[14] They knew that a crisis was approaching. Strategic orders had gone out, and vital replies were awaited at any moment of the day or night. Relays of telegraphists leaned over their machines, tightened their headsets and prepared to grip their pencils. The duty controller stood by to rush the precious pieces of paper to the teletypists who sat nervously, waiting to forward the messages to Headquarters.

Excitement at Barnes Lodge was all the higher through a sensational but puzzling incident which had occurred a week earlier. On 25 July an irregular unciphered message had been received, in the clear: 'The regiment is surrounded. They are disarming us. They are approaching us.' A most unusual exchange with Headquarters ensued. The general on duty at Upper Belgrave Street ordered Barnes Lodge over the teleprinter, 'Ask them who is disarming them?' When the reply came back, the duty general simply responded: 'It isn't true.' The transmission ended abruptly with the pathetic words 'Good-bye, brothers.'[15]

Nothing could have been more unsettling than apparently important messages sent in the clear. The rulebook stated that they should be ignored. They could easily be the work of enemy agents who had recognized the frequency of an Underground transmitter but did not know the necessary encryption procedures. German intelligence was constantly engaged in misinformation schemes.

It was all the more astonishing, therefore, that in the evening of 1 August, Barnes Lodge again received a second apparently vital message in the clear. On this occasion, the circumstances were especially disconcerting. The transmission had opened as expected at a pre-arranged time from an operator whose 'signature' was well known. It began with a call sign that by agreement had been cunningly altered from the standard 'VVV VVV VVV' to 'VVV VVV VVVE', thereby eliminating the possibility that the operator had been captured by the enemy and was transmitting under duress. And the message was preceded by the usual sort of heading. Yet the next group of letters, 'QTCO=', was totally contradictory. 'QTCO' stood for 'I am sending no messages' and = stood for 'start of message'. The receiving operator then recorded forty-six words, which, since they were not enciphered, were immediately recognizable.[16]

.--- ..- -- .-- .- .-.. -.-. --.. -.-- -- -.-- ... ..-. .-.. .- --. .-
-... .. .- .-.. --- -.-. --.. . .-. .-- --- -. .- .--. --- .-- .. . .--
.- -. .- -.. .-- .- .-. ... --.. .- .. .-- .-

The message read: 'WE ARE ALREADY FIGHTING . . .'[17] The Commanding Officer was immediately called into the Control Room. He ordered that the contents of the message be conveyed to Headquarters. There, the general who had dismissed the previous unciphered message a week earlier decided to dismiss this one likewise. Apparently, he just put it on one side. He did not inform the Chief of Staff.

During those same hours, Barnes Lodge was unwittingly involved in yet another mysterious incident. Late on 31 July, a telegram had arrived from the staff of the Commander-in-Chief, who was temporarily in Italy. At 2240 it was properly forwarded by teleprinter to HQ.[18] The Communications Company would not have understood its coded contents, which, as the post-war records show, were of absolutely crucial importance. Yet, for some reason, it had taken three days to reach London from Italy; it was never given top priority; and it was not deciphered for at least twelve hours after arrival. Even then, it was never passed on to its intended destination.[19] In other words, it was taken out of circulation in much the same way and at almost the same time as the unciphered message number (1)350. Despite the devoted work of the Communications Company, something, somewhere, was amiss.

The military events of 1 August were reported in the British newspapers on 2 August. But Wednesday's news was much the same as Tuesday's. In the West, 'US tanks cross the river into Brittany'. In the East, 'All Roads from the Baltic to East Prussia Cut' and 'Arc Drawn Around Warsaw'. The *Führer* himself was being forced to evacuate the Wolf's Lair at

Rastenburg: 'Hitler Seeks New HQ'. The *Times* leader addressed 'Britain and India'. There was even space to print a letter from Australia announcing the birth of a baby duck-billed platypus.

Just before noon, one of the receivers at Barnes Lodge crackled into action once again. The transmission began '-/xxx/999, Lavina to Martha'. The words of the following text were, as usual, unintelligible. But the staff at Barnes Lodge knew whose cryptonym Lavina was, and they could have little doubt that the long-awaited news had at last arrived. They were right. Deciphered at Headquarters in the early afternoon, and translated for wider consumption, the message was electrifying:

> . . . 1 August 1944. To the Premier and the Commander-in-Chief: The date for the beginning of a struggle to capture [the capital] was jointly fixed by us for August 1st at 1700 hours. The struggle has begun. (Signed) Home Delegate and Vice-Premier, C.O. Home Army[20]

The date was odd. The telegram appeared to be a day old. And the verb 'was' in the English translation struck some people as strange. Otherwise, everything looked genuine enough. The telegram had come through the correct channels and in the correct code. Unlike its predecessor, this one was accepted. Action was urgent. No more time could be lost. The Liberation of an Allied capital was in progress. A Rising had begun.

PART ONE

Before the Rising

CHAPTER I

THE ALLIED COALITION

THE HISTORY OF 'WESTERN ALLIANCES' in Europe is a long one. Throughout modern history, whenever one power threatened to establish a dominant position on the Continent, a coalition of states, great and small, was formed to oppose the threat. The most frequent coalitionist was Britain, whose navy ruled the seas but whose land forces were never of a size to challenge their Continental rivals. British-inspired alliances emerged in the War of the Spanish Succession against Louis XIV, in the wars against revolutionary France, and in the two world wars. In the twentieth century, they brought in the USA, whose impact on Europe rose from the peripheral to the decisive. Yet they all had one feature in common. They all sought to include at least one partner in the East. According to circumstances, that partner could be Prussia, Russia, or even Turkey. In the exceptional circumstances of 1939, it turned out to be a country which, though possessed of ancient credentials, had played little part in European power games for nearly three hundred years.

The Allied cause of the Second World War is invariably described in the simplest of terms. If ever there was a just war, one hears, this was it. The enemy was wicked. The goal of defeating that wickedness was noble. And the Allies were victorious. Most people, certainly in Britain and America, would not think that there was much more to be said. Of course, they are aware that the conduct of the war took many twists and turns. Those who have studied it know that the Allies stared defeat in the face on several occasions before victory was finally assured. But on the basic political and moral framework they harbour no misgivings. Few would contest the popular image of the wartime Allies as a band of brothers who fought for freedom and justice and saved the world from tyranny.

Several basic facts about the Allied cause, therefore, need to be emphasized from the outset. Firstly, membership of the Allied coalition was in constant flux. The band of brothers who set out to defy the Nazi threat in 1939, when the war is generally judged to have started, was not the same as that whose victory brought the war to a close six years later. Several important states changed sides in midstream; and the most powerful of the Allies stayed aloof almost until the mid-point of the conflict. Secondly, the Allied coalition contained all manner of member states, from global empires to totalitarian dictatorships, semi-constitutional monarchies, democratic republics, Governments-in-Exile, and several countries divided by civil war. Thirdly, when the fighting spread in December 1941 to the Pacific, the original war in Europe was complicated by numerous forms of interaction with the Asian theatre. In theory, the Allied cause came to be based on the undertakings of the United Nations Declaration of 1942, which obtained twenty-six signatories. The Declaration in turn was based on the terms of the earlier Atlantic Charter which, among other things, condemned territorial aggrandizement and confirmed 'the right of all peoples to choose their Governments'. In practice, the Allies were united by little except the commitment to fight the common enemy.

Throughout the war, the Alliance was clouded by the old-fashioned and highly paternalistic assumption that 'the principal Allies' were entitled to determine policy separately and in private, whilst 'the lesser Allies' were expected to accept the decisions of their betters. The assumption was not widely challenged at the time, and has rarely been challenged since by historians. But it was to have some serious consequences. Though never formally recognized, it was embodied in the workings of the 'Big Three' to which Winston Churchill, in conscious imitation of the experience of his eighteenth-century ancestor the Duke of Marlborough, gave the grand title of 'the Grand Alliance'.

The Allied cause was further complicated by the fact that most of its constituent members were caught up in their own tangled web of bilateral treaties, separate declarations, and subordinate alliances. All the 'United Nations', as they came to call themselves, were committed to cooperate in the struggle against the Axis powers. But they were not necessarily committed to defend or to assist each other. In particular, no mechanism was ever put in place to protect one ally from the depredations of another. Inter-Allied disputes that could not be readily resolved were usually deferred either to the intended post-war Peace Conference, which never happened, or to the United Nations Organisation, which did not open for business until September 1945.

On close examination, therefore, one can see that the ties binding different members of the coalition together differed widely in their nature and in their degree of commitment. The relations between Britain and the United States, for example, were largely conducted on the basis of mutual trust. With the sole exception of the Lend-Lease Agreement (February 1942), there was no formal or comprehensive British–US Treaty. British relations with France still operated on the rather imprecise understandings of the old Entente Cordiale. British relations with the USSR, in contrast, were governed by the elaborate provisions of the Anglo-Soviet Treaty signed on 12 July 1941. Soviet–American relations were similarly regulated by an agreement signed the following year. Generally speaking, the Western Allies saw diplomatic treaties as a constraining influence that limited the otherwise boundless scope for initiatives. The Soviet Union looked at them from the opposite perspective. They saw treaties with Western capitalist powers as vehicles of convenience, which enabled them to practise cooperation on a temporary and precisely defined basis, but not to modify their essentially hostile and suspicious stance.

The make-up and predispositions of the Allied coalition of 1939–45 were strongly influenced by its predecessor of 1914–18. During the First World War, France, Britain, Russia, and the USA had dominated the group of 'Entente Powers' which had challenged German hegemony. During the Second World War, the legacy of the Entente coloured the natural sympathies and alignments of the next Allied generation. Germany was taken to be a unique, unparalleled threat. France, Britain, and America imagined themselves to be paragons of democracy. The solidarity of the English-speaking world, re-established in 1917, was to be further strengthened. The Russians – as the Soviets were wrongly called – would be readily accepted as natural partners for the West, even though the old liberalizing regime of late tsardom had been replaced by a new totalitarian monster of far more sinister proclivities.

The men who rose to leadership in 1939–45 possessed a mental map of the world which had been formed thirty, forty, or even fifty years before. Churchill, for instance, born in 1874, was a Victorian who was well into adult life before the twentieth century arrived. Politics for him was the business of empires and of a hierarchy of states where clients and colonials could not aspire to equal treatment. Stalin was only five years younger, Roosevelt eight. All of them were older than Hitler or Mussolini. Almost all the top brass of the Allied military – Weygand, de Gaulle, Brooke, Montgomery, Zhukov, Rokossovsky, Patton, but *not* Eisenhower – had survived a formative experience in the First World War. They had been left not only with a searing memory of total war between massed armies but also of a particular vision of the map of Europe. They had grown up to believe that if the layout of Western Europe was rather complicated, that of Eastern Europe was rather straightforward. They knew Germany's place on the map from the Rhine to the Niemen. They knew that to the west of Germany lay a clutch of countries: Holland, Belgium, Luxembourg, France, Switzerland. But they thought that to the east of Germany there was nothing, or at least nothing of importance, except 'Russia'. After all, in the world of their youth, the German and the Russian Empires had been contiguous. Warsaw, like Riga or Vilno, had been a Russian city.

A true story nicely illustrates the mental maps that floated around in Western heads. One day in 1944 Gen. Montgomery met the commanding officer of the 1st (Polish) Armoured Division in Normandy for the first time. Looking for something to say, Montgomery asked him, 'Tell me, General, in Warsaw these days, do people speak Russian or German?'[1] It was a blunder of capital proportions, equivalent to asking whether French or Latin is the language of London. But it should not cause too much surprise. After all, when Montgomery was a young soldier, Warsaw was in Russia. He would also have known that the Germans had captured Warsaw in 1915 and had done so again in 1939. What was more natural than to think of Warsaw as a place contested by Russians and Germans? It would have been a very rare and erudite Westerner who knew that Poland had a longer independent history than Russia and traditions of freedom and democracy that were older than Britain's.[2]

For Western views of the nations of Eastern Europe, where they existed at all, often possessed a decidedly judgemental character. Winston Churchill, for example, divided the states of Europe unkindly into 'giants' and 'pygmies'. The giants were the Great Powers who had just fought the Great War. The pygmies were all those troublesome national states which had emerged through the collapse of the old empires and which had promptly started to fight each other. The dismissive approach to the New Europe was thinly disguised. And it was accompanied by a tendency to classify the pygmies as one might classify children, into the nice and the naughty. Europe's new nations were pictured as nice in Allied eyes if, like the Czechs and the Slovaks, they had won their independence by fighting against Germany or Austria. If, like the Ukrainians or the Irish, they had gained it by rebelling against an Allied power, they were naughty, not to say downright nasty. In the case of Ukraine, which had carved out its own republic with German help, it was taken to be a fiction. States which had not obtained Allied recognition did not really exist.

As for the Poles, who had dared to assert themselves both against the Central Powers and against Russia, they could be nothing other than mixed-up problem children. They were pygmies pretending to be giants. Some Polish leaders, who had spent the Great War in St Petersburg, London, or Paris, were obviously sound enough. But others, like Marshal Pilsudski, who spent years in the Austrian ranks fighting against the Russians, were clearly unreliable. The fact that Pilsudski had spent the last year of the war imprisoned in Magdeburg, having refused to swear an oath of loyalty to the Kaiser, did not remove the suspicion that he was dangerously 'pro-German'. The Marshal was dead by 1939. But the alleged ambivalence of his legacy lingered on. After all, in 1920, he had defied good sense by defeating Soviet Russia in battle, and in the 1930s he had signed non-aggression pacts with both Stalin and Hitler. His doctrine of 'two enemies' was thought very eccentric. By Allied standards, it was hard to see what the Poles were playing at.

The Allied camp evolved in several distinct stages. To begin with, in 1939, it consisted of just three states – France, the United Kingdom, and Poland. It did not include either Lithuania, whose port of Klaipeda (Memel) was seized by Germany on 23 March 1939, or Albania, which had been invaded and annexed by fascist Italy in April 1939, or indeed Finland, which was attacked by the Soviet Union in November. For Lithuania was coerced by Germany into the formal acceptance of its loss. The Italian annexation of Albania was recognized by France and Britain in a dubious diplomatic manoeuvre reminiscent of the recent Munich Agreement. And the Finno-Soviet conflict was brought to an uneasy close before any other states intervened. By Allied calculations, therefore, no significant breach of the peace occurred in Europe in 1939 other than the German assault on Poland in September. It was the Polish Crisis which brought the Allied coalition into being and gave it its first war aim. Poland had been allied to France since 1921, and to Britain by the Treaty of Mutual Assistance signed on 25 August 1939. Both France and Britain had publicly guaranteed Poland's independence on 31 March. So when the Wehrmacht poured over the Polish frontier at dawn on 1 September, the Allies possessed a clear *casus belli*.

After the fall of Poland in 1939 and the fall of France in 1940, the Allied camp is often said to have been reduced to the grand total of one, namely

Britain. This is hardly correct even if one discounts the great support of Canada, Australia, New Zealand, and South Africa. the involvement of India, and the growing band of exiled Governments, some of them with significant military contingents at their disposal. For the United States was not exactly neutral. Whilst officially pursuing a policy of non-belligerency, President Roosevelt embarked on a systematic programme of turning his country into 'the great arsenal of democracy'. Energetic efforts were made to strengthen America's military establishment, to expand industrial production, and to lay down a 'two-ocean navy'. Huge supplies and subsidies were shipped to Britain under the principle of Lend-Lease. Both the Destroyers for Bases deal and the Atlantic Charter were in place well before the USA itself took to arms.

1941 saw the Allied coalition transformed by three capital events. On 22 June, Nazi Germany invaded the USSR, thereby changing Stalin from Hitler's friend to Hitler's mortal foe. On 7 December, Japan bombed the US Pacific fleet at Pearl Harbor, thereby destroying American isolationism at one blow. Four days later, in a gesture of encouragement to its Japanese partner, Germany declared war on the USA. From then on, 'the Grand Alliance' was in place.

In the last phase of the war, as victory drew ever closer, any number of countries from Iraq to Liberia joined the Allied ranks. Former German allies such as Italy, Romania, Bulgaria, Hungary, and Finland were forced to change sides. Former neutrals such as Turkey abandoned their neutrality. Finally, on 1 March 1945, Saudi Arabia boldly declared war on both Germany and Japan.

Britain's role in this changing constellation was absolutely crucial, though not necessarily in the ways that many Britons imagined. Britain did not 'win the war'. But it did fight on the winning side and it supplied the third largest group of military forces within the Allied camp. Above all, it supplied the main strand of continuity in the Allied cause. It was the only one of the Allied principals to wage war against Germany almost from the start and right to the end. It held the coalition together after France had fallen by the wayside and until the Soviets and the Americans joined in. Thereafter, it was the great offshore 'aircraft carrier' that gave the Americans their foothold in Europe and which provided the springboard for the D-Day landings. Most importantly, it provided the heart-warming voice of defiance, which, from a position of near hopelessness, promised a triumphal outcome even in the darkest hours.

From the military point of view, Britain's role was strictly limited. For the British war machine was strangely unbalanced. On the one hand, in the Royal Navy and the RAF, the United Kingdom possessed a world-class system of defence forces that could effectively prevent any enemy from invading its island base. On the other hand, despite the largest empire on the globe, it maintained land forces of such modest proportions that they were incapable of independent action in Continental warfare. In 1939, the trained reserves of the British army were smaller than Czechoslovakia's. What is more, British finances hung on a thread. As the appeasers of the 1930s had correctly calculated, a stark choice loomed between saving the Empire or fighting a European war. If Britain were to involve itself in a major conflict, there was little chance of success without major financial assistance from the only source then available – the USA. In which case, willy-nilly, even a victorious Britain would end up as an American dependant.

As in 1914, HMG (His Majesty's Government) in 1939 could not begin to contemplate war against Germany without a principal ally in the West and a principal ally in the East, plus, ideally, a rich backer. Further, HMG's preferences were the same as they had been for thirty years – for France, for 'Russia', and for the USA. Britain was bound to France by the terms of the Treaty of Locarno (signed in 1925). She was not yet bound to the Soviet Union. Indeed, public opinion had spent more than a dozen years in revulsion against Bolshevik misdeeds. But in the 1930s, as the Nazi threat grew, the old Russophile sympathies revived. The British Left, oblivious to the criminal realities of Stalinism, was increasingly seduced by the charms of anti-fascism and increasingly advocated an Anglo-Soviet rapprochement. The British Right, oblivious to the hypocrisy of consorting with a revolutionary dictator, was driven by *Realpolitik*. Writing on 4 February 1936, Lord Beaverbrook, owner of the *Daily Express* and chief crusader of the British Empire, saw nothing wrong in advocating friendship with Moscow:

> In international affairs, the new development seems to be the big part Russia is playing in the world. The Russians have become very respectable. They wear high hats at the funeral of George V, and they please the high Tory newspapers. The truth is that, if we are to

continue to take part in the European game, we need Russia. We are united by a fear of Germany.[3]

The trouble with Britain's preferred scenario was that none of the chosen pieces would fall into place. France, though far stronger than Britain in land forces, did not seem to possess the political will to take international initiatives. During the Munich Crisis of September 1938, the Czechoslovaks were allied to France, not Britain. But it was the British Prime Minister, Neville Chamberlain, who was obliged to take the lead. Unknown to the outside world, the Soviet Union was engaged in a series of political purges and mass murders whose scale at the time was unimagined and whose paralysing effects, not least among the decimated military, rendered any major foreign involvement impossible. In 1939, the Soviet Census Office lasted just long enough (before the censors were themselves purged) to report in *Izvestia* that 17 million people had disappeared during the previous decade. The Red Army, at war in Mongolia and hard pressed by the Japanese, was only saved at the last minute by the brilliance of a young general called Zhukov, who had been rapidly promoted to replace his purged superiors. All thought of Soviet action in Europe was unrealistic until a truce could be arranged on the Mongolian front. This did not happen until after 15 September. As for the United States, though recovering from the Depression, she was still gripped by an extreme form of isolationism, which inspired Congress to block any overt intervention in Europe. In short, the Polish Crisis crept up on a continent in which the old Allied coalition could not be reconstructed. This is exactly the reason why Hitler could calculate quite correctly that, given Stalin's help, he could destroy Poland at very low cost.

The last months of peace, therefore, were filled with a great deal of diplomatic manoeuvring and a great deal of bluff. Britain's guarantee of Poland, issued on 31 March, was not supported by any credible threat of enforcement. It bound Britain to protect Poland's 'independence' and to offer 'all support in her power'. It led to some desultory staff talks between British, French, and Polish officers who agreed, somewhat disingenuously, that a German attack on Poland should be answered by a French attack on Germany. Gen. Gamelin promised to aid the Poles with 'the bulk of our forces'. But no detailed plans were laid.[4]

On 6 April 1939, the guarantee became reciprocal. During the Polish Foreign Minister's visit to London, Poland undertook to defend Britain's independence, if threatened, just as Britain had agreed to defend Poland's.[5]

The Anglo-Polish Treaty of Mutual Assistance of 25 August was even more of a stop-gap measure. It came about because Britain and France had failed to prevent Stalin from throwing in his lot with Hitler. It was signed in haste in response to the Nazi–Soviet Pact concluded only three days earlier. Everyone in Britain knew that it was not an ideal arrangement. Most people would not have hesitated to accept the Soviet Union as the eastern ally, or perhaps the Soviet Union plus Poland to balance the combination of France and Belgium in the West. But such things were simply not in the running. Once Ribbentrop and Molotov had signed their pact, the British Government had only one choice – to have Poland as the eastern ally or to have nothing. And, to put it bluntly, Poland was indisputably better than nothing. Apart from that, time was of the essence. The Wehrmacht was expected to strike at any moment. Indeed, as historians later learned, Hitler actually gave the order to march on 26 August only to countermand it and postpone it for a week.

From Poland's point of view, of course, the Treaty could be regarded as something of a success. Warsaw had feared that Poland might be attacked in isolation, and that none of the powers would bother to defend her. Poland's future could best be protected when a German–Polish conflict became a European one. To be allied to both France and Britain was not a bad prospect.

The Treaty of Mutual Assistance had talked about aggression by an unnamed 'European Power'. A secret protocol clarified the term. It identified the power concerned as Germany and it provided that, if some power other than Germany should make a similarly aggressive move, then 'the Contracting Parties will consult together on the measures to be taken in common.'[6]

Nonetheless, the British establishment did not waver in its conviction that Nazi conduct had passed the bounds of tolerance. Hitler's occupation of Prague in March was the event that brought all shades of opinion to a common conclusion. Even those like Beaverbrook, who continued to argue publicly for avoiding war, privately accepted that war was coming. 'One or the other,' he wrote to a friend in March, 'the British Empire or the German Reich must be destroyed.'[7] The only questions were when and how. The *Daily Express* was still asserting in August that 'there will be no war this year',[8] and, when the Wehrmacht finally marched, the likes of Beaverbrook were still trying to stay aloof. 'Poland', he objected, 'is no friend of ours.'[9] But by then, they were voices crying in the wilderness. The British Government, the British Parliament, and British public opinion as a whole had decided that enough was enough. Even Chamberlain, the arch-appeaser, was determined to respect his commitments. Early on 3 September, he made the fateful broadcast. 'This morning, the British Ambassador in Berlin handed the German Government a final Note stating that unless we heard from them by eleven o'clock that they were prepared at once to withdraw their troops from Poland, a state of war would exist between us. I have to tell you now that no such undertaking has been received, and that consquently this country is at war with Germany.'[10]

Britain's dilemma with its eastern allies was well illustrated by the case of Czechoslovakia, which, after Austria, was the second of Germany's neighbours to feel the heat of Hitler's attentions. In the 1930s, Britain simply had no means of intervening in Central Europe. The RAF had very few warplanes with the practical capability to fly across Germany and to return without refuelling. The Royal Navy could not steam along 'the coast of Bohemia'. The tiny British army could not contemplate marching across Germany. And to take any sort of action on the Continent without French support was unthinkable. Hence, during the Munich Crisis of September 1938, the British Government took the perfectly rational option of appeasing Nazi Germany rather than of confronting it. They did not play their hand very cleverly, and missed the chance of reaching a workable compromise. But they had already made the mistake of issuing an unenforceable guarantee to Austria and of seeing the guarantee humiliatingly sidelined by the *Anschluss*. So they were all too eager to save face and to reach a settlement. Czechoslovakia capitulated without a fight, signing an agreement that proved to be its death warrant. In less than six months, Hitler was in Prague, waving from the same window in Hradčany Castle from which Presidents Masaryk and Beneš had been wont to wave. Slovakia broke away. Bohemia and Moravia were turned into a protectorate of the Reich. President Beneš and his Czecho-Slovak Committee took up residence in Paris, and then, after the fall of France, moved to London, where they stayed until the end of the war.

Throughout the war years, the Czechs planned for the day when their people would rise against the Nazi oppressor and welcome their exiled rulers back home. They were to have many setbacks, and a long wait. Yet in the end their patience was rewarded. A rising broke out in Slovakia in late August 1944, and in the first week of May 1945 a popular rising in Prague immediately preceded Liberation. An understanding was reached between the Western Allies and the Soviets to avoid friction. It was swiftly followed by the homecoming of President Beneš and the restoration of the exiled Government with the blessing of all the Allied powers.

At the other end of the Continent, the victory of Gen. Franco's fascists in Spain had incalculable consequences for British attitudes. For three years, from 1936 to 1939, the Western powers had anxiously watched as the Spanish Republic gradually submitted to the fascist onslaught. Their sympathies undoubtedly lay with the Republic. But they could no more rejoice at the overthrow of the democratic republicans by the Communists than at the bolstering of Franco's cause by forces sent by Hitler and Mussolini. So their judgement long swung in the balance. If Stalin's proxies had triumphed in Spain, the West might well have come to see international communism as the more serious threat. As it was, the triumph of the fascists cemented the belief not only that international fascism had to be stopped but also that the Communists, for all their faults, might have to be recruited to the Allied camp.

Britain's relationship with the country where the Second World War in Europe started, its First Ally, inevitably had its ups and downs. It was born from the collapse of appeasement and of the shared determination to stand and fight against Nazi Germany. It generated a genuine comradeship-in-arms, especially in 1940–41, when Britain faced the prospect of the same national catastrophe by which the First Ally had already been engulfed. It also generated much genuine affection, especially among the diplomats, administrators, and military personnel on both sides who worked and fought in harness. At the same time, like a love affair that faded, it came under growing pressures. Britain found new and more powerful partners. The First Ally was reduced to the ever-growing company of minor clients and hopeful petitioners. It was not abandoned, but it had every right to feel increasingly neglected. In late 1944, a state of informal separation emerged. Formal divorce did not occur until July 1945.

During the September Campaign of 1939, when the First Ally was attacked by Nazi Germany and then by the Soviet Union, the weaknesses of the Allied camp were cruelly exposed. Despite their declarations of war, neither Britain nor France thought fit to activate assistance. And the First Ally was left to face its enemies alone. The RAF dropped leaflets over

Berlin urging the Nazis to desist. The French army crossed Germany's western frontier to test the response, but retreated in haste after coming under fire and advancing less than 10km (six miles). Its complicated mobilization procedures meant that Gamelin's promises could not be kept. At Franco-British staff talks on 12 September, no senior representatives of the First Ally were present, and it was decided that no major action could be taken. The First Ally's fate was thereby sealed. Fighting lasted for five weeks. A German *panzer* column reached the outskirts of the Capital, Warsaw, on 9 September; and repeated reports falsely announced that the defenders had surrendered. In fact, the First Ally continued to resist a merciless siege by land and air until the 27th. A fierce counter-attack to the west of the Capital inflicted heavy losses on the Germans in the third week of September; and some spirited skirmishes on the frontier held up the Red Army before it swarmed through the undefended eastern provinces. A joint Nazi–Soviet victory parade was held at Brest-Litovsk whilst the Capital was still holding out. The last fighting ended on 6 October in the marshland wilderness beyond the River Bug. In all, the Germans had suffered 60,000 casualties, the First Ally 216,000, and the Soviets 11,500. Two images of the conflict stand out. One is that of encircled cavalrymen charging tanks in order to escape. The other is of two Allied planes, reinforced with sticking plaster, taking off for the very last sortie of the campaign.[11]

The diplomatic fall-out of the September Campaign was considerable. Somewhat belatedly, the British Government clarified its understanding of its obligations. When pressed by the First Ally's Ambassador in London, Count R., the Foreign Office explained that according to the secret protocol, the clause in the treaty of 25 August concerning common action against an 'attack by a European Power' could not be used to refer to the attack by the USSR. It also explained that the British guarantee referred only to the First Ally's sovereign status, not to its frontiers. In other words, even if Nazi Germany were defeated, the First Ally could not expect any help in recovering its full pre-war status and territory. The mean-spirited sophistry of British diplomats on this occasion did not bode well for the future.[12]

At the end of the September Campaign, the most important development was the signing on 28 September of the German–Soviet Treaty of Friendship, Demarcation, and Cooperation, which superseded the secret protocols of the earlier Nazi–Soviet Pact. It divided the First Ally's territory into two parts and introduced a slightly modified frontier between the

German Zone in the west and the Soviet Zone in the east. This 'Peace Boundary' was the frontier that the Soviets henceforth, throughout the war, claimed to be rightfully theirs. Nazi and Soviet propaganda was obliged to present Hitler and Stalin as admiring friends and to suppress any hint of incompatibility. The security machines of the Reich and of the Soviet Union were pledged to cooperate against any attempt to resurrect the First Ally's fortunes. Himmler and Beria were handed a joint enterprise venture.

In his final report, the last British Ambassador to pre-war Poland, Sir Howard Kennard, expressed the desire that 'the whole Polish people should at the end of the war have the right to an independent life.' One might consider the sentiment fairly routine. In the event, it proved so dubious in the eyes of the British Foreign Office that the report was not published. As an official, Frank Roberts, noted in the margin: 'I see little prospect of those sections of the Polish people included in the areas taken over by Russia ever being given such an opportunity.'[13] Hence, right from the start, British support for the First Ally was less than complete.

For the majority of the 1.5 million personnel whom the First Ally had mobilized, the war ended there and then. But a considerable number escaped death or captivity, and lived to fight again. They assumed false identities, or took to the woods, or lived quietly in the countryside, biding their time. Almost all used pseudonyms. Col. Thaddeus K. (1895–1966), for example, who had been trained as an Austrian cavalry officer, had commanded a cavalry brigade in the September campaign. Speaking perfect German, he was able to give the slip both to the German military police and to the Gestapo, and lived under a series of false names in Cracow and Warsaw. In due course, he emerged in the Underground as Gen. 'Boor'. Col. Thaddeus P. (1892–1985), a recruit to Pilsudski's Legions during the First World War, had commanded the 19th Infantry Division in September 1939: he was eventually known as Gen. 'Gregory', having used numerous other pseudonyms. Lt.Col. Antoni Ch. (1895–1960) distinguished himself both in 1917–18 and in 1939, when he had commanded the 82nd Regiment of the Siberian Rifles and was then imprisoned. After release, and calling himself variously 'Adam', 'Guardian', 'Strand', 'Rice', 'Hawk', and 'X', he would emerge as Gen. 'Monter', i.e. the electrician. Lt.Col. Leopold O. (1898–1946) was the officer who, on desk duty with the General Staff on the night of 31 August/1 September 1939, had personally received the flood of telegrams from front-line units announcing the Wehrmacht's undeclared invasion. He was later involved in the siege of

Warsaw. Having lived openly as 'John Ant' and 'Johann Müller', he was known to most of his wartime comrades only as 'Yan', 'Cobra 2', 'Bullet', 'Vulture', or 'Termite'. In due course, he became the famous Brig.Gen. 'Bear Cub'. Maj. Emil F. (1895–1953) commanded the 51st Infantry Regiment in 1939. Circulating as 'Lutyk', 'May', 'Sylvester', and 'Weller', he eventually settled for the pseudonym of Gen. 'Nile'. All these men had once seen Austrian service and in 1919–20 had fought in the Polish–Soviet War. For them, to enter the wartime Resistance was simply to follow their patriotic duty and to continue their career.[14]

Western Europeans remember the winter of 1939–40 as 'the Phoney War'. But there was nothing phoney about the war in the East, where Hitler and Stalin were both actively pursuing their conquests. The Finno-Soviet Campaign, for example, began soon after the September Campaign finished, and continued until the eve of Hitler's next major venture. As usual, the Western perspective is rather partial and misleading.

The consequences for the First Ally were unspeakable. Its territory was devoured, its population enslaved, its Government separated from its people. The Nazi zone of occupation was divided into two parts. The western section was directly incorporated into the Reich, from which all 'racial undesirables', mainly Slavs and Jews, were expelled. The eastern section was set up as a separate, lawless General Government, variously dubbed 'Gestapoland' or the 'Gangster Gau'. The Soviet zone of occupation was formally annexed to the USSR, but was cordoned off and administered as a separate region. The northern section, renamed Western Byelorussia, was attached to the existing Byelorussian SSR, and the southern section, renamed Western Ukraine, was attached to the Ukrainian SSR. The Wehrmacht protected its officer prisoners from the SS, and sent them off to regular POW camps in Germany. Many common soldiers were released. The Red Army too sorted officers from other ranks. Both sides filtered the entire population through police measures, which classified different groups according to ideological principles. The Nazis used a pseudo-racial system, which hived off German 'Aryans' from Slav and Jewish 'subhumans' and introduced numerous subdivisions, which put *Reichsdeutsch* at the top of the heap and people of supposedly unmixed Jewish descent at the bottom. The Soviets introduced a pseudo-social system, where political and ethnic discrimination overruled all attempts at genuine class analysis and where Communist party membership opened the gates to the only master class. Everyone was declared a Soviet citizen. Russians and other East Slavs enjoyed preferential treatment, as did so-called 'workers and peasants'. Twenty-one categories of 'enemies of the people', varying from gamekeepers to philatelists and including all 'bourgeois' politicians, all state employees, all private employers, and all religious leaders, were targeted for elimination. In those early months, the Nazis shot 50,000 civilians in so-called reprisals, 15,000 political and religious leaders, and 2,000 Jews. They also created ghettos for Jewish settlement in each of the main cities. They founded several concentration camps, including Auschwitz, for local political suspects, removing tens of thousands of innocent people, including priests, from circulation. The Soviets were better prepared. The NKVD arrived with huge lists of names and addresses for immediate arrest. Their state concentration camp system, or Gulag, had been operating for twenty years. In that first winter, they started the vast operation of deporting 1.8 million either to the Arctic camps or to forced exile in Central Asia. Within a year, many of the deportees were dead. In line with usual Soviet practices, the entire families of persons sentenced to the Gulag were deported to distant exile from which many would never return. About 25,000 captured army and police officers, mainly reservists, were interned by the NKVD, and, after several months' investigation, shot in cold blood.

For obvious reasons, the First Ally watched events in Finland with the keenest interest. Admiration for the Finns, whose tiny army outclassed the largest military force in the world, was mixed with growing excitement at the prospect that the Western powers would intervene. If they did, then Britain and France, like the First Ally, would be simultaneously at war both with the Third Reich and with the USSR. For some time, the prospect looked imminent. After expelling the USSR in December 1939 for aggression, the League of Nations called on its members to give assistance to Finland. Britain and France made preparations for an expeditionary force to which the First Ally was asked to contribute a brigade of 5,000 men drawn from troops already in the West. They were considering an assault on northern Norway, which would have given them the dual benefit of access to Finland and control of Sweden's valuable ore exports. British planes painted with Finnish markings were already standing by on airfields near London when the Finns decided to cut their losses on 12 March 1940 and make peace. The expedition was called off. The First Ally remained in the anomalous position of being fully supported in its struggle against the German oppressor whilst being completely ignored in its struggle against the Soviet oppressor.

Three events of great importance for the First Ally occurred during the period of the Phoney War. Firstly, over 100,000 troops, who had fought in the September Campaign and had taken refuge in Romania and Hungary, undertook the perilous journey via the Balkans and the Mediterranean to southern France or to French possessions like Syria. They arrived in dribs and drabs. But there were enough of them to contemplate the re-formation of a new Allied Army under French operational control. Secondly, the First Ally's Government, which had been interned in Romania at the request of Berlin, resigned, thereby permitting the construction of a fresh Government in France, with a new president, a new national council, a new premier, and a new commander-in-chief. The reconstituted authority was established first in the Regina Hotel in Paris and then in the town of Angers. Thirdly, the original Underground Resistance movement (SZP), which had been set up on the capitulation of the Capital in September 1939, was successfully subordinated to the new exiled Government. It was replaced by a new organization, which at first was called the Union of Armed Struggle (ZWZ), and which took its orders from the new C.-in-C. It was an integral part of the First Ally's armed forces.

The political realignment of 1939–40 restored the First Ally's credentials as a legitimate member of the democratic coalition. The pre-war *Sanacja* regime had been at best a semi-democracy, being dominated by a military element that had taken on a growing nationalistic flavour and had systematically excluded and harassed its opponents. It had also been thoroughly compromised by the catastrophe of September 1939, which many people blamed on its refusal to form an all-party Government of national unity. So now was the time for inclusivity. The reconstructed, exiled Government was headed, as Premier and C.-in-C., by Gen. W. Sikorski, who had kept apart from his former comrades and had played a prominent role in the democratic opposition. Both the National Council abroad, which acted as a sort of substitute parliament, and the political bodies associated with the ZWZ at home operated on the understanding that all democratic parties would be equally respected. The principal parties, in order of their support, were the Peasants (PSL), the Socialists (PPS), the Nationalists (ND), and the Christian Democrat Labour Movement (SP). Other smaller groupings, such as the Jewish Bund, gave a measure of representation to minority interests.

Two marginal political movements, which had operated before the war, often without legal recognition, did not feature in the wartime arrangements. The extreme right-wing fascists (ONR), who admired Mussolini's Italy but hated Hitler's Germany, did not enjoy the confidence of their democratic compatriots. The extreme left-wing Communists (KPP), who never had many committed supporters, had fallen foul of their chief patron. Having established themselves on Soviet territory in the 1930s, they had been caught up in Stalin's purges. Virtually the entire party *actif*, c. 5,000 men and women, many of them Jewish, were shot on Stalin's orders. At the outbreak of war, no coherent Polish Communist movement existed.

In the spring of 1940, when Hitler unleashed a second round of Blitzkrieg, the Western powers suffered a catastrophe similar to that experienced by their First Ally the previous September. Denmark and Luxembourg surrendered in less than twenty-four hours. Holland capitulated after five days; Belgium, despite British and French assistance, after eighteen days. Norway held out for two months. In the French Campaign, which lasted for six weeks from 10 May to 22 June, the combined French and British armies performed much less effectively against the Wehrmacht than the First Ally's forces had performed against the joint attack by the Wehrmacht and the Red Army. 141 German divisions comprehensively overwhelmed the 114 French and British divisions deployed against them, a ratio of less than 3:2, compared to the ratio of 3:1 which the Wehrmacht had enjoyed in September 1939, not counting Soviet involvement. At the end of the fighting, 225,000 British and 115,000 French and Belgian troops were evacuated from Dunkirk, having lost all their arms and equipment. Over 2 million were taken prisoner.

During the debacle of 1940, the First Ally sent its forces into battle alongside the British and French. An infantry brigade went to Narvik in northern Norway, where three of the First Ally's warships also served. The First Ally contributed four infantry divisions, an armoured cavalry brigade, and an air force of four squadrons to the French Campaign. An independent Carpathian Brigade was formed under French command in Syria. The soldiers did not see action until the end of the second week in

June, when Paris was already invested. But the airmen destroyed fifty German planes for the loss of eleven pilots. On 19 June, the C.-in-C. announced that he would fight on, despite the fall of France, and ordered his men to head for Great Britain. Some 80,000 attempted to make the crossing, mainly from Brest and Bordeaux. France, under Marshal Pétain, made its peace with Germany. But the First Ally, in the steps of Churchill, refused to do so.

On 3 July 1940, at the naval port of Mers-el-Kébir in Algeria, the Royal Navy executed one of the most ruthless acts of war to that date. Having called on the French fleet either to scuttle or to surrender, British battleships opened fire at their stationary targets, sinking several vessels and killing 1,300 sailors. No one who saw that demonstration of how the British could treat their former friends could doubt the seriousness of their intent.

The First Ally's predicament at this juncture was extremely precarious. The home country was being devoured by the Nazi and Soviet Occupations. The army was posted to Scotland, whose east coast it was detailed to guard against a possible German invasion. The exiled Government was relocated to London, which was awaiting bombardment by the Luftwaffe at any moment.

It was during the darkest days in the summer of 1940 that the close relationship between Churchill's new Coalition Cabinet and the First Ally was forged. Both the individual personalities and the corporate temper of the two sides were well matched. Churchill and Sikorski formed a two-man mutual admiration society. Both had active military service and distinguished political careers behind them – Sikorski had served in the Polish Legions of the Austrian army in the First World War, had played a decisive role as a field commander during the defeat of the Red Army at Warsaw in 1920, and had been Premier of his country in 1922–23. But both men had lingered in the political doldrums in the 1930s; both were unsullied by the failed policies of their respective Governments in the run-up to war; and both had staked their all on the unequal fight against Nazi Germany. Both were leaders of multi-party coalitions, where dedication to the cause in hand counted more than factional politics.

Among the secondary figures, Churchill's deputy, Clement Attlee, leader of the Labour Party, also showed understanding for the First Ally's plight. Indeed, he was less unpredictable than Churchill. An early and outspoken critic of fascism, he also harboured a healthy reluctance to do business with Communists, whom he regarded as a danger to democratic socialism. (On this point, he had not hesitated in 1939 to expel one of his party's most prominent politicians, Sir Stafford Cripps, whom Churchill would later recall to office.) Churchill's Foreign Minister, Anthony Eden, was rather less resolute than either of them. He had risen through the diplomatic ranks as Minister to the League of Nations and as the right-hand man of Halifax and Chamberlain. He was closely associated with those in the Foreign Office who had long worked for a rapprochement with the Soviet Union; and he ended up with the reputation of being 'the Soviets' favourite British statesman'.[15] Yet he was more of a vacillator than an appeaser; as portrayed in a famous post-war cartoon, the ultimate 'sheep in wolf's clothing'. Relations with the First Ally was an issue on which he vacillated regularly.

Everyday communication between the two Governments was not facilitated by the language barrier. Most members of the exiled Government spoke French, German, or Russian, but not English. No senior Britons spoke Polish; and they had serious problems pronouncing and remembering names, which, lacking a basic knowledge of Polish diacritics and orthography, they could not even read. They could almost cope with Sikorski, and with simple names such as Stroński, Grabski, or Zaleski. But many other examples, like Śmigły-Rydz, or Bohusz-Szyszko, proved quite impossible. As a result, Britishers usually referred to their counterparts either by shortened forms or by their pseudonyms and nicknames. Hence all the Stanisławs became 'Stan'; and Mikołajczyk, even when he became Premier, was widely known as 'Mick'.

The Battle of Britain, which began on 10 July 1940 and came to an end in early October, has gone down in history, in Churchill's words, as 'their finest hour'. It took the form of a protracted air battle in which the RAF successfully thwarted the German attempt to win air supremacy over the Channel in preparation for the planned invasion of the British Isles. After some ninety days of combat, the RAF proved more resilient than Göring's Luftwaffe, forcing their adversaries to withdraw through unsustainable losses. Hitler postponed Operation Sealion indefinitely. But it was a close-run thing. By the time that the Germans disengaged, the RAF's reserves of planes and pilots were on the brink of exhaustion.

The First Ally's contribution to the victory was well appreciated at the time, but later forgotten or minimized. Their pilots served both in RAF units and in their own squadrons, operating under British command. They represented 10 per cent of the total fliers employed, and accounted for 12 per cent of the enemy aircraft destroyed.[16] Most impressively, they incurred only one-third of the average casualty rate, whilst being maintained by a ground crew ratio of only 30:1 as compared to 100:1 in the RAF and 80:1 in the Luftwaffe. Their achievements were particularly valuable in the critical days of mid-September. On the 15th, they accounted for 14 per cent of enemy losses, on the 19th, 25 per cent, and on the 26th, 48 per cent. On one occasion, British officers present were astonished to see a wing commander kissing his fitter's hands. 'Were it not for these hands,' he declared, 'I'd be dead.'[17] The last word lay with Air Chief Marshal Sir Hugh Dowding, the RAF's fighter chief. 'Had it not been for the magnificent material contributed by [the First Ally's] squadrons and their unsurpassed gallantry, I hesitate to say that the outcome of the battle would have been the same.'[18]

Mention should also be made of the key role played by the First Ally's cryptologists. Britain's near hopeless military position in 1940 was greatly strengthened by the growing ability to read most of Germany's encoded radio signals and the accompanying directives. This ability, which was to be perfected at the secret intelligence centre at Bletchley Park, had been greatly facilitated by the pioneering work of the First Ally's specialists, who had presented the British in July 1939 not only with two working replicas of the first-generation Enigma machine, but also with the mathematical formulas for reconstructing its signals.[19]

Once Britain had survived the onslaught at home, it could afford a modest show of strength abroad. In December 1940, Lt.Gen. Wavell moved against a far larger Italian army in the Libyan desert. The First Ally's Carpathian Brigade, which reached Tobruk in August 1941, formed almost one quarter of Allied troops in North Africa.

Most importantly, the American President felt confident enough to launch his clandestine programme for supplying the 'fortress of democracy'. His actions were particularly welcome to the First Ally, which, with the growing prospect of American involvement, was able to consider the possibility of ultimate liberation. The text of the Atlantic Charter, which contained a clause condemning territorial aggrandizement, looked particularly pertinent. If it meant anything at all, it meant that all the territory which had been seized in 1939 would eventually be restored under Western auspices.

Nonetheless, Stalin also felt confident enough to make further gains. Whilst Germany was preoccupied in the West, Soviet troops occupied and annexed the three Baltic states – Lithuania, Latvia, and Estonia – and large tracts of Romania. They had Berlin's approval. During the currency of the Nazi–Soviet Pact, eight countries were absorbed by German aggression and five by Soviet aggression.

On 22 June 1941, the Third Reich attacked its erstwhile associate, the Soviet Union, and with the launch of Operation Barbarossa started the German–Soviet War – the most extensive and the most savage of modern military campaigns. To begin with, the Wehrmacht carried all before it. Within a matter of weeks, millions of Soviet prisoners had been taken; Vilno, Minsk, and Kiev had been captured; and, using its hold on the Baltic states, the Wehrmacht laid siege to Leningrad. By Christmas, a Soviet collapse seemed imminent.

Almost to a man, Western commentators announced that Germany had attacked 'Russia'. The general assumption, worldwide, was that the territory seized by the Wehrmacht was somehow Russian by right or by ethnic composition. In reality, the difference between the 'Soviet Union' and 'Russia' was even greater, and every bit as important, as that between 'the United Kingdom' and 'England'. Yet it was almost universally ignored. The Nazis also ignored it, boasting that they were conquering '*Russland*'. For once, Soviet propaganda was not to blame. All the Soviet maps of the period marked a clear boundary line dividing Soviet Russia (the RSFSR) from the other Soviet republics which made up the USSR. They showed beyond any doubt that the lands which the Wehrmacht entered in June 1941 did *not* form part of Russia but of Estonia, Latvia, Lithuania, Byelorussia, and Ukraine. In the end, one can only fall back on the argument of inertia and complacency. 'Russia' had been the accepted shorthand for the Tsarist Empire during the First World War; and it now stuck as the accepted shorthand for the Soviet Union during the Second World War and after. For the peoples who inhabited the disputed region, the consequences were dire.

Even so, Operation Barbarossa brought significant benefits to the beleaguered First Ally. With Hitler and Stalin in cahoots, the First Ally had been effectively marginalized; but with Hitler and Stalin at war, she became an important player. As the Wehrmacht pressed on towards Moscow, Stalin desperately needed help. The result was a Soviet–Polish treaty signed on 30 July, and a corresponding military agreement. In essence, the USSR agreed to annul the German–Soviet treaties of 1939, to restore diplomatic relations, and to permit the formation of an army drawn from the millions of the First Ally's subjects who were being held as Soviet prisoners. For its part, the First Ally agreed to cooperate with the USSR in the prosecution of the war. The British were delighted. For the first time in the war, they had *two* eastern allies.[20]

The military agreement followed on 14 August. It stated that the First Ally's new army should be organized on Soviet soil, that it would owe allegiance to the exiled Government in London, and that it would operate on the Eastern Front under Soviet command. The army's commander was to be appointed by the exiled Government, but with Soviet approval.

Unfortunately, the frontier question was left in a state of considerable inprecision. Despite the desperate plight of the Soviets, no one on their side would accept the formula that the First Ally's eastern frontiers should return to pre-war positions. A clause in the treaty of 30 July seemed to point in that direction. The Soviet Government recognized that 'the Soviet–German treaties of 1939 relative to territorial changes . . . have lost their validity.' The British Foreign Office confirmed in a note that it did not recognize any territorial changes after August 1939. Yet that same day, when pressed in Parliament, the Foreign Secretary replied that the note 'does not involve any guarantee of frontiers by HMG.' In the midst of the double negatives and the contorted diplomatic verbiage, nothing had been properly agreed.

On 11 December 1941, in an act of supreme folly, Hitler announced in the Reichstag that Germany had declared war on the USA. He was reacting to the news from Pearl Harbor. At the time, having already caught sight of the gleaming spires of the Kremlin, a German *panzer* group was fighting on the outskirts of Moscow. Hitler was counting on the chance that the critical phase of the European war would be finished before the Americans could intervene effectively.

The creation of the Grand Alliance inevitably handed precedence to the dealings of the 'Big Three'. On the other hand, if the Red Army could avoid defeat, and if Britain could keep the Atlantic lines of communication open, there was now a real chance of constructing a winning coalition. And, as the First Ally well knew, the comprehensive defeat of Germany, which now occupied all parts of her territory, was the *sine qua non* for the restoration of the country's independence.

What is more, the Americans, unlike the British, could be expected to keep the Soviet Union's expansionist ambitions in check. They appeared to be resolutely opposed, as their spokesmen repeatedly stated, to 'all forms of expansion by conquest.' They were ruled by a Democratic president, whose party was specially sensitive to a large block of immigrant voters with close ethnic ties to the First Ally. Most importantly, since they produced a large part of the war material on which Soviet survival depended, they possessed the most powerful instrument for ensuring Stalin's good conduct.

From the psychological point of view, however, the entry of the Americans recoloured the emotional climate of the Alliance. They had none of the cynical, world-weary reserve of the British imperialists, and they had an infectious, childlike desire to see the Alliance as one great happy family. Churchill, the old anti-Bolshevik, was well aware that he had been obliged to make 'a pact with the Devil'. The British socialists, whose influence was growing, knew all about the incompatibility of communism and democracy. But few Americans shared such inhibitions. They wanted something more than a workmanlike partnership to see the war through. They wanted a moral crusade, the victory of Good over Evil. It was they who introduced the dominant mood, in which the Soviet dictator became 'Uncle Joe', in which, in discussing the Soviet Union, one talked only of the Red Army's heroism, in which 'the Russians' could be seen as 'freedom-loving democrats', and in which events before 1941 were not mentioned. Indeed, since the Americans had played no part in the first stage of the war, they were genuinely uninterested in events prior to their involvement. Nothing could have suited Stalin better.

In this new diplomatic configuration, the First Ally's Premier left London to visit both Stalin and Roosevelt. From Stalin, he obtained final details for organizing the army in Russia. But he did not obtain any credible information about his 25,000 missing officers, whom Stalin suggested might have fled to Manchuria. From Roosevelt, he received a warm welcome, and the prospect of benefiting, via Britain, from Lend-Lease. But he did not receive a separate treaty of alliance. The USA was keeping its formal commitments to a minimum.

1942 was the year in which the Grand Alliance mobilized the means of its survival. The German–Soviet War hung in the balance. The Wehrmacht had been repulsed from the gates of Moscow and had still not captured Leningrad. But in a vast summer offensive in the south, it set off for the

River Volga and the oilfields of the Caucasus. The Western powers were in no state to open a second front. The naval war in the Atlantic between the convoys and the U-boats was at its height. The 'Western Desert' in North Africa was the only place where the Allies were capable of mounting an offensive.

The fighting in the Western Desert took place over enormous distances but with tiny forces. The Italian army had been greatly strengthened by the arrival of Rommel's Afrika Korps. It faced the British Eighth Army based in Egypt. Some violent swings of fortune that brought Rommel over Egypt's borders were terminated by the second Battle of El Alamein in October, when Lt.Gen. Montgomery broke down Rommel's guard and mounted a victorious drive all the way to Tripoli. By that time, the Americans had landed in Morocco and a second British force was in Algeria. The Afrika Korps was trapped between Allied armies advancing from east and west. It surrendered in Tunis on 13 May 1943. The North African Campaign was dismissed by some as a peripheral sideshow. But it gave the beleagured Allies a great boost of morale. Churchill called it 'the end of the beginning'.

Meanwhile, the First Ally was meeting endless organizational difficulties in Russia. Its army there, which was supposed to possess 96,000 men, received rations for only 44,000. The NKVD was obstructing recruitment, especially of Jewish, Ukrainian, and Byelorussian nationals. Suitable armaments were not forthcoming, and comradely relations were soured. In due course, the commander, Gen. Anders, moved his troops from the Volga to Uzbekistan. In April 1942, convinced that the Soviets would not respect their obligations, he evacuated en masse to Persia and then in August to Palestine, where they were assigned by the British to the reserves of the Eighth Army.

Tens of thousands of civilians accompanied the evacuation of the Anders Army. Most of them were former deportees, victims of the Gulag or of forced labour. They were on the point of death from exhaustion, starvation, and disease. They included some 40,000 ragged orphans. Their first-hand knowledge of Soviet realities conflicted starkly with the rosy Anglo-American picture of Uncle Joe's heroic paradise.[21] They were told in no uncertain terms to keep their mouths shut.

The prospect of a Polish army making for Palestine reminded politicians of the Jewish issue. In January 1942, Gen. Sikorski told Eden of his hopes that the end of the war would see large numbers of Polish Jews emigrating to Palestine. The idea was not well received. The British were still aiming to keep Palestine as a predominantly Arab country. A Foreign Office minute expressed the hope that as many pre-war Polish Jews as possible would be confined in the USSR 'where Zionism is not encouraged'.[22]

1943 opened with a second inter-Allied Conference, held in January at Casablanca under the code-name of Symbol. Roosevelt and Churchill discussed grand strategy. Stalin, though invited, was unable to attend. Three capital decisions were taken. With virtually no discussion, the Grand Alliance adopted the policy of unconditional surrender. A colossal nonstop bombing offensive was to be mounted against Germany from the UK. And in place of a Second Front in France, the Western Allies were to transfer their forces from North Africa to Italy. Each decision had far-reaching implications.

The prospect of fighting on until Germany surrendered unconditionally appeared to suit the First Ally's interest. It seemed to eliminate the possibility of separate settlements in Western and Eastern Europe, and it increased the likelihood that the Western powers would be able to prevent unilateral Soviet initiatives. It greatly strengthened the will of the First Ally's exiled Government and its forces to continue their lonely struggle.

The Allied bombing offensive was controversial at the time and has caused much dissension among historians. But its destructive might is not in doubt. It culminated in the destruction of Dresden in February 1945. Once again, the contribution of the First Ally's aircrews, as in the Battle of Britain, was impressive.

The prospect of a campaign in Italy gave a sense of purpose to the Anders Army in Palestine. Training began immediately to reform as the 2nd Polish Corps and to join the 'Desert Rats' of the Eighth Army, who now had the Eternal City in their sights. For a predominantly Catholic formation, this was no mean goal. On the other hand, by postponing the major landings of the Western powers in France, it gave Stalin more time to consider his priorities.

Later in 1943, Allied fortunes were transformed by the stupendous Soviet victories at Stalingrad and Kursk. Stalingrad, where the Germans lost 250,000 men, ended in the surrender of von Paulus's Sixth Army.[23] It was the psychological turning point. Kursk, which is generally rated as the biggest armoured battle in history, destroyed the Germans' ability to mount another major offensive. Henceforth, the Red Army never lost the initiative, and moved steadily westwards on the long road to Berlin. The Soviet Union's prestige rose astronomically. Criticism of Stalin looked churlish.

Political developments were dominated by the inescapable geographical fact that in marching from Russia to Germany, the Red Army would have to cross the country in between where the war had originally started. So the problem of the First Ally re-emerged. Stalin took several relevant steps. He had already permitted the re-creation of a Polish Communist movement under a new name. He was signalling to the comrades of the Communist camp that his early policy of wiping the First Ally from the map had been reversed. He then did two things. Firstly, he set up a clutch of political and military bodies in Moscow which remained under Soviet control but which could form the basis of a surrogate post-war administration. Secondly, on 25 April 1943, he broke off diplomatic relations with the exiled Government. In retrospect, one can see that he was sounding out the limits of Western tolerance.

Berlin worked tirelessly to deepen this rift in the Allied camp. Among other things, it publicized the discovery of a mass grave, near Smolensk in Russia, containing the corpses of 4,500 of the First Ally's missing officers, and it assembled an International Committee of Enquiry, which declared the 'Katyn Forest Massacre' a Soviet crime. The First Ally appealed to the International Red Cross, thereby providing the pretext for the break in diplomatic relations with Moscow that ensued. In Allied circles, the appeal was widely thought to be 'anti-Soviet'. As historians later confirmed, the British and American Governments were well enough informed that on this occasion the Nazis had no need to lie. Yet they attributed the massacre to the Nazis all the same.[24]

The First Ally was further shaken on 4 July 1943, when its Premier and Commander-in-Chief was killed in an air crash off Gibraltar. The dead man had cooperated loyally with Stalin, was respected by Churchill, and was liked by Roosevelt. By universal consent, he was a very decent and flexible person to deal with. His removal worked only in the interest of those who wanted to disrupt the Alliance. Several candidates were suspected of murder.[25]

The most immediate effect of the Gibraltar catastrophe, however, lay in the necessary reconstitution of the exiled Government. Amidst considerable in-fighting, the post of Premier was separated from that of Commander-in-Chief. The Premiership fell to the leader of the exiled Peasant

Party, a member of the pre-war opposition, and sometime activist in the Poznan Rising against Germany, Stanislas M. The chief military post went to Gen. Casimir S., a man of a different political orientation, who had been a personal friend of the 'Great Marshal' and one of the masterminds of the victory in 1920. The new Premier was well viewed by his British allies. The new Commander-in-Chief, though a down-to-earth realist, was viewed less enthusiastically.[26]

In November 1943, the 'Big Three' met face to face for the first time. Stalin was in buoyant mood. Roosevelt and Churchill, having failed to mount a second front in Europe for the second year running, were eager to make concessions. Churchill took the initiative in proposing that the Nazi–Soviet Peace Boundary of 1939, now misleadingly renamed the 'Curzon Line', could stand as the basis for further discussions about the Soviet Union's post-war western frontier. He agreed with Stalin that the First Ally should be compensated by an unspecified slice of German territory in the west. Roosevelt put a further gloss on proceedings during a subsequent, private encounter with Stalin. But they all discussed the matter in secret, in the absence of any representative from the First Ally, and they kept the details secret.

The Italian Campaign opened in July 1943 when Allied forces landed in Sicily. The first stage was rapidly achieved. But the task of forging a path up the mountainous spine of Italy reduced progress to a crawl. Mussolini's fascist state collapsed. But the Germans conducted a brilliant fighting retreat. The 972km (604 miles) from Syracusa to Rome was to take 332 days. The largest single obstacle was encountered at the heavily fortified hill of Monte Cassino, which barred the road to Rome for the first five months of 1944.

The British Eighth Army in Italy was a wonderful microcosm of the Allied cause. Fighting alongside the US Fifth Army and commanded by Gen. Oliver Leese, it was composed of three British army corps, containing two Indian and two Canadian divisions, Gen. Juin's French Expeditionary Corps, Gen. Freyberg's New Zealand Corps, and Gen. Anders's 2nd (Polish) Corps.

Monte Cassino held out against three desperate Allied assaults, and only succumbed to the fourth attempt. In the first battle (11 January to 7 February), the French and the Americans struggled in vain against both a determined enemy and atrocious weather. In the second battle (15–18

February), which was marked by the pointless bombing of the Benedictine Monastery, the New Zealanders led the unsuccessful attack. In the third battle (15–25 March), the Indian Division tried and failed. In the fourth battle (11–18 May), the precipitous slopes of Monastery Hill were finally stormed by three frontal, uphill charges undertaken with enormous loss by two divisions of Anders's men. A British officer, later an Oxford professor, who watched them, said that he had never seen such a display of fearless courage. The victory opened the road to Rome, which was captured three weeks later. For the soldiers who had carried their red-and-white pennants to the summit of Cassino, it was celebrated as a stage on the much longer road to their own capital.

For the first six months of 1944, the Red Army was advancing across a wide stretch of politically disputed territory. It crossed the pre-war Polish–Soviet frontier on 4 January. But it did not reach the 'Peace Boundary' on the River Bug until July. Throughout that time, it was engaged in a vast and crucial military operation, namely the destruction of the German Army Group Centre. So politics, in Europe's most war-devastated zone, did not yet come to the fore. But the Red Army's highly trained political officers were fully aware of the stakes. So, too, were the First Ally's exiled Government and its local Underground representatives. The local population was not consulted. The Western powers were not specially interested. Very few of their most expert specialists would have been sufficiently well briefed to know that this was exactly the part of Europe which was home to the two divisions that were preparing to storm Monte Cassino.

Nomenclature is revealing. In Soviet usage, the lands in question were known as Western Byelorussia and Western Ukraine. In the First Ally's usage, they were known as the *Kresy*, or 'Borders'. To most British and Americans, if they could be located at all, they were known, anachronistically and quite inaccurately, as Western Russia.

Once the Red Army was approaching the Borders, the First Ally's Government in London felt obliged to react and to issue instructions to its people on the spot. It decided on a strategy under the name of Operation Tempest. The Red Army was to be welcomed. The Underground Resistance movement was to come out of hiding whenever the German–Soviet front approached, and the retreating Germans were to be attacked. Wherever possible, local officials were to take control as the Germans left and to make friendly provision for the safe passage of the Soviet forces. Nothing could have angered the Soviets more.

The D-Day Landings in Normandy on 6 June 1944 finally opened up the Second Front which the Western Allies had repeatedly postponed. Operation Overlord was the largest amphibious operation in world history. But it took almost two months for it to be firmly established. The British did not capture Caen, one of the initial D-Day objectives, until 18 July. The Americans did not break out into open country until the end of the month. The German defenders of Normandy were not forced to retreat en masse until the Battle of the Falaise Pocket (19–21 August). The signal contribution of the First Ally to these operations lay with the 1st (Polish) Armoured Division, which landed in Normandy in the second wave and which took up station to the south of Caen as the forward element of the First Canadian Army. At Falaise, they were 1,244km (773 miles) from Berlin.

The main consequences of the Normandy landings were twofold. The liberation of Paris and of northern France was at hand. And the Western armies could move into position as the second arm of the colossal pincer, which, in conjunction with the Soviets in the east, would gradually crush the Nazi Reich to death.

In the first half of 1944, the relative weight of Great Britain within the Grand Alliance declined, whilst that of the USA and the USSR increased. The American and the Soviet stars were manifestly in the ascendant. The First Ally's position was affected accordingly.

At the official level, American attitudes to the exiled Government had always been correct, and often cordial. Polish officials were warmly and frequently received in Washington. Yet, as time passed, any careful observer could have seen that the American facade of back-slapping bonhomie concealed a strong desire to avoid serious commitments. The US Government never shared the hostile political views of certain influential voices within American opinion, such as that of the publicist and commentator Walter Lippmann, who saw no reason why the First Ally's republic should be restored.[27] At the same time, it did not regard assistance to the First Ally as one of its responsibilities. Instances of prevarication multiplied. For over a year, for example, the exiled Government had been urging Washington to replace Ambassador Drexel Biddle, who had left his post in London in mid-1943. But the State Department showed little sense of urgency. A replacement, Arthur Bliss Lane, was found in July 1944; but he was kept waiting throughout the summer for confirmation by the Senate, and he never reached London in time to present his credentials.[28] Repeated delays over the supply of twelve long-range aircraft were still more frustrating. Ever since Gen. Sikorski's visit to Washington in December 1942, the exiled Government had been expecting delivery of these planes, which were intended to form an independent wing for liaison with the Polish Underground. Considering that the US was ferrying hundreds of new aircraft to Britain every month, the request was very modest. Indeed, it appears to have been accepted in principle. But it generated any number of excuses, and was never actually met. Instead, the exiled Government was informed of the availability of other types of equipment:

> S/Ops/4391 1st July 1944
> To: Maj. M. J. T. Pickles [War Office]
> From: Lt. Pudding
> We have received a signal from our representative in the USA, that he can obtain through Lendlease a Motion Picture Sound Projector, Automatic Motion Picture Camera Portable Film Recorder . . . together with single Film Recording System all 35mm, but before making further arrangements it is necessary that clearance be made through the War Office for these goods . . .[29]

This letter from Lt. 'Pudding' to Maj. Pickles needs no commentary.

When Stalin broke off diplomatic relations with the First Ally in April 1943 over the Katyn affair, he did so suddenly, brutally, and, as it later proved, on totally unjustified grounds. Since he had personally signed the order to execute the Polish officers, he knew exactly what he was doing. He was testing the political waters of the Grand Alliance to see just how far he could go. If he was right in believing that he could push the British and Americans to connive in a monstrous falsehood about the mass murder of their friends, he could be confident about pushing them to the brink on many less sensitive matters. British officialdom found itself in a quandary. The secret report on Katyn, prepared by Sir Owen O'Malley, ambassador to the exiled Government, pointed to the probability of Soviet guilt. But it proved so unpalatable to the pro-Soviet prejudices of the majority of his colleagues that they preferred to feign confusion and to admit nothing. All the Western information services were instructed to follow the Soviets and to describe Katyn as a German crime.[30]

In mid-1944, a second problem arose. It concerned Moscow's demands for the repatriation of 'Soviet citizens' who were falling into Western hands in ever-increasing numbers. Whenever British or American armies overran districts relieved of German Occupation, they invariably captured men and women from Eastern Europe who had either been used by the Nazis for slave labour or who had served under German command in one of the collaborationist formations. Some Allied officials thought the matter quite straightforward. 'The Russians want their people back, just as we want our people back.' But others could spot a trap. For one thing, many of the alleged 'Soviet citizens' were not Soviet citizens at all. For another, those who came from the First Ally's eastern provinces continued to be recognized by the Western powers as Polish citizens. And lastly, if Soviet practice were to run to form, all persons handed over to the NKVD for repatriation could be given a very short expectation of life.

The British Cabinet discussed the matter briefly on 17 July 1944, and one of the Cabinet ministers, Lord Selborne, passed his reflections to the Foreign Secretary. He talked with some distaste about 'the prospect of sending many thousands of men to die either by execution or in Siberia . . .'; and 'in the interests of humanity' he raised the possibility of 'absorbing them in some of the less populated countries of the world'. Eden gave the idea short shrift. 'If the men don't go to Russia', he minuted, 'where do they go? We don't want them here.' He then realized that numbers of British prisoners were in Soviet care, and his stance hardened:

> To refuse the Soviet Government's request for the return of their own men would lead to serious trouble with them. We have no right whatsoever to do this, and they would not understand our humanitarian motives . . . [it] would arouse their gravest suspicions.[31]

The repatriation affair had numerous repercussions. One of them was to make forceful intervention on the First Ally's behalf so much more delicate.

In early July 1944, the Soviets unleashed a ferocious offensive in the central sector of the Eastern Front. It was designed by agreement to coincide with the expected Allied break-out from Normandy and hence to prevent the

Germans from boosting their defences in France. Gen. Rokossovsky's First Byelorussian Front surged through the German front line in a hailstorm of men and machines. It rapidly reached the fortress of Brest-Litovsk, where the German–Soviet War had begun three years earlier, and surged across the River Bug. Beyond the Bug, the Vistula waited. The Red Army had reached a new territorial sphere which even Stalin did not claim as part of the Soviet Union – so it changed its name to the Soviet Army. At Lublin, they were only 650km (405 miles) from Berlin.

The military situation was very fluid. The Germans were pulling back. But they were quite capable of mounting counter-attacks, as indeed they did. Observers on the spot could hardly gauge what was happening. Column after column of weary but disciplined German soldiers trudged towards safety on the far side of the Vistula. The front-line echelons of Soviet troops pressed hard on their heels.

The political situation was particularly bewildering. The Soviets were not behaving as they had done five years before. In 1939, their main message had been 'Your country is finished.' Now, they were going out of their way to proclaim 'Your country will rise again.' Moreover, they had brought a separate army with them made up of local lads. It had been recruited from former refugees and deportees, whom no one had expected to see again; and it was commanded by a pre-war officer. The National Liberation Committee, which they also installed, did not look like the usual Communist-type organization. It was not headed by a Russian or by a known Communist, but by an unknown little man, who was presenting himself both as a local and as a non-party figure. His colleagues seemed to include a peasant, a priest, a prince, and another pre-war officer. It was all strangely moderate. Like the British Labour Party at the time, the Committee advocated the nationalization of industry and promised agrarian reform. But it did not talk of 'Five-Year Plans' or the collectivization of agriculture. Above all, it did not claim to be a Provisional Government. So the inevitable suspicions were accompanied by gaping mouths. At all their political meetings, the Committee's representatives were careful to hang the First Ally's national flag alongside the Hammer and Sickle, the Stars and Stripes, and the Union Jack.

Shortly after entering Lublin, the Soviet authorities took the front-line press corps to view a dreadful sight. Nine whole months before the Western armies could reveal the secrets of Belsen and Buchenwald, the Soviets showed the world the horrors of Maidanek. For the very first time, outside cameras zoomed in on a major Nazi concentration camp, highlighting the sinister watch-towers, the electrified wire, the piles of abandoned clothes and suitcases, and the heaps of rotting corpses. Distressed correspondents interviewed the emaciated survivors, and recounted their barely credible stories. Nothing could have given greater weight to the official Soviet contention that its army was the bearer of true Liberation.

During Gen. Sikorski's lifetime, Britain's relations with its First Ally were often conducted at the very highest level, since, to the envy of many lesser fry, the General enjoyed regular and direct access to Churchill. Contacts were greatly facilitated by the exiled Government's presence in London. The British Foreign Office was in daily touch both with the much respected ambassador to St James, Count R., and with the exiled Ministry of Foreign Affairs. Officials from the British War Office could talk directly to and arrange meetings with their opposite numbers in the exiled Ministry of National Defence. For obvious reasons, Britain's external intelligence service, MI6, enjoyed specially close relations with the II Bureau, which ran a notably far-flung and effective intelligence service of its own, particularly in the Third Reich and in the USSR.

As time went on and the First Ally organized an elaborate Resistance movement, the VI Bureau of the exiled Government's General Staff gained prominence. The VI Bureau was charged with the supervision of contacts with the occupied country in general and with underground military formations in particular. It rapidly became the focus of attention both for the British intelligence service and for the Special Operations Executive.

The ill-concealed rivalry of Britain's Intelligence Service and SOE was one of the facts of British wartime life. The former, old-established and global in scope, was officially subject to the Foreign Office. The latter, which was created by Churchill in July 1940 'to set the Continent ablaze', answered directly to the Prime Minister and was inevitably regarded as a dangerous upstart and interloper. It quickly became Britain's principal instrument for organizing secret missions into Nazi-occupied Europe.[32]

The personalities who counted most in this complicated relationship were not always the ones who held the top offices. Of course, when it came to crucial decisions, the leading figures could not be circumvented. Churchill as Prime Minister, Anthony Eden as Foreign Secretary and Gen. Brooke as CIGS (Chief of the Imperial General Staff) featured prominently on the British side throughout the war. By 1944, the most active members of the exiled Government were the Premier, Mick; the Commander-in-

Chief, Gen. S.; the Foreign Minister, Thaddeus R.; and the Chief of the General Staff, Gen. Ko.[33] It was a great misfortune that the exiled President suffered serious health problems and was unable to prevent the growing rift which developed between the Prime Minister and the Commander-in-Chief. The rift caused indecision in the First Ally's Cabinet, and bewilderment among their British friends.

Four or five Britons enjoyed close, everyday contacts with the exiled Government. Maj. Bryson of MI6 had been the original UK liaison officer in Britain's Military Mission to the First Ally in France in 1939–40. His colleague, Cmdr. Wilfred 'Biffy' Dunderdale, who reported straight to 'C', the head of MI6, ran a small unit that worked with the II Bureau. Col., later Gen. Colin Gubbins, the founder and director of SOE, had very strong Polish connections. He had worked in Warsaw in 1939 as a member of Carton de Wiart's team in the British Military Mission, spoke Polish, and sympathized strongly with the First Ally's fate. So, too, did his companion from 1939, Lt.Col. Peter Wilkinson, who became one of SOE's most influential officers. Col. Harold Perkins, the commander of SOE's Polish and Czechoslovak Section, the son of an industrial family with wide Continental interests, had actually been brought up in Silesia, had served in HM Consular Service in Warsaw, and spoke the languages fluently. Above them all was Sir Owen St Clair O'Malley, who since February 1943 had held the position of HM Ambassador to the exiled Government. O'Malley stood out in the foreign service for his secret despatch to Churchill of 24 May 1943, which demolished the Soviet case for regarding the Katyn Massacres as a Nazi crime, and for his repeated appeals for a more ethical approach to foreign policy. 'O'Malley reminded the policy-makers that the Soviet alliance was simply a matter of grim necessity: they should not deceive themselves or others that it was built on anything more fundamental, like shared values. In the circumstances prevailing . . . this was a highly inconvenient message for all concerned'.[34]

Two Polish citizens deserve special mention. Gen. Stanislas T. was widely known in London by his Underground pseudonym 'Tabor'. He only reached England in April 1944, when he surprisingly walked straight into the directorship of the VI Bureau with the high rank of Deputy Chief of the General Staff. Before that, he had been number three in the hierarchy of the First Ally's Underground Resistance movement. His background was interesting. During the First World War, having distinguished himself in the mathematical department of the Imperial Russian University in Warsaw, he had been schooled as a cadet in the Higher

Artillery School in Odessa, and had received a commission from the Tsar. Subsequently, as a graduate of the Higher Military School and of the École Superieure de Guerre in Paris, and commander of successive artillery regiments, he belonged to the cream of the pre-war military elite. At the same time, he was a passionate opponent of the *Sanacja* regime, and an unrelenting critic of Marshal Pilsudski. Brusque, arrogant and secretive, he kept many of his opinions to himself. But he came to be described by one of his biographers as that rarest of creatures – a Polish Titoist: a proponent of a national brand of Communism, independent of Moscow.[35] (It was Tabor who, as duty officer at HQ at the end of July 1944, had set aside the two controversial telegrams forwarded from Barnes Lodge.)

Joseph R., known to his friends as 'Recio', was a still more curious character. He was best known in wartime London as Gen. Sikorski's personal secretary. But his official position covered a multitude of less public connections, which all led back in one way or another to the Allied intelligence services. Born an Austrian subject in Cracow, the son of a prominent barrister, he had moved to Western Europe as a young man, studying at both the Sorbonne and, like his contemporary Lewis Namier, at the LSE. The protégé of aristocratic and influential Franco-Polish Catholic families who had taken care of his education after his father's death, he had learned to glide with ease in the highest social, political, and cultural circles. His favourite *nom de guerre* was 'Salamander'.

A polyglot and a polymath, Salamander seems to have pursued at least three careers. One, as a literary author, was helped by his long-standing connection with Joseph Conrad, who had attended the same *Gymnazium* in Cracow, and who probably introduced him to the British intelligence services. The second, as an international negotiator, began in 1917, when he was involved on the Allied side in the secret but abortive talks for a separate peace with Austria. The third, as a Latin American specialist, began shortly after, when for undisclosed reasons he left Paris in a hurry for Mexico. Thereafter, variously suspected of being an agent of the Vatican, the Bolsheviks, the Americans and the Freemasons, he cropped up time and again in all sorts of unlikely places. He played an active part in the creation of the international Trades Union movement, where he made friends with British socialists like Ernest Bevin and Stafford Cripps. He was in Spain during the Spanish Civil War. But in 1939 he was observed living in considerable poverty in a dingy one-room flat off Baker Street. His fortunes revived with the outbreak of war. It was Salamander who flew to France in July 1940, and on Churchill's express orders accompanied

Gen. Sikorski to England.[36] In 1941, he worked hard with Sikorski to forge the Polish–Soviet agreements. He even stayed on in Moscow as chargé d'affaires to oversee the establishment of the exiled Government's embassy. At this time, he became a personal acquaintance of Molotov.

Salamander's association with MI6 remains a closely guarded secret, though it is hardly in doubt. A recent study based on official sources named him as an 'agent of influence' of MI6, thereby confirming what many had always suspected.[37] But the label may not suffice. In some eyes, he was an overambitious fantasist.

After Sikorski's death in July 1943, Salamander was to some extent a faithful dog without a master. He certainly shed copious tears at the General's funeral. He was a man looking for a mission, and in due course he found one. In January 1944 he embarked on an enterprise whose exact purposes have remained obscure to the present day. He prepared to be parachuted into his home country. For a man aged fifty-six and of no great athletic ability, it was a risky step, not least because he refused to take the usual course of practice jumps for fear of losing his nerve. What is more, his task was so secret that he intended to wear a mask to hide his identity both from his companions and from the aircrew that would fly him out. He travelled to an RAF base near Brindisi to await the flight. He was repeatedly kept waiting, and read Plato to pass the time. The only person in the exiled Government who had been informed of his departure was Premier Mick. Meanwhile, rumours began to circulate in the corridors of the Rubens Hotel that Salamander had too many enemies and would be killed on arrival.[38] On present evidence, the full extent of British involvement cannot be gauged. But the mission was important in that it provided the only sign that the First Ally's British patrons were taking trouble to gather authoritative intelligence on the ground. Early in 1944, strong British missions were operating with the Underground both in Yugoslavia and in Greece, but Salamander was the only known British agent to be directed at that time to the banks of the Vistula.

The First Ally had relatively few British friends of long standing, though their number grew rapidly in the early years of the war. The most obvious circle of supporters lay within the Roman Catholic constituency and with literary people, such as the late G. K. Chesterton and Hilaire Belloc. At Court, the Duke and Duchess of Kent, who had spent their pre-war honeymoon in Warsaw, founded a coterie of well-connected sympathizers.

In Government, the War Office, which was better informed than most about the First Ally's contributions and sacrifices, could usually be counted on. So, too, could the representatives of cities and counties, especially in Scotland, where the First Ally's troops were stationed. Furthermore, an outspoken company of prominent individuals had been deeply inspired by the First Ally's determination to stand and fight. They were not always the likeliest of Polonophiles. One of them was Lord Vansittart, by then retired, but until recently the Permanent Under-Secretary at the Foreign Office. A second was Philip Noel-Baker MP, a Quaker and a pacifist, who nonetheless was often moved to defend the First Ally's interests. A third was the leading journalist J. L. Garvin, editor of the *Observer* for over thirty years, who was not impressed by the lack of impartiality adopted by many papers, especially *The Times*. Others included Maj.Gen. Sir Alfred Knox MP, sometime chief of the British Military Mission to Siberia, and Mr John McGovern, a doughty protester and Labour Party MP.

Among British residents of Polish origin, there were four prominent names. Joseph Conrad had died in 1924, and had no equivalent successor. The two men with the highest profile in the 1940s came from a very different milieu. Both were 'non-Jewish Jews' and both for different reasons had fairly jaundiced views about the land of their birth. Isaac Deutscher had been Secretary of the Polish Communist Party (KPP) before fleeing in 1932 to escape the warning signs of Stalinism. Whilst preparing ground-breaking political studies, which culminated in his biographies of *Trotsky* (1954/1959/1963) and *Stalin* (1949), he was very active in left-wing journalism. Lewis Niemirowski Bernstein, who took the surname of Namier, had carved out a career as Britain's foremost eighteenth-century historian. But he, too, wrote widely as a contemporary publicist, though arguing from a Zionist, as distinct from Deutscher's Marxist, standpoint. His collection of essays entitled *Conflicts* (1942) was an influential book of its day.

Namier, of course, had once worked in the Foreign Office, and many friends of the First Ally were tempted to think that he belonged to a deeply unsympathetic, institutional tradition. The generalization was not entirely fair. In Britain's diplomatic circles, the First Ally had both advocates and detractors. But there was a majority of British diplomats who were so preoccupied with other things that they were apt to regard the First Ally as a bit of a nuisance. Most of them were not so much hostile as otherwise engaged. Most would have agreed that the First Ally's problems should not be allowed to impinge on what they regarded as more important issues. Anthony Eden's personal secretary, Pierson Dixon, was certainly of this opinion: 'It is obvious', he recorded in his diary in February 1944,

> that no Englishman is going to war with Russia ... for Poland ... Poland as a continental power does not excite the same sympathies in English breasts as does an island power like Greece ... The consensus is clear: ... we offer to back a reasonable solution and go no further [even if the alternative is the absorption of Poland into the USSR].[39]

To people of his persuasion, the 'First Ally' was fine so long as it fitted in with their pet schemes. If it didn't, it was 'intransigent'. Intransigence was often seen as the First Ally's most prominent characteristic.

Nonetheless, Britons and Americans who were interested in learning more about the First Ally would not have been short of reading. Twenty years earlier, when the 'New Europe' had emerged from the First World War, a flood of books had been published to present the restored or newly independent countries to the English-speaking public. The quality varied. But for those who cared to explore, the libraries contained a substantial collection of titles recounting the history, geography, politics, economics and cultural life of 'The Lands Between'. A body of the First Ally's main literary works was published in English translation. And in the late 1930s, the first volume of a major history of the First Ally was produced in Cambridge to match the older volume written in Oxford by the sometime Professor of Slavonic History. No one who read either of the latter books could have retained the widespread illusion that the First Ally was a new country or that it had somehow usurped the rights of ancient German or Russian lands. It was not difficult to disabuse the readership of the illusion that the familiar map of Europe as created in the nineteenth century was somehow a permanent fixture.[40]

On the very eve of the Second World War, in the summer of 1939, a 'Penguin Special' appeared, addressing a wide public with a concise and readable summary of the First Ally's past and present. Rarely can a small book have been more topical. Starting with the crowning of the first king in the tenth century, it worked its way through the 'Golden Age' of the sixteenth century, the Partitions of the eighteenth, and the 'Ordeal' of the nineteenth. The events of 1918 were presented as 'the Restoration'. But most of the space was devoted to contemporary problems – to the struggle for democracy, to education, to economic development, to the minorities, and above all to geopolitics. The First Ally was labelled 'the most exposed country in Europe'. Its citizens were characterized as 'the coolest and least flurried of all the neighbours of the Reich – because their minds are made up': 'If attacked they will fight, asking no one for advice, and expecting no quarter. The spirit in which they are facing [the] crisis in their existence ... is beyond praise.'[41] The author was a Canadian Evangelical, and Professor of London University, William J. Rose. (See Appendix 3.)

From 1940 onwards, the exiled Government in London put out a stream of publications to keep the public informed. Apart from the Black Book[42] and the White Book,[43] which documented both the diplomatic events leading up to the outbreak of war and the Nazi atrocities that followed it, a large range of official pamphlets and statements were published. As often as not, the aim was to put the record straight with regard to the facts of history and policy. The First Ally's British friends were equally eager to take up the pen,[44] and a number of English-language newspapers and information sheets were circulated.[45] So no one with the energy to study could plead ignorance.

Britain's 'First Alliance' was also celebrated in one of the most popular films of the early war years. *Dangerous Moonlight* (1941) told the fictional story of a young pilot-pianist, Stefan, who is composing a concerto during the bombing of September 1939 and who then escapes to the West. It introduces a strong American theme when the hero leaves for a musical tour of the United States and falls in love with an American girl, Sally, before returning to fight in the Battle of Britain. Screened in the USA the following year, it conveyed the powerful message that all freedom-loving countries should bond to the common cause against Nazi Germany. Its storyline was well suited to the months preceding the USA's entry in the war. But its most durable element proved to be the music. Specially composed by Richard Addinsell, the film's concerto, which uses a number of Chopinesque and sub-Rachmaninovian effects, has remained a favourite of the piano repertoire ever since.[46]

Much confusion, however, arose from rival sources of information. Just as the First Ally had been forced to compete for its historical existence with two powerful neighbours, news and information put out by the First Ally's Government during the war now had to compete with rival information deriving from German and Soviet sources. The influence of German sources had been immensely strong in the early part of the century, and continued on pre-war issues such as Silesia, Danzig, or 'the Corridor'. But it declined precipitously with the outbreak of war. Russian and Soviet sources, in contrast, were growing rapidly in influence. And on many issues, it was hard for the uninitiated to know who or what to believe.

The First Ally's Ambassador spent much of his time contesting and correcting the misconceptions which flourished among British politicians, academics and opinion-makers. Unlike some of his compatriots, 'the Count' was immensely polite, and practised English-style understatement to masterly effect. But he crossed swords with many formidable adversaries, most of whom were blissfully unaware that their tendentious opinions on German, Russian, and sometimes Jewish matters did not necessarily represent the unadulterated truth. In 1939, he conducted a major controversy with David Lloyd George, against whose opinions he published a pamphlet. In 1941 he took on the historian Sir Bernard Pares and his views on the ethnic make-up of the Borders; and on numerous occasions he confronted Robert Barrington-Ward, the editor of *The Times*, and with various personages at the BBC. On 23 June 1944, he took on the Archbishop of York, who preaching in York Minster had pronounced in ineffable style that 'the moral issues' of the war were only now becoming apparent. In the fifth year of struggle against Nazi Germany, the Count judged this idea a trifle complacent. So he sent the Archbishop a poem:

CASUS BELLI

A sense of moral duty
Drove Britain into war,
When Hitler grabbed for booty
The Polish Corridor.
No man of honour doubted
That we were in the right.
When guarantees are flouted,
The guarantor must fight.

. . .

[For] ours is not the quarrel
By fleeting passion stirred.
For us the issue moral
Is – that we keep our word.[47]

The Count enjoyed excellent relations with Brendan Bracken, Churchill's former secretary, and later Minister of Information. In March

1943, he had been particularly outraged by a brilliant but malicious cartoon by David Low in the *Evening Standard*. Entitled 'The Irresponsibles', it was manifestly inspired by Soviet propaganda, and did much to popularize the negative stereotype of the 'First Ally' in Britain. (See Appendix 15.) Bracken's response was friendly, but not particularly helpful:

> *My dear Edward, . . . I regret very much that you should have reason to protest to me against the action of a British newspaper. I think that the cartoon by Low . . . was a deplorable piece of work, and I quite understand the difficult position in which your Government is placed . . .*
>
> *I can assure you that this Ministry is doing its utmost to restrict polemics upon Polish–Soviet disagreements. . . . On the whole, our guidance has been followed, and this makes the action of the 'Evening Standard' all the more regrettable.*
>
> *Immediately the Cartoon appeared, our chief Press Censor took the matter up with the editor of the paper and gave him the strongest possible warning to avoid inflammatory action of this kind. Under our present censorship regulations, we cannot, of course, prevent the publication of matter of this sort . . . but I am sure we shall be able to count upon their co-operation in avoiding . . . anything similar in the future.*
>
> *(signed) Brendan Bracken*[48]

In the later stages of the war, the Eastern Front did not arouse many major anxieties in the strategic calculations of the Western powers. It had been assigned by mutual consent as an undefined sphere of Soviet influence. So London and Washington were happy enough to leave the problems of Eastern Europe to their partners in Moscow. The Soviet Army was greatly admired for bearing the brunt of the fighting against the Wehrmacht and, as became increasingly clear, for making the most significant contribution to the defeat of the Reich. In Western eyes, the most worrying concern arose from the possibility that Stalin, having driven the Germans from Soviet territory, might then be tempted to make a separate peace, or still worse, to conquer a large slice of Central Europe.

Nonetheless, President Roosevelt, in particular, was well disposed to accept Soviet arguments and to leave Moscow to its own devices. The USA did not feel threatened by Soviet designs on Eastern Europe. If anything, Washington was impressed by the limited range of Soviet ambitions, which did not appear at the time to be directed against other regions, such as Persia or China, in which the Americans were more directly interested. As regards the First Ally, Washington was generally sympathetic, but inclined to pass the buck to the First Ally's formal protector – Britain.

One must always take account of the fact that in 1943–44 the ability of the Western powers to mediate in Polish–Soviet affairs was fast decreasing. Stalin's break with the First Ally would not have been so serious if other negative factors had not come into play. For one thing, American diplomacy under the guidance of Roosevelt's chief adviser, Harry Hopkins, moved steadily towards the conciliation of Moscow's ambitions, and showed ever less patience for what it regarded as peripheral causes of friction. For another, Churchill was losing something of the stature which he had initially enjoyed. Stalin could not fail to notice the inexorable rise of American influence. Churchill's discomfiture was further worsened by the departure of the former Soviet Ambassador, Maisky, with whom he had conducted frequent and friendly business for two years. His contacts with Maisky's replacement were sparse and stiff. In sum, the Americans deferred Polish matters to the British, and the British tended to evade them by telling the Poles to talk directly to Moscow, even though Stalin had cut off the normal channels for talking. The climate of embarrassment that grew in proportion to the Western powers' failure to open a second front did not provide the basis for effective problem-solving.

In the same phase of the war, the Western powers were faced with the tricky problem of Yugoslavia; and their decisions regarding the Yugoslavs reflected on their approach to Eastern Europe as a whole. From 1941 onwards, the West had supported the royal Yugoslav Government and its Serb-based Underground movement, the Chetniks. King Peter and his ministers were resident in London. But their grip on developments declined when rival elements in occupied Yugoslavia indulged in a multilateral and murderous civil war. The Chetniks appeared to be most concerned with fighting the Croat Fascists, the Ustasha, and, to assist their fight, to be willing to deal with the Italian occupiers. They were also challenged by a revolutionary partisan movement led by the Moscow-trained Josip 'Broz' Tito, who was thought to be determined both to fight the Germans and to keep Yugoslavia united. In consequence, the West switched clients. The Chetniks were abandoned. The partisans were lavishly supplied from Allied bases in Italy; and the King was pressured to reach an agreement with Tito. In February 1944, despite the protests of his ministers, the King made common cause with Tito's Anti-Fascist Council of National Liberation. It was a stop-gap measure which briefly helped the prosecution of the war, but which in due course led to the complete elimination of the King and his erstwhile adherents. It did nothing to enhance the West's reputation for political probity; and it gave the concept of 'compromise' in Eastern Europe a distinctly opportunist colouring.

Greece, in contrast, was the one East European country where Churchill was adamantly opposed to any form of compromise. In April 1939, the British Government had issued a guarantee of Greece, similar to that of the First Ally, but had not proceeded to a formal alliance. In the spring of 1944, the exiled royal Government of Greece was lodged in Cairo. The Resistance movement, which was dominated by the Communist movement, was preparing to come down from the mountains and to take over Athens as soon as the Germans withdrew. Indeed it had created a Political Committee of National Liberation that clearly harboured intentions of becoming a provisional Government. Churchill would have none of it. When mutiny threatened among Greek soldiers in Cairo, he ordered it to be snuffed out, by force if necessary. And he would not countenance a division of power. Needless to say, he could afford to take this high-handed line towards the only East European country to which the Royal Navy and British troops enjoyed direct access.

Nonetheless, it would be wrong to assume that the Western powers were totally negligent of or indifferent to their First Ally. Churchill, in particular, was acutely aware of the implications of the Soviet Army's relentless advance; and he was preoccupied by daily dealings with Polish matters. In the first half of 1944, detailed attention was paid to the political, territorial, and military issues.

On the political front, Churchill was anxious that some sort of deal be fixed up with Moscow before Stalin made his own unilateral arrangements. On 16 February 1944, he called in Premier Mick and warned him that if Stalin's wishes were not met a pro-Soviet puppet Government would be set up by the Red Army and confirmed by rigged elections. He was angered by the exiled Government's reluctance to comply. Yet he also knew that Stalin's demands were provocative, and that some form of compromise might yet be reached. The First Ally was not in the same straits as Yugoslavia. There was no Tito in the Underground; there was little popular sympathy at home for Soviet-style politics; and the First Ally's armed forces were everywhere fighting loyally for the Allied cause. What is more, there were signs that Stalin was playing a double game. Whilst demanding, outrageously, that the exiled Government purge its allegedly 'anti-Soviet' members, starting with the President of the Republic, he was also keeping unofficial feelers open though the Soviet Embassy in London. So all was not yet lost. The optimists had reason to believe that with active Western involvement they might yet be able to forge a settlement before the crunch came.

For this reason, a compromise deal on the territorial issue seemed the best way forward. Here, the counsels of the Foreign Office were divided. One view, to which Eden had initially been inclined, held that Stalin's demands would have to be met simply to keep him happy. This was the line which Eden had taken over the Baltic states in 1942 and which Churchill had favoured since Teheran, with the proviso that the First Ally must be generously compensated with land taken from Germany. But no final decision was judged to have been taken, and the Teheran discussions were kept strictly secret. The alternative view, which was not without support in London, held that the First Ally should not give way without securing some modest concessions. After all, she was being pressed to abandon the equivalent of Britain losing Scotland.

To this end, the Foreign Office put its best brains to work on the ethnic, historical, and political complexities of the First Ally's eastern borders. Between November 1943 and July 1944, four detailed memoranda were produced. Two, dated 19 and 22 November 1943, preceded the Teheran Conference. The third, dated 12 February 1944, was prepared by the world-famous historian, Director of the Royal Institute of International Affairs and Head of the FO's Research Department, Professor Arnold Toynbee. The fourth, dated 25 July 1944, was drawn up by one of Toynbee's assistants, Francis Bourdillon. The details of these memoranda will delight anyone who is fascinated by the delineation of the Suvalki Region, the location of the Borislav–Drohobich Basin, the distinction between the A and B variants of the 'Curzon Line', and the many spellings of Lwów, Lvov, L'viv, Leopolis, Lemberg, and 'City of Lions' (pronounced 'Lvoof' and here rendered as Lvuv). They are wonderful fodder for cartographic masochists. But the important fact is that all four memoranda agreed on one point – that the First Ally should at the very least retain control of Lvuv.[49]

In the minds of the British experts, these memoranda appear to have been based on the assumption of a two-stage solution: namely, that once the exiled Government had agreed to accept the Curzon Line in principle, Moscow could then be pressed to accept some relatively minor adjustments.[50] In the eyes of the exiled Government, however, the memoranda encouraged intransigence. They gave the clear impression that the game was not yet up, and that, given Western help, Lvuv represented the irreducible minimum of what could be saved.

A further distinction should be noted. The British memoranda of 1943–44, like Stalin's territorial demands, had all referred to the permanent state frontiers which were to be put in place with international recognition at the end of the war. They should not be confused with the parallel discussions held in 1944 concerning the temporary 'demarcation line', which became an urgent necessity through the Red Army's unexpectedly rapid advance. On 15 February 1944, the Premier of the exiled Government gave his consent to a demarcation line well to the east of the 'Curzon Line'. He did so on the strict understanding that negotiations on the permanent frontier would not be jeopardized. Many of his colleagues, including the Commander-in-Chief, believed that he had made a serious tactical mistake.

On the military front, the key issue centred on what would happen when the Germans finally retreated into the Reich, in particular on how the First Ally's Underground would conduct itself towards the incoming Red Army. No one needed to be told, of course, that the years of Nazi oppression were likely to end in some form of popular outburst. But the planners needed to know something rather more specific. What sort of rising might occur? Where would it be based? Who would lead it? And how could it be channelled to maximum effect?

Discussions about a possible Polish Rising against the Germans had been circulating in Allied circles for months if not years. Both London and Washington were well aware of what they called Poland's 'Secret Army' and of its potential usefulness. But no one had brought the discussions to a resolution. So Tabor now set about recovering lost time. As soon as he took up his post in the VI Bureau in April 1944 at 13 Upper Belgrave Street he pursued these questions with great energy.

At the time, the concept preferred by the exiled Government was for a 'general rising' in the rural areas, which would paralyse German communications, hinder the Wehrmacht's retreat, and speed the Red Army's advance on a broad front. Tabor's priority was to gain British backing for the enterprise. He had little success. In a number of preliminary talks, he was repeatedly told of the logistical difficulties, of the great distances involved, and of the Soviet sphere of influence. On 25 April, he met Churchill in the company of another officer, who had been flown to

England with him, but the meeting was knocked off track by a heated exchange on the frontier question. When Tabor's companion said that they would fight to the last for their rightful frontiers, Churchill responded gloomily: 'Obviously, a decision to resist, regardless of the consequences, is the privilege of every nation, and it cannot be denied even to the weakest'.[51]

Nonetheless, the British Government continued to be bombarded with queries and requests both by Tabor's team and by other Polish officials. British doubts were expressed at a variety of meetings. They conveyed a mixture of reluctance, irritation, and indecision, but not overt opposition. The definitive British answer, which was eventually issued by the Foreign Office, was constantly delayed. It had not been received by late July, when the commander of the First Ally's 'Secret Army' proposed a Rising in the immediate future and when Premier Mick's Cabinet approved the proposal.

In those same weeks, Gen. Tabor learned of two worrying developments. One of them concerned information that a colleague in London had sent a telegram to the Underground back home advising them to eliminate Salamander.[52] The other concerned news that the British wanted to transfer the First Ally's own Parachute Brigade to British command. Tabor was incensed by the alleged assassination plot, and protested to the Commander-in-Chief about 'Gestapo methods'. He was much less upset about the Parachute Brigade. He advised that the British request be granted gracefully. Assistance to the Western Allies now, he argued, would create a moral debt that would be repaid later by Western assistance to the Underground.[53]

Few of Tabor's colleagues knew much about his political views at this juncture. The report which he had prepared in the autumn of 1943, urging the Underground to work for 'friendly relations with the Soviets' 'even at the cost of major concessions', was not known in London. Nor was the conversation in which he had opined: 'The Anglo-Saxons are not interested . . . France doesn't count. So we have to show goodwill, reach an understanding with the Soviets, and go along with them.' But one junior in the VI Bureau was regularly treated to this fare:

> The Soviet Union is going to become the decisive power in all our territories. In that situation, [we] ought to enter agreements with Moscow, make the necessary concessions, and change our orientation from pro-Western to pro-Soviet.[54]

One may presume that Tabor let some of these sympathies be known when talking to British officials. If so, given the pro-Soviet attitudes then prevalent in London, he would not have caused a ripple.

Gen. Tabor's big chance came in June when he was invited to accompany Premier Mick to Washington and to present his case for help for the Underground. On three separate days, with a large map and a good translator, he was able to make a professional presentation and to answer questions. Polish–Soviet relations always came up in one form or another. On 7 June, in the White House, he met President Roosevelt in person, and elicited the greatest interest, even excitement. In response to the inevitable presidential question about Soviet views on the Polish Underground, Premier Mick intervened and explained how contacts with the Soviets had tailed off since the Katyn affair and Gen. Sikorski's death.[55] It was not the smartest move. But on 12 June, Tabor had another opportunity when he met the Combined Chiefs of Staff of the Supreme Allied Command.

A plenary session of the Combined Chiefs was held in Blair House on 12 June under the chairmanship of US Admiral William Leahy. British representatives included Gen. Redman and Lt.Gen. Macready, representative of the Chief of the Imperial General Staff. The delegation of the First Ally was ushered in when the agenda moved onto developments on the Eastern Front. It was headed by the Head of their Military Mission in the USA, who read out Gen. Tabor's paper in translation, outlining the state of affairs under the German Occupation and in the Resistance movement. The questioning was led by Gen. Macready:

MACREADY: How does Gen. Tabor envisage the execution of a general armed rising . . .? Will it take place in cooperation with the Russians?

TABOR (without an instant of hesitation): [Our Underground army] will beat the Germans in cooperation with whichever of the Allied armies reaches our territory first.

(The reply causes extraordinary excitement among the British members)

. . .

TABOR: From the military standpoint our co-operation with the Russians to date . . . has been very satisfying. In several instances, common action was agreed beforehand and gave favourable results. In one district, our commander had the opportunity of conferring directly with the commanding officer of a Soviet army group. The Soviet Command has been convinced that our [Underground army] really does possess the

> requisite forces, even in the [eastern] provinces. This state of affairs has been relayed to them by Soviet partisans who [were on our side of the German lines, but] who have now withdrawn across the front . . .[56]

A colleague of Tabor's said he wasn't sure if the Commander-in-Chief's assessment had been correctly conveyed. But Tabor did not flinch. The British delegates gave him a virtual standing ovation. They had heard exactly what they wanted.

The next morning, Gen. Tabor was the guest of the Planning Group of the Office of Strategic Services (the forerunner of the CIA), chaired by Hugh R. Wilson. Once again, he was very favourably received; and once again, among other things, he was asked about the 'Secret Army''s activities in the eastern provinces and about relations with the Soviets:

> Gen. T. pointed on the map to areas of concentration and areas of weaker activity. He referred to examples of Polish–Soviet cooperation at Kovel and Lutsk, but also to a failure by Soviet commanders to keep to the plan agreed with the [Underground army's] Volhynian Division, which resulted in the division suffering heavy casualties and the loss of its senior officer . . .[57]

The impression conveyed was that the 'Secret Army' was fighting hard, and that, in general, it was able to work with the Soviets. The Chairman closed the meeting by expressing the desire of the OSS to help the 'Secret Army' and to establish the fullest cooperation.

The visit to Washington gave a great boost to the exiled Government's confidence in all respects. Though it coincided with the D-Day landings, President Roosevelt found time to receive the Premier on four separate occasions. The climate was exceptionally cordial. The guests were attended by the highest American officials, and were made to feel genuinely welcome. The President's main message, repeatedly stated, was that the Premier should talk to Stalin directly and have 'just a human conversation'. After all, he himself got along fine with the Marshal, 'much better than my poor friend Churchill'. Stalin, he said, was 'not an imperialist', 'just a realist'. The President even made encouraging noises on the frontier issue. Lvuv might not be lost. Indeed, he 'did not entirely exclude' agreement on Vilno. The Premier noted down the President's words directly: 'Don't worry. Stalin doesn't intend to take freedom from [you]. He wouldn't dare do that because he knows that the United States Government stands solidly behind you. I shall see to it that [your country] does not come out of this war injured'.[58] At the airport, the US Secretary of State, Stettinius, made a jovial comment to the First Ally's Ambassador about the Premier. 'Our friend Stan', he remarked, 'is a regular guy; and we shall do all we can to help in his undertaking.'[59] What better assurance could a beleaguered statesman hope for?

Summing up the evidence then available, one might have drawn four firm conclusions. The First Ally appeared to have the full support of the Western powers. The Premier's prospective meeting with Stalin would be crucial, but Stalin could be expected to agree to a compromise solution. Something could still be salvaged on the frontiers. And the Rising could go ahead. The highest military authorities in the Western Alliance had been informed. And no one had said that preparations should be stopped.[60]

In short, the Premier and Tabor had good reason to congratulate themselves. What is more, their Washington visit was to bear still richer fruit. During his talks with Roosevelt, the Premier had discussed a hefty American subsidy. In due course, he learned that Roosevelt had approved a massive grant of $10m in gold – $1.5m to be spent on civilian relief and $8.5m on support for the Underground army. He could hardly have received a stronger mark of approval.

As for Tabor, he received recognition of a different sort. Soon after landing in London, he was informed that, by the personal consent of the King, he would be awarded one of Britain's most prestigious decorations – the Companion of the Order of the Bath. After months of anxiety, progress was being made.

The ceremony at which Gen. Tabor was decorated was attended by Lord Selborne, Gen. Gubbins, Air Vice Marshal Ritchie, and Lt.Col. Perkins together with Premier Mick and numerous Polish officers. In his address, Lord Selborne said that the award was being made in recognition of Tabor's services to the Underground army. In the name of the King, he wished to express his admiration for the achievements of that army, which was fighting so hard and so long in such difficult conditions. The British Government and people fully appreciated the Polish struggle for the cause of the Allied Powers:

> Seeing that there were grounds to hope that the hour of liberation was approaching, the Minister offered the General his most sincere wishes that the [First Ally's] Armed Forces . . . would be able to free their country from the enemy in the very near future.[61]

As July wore on, however, Tabor must have experienced some anxiety. He had received the strongest possible backing from Roosevelt, and the greatest possible compliment from the British. His advocacy of the 'Secret Army' certainly appeared to be on much firmer ground than before his trip to Washington. On the other hand, the Soviets were advancing with lightning speed, and the day of reckoning for the First Ally was looming rather too rapidly. Several important ends had not been tied up with the British. Furthermore, he may well have suspected that he was not always privy to the most relevant developments.

Nonetheless, his own course of action was plain enough. He was the chief representative in London of the First Ally's Underground forces; and it was his duty to continue to muster all the support he could. In this, the chief conduit to the highest British circles was SOE. Hence, as soon as he heard that his Government had approved an imminent Rising in principle, he arranged an appointment with Gubbins, the head of SOE.

Tabor's key meeting with Gubbins and other SOE officers took place on 29 July 1944. Tabor told the assembled company that a Rising was expected to break out in Warsaw as soon as the Underground leaders judged it opportune, and that, in consequence, he was looking to the Allies for immediate support. In particular, he listed six demands:

- an increased level of air drops in the Warsaw area
- the bombing of German airfields in the vicinity of Warsaw
- the transfer of Polish fighter squadrons to Poland
- the despatch of the Polish Parachute Brigade, or part of it
- recognition of the Polish secret army as an official component of the Allied forces
- the immediate despatch of an Allied military mission to Warsaw.

Gubbins reacted positively. He stated that the overall policy of the Chiefs of Staff had not changed, but that 'absolute priority' would be given to the First Ally within the existing dispositions.[62]

The details of the meeting were duly passed on to their requisite destinations. On 30 July, Gubbins sent them to the Chiefs of Staff, stressing their urgency. Most importantly, having been primed by Tabor's superior, Lord Selborne passed them to Prime Minister Churchill on 1 August, giving them his warmest endorsement:

> I should greatly rejoice if it were found possible to do anything to meet the Polish request . . . I do not think that it would be militarily very difficult to despatch now to Poland a company of Polish parachute troops . . . I also hope that it will be possible to make a declaration concerning the Polish Secret Army analogous to that just made by Gen. Eisenhower concerning the French Secret Army, i.e. that we recognise them as an Allied fighting force and combatants under international law . . . Of the two, the Polish Secret Army is certainly the best organised and most competent.[63]

Capital cities awaiting liberation were dangerous places. Everyone knew that something could erupt at any moment. After years of Nazi Occupation and repression, the populace was straining at the leash for blessed relief, and in some cases for summary revenge. The German garrisons were restless. They could see that the end of the war was coming, that it would come to a close either with an armistice as in 1918, or, if their Nazi leaders were really mad, in one last grand onslaught on the Fatherland. Either way, they had no wish to be killed on the eve of a settlement or in the retreat from some godforsaken corner of a foreign town. For ordinary soldiers at least, there was only one desire – to escape from the mess and to find their way home.

Yet the garrison commanders faced some acute dilemmas. They were trapped between the advancing Allied armies and the resentful population, who could turn on them at any moment. So above all else they needed freedom of manoeuvre – freedom to conciliate the citizens where possible, and freedom to move their troops into defensive positions. In this, they faced a mountain of troubles. As officers of the Wehrmacht, which on 20 July had been shown to harbour would-be assassins of the *Führer*, they were coming under immense suspicion. They would have known about Rommel, who had recently been given the choice between suicide and a show trial. More immediately, they were surrounded by assorted SS units, Nazi Party officials, and Gestapo types who would counsel a fight to the death. Worst of all, they were subject to a High Command that had ceased to respond to reasonable requests. As at Stalingrad, the *Führer* had always preferred a catastrophic stand to a prudent retreat. And his obstinacy was growing. If faced by open rebellion, he was more likely to sacrifice a few European cities, with everyone in them, rather than let his subordinates withdraw and prepare for the next line of defence.

The tensions in such beleaguered cities affected every single man, woman, and child. Secret resistance fighters oiled their weapons, waiting for the signal to rush out and kill Germans. Secret radio operators and encoders stood by to transmit the vital messages. German patrols stood at street corners, looking for suspicious characters, or toured the suburbs looking for illegal gatherings. Gestapo men scoured their lists of unreliable elements and prepared to pounce. Technicians crouched in their direction-finding vans, listening for unauthorized broadcasts. Policemen busied themselves with routine tasks, wondering if they would soon have new superiors. Especially at night, people hung around in their gardens, or leant out of windows, straining their ears for the rumble of distant artillery. Collaborators quaked at the thought of retribution. Women who had slept with the enemy, or worked in army brothels, feared for their lives. Criminals and profiteers racked their brains for new ways of making their ill-gotten gains. Priests witnessed a rise in weddings and confessions. Sellers of sandbags, planks, canisters, jam jars, candles, sugar, and false papers did brisk business. Prisoners and forced labourers, who rotted in cells or in Nazi camps, hoped against hope that they would be able to make a break. Jews in hiding trembled to think that their ordeal might soon be over. Parents worried themselves to distraction, knowing that their teenage sons and daughters had plans of their own. Grandparents rambled on about earlier battles and the passage of other armies. Doctors, nurses, and ambulance drivers did their rounds, knowing that their duties might suddenly increase. Patriots and oppressors alike steeled themselves for the moment of truth. They all knew what to expect. First would come the bombers, then the artillery barrage, and finally the tanks. Once someone caught sight of the first Allied tank, it would be obvious that action was about to be joined.

CHAPTER II

THE GERMAN OCCUPATION

GERMANS OF ONE SORT or another had occupied Warsaw on several occasions. In 1656, the Brandenburgers captured the capital in the course of their alliance with the Swedes during the first Northern War. In 1697, the Saxons arrived in pursuance of their Elector's elevation to the throne of Poland–Lithuania. The Polish–Saxon Union lasted sixty-six years. In 1795, the Prussians were given Warsaw as part of their deal with the Russians which ended the War of the Third Partition. They stayed for over a decade until driven out by Napoleon's great drive to the east. In 1915–18, the Kaiser's army took Warsaw as part of the victorious campaigns against the Russian Empire. Each of these occupations, whether long or short, was an episode that invariably ended badly. For the Varsovians, it helped create an important background consciousness in which the appearance of yet another conquering German army did not cause excessive surprise and in which the latest occupation was not expected to last forever.

On one point, however, most Varsovians and most of the Germans would have agreed. Despite the long periods when Polish–German relations had been harmonious,[1] both sides had been taught that the wars of the twentieth century were but the latest rounds in an endless, irreconcilable conflict between Teuton and Slav that had been in progress since the Middle Ages. Warsaw, after all, long before it became the capital of Poland, was the historic capital of the Duchy of Mazovia; and it was Conrad, Duke of Mazovia, who had taken the fatal step to call in the Teutonic Knights to help in his war against the ancient Prussians. Instead of honouring their contract and leaving, the 'Black Crusaders' stayed on to conquer Prussia for themselves, to Germanize the Prussian people, and to set up a militaristic settler state, which took over the Baltic seaboard, occupied the Vistula delta around Danzig, and blocked Mazovia's free access to the sea. In German lore, the Knights were heroes; in Polish lore they were villains.

In the era of nationalism, which began in the mid-nineteenth century, German nationalism and Polish nationalism fed off each other and produced an unprecedented degree of mutual antagonism. German nationalists, who were peacock-proud of the achievements of their new Empire, tended to look down on their eastern neighbours as the inferior relics of a defeated civilization. Polish nationalists of the variety that founded the National Democratic Party of Roman D. both hated and admired the new Germany. They sought to emulate Germany's social and economic progress. At the same time, they feared German power above all else; and they were prepared to cooperate with backward Russia in order to keep 'the Teutonic tide' at bay. Though they commanded probably the largest single opinion group in Poland they were never able to gain political control. Their rivals and opponents, the anti-Nationalists of Joseph Pilsudski, who denounced the slogans of 'Poland for the Poles', were always able to forge a dominant coalition against them. Pilsudski's disciples offered a welcome to Poland's ethnic minorities, including Jews, put a premium on winning and upholding national independence, and were the heirs of the country's historic insurrectionary tradition. They feared Russian imperialism above all else; and to this end they were prepared to envisage limited cooperation with Germany and Austria. During the First World War, Pilsudski's Legions fought on the Eastern Front in the ranks of the Austrian army. But they laid down their arms when pressed to swear an oath of allegiance to the German Kaiser. After the war, when they constituted the leading political force, they developed the 'Doctrine of Two Enemies', viewing Nazi Germany and the Soviet Union with equal contempt.

The German Occupation of 1915–18 – which had come to an end only twenty-one years before the Nazis arrived – brought many substantial benefits. In the nature of things, it could not deliver the sovereign, independent Poland for which the most ardent patriots yearned. But by the standards of the day it was markedly indulgent to local sensitivities. It was certainly much more liberal than the preceding Russian Occupation, which had persisted through much of the nineteenth century and which, for many of the decades before the First World War, had been implacably hostile to Polish national politics, to Polish culture, and to the Polish language itself. The Germans of the Kaiser's vintage, like the British and the French, were not favourable to the Wilsonian ideal of national self-determination. But they sought to exploit the weaknesses of the Tsarist Empire by making concessions to the numerous national-liberation movements in Eastern Europe. They helped create an independent Lithuania, an independent Byelorussia, and an independent Ukraine. In their part of occupied Poland, after ruling for a time through a military General Government, they restored the autonomous Kingdom of Poland, which the Russians had suppressed fifty years before. They did not have time to appoint a suitably dependent monarch or even to find a permanent regent. But they did set up a ruling Regency Council, which consisted of a Polish prince, a Polish count, and a Polish archbishop; and in the last year of the war, they permitted the regents to establish an executive Council of State or 'Government' from a mixture of appointed and elected members. This was not the heavy-handed sort of political exploitation that was practised before 1914 and after 1939.

Warsaw, in particular, had gained enormously. It gained economically, as a major logistical and industrial centre serving the German and Austrian armies on the Eastern Front. It gained politically by ceasing to be a peripheral provincial city and recovered the status of an administrative capital hosting numerous ministries, and even the headquarters of a German-run *Polnische Wehrmacht*. Above all, it gained enormously in the cultural field. The Polish language was restored both in education and in administration. The University of Warsaw was restored as a seat of Polish higher learning. National symbols and festivals, such as the celebrations of the Third of May, were reinstituted. And a serious initiative was taken to introduce Reform Judaism, thereby encouraging Jewish assimilation and easing ethnic tensions. Throughout the nineteenth century, the Jewish population had been multiplying rapidly, both in the Polish lands generally and in Warsaw in particular. Warsaw had long possessed the largest Jewish community in the world, until overtaken by New York, many of whose immigrant Jews hailed from Warsaw. By 1918, Varsovian Jews had passed the 40 per cent mark in the city's population, and seemed to be heading for an absolute majority.

Thanks to Imperial Germany's relatively benevolent stance, a group of Polish politicians was able to activate a pro-German movement. Its leading light, Ladislas S.-G., admired German culture, welcomed Germany's military strength and administrative order, feared Russia, and believed that full national independence was a pipe-dream.[2]

The end of German rule in 1918 came about in the most extraordinary way. For most of the preceding months, the German hold on the east looked unassailable. Russia had collapsed into Revolution. German troops were stationed in the Baltic states, in Byelorussia, and throughout Ukraine. The German-run Kingdom of Poland was preparing for a lengthy innings. Its opponents had been defeated. The Polish nationalist leader, Roman D., was living in exile in Paris. His lifetime rival, Pilsudski, was incarcerated as a political prisoner in Magdeburg castle, his legions disbanded. And then, with very little warning, the German Empire collapsed. Revolution broke out in Berlin. The Kaiser abdicated. The occupation regimes in Eastern Europe folded. Pilsudski was released from jail by German intelligence officers who shrewdly calculated that he was the only person left to forestall Roman D.'s pro-Western Committee. He arrived in Warsaw on the night of 10/11 November, and assumed power from the Regency Council without a shot being fired. German soldiers, who for four years had manned the most fearsome military machine in Europe, were meekly disarmed on the streets of Warsaw by small boys. No Varsovian could fail to miss this startling lesson about the fickleness of politics and the vanity of power. If it had happened once, it could happen again.

Inter-war Warsaw was the capital of a fiercely patriotic Republic. Its patriotism was greatly increased by the thrill of Pilsudski's victory in August 1920 over the Red Army, which had sought to throttle the infant republic in its cradle. Poles of that generation were naturally impressed by two imperatives. One concerned their duty to defend their country against all comers. This did not seem in the least unrealistic since they had recently seen how both Russia and Germany had feet of clay. The other was to model themselves on the Western powers, whose victory in 1918 was taken to prove not only their superiority but their invincibility.

In barely twenty years, Warsaw expanded mightily, both in population and in built-up area. The number of its citizens rose by 38 per cent from 937,000 in 1921 to 1,289,000 in 1939. The Old City and surrounding districts were refurbished and adorned with patriotic monuments forbidden by the preceding regimes. The Russian Orthodox Cathedral, which had dominated the skyline, was pulled down. New suburbs were developed to accommodate the villas and residences of the burgeoning professional and administrative classes. A new cooperative movement attacked the problems of working-class housing that were exacerbated by the rapid influx of job-seekers from the countryside. Yet despite the stresses and strains, municipal services kept pace with the expansion. Employment was provided by several large industrial enterprises in the metal-working, electrotechnical, textile, and food-processing sectors. There was a modern tramway network. A modern infrastructure supplied electricity, gas, and water, and there was a solid system of fine brick-lined sewers.

Warsaw's ethnic problems centred on the intermittent tensions between Catholics and Jews that had already come into the open before 1914. These tensions should not be exaggerated. It is important not to read history backwards and not to interpret the pre-war scene in the light of subsequent developments. For the coexistence of Catholics and Jews in Warsaw between 1918 and 1939 cannot be characterized in terms of inveterate hostility; and it cannot be seriously analysed merely by recounting the grievances of one side or the other.

Varsovian Jewry was at least five hundred years old. In the Middle Ages, the community had been excluded from the central area of municipal jurisdiction by a decree of *non tolerandis judaeis*. But it had found little difficulty in taking root, under the protection of the nobility, in the districts immediately adjacent to the city walls. As a result, since Judaic law forbade its strict observants to reside among Gentiles, substantial Jewish quarters grew up in Vola to the west and Praga to the east. Neither the pogrom of 1881, which had followed the Tsar's assassination, nor the boycott of Jewish businesses in 1911–12 had dented Jewish advancement for long.

Of course, one can easily make a list of religious, economic, social, political, and psychological grievances. But one must equally describe the considerable forces working in the direction of reconciliation and integration. The Polish Catholic Church, for example, which before 1914 had endured a long period of harassment and humiliation, was disappointed by its failure to obtain special status in the post-war constitution of the restored Republic, and some of its more militant members were willing to revive the ancient rivalry with Jews and Judaism. By the same token, the old-established authorities of Orthodox Jewry were coming under pressure from secularizing, modernizing, and in some circles, openly atheistic influences. Traditional Jewish prominence in finance, trade, and industry inevitably caused competition with newly founded businesses, especially in the Depression of the 1930s. The large-scale Jewish presence in the free professions, in the universities and among educated people in general was often felt to be a barrier to the ambitions of a Catholic lower class that was crossing the threshold of literacy exactly in those same decades. The rise of Roman D.'s nationalism, which promoted slogans of 'Poland for the Poles' and which cultivated the unsavoury association of Polishness with Catholicism, did not encourage fellow-feeling. But neither did the parallel rise of militant Zionism in the Jewish community. To objective observers, Polish and Jewish nationalisms appeared to have much in common. What is more, the deepening international crises of the 1930s could only serve to enflame anxieties. Hitler and Stalin were not seen as desirable neighbours by any but the most eccentric.

Common sense underlines the necessity for seeing pre-war Varsovian society as it really was – with its inimitable mixtures of joys and sorrows, of pleasures no less than tensions. Here one is obliged to emphasize that Pilsudski's *Sanacja* regime, which dominated inter-war politics, was fully committed to the ideal of a multinational, pluralist Poland and that it consistently excluded the nationalists from power. It welcomed Jews to its ranks, encouraged the activities of democratic Jewish parties, introduced Jewish self-government into local affairs, and drove the political extremists, whether the fascistic ONR or the Communist KPP, to the illegal margins. Its main criterion was loyalty to the republic, and most Varsovian Jews were happy to follow.

Above all, one needs to realize that the two decades of freedom between 1918 and 1939 saw many of the old barriers crumbling. They were the decades when universal schooling all but eliminated illiteracy, and the new literacy involved competence in the Polish language. Inter-war Warsaw saw a marked increase in mixed marriages and the appearance of an influential group of people who were equally at ease with their Catholic and their Jewish heritages. It saw an explosion of cultural life in theatre, literature, film, art, and music, which encouraged all Varsovians to participate and which produced a Varsovian intelligentsia where figures with varying degrees of attachment to Jewishness formed an essential element.

In this fast-changing world, it was simply not realistic to classify Varsovians as either 'Poles' or 'Jews'. Such rigid and exclusive distinctions contradict the principle of multiple identities which holds good for most modern, mobile societies. They may have been appropriate a couple of centuries earlier, when Jews had belonged to a closed, legally defined religious caste, and they were to be revived first by the pseudo-scientific racism of the Nazis and later by the fundamentalist wing of Zionism. But they cannot be reasonably applied to the complexities of inter-war society. Varsovians who had some sort of Jewish connection would have classified themselves either as 'Poles of the Mosaic faith' (if they still adhered to Judaism) or 'Poles of Jewish descent' (if they did not). There was also a shrinking category of people who, though Poles in the sense of being Polish citizens, spoke no Polish, shunned wider social contacts, and lived in closed, ultra-Orthodox Yiddish-speaking communities. These ultra-

Orthodox were dominant in the traditional *shtetln* or 'small Jewish towns' of the countryside, but less so in the larger cities, such as Warsaw.

In short, most Varsovian Jews had the same right and inclination to be regarded as Poles as New York Jews had to be regarded as Americans. One need only look at the academic world or the literary establishment. One can produce any number of names of writers who contrived to be both Polish and Jewish with no sense of contradiction. One of the best-loved lyricists, who emerged in the 1920s with the Skamander Group, Antony S., was the son of a Catholic doctor in Warsaw, whose forebears had converted some time in the nineteenth century. A cousin of his, Mikhail Leonidovitch Slonimskii, belonged to a branch of the family that had assimilated into Russian society, and became a leading Soviet writer. His colleague, Julian T., who helped found the Skamander, was also brought up in a totally assimilated and patriotic family. He formulated the concept of 'the homeland of the Polish language'. His famous verse 'Lokomotywa' ('Puffer Train', 1938) is as well known to Polish children as *Winnie the Pooh* or 'The Owl and the Pussy-cat' to their English counterparts. Dr Yanush K. came from the same milieu. A qualified physician, he made his name early in the century with a book on homeless street children; he devoted his life to the study of child psychology and to the orphanage which he founded. He was to become a true martyr to his children's cause.

Even so, a considerable degree of separateness pertained. An activist of the Socialist Jewish Bund, who vehemently opposed Zionist ideas, conceded the point:

> Outside the Jewish quarter in pre-war Warsaw, a minority of Jewish professional people and successful business men, lived as neighbours of their Catholic co-citizens. Some of them, the artists, doctors, lawyers and entrepreneurs, became linguistically, culturally, and socially assimilated, and considered themselves Poles in every respect, religion excepted. But they were only a few thousands of the 350,000 Warsaw Jews. The others spoke a different language from the rest, and remained true to an ancient and dissimilar tradition in matters of belief and behaviour.[3]

Thanks to the right of local autonomy, granted by the *Sanacja* regime, Jewish Warsaw enjoyed a wide measure of independent politics:

> Warsaw was the headquarters of Jewish parties and movements in Poland, the arena of the struggle for Jewish representation in the state [legislative assembly] and Senate, and the centre of Jewish cultural and educational activities, of the country's scholarship and literature, and of the Jewish national press. A fierce political struggle was waged over the character that Jewish life in Warsaw should assume . . . The main political struggle was between the Zionist factions and the Orthodox-hasidic groups, which combined in the Agudat Israel. Between 1926 and 1936 the direction of Warsaw's communal affairs was in the hands of Agudat Israel and the Zionists, either in coalition or alternately. However, in the 1930s the Bund gained the lead in both the elections to decide communal leadership and the Jewish representation on the Warsaw municipality. The Polish Government annulled the results of the democratically held communal elections and appointed another community board which continued in office until the German occupation in World War II.[4]

Without doubt, the most forceful opinion about Polish-Jewish identity was penned in August 1944 in London by an exile from Warsaw. Its author was none other than Julian T., who belonged to the most influential intellectual circles of his generation: Entitled *We Polish Jews*, it gives all sorts of reasons why a Jew should want to be a Pole and concludes:

> *Above all – I'm a Pole because that's how I like it*

Julian T. offered another key thought. 'I divide Poles,' he said, 'as I divide Jews and other nations,'

> into the wise and the stupid,
> the honest and the dishonest,
> the intelligent and the dim,
> the interesting and the boring,
> the oppressing and the oppressed,
> the gentlemanly and the ungentlemanly.[5]

No one before 1939 knew anything about the terrible tragedies to come. Concerns were certainly expressed on the future of Catholic–Jewish relations in Warsaw, but no one was proposing a violent solution. Public opinion was divided, on the one side between the Pilsudski-ites and the National Democrats, and on the other side between Bundists and Zionists. So it is quite unhistorical to imagine Warsaw Jewry being 'On the Edge of Destruction' or to adopt other post-war myths as the basis for discussion. Britain's leading academic on the subject at the time, in a book published in the summer of 1939, saw the existing problems largely in terms of overpopulation and socio-economic competition:

> What is the rising generation of peasants' sons and daughters to do? The amount of free land has become very small indeed. Emigration facilities are cut off. The youth on leaving school find themselves, in the American phrase, 'all dressed up with nowhere to go.'
>
> Already in the twenties, a beginning was made in the setting up of 'Christian' shops . . . as a means of challenging the monopoly of petty trading hitherto enjoyed by the Jews . . . [With this] went a certain amount of picketing of Jewish shops by the youth that provoked the use of violence on the part of those threatened, and led in places to open riot and bloodshed . . .
>
> This particular conflict has little or nothing to do with what is called anti-Semitism and is almost wholly rooted in the pinch of poverty and the congestion of population . . . Poland, one of the poorest countries of [Europe], has nearly one-quarter of all the Jews in the world . . . For generations they have been the victims of discrimination, and they deserve a better fate . . .[6]

Such contemporary opinions offer a good starting point. Ironically, the Zionists had wide support from the Polish Nationalists in holding that Jews should emigrate to Palestine. The Bundists, like the rest of the Polish Left, argued that Polish Jews should stay in the land of their birth and help build a better world for everyone.

The conflict over higher education, which surfaced in the mid-1930s, was often seen to have socio-economic causes. It stemmed, first and foremost, from the discrepancy between the educational needs of the newly literate peasantry, who until the third quarter of the nineteenth century under Russian rule had been serfs, and those of a burgeoning and increasingly assimilated Jewish bourgeoisie. Jews, though around 10 per cent of the overall population, accounted for a markedly higher percentage of the student body. In the University of Warsaw they represented a dominant element of the law and medical faculties. As a result, in certain places and at different times, as in comparable places in Britain and America, a *numerus clausus* was introduced:

> Serious objection is raised by Jewish leaders to this *numerus clausus*, and one can understand why. But not to introduce it would create worse trouble. Young men would be admitted to studies from which they would not have the slightest chance of getting a living.[7]

There can be no doubt that a degree of discrimination was involved. But the policy's advocates, like the advocates of women's advancement, saw it as a necessary form of 'positive discrimination'. Nor can the associated unpleasantness be excused. On the other hand, it would be quite out of place to regard these relatively petty disputes of the 1930s as a prelude to the generalized tyranny which would soon be implemented by the Nazis.

Warsaw Jewry enjoyed its share of affluence. In many ways, it was a vibrant, dynamic community. There were Jewish politicians of many shades, Jewish artists, Jewish actors, Jewish boxers, Jewish film-makers, Jewish millionaires . . . No doubt, there was a darker side. But to describe these people exclusively in tragic shades is a mistake, and a disservice to their memory.

Pre-war Warsaw life undoubtedly had its black spots, notably in the overcrowded slums and in the gross unemployment of the Depression years. Yet pride bloomed alongside the problems. For the Capital, whose ills until recently could always be blamed on foreigners, was now the sole responsibility of those who lived there. And there had certainly been much progress. Most of the suburbs were adorned with extensive public parks. Promenades on summer evenings in the Saxon Garden or round the lake in Lazhenki Park were extremely popular. Cafes and music halls, often with a bohemian flavour, were thriving. With universal schooling and the vogue for scout groups and sports clubs, youth had never had it so good. Young women, in particular, had never been so liberated. The standards of public hygiene were high. Hospitals were provided by a mixture of religious, charitable and municipal organizations, serving rich and poor alike. Religious life, whether at the Cathedral of St John or at one of the fifty or so parish churches, whether at the Great Synagogue on Tlomat Street or at one of the crowded Chassidic meeting-places, was strong. Generally speaking, believers respected believers. The Christian Sabbath on Sundays, and the Jewish Shabbat on Saturdays formed an age-old part of everyone's routine.

Warsaw was said to have two special treasures – its mayor and its poets. The mayor, Stefan S., a former soldier in Pilsudski's Legions, was young, energetic, eloquent, and widely respected.[8] He made his name in the crisis of September 1939, rousing the populace in daily broadcasts to defend the city, denouncing Nazi barbarism, inspiring his underlings, fortifying the firefighters, rousing the rescue squads, and comforting the victims. The poets and balladeers, who sang his virtues and those of his city, were fulsome in their praise:

And he, when the city was just a raw, red mass,
Said: 'I do not surrender.' Let the houses burn!
Let my proud achievements be bombed into dust.
So what, if a graveyard grows from my dreams?
For you, who may come here, someday recall
That some things are dearer than the finest city wall.[9]

That lost Capital was to be recalled with deep affection:

O dearest Warsaw of my youth,
Which encompassed the whole of my world!
If only for a moment and in the dark
I wish to catch a glimpse
Of the ashes and the flowers
Of that good past.[10]

Adolf Hitler hated Poland with a will. For Poland lay at the heart of the Nazis' *Lebensraum*, the ideological 'living space' into which Germany was raring to expand. It was inhabited moreover by a mixture of Slavs and Jews, both of which were classed in the Nazi handbooks as *Untermenschen*, or 'subhumans'. Hitler's priorities were shifting. In *Mein Kampf* (1925), he had poured much of his opprobrium on the Czechs. Yet when his prejudices were put to the test, the Protectorate of Bohemia and Moravia was treated far less severely. It seems that the Poles, by putting up a fight in 1939, earned themselves a special place in his demonology.[11]

From the very start, therefore, the German invasion of Poland in September 1939 had a much nastier flavour than the events of 1915–18. Hitler specifically ordered his minions to act with great cruelty. And he was fully aware of the opportunities for genocide. Briefing his generals at Obersalzburg on the eve of the invasion, he revealed his plans for the Polish nation:

> Genghis Khan had millions of women and men killed by his own will and with a gay heart. History sees him only as a great state-builder

> ... I have sent my Death's Head units to the East with the order to kill without mercy men, women and children of the Polish race or language. Only in such a way will we win the *Lebensraum* that we need. Who, after all, speaks today of the annihilation of the Armenians?[12]

Hitler's state of mind at that juncture may be judged from the fact that on the day his armies moved into Poland, he ordered a decree condemning all incurably ill persons to death.[13] One crime was to cover another.

Warsaw, as the enemy capital, attracted the Wehrmacht's special fury. It was mercilessly attacked by shrieking Stuka dive-bombers from the dawn of the very first day. And since it lay dangerously close to the frontier with East Prussia, it was immediately exposed to a German drive from the north. It was surrounded on all sides from the second week of the campaign; and on 15 September it was (wrongly) said by Berlin Radio to have fallen. This is sometimes thought to have prompted Stalin's order to invade Poland from the east, which happened two days later. Yet Warsaw fought bravely on, vainly hoping that the Western powers would honour their pledge and would bring relief by launching an offensive against western Germany. Inspired by the Mayor, who had been appointed Civilian Commissioner, the citizens threw themselves into the defence, fighting the fires, supplying the defenders, tending the homeless, and burying the dead. Capitulation only came on 28 September, by which time all water and power supplies had been cut. 50,000 citizens were dead, and 15 per cent of the urban fabric, including the Royal Castle, destroyed. In Germany, Hitler ordered all the church bells of the Reich to be rung in celebration for a week, every day between noon and one o'clock.[14]

Warsaw's defiant stand attracted many admiring descriptions:

> By September 14, Wehrmacht armor and infantry had surrounded Warsaw, and the Germans under a flag of truce delivered a demand to the Poles for unconditional surrender. But instead of giving up, the people of Warsaw began to fortify the city.
>
> Men, women and children worked into the night digging trenches in parks, playgrounds and vacant lots. Wealthy Warsaw aristocrats were chauffeured to defense sites where they toiled alongside office workers. Trolley cars were thrown across thoroughfares; barricades of cars and furniture were erected in narrow streets.
>
> When the German tanks jumped off for the attack, instead of

blitzing through as they had [done] on the Polish plains, they were stopped dead – in many cases by civilians who dashed boldly into the street to toss burning rags under the vehicles, causing them to catch fire and explode. German infantrymen, who had mopped up the Polish Army in open country, were pinned down by snipers, who seemed to have turned every house into a pillbox. Warsaw Radio helped carry on the battle in its own way. Every 30 seconds, it transmitted portions of [a Chopin Polonaise] to tell the world that the capital was still in Polish hands.

Angered by the unexpected setback, the German High Command decided to pound the stubborn citadel into submission. In round-the-clock raids, bombers knocked out flourmills, gasworks, power plants and reservoirs, then sowed the residential areas with incendiaries. One witness, passing scenes of carnage, enumerated the horrors: 'Everywhere corpses, wounded humans, dead horses . . . and hastily-dug graves.' . . .

Finally food ran out, and famished Poles, as one man put it, 'cut off flesh as soon as a horse fell, leaving only the skeleton.' On September 28, Warsaw Radio replaced the polonaise with a funeral dirge.[15]

On 5 October 1939, the *Führer* visited Warsaw for the only time in his life. Standing on a podium beside one of the broad tree-lined boulevards, he took the salute of his victorious Eighth Army. After the two-hour march-past, he visited the Belvedere Palace before hurrying back to Berlin.

In his diary entry for 10 October, after a word of appreciation for Lloyd George and a note about 'having to wait for Chamberlain', Joseph Goebbels summed up the mood of the Nazi leadership:

> The *Führer*'s verdict on the Poles is damning. More like animals than human beings, completely primitive, stupid and amorphous. And a ruling class that is the unsatisfactory result of mingling between the lower order and an Aryan master race. The Poles' dirtiness is unimaginable. Their capacity for intelligent judgement is absolutely nil . . .[16]

The military's control of conquered Poland lasted until 25 October. In that short time, according to one source, 714 mass executions were carried out, and 6,376 people, mainly Catholics, were shot.[17] Other sources put the death-toll in one town alone at 20,000. It was a taste of things to come.

The German administration of occupied Poland bore little resemblance to the occupation regimes in Western Europe, and is not to be compared to the far milder conditions in Vichy France, Denmark, or the Netherlands. The western districts annexed to the Reich were immediately cleansed of vast numbers of 'undesirables'. The central parts, adjacent to the Soviet Zone, were set up as a separate General Government, entirely subordinated to SS control, and run by Hitler's former legal expert, Hans Frank. The General Government was a police-run mini-state, where all existing laws and most institutions were abolished and where regular German administrative and judicial systems were *not* introduced. It was the lawless laboratory of Nazi racial ideology. In due course, it became the base both for the main Nazi concentration camps – Auschwitz, Maidanek, Plaschau – and of the dedicated death camps such as Treblinka, Belzec, and Sobibor. Its mission, according to Frank's précis of the *Führer*'s orders, was 'to finish off the Poles at all cost'.[18] Its nicknames included 'Gestapoland', 'the Gangster Gau', 'the Vandal Gau', and 'Frank-Reich'.

Governor Frank was a complex character, who was much more intelligent than most of his fellow Nazis, yet incapable of resisting the temptations of his post. He was one of the few close followers of Hitler to analyse his own thoughts and actions, and left a diary of thirty-eight volumes. In reflective mood, he could be remarkably honest. He admitted being two people – 'me myself, and the other Frank, the Nazi leader.' 'This one looks at the other', he would confess, 'and says "What a louse you are!"' During his trial at Nuremberg, it was Frank who declared 'Not a thousand years will cleanse Germany of its guilt.' But in office, he always gave way to his lower instincts. 'Humanity', he wrote in his diary in June 1942, 'is a word that one dares not use.' Or again, 'The power and the certainty of being able to use force without any resistance are the sweetest and most noxious poison that can be introduced into any Government.' Hence, when in time his policies did provoke resistance, he was one of the few Nazis to propose concessions. Himmler thought such weakness intolerable. 'Frank', he ranted in one outburst, 'is a traitor to the Fatherland, who is hand in glove with the Poles.'[19] This may be compared to one of Frank's own outbursts. Asked by a journalist for a comparison between the General Government and the Protectorate of Bohemia and

Moravia, he waxed lyrical. 'In Prague,' he said, 'big red posters were put up on which one could read that seven Czechs had been shot today. I said to myself, "If I had to put up a poster for every seven Poles shot, the forests of Poland would not be sufficient to manufacture the paper." '[20]

Governor Ludwig Fischer, Doctor of Jurisprudence and *SA-Gruppenführer*, ruled Warsaw for Frank from 24 October 1939 until January 1945. He had joined the NSDAP when a young law student at Heidelberg, and he was already a member of the party's 'Storm Detachments' before he had completed his PhD. As a result, he embodied two of the Nazis' worst characteristics – the zeal for administrative engineering and the acceptance of violence. Yet he appears to have been more of a compliant bureaucrat than a fanatical monster. And he does not seem to have relished the idea that the city of his charge was slated for downgrading. Talking to Hans Frank in February 1940, he complained that the population of Warsaw was not subservient and that 'it was proving impossible to play one class off against another.' He was then told, perhaps as a reassurance, that *Reichsmarschall* Göring (unlike Himmler) was opposed to Warsaw's Germanization and that the *Führer* would permit a Polish community to remain. After two years of occupation, in October 1941, Fischer claimed that Warsaw had won its 'right to existence', especially as its tax revenue was as high as that of Cracow, Radom, and Lublin combined. The trouble was that the Varsovians could not be made to love the New Order, and in later discussions with the top brass of the General Government, Fischer found himself on the defensive. At a meeting in the Belvedere Palace on 24 January 1943 he complained about public health, about the black market, and about the problem of coping with 23,000 *Reichsdeutsch* and *Volksdeutsch* who had presumably swamped the German quarter. He listened to an argument between the proponents and opponents of intensified police methods. Eight months later, on 24 September 1943, he heard an SS officer named Bierkamp describe the security situation in Warsaw as deplorable. According to the officer, 25,000 former Polish officers and 30,000 Jews were hiding in the city, were not registering for work, were operating against German interests, and ought to be shot.[21]

On close analysis, one can see that Fischer's moderation was purely tactical. He never shrank from the most inhumane aspects of creating the *Lebensraum*. He built the Warsaw Ghetto, and presided over its destruction. He transformed the Varsovians into third-rate citizens in their own town, and supervised the increasingly murderous attempts to contain them. His chilling report of 15 October 1942 says it all:

> The Jewish settlement area is essentially empty . . . It is not yet possible to say what the economic effects of decreasing Warsaw's population by about 400,000 are going to be. These economic disadvantages must be accepted however, because the extinction of Jewry is unconditionally required for political reasons.[22]

The municipal administration over which Fischer presided was run entirely by imported German officials. One may presume that some of the in-coming bureaucrats were there simply for the job and the money. But the General Government seems to have attracted more than its share of sadists, degenerates, adventurers, and committed Nazis, who willingly participated in 'the experiment in the east'. These monsters naturally gravitated to the various branches of the German police service, but they were often found in one of the more harmless-sounding resorts, like the Accommodation Office or the Labour Department, where the opportunities for excess and corruption were ubiquitous.

The police service of the Warsaw District, 1940–45, consisted of five main departments. Departments I and II dealt with administration and finance, and training. Department III (*Sicherheitsdienst*, or Security), under *SS-Stbf.* Ernst Kah, poked its fingers into all aspects of city life, and had its own police, the *Sicherheitspolizei*, or *Sipo*, whose agents often operated incognito. Department IV (*Gegner und Abwehr*, literally Opponent and Defence), under *SS-Hstuf.* Walter Stamm, linked counterintelligence and the suppression of undesirables. Its 'A-Section' (*SS-Hstuf.* Gottlieb Höhmann) was the largest in the whole service, and was directed against the Underground. Its subsections were each assigned to specific targets:

IV-A1	partisans, Communists, illegal radio transmitters
IV-A2	sabotage, armed attacks, false documents
IV-A3	1. right-wing organizations 2. courts 3. secret political organizations 4. conspiratorial resistance
IV-A4	protection service for Nazi officials
IV-A5	codes and decipherment
IV-B	religious opposition: RC Church, Freemasons, Jewish affairs
IV-C	arrests, prisons, press
IV-D	hostages, foreigners, illegals
IV-E	economic intelligence, postal security, desertion
IV-N	special Gestapo assignments (*Lt.* Wolfgang Birkner)

Department V (Crime), under *SS-Stbf.* H. Geisler, was the realm of the *Kripo* (Criminal Police). It was assisted by a large body of Polish detectives working under German orders; and it supplied the higher ranks of the municipal 'Blue Police'. Its special forces included the *Schupo* ('Guard Police') and the regular patrols of the *Orpo* ('Order Police'), whose armoured trucks always stood waiting at sensitive points in the city, their engines running and their roof-mounted machine guns primed.

As in all totalitarian systems, some of the most powerful agencies operated outside the regular structures. One of these was the *Sonderkommando der Befehlshaber der Sicherheitspolizei* of *SS-Hstuf.* Alfred Spilker, whose influence in the Warsaw Gestapo was far greater than his lowly captain's rank might have suggested. Another was the small *Rollkommando* ('Hit Squad') commanded by *SS-Ustuf.* Erich Marten. Equipped with a couple of fast cars, Marten's men were empowered to intervene with force without regard to established procedures. The people whom they arrested did not appear on the lists of either the Paviak Jail or of the Gestapo. They disappeared without trace.[23]

Excluding the Blue Police, the number and variety of armed and militarized German police units in Warsaw grew steadily. By 1943, they totalled nearly 6,000 men. Needless to say, they could call on the far better equipped and more numerous troops of the SS, the Wehrmacht, and the Luftwaffe at the least sign of trouble.

A long list of German officials earned themselves a reputation for needless nastiness, and in due course, all their names would be found on the 'Head List' of Underground revenge. Unfortunately for them, the Nazi Command judged their performance unsatisfactory. And in September 1943, one of the rising stars of the SS, *Brig.Fhr.* Franz Kutschera, was sent to Warsaw to steel their mettle. Kutschera was an Austrian, who served as a boy in the Austro-Hungarian navy, had studied in Budapest, and had lived in Czechoslovakia. So he was an East European expert. Joining the NSDAP in 1930, he was an early enthusiast who by the age of thirty-four was Gauleiter of his native Carinthia. After front-line service in France, he found his métier in the grisly business of keeping order in the east. He served successively as 'SS and Police Chief' in *Russland Mitte* and in Mogilev. Warsaw was no doubt a worthy promotion.

Warsaw's role within the General Government was intended to be a secondary one. Warsaw was to absorb large numbers of refugees and expellees from the Reich, and would then gradually decline. It lost its capital status to 'Krakau', which the Nazis declared to be an ancient

German foundation and the only one to have a future. In 1940, an architect called Pabst prepared plans for a new Warsaw with a much-reduced urban area. It was one of many Nazi plans which never came to fruition.

The Gestapo established its control over Warsaw in the early months by filtering the entire population, allocating them to racial categories and issuing them with the relevant documents. In order to live, every person required a Certificate of Racial Origin, an identity card (*Kennkarte*), and a ration card. Identity cards and ration cards were issued in accordance with the recipient's racial classification, which in doubtful cases would be established after a detailed examination by Nazi 'scientists'. The classification was drawn up in a strict hierarchy of superior and inferior groups, and with the clear intention of separating those whom the Nazis wanted to prosper from those who were doomed to fade away.

Racial Group			Daily Ration in Calories (1941)
Aryans	Germans	*Reichsdeutsch* (Germans from the Reich)	2,613
		Volksdeutsch (ethnic Germans)	2,613
	Non-Germans	suitable for Germanization	669
		Mischlings (mixed race)	669
Non-Aryan Subhumans		Non-Germans unsuitable for Germanization Jews defined by descent Homosexuals Gypsies, imbeciles, incurables	184

Later in the war, when the Nazis were desperate for recruits, they introduced a Category III, of non-Germans. These were people who in theory possessed some slight evidence of German ancestry and who were thereby qualified for military service.

Once this system was in place, Varsovians were entirely dependent on their wits and on the possession of 'correct' documents. The SS and the Gestapo who controlled it were backed up by militarized German police, by the local 'blue police', and by a ubiquitous army of informers. Anyone could be stopped on the street, arrested on suspicion, or, as increasingly happened, shot on the spot.

Even so, the Nazis possessed no ready-made plans for implementing their radical racial ambitions. In the first instance, their priorities lay with eliminating potential troublemakers, building facilities, and segregating Jews.

The *Ausserordentliche Befriedungsaktion* (*AB-Aktion*, or Extraordinary Pacification Campaign) seems to have had its origins in the Nazi–Soviet Treaty of Friendship of 28 September 1939, which foresaw common action against 'Polish agitators'. A conference attended by SS and NKVD officers took place in Cracow in March 1940, though its deliberations have not been documented. Shortly afterwards, the NKVD shot 25,000 Polish officers captured in the Soviet Zone, while the SS launched the *AB-Aktion* in the German Zone. The aim, in both cases, can only have been to kill the political and intellectual elite of the country. On this occasion, the SS could not match the performance of their Soviet partners. Some 3,500 persons were shot, and a larger consignment sent to Dachau and Sachsenhausen. In Warsaw, some 1,700 men and women were rounded up and driven 25km (fifteen miles) to an execution site at Palmiry on the edge of the Kampinos Forest. They included writers, academics, priests, Olympic athletes, parliamentary leaders, and politicians (but not Communists for the simple reason that Stalin's purges had left very few Polish Communists for the Nazis to kill).

Himmler's order to create a major concentration camp at Auschwitz for the purposes of the General Government can be dated to March 1940. It was designed to accommodate 10,000 inmates. A second camp at Auschwitz II-Birkenau began operation in October 1941 with a nominal capacity for 100,000, which was soon exceeded. Unlike Cracow and Lublin, Warsaw was not given a major concentration camp in its immediate vicinity, but in 1942 a relatively minor camp, KZ Warschau, was established in a closed-off block of streets within the city limits.

For reasons connected with its post-war fate, KZ Warschau has all but disappeared from the history books, but its grisly existence was real enough, and it features in the documentation of the Nuremberg Tribunal. Created by a series of personal directives from Himmler, it operated from October 1942 to August 1944. It consisted of a complex of five sub-camps, which were linked by a series of purpose-built railway lines. One sub-camp, in the western suburbs, had originally served in 1939 as a transit centre for POWs; two, on Goose and Bonifrater Streets, were located on the territory of the Ghetto; and two more were built in the immediate vicinity of Warsaw's Western Station. In all, the complex contained 119 barracks with space for 41,000 inmates. A set of gas chambers was constructed in a tunnel linking the two areas next to the Western Station, and three crematoria continued to function on the 'Goose Farm' site, right up to August 1944.

Attempts to ascertain the numbers and provenance of the people who died in KZ Warschau have been surrounded with unanswered questions. One estimate puts the total at 200,000, and relates the figure to the constant round-ups, executions, and collective punishments perpetrated by the SS within Warsaw itself. Some commentators have linked it to the long-standing 'Pabst Plan' of 1940, which aimed to reduce the city's population to half a million. At all events, there is every reason to separate the crimes committed in KZ Warschau from those connected with the Ghetto. And there was no shortage of eye-witness accounts:

> During the Occupation . . . [stated Adela K.] I lived about 3000 yards from the tunnel near the Western Station. We saw covered German lorries there for the first time in the autumn of 1942. They were driven by SS men in black uniforms . . . and entered the tunnel from the Armatna Street side. . . . After the arrival of each transport, one could hear screams and smell gas . . .: and the Germans ordered all the inhabitants [of the district] to draw their curtains. Any window, where the curtains were not drawn, would be shot at . . .[24]

> Many times, Felix J. personally watched as prisoners carried heaps of corpses from the tunnel and loaded them onto police trucks marked with the letters 'W.H.'. The corpses did not show any traces of bullets. Members of the *Tod-Kommando*, which was manned by Poles, told him that the remains of people who had been gassed or had otherwise died in the camp, were taken to the crematoria on the 'Goose Farm' to be burned . . .[25]

Oddly enough, Nazi policy in regard to the Catholic Church was less oppressive in the General Government than in the lands annexed directly by the Reich. In the Warthegau, for example, nine out of ten Polish parishes were closed, and the remaining clergy were subordinated to the German hierarchy. About 2,000 Polish priests were cast into Dachau alone, and with no whisper of protest from the Vatican. But in the General Government, the SS chose to let sleeping dogs lie. The primate was abroad. The bishops were docile. Other issues were more pressing.

There had been no Jewish Ghetto in pre-war Warsaw, so in November 1939 the Nazi command decided to create one. All persons who were not in possession of Ayran papers were ordered to congregate in the pre-designated area. All non-Jewish residents of the Ghetto area were expelled, and notices were posted to the effect that any Jews caught outside the Ghetto without formal permission would be killed. Within a year, the segregation of the Jews was virtually complete. The operation cut them off from the rest of the city by a continuous 6m (twenty-foot) wall topped with barbed wire and surrounded by armed guards. It had baleful consequences. It meant that the SS could apply entirely separate measures to the Jewish population. It also meant that non-Jewish Varsovians had no means of readily helping their Jewish co-citizens in their distress.

The German presence in Warsaw was stifling. Two main sections of the city centre were designated NUR FÜR DEUTSCHE – 'For Germans Only'. One of them, centred on the Adolf Hitler Platz (otherwise Pilsudski Square), contained a dense array of administrative institutions. The other, which ringed the Gestapo Headquarters on Schuch Avenue, was the official police district. Yet all the other districts and suburbs were given their military bases and fortified police stations. The pattern created by over twenty such bases and over a hundred police posts represented an even scatter rather than a limited number of large concentrations. It was admirably suited to the systematic patrolling of a quiescent populace. But it would be less effective when challenged by armed rebels. No single base was strong enough to act as a focus for offensive measures: and each base had to look to its own defences. What is more, the German military garrison was well below strength. It was designed to have 36,000 troops at its disposal; by mid-1944 it possessed barely half that.

The escalation of public violence was one of the features of German rule in Warsaw from 1943 onwards. When Nazi policies provoked open resistance both in the Ghetto and on the 'Aryan side', the Nazis did not see the causal link between oppression and defiance. Instead, they expressed astonishment at the disregard for their authority. On 10 October 1943, Varsovians listened to the pronouncement by megaphone of Governor Frank's 'Decree regarding the suppression of attacks on German reconstruction works'. Three days later, they watched helplessly as the SS started an extended programme of mass round-ups. In contrast to previous policy, the victims were not sent off to the Reich for compulsory labour or to the concentration camps. They were destined for street executions, where large groups would be shot as a collective punishment, usually for unspecified crimes. The names, ages, and addresses of the executed were posted at the site of their death, together with a second list of names of people who were held as hostages, and who would automatically be shot if anyone should dare to retaliate.

> From then on, scores of people were killed almost every day . . . most frequently people seized at random on the streets. The execution of hostages took place behind heavy police cordons . . . The manhunts were conducted with great brutality by the police and were often accompanied by the Wehrmacht, the Luftwaffe, or even by youngsters from the Hitlerjugend, who would shoot escapers or 'suspicious' passers-by. The city was transformed into a jungle, in which not just 'slave traders' and 'gangs of thugs' were at large to hand the unfortunate over. Now, nothing protected one from death – not the 'right documents', not a clean record, not a lack of contact with the Underground, not even collaborationist inclinations, neither illness nor advanced age. The inhabitants of Warsaw were turned into hunted animals, who had to go outside to live, but who were constantly on edge, lest they were pounced on. One could go out to buy a bottle of milk and not return, then be found on the list of hostages . . . to be shot [as] 'enemies of German reconstruction'. One could be grabbed in a restaurant, in a shop, in a church, or in one's own home. Life became a daily game of chance with death. The immediacy and the visibility of the threat was far greater then previously. One could see with one's own eyes the names of one's neighbours, relatives, colleagues, and loved ones on the lists of the condemned. Their blood was literally flowing in the city's gutters. The threat dominated everything. And the unseen hand had managed to write on the walls – *Mane, Tekel, Fares.*[26]

Just as conditions in the Ghetto were to deteriorate from the bad to the terminal, so conditions in the rest of the city, once the Ghetto was suppressed, deteriorated from the bad to the unbearable.[27]

Nazi cultural policy was based on the open assertion that German culture was infinitely superior to anything else. Polish cultural institutions, in so far as they were temporarily allowed to survive, were to be tailored to the needs of a semi-educated, non-executive caste of helots. In a discussion on the treatment of the Polish population on 2 October 1940, Hitler had stated his belief that 'the Poles were born just for heavy labour'.[28] As a result, all Polish universities, technical colleges, and secondary schools were shut. All museums, galleries, libraries, theatres, cinemas, concert halls, and theatres were taken over by German administrators for German use. A residue of Polish-language primary schools, newspapers, and meeting-places was permitted to function under the strict supervision of the Gestapo.

Nazi economic policy was no less ruthless. All state enterprises, all major private businesses, all factories, all professional firms, and all large or medium-sized estates were sequestrated without compensation. The country's managerial elite was dispossessed en masse, their property distributed to German companies, and their posts handed over to the incoming swarms of Schindlerite German adventurers. Agriculture was run on the basis of forced deliveries. The entire industrial production of the General Government was put at the disposal of the economic department of the RSHA ('Reich Security Main Office'). Nowhere in the whole Nazi empire was the 'Master Race' given such complete control over a conquered nation so comprehensively enslaved.

The Nazis' ideal *Lebensraum* would clearly take time to emerge. But two groups of people were subjected to extreme measures from the outset. In 1939–40, SS agents toured the General Government's hospitals, psychiatric wards, and asylums, quietly listing the mentally sick or physically sick for 'euthanasia'. At the same time, other specialist agents (often 'brown sisters' from the NSV, the Nazi welfare organization) were rounding up children for the improvement of the German gene pool. During his first visit to Poland in October 1939 aboard his special train, Heinrich Himmler had noticed that many Polish children were tall, blond, and blue-eyed. To the Nazi mind, their appearance revealed the presence of millions of inappropriately polonized youngsters of disguised German stock. So the answer was simple. 'Good blood' had to be saved, just as inferior blood had to be destroyed. Tens of thousands of suitable boys and girls were snatched from orphanages or simply kidnapped on the streets and shipped to the Reich either for adoption by German families or for the breeding programmes at *SS Lebensborn* homes. The feelings of their relatives did not come into the reckoning.[29]

Knowledge of these matters in the outside world remained sketchy. A few American correspondents, who were not yet enemy subjects, visited Warsaw in 1939–41, but their contacts were limited. The exiled Polish Government did its best to publicize the realities of Nazi rule. But it could not receive reliable information without delay, and its revelations were not universally believed. After all, horror stories about the 'pitiless Hun' were well known from the First World War, and were well known to have been exaggerated.

Historians, therefore, have a very different perspective from contemporaries. Whilst recording contemporary confusions, they are fully entitled to make assessments on the fuller information which was made available later. In this regard, they can hardly avoid the conclusion that Nazi repressions in the German Zone were not so extensive in 1939–41 as those perpetrated in Soviet Zone. For the newfound KZ-system was minuscule compared to the well-established Gulag. The social engineering of the SS was not so ambitious at this stage as that of the NKVD. And the death toll to the west of the River Bug was not yet as high as that to the east.

In the era of Hitler's partnership with Stalin, the General Government was not completely cut off from the Soviet Union. Limited traffic crossed the 'Peace Boundary'. Trains passed through Warsaw every day carrying oil, chemicals, iron ore, and steel to Germany. Selected travellers moved back and forth, and refugees from the Soviet zone, including Jewish refugees who couldn't imagine a German-run territory to be so bad, arrived every day. The news from the east was uniformly grim. Stalin's paradise was a place of terror. People in the Soviet Zone were being dispossessed, persecuted, beaten, deported, and killed.

The story of the Warsaw Ghetto has been told many times, and rightly so. It was an episode of unbounded inhumanity and sorrow. It is essential to understanding both the Jewish Holocaust and Warsaw's wider wartime tragedy. The celebrated picture of a family being led away to their deaths, hands held high, is perhaps the most stunning image of the Nazi Occupation (see 'Round-up at gunpoint' in the first plate section).

Crammed to bursting with people from outside and abroad, the Warsaw Ghetto was the largest of some eight hundred Nazi-built ghettos in the General Government. At the peak, it contained 380,000 inmates. It was completely under Nazi control, though the SS appointed a Council of Jewish Elders to administer it and a Jewish police force to do most of the dirty work. The Chairman of the Jewish Council, a Warsaw lawyer, committed suicide when the strains of his position became unbearable.[30]

The Ghetto was divided into two sections joined by a large wooden footbridge over Cool Street. The northern section, or 'Big Ghetto', was at least three times the size of the southern section, the 'Little Ghetto'. The former was dreadfully overcrowded from the start, and was undoubtedly the worst place to be. The latter, which contained more than its fair share of affluent residents and superior shops, was regarded as a haven of relative peace. The main street of the northern section ran as far as Bank Square. For two or three years, it was thronged with passers-by, with rickshaws and with its own trams mounted with a blue Star of David. It had cafes and restaurants, at number 40 a 'Soup Kitchen for Writers', and places of amusement. The Fotoplastikon at 27 Leshno Street offered a popular eye on the outside world by showing a series of still pictures of exotic places like Egypt, China, or California. A clown with a red nose stood on the pavement, cajoling people to buy a ticket for 60 groszy. At 2 Leshno Street, the Arts Coffee House laid on a daily cabaret and a stream of concerts featuring singers such as Vera G. or Marysha A., 'the Nightingale of the Ghetto', and musicians such as Ladislas S. and Arthur G. At 35 Leshno Street, the 'Femina' music hall mounted more ambitious productions from a wide Polish repertoire including the 'Princess of the Czardas' revue, and the aptly named comedy *Love Seeks an Apartment*. It was all a desperate form of escapism. As someone remarked, 'Humour is the Ghetto's only form of defence'.[31]

The Ghetto functioned from November 1939 to May 1943. In that span, it passed through five phases. At first it was open to visitors, and inmates, who were required to wear a yellow Star of David on their armband, were free to pass through the gates during the daytime. From 15 October 1941, the gates were permanently closed, inmates were subject to immediate execution if discovered outside, and the Ghetto gradually assumed the characteristics of a concentration camp. From January 1942, the Ghetto began to be emptied by regular, forced deportations to the death camps, principally to Treblinka. After an armed uprising in April and May 1943 it became a silent, smouldering graveyard inhabited only by a handful of SS guards and a body of prisoners detailed to tidy up the ruins. It was an unspoken warning of what could happen to the city as a whole.

The predicament of the Ghetto within Warsaw as a whole is not easily described. One may liken it to a sealed and watertight torture-chamber deep in the hold of a ship that had itself been hijacked by pirates. What is more, the perfidious progression of Nazi policy long prevented people from recognizing the ultimate objective. The deliberations of the Wannsee Conference in January 1942, when Nazi leaders decided to perpetrate 'the Final Solution of the Jewish Question' with all speed, were kept strictly secret. When this stage started, and victims were dragged or driven to the cattle wagons waiting on the *Umschlagplatz* (shipment centre), the Nazis used the same euphemism that was familiar from earlier Soviet deportations – 'resettlement in the east'. The gates of the Ghetto carried a health warning: 'BEWARE OF TYPHUS.'

The variety of people who were herded into the Ghetto was surprising. The native Varsovians, who spoke either Polish or Yiddish, could not easily speak to the Germans, French, and Greeks shipped in from abroad. Though Orthodox Jews probably formed a majority, there was a large group of secularized or non-religious Jews; and there was a sizeable contingent of Jewish Catholics. This last group, whose main Church of the Nativity of the Blessed Virgin Mary stood at 34 Leshno Street, had been common enough in pre-war Warsaw. They came from convert families who had shed their Jewish identity at various points over the previous two hundred years. According to reports reaching London, they were discriminated against by the Jewish police. Yet the Gestapo, when classifying people, were not interested in religion or in disputes among Jews. They were only interested in 'blood'.

The Gestapo's supervision of the Ghetto centred on a building at 13 Leshno Street, which housed the Bureau for Combating Bribery and Speculation. This agency formed the cover for an operation with much wider and more sinister functions. Universally known as 'the Thirteenth', it employed several hundred men who acted as the eyes and ears of the Gestapo and who, from their hats with green piping, attracted the label of 'gamekeepers'. Its director was a colourful figure, a pre-war journalist called Abraham G., who enjoyed complete immunity from the Ghetto Police and Jewish Council, reporting directly to Dr Ernst Kah, the Chief of Department III of the Warsaw SD.

By all accounts, Abraham G.'s motives were somewhat contorted. He was certainly an opportunist, who rapidly made a large fortune from the extortionate rents of properties which he had licensed from the SS. At the same time, he seems to have harboured a scheme for setting up a Jewish autonomous region, where he and his fellow Jews could survive. And he used his money to patronize the Ghetto's cultural and artistic activities. After a long absence in 1942, when he probably lived on the 'Aryan Side' under a false name, he briefly reappeared in the Ghetto early in 1943. He and his family are thought to have been shot in the Paviak Jail soon afterwards.

Huge discrepancies existed in the Ghetto between rich and poor. In the early days, well-heeled inmates could buy spacious properties from departing owners and bring in luxuries, valuables, and jewellery, which could later be exchanged for food and services. As late as 1943, the Ghetto still contained islands of affluence amidst the sea of starvation and misery. One honest survivor reported how his own family was able to sit down to a complete table at their annual Passover feast, even when the bombs and bullets of the Ghetto Rising were exploding outside. Dances and concerts were arranged right to the end.[32] Ghetto life was infinitely harsher for most. But the reality becomes all the more poignant when one realizes that most of that family's neighbours had already been exterminated, or had died from exhaustion on the street. Overall, the survival rate was less than 1 per cent.

By general consent, the most blood-chilling scenes in the Ghetto were those of starving, suffering children. From 1941 onwards skeletal waifs expired on the open streets, hundreds every day, and often in the vicinity of well-stocked foodstores where the wealthy spent their money. The race for survival did not encourage charity. Ragged urchins, who were thin enough to squeeze through the cracks in parts of the wooden Ghetto Wall, risked their precarious lives smuggling. Others, inured to the sight of death, played street games amid the corpses of their dead or dying fellows.[33]

Once the deportations started the pressure of sheer numbers diminished, but the murder rate increased. The agony of one day was recorded by a diarist whose account, secretly buried, survived when he did not:

> Sunday, 9 August [1942]. The 19th day of the 'action,' of which human history has not seen the like. From yesterday, the expulsion took on the character of a pogrom, or of a simple massacre. They roam through the streets and murder people in their dozens, in their hundreds. Today, they are pulling endless wagons – uncovered – full of corpses, through the streets.
>
> Everything that I have read about the events of 1918–19 pales in comparison . . . It is clear to us that 99 percent of those transported are being taken to their deaths. In addition to the atrocities, hunger haunts us . . . The 'elite' still get some [soup at a factory kitchen], but the rabble don't even get that.
>
> Twenty Ukrainians, Jewish policemen (a few dozen) and a small number of Germans lead a crowd of 3,000 Jews to the slaughter. One hears only of isolated cases of resistance. One Jew took on a German and was shot on the spot . . .

> The slaughter went on from early morning until nine and half-past nine at night. This was a pogrom with all the traits familiar from the Tsarist pogroms . . . I have heard that people are being slaughtered with bayonets . . .[34]

A fortnight after this, one of Poland's most famous couriers, Jan 'Karski', made arrangements to see the inside of the Ghetto with his own eyes. He entered through a tunnel that started in a cellar on the Aryan side:

> 'There was hardly a square yard of empty space', [Karski] recalled. 'As we picked our way across the mud and rubble, the shadows of what had once been men and women flitted by us in pursuit of someone or something, their eyes blazing with some insane hunger or greed.' The cries of the mad or hungry echoed through the streets, mingling with the voices of residents offering to barter scraps of clothing for morsels of food.
>
> [Karski] identified the stench in his nostrils, just as he discerned the unclothed corpses strewn in the gutters . . .
>
> 'What does this mean?' he asked under his breath.
>
> 'When a Jew dies,' [his guide] replied, 'the family removes the clothing and throws the body in the street. Otherwise they would have to pay a burial tax to the Germans . . .
>
> [The guide] relentlessly pointed out every macabre example of the zone's bestial conditions . . . 'Remember this', he repeated over and over, 'Remember this!'[35]

Later that year, the courier reached Washington. He was taken by the Polish Ambassador to tell his tale to a group of American Jewish leaders, including Justice Felix Frankfurter of the Supreme Court. 'I did not say that this young man is lying', Justice Frankfurter protested; 'I said I am unable to believe him.'[36]

The last sight of Warsaw for perhaps 310,000 Jews was glimpsed in the infamous *Umschlagplatz*, from which the trains left for Treblinka. Its commandant was a senior Jewish policeman called Szmerling, a 'criminal giant', 'a monster with a spiked beard and the face of a bandit.' His German superiors called him 'the Jewish Torturer'. His customers nicknamed him 'Balbo', apparently because he looked like one of Mussolini's marshals.[37] Located at the north-eastern end of the Ghetto, at the junction of Zamenhoff and Low Streets, the *Umschlagplatz* was carefully designed to mask its activities. The approaches to the specially built railway siding, where the trains waited, consisted of a labyrinthine series of pathways and open spaces, all hidden by high brick walls. The daily consignments of several thousand deportees – men, women, and children – were driven up Zamenhoff Street by the baton-wielding policemen and by heavily armed SS guards. Delay or dissent invited an instant bullet. Shuffling towards a barricade that blocked the street, the deportees were ordered to turn into a gateway on the right and then to double back along a walled trapway that led to another barricade. There they passed the observation post of the Commandant of the *Umschlagplatz* before spilling into an open square some 80m long by 30m wide (260 by 90 feet). They could see nothing but the sky, the walls, and a former hospital building that contained offices. They watched as the SS picked out a selection of strong young adults destined for slave labour in concentration camps; and they were then pushed through yet another gateway into the former hospital forecourt, where they spent the night in the open. Already hungry, cold, exhausted, and confused, they were ordered in the morning to move back through the square and through a different opening, where at last they saw the cattle trucks into which they were crammed for their last journey. Their destination, Treblinka, had no facilities except for death.

The role played by Ghetto dwellers in the mechanics of their own destruction is not always emphasized. Yet it is well understood by anyone who has been forced to live under the pressures of a totalitarian system. The life-choices which were available under Nazi rule, and still less in the Ghetto, were not those which apply in a free world. Jewish elders collaborated with the SS because, among other things, they wanted to limit their people's suffering. Jewish policemen agreed to assist the SS in the killing of Jews because they (wrongly) thought they could increase their own chances of survival.[38] All one can say is that all human beings are endowed with 'human nature', which is not, alas, spotlessly pure, and that commentators living in freedom in another age should not rush to pass judgement. Every person, and every community, has its breaking point. People will bear deprivation and humiliation with a mixture of fatalism, resignation, and fortitude. But they cannot do so indefinitely. If the maltreatment is unrelenting, the time comes when the maltreated will react violently, regardless of the consequences. In the Warsaw Ghetto, this point was reached in April 1943 when the Ghetto Rising erupted.

One should not imagine, however, that the heroism of the Ghetto should be solely attributed to those who eventually chose to fight. In this respect, there were numerous examples of heroic sacrifice by men and women who saw their prime duty in the service of others. The nurses battling impossibly painful scenes in the children's hospitals would be high on anyone's list. So, too, would be the team of medical researchers who chose for their project the mental and physical changes in their own bodies on the road to death from starvation. But many would want to honour the noble figure of Dr Yanush K., the most popular children's writer in Poland, who chose to live and die for his charges at an orphanage transferred to the Ghetto. He led his boys and girls to the *Umschlagplatz* by the hand, singing a song, and telling them that they would all enjoy 'the picnic'. There is nothing more heart-rending than to imagine Yanush K.'s kids reciting the lines of Julian T.'s 'Lokomotywa' as they listened in the dark to the rhythm of the railway track on their last journey to Treblinka: '*Tak to to, tak to to, tak to to, tak to to* . . .'[39]

Much breath has been expended condemning the alleged indifference of the Gentile population to this appalling agony. The accusers may have a point. But they are unwise to press it too harshly. For as Jewish eyewitnesses have related from their own observations, exactly the same attitudes can be found among the more affluent residents of the Ghetto:

> [The critics] don't wish to understand the behaviour of those who tried to live a 'normal' existence, and not to pay attention to the crimes being committed all around them . . . [They] limit themselves to judgements of the Poles . . . ignoring the fact that many Jews behaved in exactly the same way . . . In those conditions, Poles, Jews, and any other nationality would behave in more or less the same fashion, for such conduct forms part of what one might call 'human nature'.[40]

The question remains of how much could have been known to the world beyond the Ghetto walls. The answer must be 'a great deal', but in limited circles. The Polish Underground certainly knew what was going on, and tried to organize assistance. Some Varsovians would have met or harboured escapees from the Ghetto, and would have heard their harrowing accounts in person. Many others would not have heard, or did not want to hear, or did not know what to make of the rumours. Active sympathy was scarce; and passive antipathy was rife.[41] The real difficulty lay in publicizing the facts. The German press and radio said nothing. The German-controlled media were muzzled. Underground news-sheets did not reach the outside world. The Nazis made every effort to suppress information. Yet trams packed with Varsovians trundled every couple of minutes along Cool Street, under the bridge that connected the two parts of the Ghetto. Their occupants could see the towering walls with their own eyes, and knew that their fellow citizens were being horribly maltreated. But for two years at least they had few sure means of learning about the true scale or nature of the disaster. Nonetheless, after the Ghetto Rising, when everyone could hear the sickening silence of the ruins, no one could doubt that the Nazis had been intent on total extermination.

In London, the ordeal of the Warsaw Ghetto was known, but did not push the Powers into action. The Allied Governments were preoccupied with the War. One of the Jewish representatives in the National Council of the exiled Government committed suicide in protest. A Polish soldier-poet, then in Italy, wrote a poem in his memory. He saw a bright future:

> For us, a common sky will shine above Warsaw destroyed,
> When victory crowns our long and blood-soaked toils.
> Freedom, justice and a crust of bread will be everyone's lot.
> There will arise, supreme, a single race of noble souls.[42]

By focusing on the Ghetto, some commentators have implied that conditions 'on the Aryan Side' – as the Nazis put it – were rather plush. This is hardly the right way to describe them. The truth is the Nazi Terror raged in all parts of Warsaw, but with different degrees of intensity at different times and at different locations. The special loathing for Poles, which inspired Nazi conduct to Warsaw, cannot be repeated too often. It was well expressed by Goebbels on the day of the *Führer*'s visit:

> The *Führer* has no intention of assimilating the Poles. They are to be forced into their truncated state and left entirely to their own devices. If Henry the Lion had conquered the East . . . the result would certainly have been a stronger slavicised race of German mongrels. Better the present situation: now we know the laws of racial heredity and can handle things accordingly. The *Führer* takes a very positive view . . . We dare not lose our nerve or peace of mind.[43]

Throughout the city, the climate of fear was fostered through a mass of petty administrative measures, through a German monopoly of housing, employment, rations, and prices, and through a daily show of murderous violence. The forced Germanization of public life, and a fraught 'war of symbols', piled humiliation onto a dispossessed citizenry. German became the official language overnight in a largely non-German-speaking city. All institutions and many streets and buildings were given German names. Strict apartheid was enforced. The best wagons and compartments on all trams and trains were reserved for Germans. The sign NUR FÜR DEUTSCHE (Germans Only) appeared in parks and gardens, in apartment blocks, on benches and public toilets, in cafes, restaurants, and hotels. All national monuments were removed. The Chopin Monument was sent for scrap. The Copernicus Statue was adorned with a tablet announcing him as a famous German astronomer. Plans were drawn up to replace the Sigismund Column with something more appropriate.

Nazi policy towards the Catholic clergy of the General Government remained ambiguous. There were no mass purges like those in the Warthegau. Nine out of ten parish priests in Warsaw were allowed to keep their positions. It was said that the Nazis wanted the help of the Catholic Church in its onslaught on 'Bolshevism'. On the other hand, they did not hesitate in liquidating troublesome clerics. On 17 February 1941, for example, five Franciscan friars were taken from a priory near Warsaw, and sent to Auschwitz. One of them was Father Maximilian Kolbe, who had been known before the war for contributing to dubious journals with anti-Semitic overtones. He obviously professed the wrong brand of anti-Semitism.

Public executions, either by hanging or by firing squad, became a daily occurrence. As the condemned were driven to their fate an SS man toured the streets on a lorry and announced the event through a megaphone. The victims were guilty of something or nothing. The least hint of resistance provoked massive reprisals. In December 1939, for example, two German NCOs had been murdered by common criminals, and 120 inhabitants of the Vaver district were dragged out of their homes and shot in response. Nazi policy created bands of homeless and street orphans: they were hunted down and shot. The Nazis systematically took hostages from suspect districts or families. If anyone in the district or family offended, the hostages were killed. In autumn 1943, Governor Frank decreed that the Gestapo could shoot anyone on mere suspicion. The next year, as a gesture of conciliation, public executions were replaced by secret executions in the Ghetto ruins.

From 1942 onwards, Warsaw was subjected to a special form of random terror – the fearsome 'round-ups'. Whenever the SS needed a sizeable group of people – as hostages, reprisal fodder, candidates for forced labour, or whatever – they sealed off a church or hijacked a tramcar, and marched off their catch at gunpoint.

The 'Peacock' Jail on Pavia Street (the Paviak), and its sister prison, the adjoining 'Serbia' for women, were constructions of Tsarist vintage. From 1939, they were located in the heart of the Ghetto. These were the dens into which the Gestapo usually dragged their intended victims for interrogation, torture, and disposal. They continued to provide the same service after the Ghetto was destroyed around them. In five years, they accounted for 100,000 disposals, either shot or sent to the camps.

True to the aim of reducing the Poles to a nation of helots, the Nazis introduced a system of compulsory labour. The *Arbeitsamt* ('Labour Office') was a hated instrument of coercion, which in theory could fix the employment of every adult. In practice, it produced chaos. Its practices were barbaric, being more suited to the KZ-workgangs, which it also oversaw, than to civilian workers. Its labour relations were non-existent; and it signally failed to make sensible use of the vast pool of unemployed workers which Nazi confiscations had created. Both inside and outside the Ghetto, its priorities were for various branches of skilled and unskilled 'war work'. The best workers were drafted to Germany. In other words, good work was rewarded with deportation. Slacking and sabotage were rife. Resentment ran deep.

For many reasons, therefore, Nazi rule in Warsaw did not give rise to an efficient workforce of contented slaves. On the contrary, through its own inconsistencies, it encouraged the growth of a rebellious, pauperized, semi-employed underclass. The discrepancies, between work norms and rations, and between wages and prices, were extreme. In 1941, non-German residents were entitled to 400 grams of flour, barley, or pasta per month compared with 2,000 grams (fourteen and seventy ounces) for Germans, and 1 egg compared with 12. A quarter of the population was destitute, kept alive by soup kitchens provided largely by the Church. Employment brought few dividends. The average Warsaw worker earned 120–300 crowns per month. Yet the average cost of feeding a family of four was 1,568 crowns.[44] The black market flourished. Tuberculosis, rickets, and scarlet fever multiplied. The mortality rate soared. Frank approved a six-fold increase of grain deliveries to Germany. 'The new demand will be fulfilled exclusively at the expense of the foreign population', he stated. 'It must be done cold-bloodedly and without pity.'[45] In Nazi eyes, the Polish population of occupied Poland was 'foreign'.

Nearly 2 million Polish workers were forcibly deported, most of them from the General Government. Once in Germany, they were obliged to wear a violet letter 'P' on their arms, and were forbidden to go to church or the cinema, to use public transportation, or to engage in sexual intercourse. Sex with a German could invoke a death sentence. And Germans who showed any kindness could end up in prison. 'Germans!' they were told, 'Poles . . . are beneath all Germans whether on the farm or in the factory . . . Never forget that you belong to the *Herrenvolk*'.[46] Sooner or later, word of these outrages filtered back home.

One of three special camps for child detention was set up at Lodz, 45km (thirty miles) from Warsaw. It was filled with 'young offenders', who had been caught selling matches or railway coal perhaps, or who had not qualified for Germanization. Up to 12,000 out of 13,000 child detainees at that one camp died.[47]

Once the 'Final Solution' was drawing to a close, the SS turned to the next stage of their racial programme, the clearance of the inhabitants of good agricultural areas designated for colonization by Germans. The pilot scheme was started in November 1942 in the district of Zamost, renamed Himmlerstadt. Varsovians were well aware of the ethnic cleansing practised in 1943–44 in a neighbouring district. SS, Wehrmacht, and Ukrainian auxiliary units descended on defenceless villages. The villagers were given a few minutes to pack and leave, then sorted into four categories. Some were sent to work in the Reich. Some were sent for racial examination. Some were slated for killing. 30,000 children were seized for forcible Germanization. When word spread to Warsaw of trains carrying children to Germany, women lined the tracks offering food and water, and money to bribe the guards for ransoms. 110,000 peasants were removed in two phases. Resisters were shot, their houses burned. Tens of thousands took to the woods. The General Government saw hundreds of Lidices. Further clearances were postponed through German setbacks on the Eastern Front.

News and refugees also reached Warsaw from the *Reichskommissariat Ukraine* and the District of Galicia, where ethnic cleansing on a still grander scale had broken out. Once again, the victims were Polish peasants. The cleansers belonged to a radical branch of the Ukrainian Nationalist Movement, the UPA, encouraged, no doubt, by the Nazis. The savagery matched anything that had been seen in actions against Jewish settlements. Whole families were burned alive in their own homes or churches.

Innocent villagers had their throats cut in the middle of the night. Men, women, and children were axed to death, decapitated, and mutilated. Catholic priests were specially targeted. Babies were butchered, pregnant mothers bayoneted. The murders topped a hundred thousand, and were largely hidden to the outside world for half a century.[48] But they were well known in Warsaw from the accounts of refugees.

The overall effect of Nazi rule, therefore, was to feed the growing impression that the ultimate fate of the 'Non-Germans' could well be the same as that of Warsaw's Jews. If Germany were to lose the war against the Soviet Union, as looked increasingly likely, the Nazis were quite capable of doing what the NKVD had already done in 1941, massacring its slaves and its prisoners before withdrawing. If, on the other hand, Germany were to win the war – which in 1944 was still not impossible – the Nazis would be left in control, and would have all the time in the world to complete the racial reconstruction of their *Lebensraum*.

The number of Jews who survived the clearances of the Ghetto and the Ghetto Rising was larger than is often supposed. The *Encyclopedia Judaica* put it at 15,000 living on the Aryan side in 1944.[49] Other estimates are even higher. The Nazi policy of keeping Jews and non-Jews entirely separate had failed. The effect was to make every single Varsovian fully conscious of what the Nazis could do.[50]

Naturally, no one outside the Nazi leadership knew for certain in 1944 what Himmler and his aides were planning. But in due course, documents and witnesses were to be found showing firstly that the Final Solution was but one stage in a wider programme of racial engineering, and secondly that the worst suspicions of the Poles had been very well grounded. All original copies of the *Generalplan-Ost* seem to have been destroyed, but its contents have been reconstructed, among other things from testimony presented at Nuremberg. It was composed by officials of the RSHA in May 1942, and circulated among SS experts for comment. It contained a precise definition of the *Lebensraum* that was due for repopulation, and made detailed estimates of the number and categories of people to be relocated or eliminated. It named three 'settlement regions' – *Ingermanland* (Novgorod and Petersburg), the *Memel–Narev Gebiet* (Lithuania and Bialystok), and the *Gotengau* (Crimea and Dniepropetrovsk) – and a further thirty-six smaller 'resettlement centres', including Chenstohova, Zamost, and Lvuv. Only 14 million out of 45 million inhabitants of the *Lebensraum* were to be left untouched. Up to 85 per cent of the 19–20 million Poles deemed unsuitable for Germanization were destined either for liquidation or for expulsion to western Siberia.[51]

Totalitarian regimes can extract a measure of collaboration from all those who fall into their grasp. They can coerce people to observe deviant norms, to oppose their own best interests, to give support to undesirable goals, and to work for unwanted war efforts. Except for those who physically flee to the woods, everyone is contaminated.

Collaboration, therefore, in the sense of 'working for the enemy', does not have the same connotation that applies in free countries or under milder regimes. In Nazi-ruled Warsaw it can only be fairly applied to people who chose to assist the occupiers in ways that could otherwise have been avoided.

Furthermore, the issue of collaboration is complicated by the fact that wartime Poland was subjected to two sets of occupiers – Germans and Soviets – and hence saw two quite separate sets of collaborators. Impartial historians must take this fact into account. They must avoid the pitfall where most Western historiography flounders by regarding 'collaboration' with the Nazis as despicable and 'cooperation' with the Soviets as desirable. For moral judgements on collaboration/cooperation can only be made after consideration both of the type of regime involved and the particular circumstances of the collaborators. From the moral standpoint, voluntary assistance for mass murderers cannot be easily justified in any circumstances.

The issue becomes still more tangled when it is used to fuel inter-ethnic antagonism. During the war, for example, huge resentment was caused in Poland by the welcome afforded by *some* Jews to the Red Army in 1939, and, by implication, to the murders and deportations that followed. Those events were well documented at the time by highly respected observers such as the courier Karski, and are not in doubt.[52] Yet within a short time they were being used in certain circles to suggest, with no foundation at all, that Jews in general were Soviet sympathizers and hence that all Jews were 'anti-Polish'. On 5 May 1943, in the middle of the Ghetto Rising, an underground paper produced in Warsaw by the Nationalist Movement printed the following dubious opinion:

> With respect to the attitude of Jews to Poland . . . it is evidenced by their behaviour during the Soviet occupation, when Jews regularly

> stripped our soldiers of their arms, killed them, betrayed our community leaders, and openly crossed to the side of the occupier. In [a small town not 30km (twenty miles) from Warsaw], which in 1939 was momentarily in the hands of the Soviets . . . Jews erected a triumphal arch for the Soviet troops to pass through and all wore red armbands and cockades. That was, and is, their attitude to Poland. Everyone in Poland should remember this . . .[53]

It is not hard to see how the actions of some Jews had been inflated into a stereotypical perception about Jews as a whole.

By the same token, discussions about the actions of *some* Poles during the war have been allowed to inflate to the point where *all* Poles can be perceived as anti-Semitic. This perception is grossly unfair, but it is not uncommon. In the summer of 1941, for example, it was well known in Warsaw that massacres of Jews had begun as soon as German forces and Nazi officials moved into towns and villages recently vacated by the Soviets. It was rumoured that in one or two cases local people had participated. Yedvabne, which lies less than 160km (a hundred miles) from Warsaw, was one such country town. From 1939 to 1941, it had been the scene of murders, deportations and repressions by a Soviet-run militia. On 10 July 1941 it was the scene of a particularly brutal massacre, in which, as is now well documented, a group of locals took part, probably for reasons of collective revenge. It was a shameful event that necessarily gives pause for reflection. But it cannot be used to fuel stereotypical misconceptions about all Poles being incipient Nazi collaborators or, still worse, eager participants in the Holocaust. After all, occupied Poland contained between ten and twenty thousand towns and villages like Yedvabne. The number of reports about massacres with a similar scenario can be counted on the fingers of one hand.[54]

Nonetheless, the Nazi campaign of genocide against the Jews greatly inflamed the overall climate of fear, anxiety, and anger in the country, where the Nazis had decided to perpetrate the crime. Its special nature and full extent were becoming apparent only gradually. And the name 'Holocaust' had not been invented. But it could not fail to disturb the minds of the population. Though the involvement of locals was minimal, and though the killing usually took place behind tight military cordons, most people had a growing realization of what was happening. For Varsovians, the Warsaw Ghetto was evidence enough. And every train that pulled into Warsaw carried passengers who told stories about one town after another that had been ringed by the SS and from which all the Jewish inhabitants had disappeared. Every Varsovian who made a trip into the countryside would come across these eerie, emptied towns and villages, where half the houses were boarded up or used by squatters, and where the shops and markets had ceased to function. The face of the land was being changed beyond repair. And no respite was at hand. The Holocaust, which reached its peak in the General Government in 1943, was taking place during the years when the German–Soviet War hung in the balance. By 1944, fresh anxieties reared their head. If the Germans recovered and stopped the Soviet tide, the Nazis would turn to the further stages of constructing their *Lebensraum*. If they didn't, the Soviets would arrive and the NKVD would be given a free hand to restart the appalling murders and deportations that had marked their rule in the eastern provinces in 1939–41.

The Gestapo made wide use of 'greasers', informers and extortionists who preyed on the vulnerable. Some of these despicable types were themselves caught in a web of blackmail and exploitation. Others acted purely for money or revenge. But it is quite improper to describe them in ethnic terms, for they included Jews as well as Catholics, and they were as ready to shop a member of the Underground or an illegal trader as they were to sell a fugitive from the Ghetto. The Gestapo had a very long list of 'wanted', and a variety of shady or broken individuals were ready to supply their wants.

The police must equally be judged without ethnic bias. For the 'Blue Police' on the Aryan side found themselves in a position not totally dissimilar from that of the Jewish Police in the Ghetto. They could not refuse the orders of their German superiors; and they were subject to ferocious discipline. Nor, though bribery was rife, could they easily choose whom to favour. They helped arrange executions in their own community just as they were ordered on occasion to join in the persecution of the Jews. Nonetheless, when given the chance, they were capable of compassion. In one case, a Jewish family living outside the Ghetto under their own name was saved when a 'blue policeman' called round one evening and advised them to flee. An anonymous informer had given their address to the Gestapo, and a raid could be expected. The family moved without delay, and was not molested for the rest of the war.[55]

Very few Varsovians joined the German military. The *Waffen*-SS did not raise volunteers in the General Government, as they did in most other occupied countries, including France, Denmark, Norway, Belgium,

Holland, Hungary, and Ukraine. And the Wehrmacht did not usually attempt to raise Polish recruits, as they did as a matter of course in Silesia or Pomerania. Warsaw's small pre-war German community was the only substantial source of Varsovians serving in the *Führer*'s armed forces.

From time to time, the Nazis succeeded not only in capturing members of the Underground but also in turning them against their former comrades. Such was the origin of the Kalkstein Affair, when a group of Underground officers were somehow persuaded, apparently without torture, to work for their captors. Louis K. was a young Underground officer of the Home Army (AK), who, after being turned, recruited his fiancée and his brother-in-law to Gestapo service. Their chief catch was none other than the commanding officer of the Home Army, Gen. 'Arrow', who was trapped in an SS ambush on 30 June 1943.[56]

Thanks to their unrelentingly murderous conduct, the Nazis attracted no significant body of voluntary collaborators in the General Government, not even among the anti-Semitic tendency. There was no Polish Quisling. The National Democrats and their fascistic offshoot, the ultra-rightist, illegal pre-war ONR, were fiercely anti-German. They could have no truck whatsoever with a regime which was sworn to sever the 'eternal bond' of the Polish nation with the so-called Polish 'soil'. The sort of figures who had worked with the Germans in the First World War were no longer prepared to do so. Adolf Hitler had no more admirers on the Aryan side than in the Ghetto.

One of the very few splinter groups in which the Germans saw some potential was the 'Sword and Plough' organization. Formed in 1940 by a Catholic priest from Pomerania, it had close links with the ONR. Its activities were initially confined to clandestine propaganda that called for Poland's restoration and revival. For this its founder was quickly arrested by the Gestapo in Warsaw, and killed in Auschwitz. But then its interests shifted. As its name suggested, it was willing to take a hand both with Underground work and with armed rebellion. Its manifesto of 1942 talked of a Pan-Slavic Empire 'from sea to sea'; and its members played a distinguished role in the intelligence operations that revealed, among other things, the test sites of the V1 rockets.

The Soviet victory at Stalingrad inspired a further twist. By that time, the 'Sword and Plough' was in the hands of some extremely radical leaders. One was associated with White Russian émigrés in Warsaw; another was a professional intelligence agent who had worked in his time for various security services, possibly for the British and probably for the

Abwehr (German military intelligence). These two were now principally driven by fear of the USSR. In April 1943, they used the Japanese Embassy in Berlin as a conduit for a memorandum addressed to Hitler in person. They presented a scheme for Polish–German cooperation in fighting the Red Army, the Polish resistance, and the 'Jewish menace'. Berlin was unimpressed. Governor Frank advised the *Führer*'s office that 'Sword and Plough' had no significant support in Polish society. So, too, did Kaltenbrunner, head of the *Sipo*. More to the point, perhaps, when some rank-and-file members of the organization caught wind of the scheme, they called in their Underground partners. Three leaders of 'Sword and Plough' were condemned to death for treason by an Underground court. On 18 September 1943, in Warsaw, they were shot by a firing squad composed of the 'Sword and Plough''s own members.

The only level at which some degree of consistent collaboration took place was the local one. Some village mayors collaborated with the Germans in order to sell produce and to avoid the fearful reprisals meted out to non-cooperators. Their example could not be easily followed in the city, where the controls and the resentments were more intense.

Cultural collaboration was strictly limited. The Nazis ran a Polish-language 'reptile press' in Warsaw, they permitted a few highly controlled 'non-German' cinemas and theatres, and they did not close the lowest category of music halls and cafes, where they encouraged prostitution and pornography. For many years after the war, it was said that all these institutions were totally boycotted. Recent research shows otherwise. Yet many of those who worked for German institutions were simply going through the motions to keep themselves alive. One young man, who was ultimately destined to win a Nobel Prize, for example, has described his wartime work as a porter for the German Library Service in Warsaw. Like many intellectuals, he had no taste for insurrection. But his *marxisant* politics precluded any sympathy either for the Nazis or for the Soviets. On the face of it, his employment by a Nazi cultural enterprise might conceivably have been seen as unpatriotic. It was nothing of the sort:

> I owed my chance to become a porter to the new director of libraries, a tiny German Slavicist who had decided to protect himself at all costs from going to the front until the end of the war. With this in mind he and his adviser, a Pole, had elaborated a gigantic plan, requiring at least ten years to accomplish, that made both of them indispensable.

> With unshakable logic, the plan envisaged the rearrangement of the book collections from Warsaw's three largest libraries and the transport of millions of volumes by horse-drawn cart so that one library would contain Polish works only: the second, foreign works only; and the third, works on music, theater, and art. It was an undertaking to match moving the Alps, and in its *systematisch* approach faithfully duplicated the whole General Government – except that its madness was bloodless.[57]

The sphere of economic collaboration was equally ambiguous. Warsaw possessed probably the largest black market in Europe, yet it served both the oppressed and the oppressors. The same young man mentioned above had a second job working for 'the Firm'. It was engaged, among other things, in supplying the Wehrmacht:

> The Firm had two branches: one in Minsk, the capital of Byelorussia, and the other in Warsaw. Granted proper Nazi authorization on the ground of being 'useful for the Army,' the outfit was supplied with all sorts of passes and permits and allegedly traded in goods. In fact it dealt in the black-market purchase and sale of currency. The greater part, if not all, of the truck shipments consisted of weapons for partisan detachments. In this, the founder's talent for high diplomacy nearly reached the level of genius, because his trucks moved unharrassed through the forests of Byelorussia, which were controlled by partisans of varying colors. As a financial power The Firm secured privileges for itself from the Germans through bribery, paying out a regular bonus to a few dignitaries; it also maintained its own workshop for making false documents, and ran an effective rescue operation for those threatened with arrest – especially Jews, many of whom owe their lives to it. The Firm often transported them, carefully packaged, from city to city . . .
>
> The Firm's headquarters in Warsaw, where the major activity had shifted as the front moved gradually westward, did not look much like a commercial enterprise. In a large room, amid the disorder of tires, crates, engine parts, and drums of gasoline, truck drivers slouched with their feet up on sofas, chatting lazily in a Vilno dialect and smoking cigarettes. This brigade, composed of 'my boys' from the Vilno suburbs, knew the complex organization inside and out. It was a team of completely trustworthy men who were treated by

> their boss as equals. In the second room, the boss's partner hung on the telephone. He was a fat Latvian Jew with a black moustache, armed with Aryan birth certificates to the tenth generation.[58]

From the autumn of 1939 to the spring of 1943, Germany's *Polenpolitik* was entirely in the hands of the Nazi leadership. The *Führer* had stated his wishes. The *Reichsführer-SS* took charge. And the plans drawn up by the RSHA were implemented by the SS and their minions. Other organs of German Government were excluded. The military in particular, preoccupied with the war further to the east, did not intervene. After Stalingrad, however, the political climate began to change. Questions were asked. Alternatives were considered. Adjustments were made. Feelers were extended. As the Eastern Front recoiled inexorably back towards the heart of Poland, intelligent Germans cast around for Poles who might help them.

In February 1943, none other than Governor-General Frank advocated a change of course. He was reacting to a directive from Goebbels to all regional Gauleiters, telling them 'to stop everything that endangers the necessary cooperation of all European peoples in [the cause of] victory.'[59] He may have been crude and brutal, but he wasn't stupid. A year earlier he had mocked the policy of his superiors who were 'slaughtering the cow which they wanted to milk'.[60] So he now proposed a raft of concessions including an increase in food supplies, the re-establishment of secondary education, the restoration of Polish property rights, and the wider employment of Poles in the administration. This was not a change of heart but a tactical shift, dictated by Germany's waning fortunes. 'When we have finally won the war,' he noted optimistically in his diary, 'you can make mincemeat of the Poles and the Ukrainians and all the others as far as I'm concerned . . . But what is crucial at the moment is the maintenance of order, discipline, and diligence among a hostile population.'[61] He suggested that differentiated regimes could be introduced – a harsher one in hotbeds of resistance like Warsaw, and a milder one in the District of Galicia, where some Nazis, like Rosenberg, viewed the Ukrainians as a counterweight to the inveterate hostility of the Poles. In June 1943, for instance, Frank permitted the re-establishment of the *Polnische Hauptfilfsausschuss*, a welfare organization, which was allocated a payment from the annual budget and which, exceptionally, possessed a board of Polish directors. Less successfully, in February 1944, he tried to set up a Polish Anti-

Bolshevik League. In those same months he pressed Berlin with ideas about education, property rights, and military recruitment. At the same time, potential political partners should be sounded out, and the possibility explored of forming Polish military units, on the lines of the *SS-Galizien*. Frank even pressed for 'a statement of the future role of the Polish people in the New Europe.'[62] This last proposal came dangerously close to a categorical repudiation of the *Generalplan-Ost*.

None of Frank's proposals prospered, however. Himmler decisively overruled the idea of raising Polish military units. The Resistance put an end to the idea of political cooperation when it executed the leaders of the 'Sword and Plough' group. As reported, when representatives of the National Democrats were approached, their reply was staunchly negative: 'We regret that the German authorities have made cooperation against Bolshevism impossible for us. Now, it is too late. It should have been thought of four years ago, before millions of mistakes had been made.'[63] Frank too was unrepentant. In the light of his failure to effect a change of course, he saw fit to issue a warning. He submitted a report in which he suggested that current methods would provoke a Rising, and if such a Rising broke out, that there were no longer sufficient troops in reserve to suppress it.[64]

It may have been cynical. But at least it indicated a different approach from the moronic intransigence that Himmler was always advocating. The result was a series of limited concessions, which were put into effect, and of more far-reaching proposals, which Berlin blocked.

Meanwhile, in April 1943, Goebbels played his masterstroke. He had known for many months about the NKVD's massacre of Polish officers in the Katyn Forest, but he had waited until the information could be used to maximum effect. By demonstrating that Stalin was a mass murderer, he had high hopes of blowing the Grand Alliance apart. In the event, having told so many offensive lies in the past, he was not widely believed in Britain or America, even when he told the truth. But he caused trouble enough. The German communiqué about Katyn, from April 1943, could not be ignored by the Polish Government in London. Stalin took the opportunity to sever diplomatic relations. Though they kept their close alliance with Great Britain, the Poles had lost their formal link to the Soviet Union, whose armies were heading for Warsaw.

German-run cinemas ran a grisly documentary film showing the reopened gravesite at Katyn. It was screened on the same day that *SS-Brig.Fhr.* Jürgen Stroop launched the final assault on the Ghetto: and it attracted packed houses. Varsovians had proof of what they, unlike Western audiences, had long suspected. In some cases, they saw flickering pictures of the corpses and skulls of their loved ones, each with a tell-tale bullet hole. But they did not react as Goebbels had wished. Their sense of desolation increased. They were not unduly impressed by one gang of murderers exposing the crimes of another. They were simply confirmed in their long-standing belief in the 'doctrine of two enemies'.

About this time, American intelligence agents picked up rumours that the German High Command was trying to enlist Polish support for the war against Russia. They had heard that a Gen. von Mannheim – probably Field Marshal Erich von Manstein, who was of Polish origin – had been sent on a mission to Warsaw with a view to contacting potential partners. The rumours, almost certainly, were false. But they were indicative of the plots and possibilities which events on the Eastern Front in 1943–44 were creating.[65]

In the summer of 1944, all the vacillations in the German camp were terminated. In June, the Western powers succeeded in landing a major force in Normandy, thereby creating the war on two fronts. Then, on 20 July, the crucial Bomb Plot at the *Führer*'s field HQ in East Prussia failed. Hitler survived the explosion. The conspirators were smoked out and killed. The SS reasserted its supremacy. The Wehrmacht ceased to have ideas of its own. The Reich was going to fight to the death.

German intelligence was well aware that the Soviet advance into Poland was likely to spark a Rising.[66] They had no illusions about the ubiquitous activities of the Polish Resistance and they had great respect for its daring. Yet despite several key arrests they never obtained detailed inside knowledge. They knew neither the scale of the intended insurrection, nor its changing strategy, nor the points of its concentration. The German Command could not do more than to prepare contingency plans, to hold security forces in reserve, and to wait.

News of the Bomb Plot was widely circulated in Warsaw. The *Führer*'s field HQ was barely 160km (a hundred miles) away from Warsaw and the German garrison there was not in an enviable position. Morale was brittle. The Soviet onslaught was approaching fast. The defence of the Vistula would be left to front-line Wehrmacht formations, and the hostility of the local population was manifest. All thoughts of a political option had been dropped. The defenders of 'Warschau' were to face the fury of the Slavs with no hope of Soviet mercy and no chance of Polish assistance.

When the Soviet Army approached the Vistula, the German garrison in Warsaw prepared for the worst. There were 'Ivans' to the left of them, moving to storm the conjunction of the Vistula and the Narev. There were 'Ivans' massing in front of them. There were 'Ivans' to the right of them, aiming to create two southern bridgeheads. As a result, the order was given for partial evacuation. From 22 July, scores of trains ferried German civilians from the Central Station. Palls of smoke rose skywards as German administrators burned their files. Lines of trucks rolled out of the city carrying stores and wounded soldiers westwards. The roads were packed with retreating refugees, reserve units, and herds of livestock, which the Germans had taken in contributions.

On 27 July, Governor Fischer gave his order of the day:

> Poles! In 1920, outside this city, you repelled Bolshevism thereby demonstrating your anti-Bolshevik sentiments. Today Warsaw is again the breakwater for the Red flood and its contribution to the struggle shall be that 100,000 men and women should report for work to build defences. Gather on the main squares: Jolibord, Marszalstr., Lubliner Platz, etc. Those whose refuse will be punished.[67]

It was a risky move. If the men showed up, the Underground would be robbed of its manpower at a stroke; if they didn't, he would have a legal pretext for mass punishment. On the other hand, as happened to the Tsarist governor in 1863, he might provoke the very revolt he was trying to avoid. In the event, the order was universally ignored. In the interests of caution, no reprisals were made. The Gestapo acted more decisively. They killed the long-term political prisoners they had been holding on ice in the Paviak and who had lost their potential usefulness.

At the end of the week, the military situation seemed to stabilize. The Wehrmacht's Ninth Army was containing the southern bridgeheads. The Soviets achieved no further breakthrough. Most importantly, the defensive lines to the east of Praga were hardening. German spirits rose when strong reinforcements arrived. On the 29th, men of the Hermann Göring Panzer Division marched through the city streets in full battle array. Their tanks rumbled across the Vistula bridges, which Wehrmacht sappers were wiring for possible demolition. Tension remained high. But several of the evacuated military units returned. The defenders were given time to dig in and to brace themselves for the expected assault.

German anxieties were increased by public manifestations of Communist-led preparations. On 29 July, Soviet aircraft dropped leaflets carrying an appeal from the Soviet-controlled Committee of National Liberation calling the people to arms. In the afternoon, posters were plastered on various walls in the city announcing that the representatives of the exiled Polish Government in London had fled, and that the commander of the Communist People's Army was assuming command of all Underground units. It was more than reasonable to conclude that an imminent Soviet assault on Warsaw from outside was to be joined by a Communist-led assault within. The log of the German Ninth Army contained the following entry: '29 July 1944. Polish insurgents [were] expected to begin armed action in Warsaw district about 2300 hours . . . But nothing happened.'[68]

The 29th and 30th of July were the Saturday and Sunday of a sunny, summer weekend. Uncertain whether this was a lull before the storm, or a good chance to relax before the Bolshevik Occupation, those Varsovians who could relax, made the most of it. The churches were packed; the parks were thronged; the bathing-places on the riverside were crowded. The sound of distant artillery caused excitement, but was not sufficiently close to clear the streets. There were one or two gunfights of unknown provenance and the usual array of police cordons. No bombs were falling.

Tuesday 1 August began like any other working day during the Occupation. Heavy German patrols roamed the suburbs in trucks. Armed police were more noticeable than usual on street corners. But most people were able to go about their everyday business. The weather was fine and warm. The midday news from Radio Berlin announced that 'the Russians are planning to create a Polish statelet under their control'. Then the daily communiqué of the German News Agency issued at 1.29 p.m. stated: '*Warschau ist kalm.*'[69] As far as the German authorities could tell, the city presented an appearance of normality.

CHAPTER III

EASTERN APPROACHES

THE RED ARMY MARCHED westwards out of Russia on four separate occasions – in 1918, in 1920, in 1939, and in 1944. It did not do so simply for the greater aggrandizement of its masters but in pursuance of basic Bolshevik principles. For the Bolsheviks were internationalist revolutionaries who firmly believed that their regime could not survive in isolation. In 1918 and again in 1920, the Red Army was sent to the west by Lenin, who had hoped to exploit the revolutionary ferment in Germany. In September 1939, it was ordered to march by Stalin who was reaping the gains arranged in the recent Nazi–Soviet Pact. In 1944, in the final phase of the German–Soviet War, it was following up the colossal victories at Stalingrad and Kursk. On each occasion, the final destination was intended to be Berlin. But the early plans repeatedly went awry. In late 1918, the Red Army barely reached Lithuania before the Russian Civil War intervened. In 1920, it was held on the River Vistula and comprehensively beaten in a brilliant counter-attack by Warsaw's defenders. In 1939, it established the 'Peace Boundary' on the River Bug, from which it was driven back less than two years later by Operation Barbarossa. In 1944, therefore, at the fourth attempt, the Soviets intended to solve their 'western problem' once and for all. And they were very conscious of previous mistakes.

Bolshevik ideology, otherwise known as Marxism-Leninism or more popularly as 'Communism', played an important part in Soviet calculations, especially in the early years. Unfortunately, it did not provide any simple guidelines. Indeed, it presented the Bolsheviks with one of their most acute dilemmas. On the one hand, Marx had predicted revolution in the advanced capitalist countries, like Germany or Britain; and he was firmly convinced that peasant societies and backward economies such as Russia or China were the last place on earth for a genuine proletarian revolution. Lenin, on the other hand, had invented a set of political techniques with which a ruthless band of determined activists could seize power despite unfavourable social and economic conditions. What is more, he actually succeeded in taking control of the largest state in the world, and in setting up a totalitarian dictatorship in clear contradiction of previous Marxist precepts. Somehow the circle had to be squared. So as an adept in ideological gymnastics, he reconciled the irreconcilable by arguing that the early extension of Bolshevik power to Germany and to Western Europe in general was essential. In Bolshevik parlance, the link to be built between revolutionary Russia and Germany was known as 'the Red Bridge'.

In 1920, at a period of his career when Lenin was accusing his critics in the Bolshevik Party of 'infantile Leftism', he himself was suffering from infantile delusions on the grand scale. He really seems to have believed that crossing the 1,500km (900 miles) between Russia and Germany would be a relatively simple operation and that the advance of the Red Army across the 'Red Bridge' would be welcomed by all the peoples of the region. He ignored expert advice and learned the hard way.[1]

None of the Bolsheviks best acquainted with the problem was fully convinced by Lenin's arguments, though they were obliged to follow the party line. Leon Trotsky, the Commissar for War, knew that the fledgeling Red Army was ill prepared to face well-trained European adversaries. He recoiled from the prospect of attacking Central Europe by force, preferring instead to spread revolution into Asia. He invented the ingenious formula 'The road to London and Berlin leads through Calcutta'. Karol Radek, Lenin's special adviser on Polish affairs, told him straight that a nation consisting largely of Roman Catholic peasants was not going to fall easily for Bolshevik slogans. And Joseph Stalin, who was a Georgian and the Commissar for the Nationalities, needed no telling that most of the non-Russian peoples regarded the Bolsheviks as mere 'Red Tsars'. He was sceptical about the project throughout. As the political controller of the South-Western Front in 1920, when he signally failed to share Lenin's enthusiasm, he landed himself in serious political trouble. But in essence he was proved right. Not surprisingly, when he became supreme Soviet dictator and twice sent the Red Army back over the same ground, he had no intention of relying on popular goodwill. In 1939, he relied on his partnership with the Third Reich. In 1944, he relied on nothing else but the brute strength of his victorious forces.

The Soviet advance of 1920 was one of those episodes which have almost escaped from the history books. From the Soviet point of view, it was a shameful defeat which the Bolsheviks and their sympathizers were eager to forget and which later Communist censors would try to erase from the record. It shattered the dreams of the Congress of Comintern, which assembled in Moscow at the height of the advance; and it was not the subject of an impartial historical monograph for over fifty years. Yet it was keenly remembered by those who participated. It formed the culminating campaign of the two-year war between Soviet Russia and the Polish Republic, and it culminated with Marshal Tukhachevsky's chilling order of the day of 1 July: 'Onwards! Over the corpse of White Poland shines the road to worldwide conflagration!' Unfortunately for Tukhachevsky, the Poles proved to be anything but a corpse. After giving him a sound drubbing, they drove the Red Army back in confusion. The plan for World Revolution was postponed indefinitely.

This first modern Battle of Warsaw was closely observed by a British diplomat, who twice put his reflections to paper. On the first occasion, shortly after the battle, Lord D'Abernon summed up his impressions in truly Gibbonian style. 'If Charles Martel had not checked the Saracen conquest at the Battle of Tours,' he wrote, 'the interpretation of the Koran would be taught at the schools of Oxford . . . [And] had Pilsudski . . . failed to arrest the triumphant advance of the Soviet Army at the Battle of Warsaw, not only would Christianity have experienced a dangerous reverse, the very existence of Western civilisation would have been imperilled'.[2] A decade later, he was much less confident of the outcome:

> It may be that Communist doctrine, repelled by force of arms in 1920, will later achieve the disruption it seeks. But should this come to pass, it will be due less to the military strength of the Soviet, less to propaganda however lavish or persistent, than to disunion among its adversaries and to the strange incapacity to deal with the economic crisis, which is today so grave a reproach to the intelligence of the Western world.[3]

Stalin came out of the crisis physically safe, but politically damaged. Shortly before the Battle of Warsaw, he was ordered by Moscow to move up from the south and support Tukhachevsky's flank. If he had obeyed, he and his army group would have borne the brunt of the Polish counter-offensive and would almost certainly have been destroyed. As it was, since he disobeyed, he returned to Moscow to face Trotsky's fury and a charge of indiscipline. He was lucky that a party tribunal issued nothing more than a reprimand. But he must certainly have come away with the impression that advancing on the Vistula was a dangerous business. Seventeen years later, when he purged the Red Army's officer class, he made sure that Tukhachevsky was the leading victim. After a brief show trial, Tukhachevsky was condemned to death in the company of five other generals who had all commanded armies on the Warsaw Front under him.

The three men who signed their death warrants – Voroshilov, Yegorov, and Budyonny – had all served in 1920 on the South-Western Front with Stalin. Some people may think this is coincidence.

Equally, Stalin cannot have avoided the conviction that the Poles were not a nation to be trifled with. The Poles' fierce attachment to their independence inevitably raised his suspicions. And they never left him. Gen. de Gaulle had also fought in Poland in 1920; and when he visited Stalin in Moscow a quarter of a century later, attended by his translator Gaston P., the Soviet dictator could not refrain from a slighting remark. 'But I am a Frenchman,' protested Gaston P. 'Once a Pole, always a Pole,' was the retort.[4]

Not surprisingly, therefore, the Soviet advance of 1939 was undertaken with the greatest possible caution. It began on 17 September, two weeks later than Stalin's Nazi partners had anticipated; and it did not proceed until the Soviets had signed a truce with the Japanese in far-off Mongolia. As a result, it occurred at a juncture when the Wehrmacht had already completed most of the hard fighting and when Warsaw was already surrounded. As in 1920, the Red Army soldiers were told that their mission was one of social liberation. Their tanks rolled into towns and villages announcing to the bewildered inhabitants that they had come to save them from the fascists. This made the joint Nazi–Soviet victory parade in Brest-Litovsk a bit of an embarrassment and, in later years, yet another prime candidate for amnesia.

One thing, however, the Soviets refused to forget. The Nazi–Soviet Treaty of Friendship, Cooperation, and Demarcation, signed by Stalin's representatives on 28 September 1939, established a new Soviet frontier running along the River Bug through the middle of conquered Poland. To the east of this 'Peace Boundary', they took possession of a large tract of territory, which they henceforth treated as irrevocably theirs. For the rest of his life, Stalin never wavered, regarding the 'Peace Boundary' as the permanent and legitimate frontier of the USSR. Indeed, the view was to last as long as the Soviet Union did.

The most cynical comments about the September Campaign of 1939 were uttered by Molotov, Stalin's Commissar for Foreign Affairs. In a speech intended to justify the Soviets' contravention of their international treaties, Molotov declared shamelessly that 'Poland has ceased to exist'. The crime may be judged still more heinous when the Nazi–Soviet assault was later shown to have been planned in advance. Molotov added insult to injury. Poland, he said, was 'the Bastard of Versailles'.

The Soviet advance of 1944 was on a far grander scale than any of its predecessors. In the central sector alone, some 2.5 million troops were amassed – over three times as many as in 1920. More importantly, it came at the end of three years of indescribably brutal Nazi occupation. Many of the native peoples, who had no love either for Russia or for communism, nonetheless anticipated the Red Army's approach with a mixture of foreboding and relief.

Yet some things didn't change. The Red Army marched as always to the sound of political propaganda. Once again, the Red Army was advancing to liberate the people. So it was taken for granted that the people should rise in arms to welcome their liberators.

He would be described as 'the son of a Warsaw railwayman', 'the Marshal of Two Nations', a true proletarian and internationalist, who had chosen the services of Russia and the Revolution from his own free will. The description was not entirely true. But it served the purpose. For on the central sector of the Eastern Front in early 1944, Konstantin Konstantinovich Rokossovsky was the man of the moment. The General who had delivered the coup de grâce to the German army at Stalingrad had now been chosen to spearhead the Red Army's attack on the Reich, heading in the first instance for the Vistula. It is more than likely that he harboured ambitions to lead the subsequent attack on Berlin.

The beauty of the story, for those who wished to embroider it, was that the Soviet commander could himself be presented as a son of the Vistula Land. He had certainly spent much of his youth there. With the help of relatives, he had been able to attend the *Gymnazium* of the Merchants' Company in Warsaw. He was said to have worked as a stonemason's apprentice on the Poniatovski Bridge: and, in 1912, after participating in a revolutionary protest, to have spent time in the notorious Paviak Jail.

In reality, Rokossovsky was a typical product of the ethnically mixed borderlands of the old Tsarist Empire. He was not a full-blooded Russian; but he was not really a Pole either. His father was descended from a family of déclassé Polish nobles, who had participated in the Risings of 1831 and 1863 and who had subsequently been stripped of their lands and status. By adopting the elite profession of train driver, he travelled widely in the western provinces of the Empire, and married a Russian woman. Konstanty was their eldest son, born on 21 December 1896, when they were living at Velikie Luki, an important railway junction in north-western Russia. He apparently spoke Polish to his father's side of the family, and Russian to his mother's side. He moved with his parents to Warsaw at the age of five, and took up residence on Steel Street in the right-bank suburb of Praga. Thanks to his accent, he was reportedly teased by the local children, who called him 'Rusek' ('little Russian'). Less than two years later, when his father was killed in a railway accident, he was left with his Russian mother to struggle along as best they could. Fortunately, the boy was tall, handsome, strong, and athletic.

One should remember, of course, that the 'Варшава' of the early twentieth century, which Rokossovsky would have remembered, was in the middle of a wave of intense Russification. It was not the proud Polish city of past and future times. It was a provincial Tsarist city, full of Russian officials and of Russian soldiers, the centre of a region which had been told to forget all its previous historic connections and which had recently been renamed the 'Privislanskiy Kray' or 'Vistula Land'. Its skyline was dominated by the massive Russian Orthodox Cathedral, then under construction. As one learns from the childhood memoirs of another resident, Mme Curie, Russian was the language of instruction in all schools, even for pupils whose mother tongue was not Russian. All the main street signs were written in Russian. Russian money was in circulation, Russian weights and measures were in force, and time was measured by the old Russian calendar, thirteen days behind the rest of Europe. For Western tourists, who arrived clasping their Baedekers, this was the gateway to Tsardom:

> **Warsaw** (*Warszawa*, Варшава: Ger *Warschau*, FF. *Varsovie*; 320 ft.), the capital of the General Government of Warsaw and an important railway centre, lies on the left bank of the *Vistula*. [It is located] on the elevated edge of a valley, descending abruptly to the river, here ¼–⅓ m. in width, and gradually merging on the W. in a wide and undulating plain. The city contains 872,500 inhab. . . . and a strong garrison. Its appearance is far more like that of West Europe than of Russia. Warsaw is the seat of the Governor-General of Warsaw, . . . of [two] Archbishops, of the Commandant of the military district . . . and of a Russian university. Divided into twelve police precincts (including Praga), [it] consists of the *Old Town* (Старое Мэсто, *Stare Miasto*), the *New Town*, (Новое Мэсто, *Nove Miasto*), to the N., and of *Vola*, *Mokotóv*, and other suburbs. On the right bank of the Vistula

lies *Praga*. The river is crossed by three bridges . . . Whole quarters of the town are occupied by Jews, whose inattention to personal cleanliness has become proverbial. Warsaw is a flourishing industrial centre . . . and carries on a considerable trade.

Warsaw . . . is said to have been founded in the 12th cent., and . . . till 1526 was the residence of the Dukes of Masovia, on whose extinction it fell to Poland. King Sigismund II. Augustus fixed his residence here in 1550, and Sigismund III. [Vasa] made it the capital After the extinction of the Jagiello family in 1572, all the kings of Poland were elected on the Field of Vola. . . . Both Augustus II. and Augustus III. took great pride in the beautification of their capital . . . After the death of August III. (Oct. 5th, 1763) [it] was the scene of constant disorder, until the Russians . . . forced the electors to choose the colourless Stanislaus Poniatovski as their king. . . . Fresh disorder in 1794 ended in . . . the third partition of Poland. Poniatovski abdicated; Warsaw fell to the share of Prussia and became capital of the province of South Prussia.

On Nov. 28th, 1806, the French, under Davout and Murat, entered Warsaw. By the Peace of Tilsit (July 7th, 1807) . . . [it] was made the capital of a grand-duchy. The Congress of Vienna (1814) transferred the grand-duchy to Russia, which raised Warsaw to the rank of capital of the kingdom of Poland. The great Polish Revolution of 1830 began with an uprising in Warsaw, and ended on Sept. 7th, 1831, with the storming of the city by the Russians under Paskévitch. Warsaw was also the focus of the risings against Russian rule in 1861–64. Since the restoration of quiet the growth of Warsaw's prosperity has been continuous.

Principal Attractions (1 day) Royal [Castle]: street scenes in the [Cracow Faubourg], the Marshalkovska, and the Novy Sviat: the Saxon Garden: view from the lantern of the Lutheran Church: Aleya Uyazdovska, especially towards evening: Imperial Château of Lazienki: Cathedral of St John: Old Town: the Alexander Bridge. Those who have a little more time should not omit a visit to Villanov. . . .

To the right of [the Cracow Faubourg] rises the Greek Catholic Cathedral of St Alexander Nevski, built in the Byzantine style in 1894–1912 from the plans of Benois. It has five gilded domes and a separate belfry, 240 ft. high. To the W. stands the former Saxon

Palace, once the residence of Polish Kings . . . [now] the headquarters of the Military District. To the N. is the former Bruhl Palace, built by the favourite of Augustus III. and now the Telegraph Office. . . .

By following the Zyazd, the wide street which descends from the [Castle] Square, we obtain a good view of the water-front . . . Below the terrace lie some of the stables of the *sotnyas* (squadrons) of the Circassians and Cossacks forming the Governor-General's body-guard . . .

Praga Again starting from [Castle] Square, we follow the Zyazd towards the E. and reach the iron-girder Alexander Bridge . . . 560 yds. long and constructed by Kierbedź (1865). Smoking on the bridge is forbidden.

The bridge affords a pretty view. To the N. we see the Citadel, commanding the Vistula, the railway-bridge, and the buildings of the Old and New Towns, extending down to the brink of the river. In front of us, on the hill, lies the Royal [Castle] . . . with its terraced garden and the church of St Anne.

The bridge leads to the once fortified suburb of Praga on the right bank of the Vistula.

After the second partition of Poland, Praga . . . was captured by Suvorov, at the head of 25,000 Russians, on Nov. 5th, 1794 . . . Suvorov informed the Empress of his victory in the three words 'Hurrah, Praga, Suvorov,' and she replied, 'Bravo, F-M, Catherine.'

In the Alexandrovska, to the right is the Gothic Church of SS Florian & Michael erected in 1901; to the left the small Greek Catholic Church of Mary Magdalen with five gilded domes (1869). The Alexander Park stretching along the Vistula is frequented mainly by the lower classes.[5]

For Rokossovsky's generation, Warsaw was the epicentre of revolution and rebellion. The November Rising of 1830–31 and the January Rising of 1863–64 had both led to bitter Russo-Polish wars, and had both served as major catalysts in the growth of modern Russian nationalism. In 1905–6, Warsaw joined St Petersburg in the revolutionary disturbances; and determined strikes lasted longer in the Tsar's Polish provinces than in Russia proper. The long history of conflict had created a stereotype. In Russian eyes, Warsaw was a nest of troublemakers.

Rokossovsky's military career began in 1914 when he was conscripted into the Tsarist army at the outbreak of the Great War. Perhaps through tales of his grandfather and great-grandfather, who had both served with the Polish lancers, he chose to join the cavalry, and was drafted into the 5th Regiment of Kargopolski Dragoons. He served with distinction on the Eastern Front, winning the St George's Cross, and stayed with his regiment until it disintegrated in the revolutionary summer of 1917. At that point Konstanty, now twenty-one, made the decision to stick with a group of radical friends and to join the infant Red Army. From then on, as a professional soldier with three years' experience of active service, his prospects were extremely good. Much decorated during the Russian Civil War, he changed his patronymic to the more Russian-sounding 'Konstantinovich', obtained his membership card of the Bolshevik Party, and threw himself into the mill of campaigns and commands. In 1924–25, alongside Georgii Zhukov, he attended the Finishing School of the Red Army's General Staff. He belonged to the elite of the Red Cavalry, reaching the rank of major general by 1935. He earlier had a spell in China as a military adviser to Chiang Kai-Shek, and in 1936–37 spent a year in Spain as an adviser to the Republican Army fighting Franco. Rokossovsky had missed the Red Army's western campaign of 1920 because he was serving elsewhere. He missed the campaign of 1939 because he was a prisoner in the Gulag.

Stalin's purges defy comprehension by people who demand rational explanations. They were *not* undertaken simply to weed out opponents or unreliable elements. They were often directed against his most loyal servants, against Communists who had welcomed the earlier purges of Trotskyists and old Bolsheviks, or like Rokossovsky, who had never uttered a word of dissent. Yet they proceeded on a scale and with a ferocity unparalleled in European history. In the 1930s, Stalin ordered the deaths of more human beings than Hitler would kill in the whole of his career. And he didn't stop in 1939. He did it from motives of pure terror, to render the very idea of independent thought unthinkable. In the Red Army purge after 1937, he had 36,671 staff officers shot outright. At a time when a European war was brewing, he left a mere 303 out of 706 men in the top ranks untouched. In this light, it is surprising that Rokossovsky, who had twice been abroad, was merely sent to a concentration camp. It is even more surprising that he survived three winters in the camps when the average prisoner could only survive one. His resentment may only be imagined. At his 'trial' he was condemned on the evidence of a man who had died twenty years earlier.

Rokossovsky's war memoirs begin in the spring of 1940 when he was sunning himself on the beach at Sochi. He could not say openly why he was there. But many informed Russian readers would have correctly guessed that he was benefiting from the usual post-Gulag rehabilitation course. He waited for a posting as he recovered in the company of his Siberian wife, Julia Petrovna, and their daughter. He was to need every ounce of strength he could garner. For in the next four years, he was to receive one top operational command after another – against Operation Barbarossa, before Moscow, at Stalingrad, at Kursk, and in 1944 at the head of the conclusive Soviet drive to the West.

Rokossovsky is known to have talked in public about his years in the Gulag only once, about thirty years later when on exercises in the far north of Siberia: he reportedly ordered his command plane to circle low over the frozen tundra before uttering delphically: 'No traces left.' Nor was the experience unusual. Stalin routinely arrested the wives and relatives of his closest colleagues in order to ensure their good behaviour. The inner culture of Stalinism is all but impossible for Westerners to comprehend. But it helps to explain why the Red Army's leaders, in their heroic attempts to save the Soviet Union, were so contemptuous of the human cost. For they, like many others, were walking along the knife-edge between celebrity and extinction.[6]

During Operation Barbarossa, Rokossovsky commanded a tank brigade near the front line at Novograd Volhinsk. According to one report, his initial orders had been to attack, but when attacked himself, he conducted a skilful fighting retreat, earning himself four commendations for the Order of the Red Banner. He was then placed in command of the penal brigades made up of convicts from the Gulag, who were used for clearing minefields. One of his soldiers tried to talk to him in Polish. '*Tutaj, nie ma panów,*' he replied, 'There are no "squires" here . . . Make your report in Russian!'[7]

During the desperate Battle for Moscow in the last months of 1941, Rokossovsky was rewarded for his earlier performances by a sector command at Volokhamsk. When his troops reoccupied the town in December, after retreating to the very gates of the capital, they found the square filled with corpses swinging from gallows.

At Stalingrad, in 1942–43, Rokossovsky took control of the Don Front to the north of the besieged city, and masterminded the encirclement of the German Sixth Army. It was he who at 4 p.m. on 2 February 1943 penned the final report to Stalin, announcing that 'military operations in the city and district of Stalingrad have ceased'. Next day Rokossovsky became world-famous. *Pravda* published a full, front-page photograph of him interrogating the captured German Field Marshal, von Paulus. The only blemish in the picture was the face of the military commissar, Gen. Telegin, which for no apparent reason had been blacked out by the censor.[8]

The Battle of the Kursk Salient, in July 1943, has been described as the largest armoured battle in world history. Some 6,000 tanks, and a similar number of aircraft, mauled and blasted each other for eighteen days on the open steppe south of Moscow. The Red Army lost 600,000 men. But the T-34s saw off the German Tigers. Never again would the Wehrmacht be capable of mounting a major offensive. Rokossovsky commanded the central sector of the salient, at the heart of the cauldron.

After Kursk, the Red Army started to roll westward in a huge unstoppable tide. Rokossovsky took charge of the Central Front, pivot of the wings advancing to north and south. He broke into northern Ukraine near Glukhov and captured the ruins of Chernigov on 21 September. In October, he crossed the Dnieper, a mightily symbolic line.

Early in 1944, the Soviet Central Front was renamed the First Byelorussian Front and was designated the area of maximum concentration. Rokossovsky remained in command, and built up a crushing superiority of 2:1 in men, 3:1 in guns, more than 4:1 in tanks, and 4.5:1 in warplanes. He would be helped by a partisan force of nearly 150,000. Even so, his task was formidable. Army Group Centre had turned Byelorussia into a desert zone. Villages had been burned, crops ploughed under, towns dynamited and booby-trapped, the surviving population driven into the woods and marshes. Centres like Vitebsk and Bobruisk had been declared 'fortresses' to be defended to the last man. The principal city, Minsk, contained 4,000 delayed-action bombs. Only 19 of its 332 factories remained intact.

Nonetheless, when Operation Bagration was unleashed on 23 June, it was shattering. 100,000 German troops were quickly surrounded east of Minsk. Over half of them were marched off to Moscow to be paraded through Red Square. And the Soviet colossus kept rolling on at 10–15km (6 to 10 miles) per day. Twenty-five, or possibly twenty-eight, German divisions were annihilated. In the words of the Official Journal of the German high command, 'the rout of Army Group Centre . . . was a greater catastrophe than Stalingrad.'[9] On 18 July, Rokossovsky's men crossed the River Bug. On the 28th, they captured the fort at Brest-Litovsk where Barbarossa had begun three years earlier. Soviet territory had been cleared. On the 29th, Rokossovsky was nominated a Marshal of the Soviet Union.

That same day, his Sixty-Ninth Army raced to the Vistula and crossed to the western bank.

In spring 1944, during the Soviet build-up in Byelorussia, Rokossovsky's Front was strengthened by the arrival of Gen. Berling's 1st (Polish) Army. It was the second Polish Army to be formed in the USSR during the war, and was the military arm of the so-called Union of Polish Patriots, a political organization formed with Stalin's blessing in Moscow the previous year. Its predecessor, the army of Gen. Anders, had succeeded in extracting itself from Soviet control and had departed for the Middle East to fight for the Allied cause under British command.[10]

Berling's army, which numbered some 104,000 men when it joined Rokossovsky on 29 April 1944, was a substantial and growing force. Like the Anders Army before it, it drew on the huge pool of deportees, refugees, and POWs from Poland who found themselves in the Soviet Union, and who were now eager to fight their way home. But it was kept on the tightest of political leads. It was staffed entirely by Soviet-trained officers, and subject to the surveillance of Soviet-trained political commissars. '43,000 members of the Polish Communist forces had been transferred straight from Gulag camps', hence 'their feelings towards the Soviet Union were unlikely to be entirely fraternal.'[11] Nonetheless, it attracted more recruits than it lost in the fighting, and it grew as it marched. It now consisted of five infantry divisions, a tank brigade, four artillery brigades, and an air wing. There can be no doubt that its spirits rose with every step that it took towards home.

Little is known about Berling's relations with Rokossovsky, though the two men had much in common. They were exact contemporaries; they were both professional soldiers; and both had survived Stalin's purges by a whisker. Sigismund Berling, born 1896 near Cracow, had served in the Polish legions of the Austrian army when Rokossovsky was serving in the Tsarist army. He had joined the Polish army when Rokossovsky joined the Red Army, and had been cast into the Lubyanka Jail when Rokossovsky was lingering in the Gulag. A lieutenant colonel, he spent some months at the prison camp of Starobielsk among comrades who were later to be massacred. He belonged to the very small group of Polish officers whom Stalin kept alive, and he was the only senior member of that group to be persuaded to serve in the Soviet ranks. In the eyes of others, who stayed with Anders and eventually left the USSR, he was, to put it mildly, a turncoat.

Berling's motives were undoubtedly mixed. They seem to have included vanity, opportunism, strategic realism, fear for his skin, and resentment against his former superiors. He had left his pre-war regiment at his own request, having been reprimanded for an inappropriate romance. More to the point, there was a long tradition among people of Berling's generation which held that a war between Germany and Russia rendered a neutral stance impossible. One could work with the Russians, they thought, without sharing every Russian aim. At the time of his interrogation in the Lubyanka, Berling would not have known about the Katyn massacres. But according to various sources, including his widow, he was present at the critical meeting with Beria in October 1940, when, in response to a query about the missing officers, Beria made the chilling comment: 'We made a mistake.'[12] At all events, once Berling had agreed to cooperate, the road to fame and favour was opened. Just as Rokossovsky was sent from the Gulag to the beach at Sochi, Berling was sent from the Lubyanka to the 'Villa of Delights' at Malakhovka near Moscow. From then on, re-education and rehabilitation beckoned. Berling briefly made an appearance with the independent Anders Army – no doubt as a Soviet informer – but deserted after an altercation with one of his seniors.[13] He re-emerged in 1943–44 as commander of the Kościuszko Division, commander of the Polish Corps, and in March 1944 commander of the 1st Army. In the month when he was taking up position for the offensive in Byelorussia, Anders was covering himself in glory at the storming of Monte Cassino.

A possible clue to Berling's feelings may be gleaned from his own account of his parting with Anders in August 1942 on the shores of the Caspian Sea. He had been sent by his NKVD controllers to report for duty with his Polish superiors and to monitor their evacuation to the Middle East. He was already accompanied by the woman who would become his third wife, and he felt that his departing compatriots, by leaving Russia, were losing all chances of eventually returning home. He thought that they were even more misguided than the men of Napoleon's Polish Legions, who were sent to crush the slave revolt in San Domingo and were never seen again.

Shortly before moving to the Byelorussian Front, however, Berling and his corps were obliged to perform a highly symbolic duty. They were taken to the Katyn Forest near Smolensk, recently recaptured from the Germans, and shown the mass graves of the Polish officers murdered there. Berling knew perfectly well that the victims had disappeared in 1940, more than a year before the German Occupation of the district. Even so, since a Soviet Commission had recently pronounced the massacres to be a Nazi crime, he was obliged to make a speech confirming what he knew to be untrue. 'Our inexorable foe, the German,' he began, 'seeks to destroy our whole nation . . .'[14] Berling, like Rokossovsky, knew that Stalin's political games were every bit as deadly as the war in which they were now engaged.

Fortunately, for the sake of an easy conscience, the propaganda department of the Union of Polish Patriots pursued a comforting line in historical explanations. Pre-war Poland, it would say, had been a land of oppression run by priests and nobles. Yet the old Poland was dead. So, too, was the outdated hatred and suspicion of Russia. With the help of the Soviet Union, a new Poland would arise, full of peace and justice. What is more the Polish people had a fine tradition of fighting against oppression. Time and again, they had linked up with their Russian brothers in the long struggle against the wars. In 1793–94, in 1830, in 1863 and in 1905, their capital had risen up repeatedly. Insurrection was a Polish speciality. When the battle for the Vistula was joined, everyone knew what to expect.

There remained the key question of the 'Patriotism' on which the Union of Polish Patriots was harping at every turn. What sort of patriotism was it that required Poles not only to fight the Germans but to obey and to emulate the Soviet Union in every slavish detail? The problem was not improved by one of its early slogans: 'POLAND: THE SEVENTEENTH REPUBLIC OF THE USSR.'

One cannot repeat often enough that anyone who thinks that it was the frontier of Russia, not the Soviet Union, which the Germans crossed in June 1941 will already have lost the plot. Yet the modern history of the lands that lie between Moscow and Warsaw becomes much simpler when one realizes that *all* the interested parties without exception had their own interpretations of history, their own claims, their own propaganda and their own nomenclature. Much turns on the legacy of the Grand Duchy of Lithuania, a historic entity which occupied the enormous space between the ancient Kingdom of Poland to the west and the ancient Principality of Moscow to the east. At its greatest extent in the late sixteenth century, the

Grand Duchy included the cities of Vilno, Minsk, and Kiev, which, after many tribulations, became the capitals respectively of Lithuania, Byelorussia (Belarus), and Ukraine. (Some modern commentators refer to this region by the useful acronym of LBU (or ULB), which coincides nicely both with important ethnic divisions and with the contemporary, post-Soviet states.) (See Appendix 1.)

For most of its existence, the territory of the Grand Duchy was contested by the rival rulers of Poland and Muscovy. From 1385 to 1572 it was ruled alongside Poland by the same Yagiellonian dynasty; and from 1572–1793 it formed an integral part of the dual Polish–Lithuanian Commonwealth. Yet, from the mid-seventeenth century onwards, the tides of power were flowing in the favour of Moscow. Bit by bit, bite by bite, the Muscovites ate into the body of the Commonwealth. They swallowed Kiev in 1662, Minsk in 1773, Vilno in 1793, and Warsaw at the second or third attempt in 1815. What is more, having declared themselves Tsars of 'all the Russias', they changed the existing names. Old Muscovy had invented the name of Rossiya or 'Russia' for itself long since. 'White Ruthenia' was changed into 'White Russia'. And the other part of Ruthenia, the former southern borderland of the Commonwealth, Ukraina, was made into 'Little Russia'. In the last decades of the Tsarist Empire, historic names such as 'Poland' or 'Lithuania' or 'Ruthenia' were disappearing from official usage.

At the end of the First World War, when the Tsarist Empire fell apart, all manner of national republics claimed their independence, from Finland in the north-west to Georgia in the south-east. Most of them, like Byelorussia and Ukraine, were soon suppressed by the Bolsheviks who triumphed in the so-called Russian Civil War and were intent on recreating a new sort of empire in the form of the Soviet Union. But the Republic of Poland was one of those which resisted reincorporation. After three years of war against Germany as well as Soviet Russia, it achieved a continuous system of internationally recognized borders. Its eastern frontier, formally established by the Treaty of Riga of 1921, remained intact throughout the inter-war period and was not violated until the Soviet invasion of 17 September 1939. Though superseded in practice by the Nazi–Soviet agreements, and by the unilateral arrangements of the German Occupation regime of 1941–44, it remained in international law as the sole legitimate dividing line between the Soviet Union and Poland.

The ethnic mix of the population of Lithuania, Byelorussia, and Ukraine was no less complex than its history. The major language groups were Poles (more than 5 million), Ukrainians, Byelorussians, Lithuanians, Yiddish-speaking Jews, and, as a remnant from Tsarist days, a small number of Russians, whom the others invariably dubbed Moskale ('Muscovites'). These groups were traditionally associated with particular religions: the Poles and Lithuanians with Roman Catholicism, the Ruthenians (the Ukrainians and Byelorussians) with the Uniate (Greek Catholic) Church, the Jews with various forms of Judaism, and the Russians with Russian Orthodoxy.

This relatively straightforward picture was distorted by two acts of arbitrary policy deriving from Tsarist days. First, the Tsarist authorities absolutely refused to acknowledge the distinction between Russians and Ruthenians, or to accept that the two Ruthenian peoples belonged to separate nationalities. They held that all the East Slavs formed a single Great Russian nation and that the Byelorussian and Ukrainian languages were mere dialects of Russian. (This can be compared to the contention that the Dutch and the Deutsch belong to a single nationality whose members speak slightly different variants of the same German language.) Second, the Patriarch of Moscow categorically refused to countenance either the Greek Catholic Church or the old form of Ruthenian Orthodoxy, which had traditionally paid allegiance not to Moscow but to the Patriarch of Constantinople. As a result, wherever the Tsar's writ ran, all East Slavs were officially designated as 'Russians' and all these Russians were ascribed as Russian Orthodox. It was a grave injustice which underlay the widespread misattribution of the region as an integral part of Russia.

In reality, the outstanding characteristic of the population of these borderlands was its diversity. It was multi-ethnic, multilingual, multicultural, and multiconfessional. The same can be said of the two great cities of the region, Vilno and Lvuv, although in their case, the Polish element commanded a clear majority. Vilno, for example, served as the main cultural centre not only for Poles, but also for Lithuanians, Byelorussians, and Yiddishers of the surrounding region. Yet Lvuv was more intensely Polish than any other centre. In its whole history prior to 1939, it had never found itself in the Grand Duchy, in the Tsarist Empire, or in the USSR. Historically, it had been the eastern bastion of the Kingdom of Poland. Its motto, SEMPER FIDELIS, declared its loyalty to the Polish cause. Even under Austrian rule, as the capital of Galicia, it retained far-reaching autonomy; and Galician Poles wielded a formidable influence in Vienna. In 1918–19, it had repeatedly defended its attachment to Poland with sword in hand. It was the last place in the Borders that the Poles would willingly abandon.

In the inter-war period, both the Soviet and the Polish Governments revised the existing ethnic classifications. In the Soviet Union, Lithuanian, Byelorussian, and Ukrainian were recognized for the first time as the official national languages of their Soviet republics. In the Republic of Poland, all three were legally protected minority languages, qualifying alongside Polish as languages of instruction for schooling in the eastern provinces. Yiddish, though frowned on in various circles (including the Zionists'), continued to be the most frequent mother tongue both of Soviet and of Polish Jews. The Greek Catholic (Uniate) religion, though severely repressed on Soviet territory, was officially reinstated on the Polish side of the frontier.

During the German occupation, which in 1939–41 reached as far as the Bug and spread far to the east in 1941–44, ethnic groupings were reordered in line with the Nazis' pseudo-racial categories. The Slavs were declared to be a racial group, not just a linguistic one. They were rated as *untermenschen*, subhuman, and the differences between them were either ignored or exploited in a crude form of 'divide and rule'. They were higher in Nazi estimation than the Jews, but markedly inferior to the German master race and to the Balts, who were judged ripe for Germanization.

In the course of the war, all the nationalities of the Borders suffered grievously. The 'collateral damage' of the German–Soviet Front, which passed through twice (in 1941 and 1944), was colossal. Byelorussians and Ukrainians were vastly reduced by military and political actions. The Jews were decimated by the Nazis. The Poles were cut down by Soviet deportations, by Nazi repressions, and by a campaign of ethnic cleansing undertaken by Ukrainian nationalists. As became apparent after the war, some of the worst atrocities of the Jewish Holocaust were perpetrated by German occupying forces in these same districts. It was not Soviet practice to draw attention to any particular group.

Rokossovsky's war memoirs give no hint of these matters. But he and his men must have been keenly aware of the changing ethnic and historical complexion of the lands through which they were advancing.

Stalingrad and Kursk were both in Russia, in what in those days was called the Russian Federation of Soviet Socialist Republics (RSFSR). Stalingrad, the former Tsaritsyn renamed 'the City of Stalin', lay on the right bank of the Volga and marked the most easterly point which the Wehrmacht reached in that central sector. Kursk, 650km (400 miles) from Stalingrad, lay south of Moscow, close to the point where Russia, Byelorussia, and Ukraine meet. It was still in historic Muscovite territory, inhabited by Russians and surrounded by Russian villages where Russian peasants spoke nothing but Russian.

The RSFSR, of course, included Siberia and stretched all the way to the Pacific. It constituted 85 per cent of the territory of the Soviet Union. Even so, Russians represented only 55 per cent of the total Soviet population, though they were considerably more numerous in the army, and especially in the officer corps. As a result, they sustained a disproportionate share of military losses. At the same time, since the German occupation barely touched the fringes of Russia, their civilian losses were considerably less, both in relative and in absolute terms, than those of the Byelorussians and Ukrainians.

Ukraine, whose northern reaches were traversed by Rokossovsky's advance, was the Soviet Union's second most populous republic. It was larger than France, and with nearly 50 million inhabitants had a similar sized population to Britain or Italy. Before 1939, it had been split into two unequal parts – the smaller Western Ukraine, centred on Lvuv (L'viv), which had spent centuries in Polish or Austrian hands, and the larger swathe of Central and Eastern Ukraine, which before 1917 had been in the Tsarist Empire and from 1923 in the Soviet Union.

In the later stages of the First World War, Ukraine was benevolently treated by the occupying forces of the Kaiser's Germany, which helped to set up the short-lived independent republic. In the Second World War, it was barbarously treated by the Nazis, who rejected pleas for the restoration of the Ukrainian Republic, setting up instead the military protectorate of *Reichskommissariat Ukraine*. The estimated 3 million Ukrainians who perished at German hands in 1941–44 matched the 3 million Ukrainians who had perished ten years earlier on Stalin's orders during the artificial Terror-Famine.[15] The Ukrainians must be regarded as the nationality which suffered the largest total of civilian war dead during the war.

During the Soviet advance of 1944, Western Ukraine was in the throes of a particularly vicious campaign of ethnic cleansing. Following the murder of the region's numerous Jewish community by the Nazis, the fascistic Ukrainian Insurrectionary Army (UPA) had seized the opportunity to create a purely 'Ukrainian Ukraine' by murdering the Poles in their midst.[16] The Soviet solution was to round up all Ukrainian nationalists, whether or not they had been involved in the slaughter, then encourage the remaining Poles to leave.

Byelorussia had also been split into two distinct parts. Western Byelorussia had been in Poland. Eastern Byelorussia, otherwise the Byelorussian SSR centred on Minsk, had been a founder member of the Soviet Union. Both parts, in 1944, were suffering from extreme distress – and not only from the effects of Nazi occupation. During the war, the vast marshes and forests of Byelorussia made ideal country for partisans who were not deterred by the German threat to execute a hundred people for every German killed by 'bandits'. Soviet, Byelorussian, Polish, and even Jewish Underground groups fought and competed in the backwoods. By 1945, one quarter of the country's population had perished. Proportionately, it was the highest death toll in Europe.

Pre-war Soviet Byelorussia had suffered disaster after disaster. In the 1920s it was allowed to introduce the native language for the first time, only to find that in the 1930s the new Byelorussian intelligentsia was virtually wiped out in Stalin's purges. Sixty per cent of the professors at the Byelorussian Academy of Sciences in Minsk were liquidated. They were largely replaced by Russians. As in Ukraine, huge numbers of peasants were eliminated by forced collectivization. The entire leadership of the Polish Communist Party (KPP), which had taken refuge in Minsk, was shot. In the Kuropaty Forest, huge pits contained the bodies of several hundred thousand victims of the 'Great Terror' of 1938–39, when Stalin's security police were killing by quota. Then came the Nazis. The citizenry of Minsk, which had a particularly large Jewish community, was all but wiped out. Physical destruction followed human destruction.

Western Byelorussia, which included the towns of Novogrodek, Grodno, Brest, and Pinsk, also included the vast expanse of Polesie, better known in English as the Pripet Marshes. This was the ultimate sanctuary of primitive Slavonic folklore and of prolific birdlife. The stupendous Forest of Bialovyezha, where bison and wolves still roamed, had attracted the Tsars to their favourite hunting and shooting lodge. Under Polish rule after 1921, Byelorussian language and culture had been permitted. A strong peasant cooperative system had been formed. A Byelorussian political movement which was banned in the USSR had also functioned. Its leader had died in a Soviet prison. The towns as opposed to the countryside were overwhelmingly Polish and Jewish. Novogrodek was the birthplace of Poland's national poet, Adam M., and of Menahem Begin, a future Premier of Israel. Some towns, like Pinsk, had absolute Jewish majorities. They were notorious in the eyes of the rest of the population for having staged elaborate ceremonies of welcome for the Red Army in September 1939. But then September 1939 had seen the last days of peace. The Soviet Occupation of 1939–41 brought mass arrests, deportations, and confiscations. Operation Barbarossa brought in the Nazi regime, and endless murders and reprisals. Rokossovsky's approach brought another round of bitter fighting on the grand scale.

Byelorussia had once been the heart of the old Grand Duchy of Lithuania, and Old Byelorussian had long been used as the Grand Duchy's official language. But travelling west, as soon as one crossed the Bug, one was entering the lands of the old Kingdom of Poland, of Latin Christendom, and of predominantly Polish language and settlement. During the Nazi Occupation, one was passing from the *Reichskommissariat Ostland* to the General Government. In pre-war, and post-war terms, one would be entering the fertile Polish districts of Helm, Lublin, and Zamost, which occupied the area between the Bug and the Vistula.

Lublin, historically, is a city where West meets East. Owing to the proximity of the Grand Duchy, the Royal Castle at Lublin was chosen in 1569 as the location of the declaration of the Polish–Lithuanian Commonwealth. The Trinity Chapel in the Castle displays a wonderful mixture of Western Gothic architecture and of Eastern Byzantine frescoes. After the Partitions, the site was used for a notorious Tsarist prison. In September 1939 the Red Army advanced and crossed the Bug to Lublin, but withdrew in accordance with the Nazi–Soviet Pact. When the Germans arrived, they cleared the Jewish Community from the Old City, and set up the concentration camp of Maidanek on the city outskirts. The surrounding region was the scene of numerous conflicts. It contained both the three dedicated Nazi death camps of Treblinka, Sobibor, and Belzec and the district of Zamost, where the SS aimed to replace the entire Polish population with German settlers. Fighting in the Underground was intense. The dominant Polish Resistance movement had to hold its own not only against the German occupying forces but also against Communist rivals and Ukrainian bands from further east. Hence in July 1944, as the Soviet war machine battered its way from the Bug to the Vistula, it was driving through a population where resentments of all sorts were raw, and where politics, to put it mildly, were complex.

Rokossovsky reached Lublin on 24 July. Politics, however, were not for him. Soldiers had to stick to soldiering even when they were freshly dubbed Marshals of the Soviet Union. Two things were on his mind: as he later recalled, he had to make a public speech in Polish for the first time in his life; and he had to give serious thought to the next phase of the campaign. He was operational commander of the central sector of the Eastern Front, moving along the direct line from Moscow to Berlin. Indeed, he was already much closer to Berlin than to Moscow. One more stunning campaign of the sort which he had just pulled off in Operation Bagration would bring him to the very heart of the Reich. The Vistula would be heavily defended, and he could expect the enemy resistance to stiffen as Berlin came into his sights. He could expect counter-attacks at any point. But he held the momentum; his adversary was reeling; and it made sense to keep it going. Once his massed tanks were over the Vistula and rolling through the plains of central Poland, there was nothing much to stop them before they reached 'the lair of the Fascist Beast' itself. The final decisions would be taken by the *Stavka* ('Soviet Military Command') and by Rokossovsky's political masters. Yet, at the very least, they would surely want his professional judgement.

The history of the Russo-Polish frontier has a fearsome reputation. Like the Schleswig-Holstein Question or the Macedonian Maze, it is often said to defy rational understanding. Yet in essence, if not in detail, it is quite simple. The Polish state, which originated in the valleys of the Varta and the Vistula, spread gradually eastwards. The Russian state, which originated in the valley of the Volga, spread westwards as well as eastwards. As a result, Poles and Russians have for centuries contested the two thousand kilometres (twelve hundred miles) that separate the Vistula and the Volga. When Poland was strong, the frontier lay far to the east. When Russia was strong, as she increasingly was, it lay far to the west. When Poland was erased from the map – as in the late nineteenth century – Russia shared a frontier with Germany. (See Appendix 6.)

So-called historical claims, therefore, must all be considered with a high degree of scepticism. At the Paris Peace Conference in 1919, for instance, when the Polish representative proposed a return to the frontier of 1772, he was not widely considered to be acting reasonably. By the same token, the Russian 'Whites' who refused to budge from their claim to a return to the frontier of 1914 – which denied Poland's right to existence – were not taken seriously. The Bolsheviks, for their part, initially denounced all international frontiers as a frippery of the past. Convinced that all of Europe's territorial arrangements were soon to be overthrown by revolution, they regarded all frontier lines as temporary. Stalin, in contrast, was out to secure every inch of territory he could grab.

In the chaotic years after the First World War and the Russian Revolution, Soviet Russia and the Republic of Poland faced each other across the expanses of their predecessors' rivalries. In 1919–20, no less than three Russo-Polish frontier proposals were put forward under the auspices of the Western powers. None was accepted by the interested parties, put into force, or regarded at the time as more than an armistice or demarcation line. None made any contribution to history except to fuel the endless polemics which surround the issue. The first was the Provisional Line proposed in December 1919 by the Council of Ambassadors. The second, the Spa Line, proposed in July 1920 by the British Foreign Minister, Lord Curzon, would have left Lvuv on the Polish side. The third, the modified Spa Line, which was secretly tampered with in the British Foreign Office without Curzon's knowledge, would have put Lvuv on the Soviet side.

On 18 March 1921, in the Treaty of Riga, Polish and Soviet representatives signed the only frontier agreement between them to possess any measure of legitimacy. The Riga Line was a deliberate compromise, roughly halfway between the Spa Line and the historic frontier of 1772. It reflected Poland's victory in the recent war with Soviet Russia, but not the full extent of the territorial concessions that a desperate Lenin had been willing to make. It formed the internationally recognized frontier between Poland and the Soviet Union throughout the inter-war period. It was ratified by both sides, accepted by the League of Nations, and confirmed by the Soviet–Polish Non-aggression Pact of 25 July 1932. From then on, any unilateral abrogation of the Riga Line would be a breach of international law.

During the currency of the Nazi–Soviet Pact, 1939–41, the Soviet Union threw international law to the winds. Expelled, like Germany, from the League of Nations, Stalin put his faith in his bilateral agreements with Hitler's Reich. Moscow declared that since 'Poland no longer existed', the Riga Line had lost its validity. The Soviet Union's western frontier, 'the Peace Boundary' as negotiated in 1939, was contiguous with the Greater German Reich.

After June 1941, however, when Stalin joined the Grand Alliance, new arrangements had to be made in haste. Stalin's representatives recognized the Polish Government in London and signed the Atlantic Charter, which outlawed the principle of territorial aggrandizement. For any who were not quite so smart at the game of diplomatic chess, the Soviets were widely thought to have confessed the error of their former ways. For whilst they could not be pressed into an explicit restoration of the Riga Line, they *did* renounce their adherence to the Nazi–Soviet agreements. Hence, throughout the critical years of conflict on the Eastern Front, Western diplomats were led to believe that Stalin had abandoned the ill-gotten gains that he had obtained by collusion with his erstwhile Nazi partners. He had done nothing of the sort.

Western leaders received their first intimation of things to come during the negotiations which followed the German attack on the USSR in 1941. Eager to avoid recognition of Stalin's annexation of the Baltic states, they found to their surprise that, in spite of everything, Moscow was intent on reclaiming every inch of the territory lost during Barbarossa. Molotov made no bones of the fact that he had not rejected the substance of his territorial agreements with Ribbentrop. On Eden's advice, the British wrote off the Baltic states, although the Americans, to their credit, refrained. But there were more surprises in store. When Molotov came to England in May 1942 to sign the Anglo-Soviet Treaty, he proposed a treaty with no territorial clauses whatsoever. And so it went on.

At the first meeting of the 'Big Three' at Teheran in November 1943 – suitably code-named Eureka – the Western representatives were caught on the back foot once again. In the course of discussions about the future shape of Europe, Molotov coolly produced a copy of the British telegram dated 25.7.1920 describing what he now chose to call the 'Curzon Line'. The surprise must have been palpable. The British themselves were unsure what the Curzon Line was, and were unable to explain it satisfactorily to the Americans. As yet, they did not suspect that someone in the British Foreign Office had secretly modified Lord Curzon's proposals all those years before; nor did they seem to realize that the modified Spa Line, a.k.a. the Curzon Line, bore a striking resemblance to the Nazi–Soviet 'Peace Boundary'. In any case, they were in no mood to protest. Having signally failed to open the long promised 'Second Front' against Germany, Britain and America were highly embarrassed. So Stalin found that he was risking little by taking a hard line. He also found that Churchill and Roosevelt had no stomach either for insisting on the Atlantic Charter or for defending the interests of their First Ally. In fact, he was treated to the spectacle of the Western leaders falling over themselves to please him. At one meeting, Churchill without Roosevelt took the initiative in proposing that the Curzon Line should 'provide the basis' for the post-war frontier.

The only condition was that Poland should be compensated by the transfer of German lands in the west. At another meeting, Roosevelt without Churchill calmly assured Stalin that frontier definition would 'pose no problems'. After that, the Soviet dictator would have good grounds to feel aggrieved if the Western leaders were to insist on further quibbling or if they failed to bring their clients into line. He must have been particularly satisfied that they agreed to keep the whole thing secret.

Objectively speaking, one can only label Molotov's coup as brilliant and the Anglo-American performance as lamentable. The young American diplomat who was given the unenviable task of unravelling the intricacies of the story soon came to the conclusion that the telegram presented by Molotov was not a forgery and that the frontier line suggested by Lord Curzon at the Spa Conference had been surreptitiously altered in favour of Soviet Russia by someone in the British Foreign Office. Yet, by 1943, this was ancient history. As for the Foreign Office clerk who had apparently tampered with Curzon's proposals in 1920 and who had thereby provided the ammunition for Molotov's coup in 1943: it was almost certainly Lewis Namier. In later years, Namier boasted that he, rather than Lord Curzon, was 'the author of the Curzon Line'.[17]

For practical purposes, therefore, Stalin was free to act as he thought fit. He had been relieved by Churchill and Roosevelt from the tiresome obligation of negotiating his western frontier with Poland, so, a few weeks after Eureka, he saw no objection to making his position public. In January 1944, *Izvestia* published an article about the Soviet Union's future frontier on the Curzon Line. The accompanying map showed a thick black line running along the western confines of the LBU, leaving all the major centres on the Soviet side. In the central section, it ran along the River Bug, and in the south, in a totally arbitrary manner, it cut off Lvuv from all its historic Western connections. It was repeated in scores of press releases and Soviet propaganda brochures around the world. With Western connivance, Stalin had played his hand. His opponents were left with the formidable task of trying to unplay it. (See Appendix 13.)

The true nature of Soviet intentions towards the western frontier can best be gauged from a confidential memorandum, which did not surface for fifty years. Written by Maisky to Molotov on 10 January 1944, it was entitled 'On desirable bases for the future world'; and it proposed that Poland be kept to 'a minimal size'. As stated by the Russian historian who discovered it: 'Prejudices against Poland were not peculiar to Stalin but were characteristic of the whole Soviet elite':

> The purpose of the USSR must be the creation of an independent and viable Poland: however, we are not interested in the appearance of *too big and too strong a Poland*. [Italics in the original.] In the past, Poland was almost always Russia's enemy, and no one can be sure that the future Poland would become a genuine friend of the USSR (at least during the lifetime of the rising generation). Many doubt it, and it is fair to say that there are serious grounds for such doubts.[18]

If anyone had dared to ask Stalin or Molotov whether the Atlantic Charter could be used to justify the seizure of one ally's territory by another, they would have been mightily affronted. (They were never put to the test.) But they would have argued that there was no question of seizing a neighbour's territory. All they were doing was following the long-standing advice of Western diplomats and recovering the land which the Soviet Union had possessed before the start of the war in June 1941. (In the Soviet view, there was no war before 1941.) In any case, there is no evidence to suggest that they regarded Poland as an ally. In their heart of hearts, they still thought of her as 'the Bastard'.

All armies are the servants of their political masters. But some regimes exert a greater degree of control than others. In the Second World War, the British and American Governments possessed few instruments for keeping their armed forces in line in the event of serious mutiny or disobedience. In British and American practice, it was the general staffs themselves who controlled both the military police (who were responsible for discipline), and the military intelligence (who were responsible, among other things, for testing the pulse of morale). In France, the Government was rather better equipped, thanks to the existence of a separate force of militarized gendarmerie, and, for civilian control, of the *Compagnies Républicaines de Sécurité*. But no democratic states possessed safeguards comparable to those of their totalitarian counterparts. In the Third Reich, for instance, the Nazi Party maintained its own private military-police system, in the form of the SS, which was charged with supervising all the activities of the German state. In wartime, SS units fought alongside regular units of the Wehrmacht. Yet had the regulars at any time refused orders, the SS would certainly have been used against them.

The Soviet Army of Stalinist times was probably the most elaborately shackled force in history, for it possessed no means of independent action.

What a paradox! The fearsome war machine, which was grinding the Wehrmacht to pieces, was so organized internally that its commanders could not take the slightest step on their own initiative. Marshal Rokossovsky, who held both the highest military rank and the top command in the most important of Fronts, could not take the most trivial decisions without first obtaining the written permission of the political officers who swarmed above, alongside, and behind him. He, like all Soviet soldiers, held a subordinate position within the organization of which he was the nominal head.

Three key mechanisms must be taken into account. The first revolved round Stalin's personal dictatorship; the second concerned the Communist Party's Chief Military-Political Department, or 'Glav-Pol'; the third turned on the special status of the National Commissariat of Internal Affairs (NKVD). Not only was every single Soviet institution guarded by watchdog bodies, but every watchdog was watched by other, superior, watchdogs specifically appointed to monitor their activities.

By the mid-1940s, Stalin's personal authority was virtually total. Over the previous twenty years, he had transformed the collective party dictatorship of the Bolsheviks into a still more extreme form of totalitarianism in which the will of the Leader and the will of his party were indistinguishable. Later commentators talk politely of the 'Personality Cult': in practice it was every bit as vicious and mystical as the Nazis' *Führerprinzip*. Stalin could do no wrong. He held all the levers of power. In addition to the key post of General Secretary of the Communist Party, he was also Prime Minister and Commander-in-Chief. There were no longer any party factions. There was no 'Right Opposition' or 'Left Opposition' as had once existed in the 1920s. All there was, was one person who held the lives and deaths of 200 million at his bidding. The Soviet Army existed to execute his commands; those who failed to execute them were themselves executed. Those, like Rokossovsky or Zhukov, who carried them out with efficiency and panache risked his displeasure for being too successful.

Ever since Lenin's days, the Communist Party of the Soviet Union (CPSU) had worked on the principle that it had an absolute right to guide and direct all the activities of all state institutions (known in the jargon as 'the party's leading role'). Embodied in the constitution, it ensured that any act not authorized by the party was illegal. In practice, it worked through a complicated 'dual system' of Government in which particular party organs were designated to supervise the work of particular state bodies. Hence, the party's Politburo gave (unpublished) orders to the Council of Ministers: the International Department of the Party Secretariat controlled every aspect of Soviet foreign policy including the work of the Ministry of Foreign Affairs and of foreign Communist parties abroad; and the party's Military-Political Department controlled the armed forces. Most Western commentators came to realize that the party's General Secretary was the top executive who completely outranked the Soviet State President, but many of them never managed to notice that Soviet embassies were not necessarily run by ambassadors, that Soviet ministries were not always run by ministers: and that the Soviet Army was not really run by the marshals.

In the 1940s, Glav-Pol and the NKVD maintained a stranglehold on every aspect of the army's life. Through the NKVD chief, Lavrenti Beria, they were entirely at Stalin's disposal. They exercised their hold through indoctrination, through the dual system of military commands, and through the activities of 'special forces'.

Political indoctrination received a higher priority than military training: all Soviet soldiers were thoroughly indoctrinated, but only the elite troops were thoroughly trained. The politicos ran all the military academies, induction centres, and training camps, and were apt to hold front-line propaganda seminars on the eve of battle. They were taught to inculcate the infallibility of Marxism-Leninism, the invincibility of the Soviet Union under the leadership of Russia, and the unparalleled genius of Joseph Stalin.

On the First Byelorussian Front, however, difficulties arose. In 1944–45, a new draft of non-Russian conscripts arrived. It consisted largely of local men who had been schooled before the war outside the USSR, principally in Poland and Romania, and who were not disposed to accept the official line. 'They regarded it quite sceptically,' one political department reported with alarm. 'After the conversation on the feat of a Hero of the Soviet Union, Sgt. Varlamov, who blocked the embrasure of an enemy firepoint with his body, there were comments that this cannot be possible.'[19] At the same time, another NKVD report talked of unacceptable non-operational losses 'due to the ignorance of the officers and the bad training of soldiers.' In one division alone twenty-three troopers were killed and sixty-seven wounded in a single month through the mishandling of sub-machine guns.[20]

The tentacles of the Military-Political Department were spread through every level of the armed forces. Its agents, generally known to the outside world as 'commissars' but officially designated as *politruks*, or 'political leaders', usually held two posts. One post, that was not publicized, lay within the department's own hierarchy. The other lay with the professional hierarchy of the armed forces. In this way, it was entirely possible for a person of high military rank to be relatively low in the pecking order of power, and equally for figures of apparently mediocre military status to wield power and influence far above their formal status. At the lowest level, every Soviet company or battalion possessed both a military commander and a political officer, whose job was to report to his party superiors and thereby to keep the commander in line. At the highest level, every Soviet marshal or general was shadowed by a political officer of similar nominal rank but of superior political stature.

Marshal Rokossovsky's front-line command bunker, for example, would have been laid out to a standard pattern. It was extremely austere. The essential furniture consisted of a double bunk bed, and a table with two chairs. The Marshal would occupy the top bunk. He would be constantly watched night and day from the lower bunk by his political officer, Gen. Nikolai Bulganin, an ex-Chekist. When orders were ready for despatch, the men would sit at the same table. And both would sign – Rokossovsky first, and Bulganin second. From this set-up, it is not difficult to deduce who the real commander of the First Byelorussian Front was. And the conversation can hardly have been jocular. For Bulganin was a senior member of the service which only six or seven years earlier had put Rokossovsky on trial, shot the majority of his peers, and sent him to the Gulag. Bulganin still had a brilliant career before him. Once the war was over, it was no accident that he would rise to the very top of the system whilst Rokossovsky did not.

The All-Union NKVD – successor to the Cheka and the OGPU, and predecessor of the KGB – was an umbrella organization which controlled all branches of the Soviet security services. It was far more comprehensive than anything that existed elsewhere. Its numerous directorates controlled all manner of operations from espionage and counter-espionage to the civil police, the frontier and coast guards, the fire brigades, the prisons, the Gulag, the Ministry of the Interior, criminal investigations and prosecutions, and various corps of internal security troops. In comparison to the German model, it was like the SS, the *Waffen-SS*, the *Sicherheitsdienst*, the *Abwehr*, the *Kripo*, the Gestapo, and many other services, all rolled into one. Its three Chief Directors, G. G. Yagoda, N. I. Yezhov, and Lavrentii

Beria, were all mass-murderers on the grand scale. Each was himself murdered.

The *Smyersh* organization, whose name derived from an acronym of *smyert' shpionam* ('death to the spies'), was the ultimate wartime watchdog of the watchdogs, and the embodiment of Stalinist paranoia. Formally created in 1943 as a department of the Soviet General Staff, it was separate from both the Red Army and the NKVD, even though all its operatives were drawn from the NKVD's 3rd Directorate of Military Counter-Intelligence. Its commander was Beria's deputy. Its special duties were to root out all spies, saboteurs, subversives, and suspicious persons from the military and from the rear areas under military occupation. There were *Smyersh* units in the HQ of every front, every army, every corps, and every division.

On the First Byelorussian Front, the chief representative of *Smyersh* had several discrete units under his immediate command and could call on extra 'special forces' as needs arose. Though a mere lieutenant general, he could have obtained the authority to arrest Marshal Rokossovsky at any time. Rokossovsky could never have ordered the arrest of a senior political officer.

The NKVD's Chief Directorate of Internal Troops (GUPVO) was itself divided into six directorates, controlling the Frontier Corps, the Convoy Troops, the Industrial and State Guards, the Railway Guards, and the Intendant's Service. From 1941, a large number of NKVD rifle regiments, totalling some 100,000 men, were raised and trained for combat. They were formed into independent NKVD line divisions complete with their own armour and artillery. From these were drawn the fearsome destroyer battalions, whose task was to hunt down enemies in the rear areas, and the notorious blocking detachments, whose function was to man the cordons behind the Red Army's lines and to drive the troops into battle. Every Red Army soldier knew that if he failed to face up to enemy bullets in front of him he would be killed by an NKVD bullet in the back.

The implications of these interlocking organizations for any outsider caught up in the Soviet advance were extremely serious. The front-line soldiers, whom the outsiders were likely to meet first, were usually friendly enough. But the second line was inveterately hostile. The NKVD would routinely arrest all and sundry and would ask questions later. Since they habitually killed their own people with impunity, they thought nothing of killing foreigners. Theirs was a closed world with which it was extremely difficult to interact.

The political controls under which the Red Army laboured could be clearly seen in action by anyone who watched it on the march. As reported by eye-witnesses, it passed through each locality in three distinct waves. The front-line troops, who went first, were well clothed, well shod, well armed, and supported by huge streams of tanks, self-propelled guns, motorized AA batteries, and rocket launchers. Next came a vast horde of second-line soldiery and camp followers. These were often dressed in rags or scraps of uniform and were bootless. Scurrying to and fro like ants, or riding mangy ponies, or dragging themselves along in a tangled mass of wagons and captured farm animals, they carried their rifles on a string and their sacks of loot slung over their shoulders. At the rear, the NKVD's private security army stood attentively in their shining American jeeps as they edged forward. Dressed in smart grey uniforms with bright blue epaulettes, they toted sub-machine guns at the ready. Their task was to shoot down anyone in front who failed to keep moving.

Politics equally underlay the calculated brutality of the Soviet soldiery towards civilians. The conquered peoples were deliberately chastised with the rough edge of Soviet might. What is more, on higher orders deriving from the earlier part of the war, all Soviet people who had lived under German occupation but had not been killed resisting, were to be treated as potential traitors. Plunder was standard. Assault and battery was normal. Murder was common. Rape was ubiquitous. And the NKVD, who would pounce on the least hint of political dissent, did not think to intervene in such trivialities. A famous Russian writer, who served as an artillery officer under Rokossovsky, described the scene:

The conquerors of Europe swarm,
Russians scurrying everywhere.
Vacuum cleaners, wine, and candles,
Skirts and picture frames, and pipes
Brooches and medallions, blouses, buckles
Typewriters (not of a Russian type)
Rings of sausages and cheeses . . .
A moment later the cry of a girl,
Somewhere from behind a wall,
'I'm not a German. I'm not a German.
No! I'm – Polish. I'm a Pole.'
Grabbing what comes handy, those
Like-minded lads get in and start –

And lo, what heart
Could well oppose?[21]

Politics, above all, determined the extreme rigour directed against all non-Soviet resistance fighters. On 14 July 1944, in the week that Rokossovsky crossed the Bug, Stalin and his Chief of the General Staff, Gen. Antonov, sent a special order to all commanders on the various western fronts:

> . . . Soviet troops in Lithuanian, Byelorussian, and Ukrainian territories have encountered 'Polish military detachments run by the Polish émigré Government. These detachments have behaved suspiciously and have everywhere acted against the interests of the Red Army'. Contact with them [is] therefore forbidden. When these formations are found, 'they must be immediately disarmed and sent to specially organized collection points for investigation'.[22]

From Moscow's point of view, foreign Communist parties existed to bolster Moscow's influence abroad. To these ends, every European country was blessed, or saddled, with its resident CP. Until 1943, the worldwide network of CPs was maintained and guided by the Moscow-based Comintern organization.

Several fundamental questions are raised, therefore, by Comintern's extraordinary decision in 1938 not merely to disband the Polish Communist Party (KPP) and to kill its leaders, but also to 'suspend' it in a manner that made no provision for a replacement. Clearly, this was something more than a mere purge. Stalin had killed off the Bolshevik leadership of his own party, and in wave after wave of terror purges had created an organization that was new in almost every respect. But he never attempted to abolish the party itself, because the party held the keys to the governance of the USSR. One can only conclude that his motives for attacking the Polish Communists in such an extreme way were not confined to rooting out infiltrators or suppressing ideological dissent. Since no steps were taken to create a new body in place of the KPP, one has to suspect that Stalin had already foreseen the possibility of destroying Poland itself. For the sequence of events was remarkable. Less than a year after Comintern had declared that the KPP had been 'temporarily abolished', Molotov was declaring that Poland, too, had 'ceased to exist'.

No moves to revive the Polish Communist movement were undertaken until the second half of 1941, when the USSR had been invaded by the Wehrmacht and when Stalin, in dire straights, had been forced to admit after all that Poland *did* exist. Indeed, he did not hesitate in recognizing the exiled Polish Government. Hence, if Poland had been reinstated, a Polish Communist Party had to be reinvented as well. Comintern approved the formation of a steering committee, which went under the name of the Central Bureau of Polish Communists in the Soviet Union. This body in turn made preparations for the formation of a new party that for tactical reasons was to avoid the Communist label and call itself the Polish Workers' Party (PPR). Unfortunately, since the whole of Poland was at that time occupied by the Germans, the only way to proceed was to fly in activists from Moscow. The first 'Initiative Group' landed in December 1941. After linking up with various clandestine pro-communist grouplets, it launched the PPR at a clandestine meeting in German-occupied Warsaw on 5 January 1942.

The initial phase in the wartime history of the PPR was extremely murky. It was attended by dire intrigues, murder most foul, and near-total isolation from the rest of the world. Its first Secretary was murdered by his successor, who was duly betrayed to the Gestapo by his comrades. The third in line, Comrade 'Vyeslav' (Gomulka), was a pre-war Communist, who had not been sent by Moscow, but who, having been held in a pre-war Polish jail, had chosen in 1939 to chance his luck in the Nazi rather than the Soviet Zone. The party manifesto of November 1943, 'What are we fighting for?', was a typical piece of Marxist-Leninist analysis and of pro-Soviet propaganda.

In 1943, Moscow's network for dealing with foreign Communists was transformed. As the Red Army surged towards the complete rout of Nazi Germany, the old Bolshevik internationalism was abandoned in favour of a more narrowly Soviet and more overtly Stalinist line. Comintern was disbanded. Its functions were assumed by various organs of the Soviet party's own organization.

The new tack had serious consequences for relations with Poland and with Polish Communists. A new organization, the Union of Polish Patriots (ZPP), came into being to coordinate Soviet–Polish relations. Its leader was the wayward daughter of a well-known pre-war Foreign Minister. 'Patriotic' was a new code-word meaning 'pro-Soviet', and the Patriots were ready to receive people of almost any political persuasion so long as they were willing to follow Soviet instructions. In this way, the comrades of the PPR became just one strand among many; and the Patriotic Movement was dominated by a fine gallery of obscure opportunists unearthed by the NKVD.

Late in 1943, the PPR and the ZPP jointly sponsored the formation of the National Homeland Council (KRN), which was designed as a sort of embryo Soviet-in-waiting. The KRN claimed to be an assembly of political representatives based on the pre-war model of a Popular Front. In practice, it was unable to assemble, and enjoyed the support of no one except a handful of minuscule radical fractions. Its chairman was Comrade Boleslas B. (Bierut), a Polish-born Soviet functionary, who had been made redundant by the demise of the Comintern. Its main contribution was to lay down the principles of a domestic policy based on agrarian reform and limited industrial nationalization – i.e. on the plans of Poland's Peasant and Socialist Parties – combined with a foreign policy based on 'eternal friendship' with the Soviet Union. After a few months of shadowy existence, its organizers realized that it could exert no real influence without an executive arm that could administer Polish districts as soon as they were occupied by the Soviet military.

The formation of the Polish Committee of National Liberation (PKWN), therefore, was prompted by Rokossovsky's crossing of the River Bug and by the Red Army's entry into territory which Stalin had earmarked for the future Poland. The Committee had been formed in Moscow by activists of the PPR, ZPP, and KRN. On 21 July 1944 it was flown into the town of Helm, where on the following day it issued its pre-prepared political manifesto. Its chairman, a person of great obscurity, was presented as a socialist. Of its early decrees, one was to authorize the NKVD's control of 'rear areas', and the other to announce the restoration of a Polish Army under Soviet command. Since it moved its HQ on 1 August to Lublin, it became known to the outside world as the 'Lublin Committee'.

Though the committee was a classic case of a puppet Government imported in the baggage train of a conquering army, its long-term purposes remained extremely opaque, for it did not claim to be a provisional Government and its stance was not overtly Communist. Its manifesto contained none of the policies which constituted the norms of Soviet Government, such as the collectivization of agriculture or the command economy or the 'Dictatorship of the Proletariat'. Of its sixteen departments or 'ministries', only three were in the hands of declared Communists; and nothing was said about the surrender of Poland's eastern provinces. So if the aim was to sow confusion, the means were highly successful: it is doubtful if anyone outside the circle of political planners in Moscow could have known what was really afoot. Even to advanced political analysts, the stream of acronyms such as PPR, KPP, KRN, or PKWN was so much mumbo-jumbo. Yet if anyone had asked whether the populace was expected to rise in support of the Soviet advance, the answer would undoubtedly have been yes. Indeed, there are some grounds to suppose that the Communists were hoping to lead the coming insurrection themselves.

Once the Red Army was in striking distance of central Poland, three scouting parties were sent across German lines to report on the state of the Polish Underground. In due course, the information provided by the three group leaders was collated in Moscow by Beria and, on 23 March 1944, forwarded to Comrade Stalin. It purported to contain details of the leading Underground groupings, their military wings, their class support, and their armed activities. The most influential group, it said, was orientated towards the USSR, and had been formed by the PPR and its military wing, the People's Guard (GL). One of the Soviet scouts had made contact with 'Comrade Mechislav M.', who had outlined the GL's structure and had put its *actif* at 5,000 men. The second group was said to be called 'OZON or *Sanacja*', and was described as a 'Government party of fascist orientation', 'anti-Soviet in the extreme', and 'calling for the creation of a Greater Poland from sea to sea'. The third group was described as the 'Endek Party', formed from 'petty landowners, bourgeois and officers'. It was reportedly aiming to seize power in the name of 'the reactionary element'. The Peasant Party and its Peasant Battalions were said to be organized by 'rich peasants' – i.e. kulaks. Its lower ranks were supposed to be ignoring their leaders and fraternizing with the People's Guard. Since the autumn of 1943, the report continued, the *Sanacja* Group had succeeded in merging itself with four others to form the Home Army or AK, 'now called the Polish Armed Forces'. It was led by 'army officers and policemen'. It was not involved in fighting the Germans, but was 'preparing itself for the struggle with its enemy Nr. 1 – the USSR.'[23]

Practically every statement in this lengthy report was false. The reporters could not possibly have made so many factual mistakes if they had talked to even a modest cross-section of Underground members; and their amateur class analysis was woefully inappropriate. It is hard to believe that Stalin could fail to see that he was being fed information the sycophants wanted him to believe. Yet in Moscow there was no easy way of checking the facts. And the message was rather encouraging. It conveyed the welcome impression that the Polish Underground was predominantly pro-Soviet and that, in any case, it was numerically negligible. At that stage in the war, Stalin could hardly have wished for anything better. No one in Moscow would have pondered long on the potential consequences of such poor intelligence.

As soon as Stalin had embarked on the pursuit of the retreating Wehrmacht to the Vistula and beyond, it was clear that his ability to determine the post-war settlement of Central and Eastern Europe increased with every inch of territory taken. At the same time, it was evident that no settlement would be secure without the joint approval of the Big Three, and of the post-war Peace Conference which the Western powers were still aiming to convene. To this end, Soviet policy sought to influence the public opinion of the Western powers, and particularly of Britain. For Britain was Poland's patron: and the exiled Polish government was resident in London. Soviet pressures on Britain, therefore, were to be an important factor in the final outcome.

Soviet agents and sympathizers in Britain faced three basic tasks. First, they sought to discredit the exiled Government, and everyone who respected its authority. Second, they promoted arguments which made a Soviet takeover of the Lithuania–Byelorussia–Ukraine region look eminently reasonable. And third, to make the Poles appear responsible for the inevitable bad blood, they had to deny all of their own crimes and offences. They played their cards well.

The anti-Polish campaign had begun almost as soon as the war did. On 24 September 1939 – that is, one week after the first Soviet invasion – David Lloyd George, the former Prime Minister and war leader, put his name to a long article in the *Sunday Express*, the flagship paper of the Beaverbrook fleet, entitled 'What is Stalin up to?' He said that the class-ridden Government of Poland had deserted its people. He advocated a change in the eastern frontier because the people living there were not Poles but 'of a totally other race'. He finished by denying that the Nazis and Soviets could be contemplating a new Partition of Poland. David Lloyd George could not have served Stalin's cause better if he had asked the Soviet Press Office for guidance. His tirade did not pass uncontested. But it had set the agenda for future discussion.[24] Three days later, the new Partition was announced.

The three issues raised in Lloyd George's article recurred time and time again throughout the following years. On the Governmental issue, Poland's detractors used a battery of uncomplimentary adjectives on the 'class-ridden' theme, always implying that the country was run by a rogues' gallery of landowners, aristocrats, squires, colonels, bankers, priests, or 'blood-suckers' and that, in stark contrast to the Soviet regime, it was completely unrepresentative of the people. Even when the exiled Government was manifestly dominated by democratic elements – what in Soviet terms would have been thought of as 'workers and peasants' – Soviet apologists routinely described it as 'fascist'. On the territorial issues, they carefully avoided the complex realities, arguing instead that Russian land, inhabited by Russians, should obviously belong to 'Russia'. On the issue of the Nazi–Soviet Pact and its consequences, they preferred to say nothing. They were not willing to discuss either the partition of 1939 or the mass deportations or the Katyn Massacres. Anyone who attempted to raise such unmentionables was ipso facto 'anti-Soviet'.

No less revealing was the treatment of Poland's Ambassador, who sought to refute Lloyd George's ill-informed remarks. He wrote a long letter to *The Times*, whose columns served in those days as a forum of national debate. But he was curtly told that *The Times* had a rule not to publish correspondence on subjects initiated by other newspapers. It was the classic British brush-off. The Ambassador then published his letter as a private brochure, which probably enjoyed a circulation of hundreds. One should remember that through much of the wartime years, the foreign editorship of *The Times* was held by E. H. Carr, a historian who had been almost as ready to appease the Nazis before the war as he was to appease Stalin during and after it.[25]

Fellow-travellers, in fact, formed an important part of the Soviet lobby in Britain. They consisted largely of left-leaning intellectuals, who vociferously denied having anything in common with Marxism-Leninism or with Soviet policy, but who nonetheless saw Soviet communism as an interesting and respectable branch of the political spectrum. They were people who would not have sat at the same table as a fascist but who saw nothing wrong in welcoming Communists to their homes, or in giving space to Soviet agents in their newspapers and seminars. Their archetypes were Sidney and Beatrice Webb of the Fabian Society whose fatuous and notoriously uncritical work *Soviet Communism: a new civilisation?* (1935) had gravely misled a whole generation. Yet from G. B. Shaw and H. G Wells, to Harold Laski, the influential director of the LSE, to Victor Gollancz and

J. B. Priestley, they were everywhere. And they included no small number of MPs, such as Tom Driberg or Ellen Wilkinson.[26] One cannot do better than quote the opinion of the historian whose once unfashionable opinion on these matters has been amply vindicated. 'The selective sanctimoniousness of the Stalinophile lobbies in London and Washington', he wrote, was 'even more repulsive than their political stupidity.'[27]

Even Britain's leading historian of Russia, Sir Bernard Pares, joined the international fray, directing his heavyweight fire on a point which called the very existence of Poland's independent republic into question. Writing in the *Manchester Guardian*, he referred to the period at the end of the First World War, when Russia had supposedly lost its western provinces 'almost by accident' and when, supposedly, 'ten million Russians' found themselves on the wrong side of the inter-war frontier. Sir Bernard was no Bolshevik. He had been closely associated with the *Kadets* or 'Constitutional Democrats', who had played a prominent role in late Tsarist times and whose Provisional Government had been overthrown by the Bolsheviks. He would have classed himself as a 'liberal' and a 'constitutionalist', but like many liberal Britons of his generation, he was also an unashamed imperialist. He clearly thought it a great injustice that the Tsarist Empire had not survived intact and his definition of the 'Ten Million Russians' clearly had nothing to do with the self-identity or the self-determination of the people concerned. He evidently approved both of Stalin's occupation of eastern Poland in September 1939, and the Soviet suppression of the Baltic States in 1940. He did not mention Warsaw or Helsinki, which he would probably have put in a separate category. Yet his line of thinking was only one step removed from suggesting that their unfortunate escape from Russian rule formed part of the same, serious aberration. His intervention was a good example of the strange phenomenon whereby all sorts of well-meaning Westerners, who had nothing in common with Stalin, nonetheless aided and abetted Stalin's depredations. Once again, the Count was propelled into a damage-limitation exercise.

The British Communists formed a small group, offering a raft of mainly unpopular propositions. They were the true believers of a political sect who were sworn to absolute obedience to orders passed down from above, and ultimately from Moscow. They were ultra-sensitized to the undoubted failings of British society but institutionally oblivious to Soviet failings. Since they were trained to act on the principle that 'the party is always right', they had been totally bewildered in 1939–41, when Moscow was expressing fulsome praise for the Third Reich, which until recently they had been told to condemn. But they recovered their enthusiasm when Hitler and Stalin resumed hostilities. Indeed, 1943–44 was the time when the CPGB enjoyed its greatest (though still modest) standing in British life. It included a few intellectuals like Eric Hobsbawm, who would later claim that he knew nothing about Stalin's mass crimes,[28] but consisted predominantly of dedicated proletarian activists from 'Red Clydeside' or from London's East End who had little interest in foreign affairs.[29] Extraordinarily, they were not seen by the British wartime authorities as a dubious element. Whilst British fascists were imprisoned, the British Communists were allowed to circulate freely and to promote their subversive designs in all quarters of British life. A comrade of the wartime vintage later admitted how between 1943 and 1945, when he was a serving officer in the British army, he spent his spare time writing brochures blackening the reputation of the Polish 'militarists', 'fascists', and 'imperialists' who were supposedly sowing such unwelcome discord in the democratic ranks of the Grand Alliance.[30] There was, to quote a phrase, 'an asymmetry of indulgence'.

A British writer with a personal interest in the puzzle of Western intellectuals deluded by Stalinism, has recently asked the question 'How much did the Oxford comrades know?' Having summarized the many repellent aspects of Soviet foreign policy, from the Nazi–Soviet Pact to the attacks on Poland, Finland, Romania, and the Baltic States, he made a list of the more appalling domestic horrors of Stalinism, which had been widely reported in the 1930s and which ought to have put all reasonably decent or intelligent observers on their guard:

> There were public protests in the West about Soviet forced-labour camps as early as 1931. There were also many solid accounts of the violent chaos of Collectivisation (1929–34) and of the 1933 famine (though no suggestion, as yet, that the famine was terroristic). And there were the Moscow Show Trials of 1936–38, which were open to foreign journalists and observers, and were monitored worldwide. In these pompous and hysterical charades, renowned Old Bolsheviks 'confessed' to being career-long enemies of the regime (and to other self-evidently ridiculous charges). . . . And yet the world, on the whole, took the other view, and further accepted indignant Soviet denials of famines, enserfment of the peasantry and slave labour.[31]

As to the explanation of why the truth about Soviet reality was not believed, 'it may well be that the reality – the truth – was unbelievable.'[32]

As revelations many years later would confirm, Soviet influence in the upper reaches of the British Government was far stronger that anyone then suspected. Christopher Hill, for example, who ran the Soviet desk at the FO's Northern Department in 1944, having been seconded from Military Intelligence, was a Soviet mole and a card-carrying Communist, who had concealed his membership of the CPGB. Hill's friend Peter Smollett, who held a similar position in the Ministry of Information, was an active Soviet agent who in due course defected. In turn, Smollett's colleague Kim Philby, Soviet spy par excellence, ran the Soviet Section of counter-intelligence at MI6 under the Foreign Office, thereby disabling Britain's defences against Soviet penetration. The three of them seem to have organized an informal committee whose aim was to convince the public about the benevolence of Stalin's intentions. Their contact/controller at the Soviet Embassy was probably Grigori Saksin, who departed London in a hurry in September 1944. Their views may be judged from a book, which Hill was writing, called *Two Commonwealths: the Soviets and Ourselves*. Published in 1945, under the pseudonym of K. E. Holme, the book maintained that the USSR was a full democracy with universal suffrage, and that the purges of the 1930s, comparable to the demands of the Chartists, were 'non-violent'. The presence of such people in key positions may help to explain the strange lethargy in Polish matters which beset the Foreign Office whilst the Warsaw Rising raged.[33]

Completely unbeknown to the British Communists, the Soviet authorities maintained an extensive network of spies in Britain. They ranged from low-grade casuals like Melita Norwood, who passed on technical secrets from her employers in the metal industry, to highly trained professionals working under cover in the top echelons of the British establishment. In the mid-1940s, the Cambridge 'Five' – Burgess, Maclean, Philby, Blunt and Cairncross – who had been recruited in the 1930s, were at the height of their powers, and misinformation about Poland would have figured prominently on their task list. Yet the really amazing fact about their story is the extraordinarily unguarded and congenial climate in which they were allowed to operate. Cairncross, for example, who worked for a time at Bletchley Park and sent Ultra secrets of the highest possible sensitivity to Moscow, didn't even regard himself as a spy, but as an eccentric British patriot dutifully sharing intelligence with a British ally.[34]

The British press in 1944 contained a vociferous pro-Soviet contingent, which started with the *Daily Worker* and certainly included the Labourite *Daily Herald*. What most wartime readers did not realize was that many conservative and right-wing papers, like *The Times* or the *Daily Express*, whilst keeping their distance from ideological issues, were similarly biased.

The task of encouraging the coordination of Britain's pro-Soviet chorus fell mainly to the Soviet Embassy. The Soviet Military Mission received extensive intelligence from the British and Americans. Yet in spite of the vast quantities of Western aid flowing to the USSR, not least through the Arctic convoys, the Soviets did not reciprocate in kind. They enjoyed a virtual monopoly on information from the Eastern Front, maximizing the kudos of their military victories whilst suppressing all accurate reports of political, economic, or social conditions. The Soviet Embassy worked hand in glove with the British Communist Party (CPGB), with the Soviet spy-rings, and with all sympathetic collaborators. It was a sign of the times that the Embassy's press officer found little difficulty in obtaining an influential lectureship in Russian Studies at London University.[35]

Britain's wartime Foreign Office was to gain the reputation in later years of having been culpably soft on Stalinism. Certainly, there were a number of figures like Geoffrey Wilson, who worked in the Northern Department on Soviet and Polish affairs, who can only be described as 'tireless apologists'. Yet the unashamed Sovietophiles were not in command; and their most blatant schemes did not go unchallenged. In January 1942, for example, a memorandum was received from E. H. Carr, proposing that Britain formally recognize a Soviet sphere of influence. 'It should fall to Russia', he said, without a hint of irony, 'to interpret and apply . . . the guiding principles of the Atlantic Charter in Eastern Europe.' Reviewed by one of Eden's deputies, Sir Orme Sargent, it got short shrift. It was, minuted Sargent, 'a policy of appeasement', and 'a formula for abdication.'[36] Even at that early stage, he was not alone in warning against Soviet ambitions. His colleague, Roger Makins, the Head of the Central Department, agreed. The general trend of Soviet policy, he argued as early as 1942, 'is an extension of exclusive Russian influence in Eastern Europe to be effected by the occupation of Finland . . ., the crushing of Hungary and the encirclement of Poland.'[37]

The War Office was markedly less ambivalent, however, than the diplomats. In 1942, it published a pamphlet entitled *On Dealing with the Russians* authored by a Brig. Firebrace. It described Soviet officers as 'childish barbarians', 'inordinately proud' of the Red Army's achievements. It brought down cries of 'Russophobia' and 'anti-Russian extravagances'. True to form, the FO's Geoffrey Wilson called for the British officers responsible to be purged.[38]

Already in April 1944, a debate was launched on the make-up of post-war Europe, and a Post-hostilities Planning Committee was set up. The War Office and the Foreign Office did not present a united front. The former refused to assume that Germany would be Britain's sole conceivable enemy. And the FO's Central Department proposed keeping armament production high, to allow for a possible confrontation with the USSR. The Northern Department was vehemently opposed. Wilson called for Anglo-Soviet staff talks.[39]

The typical stance of British diplomats towards the USSR, therefore, may be likened to that of post-war 'revisionist' historians, who were not entirely devoid of knowledge, but who could not bring themselves to believe the basic facts. It may best be characterized as a state of bemusement, brought on by alternating moments of admiration and fear, and by being 'isolated from any real idea of the realities of life' in the USSR: 'There were two recurrent but mutually exclusive fears: that Russia might rest on its laurels after driving the invader back to the frontiers of 1941, or, conversely that it might defeat Germany virtually single-handed. . . .'[40] According to one critic, British diplomats preparing to improve Soviet relations with Poland were 'impelled . . . by a state of mind which was somewhere between a determination to be optimistic and pure wishful thinking'.[41]

The pro-Soviet lobby in the USA was similar in make-up to that in Britain, though it possessed some more flamboyant enthusiasts and was opposed by some fierce Conservatives. After the war it emerged that there was also a sprinkling of Soviet spies. But there was no one to match the breathtaking fatuity of Joseph E. Davies (thankfully no relation), who had served as US Ambassador to Moscow in 1936–38, at the height of Stalin's Terror, and who had learned absolutely nothing. In 1941, Davies published a memoir called *Mission to Moscow*, which, with the help of Warner Bros., he then turned into a popular film over which he retained complete control. Hiring the team of Michael Curtiz and Howard Koch, who had recently directed and scripted *Casablanca*, he set out without shame to win the American public over to his vision of a happy, prosperous, and friendly Russia. With Walter Huston as his ambassadorial self, Gene Lockhart as Molotov and Dudley Malone as Churchill, he fabricated a fable for the screen, which praised the purges, vilified the victims of the show trials, justified the Nazi–Soviet Pact, and classed the invasions of Poland and Finland as 'self-defence'. Released in April 1943, after a private preview for President Roosevelt, it opened to critical acclaim and to only a muffled chorus of protests. Stalin, when shown it a month later, presumably could not believe his eyes. He immediately ordered it to be released in a Russian version – the first American film to be passed for screening in the USSR for over a decade. One thing it did not show was Davies' luxury yacht *Sea Cloud*, which he kept moored in Leningrad and which was loaded with food and drink for himself and his family.[42]

Whilst assiduously cultivating receptive people in Britain and America, the Soviets kept the exiled Polish Government at arms' length. They appeared to stick strictly to the break in diplomatic relations, which they had maintained since the Katyn affair in April 1943. Yet it is fascinating to note that the break was not total. In June and July 1944, the Soviet Ambassador in London was conducting highly secret talks with Stanislas G., a former Polish minister. The aim was to sound out the possibility of resuming official relations. Concealed from the world at large, Stalin was keeping his options open.[43]

In the summer of 1944 the Soviet Union's prestige was approaching its peak. For three years, it had borne the brunt of the fighting against Nazi Germany with little but logistical assistance from the Western powers. Now, after superhuman sacrifices, it was coming out on top. In the eyes of many people in Britain and America, irrespective of political convictions, it had earned their unstinting gratitude.

In the last week of July 1944, the Soviet Army was not only attaining its objectives on the central sector of the Eastern Front, it was exceeding them. After forty days of relentless fighting, it had covered most of the ground between the Berezina and the Vistula, and though the tempo of the advance was slackening, the front line was moving forward inexorably. The Germans were digging in on the eastern approaches to Warsaw, where they were expected to defend the vital Vistula bridges. But on either side of those approaches, weakly held positions were waiting to be attacked and punctured. The 1st (Polish) Army had already reached the right bank of the Vistula on 25 July, and repeatedly tried to force a passage. The key breakthrough occurred on 27 July when elements of Gen. Chuikov's Eighth Guards Army scrambled across a narrow stretch of the river in armoured amphibians 50km (thirty miles) south of Warsaw near the Vistula's junction with the Pilitsa. They were the advance guard of two major river-crossings which were soon supported by tanks and which created the unplanned bonus of twin bridgeheads on the Vistula's left-hand bank. On 28 July, Rokossovsky received updated objectives for the armies of his front. The orders foresaw the capture of Praga by 2 August at the latest.

The Varka–Magnushev Bridgehead, as it came to be known, defied all the Germans' desperate attempts to dislodge it. Exposed, with his forces astride the river, Chuikov was subjected to a cunning and determined counter-attack:

> Two German divisions supposed to be to the south-east of Praga turned up on the western bank of the Vistula and forward of [his] newly-won bridgehead. Heavy attacks developed . . . and the three regiments of 47th Guards Rifle Division lived through some critical hours: at noon a regiment of Stalin heavy tanks went over to the western bank, the Tiger tanks of the Hermann Göring Division were halted and the bridgehead held.[44]

The immediate effects of the Soviet Army's appearance on the Vistula were threefold. First, the German garrison in Warsaw, threatened both from the south and the east, prepared to withdraw and the civilian administration was ordered to evacuate. Second, as Rokossovsky had suspected, the German command decided to throw in its reserves and to strengthen the defence lines to the east of the city. Third, in expectation of the decisive assault on Warsaw, almost everyone anticipated some sort of action from the citizenry, who would fall on the German defenders from the rear and thereby assist the Soviet assault.

The timing was crucial. If the German garrison pulled out too hastily it would encourage the population to rise and would greatly reduce the chances of a successful defence. If the German reserves were thrown in too late, they would not be able to save the easternmost defence lines. If the Soviet assault were launched before sufficient heavy equipment had been assembled, it stood to be repulsed. If the population rose before the Germans and Soviets became fully engaged, they would be risking their lives in vain. Each of the decision-makers, therefore, was faced with a finely balanced throw.

For once, Rokossovsky decided to move with caution. His front-line troops were exhausted. His second-line positions needed consolidating. His infantry reserves and his heavy artillery were still moving up. In the long run, he would probably gain more by holding on to the bridgeheads than by chancing his arm on a premature assault on the city. Above all, as may be safely deduced, his forward intelligence was poor. He did not know for certain what either the German command or his would-be Varsovian helpers were aiming to do. He held the overall advantage. He could afford to take a breather and regain his strength, to absorb a punch if it came, and then to launch a devastating counter-punch at his leisure. For which reason, his first priority had to be reconnaissance. So at the end of July, he ordered the tanks of his Second Army to probe the German defences. Their task was not an easy one. Driving forward into uncharted terrain, they were vulnerable to German fire. Scores of tanks and their crews were lost. But on 31 July, one daring company of T-34s found their way round or through the defence lines and entered the outskirts of Warsaw's eastern suburb. They provided the sight for which the watchers had been waiting for weeks to see.

Meanwhile, the pressmen and the propagandists were straining at the leash. Governments were pressed to state their positions. War correspondents had a duty to report action. And Allied broadcasters had a duty to encourage optimistic news. Statements, reports, and appeals were descending thick and fast from all sides.

On 25 July, the Soviet Foreign Office had issued a statement. It announced that the liberation of Polish territory had been launched by Soviet and Polish troops. It said that their sole object was 'to squash the enemy' and 'to help the Polish people to re-establish an independent, strong, and democratic state.' It explained that the Soviet Government had decided not to establish any administration of its own on Polish soil, preferring instead to make an agreement with the Polish Committee of National Liberation. 'The Soviet Government does not wish to acquire any part of Polish territory or to bring about any changes in the social order.'[45]

In those same days, both the KRN and the PKWN issued decrees, statements, and manifestos that were filtering through to the outside world. The PKWN Manifesto chose to call the exiled Government in London 'a usurper', and to denounce the 1935 Constitution as 'fascist'.[46] On 29 July, Radio Moscow broadcast an emotive appeal for the citizens of Warsaw to assist their impending liberation:

> Warsaw already hears the guns of the battle which will soon bring her liberation. Those who have never bowed their heads to the Hitlerite power will again, as in 1939, join the struggle against the Germans, this time for a decisive action ... For Warsaw which did not yield, but fought on, the hour of action has already arrived.[47]

Still more electrifying was the Polish-language broadcast of 30 July, which came from the Soviet-controlled station of the PKWN, and which was repeated four times:

> Warsaw is shaking to the foundations from the roar of the guns. Soviet forces are advancing forcefully and approaching Praga. They are coming to bring you freedom. When driven out of Praga, the Germans will try to defend themselves in Warsaw. They will want to destroy everything. In [Bialystok], they went on the rampage for six days, murdering thousands of your brothers. Let's do everything in our power to prevent them repeating the same in Warsaw.
>
> People of the Capital! To arms! May the whole population rise like a stone wall around the KRN and the capital's underground army.
>
> Strike at the Germans! Obstruct their plans to blow up public buildings. Assist the Red Army in their crossing of the Vistula. Send them information. Show them the way. May your million-strong population become a million soldiers, who will drive out the German invaders and win freedom.[48]

On 1 August, *The Times* of London reported that the Battle for Warsaw had been joined. Since all such reports from the Eastern Front had to pass through the hands of Soviet censors, it was reporting material that had been prepared two or three days previously. The BBC made similar comments.

At that juncture, as he recalled in his memoirs, Rokossovsky had established his command post in a village within eyesight of eastern Warsaw. On the morning of 2 August, he was asked to look for himself:

> Together with a group of officers I was visiting the 2nd Tank Army which was fighting on that sector of the Front. From an observation point which had been set up at the top of a tall factory chimney, we could see Warsaw. The city was covered in clouds of smoke. Here and there houses were burning. Bombs and shells were exploding. Everything indicated that a battle was in progress.[49]

CHAPTER IV

RESISTANCE

POLAND HAD A TRADITION of fighting for its freedom like no other country in Europe. Armed Polish risings against the partitioning powers were a regular and well-publicized fixture of the nineteenth-century scene. But even before the partitions, in the days of the Polish-Lithuanian Commonwealth, the nobles had steadfastly defended their right to form confederations or 'armed leagues' and to contest the policies of the kings, which they themselves had elected. The cult of the country's 'Golden Freedom', therefore, had thrived for centuries, and had been celebrated by poets and balladeers for generations. It was still strong in the early twentieth century. In December 1918, for example, a popular rising in the province of Great Poland drove out the German army and secured the province for the Polish Republic. In 1919–21, three Risings contested the German hold in Silesia. Risings in Vilno and in Lvuv secured those two cities for Poland, while the Polish–Soviet War took on the appearance of the ancient *levée en masse* in defence of Poland against Soviet Russia. For the people who grew up in the 1920s and 1930s, fighting for the country's freedom could be seen not only as a patriotic duty but also as a tradition that had brought results.[1]

No less ingrained were the non-martial forms of resistance. Indeed, Polish public opinion had always been deeply divided between the 'romantic' advocates of armed combat and their 'positivist' opponents who felt that the human and material costs of insurrection were excessive. The latter tendency, which had gained the upper hand in the late nineteenth century, mocked the macho displays of the insurrectionaries, favouring instead what they called 'Organic Work'. Their preference lay not with fighting but with a more patient strategy, which aimed to build up the oppressed nation's economic and cultural resources and, in effect, to create an alternative social system that simply sidelined official state policies.

The net result of the two strategies was a social consensus which may have disagreed on the methods but which was firmly united about the ultimate goal. Armed resistance was for the few, mainly for fit young males of a combative disposition. But it could be prepared in a supportive context where a mass of other people were engaged. The role of women was crucial. It was Polish wives, mothers, and grandmothers who guarded the traditions, provided the social infrastructure, comforted the activists, and told their menfolk where their duty lay. They could even take up arms themselves. Their attitude was immortalized in the short life of Emilia P. (1806–31), the 'Virgin-Hero' of the November Rising, who had fought against the Russian army disguised in a man's uniform and whose feats were celebrated in a poem by Adam M., 'The Death of the Colonel'.

Scores of Polish insurrections had accumulated a treasure house of romantic poetry, stirring anthems and magnificent music. The best known item in this repertoire is the famous *mazurek* of Joseph W., 'Poland has not perished yet', which was composed in 1797 and which became the national anthem in 1926. But no less stirring is *La Varsovienne*, 'The Song of Warsaw', which dates from the November Rising of 1830 and which was originally set to the words of a French poem by Casimir Delavigne:

At last the day of blood has dawned.
May it be the day of our deliverance!
See the white eagle in all its splendour
Whose eyes were fixed on the rainbow of France
When it took to the wing in the sun of July.
Now, as it soars aloft, hear its cry:
'My noble country! For thee we pledge our doom:
Either the Sun of Freedom, or the night of the Tomb!
    Poles, to the bayonet!!
    That is our chosen cry
    Relayed to the roll of the drum.
    To arms! To die!
    Long live Freedom!'[2]

Given such a background, it was entirely natural that preparations for organizing Underground Resistance were laid even before the formal military campaign in September 1939 had been lost. The clandestine 'Victory Service' (SZP) was formed on the orders of the General Staff one day prior to Warsaw's capitulation. Its commander, publicly known only as 'the Doctor', was himself a staff officer. It was designed to complement the other part of the plan, which was to send the maximum number of surviving Polish soldiers abroad. It was to remain subordinate to, and in close touch with, the regular Polish authorities even when the Government and army staff took residence in Paris, and from July 1940 in London. Its regular *Information Bulletin*, which was printed secretly in Warsaw, was published in a magnificent unbroken run throughout the war.

From the very beginning, therefore, the Polish Underground possessed an established hierarchy and an unquestioned legal framework. Its first tasks were to set up communications, to secure the secret arms dumps that military units had been ordered to conceal before surrendering, and to organize a network of cells that could later be expanded into a countrywide force.

Such were the origins of Europe's largest Resistance movement, which in January 1940 adopted the name of the Union of Armed Struggle (ZWZ) and in February 1942 the Home Army (AK). It was a branch of the regular Polish armed forces, whose special task was to fight the enemy at home through clandestine methods appropriate to an occupied country. It owed undivided allegiance to the Polish Government abroad, and took its orders from the Commander-in-Chief. In this regard, it enjoyed a much stronger political and legal framework than those within which the Resistance movements in France, Italy, or Yugoslavia operated.

Everyone assumed from the start that a national rising against the occupying powers was the ultimate goal. Paragraph 4 of the ZWZ's Instruction No. 2 of 16 January 1940 went straight to the point:

> Once the armed uprising erupts, by order of the Government, the Area Commanders have the right to issue military orders to all military personnel in their territories, and they devolve this right onto the Union's organs that are subordinate to them.[3]

For obvious reasons, the friends and families of serving officers formed the natural social constituency of the Resistance in its initial phase. The younger brothers and sisters of men who had fought in the September Campaign and who, if they hadn't been killed or incarcerated in German or Soviet prison camps, flocked to the colours in their thousands. The thrill of secret activities was enormous. The practical possibilities, for the time being, were slim. The numbers, especially in towns or suburbs that had housed pre-war military garrisons, were very impressive.

The Staff Battalion of the movement's High Command – universally known by its acronym, Bashta – was one of the very first units to take shape. Its origins went back to November 1939, when the leaders of the military resistance began to recruit young volunteers to be trained as core commanders for the expanding cadres. Its initial duties were to staff the communications network – hence the high proportion of female recruits – and to guard the General Staff. By mid-1942, however, when it was joined by its future long-term CO, Lt.Col. 'Daniel', it possessed three battalions, B(altic), K(arpaty), and O(lza), and a complement of 2,000 soldiers. Each battalion was made up of numbered companies – B1, K2, O3 etc. – which were generally identified by their commander's pseudonym. It also ran several auxiliary services of great importance. Among these was the General Staff's Bureau of Information and Propaganda (BIP), headed by two distinguished historians who published an official journal and maintained a clandestine radio broadcasting station. Yet its greatest contribution probably came from military training. In the two years prior to the summer of 1944, Bashta trained over 600 Underground officers. This figure was similar to the total number of companies that were to be put at the Home Army's disposal in Warsaw.

Early in 1944, Bashta was assigned one of the southern districts of Warsaw, in Mokotov, as its area of concentration. Buildings were allocated as defence points and secretly fortified. Plans were prepared for attacks on eleven locations around which the 2,500 men of the district's German garrison were distributed. Special attention was paid to the Handweaving School, which lodged a unit of the SS. Anxieties centred on the chronic shortage of weapons. On 1 August 1944, Bashta's 31 officers and 2,170 other ranks possessed the grand total of 1 heavy machine gun, 12 light machine guns, 187 rifles, 80 sub-machine guns, 348 revolvers, 2 PIAT anti-tank rockets, 1,750 hand grenades, and 120kg (265 lb) of explosives. One might have thought that this was no arsenal with which to confront the Wehrmacht.[4]

In the winter of 1939–40, a number of Polish military units had refused both to lay down their arms and to join the clandestine movement. In short, they fought on in the open. In the German Zone, for example, Maj. 'Hubal' kept a group of 200 cavalrymen in the field and fought several pitched battles before being hunted down by superior German forces. He was by no means alone. The survivors of his group only subordinated themselves to the Resistance after nine months of defiant adventures.[5] In the Soviet Zone, similar units headed for the forests and the marshes, where they fought off the dragnets of the Red Army and the NKVD for many months. One such group was headed by Capt. 'Lightning', who was wounded and captured by the NKVD in a skirmish on 15 March 1941.[6] At the start of Operation Barbarossa in June 1941, Red Army reports mentioned trouble with 'Polish bandits'.

Generally speaking, the Resistance found it more difficult to challenge the NKVD than the SS and the Gestapo, and for several sound reasons. First, the NKVD were extremely well prepared. They moved into Poland bringing detailed lists of hundreds of thousands of people to be summarily arrested. In this way, they paralysed many parts of the potential Resistance movement before it could be organized. Second, they took immediate precautions to deny any rebels the basic means of survival. They took control of all the major forests in eastern Poland, for example, replacing all foresters and gamekeepers with their own personnel and thereby stopping the Resistance from setting up bases. Third, they received important assistance from various sections of the local population. On this last point, the contrast with conditions on the German Zone was marked. The German invaders received very little cooperation from any Polish citizens with the sole exception of the sizeable German minority in towns such as Bielsko or Lodz. Pictures which show the Wehrmacht being welcomed by cheering crowds in Lodz, for example, don't always mention the fact that the crowds as well as the soldiers were German.[7]

Yet the Soviet invaders received a warm welcome, notably from the poorer elements of the Byelorussian and Ukrainian peasantry, who hoped to gain materially, and from a vociferous section of the Jewish population. Soviet communism did not appeal to the majority of any ethnic group. But its spokesmen made clear that all Poles, all religious leaders, all commercial and professional people, all non-Communist politicians, and all land- or property-owners were its enemies. And it did prove attractive to those who believed the claim that it had come to save them from fascism.

The Jewish response to the Soviet invasion is best described by Jewish witnesses and by Jewish scholars:

> In the Soviet military administration, it was widely (and correctly) believed at the time that the Jewish minority was one of the most reliable elements ... Jews were visible in all agencies of the civil administration as the Soviet regime consolidated itself ...
>
> A Jewish Communist who ... reached the town of [Helm], which was under Soviet rule at the time ... describes the entire town having been in Jewish hands; the mayor was Jewish, and all the policemen and municipal office-holders were Jewish with the excep-

> tion of 'a few Poles'. In [Zamost] so many Jews joined the local militia that they accounted for a majority of its ranks . . .[8]

Similar situations arose in larger places. For example, in the district of Pinsk, the chief Polish police inspector turned the town over to the local Jews before he fled:

> The local police commander appeared on the portico of the police building with his replacement, Rabbi Glick . . . and other comrades who were known to be Communists. The commander announced tersely that they were quitting the town . . . and he was handing all weapons in the police station to community representatives headed by Rabbi Glick. [The two of them] shook hands, and Rabbi Glick, speaking Russian, told the crowd that gathered, 'I'm running the town . . . from now on. Anyone who disobeys my orders will be punished very severely.'[9]

The Polish Government abroad was specially interested in receiving accurate information on conditions and attitudes in their occupied country. To this end, one of their most famous Underground couriers, Karski, was dispatched from France early in 1940; and with extraordinary enterprise managed to see many things for himself. Captured and tortured by the Gestapo, he was rescued by the Underground, and helped to fulfil his mission. His report was personally delivered to the Premier and the President and subsequently to the British Foreign Minister, to the United Nations War Crimes Commission, and to the US President himself. It had a separate chapter on 'The Jews'; and a separate subsection on Polish–Jewish relations in the Soviet Zone. Here he maintained a carefully even-handed position. He admitted that relations were 'strained'. 'It is the general opinion', he wrote, 'that the Jews have betrayed Poland . . . that they are fundamentally Communist, and that they welcomed the Bolsheviks with banners unfurled.'[10] At the same time, he weighed these opinions in the light of established facts. 'In the majority of cities, the Jews organized a welcome for the Bolsheviks with red roses, with speeches and declarations . . . [they] often denounced Poles, nationalist students, and political activists . . . It has to be admitted that these incidents are frequent, more frequent in fact than those which would indicate loyalty to the Republic.'[11] Karski went on to contrast the conduct of Communist and proletarian Jews with that of educated and prosperous Jews who usually thought of Poland with sympathy. According to a recent analyst, he conspicuously rejected the criterion of symmetry between Jewish anti-Polonism and Polish anti-Semitism.[12]

Western readers, who are so used to hearing that Jews were uniquely victimized in wartime Poland (as they certainly were under Nazi rule), need to realize that Jews were not necessarily the most vulnerable group in the Soviet Zone. What is more, one should not mince words about the duties which Soviet sympathizers and Soviet-appointed policemen and militia were required to perform. They were expected to denounce 'hostile elements' to the NKVD, to help expel houseowners from their property and peasants from their farms, to assist in the mass arrests and deportations, and to combat the Resistance. These were activities which inevitably gave all participants a bad name, and which made members of the Resistance movement justifiably wary. They also meant that when eastern Poland was evacuated by the Soviets during Operation Barbarossa in 1941, the ZWZ was obliged to restart its decimated organization virtually from scratch for a second time.

As for Karski, he freely admitted that his most chilling moment came when he tried to thank his Underground rescuers. 'Don't be too grateful to us,' one of them said. 'We had two orders concerning you. The first was to do anything in our power to help you escape. The second was to shoot you if we failed.'[13]

Adversity, in fact, was the challenge on which Polish resisters thrived. For they belonged to a hard school which had little in common with the sort of comfortable assumptions on which most British or American soldiers could rely. They had no home base to which they could safely withdraw. They could not count on technical superiority or on cautious, methodical strategy, still less on the luxury of fighting a war without sustaining heavy losses. Theirs was the chosen path of risk, loneliness, sacrifice, and ridicule, even from one's own. Like the man who had inspired the army from which the movement's organizers were drawn, they had been taught to value spiritual mastery over everything. 'Victory', the Marshal had said, 'was to suffer defeat but not to surrender'. This was no easy advice, but it was open to all patriots irrespective of race, religion, or descent:

The Legions stand for a soldier's pride
The Legions stand for a martyr's fate
The Legions stand for a beggar's song
The Legions stand for a desperado's death

We are the First Brigade.
A regiment of rapid fire.
We've put our lives at stake.
We've willed our fate.
We've cast ourselves on the pyre.[14]

In spirit, the Home Army was the heir to Pilsudski's Legions in the previous generation. Their ideals inspired the men and women who formed the core of the Polish Underground from 1939 onwards. They were the same ideals that fired the soldiers whose Catholic, Orthodox, and Jewish graves fill the hillside cemetery at Monte Cassino.

The scouting movement, which began life in 1908 in England, was specially welcome after the First World War in the newly independent countries of East Central Europe. Unlike the various youth movements that existed before 1914, it had international connections, was free from state control, and introduced a completely new ethos combining outdoor adventure with patriotic pride and religious morality. In Poland as elsewhere, it was equally popular among the boys and girls, whose scout and guide troops were typically organized in secondary schools or parish halls. After twenty years of development, a strong national organization was established in Warsaw in the shape of the national Scouting Union. Thanks, apparently, to their smart light-grey uniforms, the members of the movement were universally known as the *Szare Szeregi*, the 'Grey Ranks'. It was an appropriate name for an influential section of society, which was to enter the Underground conspiracy without hesitation.

The Grey Ranks showed their mettle as soon as the war began. They set up auxiliary fire and ambulance services in Warsaw, Poznan, and other cities, and helped the authorities to cope with the effects of German bombing. When Poznan fell, a large body of scouts left with the retreating army and marched the 270km (170 miles) to Warsaw. In this way, the Posnanians joined their Varsovian colleagues, and played a significant role in many of the subsequent operations. On 27 September 1939 – i.e. on the same day that the Victory Service was founded – a meeting established a parallel, clandestine organization that put itself at the disposal of the Underground authorities. One of the first enterprises, undertaken with the regional Scout committee in Cracow, was to organize a regular courier link over the southern mountains to Hungary and thence to the outside world. This was the route whereby Karski was brought in.

At first, the intention was to accept volunteers only above the age of seventeen. But the pressures from expanding tasks, and the pleas of the youngsters, led to the formation of a three-layer structure. The reception group took boys and girls of twelve to fourteen years, the training schools took recruits of fifteen to seventeen years, and the senior battle groups were limited to adults over eighteen. The 'scholars' were confined to non-military operations such as minor sabotage or the Underground postal service. The battle groups came to be counted amongst the foremost units of the Home Army. The sororial organization of senior guides trained girls of seventeen or more as nurses, liaison officers, radio operators, cryptographers, and intelligence agents. Unlike their pre-war civilian predecessors, the wartime Grey Ranks became paramilitaries. But their motto did not change: it was 'Be Prepared'.

The origins of the Battle Group Parasol lie in the mass of scouting circles in wartime Warsaw, which in the early days were constantly merging and splitting and which were constantly changing their cryptonyms. But as the Warsaw Standard of the scouting movement evolved, it became closely associated with the K-Div. or 'Diversionary Section' of the Home Army, and its original educational functions were gradually transformed into military ones. In June 1943, following a series of nasty clashes with the Gestapo, a discussion was held in the house of the historian Professor H., and the decision was taken to form a special unit of armed youths which would fight the German police with their own methods. Its speciality was the assassination of Nazi officials. Its name was Agat, i.e. 'Anti-Gestapo', and its commander, Maj. 'Plough', was a reserve army officer and one of the 'dark and silent'. Over the next twelve months, it grew from a company to a battalion; and it changed its name twice, from Agat to Pegasus, and from Pegasus to Parasol.[15] Its brother organization, Zoshka, grew out of a parallel scouting unit, which specialized in springing prisoners of the Gestapo from jail, and which took its name from the pseudonym of its legendary leader, killed during an attack on a German guard post in September 1943.

Pre-war Poland did not possess the vicious oppressive regime which its detractors have since thought fit to invent. In terms of the rule of law, human rights and the treatment of minorities, it was categorically superior to the mass-murdering totalitarian systems that grew up on either side in Germany and in the Soviet Union. Nonetheless, it had several manifest blemishes. Even by sympathetic critics, it was variously described either as an 'ailing democracy' or as 'an authoritarian dictatorship-in-the-making'. The model Constitution of 1921, which had been largely inspired by France's Third Republic, broke down after only five years and was violated by a military coup whose leaders were intent on excluding a right-wing nationalist Government at all cost. Xenophobia was defeated by a dubiously anti-democratic manoeuvre. The *Sanacja* regime, or 'Government of Political Healing', which resulted, did not enjoy universal support. It did not destroy the elected Parliamentary or democratic elections, but it certainly set out to manipulate them. In 1930 and again in 1936, it created a Government-backed electoral bloc, which put the traditional democratic parties at a disadvantage. In 1931, it organized a series of political trials, which cast its opponents as enemies; and in 1936, it introduced a modified constitution with marked authoritarian features. This was no 'one-party state'. But it wasn't a perfectly happy democracy either. Its policies towards the nationalities, particularly the brutal pacification of the restive Ukrainian peasantry, left much to be desired.

The defeat of September 1939, however, had discredited the *Sanacja* regime. In consequence, the wartime exiled Polish Government was largely set up by the democratic opponents of the *Sanacja*, who, like Gen. Sikorski, had often stayed clear of state politics in the 1930s. It embraced the four main democratic groupings – the Peasant Party (PSL), the Socialist Party (PPS), the National Democrats (ND), and the Christian Democrat Labour Party (SP) – which, having escaped the impositions of the *Sanacja*, were now immediately cast into the infinitely harsher environment of the German and Soviet Occupations. These four parties formed the backbone of the political Underground. Each of them sprouted a paramilitary wing actively engaged in resistance.

Oddly enough, the mild adversity which Poland's best democrats had faced before 1939 did not prove to have been the worst training school for the extreme ordeal which awaited them. They were already wary of police surveillance; they knew how to beat the censors; and they were past masters at holding secret meetings and covering their tracks. As soon as the September Campaign was lost, therefore, they went to their secret work with gusto.

The position of the Polish Government in London reached its optimum in 1942. Its base in Britain was secure, and its alliance with the British was thriving. Its contribution to the pool of trained manpower in all three armed services was greatly appreciated, especially by the Ministry of Defence; and its role in the field of intelligence was outstanding. What is more, its standing in the Allied coalition was high. Gen. Sikorski was judged to have shown great statesmanship by putting resentments aside and by signing the treaty with the Soviet Union. His relations with Churchill and Roosevelt were cordial, and markedly superior to those of the Free French. For the time being, while the Soviets fought for their lives, he was not yet confronted by a Soviet partner that could treat him unreasonably.

The institutions of the exiled Government were growing to match the growing list of its competences. The Presidency was not challenged. Sikorski's joint functions as Commander-in-Chief and Premier, though not above criticism, were working well. The Cabinet was supported by all four of the main democratic parties, who shared the ministries between them. An exiled 'parliament' of appointed representatives began work in an advisory capacity.

Once central organs were established in Britain, the principal task lay in forming, strengthening, and maintaining contact with parallel civil and military organs in the occupied country. Civilian structures were already in place in December 1940, when two Government 'Delegates' were appointed – one in Poznan for the lands annexed by the Reich, and the other for the General Government. The military structures took longer to coalesce. Yet the Home Army was formally constituted on 14 February 1942. From then on, the tentacles of the exiled Government reached out from Sikorski's HQ at the Rubens Hotel in London to every town and village and to almost every clandestine formation in Poland.

Initial attempts to organize the political Underground were hampered by the deaths or arrest of many prominent figures. The Government's first choice as 'Home Delegate', a National Democrat, was killed by the Gestapo before he could take office. Sikorski's first personal emissary died in Auschwitz. The PSL leader and former Speaker of the Parliament was shot at Palmiry; the editor of the socialist daily, the *Worker*, was also shot, but not before he had been granted a personal interview with Himmler. 'What do you want from us?' the *Reichsführer-SS* asked. 'What do you expect?' 'From you, I neither want nor demand anything; with you, I fight.' It cost him his life.[16]

Much confusion was caused by lingering rivalries from the pre-war period. The military leaders, almost inevitably, were ex-Pilsudski-ites. The political representatives tended to be their former opponents. More than one political coordination committee came and went before a measure of unity emerged. Yet the principles, as described by one of the would-be coordinators in 1940, were always clear. Firstly, 'the Poles will never agree to collaborate with the Germans. Quislings are to be eliminated at all costs.'[17] Secondly, the plans of the Underground administration were to be synchronized with the exiled Government.[18]

The Peasant Party addressed the largest social constituency in Poland, but it was never quite able to realize its potential. Warsaw was not its natural habitat. Its paramilitary Peasant Battalions (BCh) came into their own in 1942–43, when they contested the Nazi resettlement scheme in the Zamost district.

The Socialist Party, which had close links with the Jewish Bund, 'had the richest and most unbroken tradition in the fight for independence'. Once led by Pilsudski himself, it later became the most spirited opponent of the *Sanacja*. It never had any truck with the Communists, whose tyrannical methods and ambivalent attitude to national sovereignty put them beyond the pale in socialist eyes. Adopting the collective pseudonym of 'Freedom, Equality, Independence', it took a combative stance from the start. Its first military organization, the Workers' Committee for the Defence of the Capital, was formed in Warsaw in the early days of September 1939.

The spirit of the wartime PPS was evident in a flysheet prepared for May Day 1940, and distributed amongst others to the passengers of the Warsaw–Cracow express (the Nazis as well as the Soviets celebrated May Day):

> Poles, we appeal to you – workers, peasants, and intellectuals – in an hour of great distress. We raise our voice in these days of our enslavement. It is the voice of Polish socialism. In the days of independence, that voice was heard again and again condemning the policies of Poland's despotic rulers . . .
>
> We appeal to you to remember the day of independence and socialism. May First approaches. On both shores of the Bug River it will be set aside as an official holiday. You are aware that it is not a day for tribute to Stalin and Hitler but a day for concentrated preparation for an intrepid struggle . . .
>
> Poland has been defeated . . . History has taught the nation a

> dreadful lesson. For us, now, the road to freedom leads through the torture chambers of the Gestapo and the GPU, through prison and concentration camps, through mass deportations and mass executions . . .
>
> In the west, England and France are fighting Germany. The new Polish army is fighting shoulder to shoulder with our Allies. But we must understand that the destiny of Poland will not be decided on the Maginot or Siegfried Lines. The hour of decision will arrive for Poland when the Polish people themselves grapple with the invader. With stubborn patience we must wait for that hour to come. Our political acumen and wisdom must be sharpened . . . Arms must be amassed and our fighters made ready.
>
> The new Poland must repair the mistakes of the past. Land must be divided among the peasants without the indemnification of the owners. Social control must be extended over mines, banks, and factories. Freedom of speech, religion, and conscience must be ordained. Schools and universities must be opened to the children of the people. The ordeals of the Jewish people of which we are the daily witness must teach us how to live in harmony with those who suffer the persecution of the common enemy . . . We must learn to respect the aspiration to freedom of the Ukrainian and White Ruthenian people.
>
> In this period of dire oppression, without precedent . . . we come to arouse your spirit of combat and perseverance. On this first day of May, let the old revolutionary slogans reverberate . . .[19]

The socialists were regaining the role which they had pioneered before 1918 – namely the avant-garde of national independence.

The National Democrats occupied the right wing of Polish politics and enjoyed a strong following throughout the country. They stood for 'Poland for the Poles' and for a vision that all too often linked an intolerant brand of nationalism with a particular brand of mystical Catholicism. One of their press organs was called, revealingly, *Polakatolik*. Another faction professed a more secular brand of nationalism. At all events, their mood was incorrigibly truculent, not least because they never gained the political power which they believed was theirs by right. They were always complaining of conspiracies cooked up either by the Pilsudski camp or by one or other of the national minorities. Indeed, they were forever seen by their rivals as a negative force.

In wartime, however, the National Democrats had a particular disability. They had a long tradition of belittling Poland's insurrections. Hence, though they could be found everywhere in the Resistance movement, they were not the natural advocates of militant action. This explains why an important section of right-wing opinion joined a radical offshoot of the National Democrats, the ONR, which had been banned before the war but which from 1940 onwards patronized a militant Underground formation calling itself the National Armed Forces or NSZ. The NSZ did not mix well with anybody. But its determination to fight the occupying forces cannot be doubted.

The Christian Democrats formed the more moderate brand of conservatism. Their party, which propagated modern Catholic views on social justice, was called, somewhat misleadingly, the Labour Party (SP). Their stronghold lay in Upper Silesia, which formed an integral part of the Reich, rather than in the General Government.

In 1939–41, there was no Polish Communist Party. The pre-war movement's leaders had been murdered by Stalin, and the Nazis' segregation of the Jewish community eliminated the constituency from which it had drawn its largest single pool of recruits. The KPP's replacement, the PPR, did not start to function until 1942; and the PPR's military wing, the People's Guard (GL), was a marginal force in the Underground until the victory of the Soviet Red Army loomed. Some would say that its ferocity made up for its lack of numbers.

In the early years of the war, all these groups were engaged in unilateral and often localized acts of resistance. Bringing them together in the dangerous surroundings of the occupation was no easy matter. And some individuals preferred to act on their own:

> I remember a man called [Yan] who came from the province of Poznan and spoke German fluently. Before the war he had traded in pigs . . . The region from which he came endured the most atrocious sufferings . . . In Warsaw, [he] became one of the many specialists in paying back the Germans in their own coin.
>
> [Yan's] favourite activity was to spread contagious diseases . . . He carried . . . a specially constructed little box that contained lice [infected with] typhoid-bearing germs . . . He would frequent bars, enter into conversation with German soldiers and drink with them . . . At the proper moment, he would drop a louse behind the collar of his German friend [or] drop germs into the drinks. He would

introduce them to girls who had VD . . . Not one of the Germans ever escaped lightly from 'the walking germ', as he was known . . .[20]

Keeping track of the mushrooming Resistance movement poses as many headaches for historians as it no doubt did for the Gestapo. But one list of the paramilitary organizations current in Warsaw in 1943, and their diverse political connections, shows the nature of the problem. By July 1944, many of the earlier organizations had merged, or multiplied, leaving a much larger body consisting of far fewer components:

Home Army (AK): Warsaw District, 860 platoons	40,330 men
National Armed Forces (NSZ)	1,000
Polish People's Army (PAL)	500
People's Army (AL) – Communist	800
Polish Syndicalist Union (ZSP)	1,000
Polish Socialist Militia (PPS)	500
State Security Corps (PKB)	500

The figures are estimates, but the proportions are self-evident. The Home Army was ten times larger than all the other formations put together.[21]

A later analysis of the geographical distribution of the Home Army units within the Warsaw region also brings some interesting results:

Location	Platoons	Strength
District I (City Centre)	90	5,500
District II (Jolibord)	12	800
District III (Vola)	21	1,300
District IV (Ohota)	12	800
District V (Mokotov)	70	4,500
District VI (Praga)	90	6,000
District VII	6	400
Okentche	13	800
Sapper Units	11	700
Regional K-Div.	3	200
Communications	(21)	460
Military Security	146	10,000
Women's Auxiliary Service (WSK)	—	4,300
Greater Warsaw County	206	11,000
TOTAL	800	46,760[22]

Different historians give different totals, but the breakdown is informative. The largest single concentration was in Praga. The only districts to possess concentrations of similar size were in the City Centre and Mokotov. If communication with the suburbs could be maintained, the city could draw on considerable reserves located within the Greater Warsaw County.

Three factors in the General Government contributed to the extraordinary resilience of the Polish resisters. One derived from the Nazi policy of closing all centres of higher education, science, and research. At a stroke the Nazis created a ready-made pool of highly educated conspirators who could turn their energies full-time to undermining German rule.

A second factor lay in the iron principle of 'no contact upward'. No one who joined the Underground knew, or expected to know, who was running the higher levels of the organization, and everyone used impenetrable pseudonyms. The resisters were content to serve without ever learning about the links in the unseen chain that bound them to their superiors in London. Hence, despite the constant resort to dragnets, torture, and shootings, the Gestapo was never able to gain the upper hand.

The third, and perhaps most vital, factor lay in the prevalence of instinctive, spontaneous social support. As one of the most famous anti-Nazi activists recalled, 'the Underground was only able to function through the existence of the unwritten and unspoken assumption of almost universal collusion.' 'We' simply did not cooperate with 'them'. One day, he arrived in Warsaw from London after one of his hair-raising runs through Nazi-occupied Europe. As he left a secret meeting in a building in the centre of town, he was stopped by the hand of a Gestapo agent on his shoulder. 'Where have you been?' asked the agent. Looking round, he saw the brass plate of a lady dentist at the side of the doorway. 'I've been to the dentist.' So the agent immediately took him to a nearby cafe, and phoned the dentist. 'Yes,' the answer came without hesitation, 'he's just left an appointment here a few minutes ago.' The courier owed his life to that dentist, whom he'd never met. And the dentist, for the sake of someone whom she'd never met, risked the lives of herself and of her entire family.[23]

'Cultural warfare' may sound like a contradiction in terms, but in an occupied country where the invaders were openly intent on transforming the human substance of the nation, it was unavoidable. The Nazis were constructing their racial 'New Order'. The Soviets had declared their ambition to forge 'a new Soviet Man'. Everything that was most precious in the captive nation's language, literature, history, folklore, customs, and identity was in mortal danger from both sides.

Free channels of information were vital to the Underground; and the tradition of secret printing presses in Warsaw was a very old one. The teams of clandestine writers, printers, and distributors had seen off the Tsarist *Ochrana*, and they were not going to be overawed by the Gestapo. Every single political orientation and every branch of the illegal Polish authorities had their dailies, their weeklies, and their news-sheets. Runners brought in communiqués from secret radio stations listening to the BBC or to WCBX relayed from New York. Hand-presses clunked in murky cellars. Shopkeepers wrapped purchases in a German paper on the outside and an illegal paper on the inside. And the Gestapo were vastly frustrated. Fresh print-shops sprang up for every one that was closed down. In July 1942, for example, the publishers of *Poland's Voice* calmly reported the results of a raid, undeterred:

> On July 4th a villa on a fashionable street in the residential section of [Cherniakov] was surrounded by the Gestapo and SS Black Guards . . . The house sheltered one of our printing shops . . . When knocking at the door brought no response, the police threw hand grenades through the windows, blasted the doors and fired inside with machine guns . . . A few days later, the owner of the villa, his wife and sons, and the tenants of neighbouring houses were arrested and subseqeuntly shot . . . This one case has cost 83 persons their lives.[24]

It was the general practice of these fearless editors to mail copies of their product direct to Gestapo HQ 'to facilitate your research, [and] to let you know what we think of you . . .'[25]

Underground literary publishing had longer-term aims: they strove to provide an outlet for all the writers and poets affected by the occupation, and to save the population at large from the intellectual starvation to which it was condemned. The Underground even dispensed scholarships and research grants. One budding poet, for example, who didn't much care for military resistance, spent his time 'unlearning Western Civilization'. He put out his first volume of poetry 'printed on a ditto machine', edited a typewritten literary journal, collected a verse anthology called *Independent Song*, and translated both Maritain's *A travers le désastre* and

Shakespeare's *As You Like It*. 'Rightly or wrongly', he recalled, 'I considered my poems a kind of higher politics.'[26]

Without doubt, one of the chief stars of underground publishing was the dazzling young poet Christopher K. B., widely known during the war by his pseudonyms of 'Bugay' and 'Christophe'. The son of a Warsaw family where socialism mingled freely with literary criticism, he attended the Stefan Batory *Gymnazium*, and was writing verse before he left school. His first collected volume, *Closed with an echo*, was published in 1940 under a false name and a false date in seven copies. Awkward and asthmatic, he was already assuming the guise of a fatalistic, Romantic, tubercular soldier-poet before he joined the Home Army and its Parasol Battalion. His lifelong love-affair with Barbara D., whom he married in 1942, added an emotional intensity to the startling precision of his words and feelings. He loved language, nature, Poland, the good times, and his 'Basia' in equal parts; and he deplored the war and the pain of not loving enough. Above all, he felt a strange and powerful premonition of the apocalypse to come. It would give him the reputation of being a visionary, the prophet of his generation. Of 'History' he wrote:

> Jeszcze słychać śpiew i rżenie koni
> (We still can hear the singing, and the neighing of horses.)[27]

As always in grim times, religion was the great comforter. The churches were full. The clergy, both secular and monastic, exercised their influence far beyond the altar, the pulpit, or the confessional. Parish halls and church crypts offered cover for meetings of all sorts. Monasteries and convents took in fugitives, who for various reasons could not circulate freely. Not for the first or the last time, the Church in Poland acted as the great unstinting protector of people in distress, including cultural activists.

Few Varsovians disagreed with the view that top priority should be given to education. A whole generation of teenagers and students looked set to remain half-educated. So the old practices of the 'Flying University' of Tsarist times were revived. German regulations were ignored. Professors and students, teachers and pupils, who had been thrown out of their colleges and schools, began to meet in private, often at night or under cover of some harmless pastime. Small, informal study circles grew into regular courses. And the participants passed exams and received diplomas. In the 1940s, students enrolled formally in the University of Warsaw, which was officially closed, were given degree certificates dated 1938 or '39. Would-be entrants to the officially non-existent university were accepted on the strength of school-leaving certificates issued by officially non-existent schools.

In this way, teenagers were brought up to regard illegal activity as a normal part of their birthright. Nazi laws were not considered morally valid. But there was a natural progression in the conduct of youngsters who thought instinctively in that way. When they finished courses and became qualified adults, they were eager to continue in the next stage of illegal activity. The students and pupils of the early war years became the recruits of the military Underground of 1944.

Underground drama circles proliferated. Many of them were closely connected to the Home Army – a cultural counterpart to military training. They observed a stern code of conduct, which forbade participation in Nazi-licensed premises. Their performances took place in private houses and monasteries, and their attitudes were forward-looking. One workshop run by a well-known director was preparing for post-war theatre reform, and was constructing a radical new repertoire.

Warsaw's architectural legacy was desperately vulnerable after the bombing of September 1939; and all manner of schemes were hatched for its preservation and recovery. One group, for example, defied the guards surrounding the ruined Royal Castle and, through surreptitious nocturnal visits over many months, painstakingly collected fragments of the pulverized fabric and furnishings. Their efforts made possible the magnificent post-war reconstruction of the castle, which was finally completed in 1990. Another group successfully relieved the Nazi administration of the sequestrated plans of the City Planning and Development Office. Their daring escape, which involved driving two lorries in broad daylight out of a Nazi-run compound, ensured that the city could be rebuilt decades later after the Nazis had done their worst.[28]

Historians, like everyone else, put their shoulders to the wheel. Many recognized the need for chronicling the occupation and for recording Nazi crimes. Thousands kept diaries. Others set out to locate, salvage, and relocate the National Archives, which had been badly damaged by fire, dispersed for safety, or plundered by the occupiers. One such devotee stayed at his desk until the end of the Rising, totally oblivious to the battles raging around him.

Musical concerts, great and small, raised morale. The droves of unemployed talent were legion. The most usual venues were cafes and cellars.

When a nation is suffering in extremis, the symbols of its identity gain life-and-death significance. Men and women were ready to risk all to paint the anchor-sign of 'Fighting Poland' on walls and placards, tear down the new German street-names, or let a gramophone blare a recording of the banished Chopin onto the street. The simple act of wearing a white blouse over a red skirt constituted a dangerous act of defiance. Refusing to speak German, or still better speaking it very badly with an execrable accent, was a patriotic duty. The soul could sometimes smile even if the body was in chains.

In the early stages of their development, the political and military wings of Poland's 'Secret State' faced daunting obstacles. Operating in absolutely the most hostile sector of Nazi-occupied Europe, they had to take elaborate precautions, and they had to steel themselves against the constant pain of the capture, torture, and death of valued comrades. But courage and ingenuity were not in themselves enough. The 'Secret State' could not have been set up and maintained so effectively without the unstinting support of Britain's 'special services'. The Polish Underground was an Allied enterprise.

The history of the *Delegatura* ('Government Delegation'), for instance, was not an easy one. The first Delegate, a former mayor of Poznan, died in the hands of Gestapo torturers. His successor, an economist, suffered a similar fate. The third, known as 'Sable', escaped capture and established himself in Warsaw as a clandestine vice-premier.[29] In 1943, eight Underground ministries were formed, to supervise health, justice, internal affairs, industry, agriculture, transport, the economy, and communications. In 1943, a separate Directorate of Underground Struggle (KWP) was formed; and on 26 July 1944 a Council of Home Ministers came into being. Such were the elements of the 'Secret State', which had no parallel in occupied Europe and which attracted so much admiration from those familiar with it. (See Appendix 11.)

The effective functioning of the *Delegatura* relied in large measure on efficient communications. London's messages were passed by the network of short-wave radio stations that were constantly on the move to avoid detection. Messages of more weighty import, requiring discussion, were brought back and forth by couriers, who crisscrossed Nazi Europe as if by supernatural means. One Home Army courier reputedly made fourteen successful runs to Paris, always travelling in first-class carriages and always dressed as a Wehrmacht general.[30]

Travelling within the Nazi realms was one thing, but travelling back and forth between Nazi-occupied Europe and the outside world demanded ingenuity of a still higher order. Border controls were severe. Documents had to be perfectly forged. The price of discovery was death. Indeed, the couriers of the exiled Government invariably carried cyanide capsules. Their journeys could take weeks, or even months.

In the course of the war, scores of Underground couriers maintained the links between Poland and the Free World. Their usual destination was London, which they could only reach with immense ingenuity via Scandinavia or Spain and Portugal. On the return leg, they could hope for a swifter journey with the help of the RAF and a parachute. Many of them remained virtually unknown and unsung, and quite a few were simply obliterated after being caught. But some who survived, like Karski, 'Novak', 'Yur', and 'Zo', became legends in their own lifetime.

Karski was the younger brother of the last pre-war superintendent of Warsaw's police department, who, though becoming head of the Blue Police, was (rightly) suspected of contacts with the Underground, and cast into Auschwitz. A member of the PPS, Karski made three 'runs', and despite his own feelings of failure became famous for bringing the truth of the Jewish Holocaust to the West.[31]

Jan N., 'Novak', is the author of the best-selling memoir *Courier from Warsaw* (1978), which did much to popularize his and his colleagues' death-defying work. Active in the Home Army's department 'N' for psychological warfare, he, too, made three runs to London. He reached Warsaw at the end of his third run on 31 July 1944.[32]

Emissary Yur was parachuted into Poland by SOE in February 1943. He returned to England via Gibraltar in May 1944. Having evaded the Gestapo, the Vichy police and Franco's Civil Guard for some two thousand miles under the guise of a rocket engineer, he was intercepted on the platform of the last station in Spain with the inimitable greeting: 'How are you, George?' In London, he became secretary to the last premier of the exiled Government.[33]

Emissary Zo was an Underground activist for whom the trans-Continental assignment to London was but one of numerous wartime episodes. A mathematics teacher, she had joined the Women's Auxiliary Army Service in 1936, and was a natural choice to be an organizer and trainer of the Home Army's numerous women recruits. When her circuit in Silesia was betrayed to the Gestapo, her own need to disappear coincided nicely with the Home Army's search for a German-speaking courier. She left Warsaw in December 1942 as Elisabet Kubitza, administrator of a German oil company. The trip to Paris, via Strasbourg, passed off faultlessly in first-class trains, luxury hotels, and elegant restaurants, but the next stage, which involved crossing the Andorran Pyrenees alone, and waiting among snow-covered bushes for her Spanish guide, was less entertaining:

> No knowledge of Spanish ... No money ... Foggy dawn, frozen to the marrow. I am coughing, which is fortunate because Gilbert was trying to find me. We descend cautiously in the direction of Seo de Urgel. Wonderful blooms in the almond groves. We run into helpful people, a teacher who was an officer in the Catalan Commune and is now a member of the Falanga ... He sends a man to the British Consulate in Barcelona. But no one there will talk to him ... Madrid ... Gibraltar ... A 19-ship convoy ... and finally, the port of Bristol ... [Then] two nights in prison. On 3 May, an officer of the Commander-in-Chief's staff collects me ...[34]

Zo spent four months in England. Having completed her parachute training, she returned to the Warsaw district with the papers of 'Elizabeth Watson' on 10 September 1943, with one perfect jump.

The Home Army (AK) developed a complicated structure in order to cope with the large variety of tasks undertaken. Its secret HQ in Warsaw was necessarily mobile, and commanded a countrywide force estimated in early 1944 at 300–400,000. In the early stages, the strategy concentrated on recruitment and training.

In the course of 1943, the exiled Government found itself confronted with mounting difficulties that were not of its own making. In April, as a result of the Katyn revelations, the USSR broke off negotiations unilaterally; in July, Gen. Sikorski was killed in the Gibraltar air crash, and in November, the Teheran Conference opened a Pandora's box of problems that needed urgent attention.

For practical purposes, Stalin's action in breaking off Soviet relations was potentially the most damaging. It was made on grounds that were 100 per cent false; and it created the prospect that the Red Army would soon be operating in territory where the local resistance forces would be considered illegitimate. The sequence of events is vital to any judgement of the issue. The break in Soviet–Polish relations occurred in April 1943. At the time, the Red Army was still battling deep inside Russia. The decisive

Battle of Kursk was still three months away. The Teheran Conference would not convene for seven months. If the 'Big Three' had seriously wanted to pluck this thorn from international politics, they had ample time to do so.

Nonetheless, Poland's alliance with Great Britain, though strained, did not waver. And one of the fields in which Polish–British cooperation intensified was that of 'special operations'.

SOE's Polish Section was the oldest in the business. Indeed, a Polish officer was aboard the very first experimental 'special flight' that was sent to France in September 1939, long before SOE was thought of.[35] And Gubbins was talking to Sikorski in Paris before the fall of France. What is more, as *résistants de la première heure*, the Poles (like the Czechs) were to enjoy special privileges. They were allowed unrestricted use of their own radio stations in Britain, and they were left to plan missions and to select agents on their own. Almost all of the Polish Section's agents were Poles not Britons. In effect, the exiled Government used SOE for its own purposes, and not vice versa. The official historian of SOE was duly impressed by the political clout of Sikorski, who in 1941 managed to obtain a dedicated flight of Halifaxes at a time when 'heavy bombers were more esteemed by the Air Ministry than pure gold'. But the Poles returned the favours. SOE was especially indebted to their Polish partners in many fields, notably in Continental intelligence, in the design and production of clandestine wireless sets, and in forgery.

The Polish agents flown into Poland by SOE were universally known as the *cichociemni* (pronounced *cheeko-chemny*), 'the dark and silent ones'. Of the 316 despatched, only 9 failed to reach their destination. Of the nine, three were lost on 30 October 1942, when their Halifax flew into a cliff on the Norwegian coast; three more were killed on 15 September 1943, when another Halifax was shot down over Denmark; and three died individually when their chutes failed to open. Their success rate, therefore, topped 97 per cent: and they performed a priceless function.[36] They landed with weapons, and kits for making weapons. They brought plans, orders, couriers, and large amounts of money for financing the Underground. (SOE's grant to the Polish Section for its first year of operation in 1941–42 was £600,000.) Above all, they brought the knowledge that the Underground had allies, that it was not fighting alone.

The wartime airflight from Britain to Poland was never luxurious. It was cold, noisy, long, and full of uncertainties. The earliest venture was undertaken on 15 February 1941 in an ancient two-engined Whitley equipped with long-range tanks and cruising at a maximum of 120 mph (190 kph). It took $11^1/_2$ hours to drop only three men and (365kg) 800 lb of stores. After that, a regular air bridge was established using four-engined Liberators that passed over Denmark or Sweden. From December 1943, a dedicated Polish air force flight (No. 1586) began to operate from Brindisi in Italy. (The plan to create an independent wing of twelve Liberators, to be used exclusively for liaison with Poland, was never realized.)

Of all the 'dark and silent' agents whom SOE injected into the Underground, none could boast a biography to compare with that of Maj. Boleslas Kontrym, alias 'White' and 'the Samogitian'. Kontrym bore witness to many of the worst horrors of the twentieth century, from the Russian Revolution to the Blitzkrieg, from Bergen-Belsen to a Stalinist show trial. His early years resembled those of Marshal Rokossovsky. Born in Volhynia, the son of a Tsarist colonel, he was the grandson and great-grandson of Polish insurgents. He was schooled at the Russian Military Academy at Jaroslavl on the Volga, before fighting successively in the Tsarist army (1915–18) and the Red Army (1918–22). By the age of twenty-four, he held the Soviet rank of 'kombryg' (brigadier), and had been three times decorated with the Order of the Red Banner. However, when Rokossovsky chose to stay in the USSR, Kontrym chose Poland. Joining the Polish Army, he moved first to the Frontier Corps and then to the State Police. By 1939, he was the Chief Superintendent of Police in Vilno.

Kontrym's wartime career began in September 1939 with a daring mission to Stockholm and back. It continued through arrest in Lithuania, escape to Norway, service in France, a return to Scandinavia with the expeditionary force to Narvik, and an adventurous journey via Spain and Portugal to Britain. In 1942, he was training in Lincolnshire with the Polish Parachute Brigade, preparing for the jump which, on 2 September 1942, brought him home.

Kontrym's career in the Underground was no less colourful. Initially assigned to Operation Fan, the Home Army's abortive attempt to establish a conspiratorial network far to the east, he returned to Warsaw to head the Investigative Department of the State Security Corps (PKB). In this capacity, he was responsible for devising the strategy and executing the plans for contesting the sway of the SS and the Gestapo. It is said that he personally eliminated twenty-five Nazis or Nazi collaborators. Even so, the most active interlude of his remarkable life was yet to begin. Kontrym had a personal interest in the outcome of the war on the Eastern Front. In the

Nazis' eyes, he was a bandit chief with a price on his head. To the Soviets, he was a deserter.[37]

The hair-raising adventures of the 'dark and silent' are scattered through their numerous memoirs. But occasionally the mission went like clockwork:

> I was assigned to a four-man team. The cryptonym of the flight was 'Spokeshave'. My carefree comrades were 'Pawn', 'Eye', and 'Grove'. The captain of our flight was an experienced pilot born in Lida; and in his crew, apart from two brothers from [Lvuv], there was a former postman who manned the tail-gun of the Halifax of 138 Squadron . . .
>
> Our clothes and equipment were checked by both Polish and British officers. They put two heavy money-belts round my waist, filled with dollars . . . One had to remember to hand over all compromising objects, like a London bus ticket . . .
>
> At the airfield at Tempsford in eastern England, we were seen off by representatives of the VI Bureau and the Air Force and by our guardian angel, Lt.Col. Harold Perkins of British Intelligence, who as usual was in excellent humour. His cane, which never left him, often fulfilled the function of a conductor's baton. 'Tell the people in Poland,' he said, 'that here in England the Poles have faithful friends who will never abandon them . . .'
>
> In Poland, the snow was beginning to thaw, so when we took off at 18.45 on 19 February 1943 we had changed our white snow suits for green-brown overalls . . . A full moon was shining, and we first caught sight of the silver Vistula, and briefly, of cloud-covered Warsaw. Our pilot said that the sirens would certainly be blaring down below, because the Germans would not be able to tell whether we were a so-called 'little bird' or a serious bombing raid. Our plane began to descend quietly over the River Pilitsa, and then to seek the reception point. What an emotional moment it was when, in the midst of the dark forest, we saw a cross of red and white flares impudently alight in a large clearing. 'Hurray! They're here and waiting for us,' we cried. After all, the Home Army is not some sort of crackpot fantasy dreamt up by émigré propaganda . . .
>
> The 'Action Station' lights flashed. I can't remember who shouted 'Go'. But the cases of arms went first. Twelve of them. 'Grove' jumped, and I as political emissary jumped second. Soon the chutes of 'Pawn' and 'Eye' were billowing above my head.

We had jumped from a mere 300 feet, so that the dispersion would be minimal. I flew past a tall pine tree and landed like a king on my feet, without the regulation roll. I realized that I was standing in a field of rich ploughed earth . . .

After a minute or two, an unprepossessing armed man in a helmet appeared. We exchanged the password . . . and then a strong manly handshake. Somewhere on the edge of the clearing, the commander sent from Warsaw called his team together. They were all locals who had joined the AK from the pre-war Rural Youth League. They removed all the boxes, and the parachutes from which the women would sew themselves silk blouses and underwear. According to instructions, we swallowed the regulation dose of Excedrin for increased alertness . . ., leaving the cyanide pills provided in case of torture in a special pocket in our trousers. I held the enciphered message from the Commander-in-Chief to the Commandant of the Home Army in the lining of my overcoat.

Under the care of local guides, we moved off beneath the starry sky for a couple of kilometres until we reached a school building. It would have been a wonderful walk except for the barking of farm dogs who could easily have attracted the attention of a nearby German guardpost. We were welcomed by the doughty village headmistress who served up a mouth-watering omelette with tomatoes and bacon. But haste was essential. The school had to be vacated by dawn. So we handed over our weapons and our money-belts to a delegate of the Warsaw AK. In this way, I never carried a pistol again, though I hoped that the gun which I had brought from England would be used by someone else in the Underground struggle . . .[38]

The importance of SOE and of the 'dark and silent' to the growth of the Underground cannot be exaggerated. By 1944, SOE had flown in an absolute majority of the military and civilian leadership. Although Boor was not among them, many of the men surrounding him were. Boor's deputy, Bear Cub, a founding member of the 'Victory Service' and sometime prisoner in the Lubyanka, was flown in from Italy on 22 May 1944. Many of the jumpers took over regional commands in the Home Army – 'Anchor' on the Niemen, 'Forester' in Polesie, 'Gloomy' in the Holy Cross Mountains. Scores of others found themselves in the Warsaw Rising. The 'dark and silent' flew to Poland to fight the Germans. Many died. But, in many instances, it wouldn't be the Germans who killed them.

In 1943–44, the activities of the Resistance movement greatly expanded and diversified. They were facilitated on the one hand by the unified command structures which had been put into place, and on the other by the fact that the whole of the country, both west and east, was now occupied by the one Nazi enemy. The single, and singularly repugnant, adversary helped to give focus to a single-minded opposition. At the same time, the psychological horizons were slowly lifting. Before 1943, the Nazis had looked invincible. From 1943 onwards, they were in retreat. Every anti-Nazi resistance fighter on the Continent could feel that the hour of retribution was coming.

The twin branches of Poland's Underground – civilian and military – had shown remarkable resilience. Directed by their Governmental superiors in London, they now possessed a full complement of ministries, bureaux, and specialized agencies. In some fields, they worked separately; in others, they worked together. Though they paid a ceaseless toll of blood and pain from Nazi repressions, they were proving irrepressible.

Thanks to the varied origins of its constituent parts, the Home Army was destined to retain much of its original character of an umbrella organization. But it increasingly contrived to form larger military detachments, which in size and style looked less like partisan bands and more like regular army formations. This was particularly true in the former Soviet Zone in eastern Poland, where regional and district units had to be re-formed after 1941. The Home Army faced special problems in each region. In (Polish) Upper Silesia, for example, which had been reincorporated into the Reich, the AK had to contend with a hostile German population. In the provinces of Cracow and Kieltse, the combination of hilly country and sympathetic Polish neighbourhoods made for ideal conditions. In the Lublin province, where some forty separate Underground detachments were operating, both the right-wing NSZ and the Communist People's Guard were reluctant to recognize the Home Army's authority and the AK Command was sometimes obliged to intervene with lethal force. Further east, there were other complications. From mid-1943, large-scale Soviet partisan units were sent through the German lines. They regarded themselves as the sole legitimate force.

Lithuanian, Byelorussian, Ukrainian, and even Jewish partisan groups kept themselves apart from Poles and Soviets alike.

The Home Army developed a surprisingly sophisticated system of arms and explosives production. A Technical Research Bureau made dozens of inventions, including two variants of the British Sten gun, howitzers, and even a home-designed armoured car. The Sappers' Division, later the Clandestine Production Directorate, turned the inventions into real weapons. Warsaw hid three illegal grenade factories. The 1,500 or so home-produced radio receivers proved more reliable than British and American sets dropped by the SOE. But the real revelation was the *filipinka* – a mass-produced type of hand grenade packed with deadly power.

From January 1943 the Home Army's Directorate of Diversionary Operations, the K-Div., was set up. Its director was Maj.Gen. 'Nile', an officer trained by the SOE and flown in by the RAF via Cairo (hence his pseudonym). Its aims were defined in a founding order:

1. To harass the enemy ... through diversionary action, sabotage, and focused reprisals for any acts of violence committed by the enemy against the civilian population.
2. To give its members the necessary experience and strength of character for the tasks ahead, viz maintaining society in a combat-ready posture ... favourable for the future rising.[39]

In 1943–44, the units subordinated to the K-Div. grew and multiplied until it formed a formidable fighting force of trained men and women. Together with Boor's HQ Guard Battalion Bashta, it constituted the core of the Home Army's active elite. It possessed its own staff, and its own military formation, the Radoslav Grouping (named after its commander), and consisted of six major units, each with its own mysterious name. The 'Beard 53' Diversionary Brigade was made up of three sub-units, the Zoshka Battalion, the Women's Battle Company 'Discus', and the 'Poplar' Company. The Parasol Battalion was one of four similarly independent formation, including 'Watch 49', 'Broom', and 'Fist'. The 'College A' Company was a special duties unit attached to the K-Div.'s Warsaw District's headquarters.

Diversionary action was a catch-all phrase for all manner of attacks which could throw the enemy off his guard and sow confusion. It included anything from springing prisoners from jail or hijacking German lorries, to arson, bank-robbery, and planting bombs in SS barracks.

Sabotage, for instance, took many forms. It ranged from Polish workers in German factories making dud shells and faulty gun muzzles to train derailment, bridge-blowing, and arson. In 1941–44, the Underground (perhaps optimistically) claimed 25,145 such incidents.

Reprisals were aimed at German personnel and most usually at Nazi officials. In Warsaw, a whole grisly gallery of SS and Gestapo men were liquidated. Otto Schultz, a sadistic guard from the Paviak, met his end on 6 May 1943, and Otto Braun, a specialist in street round-ups, on 13 December. On 1 February 1944, an assassination squad from the 'Pegasus' unit of the Grey Ranks caught up with *SS-Brig.Fhr.* Franz Kutschera, Head of the Warsaw Police District. The cost was heavy: Nazi practice was to shoot 100 Poles for every assassination. So the AK took to following their prey on leave in Germany and killing them there. In all, 5,733 assassinations were supposedly planned. Just as the Gestapo kept a list of resistance leaders to be caught and eliminated, so too, the Resistance drew up its own 'Head List' of Nazi officials.

In September 1942, for instance, a Home Army execution squad eliminated a dangerous foe. A man variously thought to be called 'Hammer' or Schweitzer, but using the pseudonym of 'Uncle', had set up a pseudo-conspiratorial intelligence network that was passing information to the *Abwehr*. His organization masqueraded under the grandiose title of the Superintelligence Service of the Exiled Government. One of their dirtier tricks was to intercept notes that were being smuggled out of the Paviak and to hand them over to the Gestapo. Their leaders were found guilty in absentia by an Underground court, and were shot on the street by a squad led by 'Hard Tommy' from the AK's counter-intelligence department.[40]

In terms of planning and daring, the assassination of Franz Kutschera was undoubtedly in the same league as the better known killing of Reinhard Heydrich in Prague eighteen months earlier. The plan originated in the AK's K-Div. Command. The eight assassins were chosen from 1st Platoon of the Pegasus organization. The leader was Cpl. 'Flight'. The time was the morning of 1 February 1944. The place was the beautiful Uyazhdov Boulevard near the parkside junction of Chopin Street.

Kutschera's steel-grey Opel Admiral turned into the boulevard past the former British Embassy at 9.06 a.m. It was followed by an open truck filled with soldiers. Armed SS men marched alongside. As it travelled slowly north, its arrival was signalled by a woman on the roadside who pulled up the hood of her coat and crossed the street. After perhaps 140m

(150 yards), a car roared around the corner of Pius XI Street, careered onto the wrong side of the road, and smashed head on into Kutschera's convoy. Almost immediately, Flight ran down the right-hand pavement and emptied his Sten at point-blank range through the Opel's open window. An accomplice arrived from the other side and repeated the performance. Kutschera was already dying. A volley of German machine-gun fire felled the two attackers, but a fierce hail of bullets and grenades from friends posted nearby kept the enemy at bay, while the wounded were picked up and the whole team scrambled into two other waiting cars. At 9.08 a.m. both cars escaped. One of them later ran into a German checkpoint on one of the Vistula bridges, and the occupants had to jump over the balustrade into the freezing river. The other made it to the Old Town, where it met a physician, 'Dr Max', but then toured the hospitals, searching desperately for a specialist surgeon who dared to tend Flight's wounds. The operations were performed late at night. Both patients deteriorated. Their mothers were summoned before they died. Flight was given a death certificate naming tuberculosis of the liver, and he was buried in the city cemetery by a regular undertaker.

Meantime, a special investigative unit of SS and Gestapo moved in from Lublin. At Lidice, after Heydrich's death, they shot 198 men. In Warsaw, after Kutschera's death, they shot 300. They exhumed Flight's body, having kept a watch on hospital deaths, and found by post-mortem that the death certificate was false. But they failed to catch the organizers. A fine of 1 million marks was imposed on the citizens. The curfew was extended by an hour. All non-German cars and motorcycles were banned indefinitely. Kutschera's funeral cortège passed through streets that, by order, were totally empty. An action that had lasted 1 minute 40 seconds was remembered for the rest of the occupation. Hundreds of less-publicized episodes occurred.[41]

In the eyes of the Nazi hierarchy, the Underground fighters were mere 'terrorists'. But as Kutschera had himself remarked: 'There is no certain defence against people who are eager to sacrifice their own lives.'[42]

Underground justice was a matter partly for the clandestine judicial system of the Secret State and partly for the courts martial of the AK. Sessions were secretly convened. Qualified magistrates and judges presided. Witnesses were called. Sentences were passed and published. AK punishment and execution squads enforced them. Informers, 'greasers', and collaborators, as well as common criminals, were made to walk in fear. Igo S., a Warsaw actor who accepted the post of director of the City Theatre from the Germans, met a sudden death. So, too, did hundreds of others, including people condemned for maltreating Jews. In all, Warsaw's Underground courts passed 220 death sentences.[43]

As the Underground struggle intensified, incidents multiplied. Some collaborators were executed, whilst others were flogged or head-shaved. One of the larger actions, in March 1944, finished off the directors of a 'Ukrainian Welfare Committee', who were judged to be engaged in something more sinister than welfare. One of the last actions, code-named Operation Hunt, consisted of a long series of grenade and petrol-bomb attacks on vehicles of the *Sipo*, and was undertaken in the second half of June 1944. (The Underground had noticed that all *Sipo* vehicles carried a registration number starting with OST-47.) In the opening attack of the series, a much hated SS-man, *Ostuf.* Herbert Junk, sometime Acting Governor of the Paviak, was killed, together with one of his attackers bearing the splendid pseudonym of 'Nicholas II'. In revenge, the Gestapo announced that seventy-five 'Communists' had been shot.[44] The 'Communists' were not Communists.

Of course, it would be wrong to suppose the Underground had no contacts whatsoever with the Gestapo. On the contrary, both sides were only too aware of the other's activities; they were working the same patch; and, on occasion, they were obliged to cut a deal. In the autumn of 1943, for example, two men from the Home Army's security corps brazenly stole an armour-plated Super-Mercedes belonging to a Nazi dignitary from the RSHA in Berlin, who had just arrived in Warsaw. The luckless car owner's subordinates were more than eager to get it back, if only to save their own skins, so the AK decided that a suitable price would be the release of fifteen named prisoners from the Paviak. As reported, the telephone rang on the *Sipo*'s duty desk:

> Did you receive our letter?
> Yes . . .
> Do your superiors accept our proposal?
> Yes, but . . .
> All right, tomorrow at 3 p.m., all on the list must be freed.
> And the car? We'll release the prisoners when we have the car. On my word as a German officer.
> You release the prisoners . . . and after three days we tell you where the car is.

What's the guarantee?

The word of a Polish officer . . .[45]

The exchange took place as agreed.

The Council for the Rescue of Jews, which was given the deliberately misleading code-name of 'Zhegota', was created in the summer of 1942, when AK intelligence discovered the true destination of transports leaving the Ghetto. Direct intervention was virtually impossible, since the Ghetto and the transports were heavily guarded. So the emphasis was on protecting Jewish children, providing false papers, hiding them in safe houses, and passing them on to Church networks. Owing to the unusual size of Poland's Jewish community, the Nazis managed to kill more Jews in occupied Poland than elsewhere. Yet it is also true, thanks in large part to Zhegota, that more Jews were rescued in Poland than anywhere else. The figure is usually put at around 100,000.[46]

The Home Army's Bureau of Information and Propaganda was responsible at its height for a daily circulation of newspapers totalling 200,000 copies. It also published all manner of military, technical, historical, and educational manuals. The *Information Bulletin* (BI), which ran into 317 issues, was its standard-bearer. Yet some of the greatest pleasure (and success) derived from its collectors' items such as *Der Soldat*, *Der Hammer* or *Der Klabautermann*, which sowed false news in the enemy ranks and which BIP's 'N' section disguised as Wehrmacht publications. In 1943, a special sub-section called 'Antique' went into action to expose the growing threat of (rival) Communist propaganda.[47]

Intelligence and counter-intelligence was the business of the Home Army's famous II Bureau, which was a priceless asset not just to Poland but to the Allied cause in general. The II Bureau was the direct successor of the pre-war service, whose agents first broke the 'unbreakable' German Enigma system; and in 1941, it supplied London with the details of the forthcoming Operation Barbarossa, which Stalin, reportedly, did not want to believe. In the summer of 1942 it suffered a major setback when it closed down its entire network following penetration by the *Abwehr*. So it started again from scratch. Three discrete and watertight networks were established – 'Arcadius' for the General Government, 'Pawnshop' for the Reich, and 'Laundry' for the Soviet Union. All three survived to the end of the war. (It is hard to believe that their archive, which was handed to the British Foreign Office in 1945, was then destroyed by mistake.)[48]

In late July 1944, one of the II Bureau's most dazzling exploits was reaching a climax. A year earlier, Polish agents had pinpointed the research centre of Germany's rocket programme at Peenemünde on the island of Usedom, which was subsequently bombed by the RAF, and then they identified the secret test-range of the ultra-modern V2 rocket at a remote site in southern Poland. Still more excitingly, they contrived to spirit away an intact V2 rocket which had failed to explode after falling into a marsh near the River Bug. The rocket and its motor were disassembled, carted in pieces to Warsaw, copied in minutest detail onto technical drawings, and packed for shipment. Chemical specialists cracked a key problem by reconstructing the formula of the V2's fuel. After that there remained the small matter of sending this priceless cache to London.[49]

During the long months and years when the Home Army was waiting for a Rising to mature, Polish patriots had to shrug off endless uncertainties. But on 1 April 1943, on the eve of Stalin's break with Poland, the *Information Bulletin* said it all: 'A National Rising cannot be declared every three months. One rising can be staged – and only one. And such a rising must unquestionably be successful.'[50] The BBC was telling the French Resistance exactly the same thing at the same time.

The most unexpected compliment eventually emerged from the unlikeliest of sources. At the end of the war, when the Third Reich was facing defeat and occupation, the Nazi leaders turned to the head of German army intelligence in the east, Reinhard Gehlen, and asked him in desperation to advise on how to form a German Resistance movement against the Allies. Gehlen, who was not a Nazi, advised that they follow the model of the Polish Home Army.

One of the hardest burdens which the Home Army and its admirers had to bear was lodged in repeated slurs propagated by Soviet and Communist sources. Far from celebrating the Home Army's achievements, Soviet commentators started to spread the word that the AK was 'inactive', 'cowardly', or even 'pro-German'. In their enthusiasm for the Soviet Union and its victories, many elements of the British and American press unthinkingly followed suit. From the AK's point of view, the only fitting response was: 'We will show them!'

The Uprising in the Warsaw Ghetto broke out on 19 April 1943, and, to general astonishment on all sides, lasted for twenty-seven days. It was launched by two small groups of clandestine fighters, who had correctly foreseen the final liquidation of the Ghetto and had jointly decided to stand and fight, come what might. Hence, when *SS-Brig.Fhr.* Jürgen Stroop entered the Ghetto with a force of some 3,000 troops and armed police he was met with a hail of grenades and bullets. The defiance was unexpected. According to the prevailing stereotype, Jews were supposed to go like lambs to the slaughter.

The suppression of the Uprising proceeded day after day with unparalleled savagery. The fighters were well prepared. Their light weapons, which had been supplied in modest quantities by the Polish Underground, were no match for the firepower of Stroop's professionals. But they inflicted casualties. What is more, a warren of hidden bunkers and invisible escape routes had been put in place. In the end, Stroop preferred fire to the sword. Water, gas, and electricity were cut off. Buildings were torched, block by block. Occupants, when forced out, were mown down. Cellars were cleared with 'smoke candles'. Over 20,000 persons were killed. A mere 16,000 were left for transport to Treblinka. The insurgents' HQ, in a bunker on Pleasant Street, was destroyed on 8 May, together with their commander, Mordechai A. A week later, Stroop was able to report to Berlin: 'The Ghetto is no more.'[51]

One can read about the Ghetto Uprising from many sources. Stroop's report is full of reluctant admiration for his adversaries. 'Jews and Jewesses shot from two pistols at the same time . . . Jewesses carried loaded [weapons] in their clothing . . . At the last moment, they would pull out hand grenades . . . and throw them at the soldiers . . .'[52] Another participant, Mark E., a Bundist who was the only recognized leader of the Uprising to survive the war, wrote an account that is free of post-war ideology.[53] Leon Uris, meanwhile, wrote the sort of fiction that can often be mistaken for fact.[54]

Not all commentaries care to emphasize that in great part the heroes of the Ghetto were Poles. For, just as American Jews would see themselves as being American as well as Jewish, so the majority of young Polish Jews of the wartime generation would *not* have accepted the assumption that 'Poles' and 'Jews' belonged to two distinct and separate species. For they were not just Polish citizens. Unlike their elders, they had largely been educated in Polish schools; they spoke Polish; and to a high degree they shared Polish patriotic values. They had not been segregated from their non-Jewish compatriots by choice but by Nazi fiat.

When the Ghetto Uprising was being suppressed, no one on the

'Aryan Side' of Warsaw could fail to notice what was happening. They couldn't follow the action in detail, but everyone saw the flames, smelt the smoke, shuddered at the gunfire, and sometimes heard the screams. Those who caught sight of the Red-and-White flag fluttering alongside the Star of David on a high building were deeply moved. But they were largely helpless. They had been cut off from the Ghetto for two years, and were obliged to face other daily horrors on their own side of the divide. Their apparent passivity should not necessarily be equated with indifference. A poet who was present and who saw the incongruity of a fairground beside the Ghetto Wall was reminded of the lonely death of the dissident 'heretic' Giordano Bruno in Rome three centuries before:

> I thought of the Campo di Fiori
> In Warsaw by the sky carousel
> One clear spring evening
> To the strains of a carnival tune.
> The bright melody
> Drowned the salvoes from the ghetto wall,
> And couples were flying
> High in the cloudless sky.
> . . .
> Those dying here, the lonely,
> Forgotten by the world,
> Our tongues become for them
> The language of an ancient planet.
> Until, when all is legend,
> And many years have passed
> On a new Campo di Fiori
> Rage will kindle at a poet's word.[55]

The Ghetto Uprising left a residue of bitter emotions, rage, guilt, and frustration among them, but it also left a more tangible legacy for those Varsovians who had seen it happen and who were ready to learn the lessons. The moral lesson was unmistakable. It stated that some things in life are more important than life itself. The Ghetto fighters faced a more extreme predicament than many other Varsovians would face. Yet their resolve could only command respect. The cause was hopeless: their courage magnificent. They set an example: some would say, a very Polish example.

The political lesson concerned the inaction of people who might have rendered assistance. By 1943, the outside world knew a great deal about Nazi treatment of the Jews. The problem was to find someone who might give it priority. For Great Powers have 'interests'. They were in the middle of a vast war; they couldn't be persuaded to set their own plans aside for something which, from their point of view, was a local sideline.[56] The Polish Underground had its own pressing problems. It was ready to extend limited assistance but not to put its entire operation at risk. The Ghetto fighters, through no fault of their own, were left to wage their battle in terrible isolation.

The military lesson centred on the extraordinary effectiveness of urban guerrilla warfare, of which the Ghetto was one of the earliest examples. The half-armed, poorly trained but unusually resourceful and motivated fighters were only defeated with great difficulty. They had successfully held out against all the heavy weaponry used against them, not for days but for weeks. They were only overcome when the enemy demolished the entire urban environment in which they operated. These facts prompted reflections. If a few hundred fighters could hold up the Nazi war machine for nearly a month, it was not unrealistic to calculate that a force thirty or forty times their size, in a battleground twenty times bigger, might conceivably achieve still more extensive results.

A final coda to the story of the Ghetto Uprising can be found in the fate of its chief chronicler, Dr Emanuel R. He had been smuggled out of the Ghetto in March 1943. For twelve months, living in a hideout on 'the Aryan Side', he devoted himself to his writings. The hideout was then discovered. Dr Emanuel R., his family, and the Catholics who had been sheltering him, were hauled off to the Paviak and shot.[57]

For Polish officialdom, a national Rising was always on the agenda. It was discussed from the day the country was forced to surrender in 1939. Some civilians did not like the idea, and many military men questioned its practicality. But the Government never wavered; and the majority followed their lead. Throughout the war, therefore, the main questions were simply when and how. Three distinct variants were proposed: a general Rising, Operation Tempest, and 'the Battle for the Capital'.

When Gen. Sikorski first came to London in October 1940, he authorized a plan for a general Rising, which would coincide with a major landing of regular forces. He had included this sort of scheme in the founding statute of the 'Union of Armed Struggle', which was ordered to prepare for an armed Rising as soon as it was appropriate.[58] The assumption seems to have been that the Royal Navy or the Royal Air Force would be strong enough to ferry the landing force to a suitable point on the Continent, and that the insurgents, operating principally in rural areas, would be able to obstruct German counter-measures.

Plans inevitably changed once the German–Soviet War had broken out. Operational Report Nr. 54, in autumn 1942, foresaw a general Rising in central Poland but not in the western or eastern provinces. The signal was to be preceded by a fourteen-day 'period of vigilance', and was to be decided on by the Commander of the Home Army. The long list of aims was headed by the toppling of the German occupants, and the capture of arms and ammunition to permit the further expansion of the Rising.[59] Regarding the USSR, Gen. Arrow noted: 'I only include [Russia] among the allied states for formal reasons. In reality, I maintain the view that Russia will assume a clearly hostile posture towards us . . . and will camouflage this posture so long as she remains feeble.'[60]

None of these plans was withheld from the British and Americans. On the contrary, Poland's military missions in London and Washington were constantly pestering their British and American counterparts for material support. On 2 July 1943, for example, a summary of the Home Army's intended action was placed before the Combined Chiefs of Staff, together with an accompanying shopping list. Col. M., the head of the military mission in Washington, was duly grilled by Lt.Gen. Gordon Macready, a British member of the Combined Chiefs of Staff. In answer to a question about the best moment for launching the Rising, Col. M. replied that the entry of Allied armies into the Hungarian Plain would suit well. He was obviously aware of Churchill's dream of a lightning march from Italy and through the so-called Ljubljana Gap. In answer to a question about the implications of a possible Soviet offensive into Poland, the reply was unequivocal. 'In that case there would be no Rising, and the Home Army would stay in the Underground.'[61]

At Poland's insistence, inter-Allied discussions regarding the 'Secret Army' in Poland proceeded through 1943 and into 1944. As shown by the voluminous papers of Col. M. in Washington, they were based on two assumptions – that the 'Secret Army' would at the least receive Western air support, and that Poland's Parachute Brigade, which was being trained in Britain under the direct command of the exiled Government, would be made available.[62]

By the autumn of 1943, however, the Western powers had still not established a military presence on the Continent outside Italy, whilst the victory of the Red Army on the Eastern Front was forging rapidly ahead. After Kursk in July, the exiled Government had to face the likelihood that its territory would not be liberated by the Western powers, but by Stalin's armies. The result was Operation Tempest.

Proof that knowledge about Poland's plans for a Rising were circulating at the very top of the Coalition is contained in a telegram from Secretary of State Hull to President Roosevelt dated 23 November 1943. Hull was passing on information that had been received from Premier Mick. 'A rising in Poland against Germany', he wrote, 'is being planned to break out at a moment mutually agreed upon with our Allies either before or at the very moment of the entry of Soviet troops into Poland.'[63] The statement is there for all to see. It was produced in advance of Teheran, two months prior to the Red Army's entry into Poland, nine months prior to its advance on the Vistula. A key phrase was 'a moment mutually agreed upon'. A key question for historians is what happened to this information in subsequent months.

On 26 October 1943, the exiled Government had sent an elaborate Instruction to the AK Commander and to the Delegate, which reviewed a series of possible variants for the future Rising. As previously, the first variant postulated a widespread general Rising pursued in conjunction with the Western powers. The second proposed scaled-down diversionary activities, in the event that a general Rising was not approved by the Western powers. The third and fourth analysed actions to be taken if the Red Army intervened. The exiled Government reserved for itself the decision about steps to be taken if diplomatic relations with the Soviets had not been resumed.[64]

A month later, having pondered his Government's Instruction, Gen. Boor decided to pursue a variant of his own. His Order Nr. 1300/111 of 20 November 1943 contained a basic outline of Operation Tempest. In some aspects, it varied from the Instruction. It was influenced by the consideration that various ethnic groups in eastern Poland might react unpredictably and that a much weakened Polish community in the Borders was in no condition to underpin a general insurgency. It had also to take account of the recent break in Polish–Soviet diplomatic relations. In the circumstances, it determined to use the re-established military formations of the Underground but to do so in a manner which made Soviet forces welcome as 'allies of allies' and to stress their partnership in the common fight against Nazi Germany. Much latitude was left to the judgement of local commanders. Their orders were to take the Wehrmacht in the rear whenever the Front approached their locality, to assist Soviet commanders by all means possible, then to act as genial hosts to incoming Soviet formations. Tempest was envisaged as a rash or scatter of limited local actions, as opposed to one large, coordinated insurrection.

In a covering note to the C.-in-C., Boor explained how his order diverged from the Government's advice of the previous month:

> I have ordered the commanders and units which are to participate in fighting the retreating Germans to reveal themselves to in-coming Russians. Their task at this stage will be to assert the existence of the Polish Republic. On this point, my order is at variance with the Government's Instruction.[65]

He clarified the principles on which his decision was based:

> All our war preparations are aimed at armed action against the Germans. In no circumstances can they result in armed action against the [Soviets] who are entering our territories in hot pursuit of the Germans . . . The exception is in essential acts of self-defence, which is the right of every human being.[66]

The Tempest plan assumed that a general Rising remained a definite possibility, particularly in the more central and westerly provinces of the country. To this end, Boor issued a three-stage procedure of readiness. The first stage foresaw a 'state of intensified monitoring', the second a formal 'state of alert', the third a 'state of stand-by' that would immediately precede action.

Consideration was also given to Warsaw's role. In the event of a general Rising, Warsaw was to be excluded in favour of rural concentrations. But if Operation Tempest spread as far as the Vistula, Warsaw was to be included as one local element.

Historians have questioned the competence and even the loyalty of the Home Army leadership who put Tempest into effect. Some have drawn attention to the alleged insubordination of Gen. Boor, whose orders for Tempest drew very selectively on the Government's guidelines. Yet few people at the time noticed the most sinister prospect – namely, that if the Underground leaders ever fell out of step with their superiors in London, the task of successfully coordinating their plans with the Western powers could be seriously compromised.

The affair of the October Instruction revealed the conflicting positions that were developing within the exiled Government and would eventually lead to an open rift. Yet the conflict has rarely been presented accurately. In the conventional view, which largely derived from ill-informed Soviet sources, a 'hardline' faction, led by the Commander-in-Chief, was planning a diehard Rising whose main purpose was to prevent a Soviet takeover. Throughout 1944, the Soviets were demanding the dismissal of these 'anti-Soviet elements' as one of their preconditions for resuming relations. A faction led by the Premier, in contrast, was supposed to favour compromise with the Soviets, and was hence assumed to oppose precipitate action. Practically nothing in this scenario corresponded with reality. Almost everyone within the exiled Government was 'anti-Soviet' in the sense that they valued national independence and were strongly opposed to Stalin's arbitrary schemes. Almost everyone favoured a Rising in principle, regarding it as a legitimate instrument for overthrowing foreign oppression and an established feature of the national tradition. The differences arose in part over the practicalities of a Rising and in particular over divergent assessments of the intentions of the 'Big Three'. The Commander-in-Chief's group, who might best be called the 'sceptics', believed firstly that Stalin was not a person to compromise willingly, and secondly that the Western powers lacked the nerve to confront him. As shown by the October Instruction, they doubted whether an isolated Rising against the Germans was likely to succeed. The Premier's group, in contrast, who may best be characterized as the 'optimists', were determined to accept Western assurances as good coin. They believed the promises about Western brokerage of a deal with Stalin, and they counted, in the last resort, on active Western assistance. Paradoxically, therefore, it was the men who were thought in Whitehall and Washington to be the most 'anti-Soviet' who in reality were the Rising's most outspoken opponents.

None of the leading 'optimists' had any personal knowledge of Russia. The Premier came from western Poland, where the traditional stance was to fear the Germans and hence, reluctantly, to look for help from the east. In any case, as leader of the Peasant Party, he felt less at home with international relations than with domestic affairs. Interestingly, all the leading commanders of the Underground to whom the Government would ultimately delegate responsibility for the Rising – Boor, Sable, Monter, and Bear Cub – had originally been trained as Austrian officers or had served under Austrian command. The leading 'cynics', on the other hand, were all men very familiar with Russian ways. The Commander-in-Chief, born a subject of the Tsar, had served in 1920 as Pilsudski's right-hand man in the defeat of the Red Army. His colleague, Gen. Anders, had been both a Tsarist officer and a prisoner of the Lubyanka. There were obvious exceptions. Gen. Tabor, a former Russian officer, probably wished to launch the Rising at all costs simply because the C-in-C opposed it. Even so, it does seem that those who were most sceptical about the Rising and about the prospects of Soviet and Western aid were often those whose scepticism had Russian roots.

Time and again Polish representatives appealed to the British and the Americans for help. All the British told them was that the logistical problems of intervening in the east were enormous. The Americans repeatedly emphasized that the Eastern Front had been designated as the theatre of Soviet operations and that the Poles must somehow make a deal with the Soviet Command.

The exiled Government, knowing the dilemmas to be faced and the imminence of Tempest, made repeated requests to the Western powers to send a military mission to the Home Army to observe the Underground at first hand. The first was made by Premier Mick to Winston Churchill on 22 February 1944. It was followed by a similar proposal to the American chargé d'affaires in London on the 23rd. The idea would have been mutually advantageous. The Western powers would have gained their own channel of reliable information, and Poland would have been relieved of the suspicion that its officials were spreading biased or alarmist stories. But neither the British nor the Americans were in any hurry to oblige. They did not say yes, and they did not say no. Despite regular reminders, the weeks and months were allowed to pass. Nothing was arranged.

Such was the situation in mid-July 1944, when Rokossovsky's advance began to impinge on Warsaw itself. At a council of war held on 21 July, the Home Army's top brass unanimously agreed that the rout of the Wehrmacht's Army Group Centre was creating the pre-conditions for a successful rising in the Capital. Notice was given for a 'state of alert' to start on the 25th. Urgent radio calls were sent to London requesting a final decision at the highest level.

Given the tremendous strain, it was only to be expected that Polish Government circles in London were deeply divided. But it is greatly to their credit that decisions were quickly made on the two most burning issues of the day – policy towards the Soviet Union and on the Home Army's advice to unleash the long-awaited Rising. (It may have helped that the Commander-in-Chief was absent on a tour of the troops in Italy.) The crucial Cabinet meeting was convened on 25 July.

Polish attitudes to the USSR had crystallized into three distinct positions. One group, typified by Gen. Berling, held the view that Stalin's every wish must be accommodated. Their stance was mirrored in that of the reviving Communist movement, whose long-despised subservience was now becoming more comprehensible. A second group, typified by the Commander-in-Chief, took the line that any attempt to negotiate with the Soviets would end in humiliation. The best course of action was to do nothing rash, to watch developments, to keep one's powder dry, and, if Rokossovsky entered Warsaw, to hold the Home Army in concealment. The dominant group, typified by the Peasant Party and Premier, however, held that these counsels of despair were self-defeating and that, with the help of the Western powers, some sort of modus vivendi was both desirable and possible. They knew that Poland's hand was weak and was growing weaker. But they also knew that Stalin was receiving vast quantities of Western aid; and they couldn't contemplate the possibility that Churchill and Roosevelt would throw them to the wolves. In consequence, they found little difficulty in trusting Roosevelt's promises, in acquiescing to Churchill's demands, and in agreeing to send Premier Mick to Moscow for a face-to-face encounter with Stalin.

The other decision was not so straightforward. Everyone could see from the map that Rokossovsky's offensive was heading in a direct line for Warsaw, where all the command posts of the Home Army and Secret State were concentrated. So there was no time to be lost. On the other hand, the German occupation forces in central Poland did not appear on the point of collapse. Hence, it was impossible in London to gauge the optimum moment to strike; and it was important to balance the countervalent demands both for action and for caution. Three points were agreed. The Home Army's advice to unleash a Rising should be accepted; the Rising should be limited to the Capital in the form of a localized action to be described as 'the Battle for Warsaw'; and third, since the pace of events could not be foreseen, the exact timing of the final order would be left to the Government's representatives on the spot. The Premier in London signalled the Delegate in Warsaw on the morning of 26 July: 'The Government of the Republic has unanimously resolved to empower you to pronounce the Rising at a time to be determined by you. If possible, advise us beforehand. Copy through army channels to the Commander of the Home Army.'[67]

That same day, Premier Mick left London en route for Moscow via Gibraltar, Cairo, and Teheran. He was not due to arrive in Russia for four or five days. His bid to placate Stalin, to win approval for the Rising, and to lay the most practical conditions for the Soviets' entry into Warsaw, were complementary elements of the same strategy.

Poland's Commander-in-Chief was deeply perturbed by the turn of events in June and July. A firm disciple of the 'Doctrine of Two Enemies', he was as committed as anyone to the war against Germany. But, unlike the Premier's British and American patrons, he was sorely troubled by the Red Army's rapid advance and, above all, by what he took to be Allied complacency regarding Soviet realities. He was particularly incensed by the Premier's plans to travel to Moscow without clear proposals and with no concrete guarantees of Western support. And he suspected worse. He suspected that Britain and America had secretly endorsed Stalin's ambitions and that the Premier would be forced to capitulate.

On 3 July, the Minister for War arranged for the Commander-in-Chief and the Premier to meet over dinner in London, and to discuss their differences. All three diners realized that the Underground leaders would soon be calling on them for guidance. None was thinking of an imminent insurrection in Warsaw. Premier Mick's position had been bolstered by his recent talks with Roosevelt. He accepted the Western view that the Soviet annexation of Poland was not a foregone conclusion, and that Stalin, who was dependent on Western aid, was not bent on spreading communism or on endangering his relations with the West.

The Commander-in-Chief did not share his optimism either about Stalin's restraint or about Western benevolence. His advice may be summarized under four headings: 1. that the war against Germany be continued: 2. that armed resistance against the Soviets be forbidden: 3. that in the event of the Soviets refusing to recognize representatives of the exiled Government, the Home Army should transfer its cadres into the German-occupied zone; and 4. that barring a Soviet–Polish agreement a general insurrection against the Germans be excluded. This last point deserves to be underlined with a direct quotation. 'Insurrection without a fair understanding with the USSR and honest and real cooperation with the Red Army would be politically unjustified and militarily nothing more than an act of despair.'[68] Nothing could be more categorical. Anyone who believes that the Commander-in-Chief can be counted among the instigators of the Rising is plain wrong.

At the end of the dinner, the Commander-in-Chief confirmed his intention of leaving shortly for an extended tour of the troops in Italy. The Premier and the Minister protested in vain. He left on 11 July, and played no further part in the decisions that were made that month.[69]

Before departing, he exercised his right to advise Gen. Boor in Warsaw. His despatch of 7 July confirmed the line of argument put to the Premier, but it contained a twist in the tail. The Red Army, he said, would soon overrun most of Poland, and the Kremlin would be reluctant 'even to enter into talks with our Government. In such conditions, a national armed rising would be unjustifiable . . .' However, circumstances could change, a state of readiness should be maintained, and 'In the last moments of the German retreat and before the entry of the Red units, if the chance should arise even of the temporary occupation of [Vilno], [Lvuv], or any other important centre . . ., this should be accomplished and we should act as rightful hosts [to the Soviets].'[70] Boor would have noticed that Warsaw could be seen as 'another important centre'.

The Commander-in-Chief also briefed the courier 'Novak', who was setting out for Warsaw, telling him that a conflict between the West and the USSR would occur within five years. The Premier said the opposite, telling him to impress on the Underground leaders that the most urgent necessity was to reach an understanding in Moscow with the diplomatic backing of Roosevelt and Churchill.

It seems that the Comander-in-Chief's opinions were soon reinforced by long talks with Gen. Anders. Anders had been in the claws of the NKVD only three years earlier, and he had the strongest possible view of what to expect:

> [The Commander-in-Chief believed] that a general rising could not succeed without help from outside the country, and the only real possibilities for this were from the Soviet Union. But, knowing the Russians as I did, I was certain that no assistance could be counted upon from her; Russia had her own plans . . . I was of the opinion

that any action taken against the Germans could only lead to useless bloodshed . . .[71]

Once in Italy, the Commander-in-Chief stayed in touch by radio with his Chief-of-Staff, through whom he sought to continue to advise Gen. Boor. One directive did get through. The Underground leadership was ordered to divide itself into two sections. One section, under Boor, was to stay in being and to lead the Rising. The other section, under Boor's deputy, Bear Cub, was to take one third of HQ staff and the top civilian echelons of the Secret State and go into deep hiding. They were to merge with the passive elements of the Capital's population; they were to avoid all aspects of the fighting; and they were not to emerge unless their comrades in the active section were killed, captured, or otherwise disabled.[72] The text of the directive leaves no doubt that the Commander-in-Chief was taking practical precautions against the expected Soviet Occupation of Warsaw.

Yet, as the Commander-in-Chief would later discover, the rest of his communications were either blocked or filtered. His despatch to Boor from Ancona on 25 July, for example, was reacting to news of the round-up of the Home Army in Vilno and the formation of the Polish Committee of National Liberation. 'Moscow', it said, 'has chosen the path of violence, pressure and faits accomplis.' It reached its destination in Warsaw with three days' delay, and shorn of three offending passages. One of these had read: 'In the light of the rapid advances of the Soviet Occupation, it is imperative to strive for the preservation of the biological substance of the nation, given the double threat of extermination.' The censoring had been done by his own colleagues.[73] His despatch to Boor from 'the Italian Front' on 28 July was reacting to the news that the Home Army had been put in a state of readiness. It contained the sentence: 'an armed rising would be an act devoid of political sense, capable of causing needless victims.'[74] It was not forwarded, because it contravened the Government's decision taken without his paricipation three days earlier. According to the record, it was not even deciphered and read until 1 August. The culprit, without doubt, was Tabor.

Salamander's mission to Poland in the spring of 1944, though much discussed, remains one of the most mysterious episodes in the history of the Underground. Readers of his biography are invited to believe that this super-*éminence grise* was solely responsible for the scheme to fly him into Nazi-occupied Europe and that his sole purpose was to test political opinion in the occupied country. Any assessment must take several known facts into consideration. One: Salamander left London for Bari in Italy in January 1944, but did not get a flight until April. Two: with the exception of the Premier, he left without telling anyone in the exiled Government or their Supreme Command where he was going or what he was doing. Three: on the flight to Poland, organized by SOE, he wore a mask to conceal his identity. Four: the flight did not go to one of the more usual dropping sites. Five: when in Poland, Salamander was the object of an assassination attempt. Six: when he finally arrived back in London, his very first visitor was the Foreign Secretary, Anthony Eden. Seven: as revealed in official British documents many years later, he was an MI6 'asset': that is, whilst not a formal employee, he was regarded as a valuable source of information. Eight: thanks to his diplomatic tour in Moscow in 1941, he was personally acquainted with the top Soviet leaders, especially Molotov. Nine: he was in favour of Polish–Soviet reconciliation.

Salamander must have been acutely aware of the political crisis that was looming at the turn of 1943–44. The Red Army was driving inexorably westwards. The frontier question remained unresolved. Moscow was schooling its own Polish clients for a possible takeover. And, as the Germans were driven back, the Polish Underground was planning a rising. Yet the Soviet Union had broken off relations. So much was public knowledge. What is more, ever since his years as Sikorski's secretary, Salamander had made no secret of his advocacy for Polish–Soviet reconciliation. One might have thought him an excellent candidate not only for sounding out like-minded people back home, but also for preparing some sort of a solution.

When he belatedly wrote to the President to explain his sudden departure, he said that it was 'the British' who had insisted on keeping his mission secret. 'The British' almost certainly meant MI6. But what game were MI6, and their political masters in the Foreign Office, playing? One can only speculate. (Speculation is no sin.)

At the turn of 1943–44, the Foreign Office was being fed two contradictory stories about Polish–Soviet relations. The British Embassy in Moscow was passing on the Soviet line, which held that the Polish people were longing to be liberated by the Red Army, and that the only obstacle lay with the exiled Government and its reactionary policies. The exiled Government, in contrast, was telling them something completely different.

August 1944

Barnes Lodge, King's Langley

The Prudential Building, Warsaw

Britain's First Allies

Gen. Sikorski, †1943

The President

Premier 'Mick'

The Commander-in-Chief

Gen. Tatar, 'Tabor'

Count Raczyński, Ambassador (left), with Foreign Minister Romer

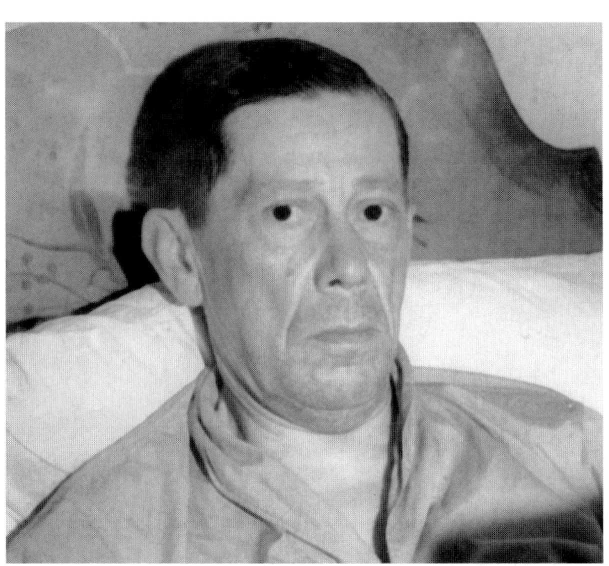

'Salamander', convalescent after poisoning

Poland's British Allies

Anthony Eden, Foreign Secretary

Colin Gubbins, Head of SOE

Air Marshal Sir John Slessor

Sgt. John Ward RAF, the only Briton in Warsaw

Moscow's Polish Servants

Marshal Konstanty Rokossovsky

Gen. Zygmunt Berling

Bolesław Bierut

Comrade 'Vyeslav' (Gomulka)

Pre-war Warsaw

The Cracow Faubourg

The Saxon Palace

October 1939

Adolf Hitler in Warsaw

German troops on Uyazdov Avenue

Nazi Barbarity

Street execution

The Nazi-built Ghetto at Cool Street

The Warsaw Ghetto Tragedy

Round-up at gunpoint

The Ghetto Rising, April 1943

Polish Forces in Britain

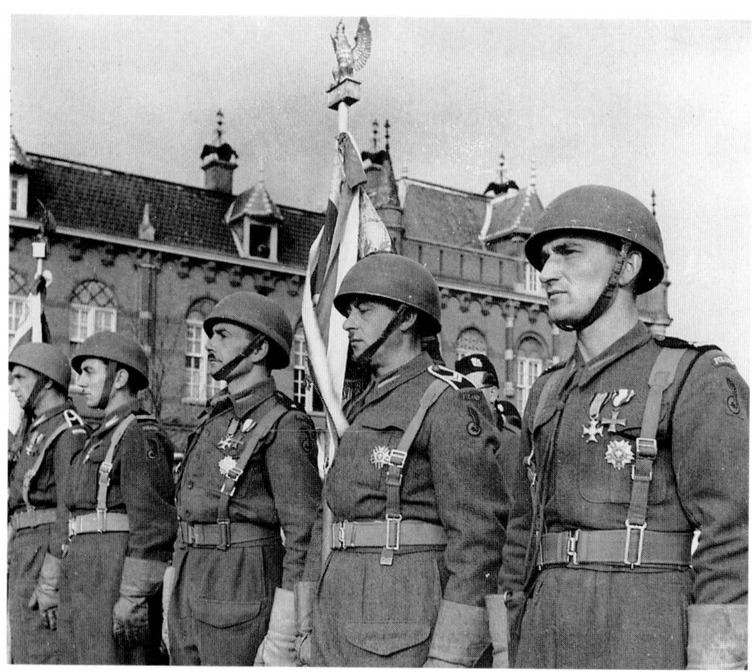

The Polish Parachute Brigade, trained to fly to Warsaw

The 1st (Polish) Armoured Division

Soviet Forces Heading West

Rokossovsky, Victor of Stalingrad

Gunners of Berling's 1st (Polish) Army

The Secret Home Army

On patrol in the countryside

The 'Bashta' Battalion on exercises

above: Presenting the standard (27th Volhynian Infantry Division)

right: Maj. 'Gloomy', one of SOE's 'Dark and Silent'

The Allied Coalition

London, 5 August 1940: signing of the Anglo-Polish Treaty

Teheran, 1943: the Big Three: Churchill and Roosevelt give Stalin secret assurances

London, 1943–44: the Exiled Polish Government

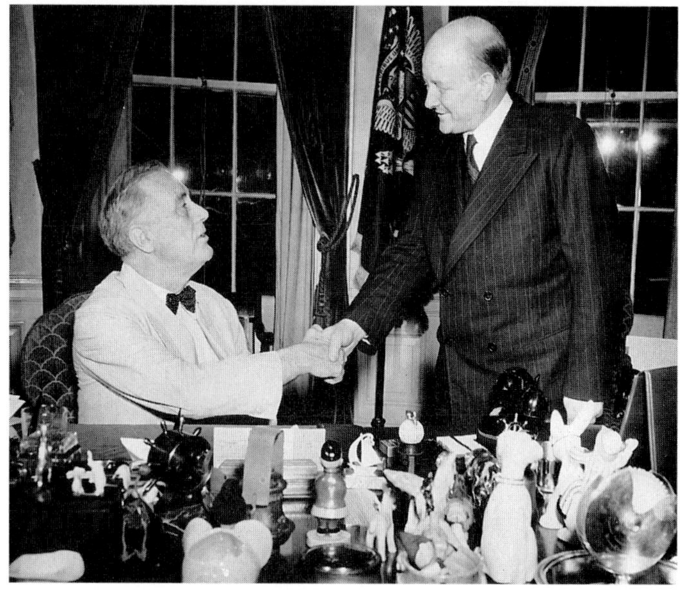

Washington, June 1944: FDR to Premier 'Mick',
'Your country will emerge undiminished'

Anti-German Risings, August 1944

Paris

Slovakia

Polish circles in London were thought notorious for their tall tales about Soviet camps and Soviet mass murders and for their obstinate conviction that few of their compatriots were disposed to welcome the Soviets. So an independent figure had to go to find out where the truth really lay. And who was better qualified than Salamander? Put another way, he was being sent behind the backs of the exiled Government to report on the veracity of their statements. In particular, he would have been asked to explore three aspects: the level of popular support for the Communist and pro-Communist organizations; the chances of cooperation between the Communists and the democratic parties; and the likely reaction of the population to the outbreak of a Rising. It is a credible scenario.

Salamander waited for a flight from Bari for three months. His presence was not advertised. The delay was blamed improbably on poor weather. In the end, he boarded an SOE plane at Bari on 22 April, and six hours later, he jumped into the dawn, landing safely. He was met by a personal welcome party, who spirited him off for tasks and destinations about which his companions on the flight could not even guess. The known details of his activities in Poland do not add up to much. At some point, he took up residence in Warsaw and talked to the Underground leaders. He met Gen. Boor. He met the Government Delegate, Sable, and other political figures, who could only have repeated what they had already relayed to London. For a time, he was provided with a bodyguard by the AK security services, which saw him installed in a safe house. There is nothing in the record to show that he made contact with the Communists, though both Boleslas B. and Comrade Vyeslav were holed up in the vicinity. They would certainly have known who he was, and would certainly have had the means, through intermediaries, to arrange a meeting. Yet the Communists represented a tiny isolated minority, and they had little scope for independent action. Their first instinct would have been to refer all enquiries to Moscow.

Salamander's personal papers, which have survived in part in London, confirm that he met Boor and Sable. They confirm the impression that the Gestapo knew of his arrival. And they confirm that he resented being thought of as a spy. 'I have always been opposed to the idea of professional intelligence . . .' he wrote, '[and] for this reason, I have encountered the hostility of the Intelligence Service or Deuxième Bureau of every country with which I have been familiar.'[75] Nonetheless, there are indications that he was specially interested in the strength of the Underground, and that his assessment was not entirely favourable. 'Poland was Polish at night' was one comment. The role of the NSZ and the Peasant Party was noted, but not, apparently, the presence of the Communists. In comments that seem to have been recorded at a later date, he was impressed by the authority of the Secret State in civilian matters, but not to any obvious degree by the military capacity of the Home Army. He estimated that 27 per cent of British agents sent to Poland had been put out of circulation. The orders of the Home Army Command were accepted by 40 per cent of adults of military age in Warsaw, but by a mere 5 per cent of the population as a whole.[76]

The attempt to kill Salamander was undertaken by a young woman who was acting on the direct orders of her Home Army superiors. By her own account, she had already executed a score of Nazis and collaborators; but she was never told the exact grounds on which she was ordered to eliminate them. As she later recalled, her orders on this occasion came directly from Boor's intelligence chief, Heller, though the point has been fiercely contested. At all events, there is little doubt that the attempt took place, and that the chosen method was poison. The would-be executioner gained entry to Salamander's apartment, laced a bottle of medicine that she found, and withdrew to observe the effects. The would-be victim duly returned, drank his medicine, and fell violently ill. But since he recovered, he suspected nothing more than a stomach bug. Shortly afterwards, however, he was struck down with polyneuritis, an acute condition which can follow poisoning and is marked by paralysis of the arms and legs.[77] His mission, whatever it was, was over. Friends deposited him under a false name in a German clinic, where he was cared for by a sympathetic Polish doctor, and where he no doubt pondered his chances of survival. After six months of desultory intelligence-gathering, MI6 was no wiser than before about what it wanted to know.

Fortune, however, grinned. It was Salamander's good luck that in July 1944 SOE was planning a special flight to take out the V2 rocket which the Home Army had captured. Exceptionally, it was a flight where the plane would have to land. So the paralysed *éminence grise* was added to the cargo list. The conditions were strict. The crew was told that the dismantled rocket had to be taken on board at all costs. Their next priority was to bring out the Underground engineer who had supervised the technical examination of the rocket. The paralytic was given the lowest priority. He was due to be carried on the back of a young soldier, who would also travel with him, but if their disabilities were in any way to obstruct the plane's departure, they were to be left behind.

The airfield chosen for the operation was one abandoned by the Germans in southern Poland. It had been given the code-name of 'Butterfly', and all the passengers [had] gathered in secret quarters nearby . . . The flight could not be fixed for a definite night, because of the weather.

On 25 July, the weather report at 8 p.m. was good enough for a Dakota to take off from Brindisi . . . The crew was British, but the pilot was a New Zealander, while the co-pilot and interpreter were Poles . . .

The flight was uneventful, yet the whole operation was nearly called off. The Eastern Front now ran through the very centre of Poland, and the territory still in German hands was crowded with units retreating westward . . . Two German Storch reconnaissance planes landed on the airstrip. They took off again shortly afterwards, but there was no certainty that they would not return . . .

Twice the Dakota had to overfly the landing-ground which it lit up in the sharp glare of its twin searchlights, and when it climbed after its first unsuccessful run, the roar of its engines shattered the night silence. When it finally landed, it was surrounded by a crowd of underground soldiers and of local boys, some of them barefoot . . .

Haste was necessary. The incoming passengers climbed out and vanished into the night, and then the westbound group began to get aboard. . . . The engines roared, the aircraft vibrated, moved a few inches and stopped. . . . The wheels had sunk in and made take-off impossible.

After discussing matters with the despatch officer, [the pilots] ordered all the passengers to get out and the baggage to be unloaded . . . The soldiers of the reception team were ordered to dig small trenches in front of the aircraft's wheels and fill them with straw.

Once this was done, [Salamander] was again carried on board, the bag of V2 parts was loaded, the remaining passengers climbed in and the luggage was thrown in behind them. The shrieking engines rang out over the slumbering fields, and must have awakened every German for miles around . . . The plane still refused to move . . .

The crew was now faced with the prospect of following instructions to set fire to the aircraft, if take-off was not possible. But . . .

> [the officers] decided to make one more attempt. The soldiers laid boards under the wheels. For a third time, the wretched passengers were told to board . . . The short July night was beginning to brighten into dawn.
>
> This time, at last, the Dakota began to move. Its take-off was accompanied by the joyful shouts of the soldiers who ran alongside waving their weapons and caps.
>
> The flight to Brindisi was without incident. But, . . . on take off, believing the brakes to have jammed, they had cut the cables . . . They landed at Brindisi without brakes.[78]

At Brindisi, Salamander and two others left the flight. The Dakota was repaired, and flew off to London, via Rabat and Gibraltar, arriving on the 28th. According to his own account, the emissary carrying the V2 bag was approached by two British officers who threatened to shoot him if he did not surrender the bag immediately. 'Mr Churchill has been waiting for this package for several days,' they said. The emissary drew a knife, told them that the bag was destined for his own superiors, and retorted: '*We* have been waiting for Mr Churchill for four years.'[79]

Meanwhile, the paralysed Salamander was deposited in the base commander's quarters at Brindisi. A British woman auxiliary (FANY), attached to SOE's Polish Section, was ordered to tend to his needs:

> It was all terribly hush, hush. The commander of the base [Terry Roper-Caldbeck] asked me to look after a visitor, who was not at all well. I was told that the visitor had polio, but I didn't even know that he was a Pole until afterwards, let alone who he was. In those days, one didn't talk about those things, and certainly didn't chat. He was with us for twenty-four hours, and was said to be on a mission to Churchill . . . I had to help him eat . . . He couldn't even walk . . . And he had this enormous sergeant with him . . . I was scared, I can tell you . . . I kept my revolver, a Luger, on the table . . .[80]

Salamander was not on a mission to Churchill. He was hoping to meet his own Prime Minister, Mick, who would soon be passing through Egypt on his way to meet Stalin in Moscow. So, after the briefest convalescence, he flew off again for Cairo.[81]

The last leg of his mission took him back to London. Twenty hours of flying in a bumpy, unheated Liberator must have been a major ordeal for an exhausted and paralysed man. But he made it. A luxurious apartment in the Dorchester Hotel was waiting. So, too, was the British Foreign Secretary. Their conversation does not appear to have been recorded. But it cannot have differed much from Salamander's talk with the Premier. The exiled Government was not exaggerating. The Soviets were well nigh impossible to deal with. The Polish people were no more eager to be occupied by the Communists than by the fascists. So the one gleam of hope lay in the Premier's appointment with Stalin.

Contact between the Home Army and the advancing Soviet fronts was first established in Volhynia in February. Spearheads of Rokossovsky's First Byelorussian Front briefly encountered elements of the AK's 27th Infantry Division, and the local military commanders agreed the principle of tactical cooperation. Large-scale confrontation did not occur until early July, when Operation Tempest was put into full operation. Apart from the 27th Division in Volhynia, which numbered some 6,000 soldiers, under Lt.Col. 'Oliva', the two formations most actively engaged were, the consolidated Vilno Brigade of 12,000 men under Col. 'Wolf' in the north, and the 5th Infantry Division of 11,000 men under Col. 'Yanka' to the south. These formations were far inferior to the vast German and Soviet forces deployed around them, but they were strong enough to make their presence felt in local sectors.

In view of later developments, it was misleading when the very first contacts between the AK and the Soviets proved unexpectedly positive. On 23 March, Boor was able to inform London that the deputy AK commander in Volhynia had been received by Soviet officers 'with demonstrative cordiality'. Three days later, Oliva succeeded in signing a detailed memorandum of cooperation with Gen. Sergeev, in which the 27th Division was described as a unit owing allegiance to its higher authorities in Warsaw and London. This memorandum would have been known to Gen. Tabor and was the inspiration for his optimistic remarks in Washington. Critics point out that clause five of the memorandum, which stated clearly that 'the Soviet Command will not allow any partisan units in their rear', was foolishly ignored by the Polish side.[82]

Of course, as soon as the Soviet Army occupied a district, the NKVD were not far behind. Their first task was to find out what underground units might be present. In this connection, a fascinating document was drawn up on 15 July in Vilno by Col. Serov, the head of NKVD forces, for immediate despatch to Beria and Stalin. Serov's report, relates everything from the weapons and uniforms of the Home Army to the attitude of the local population. But its most interesting characteristic is that practically every detail is either false or skewed. It starts by wrongly giving Col. Wolf's surname as Kasplitski, and by saying that during the German occupation 'he arrived here illegally from Warsaw by aeroplane as a representative of the London Government.' Its description of the Home Army men's appearance, was, to say the least, curious:

> All soldiers of this Polish Army are dressed in uniforms *of the Polish-German type* [translator's italics], with epaulettes and marks of rank; and they wear either *konfederatki* or forage caps on their heads, the majority with an eagle badge, and with a red-and-white brassard on their arms . . . Every soldier carries a printed certificate that he is a member of the Polish Home Army and belongs to a particular unit . . . The population (Polish) behaves in a very favourable and friendly fashion to these units; many of them wear a white and yellow cockade, the sign of a Polish patriot.[83]

Serov invented his own explanation of the fact that the Home Army commander had taken care to obtain a written recommendation from the Soviet general, with whom he had recently cooperated:

> I, General Bielkin, confirm that the Polish soldiers fought well in the capture of Vilno. I express the gratitude of the [Soviet] Army. The [Polish] Brigade has earned the right to benefit from all necessary privileges.[84]

Serov thought that the recommendation was being used for some ulterior purpose, such as the claim that Vilno had been captured in a joint operation. It never struck him that it might have been obtained to defend the brigade against himself. He concluded by reporting that the NKVD regiments in the district totalled 12,000 men.

Nothing could better illustrate the mindset of the Stalinist bureaucracy. Everyone outside their own closed world was an alien and a potential enemy. The Germans were enemies; and these Poles had just arrived from the German-dominated planet. Ergo, the Poles and the Germans were essentially the same sort of alien, and must be wearing the same type of 'Polish-German' uniforms. Ergo, Polish resistance leaders could not be really engaged in resistance, and were free to fly around Nazi-occupied Europe in aeroplanes which they had presumably borrowed from the Luftwaffe. Or perhaps the Home Army possessed its own air force, for which the Germans provided the facilities. The flight was inevitably 'illegal', since it had no clearance from the NKVD. Serov did not question that Wolf had been sent by the exiled Government in London. But he did not make the connection that London was the capital of Great Britain; that Great Britain was at war with Germany; and hence, that the exiled Government might be a British ally that was also at war with Germany. To the Soviet mind, the only war that counted was the 'Great Patriotic War'. Ergo, anywhere beyond the Eastern Front must be in a state of relative peace. So there was no more problem in flying from London to Warsaw in 1943 or 1944 than in flying from Warsaw to Lithuania.[85] One can read it in black and white.

Since Soviet intelligence was obliged to rely on analysis of this sort, it is not difficult to see how decision-making in Moscow must often have been based on false premises. But it is also fair to say that most British and American officials were little better informed. They, too, had serious problems in grasping the realities of a different world. They were pushing their First Ally to reconcile itself to a system whose outlook was so completely at odds with their own. Even the Poles who had been born in the Tsarist Empire and who could speak Russian were constantly taken aback by the apparently senseless hostility of the Soviet formations whom they met. [**NKVD**, p. 222]

In this situation, Operation Tempest appears to have been doomed before it began. The Home Army commanders were obliged to reveal their units to the Soviets. The Soviet military could welcome their appearance, and use their services. But the NKVD would treat them with the utmost suspicion. The AK's Vilno Brigade, for example, made contact with Gen. Bielkin, and on 12–13 July mounted an assault on the Germans, playing their part in the capture of the city. They participated in a parade, which was led by a Red Army man, a Berling trooper, and an AK soldier, and for a couple of days, whilst Serov was preparing his report, they circulated freely. Then, suddenly, they were ordered to attend a meeting outside the city, and found themselves surrounded. They were unceremoniously disarmed at gunpoint. The officers were separated from the men. The former were marched off under guard; the latter were told that they were being sent to join Berling's Army. The AK's 5th Division experienced something very similiar following the capture of Lvuv on 27 July.

The fate of the 27th Volhynian Division was somewhat more protracted. In the spring, it had been a formidable force of some 10,000 men

NKVD

A Home Army unit meets 'friends of friends' outside Warsaw

. . . the first T34s rumbled by the manor house. It was the spearhead of the 117th Stalin Guards Armoured Brigade . . . Meeting the Russian front-line troops was like meeting comrades-in-arms . . . [But] if one touched on non-military subjects, an invisible wall would arise.

Except for the tanks, all the heavy equipment was American, visibly stamped 'U.S.A.'. The Russian explanation invariably was that they had stamped the equipment in this way because it was being shipped to the USA to help the war effort . . . It was no use trying to convince them [otherwise].

After the armour, the infantry came like lice, a mass of men moving on foot along every road and track. And with the rear echelons came the NKVD. The soldiers then stopped talking altogether . . .

[Our] rendezvous before crossing the mountains had been fixed for 1600 hours in a forester's hut. Our sentries reported that a Russian major had come . . . with a message inviting all officers of [our] 2nd Division to attend a special meeting . . . 'Raven' asked me to accompany him [because] I spoke Russian . . .

At about 1930 we arrived at the [Soviet] Command Post. Two officers met us, both in field-brown uniform with NKVD collar flashes . . . They introduced themselves as *Politruks* . . . The older, a tall stout Jew, mentioned that he was from Bialystock in the north-east of Poland. The younger was from Kharkhov in Ukraine.

At once they asked Raven why the other [AK] officers . . . had not come. Raven explained that orders had been received to move to the German side of the front. The Russians did not like this at all.

One of the runners sat behind me and Raven's runner stood under a nearby tree. Light was provided by a candle stuck in the neck of a bottle. Armed men could be seen moving around like ghosts. We were offered vodka. Raven [lied], saying that we were not used to drinking on duty . . . Cigarettes were then passed around, [amid comments about] their high quality and low price in Russia.

The elder of the two Russians was trying to pump us about . . . our numbers, equipment, ammunition, morale, and social class . . . And the younger [one] would interject questions about the Germans . . . With great aplomb, I told them that the Home Army was very well equipped from air-drops with PIAT anti-tank weapons. I told them that officers and other ranks all belonged to the working or peasant class . . . We implied that every battalion was in touch with Raven who in turn was in direct contact with London four times a day. (Actually the contact was via the Dawn Station somewhere in Sweden.) . . .

Then they changed tactics. 'Would you be willing to recognize the Lublin Committee [which is] truly representative of the masses?'

'We know nothing of the Lublin Committee. We obey orders from the Polish government in London.'

'But can you imagine fighting side by side with us without being under our command and members of General Berling's Polish Army?'

'The [former plan] has been superseded by an order to go to the rescue of Warsaw . . .' I answered.

A plane droned overhead. The lights went out. I waited to pull my boot up. A torch at once shone on my hands.

The Russians now produced a huge poster [showing] twelve members of the Lublin Committee.

'Do you know who he is? And this one?' And so on.

'We do not know any of them,' I said. 'But [wait] . . . [This] looks like an inmate from the Holy Cross Jail. I hope I'm wrong.'

On and on it went. The tension was becoming unbearable. Eventually one last question was put: 'And if we give you an explicit command to join us, what will you do?'

'We have our orders. And if you don't mind, we have to leave . . .'

A heavy silence fell, broken only by the occasional explosion of heavy German artillery shells in the distance. The corner of my eye caught the slight movement of my runner's hand towards the safety catch of his Sten. My own fingers slid to the safety catch of my Udet . . . If we have to go, I thought, the two of them will go first.

The two NKVD men looked at each other in silence for what seemed like an eternity. Eventually, the older one said, '*Nu chtosh. Puskay yedut.*' (Well, nothing. Let them go!)

We all shook hands and said a very formal goodbye . . . We mounted our horses. Unaccompanied, we galloped into the darkness of the forest.[1]

---

supported by cavalry and artillery. Mobile and well-armed, it had fought a pitched battle with the *Waffen-SS* in the vicinity of Kovel. Its commander, Oliva, was killed and much of its heavy equipment was lost. But it was not broken, and was able to withdraw in good order. After seeking in vain to replace its lost weapons from the Soviets, it decided on a fighting withdrawal to the west, moving in the dangerous no-man's-land that separated retreating Germans from the advancing Soviets. The country was covered with alternating forest and marshland. The few villages of the region were either burned to the ground or full of Germans. Supplies ran short. Constant skirmishes were fought both at the front and the rear. At one point a strong German anti-partisan expeditionary force was narrowly avoided. At another, on the edge of the Pripet Marshes, they were fired on and trapped by the Soviets. After 300km (190 miles), and eight weeks, some 6,000 stragglers crossed the River Bug and entered the province of Lublin.

The 27th no doubt hoped to find refuge in Lublin. The peasants were friendly. Numerous other AK units were operating. Warsaw was on the horizon. As luck would have it, however, they arrived in the same week as Rokossovsky. Hostile Communist partisans were emboldened by the Red Army. On 24 July, the 27th engaged a group of Germans. And they liberated a couple of towns. Moving on, they suddenly found themselves surrounded. They had walked into a Soviet trap. Their radio operator had no time to encode the message that was picked up at Barnes Lodge *en clair*. 'They are disarming us. They are approaching us . . .' The last substantial unit from the east had been eliminated. Once again, they had fallen not to the Germans, but to 'the ally of the allies'. In little more than a week, 20–30,000 Home Army soldiers had been removed from the scene.

As usual, streams of reports from the NKVD were flowing back to Moscow. Yet the language was shifting. In his report of 15 July, Serov had used the proper name 'Polish Home Army'. But now, Stalin had issued the decree that had made his displeasure plain. So now the NKVD reports talked disparagingly of 'White Poles', 'illegal formations', 'rebels', and most frequently, 'bandits'.

Events were moving extremely fast. Key decisions had to be made before the full significance of the developments could be clarified. The AK Command in Warsaw felt obliged to recommend adoption of the plan for a 'Battle for Warsaw' on 21 July, only days after the first major round-up in Vilno had occurred. The critical meeting of Premier Mick's Cabinet on 25 July, when the decision was taken to approve Boor's plan, took place *before* the reservations of the Commander-in-Chief were received, *before* news of the 27th Division's fate had come in, and four days *before* the attempted round-up of the 5th Division. In any case, Premier Mick was swayed at this juncture by two particular considerations:

by the hope that the Soviets might behave with greater generosity on territory which Moscow regarded as Polish, and by the conviction that nothing could be resolved without a face-to-face meeting with Stalin. For this reason, he had given absolute priority to his journey to Moscow, and had left London in haste without waiting for all the loose ends to be tied up.

Nonetheless, the dramatic SOS from the 27th Division at the moment of its disarming could not fail to make a strong impression in London. It came too late to influence Premier Mick's Cabinet. But it provided suitable ammunition for urgent intervention with the Western powers. On 26 July, the Polish Ambassador in London requested an interview with Churchill. Instead, he was granted a short meeting with Anthony Eden, deputizing for the PM, on the following day.

> I raised the matter of the disarming of the 27th (Volhynian) DI of the AK, handing Mr Eden a memorandum about it. The Foreign Secretary replied that he would take it up with [Soviet] Ambassador Gusev . . .[86]

Next, the Count returned to his frequent earlier requests regarding assistance from the RAF for the Polish Underground, but with explicit reference to Warsaw. Lastly, he moved to the important matter of combatant rights, which the Home Army wished to secure before engaging in battle with the Germans:

> The Foreign Secretary took note of the AK Commander's argument for a radio broadcast to be transmitted [by the BBC] in German and Polish with a view to guaranteeing combatant rights for AK soldiers fighting the Germans, and threatening retaliation if the German authorities perpetrated further atrocities . . . It was evident that this last point aroused doubts on the British side, which has found itself in difficulties more than once with games of this sort . . .[87]

The meeting closed after Eden had expressed his 'strong displeasure' that American news agencies had released details of Premier Mick's journey to Moscow. Eden complained that this 'indiscretion could provoke a brutal reaction from the Soviet Government.'[88] Whether or not he knew that Tabor was about to meet the leaders of SOE in a totally different climate is a matter of conjecture.

In the light of subsequent developments, or lack of them, one may assume that Eden did not pursue the Ambassador's points with any great energy. But he did order one of his subordinates to reply immediately, and in the negative, to his request for RAF support, and to give noncommittal answers to his other requests. The letter, written on 28 July, says nothing new about British policy. It would not be remarkable but for the fact that it refers unmistakably to 'A Rising in Warsaw'.[89] It destroys at a stroke all later claims that the Western powers had not been informed about the Rising in advance. (See Appendix 16.)

The last week of July 1944 was, for the leaders of the Resistance in Warsaw, the week of painful decision. Responsibility for launching the 'Battle for Warsaw' had been thrust onto their shoulders; and none of the available options was particularly attractive. To judge from the evidence of Operation Tempest, doing nothing was to invite automatic defeat. Yet to launch a rising which the Germans were able to crush would be catastrophic.

Underground leaders had to think deeply about what 'success' actually meant. They certainly could not hope to smash the Wehrmacht single-handedly. At the most, they could aim to seize the city, or large parts of it, and then to hold on for long enough to allow other critical developments to occur. They estimated that five to seven days would suffice. Within that time, the Premier should be able to strike a deal with Stalin in Moscow. The Western powers should be able to fly in arms, and possibly reinforcements. The Underground authorities would be able to come into the open and establish their own administration. And the Soviet Army would be in position to mount the conclusive assault and to drive the Germans from the scene.

Thought had equally to be given to the consequences of a delayed result. What would happen if the planned five to seven days were to be prolonged to ten days or even twenty? Logically, a prolongation would give more time for the Premier to negotiate in Moscow, more time for the West to organize assistance, more time for the Underground to consolidate their administration, and more time for the Soviet build-up to assume dominant proportions. On the other hand, it would also give the Germans space to organize their counter-measures and it would stretch Underground resources to the limit. It was hard to imagine the Home Army holding out for two to three weeks. [**RECRUIT**, p. 228]

Much had happened in the preceding days. The Soviet Army had raced to the Vistula and beyond. The PKWN had been set up in Helm, and was claiming general authority over the liberated areas. Reports were multiplying of resistance units being disarmed. The number of SOE missions was increasing. The world was digesting the news about the bomb plot on the *Führer*'s life at Rastenburg. The Nazi giant was reeling. Its enemies rejoiced. The psychological pressure for striking another blow and for adding to Germany's discomfiture was enormous.

Anyone who analysed the Home Army's predicament would have identified four or five major considerations. Each factor played its part in the total equation. None was a determinant in itself.

For one thing, the civilian population was restless. There were fears that they might take matters into their own hands. After nearly five years of Nazi occupation, many people were longing for revenge. They had not reacted on the 29th when the Germans called for 100,000 recruits to report for ditch-digging. But they might not stay passive indefinitely. The mood was volatile.

For another, the Communists were plotting some sort of action of their own. The Home Army had no means of learning the Communist plans – and historians have had little more luck. But it was reasonable to suspect that they were in contact with the PKWN and that Moscow's repeated appeals for a popular rising were mainly directed at them. On the 29th, the military wing of the Communist PPR was renamed the 'People's Army'; and on the 30th, posters in the streets appeared denouncing the exiled Government as usurpers. For the time being, no one in Warsaw took much notice. But delay could work to the Communists' advantage. In which case, all hopes for building a democratic country would be lost.

Western reactions to the Rising were very difficult to predict. By late July, the Home Army leaders were aware that the British had shown no enthusiasm for requests to fly in the Polish Parachute Brigade or to bomb German airfields. The logistics were simply too difficult. And Novak was on his way from London to confirm depressing news that Polish affairs were not a top priority in Anglo-American eyes. He was to warn them that a Warsaw Rising would be seen as a 'storm in a teacup'. On the other hand, Underground leaders in touch with Tabor had grounds to think that

RECRUIT

A Jewish lad, who had escaped from the Ghetto, joins the Home Army

I was born in Warsaw on 6 May 1925 to a well-to-do Polish-Jewish family. My parents and my older and only sister perished in the Holocaust. I attended secondary school in Lodz. A few days after the war broke out, we left Lodz and proceeded by car eastwards to the vicinity of Ruvno, where our relatives owned a large estate . . . We never reached [our destination] . . .

We arrived in the Warsaw Ghetto before the Germans started mass liquidations. Life was still bearable and people with means could survive. I continued my last year of secondary school in one of the Underground schools, and even took some exams. At the same time I worked, first in a German factory that assembled Astra adding machines in the Ghetto, and later on . . . in a work gang outside the Ghetto. We left early in the morning every day and returned in the afternoon . . . The important thing was that we were fed and it kept me in very good physical condition.

In January 1943, the Germans rounded up my parents, my sister, and myself, and took us to the *Umschlagplatz* . . . There the SS separated me from my family, beat me up, and put me in a transport to one of the concentration camps. The freight train was standing in the Danzig Railway Station. We were pushed into the freight cars and were so tightly packed it was impossible to move or breathe. Near the roof of the car I noticed a small opening that was narrow but not fastened . . . I decided that whatever the consequences, if I could squeeze through that opening, I would jump out . . .

After a few hours, around four or five o'clock in the morning, the train at last started moving . . . We had travelled maybe fifteen minutes when it stopped. At that moment I pulled myself up and with great difficulty squeezed through the opening. Everyone in the wagon tried to stop me, fearing reprisals by the Germans, but I was too quick and in a few seconds I was outside and jumped . . .

First I lay under the train. It was a cold winter's day, but the snow was not very deep. I observed the SS combing the field round the train with searchlights. As soon as they changed direction, I ran a couple of hundred metres in record time . . .

When the train left, I got up and started to walk in the direction of some woods. After a few minutes I came to a small chapel and went in. Later in the morning I walked towards some houses. I knocked on a door. A farmer came out and I asked him the way to Warsaw. He invited me in, served breakfast, and didn't ask any questions – he understood. Afterwards he took me to a small train station. Within twenty minutes I was in the centre of Warsaw . . .

In Warsaw, I went to see a very close friend of my sister . . . Within a few hours, she arranged for me to stay with an aunt of hers who was of German origin and above suspicion . . . This woman organised papers, lodging and work, and my first contact with the Underground . . . At first I was only doing sabotage on railway equipment . . . [But] after [four] months, I was transferred to Lt. 'Wildcat''s Cherniakov combat team. This meant that I had passed the initiation. The unit which I joined was one of the [Home Army's] Special Operation Commando units known as 'K-Div. College A' . . . We knew each other very well and became close friends . . . [But] we were all kept totally in the dark about one thing – the names and address of our superiors . . .

Sometime in mid-1943, my Home Army superior, Wildcat, approached me and asked me out of the blue if I was a Jew. For a moment I hesitated, and then confirmed it. Till then I had told everyone that I was from Lvov because my documents were from there. Wildcat explained that they had checked that my family didn't exist in Lvuv. This aroused the suspicion that I was either a Ukrainian or a Jew.

The same day Wildcat informed André, the CO of Special Operations in the Warsaw district, that I was a Jew, and asked him if the safety of the unit might be endangered, since I could be recognized . . . However, as I hadn't lived in Warsaw since the age of six, the possibility was disregarded. If I had attended school there, the risk would have been unacceptable and I would have been transferred to a partisan unit in the forest.

Wildcat asked me not to tell anyone about my being Jewish, but 'Elephant' already knew because Wildcat had questioned him, knowing we were very close. Wildcat immediately arranged new papers for me, and instead of 'Richard Zhuravski', I became 'Richard Zhukovski'.[1]

S. Aronson

---

the last word from London and Washington had yet to be spoken. The more bullish among them could guess that Western enthusiasm would increase once a Rising had been launched. It would certainly increase if the Premier reached agreement with Stalin.

German reactions were going to be brutal whatever happened. Armed resistance would provoke a massive and murderous response from the SS. On the other hand, if the Rising were timed to coincide with a Soviet assault, the SS would not have the leisure to respond as they wished. In any case, the prospects were hardly less bleak if the Germans were allowed to prepare defences uninterrupted. For their established policy throughout the retreat on the Eastern Front was to declare strong points, like Warsaw, a 'fortress', to evacuate all civilians, to dig in, and then to watch the physical destruction of the city from the ensuing bombardments. From the

Varsovians' viewpoint, to do nothing was simply to invite a different form of disaster. It was to invite a repeat of the disaster that had recently been inflicted on Minsk. [**MELECH**, p. 231]

Soviet reactions were the most inscrutable of all. The Soviet Command did not reveal their secrets to anyone; and their further intentions could only be guessed at. It was perfectly possible to argue that Rokossovsky would call a halt on the Vistula and take a breather. After all, his front-line forces were bound to be exhausted after the long slog through Byelorussia, and everyone could see that the Wehrmacht was taking steps to counter-attack. At the same time, Home Army intelligence had been counting the ceaseless procession of German hospital trains that had been rolling through Warsaw in recent months, and they had a good idea of the massive superiority in men and materiel which the Soviets had accumulated. What is more, they cannot have failed to notice how the Soviets had learned to bring their numbers to bear through a seamless strategy of rolling offensives that never let the Germans rest. From purely military calculations, therefore, it was possible to deduce that Rokossovsky would not wish to tarry on the Vistula, but would prefer to draw on his seemingly endless reserves and to exploit the bridgeheads that he had already created. It was not for nothing that the Home Army analysts had concluded that the appearance of Soviet armour on Warsaw's eastern approaches would herald an assault.

As for Stalin, his reactions or non-reactions lay far above the field of vision of local military commanders. He did not have to be swayed by the advice of his own marshals, let alone by the dispositions of an ally of allies on just one sector of one front. The Polish Resistance leaders had seen how Stalin had shown no generosity during Operation Tempest when their colleagues had approached the Soviets in a spirit of partnership. So their chances of a better outcome could hardly be further reduced if they now aimed to deal from a position of local strength. If the whole democratic world were to learn that the Polish capital had been recaptured by Polish democrats, Stalin would really be straining the Grand Alliance if he subsequently tried to dislodge them by force.

Such was the sum total of knowledge and surmise when the General Staff of the Home Army met for its final deliberations in the last days of July. The first of their key meetings, on the morning of the 29th, was with members of the Council of National Unity, the Underground parliament. In effect, the military were asking the democratic representatives to legitimize the proposed Rising. They received unanimous consent.

MELECH

A Warsaw journalist, who has been trying to learn English, starts a diary

'It came nearly the time, when the Germans dis-continued to be here as the masters, though they were never the [real] master on Polish territory . . . I remember very well the speech of Dr. Frank in 1939 year, who took office in [General Government] . . . He said: 'Germans will never leave these terrains. Sooner the ground will fall down than Germans will go out from here.' *Tempora mutantur!* . . . Germans fly, they fly in great disorder and panic . . .

We are ready to only fight with cruel occupant, the fight which it is not necessary to encourage, because the enemy during five years assembled such a sea of hatred which can overflow him in the moment of his defeat . . .

We shall treat the Soviet forces as the forces which fight with common enemy . . . We expect that military Soviet authorities will honour our sovereignty, from which arise the rights to the administration with freed terrains . . . From our sovereignty arise the rights of restoration of political, social, cultural and economic life, according to our own plans . . .[1]

Tuesday, the first of August, 1944

From three days, I cannot sleep, because I know that from twenty and eight July it began the hard readiness for Polish Underground Army . . . I awake myself very earlier, and think about . . . the armed action, which can follow in sooner time.

My brother [Bohdan] officer, my friends Stanislas and Vladimir D. policeman and ensign, and many, many other friends belong to the Polish army. The last week passed for them laboriously. They transported to the different important points the military implements as the grenades, ammunition, revolvers.

Today, when I left my flat and went to the town, I saw completely other life. The traffic is no great. Only through Warsaw go in the western course the German military transports. The shops are mostly shut. It is strange excitement. The strange quite before the storm . . .'[2]

The mangled grammar, curious spelling, and quaint vocabulary undoubtedly increase the peculiar eloquence of the diarist's sentiments.

The second key meeting took place two days later. The time was 6 p.m. on a sunny Monday evening. The place was a safe apartment in the very heart of Warsaw. Present, in a motley array of workmen's disguises, were the Home Army Commander, Gen. Boor, the Commander's two deputies, Bear Cub and 'Gregory', and the Head of AK's Warsaw Region, Col. Monter. The Government Delegate was waiting in an adjacent room. A notable absentee was the Head of AK Intelligence, Heller, who had been delayed by a German roadblock. Nonetheless, since the Vistula bridges were heavily guarded but still open, Monter had been able to take a bicycle that afternoon and ride out for a few miles beyond the eastern suburbs. He now reported that the Germans had abandoned several localities on the immediate periphery, and that Soviet tanks had been sighted on the road to Praga. His report was accepted. Boor concluded that the time for action had come. He advised that the state of 'stand-by' should be instituted without delay.

In his memoirs, Boor justified his decision by explaining the expected consequences of delay:

> That afternoon, a communiqué of the Wehrmacht's High Command had announced [that] the Russians had launched 'a general assault on Warsaw from the south-east.' It also said that the commander of the [German] 73rd Infantry Division, stationed across the river from Warsaw, had been taken prisoner . . . In my view, if we unleashed our struggle then, we would prevent the Germans from bringing up reserves and cut off their supply lines . . . If, on the other hand, the Germans were forced back across the river under Soviet pressure, as could be expected at any moment, their troops would crowd into the city in great numbers and would paralyse any chance of action by us. The city would become a battlefield between Germans and Russians, and would be reduced to ruins. [Hence], in my opinion, the right time for starting had arrived . . .[90]

Gen. Monter was then asked to put the necessary order into writing for distribution to his subordinates. Teams of runners were at hand to carry the order to every Underground unit in Warsaw:

> Alarm – by hand! 31 July, 1900hrs. I am fixing L-Hour for 5 p.m. on 1 August. My address, valid from L-Hour, is at 22 [Bright Street], apt 20. Acknowledge receipt of this order. X[91]

As a last step, the Chief Delegate was called in to give the order his blessing. After asking a few questions, he said: 'Very well. Go ahead!' [**IRKA I**, p. 234]

In the high summer of 1944, Paris, like Warsaw, was looking to liberation. At one level, the ferment brewing in the French capital possessed many features that were absent in the Polish capital. There were the institutions and politicians of a collaborationist Government, for example; there was a strong Communist contingent in the Resistance; and there was a powerful, 20,000-strong armed French police force, whose loyalties would be crucial. Yet in the general set-up, there were many similarities. Victorious Allied armies were approaching. The Germans were reeling. After a cruel occupation, many citizens were longing for retribution. And the resisters were hoping not only to strike the decisive blow, but also to reap the post-war political rewards. From the organizational viewpoint, however, the most interesting feature was the almost total lack of advance planning or prior consultation. The US Army, when it swept out of Normandy, had no plans whatsoever to capture Paris. Gen. Leclerc, who commanded a French armoured division under American command, had no orders to break away and to help the Parisian Resistance. Gen. de Gaulle, the head of the Free French, was abroad until the very last minute. He had reached no firm understanding either with his Vichy adversaries or with his Communist rivals. He was not yet formally recognized by the Americans as France's leader-in-waiting.[92] Objectively speaking, it might be described as being *pas mal de pagaille, un beau gâchis*, 'a bit of a shambles'. Yet there was still space for optimism. War has always been accompanied by mix-ups, messes, and confusion. Landing on Utah Beach in Normandy, Gen. Leclerc had declared:

> We wish to join up with those good French people who, for the last four years, have been carrying on the same struggle at home that we were pursuing abroad. Hail to those who have already taken to arms. Together, we constitute one and the same army, the army of Liberation.[93]

Here was a sentiment that all Varsovians would have understood. The date was 1 August 1944.

*

IRKA I

The young wife of a Home Army officer says farewell to her husband

A schoolfriend had recruited my sister and me to the Underground . . . in the winter of 1940. We were sworn in with six young girls (the youngest only twelve), as messengers for the *Information Bulletin*. After eight months, the Gestapo came to the *Bulletin*'s editorial office at night. All the workers were taken to Shuch Street and subjected to cruel interrogation. Next day we messengers were also arrested and sent to the Paviak [Jail] . . .

We ended up in a vast cell for minors, swearing that we would never admit our guilt. In a kitchen, where female prisoners peeled potatoes, we met one of our friends, Josephine K., who was frightened because, under extreme interrogation, she had incriminated us. She promised to retract her confession.

It was July 1941 before they interrogated us again. The Germans had declared war on the Soviet Union and were 'cleansing' the prison of less important prisoners. We were taken by truck to Shuch Street and were placed in the so-called 'trams', whence prisoners were summoned in turn for questioning, often returning beaten and bloodied. A wonderful guard, Sophie K., a member of the Underground, made contact with the first love of my life, André F., smuggling our love letters back and forth and informing him when I was to be interrogated. I sat in the back of the truck, André waited on a given street corner [of New World Street and Jerusalem Avenue], and in that way we were able to see each other . . . The same guard carried the holy Eucharist in a little compact to those sentenced to death or to Auschwitz . . .

My own life was saved by Josephine K., who resolutely maintained to the Gestapo that she had only given the names of her schoolfriends in order to stop being tortured. In my presence a German officer asked her if she realized that by admitting to lying she would earn more severe punishment. 'I know,' she replied, 'but I could not live knowing that I had harmed so many innocent people.' I had fallen ill in the Paviak, with inflamed lungs and tuberculosis. But all the messengers were then freed. Josephine perished in Auschwitz . . .

We then returned to my parents, who were sharing an apartment very close to the Ghetto where famine was raging. Everyday, two tiny starving urchins would visit our house to receive a bowl of hot soup and a bit of food. One day I saw something that has been burned into my memory. Walking across the square, I saw two Gestapo agents standing over a couple of emaciated boys who could hardly stand on their little legs. One of the agents grabbed the first boy by the ankles and smashed his head against the wall. Then he grabbed the other and did the same. That event affected my later life very deeply and means more than anything that I would later read about the Holocaust. From then on, our two urchins did not visit us.

On 30 July 1944, André F., whom I had married in the meantime, received an order to break off his secret military exercises with Home Army conscripts in the Kieltse region, and he returned to me in Warsaw. I was in the ninth month of pregnancy. 'Tomorrow at five in the afternoon we will start the Rising,' he said. He looked at me and our one-year-old daughter, Magdalena. I remember his every word exactly. 'I must believe that we will be victorious, but I will rest easier if I can leave you at your uncle's place' – fifty kilometres away from Warsaw. 'We do not know how the Soviet Army will behave – our parting may last a long time . . .'[1]

A writer whose diary would become a famous literary work recalled those same heady days

Tuesday 1 August 1944 was not sunny, but wet, and not too warm. In the afternoon, perhaps, I went to Cool Street – I lived at number 40 – and saw that there were lots of trams, cars, and people. Suddenly, on the corner of Iron Street, I remembered what the date was – '1 August – Sunflower Day' . . . What made me think of sunflowers? That's when they mature . . . And I was still young and sentimental. After all, those times were naive, primitive, carefree, romantic, conspiratorial. Even so, that yellow colour had to come from somewhere, perhaps from the light of the inclement weather or from its reflection on Warsaw's red trams . . .[2]

Twenty-two hours separated the departure of the Home Army runners from their Sunday afternoon meeting and the arrival of 'L-Hour'. Eight of the twenty-two would be taken up by the night curfew, when free movement in the streets was forbidden and the use of radios impossibly dangerous. Telephones were tapped and off limits. Most of the runners barely had time to go home before the curfew fell. Many were not able to inform their units of the 'stand-by' until the Monday morning. The Commander of the Bashta Battalion, for example, heard of Boor's order at 9.15 a.m. The scramble to make preparations before the 5 p.m. deadline was hectic.

Soon after the runners left, the Chief of AK Intelligence finally arrived. He was convinced that Monter's report about Soviet tanks on the road to

Praga was false. One can only imagine the sinking feeling in Gen. Boor's stomach. For the second time in as many days he had received crucial information which, if presented earlier, might have changed his decision. But, once again, it was too late. There was nothing he could do. The runners could not be recalled. The order could not be rescinded. In any case, there was no way of checking quickly whether Monter was right or wrong. From what was later learned about the Second Guards Tank Army, if its vanguard units had not been operating near Praga in the afternoon of the 31st, they were almost certainly operating there later in the day. The log of the German Ninth Army on the 30th and 31st noted that Praga had been 'exposed and defenceless' and that little progress had been made in retaking Radzymin.[94] So Monter's report, even if he had invented it, was not very wide of the mark.

Nonetheless, the deficiencies of Boor's hasty plans were soon making themselves manifest. As the Monter incident showed, there were grave gaps in intelligence. There was also a serious shortage of weapons. Many arms caches had been removed from Warsaw in preparation for a general Rising in the countryside. Barely one quarter of Boor's men could hope to go to war with a weapon in their hands. Boor's own command post was being relocated to a reinforced concrete building, where radio signals could neither be received nor sent. The insurgents were dispersed into a large number of small groups which could not easily communicate. And there was no fall-back plan if initial objectives were not achieved. It can all be made to look hopelessly incompetent. The real question is whether the flaws in Boor's dispositions were so dire that they would condemn the Rising to instant failure. Only time would tell.

No warning could be given to the civilian population. The 40–50,000 members of the AK who had been put on stand-by were sworn to secrecy. Twenty or thirty times that number of civilians were in the same fix as the Germans. They sensed that something was afoot, without knowing exactly what. As 1 August wore on, they occasionally caught sight of small bunches of youngsters gathering in courtyards or mysteriously disappearing into cellars or empty buildings. They saw intensified German patrols. But they simply didn't ask. There was little panic buying, for the simple reason that food could only be bought on ration cards and such stores as were available had been stockpiled long since. At the most, people went out for a few last-minute purchases. Rumours of an imminent Rising were not the only source of anxiety. For ordinary men and women, it was just as worrying to think that 'the Russians' might start a bombardment, or that the Germans might order an evacuation or, worst of all, both. Even when bursts of gunfire were heard in the course of the afternoon, no one paid special attention. The Germans were nervous, and were notorious for shooting at anything and everything.

The fortunes of the would-be insurgents on the eve of the Rising were far from uniform. A few received their orders early, and made for their assembly points in good time. Most received their orders late. Many took up positions at the very last moment or after the 5 p.m. deadline. Some never made it at all. 'Everything in war is simple,' wrote the great Clausewitz, 'but the simplest thing is difficult.' [**PROSPECTS**, p. 238]

Several of the units that didn't make it were outside Warsaw and unable to cross the German or Soviet cordons. One had been roaming the woods in the Holy Cross Mountains well to the south of Warsaw. A few days earlier, their commander had picked up word of Boor's state of alert on their radio, and had decided on his own initiative to join in. But the cross-country journey proved impossible. He was separated from Warsaw by the area in which the Wehrmacht was massing to contain the Soviet bridgeheads, and he counted eleven separate defence lines. In the end, after much night wandering, and repeated delays, he realized that he was in the middle of the advancing Soviets. That unit, though it escaped from the NKVD, was never able to join the Rising.[95]

In Warsaw, meanwhile, over 600 companies of AK soldiers were striving to wend their way to their muster stations as inconspicuously as possible. Some reported the street traffic to be heavy; others said it was light. All noticed the ominous air of expectation:

> In the morning, walking along the streets, I joined a strong stream of people among whom youngsters predominated. I observed the tension and seriousness in their faces. Each of them, through some detail of clothing, was trying to look like a soldier. Some were wearing officers' boots, others military belts . . . Horse-drawn carriages and rickshaws were ferrying them and their baggage in all directions . . . I was well aware that the storm was about to break in Warsaw, and that we would be defenceless. When were the Soviet forces going to enter – tomorrow?, or at the most in a couple of days' time? . . . On my way, I looked into the Church of St Charles Borromeo, where many young people were kneeling in prayer in complete silence. Outside, I met a group of youths dressed mainly in raincoats. Walking behind them, I could see from their silhouettes

PROSPECTS

Underground soldiers debate the prospects of a Rising as life in Warsaw deteriorates

By July 1944 the Front was rapidly approaching Warsaw. The inhabitants of the city watched the German troops retreat with their Hungarian toadies: not without *Schadenfreude*. Yesterday's conquerors presented a sorry sight. There was no hint of the arrogance and haughtiness so blatant in 1939 at the time of their invasion of Poland, and again in 1941 when they were preparing to attack the USSR. The Warsaw sky became the scene of repeated dogfights between German and Soviet planes. In short, it became obvious that the end of German rule in Warsaw was in sight.[1]

'Warsaw's economy is in a siege situation because supplies have been cut off,' declares the AK command. The price of basic foodstuffs is going up. And so are the prices of foreign currency on the black market. Pork belly costs 600 zloties, butter 500 zloties, dollar bills are 300–400 zloties and a dollar in gold is worth 2000 zloties. A number of shops are closed.

Today the Germans released about 150 men and 50 women from the Paviak Jail. They are mainly the sick and mothers with small children, but also doctors and nurses. During their years in the prison they were all engaged in conspiracy. They helped their co-prisoners and delivered messages from them to their relatives. Over 100 Jewish men and women from the Paviak have been transported to the nearby Goose Farm concentration camp.

On 31 July General Rainer Stahel arrived in Warsaw. He has been made directly responsible by Hitler for the defence of Warsaw's railway junctions, in case of an uprising. Stahel is considered a determined and energetic commander, who knows how to crush any insurrection. Several units were put at his disposal.[2]

In our K-Div. unit, the chances of a successful Rising against the Germans are not highly rated. 'Stan' and 'Alder' are staunchly pessimistic. We know only too well that while K-Div. possesses some light weapons, other units are very short of arms and especially of anti-tank weapons. Our Home Army, with roughly one grenade per five soldiers, has to face an enemy still armed to the teeth.

My friend, Roman M. (later known as Roman Bratny, the celebrated writer), came to see me several days before the Rising. 'Mark my words,' he said. 'The Russians will provoke an insurrection in Warsaw and when we start fighting, they'll stop their advance and let the Germans finish us off.' 'If you and I know that,' I replied, 'so must our leaders. I don't believe that an order to start a general Rising would be given without the prior approval of the British and the Soviets.'[3]

Nobody in Warsaw, during those sunny July days when we could hear the roll of artillery, was aware that the worst was still to come. Nobody dared to think that the agony of the city and its residents was only beginning.[4]

> that they were carrying guns under their coats . . . In the roadway, lorries filled with German soldiers were cruising around, ready to shoot. The fingers of the clock were moving inexorably. L-Hour was approaching.[96]

Dozens of diarists, similarly conscious of the drama, put pen to paper. Poets and balladeers, too, were at work. Would-be insurgents, waiting in their cellars and collecting centres, already had suitable songs to sing:

> The hour of revenge has resounded
> For our wrongs, our blood, our tears.
> We soldiers are summoned to fight.
> O Yezus Maria! To arms! To arms!
> The dawn sky of freedom is burning
> For our country and all that she'll be.
> As a new world is thrust into life,
> Our might will cast off slavery.[97]

As Warsaw steeled itself, SOE was busy as usual. At 7 p.m. on the last Sunday evening of July, an RAF Liberator took off from Campo Casale in southern Italy. It had a Polish captain, a Polish crew, and a passenger list of six Polish parachutists. Its destination, revealed only at the last minute, was Warsaw.

The parachutists had waited all day in the burning sun at the holding station in Lauretto. The news of their imminent takeoff barely gave them time to shed their tropical shorts and shirts, to dress in civilian clothes, and to drive to the airfield. There, they were issued with false German *kennkarte* and other papers, and were given different pseudonyms from those they had used previously. They were now 'Axe', 'Lightning', 'Elk', 'Hawk', 'Revere', and 'Cyprus'.

The night flight did not pass without incident. Having rounded Budapest and crossed the Tatras, the Liberator was picked up near Cracow by two German night fighters. One of the fighters was hit by the tail-gunner. But the other stayed with them almost until arrival:

> They landed happily c. 1 am on 31 July, about 7 km [four miles] to the south of Grodzisk at a site called 'Salt-pot'. The commander of the technical team was Lt. 'Flash'. Exchange of passwords. Embraces. A quick transfer to the base, where they were greeted by the HQ representative, Lt. 'Christopher'. Handing over of weapons, money-belts. Examination of documents, and talking until dawn.
>
> 1 August 1944. 'Revere' was taken to Grodzisk in a peasant cart carrying vegetables. According to his documents, he was a gardener's assistant by the name of Julian B. In case of trouble, he had learned his biography by heart. A short journey on the electric train [to Warsaw] brought him into contact with the reality of Occupation. Before 2 p.m., he crossed the threshold of a house at Natolin Street, 6. Another exchange of passwords, and once the door was shut, a warm hug from the lady owner of the 'London contact house', who went by the name of 'Stefa'.
>
> Stefa informed them that they had arrived at the very last minute. For that day, at five o'clock, battle would be joined. The Rising! They were shocked.
>
> Axe stroked his chin. 'I'm sure that our people have reached an arrangement with the Soviets,' he said. 'If not,' asked Revere, 'what then?'[98]

PART TWO

The Rising

CHAPTER V

THE WARSAW RISING

Outbreak

'L-Hour' had been fixed for 5 p.m. on 1 August. But at 1.50, in the suburb of Jolibord, a young Home Army captain known as 'Mark', later to become a prominent music critic, had the distinction of launching the Rising prematurely. Leading his company towards their rendezvous point, he ran into a motorized German patrol:

> There was a moment when we watched each other with absolute clarity. The Germans were obviously calculating the possible gains and losses, whether to challenge us or whether to pretend that they hadn't seen this group of youngsters wearing half-concealed uniforms and carrying sub-machine guns under their coats . . . Then they decided to start a fight from which we emerged unscathed. We threw our grenades into their lorry, which exploded . . . and we managed to run across the street and to take cover with the rest of our unit.[1]

At five o'clock, as arranged, the main German strongpoints were rushed, infiltrated, or bombarded by groups of dashing young men wearing red-and-white armbands. Civilians were still on the streets. Some were hit in the crossfire, or cut off from their homes for life. Soon, the red-and-white banner was waving atop the Prudential Building, the city's tallest. A major German arsenal and storehouse was captured. So, too, were the main post office, the power station, the railway office in Praga, and wide swathes of the city. The cost was 2,500 lives – 80 per cent of them from the Home Army. It was a similar total to that of Allied losses on the Normandy beaches on D-Day. [**BAPTISM OF FIRE**, p. 246]

It is impossible to establish who was the first insurgent to die. Several were killed before the fighting officially began. But 'Sadovski', the fifteen-year-old ex-Premier's son, must have been one of the very earliest casualties. Shortly after 5 p.m. on 1 August, 'he was mortally wounded on Flora Street opposite the Dakovski coffee-house. According to his

BAPTISM OF FIRE

A young recruit meets his comrades for the first time, and goes into combat

I had spent the last days of July next to a telephone, as a sort of duty officer, awaiting the call to activate the platoon . . . The call came in the morning hours of 1 August and we set out in pairs to our unit assembly point in the customs house next to the Danzig Railway Station. I arrived there quite early, but by about 3 o'clock all were there – some seventy to seventy-five men. This was the first time that we had all met together in the open . . .

We were designated to operate in the Rising as a company. Our commander was Stan, whom I had met previously when he was commanding Underground actions . . . We knew him as a very brave officer and an excellent leader . . .

After warm greetings, a lot of chattering, and great excitement, Stan assembled us and gave a short speech. We were lined up in two files in the main hall of the customs house, and put on white-and-red armbands, and rank insignia. After eighteen months of conspiracy it was our first military ceremony . . .

At exactly 5 p.m. our unit, the 'College A' of the K-Div. organization, jumped out of the customs building and advanced towards our first objective. We headed for the *Umschlagplatz*, which had been the loading centre for Jews from the entire Warsaw district on the way to extermination camps. It was the same building where I myself had waited to be transported nearly two years earlier. It was defended by an SS unit, which had been alerted for an attack in the morning when some Home Army soldiers were caught by the Germans transferring arms. During the first hour of fighting, we suffered a number of casualties – both wounded and killed.

After capturing the *Umschlagplatz*, however, where we liberated fifty Jews employed by the SS as slaves, we remained in the building overnight. We found enormous stores of food and uniforms and some arms. We immediately changed from half-civilian clothes into the SS uniforms and boots. But to distinguish ourselves from the Germans, we wore our armbands, insignia of rank, and eagles on our new hats.

2 August was the second day of the Rising and we marched from the *Umschlagplatz* to Vola (a nearby district in Warsaw). This distance of one or two kilometres was free of Germans, and thousands of people lined the streets, throwing flowers and crying. It was a very moving scene . . .[1]

S. Aronson

colleague, who was urging flight, he said: "That's not why they placed me here." ' Then, while attacking a German tank, he was burned by a flame thrower.[2]

That same evening, another member of Sadovski's 'Stag' Group died of her wounds in a field hospital. The thirty-year-old nurse nr. 1108, 'Danuta', had been shot when she rushed out to tend a wounded soldier during the attack on the Press House. A singer and composer, she was the author of the Rising's most popular song, 'Fix bayonets, lads'. She had also been the model for Warsaw's famous Siren Statue, which the Germans carried off.[3]

The Home Army Command had been relocated in the Kammler furniture factory in Vola. That night, evaluating reports, they learned that many key objectives had *not* been won. The insurgents had met with little success in Castle Square, in the Police District, and at the airport, where they had suffered heavy losses. Above all, they had not been able to seize control either of the western or the eastern ends of the two main bridges across the river. They already knew that they could be in for a very long fight.

On 2 August, AK Command re-established the radio link with London that they had lost during the move to the Kammler factory. The message sent improperly *en clair* the previous day was repeated properly in code. 'The struggle for Warsaw has begun'.[4] On each of the following days, Gen. Boor begged London time and again for airdrops, ammunition, and the despatch of the Parachute Brigade, whose release from British command he still clearly expected.

On the first full day of fighting, paperboys appeared on the streets, openly distributing the Home Army's *Information Bulletin*. The underground press carried declarations from the military and the political authorities, and severe instructions from the Civilian Commissioner:

1. All the dead, both German and Polish, are to be given temporary burial, and all personal documents preserved.
2. All self-appointed courts are banned.
3. All enemies of the Polish nation, Germans, or *Volksdeutsche* are to be protected pending trial.
4. All property belonging to German citizens or to the German state is to be guarded and inventarized . . .[5]

On 3 August, the insurgents not only captured their first German tank, they repaired it and drove it into action against its former owners. An early target was the SS 'Goose Farm' concentration camp. Their resourcefulness revealed some of the unforeseen difficulties which the Germans were already facing, despite their deployment of special units.

During the night of 4/5 August, the first RAF bombers appeared in the skies over Warsaw, having flown from Italy. They made successful drops over Krashinski Square and Vola. The insurgents could not know how many other planes had taken off and had been lost. But they took heart. They were not totally forgotten. There were part of a coalition.

On 5 August, *SS-Ogruf.* Erich von dem Bach reached Warsaw, to take charge of all anti-insurgent operations. His arrival coincided with the news of mass murders of civilians, the flight of refugees, and heavy bombardments.

Sunday 6 August was the sixth day of the Rising. The insurgents had intended to hold out ideally for forty-eight hours and at the most for five to six days. The limit had now been reached. But there was no sign whatsoever of a resolution. They had taken control of much of the capital, but they had not driven the Germans out. They had always understood that German counter-attacks to the east of the Vistula might upset their calculations, but they had no means of telling how the renewed armoured clashes between Germans and Soviets were faring. They held high hopes for their Premier's mission to Moscow, but they were not yet aware of an outcome. They had sent off their appeals to the Western Allies, but as yet they had not received a clear response. They had no choice but to fight on. They had met neither defeat nor victory. [**L-HOUR**, p. 250]

The German reaction to the Rising was at once complacent and vicious. Governor Fischer, having heard of several premature clashes in the afternoon of the 1st, put the garrison on full alert at 4.30 p.m., and reported to his superiors. Loudspeakers on the streets blared out the warning that bandits were operating and that action against them was starting: 'any civilian found on the street would be fired on.'[6] That evening, Wehrmacht officers met at the HQ of Gen. von Vormann. The Ninth Army logbook calmly noted 'the outbreak of the expected insurgency': 'Battles are in progress in all parts of Warsaw. The direct supply line of the 39th Armoured Corps has been cut. Fortunately, control of the telephone exchange is facilitating communication . . . Ninth Army Command has requested police formations [to be brought in] for crushing the Rising.'[7] In other words, the hard-pressed Wehrmacht saw no reason to redirect its own forces. The SS had created the mess in Warsaw, and the SS could sort it out.

The Nazi leaders reacted with savage delight. The Rising gave them the pretext for punishing Warsaw once and for all. Himmler was informed by radio at 5.30 p.m. He immediately flew into a rage, firing off a telegram to the Commandant of KZ Sachsenhausen and ordering him to kill Gen. Arrow. An initial report spoke merely of 'disturbances' in Warsaw and of the false supposition that the rebels were Communists. Gen. Hahn corrected his mistake in the evening, informing Berlin that the rebels belonged to the 'national Resistance movement, the Home Army', and that they were wearing red-and-white armbands, not red ones.

In due course, Himmler took the news to Hitler. *'Mein Führer!'* he said, according to his later recollection,

> The moment is a difficult one. [But] from the historical point of view, the action of the Poles is a blessing. We shall finish them off . . . Warsaw will be liquidated; and this city, which is the intellectual capital of a sixteen- to seventeen-million-strong nation that has blocked our path to the east for seven hundred years, ever since the first battle of Tannenberg, will have ceased to exist. By the same token, the . . . Poles themselves will cease to be a problem for our children and for all who will follow us . . .[8]

Hitler's response was not directly recorded. But it was undoubtedly reflected in Himmler's subsequent orders, which talked of 'every inhabitant to be killed', 'no prisoners to be taken', and 'every single house to be blown up and burned'.[9]

On 3 August, the *Reichsführer-SS* was visiting Poznan and was addressing a conference of Nazi Gauleiters. It would seem that he was asked whether the latest events in Warsaw might upset the Nazis' strategic plans. His reply was uncompromising. The most important aspect of strategy concerned 'racial reconstruction'. 'The programme is irreversible. We have extended our [racial] frontier far to the East, and that, too, is irreversible . . . It is irreversible that we fill this settlement area, that we create a garden of Germanic blood in the East.'[10] To the Nazi mind, the irreversibility of changes to the population was a victory from which no military setback could detract.

Governor-General Frank telexed the Reich Chancellery on 5 August in similar vein:

L-HOUR

A soldier of the K-Div. goes into battle

We received our orders on 31 July and Home Army detachments assembled at their designated points. The first objective was the German army stores in the district of Stavki. We, in K-Div., were relatively well armed with captured weapons and a few Thompson guns from parachute drops. We were also battle-hardened. According to the plan, having secured the stores, we were to march to the [PKO] Savings Bank building in the City Centre and place ourselves at the disposal of General Monter, the commander of the Rising. The battle order stipulated that once the capital had been liberated we were . . . to secure all weapons in arms caches and to remain prepared for possible further clandestine activity under Soviet occupation . . .

In my mind's eye I saw a victory parade in full glory. I was only twenty-one, and after years of stressful Underground work I was hoping for some recognition. We were overdue for celebrations, and were full of hope that our equally patriotic girls would recognize our valour and succumb to the charms of the uniform . . .

On 1 August, on leaving our base, I saw my old friend Alex T. at the head of his platoon. There was no time to talk and we just waved. Several minutes later, about 3 p.m., as they were crossing [Mitskevich Street], a German tank opened fire and Alex was hit in the forehead. He died instantly. He may have been the first casualty of the insurrection . . .

Our [Jolibord] detachment reached its jump-off point in a covered lorry driven by 'Columbus'. It was in the grounds of a school bordering the Stavki stores . . . we seized the school at 3.30 p.m. Columbus and I went to move our lorry to a safer location. We travelled maybe ten metres when an artillery shell exploded at the very place we had just vacated . . .

Our attack evolved according to plan. At exactly 5 p.m. we jumped over the fence at the back of the stores. We shot several SS men dead . . . Two Krauts who tried to escape into the ruins of the ghetto on the other side . . . were also killed. Suddenly, inside the stores, a group of about fifty men ran towards us, wearing the striped garb of concentration-camp prisoners. They called out to us, but we couldn't understand a single word. They were Greek Jews from Salonika who had been put to work there. With difficulty, we explained to them . . . that they were now free.

A young SS officer who survived our initial assault had built a barricade of packing cases on the first floor. He must have amassed a large amount of ammunition, as he kept us under almost constant fire. Columbus was wounded in the hand. So we decided to blow up another door next to the officer's hideout. Tony Flamethrower did it with an impact grenade. In his hate-fired eagerness, he did not take cover in time and his legs stopped a number of fragments. After Columbus, he was our second casualty.

As I learned after the war, the inhabitants of the Old Town later managed to remove tons of provisions from the stores: flour, sugar, cereals, etc. They carried the bags and boxes on their backs. These supplies helped them to survive the next three weeks of savage fighting, when the Old Town was completely cut off from the outside world.

We spent the night in the stores. We found a large stock of camouflage jackets worn by German paratroopers, and naturally we put them on. As many of us had joined the Rising in civvies, it was only now that we began to look like soldiers. I was wearing a smart pair of high boots, a Polish officer's tunic . . . and the newly acquired camouflage jacket. I was very proud of it.[1]

Stanisław Likiernik

A German military administrator, who later fell into Polish hands, describes the chaos that day in his office

'The Cracow office of the *Befehlshaber der Sicherheitspolizei und des SD* contained a file on the expected Polish Rising. It grouped all our experts' major studies, opinions, and forecasts, as well as reports from our secret agents. The dossier was kept in a special safe. As an archivist, it was my duty to check the file page-by-page monthly – an extremely boring job. Occasionally some big-shot would request one of the 'insurrectional' documents *sofort*. We had hundreds of people working at decoding your group's secret papers. And what did it all add up to, [do you think]? Fuck all! That's right, fuck all!'

'Why fuck all?' I asked.

'Because in spite of our preparations, the Warsaw Rising caught us by surprise. The office was a madhouse. Telephone, telegraph, and telex lines were jammed. Dozens of "experts" started pawing through my archives. They concluded that our intelligence reports were outdated, and that the [frequent] rumours of an impending Rising were plants from the Home Army and designed to mislead us. That doesn't mean that we knew nothing of what was coming. Far from it. But our information was completely inadequate . . .'[2]

For the most part, Warsaw is in flames. Burning down the houses is the most reliable means of liquidating the insurgents' hideouts . . . Indescribable poverty reigns among the million inhabitants. Warsaw

> will be punished with complete destruction after the suppression or collapse of the rising. Unfortunately, our own losses are considerable. But thanks to the improved situation [on the Soviet front] one can count on the total crushing of the insurrection by the continuing siege within a few days.[11]

Inimitably, the Nazis' instinct was to think of flattening the rebel city and all its inhabitants by aerial bombardment. But the VI Air Fleet had better things to do. And in any case the German troops that were engaged in the city could not be safely withdrawn.

So, to achieve his aim, Himmler ordered the mobilization of a special anti-insurgent corps to be commanded by von dem Bach. He had the full approval of the Chief of Staff, Guderian. The various elements of the corps reached Warsaw by rail in the course of the first week of August. By that time, the main units at the disposal of von dem Bach's chief of operations, *SS-Gruf.* Heinz Reinefarth, formed a powerful if somewhat motley array.

— the SS RONA Brigade from the Russian National Liberation Army under *Brig.Fhr.* Mechislav Kaminski: an advance party of 2,000 men
— the SS Brigade of *SS-Staf.* Oskar Dirlewanger (two battalions, 3,381 men), including the 111th Azerbaijani Regiment
— the 572nd and 580th Cossack Battalions
— the 608th Special Defence Battalion (under Col. Willy Schmidt) from Breslau
— a Posnanian militarized police battalion
— a Luftwaffe guard regiment
— a reserve battalion of the Hermann Göring Panzer-Parachute Division that was operating to the east of Warsaw.

These units were added to the existing German garrison, and formed into a dedicated Attack Group. They moved into position on the 4th, with a full-scale assault on the western suburbs starting at dawn on the 5th. They were taking Himmler's orders literally. Their skirmishes with Home Army defenders were almost a sideline, since for two days they concentrated on massacring every man, woman, and child in sight. No one was spared – not even nuns, nurses, hospital patients, doctors, invalids, or babies. Estimates of their non-combatant victims in the suburbs of Ohota and Vola vary from 20,000 to 50,000.

On the 6th, von dem Bach instituted a new policy. Only men were to be shot. Captured civilians were to be sent to a transit camp newly set up 16km (ten miles) outside the city. Executions were to be handled by specialized *Einsatzkommandos* (task forces). The Attack Group was to concentrate on attacking the rebels. The chaos was so immense that it obstructed the Germans' own operations. The main strategic west–east thoroughfare was still blocked. On 4 August, the 19th Panzer Division, whilst redeploying from Praga towards the Soviets' southern bridgehead, took numerous casualties as it passed through the besieged city. To cap it all, the Luftwaffe had started to bomb rebel-held districts. Relays of Junkers Ju87 and Messerschmitt Me-109 fighter-bombers were operating from the airport.

Facing this formidable war machine, the Home Army had no air force, no heavy artillery, and few fully armed units. But it immediately proved to be no mean adversary. Its command structure was divided into eight city districts, and each district into wards. Its military formations were based on large groupings, which in turn were composed of battalions, companies, and platoons. But in practice, given the demands of urban warfare, in which relatively small forces were often required to operate on a semi-autonomous basis, the company of 50–100 men, usually named after the pseudonym of its commanding officer, became the basic unit. Over 600 such companies had fanned out into the city on 1 August, each with a specific street or building to defend. Their geographical diffusion, together with their ability to merge or to separate at will, made them extremely difficult to pin down and winkle out. They quickly exposed the Germans' failings.

Meanwhile, in Cracow, the authorities of the General Government reacted by ordering a pre-emptive round-up of young men, similar to the one that had misfired the previous week in Warsaw. On this occasion, the Gestapo took no chances. After sweeping the streets on the afternoon of Sunday 6 August, they then searched the houses of suspect youngsters. At 10 Tyniets Street, they broke in, but failed to find the twenty-four-year-old Underground actor and aspirant priest who was praying on his knees, 'heart pounding', in a hidden compartment in the cellar. His close colleague had been shot as a hostage only shortly before. When they left, a young woman guided the fugitive to the archbishop's palace. He was taken in, given a cassock to wear, and was told to present himself as one of the archbishop's 'secretaries'.[12] In this way, Karol Wojtyła took a major step towards ordination, and in the long term, towards the Throne of St Peter.

In the considered opinion of professional soldiers, both German and Polish, an insurrection by ill-armed irregulars in a large urban area had no chance of long-term success. In military terms, it could only be considered a short-term, stop-gap measure. There were few places to hide, and no way to escape. In street fighting, as distinct from the guerrilla-friendly environment of forests and countryside, the superior discipline and firepower of regular units supported by armour and artillery was thought to be invincible. It was for these reasons that the Home Army had originally planned to stage a rising outside the towns, and that the SS in Warsaw anticipated a quick victory. [**TRAPPED**, p. 255]

Nonetheless, despite the deployment of some 50,000 troops, the German concentration of forces hardly reached the density required by an urban battlefield of some 250km² (100 square miles). The perimeter of the three main insurgent positions which had stabilized by the end of the first week, in the Old Town, the City Centre, and the Southern Suburbs, totalled over 80km (fifty miles), and it was too long to be attacked except in local segments at any one time. The insurgents proved capable of surviving the heaviest bombardments, and they were extremely adept at repeatedly reoccupying the strongpoints which they had lost. They also enjoyed interior lines of communication whereby they could reinforce sectors under assault. They showed themselves far superior in the arts of entrapment and surprise, frequently nullifying or reversing laborious German offensives that were highly predictable. Nor, amazingly, did they ever run out of arms and ammunition. They became past masters at seizing their requirements from a bewildered enemy who, like the large but clumsy opponent of an expert judo player, found great difficulty in bringing his weight and bulk to bear.

After the first week, therefore, when neither side had gained a decisive advantage, Warsaw became the scene of long, relentless battles of attrition. Every day, usually at dawn, the Germans would return to their chosen sectors like workmen returning to a building site. Unable to dislodge their adversary by standard infantry tactics, they would call up the bombers and the heavy guns, pound the insurgent positions into mounds of rubble, demolish a few barricades, and gain a few yards or a couple of streets. Next morning they would find that half the barricades had been rebuilt

TRAPPED

Thousands of civilians are trapped by the outbreak of the Rising

The time was drawing near for the destruction of Warsaw. The Uprising was a blameworthy, lightheaded enterprise; it completely confirmed 'Tiger''s diagnosis – although no one can tell what shapes the legend may take, or what influence it may exert during the decades and centuries to come. You could already hear Russian artillery fire. Rumours of an insurrection were greeted joyfully: a chance to throw oneself at one's tormentors and take revenge . . . Soon, however, came news that there would be no Uprising. One of my socialist colleagues told me that to take action now, when the premier of the London government was flying to Moscow, would be nonsense. Stalin was too clever to negotiate with anyone using such a trump card . . .

That day, 1 August, [Yanka] and I were walking over to Tiger's for an after-dinner chat and a cup of tea. I had something terribly important to discuss; namely, my new translation of an English poem. On leaving for a walk one should never be too sure of returning home, not only because something may happen to one personally, but also because the house may cease to exist. Our walk was to last a long time.

Ten carefree minutes under a cloudless sky. Then, unexpectedly, everything burst, and my angle of vision changed as I found myself advancing on all fours. This outer-city district, where vegetable gardens and sparsely scattered houses bordered the fields, was thickly planted with SS troops. Machine guns fired at anything that moved. Not far away some friends lived; but when neither running nor walking is possible, three hundred feet becomes a whole journey . . . In spite of this I never let go of my book – first of all out of respect for social ownership, since the book bore a call number of the University Library; secondly I needed it (although I could stop needing it). Its title: *The Collected Poems of T. S. Eliot*, in the Faber & Faber edition.

It was dawn of the next day by the time we crawled up to the island; that is, to a small modern flat with beautiful flowers in the courtyard; the open spaces around it made it seem completely cut off from the outside world.

Czesław Miłosz[1]

When the Rising broke out I was in the flat with my mother and our maid. My father was somewhere in town, we wouldn't see him for many months, but he is my strongest memory of the first days of the Rising. Telephones were still working, so my father called from nearby, saying he would climb to the top of the roof and if we climbed our roof we would see him. I clearly remember climbing carefully, hiding among the chimneys to avoid being spotted and fired at. My memory is confused – was it that my mother told us to do this to make it stick in our minds, or did we assume little chance of seeing him again? In winter, when he was discovered in Cracow, it was like a miracle because we thought he was dead. I already thought of myself as a little boy without a father.

Krzysztof Zanussi[2]

Christine and I were living in a room across the street from the Opera House. On 1 August we suddenly heard shooting throughout the city. We knew what it was: the Russians were already on the other side of the Vistula; we could see their tanks in Praga from the third floor of our building.

We attempted to make our way to the Old Town but were not allowed out in the street. We made our way from our basement through those of the next four houses. Then we needed to go above ground, to run across a street. I gave Christine instructions: 'When I say "run", then run! Then flat on your belly! Down here you're going to die,' I said. 'The house will collapse and we'll be buried. If we go up we still have a chance.' Somehow I got her out of that basement, the moment before a bomb fell on the building.

The Germans started burning out the houses. Our building was already on fire. We were trying to extinguish the flames, but I couldn't keep it up for long . . . We moved to the next building, then that house burned out. We saw what was the remains of a garden plot; somebody had dug a hole, just large enough for the two of us to slide into. Cinders were flying everywhere. You couldn't see the sun for all the ashes; it was like a huge orange ball. All of Warsaw was burning. I had to urinate on my handkerchief and cover Christine's head with it, to keep her hair from burning. We stayed in that hole for three days . . .

John Damski[3]

---

during the night and booby-trapped, and that the shattered buildings provided perfect cover for unseen snipers and grenade throwers. In this way, practically every building and cellar had to be fought over time and time again before the Germans could secure a disputed sector. Every delay played straight into the insurgents' hands. The days became weeks; and, eventually, to the common dismay of all combatants, the weeks became months.

Much was due to the resourcefulness of the insurgents, to brilliant improvisations, to their auxiliary services largely run by women, and, above all, to their unbreakable spirit. Where AK platoons possessed only one gun for every two men, the night watch would take over the weapons of the day watch. So long as the guns of the dead and wounded could be recovered, the ratio of guns to men was actually increasing. Weapons and ammunition had often to be won from enemy stores. Communications were maintained through warrens of deep trenches and sewers. Underground kitchens, hospitals, workshops, and command posts continued to function in the deep, impenetrable levels of Warsaw's multi-storeyed cellars. The men and women of the AK fought like tigers at bay, undeterred by horrendous casualties and undiverted by hopes of survival after capture. It was a long time before the German command realized that instead of trying to kill them, there might be a better chance of persuading them to capitulate with honour.

The weapons used during the Rising were extraordinarily one-sided. The insurgents relied to a large extent on small arms, on old army rifles, and on hand grenades, especially the homemade *filipinki*. They quickly organized a network of underground factories and repair shops which kept up the flow of these basic armaments. They were desperately short of automatic weapons, although they collected a modest arsenal of machine-guns, Stens, rocket-launchers, and anti-tank guns from airdrops, from enemy stores, from their own production lines, and from the enemy. Their street barricades ranged from the frivolously flimsy to the super-solid, especially when constructed of heavy flagstones. They were numerous enough to prevent free access to any district; and even when approached by German armour, they could slow the tanks down sufficiently for the attackers to be attacked. (See Appendix 30.)

The Germans, in contrast, possessed all manner of small, light, medium, heavy, and ultra-heavy weapons, and limitless supplies of ammunition. Their infantry carried modern Schmeisser sub-machine guns and rode in APCs. Their armoured formations used a variety of vehicles, from the massive sixty-eight-tonne Tiger II to the small Hetzer self-propelled anti-tank gun. Their artillery was supplied with a wide range of equipment including Rheinmetall Le-FH18 field-guns, 81mm mortars, and the famous 88mm AA gun. They also used grossly oversized anti-siege guns such as the 60cm 'Karl' howitzer or the long-range Bertha cannon firing 38cm shells. Their armoured trains rolled round suburban railway lines, seeking out the best locations for their salvoes of high explosive. [**MASSACRE**, p. 258]

Two items in the German armoury gained special notoriety. One, the

MASSACRE

A religious order attracts the attention of the Nazis

From dawn on 2 August, the Jesuit fathers have been celebrating a perpetual Mass in their chapel . . . Explosions shake the walls. Plaster and rubble rain down. Violent gunfire continues until the *Agnus Dei.* Father Henryk Wi., oblivious, celebrates the Mass calmly to its conclusion.

Around ten o'clock, there is a violent knocking at the main entrance. A band of armed SS men burst in.

'*Wer hat hier geschossen?*' they ask . . .

The Porter, who is a friar, waves his arms . . .

'*Ja verfluchten Polen! Wo sind Banditen?*'

The SS men carry out a search and return.

'Everything in order,' they say to the Father Superior. 'But come with us.' . . .

The clock strikes eleven o'clock. Again soldiers' boots reverberate. The SS men return. Father S. asks, 'Where is the Father Superior?'

'Go downstairs.'

The German voices bring Father Ko. downstairs.

'What is going on?' he asks in excellent German.

'Shots were fired from this house.'

'That is impossible. No one has a weapon!'

'But someone fired from this building!' screams one of the SS men.

'We have been in the basement the whole time. I would stake my life that no one fired. This is a closed house.'

'Everyone to the boiler room!' screams an SS man.

An SS man stands at the doors of the boiler room, with a sub-machine gun in his hand and grenades in his belt. Suddenly he points his finger at Father Wi., who is closest, and orders him into the corridor. He appears again . . . and signals to Father L., sitting in a chair. The old man gets up with difficulty. 'I suffer from rheumatism,' he says in German. The SS man nods. He stops the priest in the corridor and asks him the time. The priest takes off his watch, gives it to the thief, and carries on. Another SS man indicates a door to him. More and more priests and brothers flow into one small room.

Father W. says: 'This is our last hour . . . Soon we will find ourselves before the Lord Jesus. We must be prepared . . . Everyone can make their confessions.' Father M. reads from the breviary of apostolic blessings for the hour of death. The doors open and an SS officer appears, gathers everyone's attention, and issues an order.

'*Los.*' The SS men pull out the pins of the grenades and throw them into the crowd. Awful explosions follow. Bricks, plaster, wood, and glass fly, and awful cries ring out. As if in reply, SS men stand in the doorway and spray bullets into the swirl of bodies, which slowly becomes silent.

Father K. lies face to the ground and tries to free himself from the weight of the dead. Father S. is also alive. Next to him, Father Wi. is moaning. Father Wr. is in the throes of death. Father L. raises a hand, as though administering the Last Rites. The voices and moans bring the SS men back. They shoot at those who are still moving.

A young boy from a German family darts in. He has attached himself to the SS men and never leaves their side. His childish voice rings out.

'*Achtung! Der lebt noch! O hier, hier, er atmet noch!*'

The SS men return and more rounds ring out, accompanied by childish laughter and applause.

'I hold my breath,' remembers Father R. 'My eyes are closed, I do not see his face but I wait for the shot and darkness, letting my head drop like a corpse's.' Father S. also feels the breath of an SS man. 'How can I pretend to be dead when my heart is beating like a hammer?'

The retreating footsteps of the SS grow distant. The living extricate themselves from under the pile of bodies. 'Father, please take care not to tread on my face.' It is Father K. So he is alive! His face is streaming with blood.

Father K. sees two women, lighting their way along the corridor with a torch. 'The torch, please.'

One of the women gives it to him silently.

'And who are you?'

'Nurses. From the state medical point of Professor L.'

'Can we leave here?'

'Yes, the boys are nearby. There are no Germans. We are caring for the wounded.'[1]

Goliath, was an unmanned, remote-controlled miniature tank, which could serve as a platform for cameras and listening devices but was primarily employed as a transporter of explosives. Its only weakness was its long electric cable which was susceptible to the attention of daring soldiers and small boys who learned how to crawl out among the rubble with a pair of pincers and cut the Goliath dead with a single snip. The other, the *Nebelwerfer*, was a mobile, multiple rocket-launcher which fired a mixed salvo of incendiaries and explosives. Its nicknames, of 'Cupboard' and 'Cow', derived from the terrifying noises that accompanied each firing, and that were variously described as the grating of heavy furniture on a stone floor or as the bellowing of a wounded cow.

German sources soon reported that nothing resembling the Warsaw Rising had been seen since Stalingrad. But there was a fundamental difference. Stalingrad had been contested by two professional armies, each possessing a full complement of aerial and armoured weapons. Warsaw was being contested by a professional army and a dedicated band of irregulars.

In London, the exiled Government had waited for news of the Rising for over a week. They had known it was coming, but hadn't known when. But after the delayed message from Gen. Boor was properly received on 2 August, they sprang into action. They had two priorities. The first was to obtain the full support of the Western powers. The second was to organize a favourable outcome of the Premier's talks in Moscow that were due to commence at any time. [**GOOSE FARM**, p. 261]

In its Cabinet meeting at 15.30 on 2 August, the exiled Government – minus its Premier – agreed the text of a communiqué and received a report from the socialist leader, 'Thomas', who had recently left Poland with Salamander. They also discussed the criticisms of the Rising contained in the Commander-in-Chief's delayed telegram from Italy. They declared them invalid, and contrary to the Government's decision of 25 July.[13]

The British public woke up to news of the Rising on 3 August. A small paragraph in *The Times* that morning was typical:

> The Polish Government in London issued the following communiqué yesterday afternoon: – 'The Delegate of the Polish Government in Poland and the Commander-in-Chief of the Underground Army report that at 1700 hours on August 1 units of the Polish Underground Army in Warsaw started open fighting for the seizure of the capital from the Germans.[14]

The Government served as the main channel of information about the Rising for the Western Allies, and Gen. Boor sent daily reports by radio. But there were considerable delays between messages being sent, and being deciphered, discussed, and forwarded to their final destination. Two whole days passed, for example, before the President could officially inform Churchill:

GOOSE FARM

The officer commanding Zoshka's Storm Battalion liberates a death camp inside the walls of the former Ghetto

During the Rising, we did not know the history of the Goose Farm Camp. All we knew was that an extermination camp lay in front of our lines, and that the prisoners had to be rescued. The camp consisted of two sections. One abutted Trench Street and had been partly captured on the Rising's first day. But the Germans had retreated to the other section, which was unusually well fortified. It was surrounded by a high brick wall, and about a dozen watchtowers, armed with heavy machine guns, had been built into the wall. From these towers, German 'storks' – as we called them – had an excellent view over the surrounding terrain.

The attack on the Goose Farm began about 2 p.m. on the 5th. 'Alek''s platoon . . . engaged the watchtowers from a position on Trench Street, drawing the Germans' attention in that direction. 'Felek''s platoon then approached the first watchtower on the left unobserved. The tower was to be destroyed by two rounds from our tank; and the second round was to be the signal for the assault. The tank, under my command, was to proceed slowly down Goose Street from the Trench Street end. It was to make a sharp left turn opposite the main entrance to the camp which was blocked by an enormous barricade . . .

When we approached the barricade, which was built of concrete blocks, railway tracks, and other metal objects and which was at least one storey high, I realized the size of the risk that we were taking. Fortunately, we had a fantastic driver, called 'Roar'. He pressed the accelerator to the floorboard, the engine roared at full rev, and bit by bit the tank edged its way to the top. Suddenly, it tipped over and dropped down on the far side. It wasn't damaged, though we were all thoroughly shaken . . . The Germans hurled a cluster of grenades, but the tracks still held even though the vehicle was momentarily blown off the ground. A quick turn to the right, and we were already standing beside the second barricade. We fired the agreed two shots; the corner watchtower was demolished and the way was open for the assault. Some of our boys literally jumped the gun, and stormed one of the towers after the first of our shots . . .

All the watchtowers were under direct fire from our tank. As soon as anything moved, we demolished it . . . At one moment, I saw a lad riding at full speed through the middle of the camp on a bicycle. I was sure that he would be brought down. But he jumped off at the end of the alley, turned round, and started firing his Sten gun at one of the towers. The Germans had either to run, to surrender, or to perish.

Our lads were dressed in captured German uniforms and German helmets. And they shouted in German to the prisoners who were of various nationalities. The prisoners thought that their last hour had come. It's hard to imagine the emotion when they realized that we brought them freedom not death. I remembered Radoslav's words: 'The Germans are capable of killing the prisoners even after you capture the camp.' So I threw open the lid of the tank and shouted, 'For God's sake, get down and take cover.' But no one paid any attention whatsoever . . .

The camp had been captured. Our nurses appeared. Since the tank's ventilation had not been working very well, we were more or less suffocated; and I went for a stroll to recover. I saw the most extraordinary sight. In the middle of the camp square, at least a hundred prisoners had been drawn up military-style in two long ranks. As I went to them, a voice called out, 'Attention! Eyes left.' And one of them came up to me and saluted: 'Sergeant Henryk Lederman, sir,' he reported, 'and the Jewish Battalion ready for action.' My wonder at these people knew no bounds. Not only had they not been broken by Nazi savagery, they had managed to organize themselves, despite the conditions of the camp, and to ready themselves as soon as an opportunity occurred.

Radoslav gave me permission to take these Jewish soldiers into our ranks. Some of them went to Parasol, others to 'Fila' . . . Many died in combat. Our losses were horrendous. But those soldier-Jews left behind them the reputation of exceptionally brave, ingenious, and faithful people. Many of their names or pseudonyms can be seen in Zoshka's enclosure in Warsaw's Military Cemetery.[1]

W. Micuta

London 3 August 1944

My dear Prime Minister,

For the last two days Warsaw fights. To save the city, it is indispensable that a large quantity of equipment be dropped this very night in places indicated . . . It is to be feared that without your decision giving this operation priority for tonight (3rd to 4th August) it may fail to take place [and] my Nation . . . would never forget that it was left unaided at a most critical moment by its British ally. I appeal to your friendship . . . and your deep understanding of soldierly solidarity.

Yours very sincerely[15]

Considerable difficulties were also created by the fact that the Commander-in-Chief was still in Italy. His subordinates were left scrambling to make the necessary contacts on his behalf. His Chief of Staff and the Minister of Defence were trying desperately to find out from the British military whether their various requests were feasible. The Chief of Section VI was in constant touch with the Polish squadrons in the Mediterranean, asking them whether they were ready to fly.

As often as not, the British response was deeply distressing to their allies. In many instances, it showed little sense of urgency or commitment. It took five days, for example, for Churchill's Chief of Staff, Gen. Hastings Ismay, to say (incorrectly) that the use of RAF bombers in Poland could only be considered in conjunction with the expected Soviet assault. Other proposals, such as the use of fighters, were again dismissed as unrealistic. Matters like the Home Army's combatant rights remained 'under discussion'. On 2 August, the Chief of the VI Bureau informed Gen. Boor by radio: 'The English are making all significant assistance for you dependent on the results of the Moscow talks.' He also said that the long-delayed issue of a British mission to the Home Army was waiting for Soviet approval.[16]

Diplomacy was brought into play, therefore, with maximum urgency. The Ambassador to Britain had been told by the Foreign Office a week earlier that British diplomats would intervene in Moscow in order to ensure maximum cooperation. He now wanted to learn what effect such intervention had achieved.

The Ambassador to the USA turned to the State Department. He received a sympathetic hearing from the acting Secretary of State, Edward Stettinius, at 11.30 on the morning of Sunday the 6th, before moving on to Gen. Joseph T. McNarney at the Department of War. Stettinius immediately saw the point of instructing Ambassador Harriman in Moscow to facilitate the Premier's talks with Stalin, and promised 'to set the wheels to work within the hour'. Gen. McNarney similarly understood the gravity of the moment and the vital importance of Soviet cooperation. The Ambassador had specifically requested that Gen. Eisenhower become involved.[17]

As the days passed, Gen. Boor's reports, whilst desperately pleading for assistance, nonetheless indicated that the Rising might continue 'for several days'. So there was still a chance. Yet the 'deathly silence' of the Soviet Army, and still worse the continuing arrests of AK soldiers by the Soviets outside Warsaw, were causes of intense anxiety. On 4 August, Boor was obliged to deny the content of a BBC broadcast which had stated that the Soviets were cooperating fully. For his superiors, it was a painful experience to see the difference between the first-hand information in their possession and the complacent stories that filled the Western press.

Almost without exception, the British newspapers carried optimistic accounts. The *News Chronicle* of 1 August had reported that Warsaw was on the verge of 'complete liberation'. On 4 August, the *Daily Mail* mentioned 'street fighting'. The *Daily Express* spread the news that members of the Polish Underground were fighting 'shoulder to shoulder with the Russians'.[18]

The Western Governments in London and Washington could not honestly claim that they were taken completely by surprise. They had long known that a Rising was on the cards, though they knew nothing of the timing. They were preoccupied with the campaign in Normandy, and they took it as read that events on the Eastern Front in the Soviet sphere were not their business. On the other hand, they could hardly turn a deaf ear to the appeals of a close ally in distress; and they had a prime interest in keeping the Soviets sweet. So their priorities were twofold: to send such aid for the Rising as could be quickly improvised and to assure a congenial climate for the Polish–Soviet talks in Moscow.

Churchill had made a measured statement to the House of Commons on the evening of 2 August, before news of the Rising was generally known. He announced: 'The Russian armies now stand before the gates of Warsaw.' He made one gesture to the courage of the Poles, and another to 'Russia's need for friendly neighbours'. And he made an appeal for the 'union of different Polish forces':

> [The Russian armies] offer freedom, sovereignty and independence to the Poles friendly to Russia. This seems to me very reasonable, considering the injuries which Russia has suffered . . . The Allies would welcome any general rally or fusion of Polish forces, both those who are working with the Western powers and those who are working with the Soviet . . . Let them come together. We desire this union, and it would be a marvellous thing if it could be proclaimed or at least its foundations laid, at the moment when the famous capital of Poland . . . has been liberated by the bravery of Russian Armies . . .[19]

His words were well received. On the face of it, they sounded perfectly reasonable. Yet in reality they begged some essential questions: what exactly did 'friendly neighbours' mean, and whose definition of 'friendliness' did Churchill intend to accept? His Polish listeners would have noticed that he did not say that Poland, too, needed friendly neighbours. Indeed, they might have argued, since Poland's injuries were proportionately greater than the Soviet Union's, that some Allied powers were in very special need of good neighbours. [**PROFESSOR**, p. 266]

Incidentally, Churchill's preoccupation with Poland irritated some members of his own Government. Sir Alexander Cadogan, for one, was kept waiting at 10 Downing Street in the hope of joining the cabinet on 2 August, and was then told that he wasn't wanted when Churchill headed off for the Commons. 'It's terrible that we have a P.M., who simply can't conduct business,' he noted in his diary. 'It's all hot air!'[20]

Churchill certainly reacted energetically. Despite the predictable feet-dragging by British officials, he authorized RAF flights to Warsaw to be prepared without delay. One should note that in this same period, British and American officials were resisting requests for flights of similar difficulty to be sent to destroy the rail-lines to Auschwitz. There were delays, perhaps unavoidable. But the operation started at Churchill's specific request.

On 4 August, the Prime Minister telegraphed Stalin:

> At the urgent request of the Polish underground army, we are dropping subject to the weather about 60 tons of equipment and ammunition into the south-western quarter of the city, where, it is said, a Polish revolt against the Germans is in fierce struggle. They also say that they appeal for Russian aid, which seems very near. They are being attacked by one-and-a-half German divisions. This may be of help to your operations.[21]

Stalin's reply was received the next day. It was not encouraging, but neither was it overtly hostile:

> I think that the information given to you by the Poles is greatly exaggerated and unreliable . . . The Home Army consists of a few detachments misnamed divisions. They have neither guns, aircraft, nor tanks. I cannot imagine detachments like those taking Warsaw.[22]

From the Western standpoint, it was important that Stalin had not rebuffed Churchill's approach outright. Great hopes were riding on the Moscow talks, whose result was not yet known.

It is perhaps worth repeating that the Western leaders were still headed on the path of 'compromise' with Stalin over Poland and that they

PROFESSOR

A German law professor, conscripted by the Wehrmacht, discovers the realities of Nazi warfare

I regarded our mission to Warsaw with immediate mistrust. We did not know exactly what had happened there, but we could guess. I already knew more than enough about SS terror. We did not want to be dragged into brutality at five to midnight.

It must have been early in the morning on 5 or 6 August 1944, when, after travelling through Kutno–Lowitsch (names famous from 1939), we reached Warsaw West Station. A thick smoke rose above the city. Artillery fire could be heard. The station was virtually empty. Polish railwaymen were still working under German supervision. No one knew what to do with us. It was extremely difficult to find Colonel Schmidt from 608, with whom we were supposed to work. We were transported to a suburban station [in the direction of Sohachev-Vlohy]. There, far from the centre, it seemed that life continued almost as normal. Except that a very large army was present, and lorryloads of police from Azerbaijan . . .

We commandeered a large farm [near Vlohy] for the artillery troop, a few small houses for our HQ, and a humble dwelling designated for women of German descent, for the Major and myself. Finally we drove into the unlucky city. Policemen blocked the approach road. In the middle of the cemetery on Lodz Street stood an Orthodox church, quite modern, solidly built and beautifully furnished. Plundered suitcases, clothes, beds, and other things lay scattered outside, but where were the people? I walked around the church to one of the family vaults. This is where the people were! Men, women, children, and old people – obviously innocent refugees who had been rounded up and shot, every last one of them. Flies swarmed round the corpses and the pools of blood. Other bodies were piled up on barrows . . . During the first three or five days of the Rising they shot all Poles, on the personal order of Hitler, without regard to age or gender. Now they had changed tack. But not for humanitarian reasons. They were still shooting men. They had ordered them to go to the wooden fence and tear out a railing. Then they shot the whole line, poured petrol over them, and set them on fire. The railings were to make people burn better. I had never seen anything like it.

We continued in the direction of the city centre, but travelled only a few metres, because of the intense fighting . . . A never-ending column of miserable people shuffled by. It was the most shocking sight. Women, children, old people. Deadly tired faces without a shadow of hope, eyes swollen from smoke and tears, faces covered with soot, a picture of despair and doubt. Policemen with machine guns walked beside them. It struck us, unlike in Russia, that these were not impoverished or marginal people. They were from our own social level: women in fur coats, and beautiful children, who two days ago were still being well cared for.

The Azerbaijan Battalion was engaged in battle – together with 'Kaminski's infamous bandit brigade', which was made up of wild individuals, who inflicted their rage on civilians. A terrified woman ran up to us from a family house [in the respectable suburb of Vlohy]. She had been attacked by two thugs wearing just shirts and trousers and brandishing revolvers. I went there with a few men and took the thugs with me. First I came across an SS officer. I told him that we should be ashamed of such an auxiliary army in front of the Poles. He replied that it was very good for the Poles to see what would have happened had we not saved them from the Asiatics. Then I led them to 'Colonel' Kaminski, who slapped them in the face and led them away. What a bizarre individual for a Caucasian!

At Hitler's command, Warsaw was to be razed. All movables were to be taken away. We carried off a large amount of eggs and sugar that could be put into sacks, and my office was equipped with a new typewriter, which Major Weiss lifted from an abandoned house. Lieutenant Johann 'acquired' a huge brand-new six-lamp Telefunken radio for himself, and he wore a gold signet ring, which could only have been stolen. He got drunk with his sergeant, *Owm.* Muhle, and some Polish 'ladies', with whom they had spent the night . . . Hitler's permission to loot, issued to all the units fighting in Warsaw, was spreading demoralization.[1]

---

had left the Premier in no doubt about 'compromise' being absolutely essential. What is more, they had made no bones about the fact that, in their view, the 'compromise' would have to be rather one-sided. Stalin's demands could not be minimized. Major concessions were unavoidable. The Soviet Union had gained a position of strength. The exiled Government could not hope to hang on to its pre-war frontiers intact; and sooner or later it would have to share some power with the Communists. Yet if reasonable steps were taken, the accompanying assumption held that Stalin, too, would be reasonable. Such, after all, was the Westerners' idea of a political deal.

In Washington, both the Polish Mission and the US Government were taken unawares by news of the Rising, which, thanks to the time difference with Europe, was already announced in the morning papers of 2 August. The director of the mission said that everyone was 'thunderstruck, bewildered, and depressed'. He reported one of his colleagues saying, 'This is capital stupidity.' He also maintained that according to Gen. Tabor's statements to them in June no one had expected Warsaw to be the scene of fighting. 'The surprise of the Combined Chiefs of Staff and of the American Staff', he would recall, 'was no less than our own.'[23]

For many reasons the initial Soviet reaction to the Warsaw Rising was characterized by caution. On the ground, as is now known for certain, the Soviet Army was running into a determined German counter-attack to the east of the Vistula, and the High Command would not have been able to tell how quickly the front might be stabilized. Certainly in the first week of August, there was little chance that Rokossovsky could easily have crossed the Vistula in force. On the diplomatic front, the key talks with the Polish Premier were yet to take place. It was not yet clear what proposals he would make or how resolutely he would be backed by Churchill and Roosevelt. Above all, Moscow was in acute need of accurate intelligence. Stalin would have wanted to know who was running the Rising, how it might affect his Polish protégés, and how long it could be expected to last. If the insurgents were likely to surrender before Rokossovsky could think of helping them, there would be nothing to worry about. Hence on 2 August, in an order later concealed, Stalin called the First Byelorussian Front to a halt. He had decided to wait and see. As Boor informed London on 2, 3, and 4 August, there were no signs of a Soviet attack developing. [**SEWER I**, p. 269]

Neither the British nor the Soviets had intelligence officers in Warsaw. The British were to find that an RAF POW, John Ward, had escaped German detention and had joined the Home Army. And the Soviets, too, would find that one of their own men was in a similar position. Capt. Konstanty Kalugin had found his way into Warsaw after evading his German captors, and, with the help of the Home Army, was desperate to contact his superiors. The irony was, though Rokossovsky's forces were only a few miles away, there was apparently no means of communicating with them except by radio via London and Moscow. On 5 August, Kalugin sent a personal message addressed to Stalin and tapped out on the airwaves to Barnes Lodge:

> I have established personal contact with the commander of the Warsaw garrison [Monter], which is conducting the nation's heroic battle against the Hitlerite bandits . . . I have come to the conclusion that the following deliveries need to be made . . . in order to

SEWER I

Lieutenant 'Marten', an engineer, organizes the Home Army's network of sewers

By 6 August, a project had been set up to make use of the sewers. Among the Jews liberated from the Goose Farm Camp, there was a man who knew the sewers from the battle in the Ghetto; and he gave us the first valuable instructions. On 6 August, two messengers arrived in the City Centre via the sewers from Mokotov. By the 15th, a telephone line had been laid from the City Centre to the Old Town . . .

The Warsaw sewerage system was based on three main drains. Drain A ran along Commodity and Trench Streets, Drain B ran under Marshal Street, and Drain C under New World Street and the Cracow Faubourg. They all joined up near the Danzig Station and then ran on north to Jolibord. The main drains collected effluent from side sewers, whilst storm-channels led excess water off to the Vistula.

I became acquainted with the battle in the sewers [later in the month], when I received orders to go from the Old Town to Jolibord. It was supposed to be a short expedition to replenish anti-tank ammunition, but fate decided that I would remain permanently on sewer service. In Jolibord I sought out employees of the Warsaw sanitation department, who instructed us how to move through the smaller sewers on all fours, holding a wooden stick against the sides for support. The principal sewer route from Jolibord to Ohota measured 5–6 kilometres.[1]

Commander 'Ela' opens up the route from the City Centre to Mokotov

The bitter smell of hydrogen sulphate, mixed with that stagnant odour of rotting slime and mouldering plants assaulted the nostrils. The yellow, concentrated light of the lanterns fell a few metres before us, sliding along the lichen-covered oval vault. The surface of the mud shone in the light like black, shiny metal. The height of the sewer did not exceed one and a half metres. We had to bend our legs at the knees, to stoop even lower . . . and to rest our arms on the slippery wall.

It was not hard to guess that we were under Crossroads Square. To the left stretched Jerusalem Avenue, to the right was Schuch Avenue with its dense concentration of SS men . . . The sewer there became narrower and lower . . .

Crunch! Crash! With the jarring of iron and the cracking of crushed stones, a tank was moving over the top of us . . . But then it passed! . . . 'It isn't even worth trying under Pulavy Street,' my companion remarked . . . The whole area could have remained in enemy hands . . .

The mud stuck to our legs. Sultry weather, lack of expertise, and failure to conserve our strength intensified the exhaustion ... We had to crawl. We groaned from fear ... It would only take a shower of rain to block the exits and drown us ... We had to slither on elbows and knees, holding our breath.

A catchment chamber. We could sit on the bottom, straighten our backs, and rest. [But] the manhole above was closed ... Where were we? At the next chamber it was the same story. The sewer stretched on and on. Our strength was spent. We could not get out and we would not make it back!

There was no way of understanding how it happened. An imperceptible draught of cool air revived us; and we noticed a pale glow like a half moon in the sky. Swiftly we made for the metal climbing irons! Up and up we climbed. I raised my head gingerly above the surface ... No light, not a living soul.

'*Stoi!* Hands up!'

My tension eased. They are ours!

'From the City Centre,' I cried. 'From Commander Monter.'[2]

Eighteen-year-old 'Rake', a future literary critic, went in the opposite direction

I entered the sewers seriously wounded and feverish ... Our platoon no longer existed ... I spent the most horrendous day of my life down there ... The Germans were throwing in carbide gas. They waited by every manhole with grenades ... People could not cope psychologically; they were constantly stepping on corpses ...

Yet, after a series of hallucinations caused by gas poisoning, the strangest thing happened. With the use of my one arm, I managed to scramble out of a manhole, only to be grabbed by the neck by two SS men. If they had shot me, it would have been fully expected. I was almost unconscious and totally indifferent. But seeing that I was wounded, they lifted my shattered arm from the board to which it was tied, washed it with water from a flask and led me to a dressing station. I guess that the meeting was rather untypical.[3]

---

ensure victory over the common enemy – automatic weapons, ammunition, grenades, anti-tank guns. Drop the weapons in Wilson Square, Napoleon Square, the Ghetto ... Reception points can be recognized by their red-and-white marking. ... Direct the artillery against the main German positions on the Vistula bridges, in the Saxon Garden, and Jerusalem Avenue ... The heroic population of Warsaw believes that you will provide effective armed assistance

> within the next few hours. Please arrange a link-up for me with Marshal Rokossovsky.
>
> From the Black Group, Kalugin Konstanty, Warsaw 66804[24]

The enthusiastic reaction of the Communist propaganda organs contrasted strongly with the caution of the Soviet High Command. On 3 August, Moscow Radio's Polish Service announced: 'The Red Army is approaching Warsaw. Polish units are located in the immediate vicinity of Warsaw.'[25] The Polish Communist station went further:

> The People's Army has taken to arms in Warsaw. German blood is flowing on the streets . . . The German garrison is threatened from the front and from the rear. Battles are in progress at Anin between German units and the People's Army.
>
> A great battle is raging at Bielany and on the right bank of the Vistula, where Polish units are opening the way for the Red Army that is attacking Warsaw. Fierce fighting is taking place on the Cracow Faubourg. The capital's population is assisting the People's Army.
>
> Soldiers of the Polish Home Army have joined up with the action of the People's Army.[26]

Much of this bulletin was pure fiction, invented by overeager activists who had not yet heard of Stalin's latest posture. The Soviet press indulged in still wilder fantasies. An article in the military paper, *Red Star*, quoted by Moscow Radio, was entitled 'General Sosnkowski's Black Hundreds at Work' (the Black Hundreds were the most notorious of the Tsarist regime's most repressive formations).[27]

Stalin faced a weighty strategic problem. Once his armies had occupied all the territory he was claiming for the USSR, he had to decide whether to keep them moving westwards on the direct road to Berlin or turn south into the Balkans. The Soviets stood a fair chance of conquering the capital of the Reich before the Wehrmacht could marshal its defences and before the Western powers could participate. If they turned south, they could probably overrun three or four countries in rapid succession, thereby denying the West access and ensuring Soviet control over half of Europe. In the best of circumstances, they might conceivably find the resources to do both. In the first week of August, however, Moscow could have had no certain information either about the roadblock in Warsaw or about

Rokossovsky's exact predicament. So it was not unwise to stall until all aspects of the problem clarified.

Moscow was eager to hear news from its own political and security organs. On 3 August, for example, Beria forwarded an NKVD report to Stalin regarding the recent operation to disarm 'so-called Polish Home Army units' captured in Lithuania.[28] Among other things, he was at pains to show not only that 'the Polish nationalists are fomenting anti-Soviet activity' but also that the captured men had little inclination to cooperate. Of the 7,924 persons arrested in that particular operation, only 440 had agreed to join the Berling Army. Not a single AK officer had offered his services. One may deduce that the Soviet High Command was not encouraged to rush into an involvement in Warsaw, where the Home Army might be much more numerous.

Beria's correspondence is sufficient to show that Soviet policy was ruthless, inhumane, and coldly calculating. Yet one must also consider the possibility that another factor was coming into play: that Soviet calculations were simply confused. As Soviet forces moved into Poland, they were leaving the bubble of their rigid ideological world, and were finding that reality did not conform to existing analyses. Their hesitations may have been inspired as much by disorientation as by deliberate policy.

Poland's Premier had arrived in Moscow on 30 July, and looked to an early meeting with Stalin. He was a man of determination and moderation, who was staking his career on striking a deal with the Soviets and their protégés. Unlike some of his colleagues, he was not assertively anti-Communist. Nor had he any connection with the pre-war *Sanacja* regime. He was a middle-of-the-road democrat, who, as head of the Peasant Party, could be confident of commanding the largest block of votes in a free, post-war parliament. Balding, rosy-cheeked, undemonstrative, he was known, as befitted a representative of the peasantry, for his stubbornness. He was under no illusion that his Western partners were anxious to see the deal clinched.

In judging the Premier's mission, however, it is essential to consider what he knew in advance, what he learned in the course of his trip, and what he could not have known. For example, he knew that Stalin had been pressing for months for the restoration of the 'Peace Boundary' of 1939–41, that the Lublin Committee had been installed as an acting administration, and that the 'Big Three' had already discussed Polish matters at Teheran. He did not know how far Stalin might be prepared to compromise on frontier matters, nor whether the PKWN was viewed in Moscow as Poland's future Government, nor whether the Teheran Conference had reached any concrete decisions. He knew on departure that the Warsaw Rising was due to take place, that the Home Army was the only serious fighting force in the Polish Underground, and that the Home Army's aim was to welcome the Soviet Army into Warsaw. He did not know how the Rising was faring. He had no information about the likely stance of the Communist Underground, nor about Rokossovsky's intentions. Unlike many of his colleagues, he had no personal experience of Russia and Russian methods. But he would have heard far more hard fact about Stalin and Stalin's country than any other Western statesman of the day. Above all, he would have been conscious of his Cabinet's feelings, which were not as evenly optimistic as his own.

Stalin's views of the Premier have not been recorded, but they can be surmised. He would have known that the visitor was 'a peasant politician'. This can only have meant in Stalin's eyes that he was a kulak – a member of the class of rural bourgeois which was destined to extinction and of which, at Stalin's bidding, some 10–20 million had perished in the previous decade. He would also have known that the exiled Polish Government was resident in London, hence ultimately subject to British control. In Stalin's view, this undoubtedly meant that the Premier's proposals, whatever they were, would be rather less important than the strength of Churchill's backing. It would have been in Stalin's nature to act provocatively and to put these issues to the test.

From the start, therefore, Premier Mick and his entourage were left in no doubt about the pains of their task:

> From the moment of their arrival in Moscow, [they] were ostentatiously snubbed. No one of importance greeted them at the airport, and while their own visit was not once mentioned in the press, they read in *Pravda* a long article about the official exchange of representatives between the Lublin Committee and the Soviet Government. As soon as he arrived, [the Premier], anxious to obtain some briefing, called on the British ambassador, Clerk Kerr. He did not get much information, but he did receive significant advice. The best way to strengthen his position vis-à-vis Stalin was to purge his Government of 'reactionary' and 'anti-Soviet' elements, to accept the Curzon Line as a basis for negotiations, to recognize the Soviet findings on the

> [Katyn] massacre as conclusive, and to come to a 'working arrangement' with the Lublin Committee. This, of course, meant acceptance of all Stalin's demands.[29]

The visitor was received by Molotov on 31 July. 'Why have you come here?' he was asked, as if Molotov didn't know. He was then told that Stalin was very busy, and that it would be better to talk to representatives of the Lublin Committee, who happened to be in Moscow. The Premier declined.

The Premier learned of the outbreak of the Rising by radio, sometime towards the end of the three days when he was kept waiting for his audience with Stalin. The development made him all the more beholden to Stalin's goodwill. He would undoubtedly have preferred to negotiate with Stalin before the complications of the Rising arose.

Stalin finally received his visitor on 3 August. The Premier set out his agenda, including his wish to discuss the frontier issue. Stalin took the line that he was caught between the conflicting demands of two rival Polish bodies and that he could not deal with them properly until they had settled their differences. He was not inclined to listen to the Premier's outline of frontier proposals as worked out with the British Foreign Office; but he intimated that Poland would receive land up to the Oder and Neisse in compensation. On the question of aid for the Warsaw Rising, he sounded sympathetic at first and then turned truculent:

PREMIER: Marshal, I have a request to make to you, to give orders for providing assistance for our units fighting in Warsaw.
STALIN: I shall give those orders . . .
PREMIER: I wish to ask you to facilitate my journey to Warsaw.
STALIN: But, surely, the Germans are there.
PREMIER: Warsaw will be free any day now.
STALIN: Please God that it will be so . . . But I don't see how your units could drive the Germans out. After all, they have not been fighting the Germans, but have been skulking in the woods . . .
PREMIER: Will you supply those people with weapons?
STALIN: I will not permit any operation beyond our lines. You will have to talk to the Lublin Committee.[30]

The two men parted without it being clear whether substantial Soviet aid would be given to the Rising or not. But Premier Mick, as always, looked for something positive. He told the British Embassy that Stalin had undertaken to give orders for providing assistance to Warsaw.

In the light of these difficulties, the Premier reluctantly agreed to meet the representatives from Lublin, headed by Boleslas B. and Vanda W. He saw them twice. On the 6th, they solemnly told him that there was no fighting in Warsaw, thereby contradicting their own communiqués. Vanda W. had supposedly talked to a person who had been in Warsaw only two days previously and who had not seen any fighting at all. On the 7th, the commander of the Polish People's Army complained that the AK had created a terrible situation by starting the Rising without prior consultation with the Soviets. At least he was not denying the reality of the Rising. Boleslas B. then calmly suggested that the Premier should resign so that the Lublin Committee could officially become the Government and Boleslas B. could become the president. When the Premier hinted that he might return to Poland as a private citizen, Boleslas B. told him bluntly that he would be arrested. The Communist cat was playing with a poor and lonely mouse. In the absence of even symbolic support from British or American diplomats, the mission was going nowhere. The Premier prepared to pack his bags. Nothing had been achieved.

At least Premier Mick had succeeded in extracting from Stalin that one, rather ambiguous undertaking about Soviet assistance. And it was his duty to stay in Moscow to see if this important point could be clarified. He requested a second meeting.

Behind the scenes, the wheels were turning. On 5 August, the Soviet General Staff received a letter from the head of the British Military Mission, Col. Turner, requesting information about 'the decision' to fly in arms and ammunition to Warsaw. The Colonel was passing on requests which he himself had received both from London and, presumably, from Premier Mick. The next day, his letter was forwarded to the National Commissar for the Defence of the USSR. This Anglo-Soviet correspondence is curious on two scores. Firstly, in the Russian versions of the exchange, both sides use the formula 'assistance for the illegal Polish Army in Warsaw'. Secondly, the National Commissar for the Defence of the USSR was Stalin.[31] All paths led back to him. [**BARRICADE**, p. 276]

In the first days of the Rising, the insurgents learned the hard way about the effective methods of attack and defence. In some instances, the pent-up urge to mount a frontal assault on German positions proved cata-

BARRICADE

A woman poet who helped build a barricade apologizes for her modest role

Let me tell you, dear daughter,
That I was no heroine.
Everyone was building the barricades under fire.
But I did see heroes;
And I must tell you about them.

The publican, the jeweller's lover, the hairdresser –
All were cowards.
A waitress fell to the ground
Hoisting a flagstone from the pavement.
We were all scared, all cowards –
The manager, the stall-holder, the pensioner . . .
No one forced us.
But we built the barricade
Under fire.

The museum is alight. It burns
As beautifully as straw,
Adored by generations,
Priceless,
Like a human body.

They thought that I had been felled
On the corner of the street by a bullet.
And they wept.

They sneaked into the warehouse at night
Dragging meat off the shelves.
The Germans shot them at night
On the meat shelves.

The son forgot his mother.
She was dying in the cellar,
Lying on coal bags.
She called for water.
She called for her son.
No one came.
He was cleaning his automatic,

Counting the rounds of ammunition
Before the battle.

Come with me, General,
Let us go together
To capture machine guns and cannon
With our bare knuckles.

The child is two months old.
The doctor says:
It will die without milk . . .
He brings three spoonfuls of milk
The child lives
An hour longer.

I slept with corpses under the same blanket,
I apologized to the corpses
For being alive.

He was perhaps two metres tall
That young ragamuffin,
A happy-go-lucky worker from Riverside,
Who fought
In the hell of Herb Street,
In the telephone building.
When I bandaged
His lacerated leg
He grimaced, he laughed.
'When the war ends,' he said,
'Let's go and dance, lass;
It's on me.'
I waited for him
For thirty years.

There were so many noises then:
The roar of planes, of fire of despair,
Rising up to the clouds, screaming.
Now the earth and the sky
Are silent.[1]

Anna Świrczyńska

strophic. At exactly 5 p.m. on 1 August, for example, ninety-eight men of the Stag Battalion, a mixture of pre-war cavalrymen and raw recruits armed only with revolvers, poured out of a tenement on the corner of Bagatelle Street and attempted to rush a complex of bunkers guarding the SS and Gestapo buildings on nearby Schuch Avenue. Only their commander and six men survived. During their retreat, they ambushed a German patrol, which had been searching some houses, and shot several soldiers. In revenge, the Germans returned that evening to kill every inhabitant of the houses concerned. Insurgent losses were approximately twenty times higher than those of the Germans.

Elsewhere, more circumspect tactics brought more effective results. Five companies of the elite Parasol Battalion, for instance, already hardened by action in the underground K-Div. organization, took up positions on 1 August on the western side of the adjoining Jewish, Lutheran, and Calvinist cemeteries. Their HQ and observation post was located in an old folks' home. On the morning of the 2nd, they were unable to stop a column of Panthers, which drove past into the positions of their comrades of the Zoshka Battalion. That afternoon, however, they were confronted by a major German attack directed from the western suburbs. They faced a column of Tiger tanks of the Hermann Göring Panzer Division, supported by elements of the 2nd Regiment of Grenadiers and an armoured artillery regiment. Whilst the tanks were smashing their way up front through a complex of barricades manned by the Communist AL, an assortment of Home Army units fell on the trailing German infantry. In this way, the attack was brought to a halt some 200 metres (650 feet) short of Parasol's main defence line. Next day, the cemetery district was subjected to heavy bombardments from an armoured train. Parasol suffered its first serious casualties in the evening, when its HQ took a direct hit from bombs dropped by a score of Heinkel 111s. The command post was relocated a few streets away. On the 4th, Parasol captured three armoured cars, a large cache of guns and ammunition, and a band of prisoners. And, amidst considerable rejoicing, it received two PIAT anti-tank rockets and two machine guns as its share of the drop by the first RAF Liberator. The night was spent burying the dead, rebuilding barricades, and strengthening defences. After four days of hard fighting the battalion had lost only 8 per cent of its effectives in dead and wounded. At that rate, they would not be annihilated for some time. They had passed their baptism of fire.[32]

In one incident, when Parasol had begun to prepare a strongpoint near the Hospital of St Stanislas Kostka, a white-coated doctor came out and asked them to move on, for fear of German reprisals. They obliged. Next day, the doctor and all his staff and patients were massacred.

The 5th and 6th of August saw two of the blackest days in Warsaw's history. The principal reinforcements of the German garrison had arrived, and *SS-Gruf.* Reinefarth launched his grand assault on Vola. The insurgents were gradually forced back towards the City Centre. Hand-to-hand fighting persisted in the cemeteries, even when the main insurgent units had been ordered to retreat through the ruins of the Ghetto. Rheinefarth complained about a shortage of ammuition. 'We just can't kill them all,' he grumbled.[33] The price was paid by civilians. On 5 August alone, an estimated 35,000 men, women, and children were shot by the SS in cold blood.

The first week of the Rising brought little satisfaction to either side. The insurgents had not seized full control of the capital. The Germans had not crushed the insurgents. Both the opening assault by the Home Army and the subsequent German counter-attack had fallen short of their goals. Far more civilians had been killed than combatants. Indeed, the obsession of the SS with slaughtering innocents was seriously hampering the German military effort. Neither side had been brought to its knees. So neither side was willing to call a halt.

Impasse

The fighting continued with unrelenting intensity. The Soviet Army was clinging on to its bridgeheads far to the south of the city, but it had been driven back in the central sector and had not achieved its original objective of establishing the front right along the line of the Vistula. The Wehrmacht had contained the Soviet pincers on either side of Warsaw, but the SS had not suppressed the Rising.

Given his overall supremacy in men and materiel, Rokossovsky must have been confident that his setback on the central sector would prove temporary. But he estimated the delay at two to three weeks, and it was not until 8 August that he drew up his plan for the next stage of the campaign. The plan, which was agreed with Zhukov and submitted for *Stavka*'s approval, assumed that the German salient east of Warsaw would be eliminated by the third week of August. After that would come a massive new offensive across the Vistula from the 25th, liberating Warsaw in the opening stage and driving westwards towards the Oder, 450km (280 miles) distant.[34]

German strategy, whilst stubbornly blocking the Soviet advance, gave priority to separating the Rising from operations at the front. To this end, a cordon was thrown round Warsaw on all sides, and two reserve Hungarian divisions were brought in to strengthen it. Systematic measures were taken to open the west–east supply line through the city and keep it open; the guard on the Vistula bridges was strengthened; the eastern suburb of Praga, where the insurgents had already been defeated, was heavily garrisoned; and the southern Soviet bridgeheads were surrounded by rings of steel. Von dem Bach kept his forces in the city busy, pounding insurgent positions and chipping away at vulnerable sectors, especially in the western suburbs. But it was not until 19 August, towards the end of the third week, that *SS-Gruf.* Reinefarth received orders to mount a concerted attack on one of the smallest sectors in the insurgent enclaves, in the Old Town. The Ninth Army log book repeatedly reported that the resistance was 'ferocious', 'fanatical', 'extremely determined', and that prospects for a rapid result were not good.

Home Army strategy turned almost exclusively to active defence. Lacking heavy weapons and having spent the element of surprise, the insurgents could only mount limited local counter-attacks and were constantly forced to make tactical withdrawals. On the other hand, they daily witnessed their enemy's inability to strike a knock-out blow. Allied airdrops were frustratingly scarce; but they raised hopes of more to come. Soviet intentions were sinisterly opaque; but as Rokossovsky steadily reasserted his supremacy his arrival on the far side of the river grew tantalizingly imminent. Death from surrender was seen as more likely than death in combat. So combat continued. [**PANTHER**, p. 281]

Once the initial fighting stabilized, the insurgents found themselves in control of three main areas – in the north, in the Centre, and the south – and in full command of two dense forests beyond the German cordon, one at Kampinos to the north and another in the Kabaty Woods to the south. Surface communication between these five areas was virtually impossible during daylight, but movement was feasible at night, and sewers and irrigation channels provided a ready-made network for the unsqueamish. German armoured columns were eventually able to roll along the main east–west boulevard between dawn and dusk, but they spent over two weeks securing this vital thoroughfare, and even then they did not usually venture out after nightfall. In the City Centre, the

PANTHER

A soldier from 'Dyon 1806', with three colleagues, achieves the impossible

The German Panther tanks were extremely heavily armoured, and I know from later experience that neither the American Shermans nor the British Cromwells with their 75mm cannon were strong enough to pierce the Panther's armour. For our part, we had nothing more than small-calibre weapons; and our bullets bounced off the Panthers like peas off a wall. Hence we only captured a second Panther by a sort of freak chance. There were three of us from our unit, together with 'Power', a man of unheard-of valour, about whom much has been written.

In the instant when the tank was driving through the barricade, Power leaped out of a gateway, ran up to the tank and pushed an enormous petrol bomb through the driver's visor. The bomb was too weak to damage the armour-plating. But by exploding right in front of the driver's face, it blinded him and caused him to lose control. He must have pulled the right-hand guidance lever, because the tank lurched suddenly to the right, ran off the roadway, and drove down into a garden ditch that was five or six feet lower. The driver tried to reverse; but the tank only dug itself in even deeper. After gathering our senses for a couple of seconds, either Mark or I, since both of us speak German well, shouted, '*Alle aussteigen!*', i.e., 'Everyone out'; and sure enough, after a short delay, the tank's upper cover opened, and the Germans began to climb out. Shouting, '*Hände hoch!*', we then jumped on top of the tank to disarm the Germans. Since it was damaged, the second tank had to be towed away by the first one.

At which point, a man in civilian clothes wearing a hat and coat (probably Radoslav in person) appeared from nowhere, introduced himself as a colonel, and demanded that we hand everything over. An argument ensued, and nearly led to shots being fired. But Power, as a pre-war officer, eventually gave in, and we had to surrender our captured weapons. All we kept was one brand-new carbine and its ammunition, which I hung on to, and a crate of anti-tank mines. There's no doubt that the petrol bomb inserted by Power provided the decisive element. And that's how we captured a tank![1]

Andrzej Nowakowski

insurgents were under pressure from the west, losing the cemeteries and most of the Ghetto by 12 August. But they fell back in orderly fashion; and in the middle of the month they were still holding the Old Town and the Riverside District in strength. In the northern suburbs, they re-entered districts that had been evacuated during the first week, and they were not seriously troubled there for the rest of the month.

On 15 August, Gen. Boor ordered all Home Army units in the vicinity of Warsaw to come to the capital's rescue. Fierce but abortive attempts were made to break through the German cordon from the Kampinos Forest. Similarly fierce and unsuccessful attempts were launched against German positions at the Danzig Station, to cut the main east–west railway line and relink the City Centre with the northern suburbs. No major ground was won or lost, but both sides exhausted themselves. In the southern suburbs the Home Army enjoyed greater success, holding on strongly to Mokotov opening up a pathway to the Kabaty Woods, and occupying a stretch of the Vistula foreshore facing Praga. This last conquest, which brought the insurgent strongholds to their maximum extent, was particularly valuable since it provided a prospective landing-stage for Soviet forces approaching from the east.

Reinefarth's assault on the Old Town relied increasingly on mass bombardments than to waves of infantry. It gradually reduced the insurgents' redoubt to an oblong of streets roughly 1200m by 600m (1,300 yards by 650), where life of any sort among the mountainous ruins became increasingly perilous. By the fourth week of August, Gen. Boor was forced to prepare a military withdrawal through the sewers.

Yet the SS looked incapable of inducing the total collapse which they so earnestly sought. The anger of the Ninth Army Command was mounting. On 29 August, von dem Bach admitted to them that the Rising was unlikely to be terminated by existing methods. He requested the transfer of an extra division possessing fully trained and battle-hardened infantrymen, not 'the rag-bag of assorted units' which he had at his disposal at present. On 30 August, the Ninth's log showed how difficult it was to fight both the Soviets and the insurgents simultaneously. The Soviets had just taken the town of Radzymin, 20km (twelve miles) to the east of Warsaw, so German reinforcements had to be brought in, and a battalion of sappers, which was vital to the final attack on the Old Town, was pulled out during the night in order to guard the Vistula bridges.[35]

*

As August wore on, German reactions to the Rising were conditioned by setbacks on other fronts. The Allies held Rome. The Americans were driving across France. The Soviets, though slowed before Warsaw, were gearing up for renewed offensives in East Prussia and the Balkans. Warsaw was annoying, even humiliating, but it was not Berlin's most pressing problem. Indeed, the impasse on the Vistula rather suited the Wehrmacht's purposes.

The German counter-attack east of the Vistula by four *panzer* divisions had proved surprisingly effective. When launched on 2 August, it was conceived as a last-minute move to staunch the gaping wound caused by Operation Bagration and the collapse of Army Group Centre. But instead it made headway, and Rokossovsky, who had literally been within sight of Warsaw, was pushed back halfway to the Bug. With the Wehrmacht in full retreat in most other places, this must be reckoned an exceptional German achievement.

All German sources of the time took it for granted that the Soviet Army was seeking to link up with the insurgents. In its log of 8 August, the Ninth Army took satisfaction from the fact that 'the Russian attempt to seize Warsaw by a coup de main had been defeated by our defence' and that 'from the enemy's point of view, [the Rising] had started too soon'. Guderian later commented: 'We Germans had the impression that it was our defence which halted the enemy rather than a Russian desire to sabotage the Warsaw Rising.'[36]

In the meantime, the most imminent threat, from the German point of view, lay to the north. Whilst Rokossovsky had been advancing towards the Vistula, the First and Second Baltic Fronts and the Third Byelorussian Front had invaded the Baltic states. One mighty thrust was aimed at the Gulf of Riga and the other at Lithuania and the Baltic coast round Memel. The latter operation, which made great progress in August but was not completed until October, was particularly dangerous since it gradually cut off a whole German army group in Courland. It also promised to lead the Soviet Army for the first time onto the territory of the Reich, in East Prussia. One effect of these developments was the decision by the Government of Finland on 25 August to sue for an armistice. A second was to sow the seeds of panic among the population of East Prussia. For the time being, however, they were relieved to learn that the latest Soviet offensive had been directed into the Balkans.

German propaganda inevitably tried to exploit developments to their own advantage. On 19 August the *Völkische Beobachter*, the principal organ of the NSDAP, published a major article on the Rising. Entitled 'The Satanic Game with Warsaw', it concluded that 'London and Moscow have rushed the Poles into a Rising and have left them in the lurch.' The clear implication was that Churchill and Stalin were working in cahoots.[37]

By 21 August, the Germans had lost over 9,000 soldiers killed in Warsaw, with still more wounded or missing. They clearly had cause for reflection. Their tactics were not working. They were not making rapid inroads into the insurgent-held districts; and they were paying a heavy price. [**NIGHT PATROL**, p. 285]

All standard accounts of the Warsaw Rising present the picture of a deeply polarized conflict between two sides – 'the Germans' and 'the Poles'. If they discuss the third, but largely passive, party in the conflict, they usually talk about 'the Russians'. Each of these generalizations calls for examination.

On the German side, a large if not predominant part of the soldiery was made up of what were often called 'collaborationist forces'. By 1944, both the Wehrmacht and the SS were accepting recruits from almost any source available. (The two obvious exceptions were Poles and Jews.) In Warsaw, the largest single group of non-Germans were Russians from the RONA Brigade, whose origins lay in the province of Briansk. The Azeris of the 111th Regiment formed a distinct formation, as did the Oriental Muslim Regiment. The two Cossack units came from the 15th Cossack Cavalry Corps, which consisted of Tsarist émigrés of post-1917 vintage and which, having been largely raised in the Balkans, contained a smattering of Bulgars, Serbs, and other Orthodox. (They were eventually handed over to the Soviets by the British in Austria.) The 2nd Hungarian Corps were particularly reluctant to serve. Indeed, they seriously considered joining the insurgents. They were told by their Government in Budapest, 'not to join the Poles, but . . . not to fight them.'[38]

On this issue, two major misconceptions can be identified. It is often said that the collaborationist forces in Warsaw included 'Vlassovites' and also Ukrainians from the 14th *Waffen-SS Galizien* Division. Neither statement is true. Vlassov was not in Warsaw. Indeed the Vlassov Army was not formally constituted until the winter of 1944–45. The source of the mistake seems to derive from the fact that part of the RONA Brigade, which was broken up after the Rising, was transferred to the Vlassov

NIGHT PATROL

A member of the Home Army's Information Department is asked to witness a vital operation

On Wednesday 30 August, I was summoned to Monter, who announced that our forces were going to retreat from the Old Town that same night. All the elite formations in the City Centre had been concentrated for an attack on the German-held corridor, which ran from the Saxon Garden to the Iron Gate Square. The Germans were to be pinned down by two lines of fire. We were to give cover to units crossing over to us from the Old Town. 'I want to have you with me as a reporter,' said Monter, 'to broadcast about it in English and Polish.' He was in a good mood, confident of success.

Around ten at night, we moved off . . . The closer we got to the target, the more difficult it was to find our bearings. I was brought up in this town. I knew every corner. But we were advancing through a forest of stone ruins along twisting paths trodden into the rubble, climbing over mounds of bricks. Somewhere not far from the Square, we stopped in a courtyard surrounded by the burnt-out remnants of its walls. Soldiers sat by the wall waiting for action to begin. Officers were reporting to Monter every few minutes . . .

Sometime after midnight Monter ordered the firing of a green flare, the agreed signal for those in the Old Town to commence. For a long time we looked up into the sky, watching for the reply, which did not come. I asked the Colonel about enemy strength. 'Three battalions,' he replied, 'and probably seven or eight tanks.' He explained how the plan was to work. There would be a diversionary attack in the Saxon Garden. During that time our men would smash holes in the walls of the tenement houses facing onto Iron Gate Square and the Mirov Hall, and would carry out a raid in the direction of Elector Street where they would meet up with the others. So as not to mistake each other for Germans, they were to use the password *sosna*, meaning 'pine tree'. The most dangerous moment would come when they broke into the Mirov Hall.

About one o'clock, shots were fired in the region of the Saxon Garden. Bursts from machine pistols could be heard, and exploding grenades. An orange flare roared into the sky. The Germans were summoning help. They were answered by the thunder of their tanks arriving from the direction of Cool Street.

All the time I was at Monter's side, listening to reports being delivered and orders being issued. After half an hour the Colonel grew uneasy. For some reason, our main attack could not get started. He decided to go forward to see what was happening.

We climbed up fire-damaged stairs; we jumped from one piece of wall to another . . . Eventually we reached a line of destroyed houses [on Starch Street], right opposite the Mirov Hall. In front of the Colonel loomed the silhouette of a young officer, Lieutenant 'Yanush' Z.

'Colonel. Our girl sappers are blowing a hole in the wall. [But] there is no way out. The German howitzers have found the range both of the opening and of the courtyard.'

Monter, who till that point had been silent, spoke up.

'Execute the order. You are to attack immediately. We will not leave our people on the other side without support.'

'Understood, Colonel,' replied the lieutenant grimly.

Again, I climbed behind Monter up something that was once a stairwell, and we stood on a scorched window, which looked out to the left onto the Mirov Hall. Two floors below was a courtyard gradually filling with youngsters round the well. I recognized the group of girls from the sapper patrol. Suddenly, a mortar landed in the crowd, followed by a second and a third. They set off our petrol bombs. I heard the screams of shock and pain, mainly from girls' voices. Flames lit up a hellish scene of wounded and burning bodies . . .

I crossed the whole sector with Monter . . . In the morning, the units returned to their jumping-off points. I was with him when he received their reports. That night around one hundred young people had died.[1]

J. 'Novak'

Army and fought with them to the end of the war. The term 'Vlassovites' was used by the post-war Communists as pejorative shorthand for all Russians serving in the German military. What is true, therefore, is that the 'Vlassovites' of 1945 did include men who had served under Kaminski in Warsaw.

A similar misunderstanding surrounds the Ukrainians. The *SS-Galizien* was never in Warsaw, and cannot be fairly accused of atrocities there. Nonetheless, a certain number of ethnic Ukrainians *were* present. Some served alongside Russians in RONA. Others served in a variety of German police units, both as distinct formations and in conjunction with policemen of other nationalities. It was said that the Nazi execution squads commanded by *SS-Hstuf.* Spilker, for example, were largely manned by Ukrainians. The Volhynian Self-Defence Legion made a brief appearance late on. What *is* true is that one or more of the Ukrainian police units were transferred to the *SS-Galizien* after the Rising. In this way, the *SS-Galizien* came to include men who had earlier served in Warsaw.

On the Polish side, discussions can be found on the role of Jews in the Rising. In the eyes of most Jewish insurgents this is a non-issue, since they were accustomed to regard themselves as patriotic Poles like anyone else. They have no sympathy for the post-war Zionist convention which regards 'Poles' and 'Jews' as two completely separate ethnic or national groups, and which tries to magnify the friction between the two. They are particularly incensed by the false accusation that the Home Army did not accept Jews, and by even wilder talk about it being an 'anti-Semitic organization'. The fact is, Jews with various religious or political connections served with distinction both in the Home Army and in the People's Army. The latter, which was particularly short of recruits, agreed to organize a separate Jewish section that was mainly composed of surviving Ghetto fighters. There was also an assortment of foreign Jews, especially Hungarians, who had been liberated from their German captors and who volunteered to join their Polish liberators.

This is not to say that occasional problems did not arise. Many years after the war, certain Jewish historians produced the accusation that Jews had been murdered during the Rising by the AK and NSZ. On reflection, the accusation was duly modified and redirected against individuals who may have belonged to the AK or the NSZ. Close examination revealed both a large number of misunderstandings and a small number of rapes and murders of which Jews had been the victims. The difficulty was to know whether these 'black pages of the Rising' were racially motivated and whether they were qualitatively different from the numerous other crimes which occurred as a matter of course in a starving city of nearly a million people. Certainly, they were not ignored by the Home Army's security organs. What the investigations did underline was firstly that Warsaw in 1944 still harboured a very sizeable Jewish community and secondly that Jews served with distinction in the insurgent ranks. Samuel Willenberg, for example, who was a survivor of the rising in Treblinka, contrived to serve during the Warsaw Rising both in the AK's 'Brooke' Battalion and in the socialist PAL group.[39]

Like any major pre-war city, Warsaw contained a large variety of foreign communities. As a result, the Home Army attracted a corresponding variety of non-Polish fighters, among them Turks, Serbs, Georgians, Slovenes, Russians, Britons, Irish, and even Germans. One AK battalion contained a distinct platoon of Slovaks who had fled from the fascistic regime in their own country.[40]

On the Soviet side of the front, the array of nationalities was particularly diverse: and the ingrained habit of calling everyone a 'Russian' was particularly inappropriate. Russians formed only slightly more than half of the Soviet Union's population. The rest were drawn from seventy official nationalities, most of whom would have been represented in Rokossovsky's armies approaching the Vistula. [**MAGYAR**, p. 289]

Despite later legends, the civilian population did not support the Rising with uniform enthusiasm. It is probably accurate to say that the majority of Varsovians felt common cause with the insurgents, yet there was a significant sector which held aloof, seeking merely to survive. And, as always, there were groups and individuals who expressed opposition. After all, Poland's insurrectionary tradition had never failed to provoke a chorus of critics who mocked the record of lost causes and romantic catastrophes. In consequence, the civilian mood in Warsaw rose and fell considerably, according to time and place. Nonetheless, one can state with confidence that there was no substantial group of Varsovians actively prepared to assist the Germans against the insurgents.

Objectively, one would have thought that it was in the German interest to discourage civilian sympathy for the insurgents. Yet the mass killings of tens of thousands of innocents during the early days had exactly the opposite effect. What is more, the recurrent flight of people from their homes either to the insurgent enclaves or to the evacuation points provided by the Germans tended to concentrate the supporters and to disperse the discontented. Home Army propaganda, which ridiculed German promises of humane treatment, was more credible than the German appeals constantly urging civilians to leave. So long as the food stocks remained, therefore, most Varsovians were prepared to sit it out.

On 24 August, one of the few British observers of the Rising, John Ward, sent a radio message to London trying to explain the nature of the conflict:

> Today, a battle is going on that I think is very difficult for the British nation to understand. It is a battle that is being carried on by the civilian population as well as by the AK . . . It is total warfare. Every street in the city has been a battlefield . . . The enemy minethrowers, artillery and aircraft are taking a heavy toll of human life. The damage to property is incalculable. Normal life . . . is at a complete standstill.[41]

MAGYAR

It is evident that relations between the Germans and their allies are not ideal

The approaching column of Hungarian infantry was beset by passers-by, and was forced to stop. We were standing right on Krashinski Square and from all sides we threw questions at the soldiers in different languages. Earlier they had smiled at us rather sheepishly. But lately, they expressed their sympathies quite openly. Traditional Polish–Hungarian cordiality was breaking through the walls of the enemy camp, and the chasm that had divided the enemies of Hitler, like us, from his allies, was crumbling.

'Long live Poland!' shouted one of the Hungarian soldiers. He was a Slovak and had correctly mastered the Polish language. 'Keep yourselves hale and hearty, the devils have already taken Hitler . . .'

We were able to discover the details of the latest events on the Eastern Front. The Red Army was less than fifty kilometres from Warsaw. The German army had been shattered. Garrisons, administrators, and the German civilian population were rapidly retreating to the west.

At this moment, I saw a [German] gendarmerie patrol approaching from Long Street. Heavy blows from metal rifle butts rained down on the backs of the people who had been talking to the Hungarians. Fear of German brutality, which had kept a strong grip on us throughout the Occupation, had been recently replaced by greater boldness . . . In the eyes of the whole of Warsaw, the Germans had lost their victors' strength.

One of the furious gendarmes fell upon the Slovak and began to tug at his uniform. The Hungarian soldiers and the German gendarmerie stared at each other, sizing each other up. But the stand-off did not deteriorate into open hostilities, because a Hungarian officer appeared [from Honey Street] on a beautiful dun horse, rode towards the group at a light gallop, and without a word whipped the German gendarme until bloody stripes ran along the length of his hands. The Hungarians immediately marched forward, and the gendarme stepped back onto the pavement.[1]

From the log of the German Ninth Army

The Hungarian Corps has been transferred to the north wing of the SS Panzer Corps. However, the general commanding the Hungarian Corps has reported quite openly to Ninth Army that no purpose is served by using his reserve division to block the flow of Polish reserves into Warsaw. The Polish population has always had very warm relations with the Hungarians thanks to their centuries-old tradition of friendship. The general's troops are inclined to fraternize with the locals; and it cannot be said how long they will remain under their officers' control. Their equipment is minimal, and consequently their effectiveness in combat is virtually nil. The Ninth Army command has taken the decision not to employ the 12th Reserve Division in a security role.[2]

Still harder to describe to outsiders was the scene in which every part of the city controlled by the insurgents possessed its own self-governing administration. Each municipal district had its mayor, just as each street had its self-help committee and each tenement block its prefect. These organizations sprang to life spontaneously in a society whose loyalty had in large measure been won before the Rising by the secret 'Underground State'. They ran communal kitchens, built barricades, cleared rubble, buried the dead, cared for the sick, extinguished fires. In close association with the Home Army and the Government delegates, they maintained a postal service, a widespread system of press distribution, and a fully fledged Public Security Corps (PKB) with police, judicial, and investigatory functions.[42] Each of the main political groupings organized its own district militias.

Insurgent justice was supposed to follow strict procedures, with regular court trials and verdicts. Executions of convicted spies, murderers, traitors, looters, and informers were carried out by AK police units. But lynchings were not unknown. *Volksdeutsche* were in constant danger, as were prostitutes who serviced the German military. German sources complained, among other things, that German civilians were robbed and murdered.[43]

Civilian morale was affected by a wide variety of factors, both political and material, and it passed through several phases. It was high after the outbreak, gradually declined during August, survived a crisis in early September, and revived again thereafter. Like military morale, it was strongly influenced by the hopes and fears surrounding Western aid and Soviet intervention.[44]

Nonetheless, it is a simple fact that a large body of Varsovians chose to stay, and to share the fate of the fighters. It was their unstinting support that enabled the insurgents to keep fighting. The Rising would have collapsed at any point if the civilians had decided en masse to heed

German orders and surrender. The leading study of the subject concludes by describing insurgent Warsaw as a 'city of contrasts':

> Alongside the superhuman sacrifice and selflessness, there was selfishness and shirking; where many gave everything they possessed, others hoarded and capitalised; unprecedented communal solidarity was marred by intrigue and betrayal. Whilst some people treated the insurgents as faultless heroes, others regarded them as the instigators of their suffering and the murderers of their families and children.[45]

F-M Montgomery's account of the Battle of the Falaise Gap, in August 1944, is a wonderful piece of post-hoc self-justification. Readers of his memoirs may be forgiven for thinking of the battle as a melange of superlative planning and masterly execution. Participants tended to think the opposite. They remember it more as a fine example of Clausewitz's remark about 'the fog of war'. Allied units were bombed by their own side. Others got lost, after confusing French villages with similar names. Coordination between Montgomery's armies to the north and Omar Bradley's American forces to the south was virtually non-existent. At one point, offended by the future Field Marshal's habitual arrogance, Bradley remarked: 'Montgomery can have our support if he *asks* for it.' The decisive conjunction of the British and American offensives on 18–20 August 1944, which sealed the fate of the German Seventh Army and ended the campaign in Normandy, seems to have happened as much by good fortune as by design. [**REFLECTIONS**, p. 292]

In those crucial August days, a key role fell to the 1st (Polish) Armoured Division of Maj.Gen. M., which formed the spearhead of the 2nd Canadian Corps on the flank of Montgomery's command. Probing southwards from Falaise, the division linked up with the Americans, who were moving north from Argentan, and, by occupying a strategic ridge, blocked the Seventh Army's line of retreat. It has been described as 'the cork in the bottle neck'. Maj.Gen. M.'s tankmen found themselves in the very hottest cauldron of the battle. Whilst fending off the ever more desperate attacks of the German divisions who were trapped on one side of the ridge, they wrestled with similarly desperate rescue attempts mounted by German units from the other side. But they held out; and Montgomery was able to claim the Falaise Gap as one of the greatest victories of his career. Indeed, it was the victory which preceded his

REFLECTIONS

A German officer and former schoolteacher posted to Warsaw enters desperate thoughts into his diary

The National Socialist revolution seems half-hearted in every way. History tells us of dreadful deeds and appalling barbarities during the French Revolution. And the Bolshevik Revolution too allowed terrible atrocities to be perpetrated . . . Both the Jacobins and the Bolsheviks butchered the ruling upper classes and executed their royal families. They broke with Christianity and waged war on it, intending to wipe it off the face of the earth . . .

The methods of the National Socialists are different, but basically they too pursue a single idea: the extermination and annihilation of people who think differently from them. Now and then a certain number of Germans are shot . . . People are imprisoned in concentration camps . . . The public hears nothing about it.

On the one hand, they ally themselves with the ruling classes in capital and industry . . . on the other they preach socialism. They declare themselves in favour of the right to personal and religious freedom, but they destroy the Christian churches and conduct a secret, underground battle against them. They speak of the Führer principle and the rights of capable people to develop their talents freely, but they make everything dependent on party membership . . .

And look at the National Socialists themselves – see how far they really live by National Socialist principles . . . Who faces the enemy? The people, not the party. Now they are calling up the physically infirm to serve in the army, while you see healthy, fit young men working in party offices and the police, far from the firing line. Why are they exempt?

They seize Polish and Jewish property to enjoy it themselves. Now the Poles and the Jews have nothing to eat, they live in want, they are freezing, and the National Socialists see nothing wrong in taking everything for themselves . . .

If you read the newspapers and listen to the news on the radio you might think everything was going very well, peace was certain, the war already won and the future of the German people full of hope. However, I just can't believe it, if only because injustice cannot prevail in the long run . . .[1]

The last year has been one setback after another . . .

No one in Germany believes we will win the war any more either, but what way out is there? There'll be no revolution at home because no one has the courage to risk his life by standing up to the Gestapo . . . And we can't expect an army coup. The army is willingly being driven to its death, and any idea of opposition that might set off a mass movement is quickly suppressed there too. So we must go on to the bitter end. Our entire nation will have to pay for all these wrongs and this unhappiness, all the crimes we have committed . . .

11 August 1944

The Führer is to issue a decree that Warsaw is to be razed to the ground. A start has been made already. All the streets liberated in the Uprising are being destroyed by fire. The inhabitants have to leave the city, and are going westward in crowds of many thousands. If the news of this decree is true then it's clear to me that we have lost Warsaw, and with it Poland and the war itself. We are giving up a place we held for five years, extending it and telling the world it was a forfeit of war. Monstrous methods were used here. We acted as if we were the masters and would never go away. Now we can't help seeing that all is lost, we're destroying our own work . . . Our policy in the East is bankrupt, and we are erecting a final memorial to it with the destruction of Warsaw.

Captain Wilm Hosenfeld*

* The officer who saved Władysław Szpilman, 'The Pianist'.

---

promotion to field marshal. In the course of the action, Maj.Gen. M.'s division suffered 20 per cent casualties.

Thanks to the radio link via London, the Home Army leaders in Warsaw were kept abreast of their comrades' fortunes in Normandy. Their view of the matter was simple. It held that, since Poles were laying down their lives for the Allied cause in the West, the Allies should find a way of assisting the Poles who were fighting the same German enemy in the East.

In London, reliable news about Warsaw's predicament was in short supply. The exiled Government received daily bulletins from Gen. Boor, who was the principal source of information for all and sundry. But his comments were generally thought to be exaggerated and (to critics) motivated by the desire to extract large amounts of Western aid. The official German broadcasts were worse than useless. The *Deutsche Nachrichten Bureau* news agency did not even mention the Rising until 15 August, and then only to say that it had collapsed. Soviet sources were little better. They also kept silent about the Rising for many days, and once they had admitted its existence, they limited their comments to political denunciations. They simply did not discuss the key question, whether Soviet forces would or would not come to the insurgents' rescue. British commentators largely took their cue from Moscow.

Officials of the Polish Government and army continued to rush to and fro in their efforts to shake up what seemed to them like British 'passivity'. On 8 August, after returning from Italy, the Commander-in-Chief signalled to Boor that Churchill had agreed to restart RAF relief flights. He had spoken to Gen. Ismay, F-M Brooke, Air Vice Marshal Wilson, and the Secretary for Air, Archibald Sinclair. He reported 'considerable resistance'. When he read out Boor's earlier telegram about the balance sheet of Allied cooperation showing nothing except Polish sacrifices on behalf of the West, he received 'a violent and sharp protest about insulting the Empire'.[46] Eden, the Foreign Secretary, attempted to calm the troubled waters, but without making specific commitments.

The position of the Commander-in-Chief, however, had been seriously damaged. He now found out that his advice about the Rising had been ignored or overruled by his own collegues and that his telegrams on the subject had been tampered with. Not surprisingly, he protested very forcefully to the President.[47] His closest followers were aghast. The National Council was riven with splits, and spent hours in fruitless attempts to pass the simplest of resolutions.[48] [**TRADER**, p. 295]

When the Premier arrived back in London from Moscow, he, too, joined the fray. He thought he had benefited from Stalin's apparent promise of aid, but his difficulties grew when he made a full report to his Cabinet. The political dimensions of the looming disaster were fast becoming apparent. Intense negotiations began both within the Government and between the Government, the 'National Council', and the underground authorities in Warsaw. One way or another, a definitive response had to be made to Stalin's demands. The aim was to thrash out a plan, which, with the backing of the Western Allies, would finally reconcile Polish and Soviet positions. It would obviously be required to address all the main criticisms of the pre-war Republic; it would have to find a place for the Communists in the new order; and it could not possibly avoid far-reaching territorial concessions to the USSR. The discussions were fierce. Some observers believed that the Premier was being pushed not to a genuine compromise but to an ill-disguised sell-out.

In those same weeks, intense lobbying was directed at all known and potential friends of Poland. A delegation of Polish socialists went to see Clement Attlee. Polish Jews lobbied British Jews. A group of Polish trade

TRADER

A man with marked commercial talents manages to escape from the Rising, and to take his Jewish girlfriend with him

Knowing the dangers, I had arranged to meet Christine and her mother, Helen Rozen, in Warsaw, to help them get Aryan identification papers. I had some connections in the Underground, and was able to get them genuine birth certificates of people whose deaths had not been recorded. Her mother, who was very Jewish-looking, became Sophie O., while Sara, who didn't look Jewish at all, became Christine P. Sophie became my 'aunt' and Christine my 'wife'. We even had a false marriage certificate. Whilst waiting for their papers, Christine and her mother stayed with a woman who was making some very nasty remarks about the Jews being killed by the Germans 'like bedbugs'. Perhaps she said that intentionally, to warn me; I don't know . . .

In August people came around asking for helpers for a makeshift hospital they were setting up in the basement of the Foreign Ministry building. They took Christine, a few other women, and me. We stayed there a couple of days, until a fellow came along whom I'll always remember: an SS man, tall, cross-eyed, carrying a basket loaded with fine crystal glassware, obviously stolen; the Germans were looting all the houses. He looked at me and said, 'You Polish swine, why are you looking at me like that?' I replied in German, 'I'm sorry, but I'm not Polish.' 'Oh, forgive me. What are you doing over here?' I told him my business story, that I got caught by the Rising. Then he said, 'Look, every day at four o'clock we take our packages for Germany to Jablonna. You and your wife can come with us tomorrow.' Well, it was a chance to get out.

The next day at four o'clock they showed up, drunk. 'Come on!' they yelled. They gave me a bottle, and I had to have a drink too. Then they warned us, 'When the truck turns the corner, duck as low as you can. They are going to shoot.' They explained that the partisans' guns were aimed at a certain height; if we got down, they couldn't hit us.

They made a stop about 25 kilometres from Warsaw, in a place called Bielany. Everyone in the village was scared; they didn't know what was going on in Warsaw. They had set up beds in the church basement and were all staying there. The next day we decided to strike out on our own.

Walking through the woods we came upon a large villa. Everybody there wanted to know our story – how we got out of Warsaw. Some of them thought we were traitors, not because we didn't stay to fight, but because I was not in favour of the

Rising. I said that it was unwise, in fact suicidal, for the Poles to attempt a Rising; we didn't stand a chance; we should let the Russian army finish the Germans off.

We stayed on for a week or two. One day, in the daytime, someone called to me, 'Mr Damski! Germans are coming! Try to talk to them.' They were a group of German officers – medical doctors – who were looking for a place to put a hospital. They were all from Bavaria, from a regiment that had retreated from Stalingrad. Hitler had blocked all promotions in their division for not fighting. They said something to me about 'Polish bandits'. I said I didn't consider them outlaws, just Home Army fighters . . .

After they had gone, I found why the people in the villa had wanted me to stall the Germans: they were operating a secret hospital for Polish partisans hiding in the nearby forest. While I was talking to the Germans in the front, they were taking the wounded partisans out of the back door.

A few days later, one of the doctors came back, saying they were organizing the collection and delivery of farm produce and needed a translator. So Christine and I moved to the little town of Ozharov, where I organized a wholesale business which grew very quickly. We employed 119 people and at peak time we were selling 4,000 tons of vegetables. I could get the trucks from the Germans . . . Every month we loaded between twelve and fifteen railway carriages with vegetables that were shipped to Hamburg, to Brussels, everywhere. It was a terrific success.[1]

John Damski

---

unionists addressed the British TUC. Grandees like Vansittart and Lord Selborne spoke up in Parliament, or wrote to the Foreign Office. The impact was negligible. Resentments inevitably grew.

Few signs of this activity were visible in the British press. The first serious comments about the Rising surfaced on 10–11 August. 'The third battle for Warsaw', wrote the *Scotsman*, 'is being waged without the Allies, and without the material support that could have been expected. The situation is desperate but not beyond repair. The inhabitants of Warsaw are right to ask "where are our friends?"' The left-wing *New Statesman* opined that 'true to their Romantic traditions', the Poles were 'probably' inspired by 'the hope of liberating the capital before the Russians'.

On 11 August, debates in the world press took a new turn when an article in the Vatican's *Osservatore Romano* stated baldly that the Russians' approach to the Rising was a purely political game. The *News Chronicle* quickly dismissed this view as a blatant attempt to split the Alliance. For the time being, other British journalists held their tongues.

The first serious piece to analyse sources of public information and to criticize the gullibility of the British press was written by the diplomatic correspondent of the *Manchester Guardian* and published on 22 August. Headlined 'The Warsaw Rising: the Question of Responsibility', it poured scorn on the notion that the Allies had not been aware of the impending Rising:

> It has been argued recently that it was impossible to organise the provision of adequate supplies to Warsaw because the battle arose spontaneously – or, at any rate, not in synchronisation with the Russian military plans. Such statements seem surprising in view of the systematic appeals for armed Resistance broadcast from Russia . . . long before and during the first stages of the battle from Warsaw. These appeals can hardly have escaped Allied military attention.

There followed a series of long quotations from broadcasts transmitted in Polish by the Communist-run 'Kościuszko Station' in Moscow between 2 June and 30 July. One of the quotes, from 15 June, talked of alleged 'discontent' with the orders of the Commander-in-Chief and of Gen. Boor, who were supposedly out of step with the popular will. 'The will to fight has grown within the home army [sic]', it said, 'it is generally believed that it is time to act.' Two weeks earlier, i.e. two whole months before the outbreak of the Rising, the voice from Moscow had argued unequivocally for action:

> The armed Resistance movement has saved tens of thousands from death, and has inflicted great losses on the Germans. These battles have shown that a mass armed Resistance movement is possible, and that the losses are smaller than in submitting passively to terrorism. Today, no one should dare to say that the Poles are mad.[49]

The persistence of the Warsaw Rising placed the British and American Governments in a bind. If the insurgents had been defeated quickly, they would have been lavishly praised for their courage, but would not have become a major embarrassment. As it was, they fought on inexplicably, forcing issues into the open which many Allied leaders would have preferred to ignore. Sensitive people squirmed uncomfortably.

All the indications are that Churchill was genuinely alert to the desirability of giving the Rising all possible assistance. So, too, were many

British officials, especially in the RAF, SOE, and War Ministry. But the same cannot be said of Stalin, of Roosevelt, or of key American advisers; and it cannot be said of the Foreign Office. Immense frustrations ensued.

Certainly, the British Military Mission in Moscow kept up a stream of daily requests, pressing their Soviet counterparts to help Warsaw. Whilst informing the Soviets that RAF flights were being sent from Italy, they pointed out that Rokossovsky's forces were in 'a much better position'. On 9 August, Col. Brinkman mentioned Capt. Kalugin's appeal, and passed on detailed instructions from the Polish Commander-in-Chief about the exact locations for airdrops and artillery fire. On 10 August, the British Ambassador, Clerk Kerr, reminded Molotov of Stalin's promise to the Polish Premier, whilst his Counsellor, 'P. M. Krostveit' (Crosthwaite), provided exact map references for the village of Truskav, where a reception committee was waiting to receive a Soviet liaison officer.

Examination of these files provides many surprises. One is that, as is evident from the place names used, the British Military Mission was using German maps. Another shows how repeated translations of the same documents distorted their meaning significantly. For example, writing in English, a British official would use the term 'Polish Home Army'. After the first translation into Russian, this becomes the 'Polish Internal Army'. By the time it reaches Stalin, it has become the 'Polish Illegal Army'.[50]

After re-authorizing RAF flights from Italy, Churchill repeated his earlier request to Stalin. 'I expect from you', he wrote on 12 August, 'the greatest efforts in this respect.'[51] He also expressed his suspicions to Eden. 'It is certainly very curious that at the moment the Underground Army has revolted, the Russians should have halted that offensive against Warsaw and withdrawn some distance. For them to send in all the quantities of machine-guns and ammunition required by the Poles for their heroic fight would involve a flight of only 100 miles.' He smelt a rat. He was equally disappointed by 'the lukewarm telegram' which the US Chief of Staff had sent to Gen. Eisenhower and by the question of American overflights to Warsaw and of landing them in the bases on Soviet territory where the USAAF was already operating. [**SAVAGERY**, p. 299]

At a lower level, Britain's relations with Poland were experiencing a number of severe shocks. Polish officials in London were outraged not only to find that their desperate appeals inspired little sense of urgency but also to discover that different British agencies had been following different policies and issuing contradictory advice. Gen. Tabor, for example, must have been mortified to learn that SOE's assurances of

SAVAGERY

A wounded insurgent nurse escapes a massacre at the very last minute

The German tanks were approaching Kilinski Square. Thirteen- and fourteen-year-olds were throwing petrol-filled bottles, and managed to set fire to a tank almost every time. On the 18th, the Germans deliberately left a tank loaded with explosives in the square. Our boys had no idea. When they approached it, there was an explosion causing many deaths, especially amongst the youngsters . . .

Hatred of these villains grew with every atrocity. They would round up Poles and place them in front of the tanks, so that the insurgents couldn't shoot. It was a ghastly sight – you couldn't fire at your own, and it was even worse to see the bastards pressing on ahead. They would kill the poor wretches, despite sustaining many casualties themselves. That's how it was on Leshno Street, where both the hostages and the tank and its crew were destroyed. The Germans often went through a routine of running over several dozen hostages at a time with their tanks.

One evening at around eight we were sitting by the entrance to our courtyard. It was a safe collection-point and we kept a well-staffed night shift there. Suddenly we heard the drone of an aeroplane. We realized that it must be a British Wellington bomber, the so-called 'flying coffin', which was circling Kilinski Square and waiting for the signal to drop weapons. Thousands of smoke trails in the darkness made an indescribable sight. The barrage looked like a firework display. The Germans were firing furiously. They turned on the spotlights . . . Eventually the plane's wing clipped a chimney, and it came down somewhere in the Old Town. We were badly affected. Both of the airmen were Canadians serving in the RAF. They had wanted to help us with all their hearts, taking the long, long road to our city and to their graves.

The Germans and Ukrainians fell on the insurgent hospital, kicking and beating the wounded who were lying on the floor and calling them sons of bitches and Polish bandits. They dashed the heads of those lying on the ground with their boots, screaming horribly as they did it. Blood and brains were spattered in all directions . . . A contingent of German soldiers with an officer at its head came in. '*Was ist hier los?*' the officer asked. After driving out the murderers, he gave orders to clear up the dead bodies, and calmly requested those who had survived and could walk to get up and go to the courtyard. We were certain they would be shot.

After an hour or two another German-Ukrainian horde came in. Once again they started screaming and this time ran out again. One older German remained, wandering here and there in quite a state. Knowing German, I said:

'Can you tell me what is going to happen us? We're seriously ill.'

'Are you German by birth or are you a *Volksdeutsch*?'

'I'm Polish.'

'How come your German is so good?'

'I studied in Vienna.'

'Are you from Vienna? I am too. Which district are you from?'

'Hutteldorf XV.'

At this the German broke down and started shouting like one demented:

'My dearest, get out of here, get out quickly!'

Yanek picked me up and I hung on to his neck. The German walked the other side of me and together they took me to the exit where I was able to clutch a handrail on the staircase. Other Germans were arriving, carrying straw. One of them poured some petrol over it . . . There was a blast, and a terrible cry – the fire was right behind us. The Germans had torched the hospital and were shooting the wounded. Were it not for my conversation with the German soldier, I would have shared their fate.[1]

Kamila M.

---

29 July concerning the 'absolute priority' to be given to the Rising had already been contradicted by the Foreign Office even before they were given. Eden's negative letter of 28 July had apparently been delivered to the Count on the same day that Gen. Gubbins made such positive noises to Tabor. The resultant confusion could not have been sorted out quickly, especially as the sluggishness of the Foreign Office seemed to be winning out. The bitter pill became still more bitter when SOE abandoned its initial optimism, and began to spout the Foreign Office line. Gen. Gubbins had left London for Normandy on French Section business, and was not to be seen again for some weeks; and his deputy Lt.Col. Perkins strangely lost his former sympathy for Poland's predicament. Meeting Tabor and other Polish generals on 16 August, Perkins delivered a tirade of recriminations which placed all the blame on the Poles and none whatsoever on the British:

> I gave them as my personal opinion that it was criminal for them to plan the supply of relief to Warsaw on such risky operations as they were doing at present . . . I told them quite plainly that I considered it their duty to inform Gen. [Boor] exactly what the situation was and to stop leading him any further up the garden path. I myself am convinced that they have passed all sorts of promises to [Boor] . . . and now, when their promises are not being fulfilled, they are

> blaming the British to cover themselves . . . The outcome of the meeting was that the Poles were left in no doubt regarding the difficulties of the situation and the futility of continually making approaches and demands for the impossible.[52]

The use of the word 'criminal' at this early date is curious. It suggests that Perkins had been in touch with the Foreign Office, which in turn was in touch with Moscow. At all events, the British historian who has analysed these documents in detail has characterized Perkins's outburst as 'remarkably arrogant and unsympathetic.'[53]

Throughout this stage of the proceedings, President Roosevelt's entourage was largely concerned with trying to establish the facts. They were repeatedly in touch with the Chiefs of Staff, the State Department, and Ambassador Harriman in Moscow. The information was conflicting. A cable from Harriman dated 4 August threw doubt on earlier assurances which FDR had received about Stalin's readiness to help the Poles (e.g. from Oskar Lange). Subsequent cables seemed to rectify the impression. On 10 August, Harriman reported that Stalin had promised the Polish Premier to organize airdrops. The next day he related a long conversation with Molotov, who, whilst bemoaning the unilateral nature of the Rising, looked forward both to airdrops and to an offensive by the Soviet Army. Molotov said that the authorities had been unable to identify Capt. Kalugin. US military intelligence was not helpful. On 12 August, it advised the President that 'the Polish Underground . . . is believed to be slowly disintegrating.' Stettinius took another tack. 'If it is militarily feasible, I feel we have moral and other obligations to do what we can to help get aid to the Polish Underground in full battle against the Nazis.'[54] Then the Joint Chiefs of Staff advised that American aid was 'almost impracticable'.[55] Yet none of these differences prevented the President from urging Stalin to make provision for shuttle flights over Soviet territory.

On the 18th, the rat which Churchill had smelt duly emerged in the person of M. Vyshinsky, Soviet Deputy Commissar for Foreign Affairs, who 'to avoid the possibility of misunderstanding' read out a prepared statement to the US Ambassador in Moscow:

> The Soviet Government cannot of course object to English or American aircraft dropping arms in the region of Warsaw, since this is an American and British affair. But they decidedly object to British or American aircraft, after dropping arms in the region of Warsaw, landing on Soviet territory, since the Soviet Government do not wish

to associate themselves either directly or indirectly with the adventure in Warsaw.[56]

For the next two weeks, Churchill was preoccupied with the problem of countering Stalin's obstructionism and of badgering Roosevelt into joint action. He was to call it 'an episode of profound and far-reaching gravity'. (Later historians would think of it as the start of the Cold War.) In the first round, he persuaded the President to formulate a joint request. 'We are thinking of world opinion if the anti-Nazis in Warsaw are in effect abandoned,' they wrote on the 20th. 'We believe that all three of us should do the utmost to save as many of the patriots there as possible.'[57] But in the second round, after Stalin had responded with a crude denunciation of 'the group of criminals' in Warsaw, Churchill was unable to keep Roosevelt on track. He wanted to remind Stalin that Moscow Radio had encouraged Warsaw to rise. He was even inclined 'to send the planes and see what happens'. Nonetheless, 'I do not see what further steps we can take at the present time . . .' Roosevelt replied. And on the 26th, he was still more dismissive. 'I do not consider it would prove advantageous to the long-range general war prospect for me to join you in the proposed message to Stalin.'[58] Roosevelt appeared to be switching off. [**PAST**, p. 303]

Churchill was regularly informed by his Polish allies about events in Warsaw; and he thought that 'some of this tale of villainy and horror should reach the world.' Yet, here again, he found that the British press was not always willing to report it. So he wrote to the Minister of Information:

> Is there any stop on the publicity for the facts about the agony of Warsaw, which seem, from the papers, to have been practically suppressed? It is not for us to cast reproaches on the Soviet Government, but surely the facts should be allowed to speak for themselves. There is no need to mention the strange and sinister behaviour of the Russians, but is there any reason why the consequences of such behaviour should not be made public?[59]

This letter was included in Churchill's war memoirs. The Minister's reply was not, but it deserves to be prominently quoted:

> There is nothing to stop the British press from publishing anything on the subject of Warsaw. But you must understand that the press here does not have the means for finding out what is really happening

PAST

After the capture of the PAST Building, a German soldier's notebook falls into insurgent hands and is translated into a sort of English

The notebook of soldier Kurt Heller belongs to all German soldiers, because in this notebook are disclosed the thoughts of all Germans, who are tired by the long war. Germans . . . want to be in Germany, at home. In Germany they have their families, their houses, their wives, mothers, fathers, and children . . . Here is the contents:

1.VIII. After noon the beginning of fights on the streets in Warsaw. We are [already] closed [in] on the second of August.

3.VIII. Ulrich was killed. S.S. Sturm-führer and many other dies.

4.VIII. We are further closed [in]. No support from the outside. We expect today or tomorrow the help. We have not the food. Water lacking.

5.VIII. Rudolph is killed. Except him are killed my other friends. I am at the limit of vigours. Luttewitz fell. Hollweg is hard wounded.

6.VIII. In the morning I have a little dream . . . a little coffee with sugar. From all sides lurks the death. I should like to live. My three friends fulfilled the suicide by the shooting.

7.VIII. At noon we were shot by our own artillery, but without losses. The experiment of sally did not bring us the result. During this sally one was killed, four was hard wounded, one from those died. Our killed soldier in the number of fourteen persons were buried today at eight o'clock on the court-yard. The air is very bad, because the corpses of our killed soldiers stink.

8.VIII. Our sections there are in the distance of two hundred metres, but the resistance of bandits is hard and great.

9.VIII. With the food is very niggardly.

11.VIII. All the rests of food took from us the police, also the cigarettes. The situation does not suit to the resistance.

12.VIII. My hunger is great. Every day I have only the soup and six cigarettes. The police took from us all. Even not a whit of marmalade he did not leave to us. When will end this misery and pain?

13.VIII. The hard German fire from tanks at positions of Poles. The hits in our tower are more often, but without the losses. The tank brought to us the food on five days. My health began to decline. I have the ill stomach, and scarcely I can keep on the feet. When will come the freedom?

14.VIII.–15.VIII.–16.VIII. Terrible hunger. In the night involves us the fear. When the first star comes forth in the sky – I think about my house, my wife, and my boy, who lives in the earth of Stettin. I cannot contain this with my mind, and now I am in this same situation.

17.VIII. Poles want to drive away us with the fire and with the bottles of benzine. Anew several men lost the nerves and committed the suicide. Terible stink from the bodies, who are lying on the streets.

18.VIII. We are completely isolated from the exterior world.

19.VIII. I cannot think about the delivery. Around us there are Poles. Who will be first from us, who will go to the massy grave on the courtyard?[1]

On the nineteenth day German soldier ended his annotations. Next day the building of PAST was attained by our soldiers, and Kurt Heller found himself in Polish slavery.[1]

> ... Furthermore, apart from the good news from the [Eastern] Front, the readers are not specially interested in the Warsaw events. The Polish Government is not short of good writers who could report on Warsaw's agony. But their activities to date undermine their credibility. Fleet Street considers their Ministry of Information to be an incompetent ass.
>
> If HMG were willing to make Ward's reports public, I've little doubt that the newspapers could be persuaded to print them. But I can't say what effect they might have on public opinion, which tends to regard the Poles as a pretty inept race. What is more, the supporters of Uncle Joe, who are not lacking in the press, would be provoked into further attacks on the Poles.
>
> [The Polish Premier] has raised the matter of [his Government's] official reports from Warsaw and of the way in which they are ignored by the press and mistrusted by Eden. The [Foreign Office's] News Department, whilst not questioning these reports, is reluctant to hand them to the press for fear of exciting interest in the troubled state of Polish–Soviet relations.[60]

One is tempted to characterize this statement as damning. Not only did the British have no independent source of information of their own, they were unwilling to use the one authoritative source that was available.

The difficulties were obviously deeper than Churchill had imagined.

They became still more apparent in the week that Paris was liberated by a Polish-style Rising.

In the last week of August, news spread that the French Resistance had pulled off exactly the sort of coup in Paris that the Home Army had sprung in Warsaw. Not waiting for the arrival of the US Army, elements of the Underground had attacked the remnants of the German garrison on the 19th and had provoked several days of chaotic and vicious street fighting. There had been no question of synchronizing action with the advancing Allies, even when the Germans had begun to withdraw. There was no pre-arranged plan. A general strike had broken out on the 18th. The French police rebelled against their German masters. Shots were fired in anger. Civilians joined in. Barricades were thrown up. The fighting spread. Isolated German outposts were attacked. It was later learned that the military Governor of Paris, Gen. von Choltitz, had ignored orders to raze the city. But the decisive move was made by the American Command, which reacted promptly to divert Gen. Leclerc's 2nd (French) Armoured Division towards Paris. Even so, the commander of the US 5th Corps was furious when he learned that Leclerc had unilaterally ordered a column to advance from Versailles. The leading echelon of three tanks, eleven APCs, and a sapper company reached the Hôtel de Ville at 21.22 on the 24th. It was commanded by a French colonial officer, Capt. Dronne of the 9th Tchad Infantry Regiment, and, from the presence of numerous Spaniards, was known as 'La Nueve'. They were received by a tearful Georges Bidault, Chairman of the National Resistance Committee. The German *Kommandatur* at the Place de L'Opéra surrendered at 14.30 on the 26th. Apart from its improvised nature, the liberation of Paris was notable in two other important respects. One, despite the extreme political complexity of the French Resistance, was the unbroken unity of all participants. The other was the unwavering support of the Allies.

The complexity can be seen from the fact that the principal clandestine military organization in Paris, the *Forces Françaises de l'Intérieur* (FFI), was commanded by a Communist, Col. 'Rol' Tanguy. Gen. de Gaulle, the head of the Free French, the largest Resistance body, only took overall charge after his legendary stroll down the Champs-Elysées under fire on the 27th. Gen. Leclerc and his men were directly subordinated to the Americans. When Bidault asked de Gaulle to declare the re-founding of the Republic, de Gaulle refused. '*Non,*' he retorted, '*la République n'a jamais cessé d'être.*'[61]

The Allies, engaged in a strenuous campaign, might easily have left Paris to fend for itself. On the very first day, however, they were implored to establish contact with the insurgents via the BBC 'in order to avoid the fate of Warsaw'.[62] They adjusted quickly. On 29 August, the Supreme Allied Commander, Gen. Eisenhower, accompanied by British Air Vice-Marshal Tedder, paid personal homage at the Arc de Triomphe, thereby giving his blessing to Gen. de Gaulle's authority.

The cost of liberation was not insignificant. The FFI suffered 2,500 casualties, the 2nd Armoured Division 400. The civil population lost 582 dead and over 2,000 injured. The Germans lost 3,200 dead and 12,800 prisoners.

The Home Army in Warsaw saluted the success of their French comrades. The underground *Information Bulletin* described the liberation of Paris as a event of 'exceptionally exalted significance':

> It is the symbol of the end of Germany's military dominance on the continent of Europe. It is a witness to France's return to the ranks of the great powers . . . Morally, it underlines the disgrace of the defeat and capitulation of 1940 . . . In the midst of our own struggle, we greet the news of the liberation of Paris with profound and sincere joy . . .[63]

Inevitably, close parallels with the Rising in Warsaw were noted with approval. 'As in Warsaw,' the *Bulletin* remarked, 'the French Underground did not wait for the moment when the capital would have been liberated by external forces. The people of Paris undertook the struggle on their own account, and brought it to a victorious conclusion after three days.'[64]

Radio Lightning contrived to broadcast its congratulations in French:

> Comrades-in-arms!
>
> On this occasion, when Paris, the capital of Freedom and the heart of European civilization, has cast off its shackles . . . We, the soldiers of Poland's Home Army, who have been fighting in Warsaw for three weeks, send you our most heartfelt felicitations . . .[65]

For those who knew, the broadcast was all the more moving because it was read by the unlikeliest of broadcasters – a Belgian diamond smuggler, who had been accidentally trapped in Warsaw by the Rising, and who had now been pulled from his refuge in a cellar to give the message an authentic flavour. By all accounts, the smuggler adorned his performance with a fervour and passion worthy of a professional actor.

The Warsaw Airlift of 1944 is one of the great unsung sagas of the Second World War. In theory it had three participants – the Soviets, Americans, and British. In reality, only the British and their partners made a significant contribution. Soviet warplanes, which had been flying over Warsaw in late July, disappeared from the skies after the outbreak of the Rising and failed to reappear for the best part of six weeks. American planes, which were supposed to fly out from England in August, did not manage to take off until mid-September, and then only once. As a result, it was RAF squadrons operating from Italy which assumed the overwhelming brunt of the missions. They did so at a juncture when RAF Bomber Command was regularly pounding targets on the Baltic coast not far from Warsaw. On two nights at the end of August, for example, nearly 200 Lancasters from Britain attacked Königsberg, suffering only 7.5 per cent losses. [**NAVIGATOR**, p. 308]

Warsaw lay 1,311km (815 miles) from the RAF base at Brindisi in Apulia. The chosen route to Poland took the form of an elongated lozenge with Brindisi at the southern end and Warsaw at the northern tip. The planes took off in the evening over the Adriatic, crossed the Croatian coast in the last rays of the setting sun, overflew the Danube in Hungary in darkness, and climbed north-east over the Carpathians before approaching Warsaw from the east over Soviet-held territory. The return journey, which brought the fliers back to Brindisi in midmorning after twelve to fourteen hours in the air, was spent in large part over Germany and Austria. It descended from the Austrian Alps into full daylight over Italy.

The airmen faced manifold dangers. They had no fighter escort, and had nothing but their own guns to ward off German planes sent up in ground-controlled interception areas. They were fully visible crossing the Adriatic coast in both directions, and a Luftwaffe night-fighter training centre near Cracow presented a constant hazard. Visibility over Warsaw was severely limited by clouds of smoke, whilst their approach run, which was made at only 45 metres (150 feet) and at a mere 200kmh (125 mph), made them specially vulnerable to ground fire. Electric storms were a common summer occurrence over the Alps and Carpathians. Pilots frequently reported instances of St Elmo's fire, when blue flames trailed from wingtips and propeller blades.

NAVIGATOR

'For the RAF and SAAF squadrons of No. 205 Group operating from bases in the Foggian Plain, the call to assist the Balkan Air Force squadrons came out of the blue.'[1]

In the forenoon of 13 August, 205 Group air crews were told that a maximum effort was to be flown against an unknown target that night. 2,300 gallons of fuel were to be taken on by each aircraft, and would be topped up for extreme range at Brindisi where the operational briefing would take place. Normally the fuel load for a target in northern Austria used around 1,800 gallons.

The target only became known at Brindisi, when, on entering the briefing room, the aircrews sighted a wall covered with international modified polyconic maps, extending from floor to ceiling. A red line extended from Brindisi at the bottom to Warsaw at the top. A sobering revelation for those about to go out into the night.

The briefing officer was Lieutenant George Z. His briefing was a model: compelling, honest, accurate, comprehensive, in a situation in which the aircrews needed to know the political, military, and tactical situation of the Polish Home Army in Warsaw; the German army in Warsaw; the Red Army sitting on its hands across the Vistula at Praga; and the advance of the Red Front.

For accuracy, a low-level drop was essential: height not above 500 feet, speed not above 150 m.p.h. Target maps and photographs were available. Three aligning points (Mokotov in the south, the Old City in the centre, and the Citadel in the north) were given. Take-off time for 178 Squadron was 19:45; estimated time on target 01:30. The twilight was critical for returning aircraft, which would have little chance of survival in daylight over enemy territory extending from Albania to the Baltic Sea.

At the start of the operation in support of the Warsaw Uprising, RAF aircrews were issued with blood chits. They were silk with a Union Jack on the obverse and something along the lines of 'This chap is a British officer. Return him in good shape and in working order and you will be rewarded' – on the reverse side, the same in Russian. Since for the Warsaw operations we were briefed to give nothing other than number, rank, and name, if we fell into Russian hands (the same as if captured by the Germans) the blood chits were ominous rather than comforting. After difficult, protracted high-level negotiations, the Russians agreed to allow a free passage route over Russian-held territory; for specifically agreed missions.

Warsaw was burning: not in the manner of fire storms which British and Polish Bomber Command aircrews remember; but as a great city in which a land battle to destruction is going on. Approaching at low altitude in the darkness, it was as if the city was covered by an inverted fish-bowl inside which the night was a dull red. Individual fires and gun flashes showed up as bright sparks; flak streamed across the area or burst above the dome amidst the coning searchlight. Inside the red dome, aircraft were seen in silhouette against the fiery city as they made their low-level dropping run.

That night, 13/14 August, over Warsaw, my crew sighted a four-engined aircraft, lower than our own, silhouetted against the fires of the city. It was in a nose-down attitude as if coming in to land, very low, and engaged in a gun battle with a German light flak battery and a nearby searchlight. It could only be one of the Halifax aircraft of 1586 (Polish) Special Duties Flight flown from Brindisi five and a half hours earlier. Almost certainly the aircraft had already dropped its load of arms and ammunition and its crew was now joining the land battle while they still had something left to give. Such was the spirit of the Polish aviators who flew in support of the Warsaw Uprising.

On my crew's last sortie to Warsaw (night of 10/11 September 1944) we were engaged by Russian AA fire and Russian night fighters along much of the two-and-a-half hour route. Disenchanted by this, our South African pilots and Australian navigator, at about 12,000 feet and outside gun-range from Lublin, rapidly decided that if we survived the drop on Warsaw and were fated to be shot down on the way home, it would be by the enemy and not by our Russian 'friends'. On climbing away from Warsaw, therefore we followed the direct route through enemy territory, rather than putting our Russian blood chits to the test. Some crews of our force were not so lucky.

With the benefit of hindsight, one wonders what our masters knew (and how much they chose to tell) about our Russian 'Allies'.[2]

Alan McIntosh

The aircraft most usually employed in the Warsaw Airlift was the Consolidated B24 Liberator. It had more speed and payload than the Boeing B17 Flying Fortress and a greater range than the Avro Lancaster. Its four Pratt and Whitney double-banked radial engines were boosted by a super-charger. They permitted a payload of 5½ tons and a cruising speed of 210 mph. Fully loaded with 2,300 gallons of fuel and with twelve parachute-controlled containers in the bomb racks, take-off had to be undertaken overweight. The modern electronic equipment included a GEE box (a navigational radio-triangulation system) and a radio altimeter. Armament consisted of ten 0.5 in heavy machine guns. There was a crew of ten.

205 Group RAF in Italy, commanded by Maj.Gen. Durrant, consisted of five wings: three RAF and two South African Air Force. In the summer of 1944, the RAF's 334 Special Operations Wing was attached to the newly formed 'Balkan Airforce', whose principal task was liaison with Yugoslavia. It included 148 and 624 Squadrons RAF, each equipped with fourteen Halifaxes, and the independent (Polish) 1586 Special Duties Flight with ten aircrews flying a mixture of Halifaxes and Liberators. 2 Wing of the SAAF consisted of 24, 31, and 34 Squadrons, all equipped with Liberators.

The first flight to Warsaw had been undertaken on 4–5 August by 1586 SDF accompanied by seven Halifaxes of 148 Squadron. It provided a grim warning of things to come. The orders mentioned drops in the Kampinos and Kabaty forests; and senior officers were unaware that four Polish crews had secretly volunteered to fly directly over Warsaw. On return, one Polish Liberator made a miraculous crash-landing on two engines with no undercarriage, stopping ten yards short of the sea. But five RAF planes were lost, and only two successful drops were made. Senior RAF commanders intervened, and flights were suspended.

At this point, the Warsaw Rising forced itself onto the agenda of Allied planners who were meeting at Naples to discuss the landings on the French Riviera:

> The Polish Question was on [Churchill's mind] as he contemplated the beauty of Naples Bay and the slopes of Vesuvius from his quarters at the Villa Rivalta . . . He was expecting Marshal Tito for discussions on the situation in Yugoslavia. It was 12 August, and Churchill must have sensed that Warsaw could expect no help from Moscow. He agreed with Field Marshal Smuts that the airlift was of little military value. Gen. Mark Clark of the US Fifth Army in Italy could not understand the reasoning of the Combined Chiefs in supporting the operation, and Churchill wondered whether the latest news from Warsaw could mean much in the long run. Nonetheless, he sent off another signal to Stalin . . .
>
> Churchill discussed the matter again with Air Marshal Slessor. The RAF commander reiterated his conviction that the Russians would not drop supplies in Warsaw. The only feasible way to assist the AK adequately was for the US Eighth Airforce to fly the aircraft from Britain. The planes would have to land at Russian bases to refuel, as had been arranged for their bomber offensive. But the

> Polish appeal, of course, had been made to the British, not to the Americans. Churchill weighed the matter up carefully, knowing that the Russians would not help, and came to a painful decision. Help *must* be sent, he declared, even at the risk of heavy losses.[66]

As a result, 205 Group was ordered to maintain a regular supply line to Warsaw. In actual fact, 1586 SDF, 148 and 178 Squadrons RAF, and 31 Squadron SAAF had already made several extra flights to Poland, presumably on their own account, or on their local commander's responsibility. In all, they took off from Brindisi for Warsaw on 4, 8, 11–18, and 20–28 August, on a total of nineteen nights.

The supplies which reached the Home Army were not inconsiderable. Early in September, Gen. Boor acknowledged receipt of 250 PIAT anti-tank weapons, 1,000 Sten guns, 19,000 grenades, and 2 million rounds of ammunition. [**'1586'**, p. 312]

But the losses were horrendous. Air Marshal Slessor calculated that one bomber was lost for every ton of supplies delivered. The sacrifices of 1586 SDF were particularly severe. On 1 August they had just completed a tour of duty and were due for a period of rest. Only five aircraft and five air crews were available. By the end of the month, only of those five crews survived.[67]

Appeals were equally directed to the USAAF, and the possibility of using high-flying American B-17 Flying Fortresses based in Ukraine was under discussion for several weeks. After many delays, an inter-Allied system code-named Frantic had begun to operate in June 1944, Stalin having been sweetened with the gift of a top-secret Norden bombsight. Using Poltava, Mirogrod and a nearby fighter base, massive fleets of up to 200 US planes were able to shuttle back and forward between the USSR and either Italy or Britain. On each leg, they dropped huge bomb-loads on pre-arranged targets in the Reich or in German-held territory. In July and August 1944, their main destinations were in Romania, though two were in Germany, and three were in German-occupied Poland.

A report about one of these flights appeared in *The Times* on 8 August:

> Heavy bombers of the 8th Air Force from England have attacked a German aircraft plant at Rahmel, 10 miles NW of Gdynia in Poland, and have landed safely at American bases in the Soviet Union. The bombers were escorted throughout by P51 Mustangs . . . No airplane

'1586'

Pilots of 1586 Special Duties Flight, based at Brindisi, experience moments of hope and weeks of despair

The Warsaw Rising broke out on 1 August 1944, between four and five in the afternoon. For us, listening to the loudspeakers, the only vital question was: Warsaw is fighting – when do we fly to help them? . . . The announcer was finding it difficult to keep his voice properly calm and impersonal . . . I looked round: every face was set and stern. . . . We were to take off at midnight. Stan, my tail gunner, rapped out a curse, banging the table with his fist and went out, slamming the door. Of course our flight was unimportant. Just as everything not taking place in Warsaw was unimportant.

20 August 1944

We had been ordered to carry out the sortie regardless of weather conditions. So, though the met. forecast was exceptionally despondent, we took off . . . Sure enough, right from the Yugoslav coast fog stretched from the ground to 6,000 feet. Fog was hardly the word for it – water vapour or steam would be more appropriate. We had no ground-based navigational aid; I tried map reading . . . but we finally flew on solely with star 'fixes'.

We had similar weather all the way until over Poland we saw a Jerry fighter shoot down one of our Halifaxes. (There had been a lot of flak over Yugoslavia and the Danube.) We pushed on and got a decent 'fix' by the time we reached the Pilitsa River. After that we flew on guided by the distant glow . . .

We dropped to some 700 feet, got through a very dense barrage [near Sluzhev] over the Vistula. Fires were blazing in every district of Warsaw. The dark spots were places occupied by the Jerries. Everything was smothered in smoke through which ruddy-orange flames flickered. It was terrible and must have been hell for everybody down there.

The German flak was the hottest I have ever been through, so we got down to just 70 or 100 feet . . . The flicks in the Praga and Mokotov suburbs kept us constantly lit up – there was nothing we would do about it. We nearly hit the Poniatovski Bridge as we cracked along the Vistula: the pilot hopped over it by the skin of his teeth.

Our reception point was Krashinski Square. So, when we passed the [Kerbeds] iron-girder bridge, we turned sharp to port and made ready for the run-in. The whole southern side of the Square was blazing and wind was blowing the smoke south, much to our satisfaction. We dropped the containers and knew we had made a good job.

It was time to clear out. The pilot came down still lower, keeping an eye for steeples and high buildings. The cabin was full of smoke, which got into our eyes and made them smart. We could feel the heat . . . We ripped along the railway line leading west [to Prushkov and Skiernievitse]. Some flak from an anti-aircraft train tried to hit us, so we let go some bursts. We had a breathing space until flicks near Bohnia picked us up again, and the flak got uncomfortably close. We passed over the crashed bomber in the foothills, which was now burning itself out. (Five Halifaxes that had taken off with us never returned.) The Home Army people signaled that a supply was received on Krashinski Square at the time we noted in our logbook. So we knew that at least our flight had not been in vain.

2 October 1944

As we were climbing out of our bombers one day after an op., an aircraftman came up and told me [the news]. Stanley was just behind me. He's what you'd call a Warsaw cockney with all a cockney's affection for his city. He stopped short and dumped his 'chute on the ground. He just stood there, turning his head from side to side helplessly . . . He shuffled off without a word. Later, he came up to me in the Ops. Room as I was studying the maps. His eyes were sunken and lifeless. 'Sir, what's the use?' he asked in a hoarse, unfamiliar voice. 'What's the use, sir?' He pressed his face against the [window] and looked out through the panes where the drops of mist were trickling down like tears.[1]

---

was lost . . . Today's attack was the twentieth operation in which Eastern Command bases have figured.[68]

The headline ran 'Poland Bombed by U.S. Airforce'. It would have been read in conjunction with another piece immediately below headed 'Furious Fighting in Warsaw: More Ground Gained by Patriots'. Ordinary readers must have drawn the obvious conclusion. If the Allies were bombing Gdynia, the bombing of German positions in Warsaw could not be far behind.

During these operations, the Americans frequently reported incidents of 'friendly fire'. It was assumed that Soviet anti-aircraft gunners had standing orders to fire on any unauthorized flights. But that was only part of the explanation. On 15–16 June, Soviet Yak fighters had attacked two American F-5 reconnaissance planes, damaging one and destroying the other.[69]

Throughout August, Churchill and to a lesser extent Roosevelt strove to persuade Stalin to give landing rights in the USSR to Allied flights heading for Warsaw. Stalin's responses were uniformly hostile. Roosevelt's interest was, at best, lukewarm. Churchill's message to Moscow on 12 August was phrased in strong language:

> We have practically no news from you, no information on the political situation, no advice and no instruction. Have you discussed in Moscow help for Warsaw? I repeat emphatically that without immediate support, consisting of drops of arms and ammunition, bombing of objectives held by the enemy, and air landing, our fight will collapse in a few days . . . I expect from you the greatest effort in this respect.[70]

This was countered by the extraordinary dressing-down of the US Ambassador in Moscow mentioned earlier. But Churchill persisted. On the 18th, he told Eden to check out the technical feasibility of the overflights, and he appealed to Roosevelt for joint action. Their message to Stalin, which Roosevelt drafted, was deliberately mild in tone. It started: 'We are thinking of world opinion'. And it ended, 'The time element is of the greatest importance.' It did not evoke a definite reply. What was worse, at the next round Roosevelt casually told Churchill: 'I do not see what further steps we can take at the present time which promise results.'[71] Churchill was roused to undisguised anger. He proposed a draft message which commented less than diplomatically on Stalin's earlier replies. 'Our sympathies are aroused for these "almost unarmed people" whose special faith has led them to attack German tanks, guns and planes,' he said; also 'the [Warsaw] Rising was certainly called for repeatedly by Moscow Radio'; and 'we propose to send the aircraft unless you directly forbid it.'[72] This time, the President refused to join in. September arrived; and the question of using the Frantic system was unresolved.

Once the conflict inside Warsaw had reached virtual stalemate, and Western assistance was failing, all eyes turned to Moscow. Historians must equally turn their attention to the Kremlin, for the simple reason that Moscow was rapidly becoming the key player in deciding the Rising's fate. Yet the task is a tricky one. All arguments are necessarily based on inadequate documentation, on deduction, and to some extent on speculation. At no point in the remaining decades of the twentieth century would all parts of the relevant archives in Moscow be freely opened to independent enquiry.

In mid-August 1944, Stalin's approach to the Warsaw Rising would have been formed within the context of six factors – the news from Warsaw, the talks with the Polish Premier, Rokossovsky's fortunes at the front, relations with the Lublin Committee, security assessments from the NKVD, and grand strategy. One can only surmise which might have been the determinant. For if Stalin's actions may be discussed in outline, the exact timing and motives remain opaque. In essence, the sequence of Stalin's decisions seems to have been first to wait and see, second to dissociate himself from the Rising's political leadership, and last to withhold the Soviet Army. Why or precisely when he took these steps, it is impossible to say.

From Moscow's standpoint, the news from Warsaw was baffling. The Rising had not been suppressed, even though it had received no significant reinforcements. This could only mean that early Soviet assessments were faulty, and that the Polish Communists had been telling stories. It did not provide the basis for confident decisions. Above all, it meant that the Home Army was a much stronger force then the Kremlin had reckoned on. From the Kremlin's viewpoint, it was unsettling.

The Polish Premier, who had stayed on, was granted a second hour-long audience with Stalin on the evening of 9 August. Some accounts of the meeting suggest that Stalin turned nasty, repeating the outrageous claims of Bierut and Co. that 'there was no fighting in Warsaw at all'.[73] The protocol of the conversation, however, does not support such an interpretation. On the contrary, it shows that Stalin was unusually genial. In response to various comments, he repeatedly said: 'That would be very nice.' With respect to aid for the Rising, he did say at its first mention that the suggested moves 'looked unrealistic'. He explained that Rokossovsky's front had been pushed back and that Soviet capabilities were limited. But he appeared to take a detailed interest in the technicalities of airdrops. And he waxed quite lyrical on the subject of Polish–Soviet relations. He said that the aim of Soviet policy was 'to have friendship between us'. He wanted 'all Poles to understand that the present leadership of Soviet Russia differed from the leadership of Tsarist Russia'. In his conviction, 'the Polish nation should go hand in hand with the Soviet Union, not against it.' He even said that he had been in Warsaw, and knew the narrow streets of the Old Town. The Premier had stated that everyone fighting in Warsaw was united, both in the Home Army and the People's Army. And Stalin twice confirmed his readiness to provide Warsaw 'with the most rapid assistance possible'. The two men warmed to the theme of the German menace. Stalin expressed his pleasure that the Premier was 'so anti-German'. And, in closing, made his famous comment about communism suiting Germany 'like a saddle fits a cow'. Contrary to later accounts, this meeting was not a sullen confrontation. If anything, it was suspiciously hearty. The two men passed an hour amidst a cloud of pleasant platitudes.[74] The Premier believed that he had extracted Stalin's 'promise' about the Rising. He left Moscow immediately. [**REFUGEE**, p. 317]

Rokossovsky had clearly suffered some sort of setback, whose political implications could be no doubt exaggerated and exploited in Moscow. But the setback was not critical. His plan of 8 August, for restarting the Western offensive, was approved by Zhukov and showed that there was no serious military obstacle to crossing the Vistula and rescuing the Rising. The capture of Warsaw would be the first step on the road towards Berlin. Stalin was being offered the means of striking a war-winning blow in record time; and the advice was proffered by the two men whose knowledge of the Eastern Front was unrivalled.[75]

Stalin's own clients, in the Lublin Committee, were almost more trouble than they were worth. They were slavishly obsequious but they had no discernible standing either in Poland or abroad. And they did not always stay in line. On 13 August, in Order nr. 6, the Committee's Army Commander gave an unmistakable signal to his soldiers that they would be marching into Warsaw in the very near future:

> Soldiers! The moment has arrived for the liberation of our capital. Warsaw, the symbol of the unbending, five-year struggle of the Polish nation, is watching you ... The great honour of taking part in the liberation battle and of ending the torment of your murdered compatriots has fallen to you ...
>
> The whole world is waiting for Warsaw's liberation, for the victory which you will win, arm in arm with the greatest fighting force in the world, the Red Army ... You must show the world that Poles are fighting for their capital. Forward to Warsaw! For Poland![76]

All the indications are that the Lublin Committee and its generals had been talking with Rokossovsky.

One reason for Moscow's caution might be found in the torrent of vitriol that was pouring out of the Lublin Committee and its associated bodies. At the very time that the Committee's leaders had been pretending in Moscow that there was no such thing as a Warsaw Rising, their

REFUGEE

Refugees unable to return home take cover for many days then decide to flee

During our two weeks of forced internment . . . I dug out a volume of sociological essays about prewar Poland, *The Young Generation of Peasants*, and plunged into a sorry reckoning with my own and my country's past, from time to time dropping flat on the floor as bullets traced long patterns across the plaster.

[We found] a kind of well in the cellar . . . big enough for two to stand in comfortably. But there were eleven . . . men in the house. We hid in it when the rumble of huge SS tanks sounded in the vicinity. The women closed the metal cover over us, and . . . we immediately began to suffocate. It was quite theatrical. In the light from the electric bulb I saw the mouths of fish thrown up on the sand and heads withering on stems of necks. A struggle also went on between those who preferred to suffocate and those who wanted to lift the cover. I suffocated, but with a nervous giggle. And anyway I did not know how real the danger was until one of us was picked up by the SS one day. He died running with upraised arms in front of a tank . . . as a human buffer in an attack on the insurrectionists' barricades.

Then the houses nearby caught fire . . . The only logical way out was across the fields. After much debate . . . our group, having made it over vegetable gardens, oat fields, and stubble, took shelter in an isolated grain store not far from the airport . . . From the attic, we had a magnificent panorama of a white city on a plain over which masses of black smoke billowed, pierced through with red tongues of flame. The noise of battle reached even to where we were: the rattle of machine guns, the laborious hammering of tank artillery, the flat sound of anti-aircraft guns, bomb explosions.

Since our home neighbourhood was very close . . . I could make out our house, where my desk, the witness of so many inner struggles, stood. Under the artillery fire its facade wrinkled like a face rapidly growing old. It was probably then that all my worldly goods fell through to the floor below.

At night, dots of varicoloured lights moved over the city: they were Germans firing . . . at [the] Polish and British planes . . . [which were] flying in to drop supplies . . . We passed several days and nights in the granary, while the nearby highway was patrolled by so-called 'Vlasovians' (soldiers from auxiliary German army divisions) recruited from various nationalities of the Soviet Union . . . They were taking advantage of their idleness to learn how to ride the bicycles they had captured. Of all things on earth, this, for some reason, seemed to me the most extravagant. They had chosen the slaughter of civilians as their vocation because, as their officers had told them, Warsaw was a 'bourgeois city'. Those bodies of dead women we had passed in the fields were their work.

Among our group . . . there was one specimen who looked as if he had just emerged from the Tertiary, or at least the Victorian, era. A corpulent man with a short black moustache . . . a black suit and a bowler. He raised his finger, sniffed, and said: 'Bad. It smells of a corpse in here.' And he was right. We could not prolong our rodent's life, flattened out between the sacks of grain . . . Some held that it was worse to go, others that it was worse to wait. Since we belonged to the latter, we set out whilst the grasshoppers were singing . . . in the warmth of a sunny afternoon.

Is it possible to surround a city of over a million with a cordon of guards? We found out that it was when we were caught and put behind the barbed-wire fence of a camp. 'Camp' is saying too much: it was nothing more than the yard of some construction firm, with sleepy German soldiers guarding the gates. Every morning the daily catch was sent to another camp in nearby . . . [Prushkov]. There people were sorted into transports . . . [for] concentration camps in Germany. We had to get out of there at all costs. I wrote secret notes . . . handing my appeals for help through the fence and trusting to the local children . . .

Human solidarity. Rescue showed up that evening in the form of a majestic nun. She commanded me severely to remember that I was her nephew. Her quiet, authoritative tone and the fluency of her German forced the soldiers into unwilling respect. Her conversation with the officer lasted an hour. Finally she appeared on the threshold: 'Hurry up, hurry up.' We passed through the main gate. I had never met her before and I never met her again. Nor did I ever know her name.[1]

Czesław Miłosz

---

comrades in Lublin had been preparing to denounce the Home Army for supposedly usurping control of it. A decree to this effect was published on 8 August by the Central Executive of the Communist PPR:

> First Revolutionary Decree to the Fighters and Citizens of Warsaw
>
> [Boor], the chief commandant of the so-called Home Army, has betrayed the Rising in Warsaw against the Hitlerite murderers. The coward and traitor Boor has dared to swindle the fighters. He wants to capitulate!
>
> Hence, as from today, the Central Executive Committee of the PPR has assumed leadership of the insurrectionary movement in Warsaw. It is the only genuine and responsible source of authority before the people.

> To this end . . .
>
> 1. All orders of the so-called Home Army must be disobeyed.
> 2. All officers of the so-called Home Army must be arrested and handed over to the incoming Red Army. Any officer who resists must be shot.
> 3. All insurgents must immediately replace their red-and-white armbands with red armbands.
> 4. As from 12.00 noon, units of the People's Army and PPR will shoot anyone still wearing red-and-white armbands.
> 5. After entering Warsaw, the Red Army will also treat all such fighters with red-and-white armbands as traitors . . .
>
> The Bloody Scourge of Fascism must be denounced.
>
> Long Live Marshal Stalin! Long Live a free socialist Poland![77]

Whoever penned this choice piece of prose was convinced of two things: the Rising was definitely in progress, and the Soviet Army was going to arrive any day.

Back in London, the Foreign Office officials charged with monitoring these developments were none too happy:

> August 13. Mick in Moscow had a series of talks with Stalin, Molotov and the Polish National Committee. They were all friendly and well-disposed . . . The PNC delegation was headed by an entirely new and hitherto unheard-of Pole called Berut – a pseudonym – whom Mick described as a sort of Polish Tito. Finally Mick decided he must come back to London to report. We telegraphed . . . to urge him to stop on . . . But he had already started, and in fact he reached London today.
>
> Meanwhile the Poles in London who control the Underground have set off a general Rising in Warsaw. They had not timed this with Russian plans, and we told them we could accept no responsibility for advising them on operations in the Russian sphere. The Russian forces have been held up outside Warsaw . . . and the Poles are now blaming everybody for not sending them help . . . As usual, they impute sinister motives to the Russians, such as that they are deliberately not helping, and not pressing their assault on Warsaw because they wish the Poles to be exterminated . . .[78]

Imputing sinister motives to the Russians was clearly bad form. Impugning the motives of the Poles, in contrast, was fair comment.

At this juncture, both the NKVD and *Smyersh* were hard at work filtering the population of the Soviet Army's rear areas. Lt.Gen. Serov was already in Lublin. Judging by the mountain of paper which he sent back to Beria, and which Beria summarized for Stalin, he can only have been aghast at the size of his task. Supporters of the Home Army apparently filled every town and village. Every woman, every priest, every boy scout whom they interrogated was firmly in favour of the exiled Government. Thousands upon thousands of arrests were barely scratching the surface. Stalin could not have been given the impression that it was specially safe to risk an immediate advance in that sector.

The prospect of invading the Balkans, in contrast, offered many rich rewards. In the larger strategic game, it was extremely attractive. It would put a stop to Churchill's dreams about winning Europe's 'soft underbelly' for the West; and it would open up an alternative route into the Reich via Budapest and Vienna. It did not preclude an offensive against Berlin at a later stage. Hence, at some point in mid-August Stalin gave orders for Marshal Tolbukhin to storm into Romania on the 20th. All other operations would have to fit in with this priority. Rokossovsky's and Zhukov's plan was shelved.

By reading the implications of numerous small shifts and signs, historians have reached the conclusion that Stalin issued Warsaw's death warrant on 13 August.[79] The deduction is not necessarily invalid, but it is unlikely to be accurate in all respects. In particular, the decision may not have been quite as final as has been suggested. It may have left the possibility open for a further change of tack. What is certain: Stalin dismissed the opportunity to help the Rising when assistance would have been most effective. What is more, after a long period of silence, he chose to condemn the Rising in the most callous terms. On 13 August, the TASS agency issued an authoritative communiqué:

> In recent days, information has appeared in the foreign press ... regarding an armed insurrection launched in Warsaw on 1 August on the orders of Polish émigrés in London and continuing to the present time. The press and radio of the Polish émigré Government have made allusions whereby the insurgents are said to have stayed in contact with the Soviet Command and whereby the Soviet Command has denied them suitable assistance.
>
> TASS is authorized to state that these allusions are either the result of a misunderstanding or else are a foul insult against the

> Soviet Command. TASS is informed that no attempt was made by the London Poles to inform the Soviet Command of their intentions in good time or to coordinate their actions in Warsaw. In consequence, full responsibility for the events in Warsaw will fall exclusively on Polish émigré circles in London.[80]

This communiqué clarified the negative position, which Moscow had now taken and which was reflected in the language of subsequent correspondence both with Churchill and with the Polish Premier. Stalin lost all his inhibitions, ranting openly about 'the reckless adventure' in Warsaw and 'the gang of criminals' who started it.

More surprisingly perhaps, the Kremlin permitted its underlings to show their teeth to Western representatives. On the night of 15/16 August, in their meeting with Vyshinsky, the British and US Ambassadors in Moscow were treated to a performance of savage delight such as they had never before witnessed. Harriman's telegram reported: 'the Soviet Government's refusal [to help Warsaw] is not based on operational difficulties, nor on a denial of the conflict, but on ruthless political calculations.' George Kennan, the US chargé d'affaires in Moscow, recalled the moment:

> I was personally not present at this fateful meeting with Stalin and Molotov; but I can recall the appearance of the ambassador and Gen. Deane as they returned, in the wee hours of the night, shattered by the experience. There was no doubt in any of our minds as to the implications of the position the Soviet leaders had taken. This was a gauntlet thrown down, in a spirit of malicious glee, before the Western powers. What it was meant to imply was: 'We intend to have Poland, lock, stock and barrel. We don't care a fig for those Polish underground fighters who have not accepted Communist authority. To us, they are no better than the Germans; and if they and the Germans slaughter each other off, so much the better. It is a matter of indifference to us what you Americans think of all this. You are going to have no part in determining the affairs of Poland from here on out, and it is time you realized this.'[81]

Of course, none of this was known at the time in Warsaw.

Yet the story was worse than even Kennan knew. For, unbeknown to the Western Allies, Soviet policy towards the Rising had moved from a passive to an actively hostile stance. On 22 August, the NKVD was ordered to arrest and disarm all captured insurgents who fell into its hands.[82] In the last week of the month, after Rokossovsky had rebuffed the German counter-attack, he was not merely ordered to resume defensive positions, he was ordered to transfer his Forty-Eighth Tank Army to the neighbouring sector facing East Prussia. Henceforth, unless new dispositions were made, he would find great difficulty in storming Warsaw, even if he had wanted to do so.

Some of the tensions of the moment were reflected in an off-the-record interview which Rokossovsky gave to a Western correspondent on 26 August:

ROKOSSOVSKY: I can't go into any details, but I'll tell you this. After several weeks of heavy fighting . . . we finally reached the outskirts of Praga about the 1st of August. At this point, the Germans threw in four armoured divisions, and we were driven back.

WERTH: How far back?

ROKOSSOVSKY: I can't tell you exactly, but let's say nearly 100km [sixty miles].

WERTH: Are you still retreating?

ROKOSSOVSKY: No – we are now advancing – but slowly . . .

WERTH: Wasn't the Warsaw Rising justified in the circumstances?

ROKOSSOVSKY: No, it was a bad mistake . . .

WERTH: There was that broadcast from Moscow calling on them to rise.

ROKOSSOVSKY: That was routine stuff . . .

WERTH: What prospect is there of your getting back to Praga in the next few weeks?

ROKOSSOVSKY: I can't go into that. All I can say is that we shall try to capture both Praga and Warsaw, but it won't be easy . . .

WERTH: Why can't you let British and American planes land behind Russian lines . . . There's been an awful stink in England and America about your refusal.

ROKOSSOVSKY: The military situation is more complicated than you realize. And we just don't want any British and American planes mucking around here at the moment . . .

WERTH: Isn't all this massacre and destruction in Warsaw having a terribly depressing effect on the Polish people here?

ROKOSSOVSKY: Of course it has. But a fearful mistake was made by the AK leadership. *We* [the Soviet Army] are responsible for the war in Poland: *we* are the force that will liberate the whole of the country within the next few months. And [Gen. Boor] and the people round him have

> butted in *kak ryzhy v tsirke* – like the clown in the circus who pops up at the wrong moment and only gets wrapped up in the carpet . . . If it were only a piece of clowning, it wouldn't matter, but the political stunt is going to cost hundreds of thousands of lives. It is an appalling tragedy, and they are now trying to put the blame on us . . .[83]

'And do you think', Rokossovsky concluded, 'that we would not have taken Warsaw if we had been able to do it? The whole idea that we are in any sense afraid of the AK is too idiotically absurd.'

Such was the Soviet attitude towards the workings of the Allied coalition. No one in the outside world had ever suggested that the Home Army was something of which the Soviets might be afraid. [**WARD**, p. 324]

The inconclusive operations in Warsaw in August were largely determined by the contrasting objectives of the combatants. The Germans' top priority was to prevent the insurgents from interfering with the front. The Home Army's only priority was to keep going for as long as possible until relief arrived.

One reason why von dem Bach took so long to mount a concerted assault on the insurgent enclaves lies with his protracted failures to close down attacks on the west–east thoroughfares. In one particular spot on the Jerusalem Avenue, for example, a company led by Capt. 'Roman' repeatedly invested a strategic building which overlooked the traffic on the boulevard. Roman, who was one of the very few people to have escaped from Auschwitz, was an unusually determined soldier. Almost every day during the first two weeks of the month, he captured, lost, and recaptured this building. Repeatedly driven out, he repeatedly returned and with deadly cunning repeatedly expelled the German defenders. He lived to fight elsewhere. But so long as he threatened this one vital pressure point, the German command was constantly made to feel insecure. One is tempted to suggest that a single company could have won the Rising a fortnight's reprieve.[84]

Having exceeded the Rising's expected duration by 200 per cent, Gen. Boor then called in his reserves. On 15 August, he summonded all Home Army units within reach of Warsaw to march to the capital's aid.[85] It was a tall order. For no one could join Gen. Boor without first crossing either the German lines or the Soviet lines or both.

WARD

Britain's Foreign Secretary tells the Prime Minister about their only direct source of information in Warsaw

Printed for the War Cabinet. August 1944

The circulation of this paper has been strictly limited. It is issued for the personal use of the Prime Minister.

TOP SECRET Copy No 2
W.P. (44) 461 22nd August, 1944

WAR CABINET.

SITUATION IN WARSAW.

MEMORANDUM BY THE SECRETARY OF STATE FOR FOREIGN AFFAIRS.

I circulate to my colleagues herewith (1) a translation of the latest message received by the Polish Government . . . together with (2) the text of the six latest messages from an escaped British R.A.F. prisoner of war, Sergeant Ward, who is . . . in Warsaw.

A.E.

Foreign Office, 22nd August, 1944

(1) Telegram from Warsaw

The lack of effective help, with the exception of a few droppings, is the main reason why Warsaw has become a beleaguered city and the Home Army is forced to a defensive position. The liquidation of the numerous points which the Germans hold in the capital is impossible in view of the lack of offensive weapons and ammunition . . . The Soviet Army is again standing again inactive at the gates of Warsaw.

The breaking of the deadlock . . . is not possible without serious droppings of arms and ammunition. The prolongation of the present phase leads to the total obliteration of Warsaw . . .

(2)

(No. 625.) • 18th August, 1944 • From J. Ward, No. 542939.

The main situation has not changed. In the centre fighting continues to be very heavy. The enemy continues with the ruthless destruction by air bombardment, by 75 mm. tank artillery, and by mine throwers. About 40 per cent. of the city centre is already completely destroyed and another 20 per cent. badly damaged . . . The Germans are carrying out their attempt to destroy Warsaw. Loss of life among civil population and the A.K. is very high.

(No. 626.) • 19th August, 1944 • From J. Ward.

The people of Warsaw call the Germans' minethrower 'the moving cupboard' on account of the fact that it gives a sound like that of a heavy piece of furniture being moved, followed a few seconds later by a number of terrific explosions. The Prudential Building on Sq. Napoleon, the highest building in Warsaw, was hit three times by mines and once by bombs [and] completely burnt out. The pavements in Warsaw have been turned into grave-yards . . .

(No. 627.) • 19th August, 1944 • Addressed to Espe. From J. Ward.

Sir, reply to my telegram received. I was born in Birmingham. Maiden name of mother Anne Elizabeth Margewws [sic], father's John Ward. Address, 54 Madison Avenue, Wardend, Birmingham, 8.

Sir, I beg for more detailed orders. For three years I have worked in Polish underground army. Now, acting on advice of the Polish staff here, am combining my military duties as acting lt. in A.K. with that of War Correspondent. All my telegrams are without censure.

(No. 634.) • 20th August, 1944 • From J. Ward, No. 542939, R.A.F.

Thousands of people are each day rendered homeless in Warsaw and hundreds killed . . . There are thousands of wounded men, women and children suffering from the most horrible burns and in some cases from shrapnel and bullet wounds. Each day battle . . . is prolonged the cost mounting higher. But the determination of the population to fight to the last man is only strengthened by this German barbarism.

(No. 635.) • 20th August, 1944 • From J. Ward, No. 542939, R.A.F.

On practically every open piece of ground . . . wells are being dug. Shortage of water is starting to be serious. If in ten days the city receives no relief then the (?) food will also give out. Rations are already very short. Situation Warsaw desperate. On the outskirts, huge concentration camps full of women and children living in the open air without food or help. They are dying of hunger and disease . . . The Germans show no mercy . . . The men were shot when the women and children were taken prisoners.

(No. 636.) • 20th August, 1944 • From J. Ward, No. 542939, R.A.F.

The Germans have in many areas got over from the defensive to the attack. The high school on Novakovski street was taken by Germans at 5 hours on the 19th. The attack was carried out under a heavy artillery barrage . . . Despite these drawbacks, the troops of A.K. continue to fight with magnificent courage. Other attacks from the German forces on the night of the 19th August south of Av. Sikorski were firmly held.[1]

Several such groups were already on the march, retreating as best they could from the East. Others were located in the province of Lublin or to the south in the Holy Cross Mountains. None of them made the perilous journey all the way to Warsaw, though a few got as far as the Kampinos Forest. The 30th Infantry Division of the Home Army, which hailed from the district of Pinsk, followed a familiar course. Under its commander, Maj. 'Thunder', it had recently participated with the Soviet Sixty-Fifth Army in the siege of Brest, and had crossed the River Bug undisturbed. In mid-August, it moved off with about 150km (90 miles) to cover. It reached a point within sight of the Vistula. There it was trapped by the Soviets, and disarmed.

Few accounts of those turbulent days care to mention the fact that some Home Army units continued to put Operation Tempest into effect wherever possible, even in the immediate environs of the capital. An overhead snapshot taken in mid-August in the Warsaw District would have shown the main element of the Home Army engaged with the Germans in the city, a second element being interned by the NKVD, and a third element still battling alongside Rokossovsky in the fighting for several small towns.[86]

Inside the city, the Battle of the PAST Building was one of slow, dogged, hand-to-hand fighting. The multistorey tower of the State Telephone Company (PAST) was, after the Prudential, the second highest structure in Warsaw, and in pre-war terms counted as a skyscraper. It was one of the places where a substantial German garrison, though cut off and surrounded since 1 August, had refused to surrender. The Home Army had none of the heavy artillery the Germans would have used, so they had to storm the lower part of the building, then fight their way up, room by room, floor by floor. The action moved from an indecisive siege to the terminal attack on 20 August. Headed by Maj. 'Leliva' of the Kilinski Battalion, it was systematically prepared. The captured diaries of German soldiers, trapped on the upper floor, gave proof of extreme privation. First, the surrounding streets were reinforced with units which could block the forays of German tanks that had been bringing food and ammunition for the besieged. But then the attackers took serious measures. A team of women sappers – the famous *minerki* – placed explosives in the basement; and the building was set alight with flame-throwers. An early example of the 'towering inferno' ensued. Germans jumped from the upper windows, were killed attempting to descend the staircases, or simply shot themselves. A white flag finally emerged on 22 August. 115 prisoners were taken. If anyone on the German side had thought that the Home Army was simply holding out, they could think again. [**PAST**, p. 303]

Monday 28 August marked the end of the fourth week, and the Rising was still going strong. In the previous days, as noted with dismay by the Ninth Army Command, the insurgents had launched some local counter-attacks both in the north and in the south. A verse written on the 28th by a soldier of the Kilinski Battalion bore witness to their unbroken spirit:

> Remember, you cannot doubt in Freedom / Whatever comes, even if you fail. / Remember that the whole wide world Is watching you in wonderment. / Though all assistance crumble And hunger and pain set in. / We shall not lose our wager – / The wager of honour.[87]

The Wehrmacht Command was well aware of the insurgents' success. The entry for 29 August in the Ninth Army's log stated that the Home Army was maintaining its strength in critical sectors by the brilliant use of the sewers and other underground passages. The besieging forces were unlikely to make decisive progress without the addition of another whole division of experienced infantry. 'The crushing of the Rising is becoming a very difficult task,' it concluded; 'and its completion is ever more doubtful with every day that passes.'[88]

Attrition

By the end of August, both sides in the struggle for Warsaw were sensing the sour smell of failure. Von dem Bach's hard-pressed men must have been painfully aware that their colleagues in the Wehrmacht were smirking at their inability to finish off a gang of bandits. Gen. Boor's subordinates were sick with anxiety that their stupendous sacrifices might yet be in vain. Their anxiety was fuelled by the realization of three bitter truths: that the Old Town would soon have to be abandoned; that the Western allies could not supply effective assistance; and that the silence of the Soviet Army could no longer be due to practical difficulties.

Warsaw's Old Town consisted of a maze of narrow, ancient streets clustered round St John's Cathedral, the Royal Castle, and the stately Old Town Square. Surrounded by medieval battlements and defended by some 8,000 insurgents, it had provided a secure base for the guerrilla fighting in which the Home Army excelled. But it was a sitting duck for the mass bombardments which were directed against it by Gen. Rohr from the last week of August onwards, and against which there was no satisfactory defence. The toll both in fighters and civilians was becoming intolerable. When the number of defenders dropped to one quarter of their original strength, the AK Command knew that the remainder would somehow have to be evacuated into the City Centre, perhaps a kilometre to the south. They also knew, if the defenders left, that the vulnerable civilian population would be left to the tender mercy of the Nazis.

The Old Town, moreover, was an important symbol of the city's history and heritage. The figure of King Sigismund III stood atop his marble column in Castle Square much as the figure of Admiral Nelson stands above Trafalgar Square in London. In late August, the Sigismund Column was still standing proudly intact among the ruins. If it should fall, the hearts of the defenders would inevitably sink with it. [**BATTLE**, p. 329]

The British airlift from Italy, which had resumed on 8 August and extended on Churchill's orders from the 13th, persisted against all the odds. Losses were disproportionate to the benefits. Many planes were shot down before reaching Warsaw. Many were unable to make their drops in the designated areas. Many failed to return to base. But every crate of Sten guns, of ammunition, or especially of PIAT anti-tank weapons was worth its weight in gold. It raised morale, as well as the insurgents' armoury. Yet doubts inevitably multiplied. From the insurgent side, it was not hard to calculate that military, medical, and food stores were declining faster than they could be replaced. From the standpoint of the aircrews, it was extremely difficult to understand why they should risk so much to deliver so little when their Soviet allies, virtually on the spot, were not lifting a finger. And another sickening puzzle arose. Reports grew not only about the Soviets refusing to cooperate but also about them actively firing on British planes.

Throughout August, many explanations had been tendered about Soviet inactivity on the Vistula front. The Wehrmacht's Panzer force had delivered a devastating counter-attack. Rokossovsky's soldiers were disoriented and had been obliged to withdraw and regroup. Soviet reserves had been transferred from the Vistula to the Balkan front. Yet by the end of the month, all these arguments were wearing thin. When the German Ninth Army was forced to retreat in early September to the line of the Vistula, preparing new defences, it was crystal clear that Rokossovsky had fully recovered. There was no military reason why he could not at least

BATTLE

A German journalist, correspondent of *Das Reich*, sees for himself the efforts required to overcome insurgent resistance

Flame-throwers, Schmeissers, and heavy ordnance shattered the walls of reinforced concrete into thick pieces. Intensive bombing from the air destroyed the courtyards, whilst unmanned Goliaths, long-distance shelling, and anti-tank artillery drove the defenders from the upper floors with murderous fire. But in the labyrinthine cellars, vaults, and passages, battles raged on, even when large buildings were reduced to heaps of rubble emitting clouds of smoke and dust. It was only when divisions of Wehrmacht soldiers, police, and gendarmerie advanced into the final attack with a battalion of flame-throwers that grenadiers managed to enter the underground labyrinth, and the commander of Colonel Schmidt's section could report on the capture of these splendid ruins.[1]

A Polish journalist working for an Underground socialist paper assesses the effect of different weapons

[. . .] 'The bellowing cow' – a horrendous machine throwing out a series of incendiary and demolition missiles spread devastation. We felt its hellish breath in our editorial office. Two or three of its rockets fell into a room on the first floor, one of the offices of the Department of Information. In the wink of an eye everything burst into flames. A messenger, who happened to be in the office, was turned into a living torch. Admittedly the fire was overcome by the immediate emergency aid of a PPS militia division, quartered on the ground floor, but the girl died after a few hours of awful suffering.

The 'bellowing cow', also known as the 'musical box', could provoke a stampede. The sound, which it emitted before it threw a missile, made an incredible impression . . . That machine's actions always evoked a picture of some kind of monster from before the Flood, which had come out of its lair for food making its presence known in the wilderness and its desire for blood and fresh meat. At the sound of it, blood froze in the veins, and all the animals escaped in panic. In the same way people fled at the sound of the 'bellowing cow', so that after the explosion, which followed, people emerged again with a latent feeling of relief that the monster had found its victim elsewhere.

Other machines of destruction were deployed. The Big Bertha was introduced. This huge rail ordnance emitted enormous missiles almost a metre long, which could shatter a house; on explosion, they threw into the air the most powerful reinforced concrete constructions . . . On the edges of the junction point with the surrounding German army, Goliaths appeared – demolition mines, on wheels like small tanks, which the Germans had directed from a distance towards the barricades or houses on the banks of the river which had been turned into fortresses; they exploded on contact with any obstacle.

Neither the Tigers nor the Big Berthas, not even the Goliaths, however, could overpower the insurgent city. Petrol bombs and other missiles fell upon the Tigers. The missiles of the Big Bertha, as unexpected as bad luck, fortunately rarely met with success. The 'bellowing cow' destroyed houses, but mainly the higher floors, it was possible to survive on the ground floor or in the basements. The soldiers built shields against Goliaths from the street pavements. They were a few metres long and located in front of defended positions. These shields, which the Goliaths smashed into, far from the barricades or houses, gained the fitting name of 'Little Davids'.

However, there was no help against planes, no way of fighting. [. . .] Therefore planes systematically threw missiles on one block of houses after another, with no chance of reply.[2]

Z. Zaremba

---

establish radio contact with the insurgents or why Soviet aerial and artillery support could not come into play. There could be little question that all further lack of urgency must be due to Stalin's politics, not to military setbacks.

As a result, both the German and the Home Army Commands began to reflect on a possible escape route. In German calculations, progress against the Rising was so slow that the insurgency could continue for weeks and seriously obstruct plans to turn Warsaw into a front-line fortress. In Polish calculations, the cost in lives and suffering was so high that endless resistance could not be justified, unless Rokossovsky made a move. So both sides put out feelers for a capitulation by agreement. The Germans would not agree to a settlement if the entire population were not removed. The Home Army would not settle if their people were not guaranteed a safe passage. General Rohr formally proposed negotiations on 7 September. On the 8th, General Boor accepted. Meanwhile, for week after week, the war of attrition persisted.

*

In September 1944, the German High Command had more to think about than the festering battle in Warsaw. Ever since Rokossovsky's obliteration of Army Group Centre, the Soviet Army's presence on the central stretch of the Vistula continued to pose a threat pointing directly at Berlin. Yet Soviet movement on that front was strangely sluggish, even when the Panzers' counter-attack had been neutralized. Moscow was diverting much greater resources to the northern front in the Baltic and to the southern campaign in the Balkans. At the same time, France had fallen to the Anglo-Americans; the Low Countries were under attack: and Operation Market Garden, the attack on Arnhem, though abortive, suggested that Allied strategists were cooking up a series of knock-out blows. The prime task in mid-September, therefore, was to calculate the most likely contours of the Allies' grand offensive and to deploy the Reich's dwindling defences accordingly.

German military planners did not fail to notice the odd situation that had developed round Warsaw. They were no less mystified by the failure of the SS to crush the Rising than by the Soviets' apparent inability to join up with the insurgents and to create a truly menacing stance on the Vistula's western bank. German thoughts on this matter did not entertain the possibility that Rokossovsky was deliberately holding back. Indeed, the log of the Ninth Army on 2 September interpreted the Soviet attack on Radzymin as an attempt to break through and to relieve the impending collapse of the insurgents in the Old Town. So a solid defence of the front to the east of Warsaw was an essential corollary to the operations against the Rising, and von dem Bach was to receive the requested reinforcement. The battle-hardened 542nd Grenadier Regiment was to be transferred to Warsaw from the Fourth Army on the River Biebra. The overstretched Wehrmacht was only meeting its needs with difficulty. Even the *Waffen-SS* had been forced to make concessions. Its recruitment policy, for example, had been completely transformed. An elite formation that in its early days had screened all applicants for the purest 'German blood' was now accepting volunteers with no German credentials at all. Indeed, the point was approaching when non-Germans would numerically predominate. In a speech to the SS Latvian Legion in September 1944, Himmler presented his new vision of a multinational Europe, whose world mission would be to stem the threat of the black and yellow races.[89] Yet, in essence, the ultimate aim remained German domination or nothing.

There can be few cases where the Nazis condemned one of their own leading thugs to death on the grounds of 'perpetrating excesses'.

Such, however, was the fate of *SS-Brig.Fhr.* Kaminski, whose troops had been running wild in Warsaw for a month without achieving any notable military successes. The chief of the RONA Brigade paid with his life for von dem Bach's failures. In the eyes of the Nazis, he was a low-grade Slav who had overstayed his welcome in the ranks of his German masters. The decision to dispose of him was taken at the end of August. He was out of Warsaw on leave. A fake car accident was staged near Lodz either to kill him or to cover the traces of his earlier execution. A delegation of his own men were taken to the site to pay their respects. After the war, von dem Bach claimed this action as proof of his own moderation and humanity.

The Ninth Army's plan of 2 September held off the Soviets for barely two weeks. By the 13th, German sappers were blowing up the four remaining bridges in Warsaw. By so doing, they severed the supply lines to the east by their own hand, and demonstrated to the world that the Wehrmacht was about to abandon all its positions beyond the Vistula.

Much German effort and ingenuity was put into schemes for persuading the civilian population to pack their bags and leave. Clouds of leaflets were dropped from the air: 'Do you wish to live or die?' Anyone who left, other than active insurgents, was promised fair treatment and medical aid. The *Delegatura* countered by urging people not to believe German promises, but rather to reflect on the fresh news of mass murders. Gen. Boor was in two minds. He did not wish to concede to German demands. On the other hand, he accepted that he had no means of mitigating civilian distress and that the evacuation of civilians would leave the Home Army more space to fight.

Negotiations proceeded, therefore, between German representatives and the Polish Red Cross. And on 8, 9, and 10 September, three consecutive evacuations took place involving 20–25,000 persons.[90] The majority who left were women, children, the elderly, and the poor. In some cases, AK men escorted their wives and families to the assembly point. Scuffles broke out between soldiers and healthy youths who were observed leaving. The Red Cross reported that men were being separated from the rest at Prushkov, and that the women and children 'were being sent west'. [**HOSPITAL**, p. 333]

With the evacuations underway, Gen. Rohr pressed hard for a swift capitulation. Boor responded with a request for clarification on three points: the recognition of full combatant rights for all Home Army soldiers; the destination of civilians remaining in the city; and German intentions

HOSPITAL

Patients and practitioners of the medical services both show their mettle

After the death of Lieutenant 'Girder' I took command of 1147 Platoon, an assault unit in the central district. I took part in the attack on the PAST Building . . . led by Captain Kontrym (who was murdered after the war in the Mokotov prison).

As I was wounded in the leg, I was carried to a dressing station and then to a hospital, where the ward head was Professor K. They wanted to amputate my leg, which had two shattered bones. I did not agree. Not surprisingly the Professor was angry. He was a wonderful man and said that *he* was in charge and knew what to do. I replied that it was my leg and that I was in charge. Since I was still wearing my revolver, I could stop them giving me an intravenous injection. I was afraid they would anaesthetize me completely. At every procedure, I ordered the sister to lift me up from behind, so that, pistol in hand, I could watch what they were doing. The doctors laughed – what a patient!

Thanks to the run-in with Professor K., I sent word to my colonel ['Radvan'], requesting to be transferred elsewhere. They sent me to the Home Army infirmary on Marian Street, formerly a National Health Service clinic, where the commander was Dr P. Naturally it was a temporary hospital. Beds had been collected from neighbouring houses and local people assisted in its organization.

The medical staff were immensely skilled. After the war, many of us worked in the health service. But never did we see such a high level of sterilization, or care over cleanliness as in those insurrectionary conditions, where everything could be contaminated by the constant explosions. There was a whole group of nurses trained in the Underground, who carried out the bleakest work with a smile. I take my hat off to those girls, but above all to the medical staff, who performed the most difficult operations in madly difficult circumstances. Decisions had to be taken instantly. Skull trepanations, eye removals, and limb amputations were routine. Even so, the death rate was relatively low. Throughout my stay on Marian Street, a dozen or twenty patients at the most died from the 500 or so who passed through.

The Home Army authorities concluded that the hospital, in accordance with international convention, should be clearly marked on the roof with a Red Cross. It precipitated an immediate bombardment by German Stukas and by extremely heavy rocket fire. The hospital began to burn, the upper floors to collapse . . . Immediate evacuation was essential.

My platoon was directed into emergency action . . . We had to jump with our stretchers into an area where missiles were exploding. The evacuation parties were being strafed from the air . . . We loaded up the injured then waited a moment for the end of a salvo and rushed to the safe area. Unfortunately, there were many casualties . . .

Whenever an approaching missile could be heard, we did not lie down but stood the stretchers on their legs and knelt beside them, so that the patients did not feel worse than we did. None of my colleagues left their stretchers, even though we had wounded men who were now wounded for a second time . . . I saw truly awful things, especially people set alight by incendiaries.

Of those present, I best remembered the commander of the AK medical service in Mokotov, Professor L., who held the rank of colonel and had served in the Polish Army in 1920. He was an exceptionally heroic person, I must say. His self-control, energy, and authority were astounding . . . Everyone carried out his instructions unquestioningly. Alas, he did not long survive the evacuation of his hospital.

Still, I did rescue people. It was worthwhile; and everything that I survived after the Rising somehow seemed less important.[1]

J. J. Lipski

---

regarding the Underground's non-military personnel. Rohr replied immediately, conceding 'combatant rights' and promising 'no reprisals'. But he also demanded instant capitulation by 4 p.m. on the same day. This ultimatum could not be met.

Sometime in early September, the *Reichsführer-SS* returned to the subject of the Rising, and issued one of his infrequent pronouncements. 'For five weeks we have been fighting for Warsaw . . .' he complained. 'It is the hardest battle we have fought . . . This Gen. [Boor] has been betrayed by the Russians, for they have not relieved him; and they are now pretending they would like to capitulate. He was egged on and set up by the English.'[91]

The stresses and strains of the Warsaw Rising had a demoralizing effect on the exiled Polish Government in London. Splits and recriminations broke out at various levels, and they were not ameliorated by the climate of mistrust generated by the ill-informed reporting in the British press. When the Premier returned empty-handed from Moscow, his declared policy of seeking Soviet cooperation through Western support was inevitably called into question. But there was no ready alternative. Bitter frustration at the impossibility of relieving Warsaw's distress was joined by deep resentment both at the empty promises of the Western Allies and at the cruel intransigence of the Soviets.

The Commander-in-Chief was the principal target of these tensions. A close associate of Marshal Pilsudski in the victory over the Red Army in 1920, he was the bête noire of Soviet propaganda. A firm opponent of the Rising, who had been overruled by his colleagues in July, he was nonetheless held to be responsible by virtue of his office. He was now being blamed, both by the Soviets and by Soviet sympathizers, for developments to which he had been long opposed. Absent in Italy in early August, he was accused of dereliction of duty by allowing his subordinates to engineer a supposedly premature outbreak. He came under pressure from all sides to resign.

The Premier, meanwhile, had been patiently working away to sell his plan for reconciliation with the Soviets, first to his own Cabinet and (via radio) to the Underground leaders in Warsaw. It was finally unveiled on 30 August:

1. The post-war Government would be reconstructed to offer the Communist Party (PPR) the same number of representatives as each of the four main democratic parties: Peasant, Socialist, National, and Christian Democrat.
2. Diplomatic relations would be re-established with the USSR.
3. All foreign troops would leave Poland at the end of hostilities.
4. Early elections to a constituent assembly would take place by secret and universal suffrage, and a new Constitution would be passed.
5. Social, economic, and especially agrarian reforms would be implemented.
6. A Polish–Soviet alliance would be concluded on the basis of the respect for sovereignty and for non-interference.
7. On the territorial issue: 'Poland, which has made so many sacrifices, cannot emerge diminished in territory. In the east, the main centres of Polish cultural [and economic] life shall remain within Polish boundaries. A final settlement . . . will be made by the Constituent Assembly in accordance with democratic principles.'[92]

The last clause implied concessions to the USSR, although the 'Curzon Line' was not mentioned. The British Foreign Minister was said to be satisfied, although he also said that Stalin would probably 'play for time'.

The Premier would have been aware, however, that his plan did not meet the approval of the leaders of the Rising. Gen. Boor, when consulted, made his views very plain:

> The plan is tantamount to total capitulation, and anticipates a whole series of political moves based on the goodwill of the Soviets, without any prior guarantees from the USSR and the Allies . . . At such a momentous time, . . . I consider it my duty to state, in the name of the Home Army which I command, . . . that Poland has not been fighting the Germans for five years, bearing the greatest losses, just to capitulate to Russia . . .
>
> Our fight against the Germans has shown that . . . we love freedom more than life. If necessary, we shall repeat that manifestation for anyone who wants to destroy our independence . . .[93]

The very next day, 1 September, on the fifth anniversary of the outbreak of war, the Commander-in-Chief cast prudence to the winds and spoke his mind. His Order nr. 19 to the Home Army was an open, unrestrained indictment of the Allies' complacency and ingratitude:

> Five years have passed since the day when, encouraged by the British Government and its guarantee, Poland stood up to its lonely struggle with German might. For the last month, the soldiers of the Home Army and the people of Warsaw have again been abandoned in another bloody and lonely fight. This is a tragic and repeated puzzle which we Poles cannot decipher . . . We hear arguments about gains and losses. But we remember that in the Battle of Britain Polish pilots suffered over 40 per cent casualties, whilst the loss of planes and aircrew in the flights to Poland is 15 per cent . . . If the population of our capital is to be condemned to perish in mass slaughter under the rubble of their homes through [Britain's] calculated passivity and indifference, the conscience of the world will be burdened by this terrible and unparalleled sin.[94]

With the exception of *The Times*, no London newspapers repeated the Commander-in-Chief's order in full, or mentioned his statistics. But British opinion was outraged. Britain's good faith was being openly questioned. From that day on, the C-in-C's days in office were numbered.

As it happened, 1 September 1944 also saw the publication of the most trenchant, and probably the most insightful, article ever written in Britain about the Warsaw Rising. Its author was Eric Blair, alias George Orwell.

At the time, Orwell was writing *Animal Farm*, an allegorical fiction about totalitarianism that would soon make him a household name around the world. But he was also the literary editor of *Tribune*, an independent socialist journal to which he contributed a weekly column called 'As I please'. The previous week, *Tribune* had published a long, carping letter from Geoffrey Barraclough, a young Cambridge historian who had special interests in Central Europe and a part-time job with the Foreign Office. Orwell decided to take Barraclough apart, and thereby to expose everything he thought wrong about 'the British intelligentsia'.[95]

Barraclough had made four basic charges: the Warsaw Rising was not 'spontaneous'; the order to rise was given without consultation; the Polish Resistance movement was as divided as its counterpart in Greece; and the *soi-disant* Polish Government precipitated the Rising in order to get hold of Warsaw before the Russians arrived. Orwell took these arguments to be symptomatic of the 'mean, cowardly and slavish' attitude of the British press in general and set out to demolish them. He attacked the biased language. He pointed to the lack of proof. He deplored the intellectual dishonesty: 'once a whore, always a whore.' And he argued that 'Anglo-Russian friendship' would never be attained without 'plain speaking'. It was a passionate tour de force.

Orwell's most telling point concerned the dubious motives of Stalin's admirers, who mimicked his slogans 'like a troop of parrots' and who defended them 'if at all, solely on grounds of power':

> [The] attitude . . . is not 'Is this policy right or wrong?' but 'This is Russian policy; how can we make it appear right?' . . . The Russians are powerful in Eastern Europe, we are not; therefore we must not oppose them. This involves the principle, of its nature alien to Socialism, that you must not protest against an evil which you cannot prevent.[96]

A genuine socialist was exposing the roots of pseudo-socialism. In the process, he showed why much of the prevailing comment on the Warsaw Rising was so desperately unfair. (See Appendix 26.)

Nonetheless, the British press showed only moderate signs of contrition, indeed of close interest. Orwell's stand was strengthened to some extent by Vernon Bartlett of the *News Chronicle*, who started to query Soviet policy on the Rising about the same time. A real stir was raised by Bartlett's article on 11 September, which belatedly publicized the news released a month earlier by the Vatican about Moscow's refusal to grant landing rights to the RAF. Even the left-leaning *Daily Herald* reluctantly admitted that 'Unfortunately, it [the denial of landing rights] was a fact . . .' Many journalists followed the *Scotsman*'s lead in demanding fuller information. Many, like the *Economist* and the *Spectator*, drew telling contrast between events in Paris and Warsaw. But they were put down by the usual claque of Soviet sympathizers. According to the *New Statesman*, the leaders of the Warsaw Rising were 'Machiavellian *dilettanti*'. According to *The Times*, 'it is not difficult to understand Russian unwillingness to supply arms to people, who are opposed to friendly relations with Russia'. One need not have asked whence the concept of 'friendly relations with Russia' originated. In fact, even damaged RAF planes were forbidden to land. [**FATHER**, p. 339]

In this fraught climate the British public lost much of its former confidence in the exiled Government, whilst relations between the Premier and the Commander-in-Chief spiralled out of control. They sent conflicting information to Gen. Boor concerning talks on the intended American airlift and on attempts to contact Rokossovsky. In his telegram of 13 September, the Premier let it be known that Gen. Tabor was keeping him informed on Boor's correspondence with the Commander-in-Chief. For his part, the Commander-in-Chief had let it be known that the Premier was pressing for his dismissal – 'which is exactly what the Russians want'.

To say that the Warsaw Rising drove the British and Americans 'to their wits' end' may be something of an exaggeration. Westminster and Washington had many other worries, generated both by American problems in the Far East and by the frightening rate of Soviet advances in the Balkans. On 30 August the Soviet Army entered Bucharest, and quickly moved on from Romania to Bulgaria. What was worse, the Western Allies had so underrated events in the East, they had few sure sources of independent intelligence. When told by Soviet diplomats that everything possible was being done to relieve Warsaw, they had no way – other than by asking the Poles – of verifying the facts. Needless to say, the Poles could hardly be regarded as impartial concerning the affairs of their own country.

Allied grand strategy was the subject of a meeting code-named Octagon, which was convened in Quebec, and attended by Roosevelt and Churchill between 12 and 16 September 1944. Pacific affairs came to the fore for the first time. The Allied leaders had been briefed to the effect that the war against Germany could be completed as early as December

FATHER

An insurgent soldier, an escaper from the Ghetto, sets out in search of his parents

When our sector was reasonably quiet I asked for time off to look for my father in hospital. So, with one arm in a sling and a large loaf of bread (a great luxury) under the other, I started on the arduous journey. The streets had become no-go areas. Pedestrians were restricted to cellars linked by holes hacked in the walls between them. Most of these cellars had low ceilings and were crowded beyond description. People had made them home while the battles raged above. Sick and wounded lay on the floor awaiting medical attention. Flickering candles and paraffin lamps and the pervading smell of damp added to the eerie atmosphere created by ghostlike silhouettes moving around aimlessly, by the walking wounded, and by the occasional unit of soldiers in transit to new positions. A multitude of people lived, ate, and slept here for weeks on end.

I could often only walk in a crouching position. But at the end of each block I had to emerge into the open, at times in plain view of German tanks. Bent in half, I had to run across the road making the best use of the flimsy protection offered by low barricades. Hence what in normal times would have been a thirty-minute walk along pleasant streets had become a perilous endeavour taking several hours.

The greatest hazard was crossing Marshal Street, the capital's main thoroughfare. It was some thirty metres wide, and intense German fire was repeatedly wrecking the two barricades erected across it. Constructed of paving stones, rubble, tram carriages, furniture, and anything to hand, the barricades were not strong enough to withstand the ceaseless cannonade. As I came out of a basement I took a deep breath, jack-knifed as low as I could, and dashed across. A few minutes later I was standing at the hospital reception desk, anxiously asking for Yan Malinowski, my father's assumed name. The receptionist took ages going through the register, and I lost patience. At last she found the right entry.

But was it Father or some other Yan Malinowski? Climbing the wide staircase on the way to the ward I tried to rein in my expectations. If it *was* Father, how bad would his wounds be? Inside a vast ward, between closely packed beds, a nurse led me to one of them and I sighed with relief when I recognized Father. He looked pale and gaunt. His head was heavily bandaged. He was clearly taken aback . . . His lips trembled . . . I kissed him.

'How did you get here?' I asked.

'Our house was hit by a bomb,' he answered. 'I lost consciousness and when I regained it I was lying in this hospital bed. I don't know what happened to everyone else.' He looked unsure whether he was dreaming or not.

'Do you know what happened to Mother?' He was most anxious.

'No.' I could offer no consolation. The area [around Narutovich Square], where Mother and Hela were living, had remained in German hands throughout the Rising and neither of us had heard from them . . .

'Are you in pain?' I asked.

'They might be able to remove the bandage soon.'

With a semi-theatrical gesture I put the loaf of bread in front of Father and his eyes lit up. 'I haven't seen a piece of bread since I got here. I am hungry all the time. I don't know how to thank you.' He looked at my helmet and at the Luger hanging from my belt.

'Did you risk your life to get here?'

'Don't worry. Whatever is meant to happen will happen.'

It was hard to tear myself away. I saw an anxious look clouding the unbandaged part of his face, and he could hardly control the tears. It was to be our last parting . . .[1]

---

whilst the war against Japan might continue for eighteen months to two years. In consequence, questions were now asked about slow progress in the Pacific war and about Soviet intentions towards China and Japan. One way or another it was assumed that the final showdown against Germany was imminent. In which case, it was becoming eminently desirable to obtain Soviet cooperation, both in plans for the occupation of Germany and in the final phase of the Pacific war.

Little was said about Warsaw, therefore, though the Rising was reaching its critical phase. The Western leaders' dismay at the show of Soviet hostility in Poland fitted into a wider picture of unease. Roosevelt had been pressing Stalin in vain ever since Teheran on the issue of joint staff planning. But nothing much had materialized. The Western military were not able to communicate with their Soviet counterparts except through the cumbersome channels of their respective military missions. Ambassador Harriman became so frustrated by Soviet obstructions that he recommended suspending non-military supplies to the USSR.[97]

Britain and America were much exercised at this time about plans to eliminate German economic power. On this, Roosevelt was supremely ruthless. At Quebec, he and Churchill initialled a proposal presented by Henry Morgenthau of the US Treasury for 'converting Germany into a country primarily agricultural and pastoral in character.' The conversion was to be effected partly by dismantling the Ruhr and partly by handing Silesia to Poland. An implicit deal was in the making. The Western powers could not save Warsaw. But they might find some compensation for Poland by carving up Germany's assets.

It is significant that no Polish or Soviet representatives were present at Quebec. The Poles were not invited; Stalin was invited but declined through pressure of business. As a result, the urgent issue of Polish–Soviet relations was *not* discussed. The Polish Premier's plan was not on the agenda. Another opportunity was missed.

In the autumn of 1944, US policy towards Poland came increasingly under the shadow of the approaching elections. The President was at great pains to avoid any offence to the millions of Polish-American voters who would determine the result of several Midwestern cities of key importance to the Democratic Party. Behind the scenes, however, it is clear that his closest advisers were not encouraging him to take energetic measures over Warsaw. Early in September, the US Ambassador in London, John G. Winant, following contacts with Britain's Catholic clergy, suggested that the President might speak to the Archbishop of Chicago to allay Polish-American and US Catholic concerns. Harry Hopkins responded with irritation. 'I confess I have no great patience with the efforts which the Church inspires by what amounts to almost secret and devious methods to control the political affairs of the world.' And he continued with what amounted to a counsel of inaction. 'I think that the problem of Warsaw itself', he commented, 'will be handled by the sure [Soviet] victories on Germany's eastern front.'[98]

Yet it was Adm. Leahy – FDR's personal chief of staff – who was the source of the extraordinary piece of misinformation which the President relayed virtually verbatim to Churchill on 5 September. Leahy prepared 'the following reply to the Prime Minister's messages in regard to the relief of Polish patriots in Warsaw':

> PRESIDENT TO PRIME: Replying to your 779, 780 and 781, I am informed by my office of Military Intelligence that the fighting Poles have departed from Warsaw and that the Germans are now in full control.
>
> The problem of relief for the Poles in Warsaw has therefore, unfortunately, been solved by delay and by German action and there appears now to be nothing we can do to assist them.

> I have long been deeply distressed by our inability to give adequate assistance to the heroic defenders of Warsaw, and I hope that we may together still be able to help Poland be among the victors in this war with the Nazis.
>
> State Department approves
>
> LEAHY[99]

Churchill, understandably, was aghast. Despite the rhetorical flourishes, the President was effectively washing his hands of Warsaw. One can only wonder where Leahy's misinformation came from. It may well be that US Military Intelligence had already heard of the fall of the Old Town two days previously, but that they did not have sufficient wit to distinguish between the Old Town and the city of Warsaw as a whole. On the other hand, the episode is horribly reminiscent of the gormless reaction which Western enquirers had frequently encountered in Moscow: 'Rising! What Rising?'

Nonetheless, some US officials did not abandon their long-standing efforts to organize an airdrop to Warsaw via the Frantic mission. Ambassador Winant was particularly energetic in this respect, knowing that Churchill himself had not given up. On 11 September, they finally heard that Stalin had relented. The next day, Secretary of State Cordell Hull informed Ambassador Harriman in Moscow that it was politically expedient for the Americans to work with the British and the Soviets in dropping aid to Warsaw. 'From the political point of view,' he wrote, 'we feel that it is of the highest importance that there should be no hesitation on our part . . . in order to avoid the possibility of our being blamed in the event that the aid does not arrive in time.'[100] [**CHILDHOOD**, p. 343]

On 2 September 1944, the day that the Old Town fell, the Polish 2nd Corps, which was fighting in Italy in the ranks of the British Eighth Army, was pulled out of the front line and ordered to rest in the region of Ancona. It had been engaged in continuous combat in the Adriatic sector for the previous three months. As Gen. Anders would recall, this was a time for convalescence and reflection.

Gen. Anders, the victor of Monte Cassino, stood high in Allied esteem. He was loaded with honours, having been decorated by President Roosevelt, King George VI, and the Pope. The award of the US Legion of Merit gave him special pleasure since it was made in the presence of nearly all

CHILDHOOD

A five-year-old left alone with his mother stores up selective memories

I did not become a typical child of war. If I wanted a drink, I was given rainwater from a puddle boiled on a candle. (It sounds more romantic than it really was.) Our apartment on Jerusalem Avenue looked out onto a courtyard, and at first we lived on the third floor. The neighbouring house had been burnt down in 1939, so one side of the courtyard was open to the sky.

After a certain time, [since our district had remained in German hands] all the tenants were rounded up and herded into the cellar. Part of the building was taken over by a hotel called the Central that was empty during the Rising. There was no owner, so we all had equal rights. Everything was decided by the one German, who lived there. I don't know why he was the only one. But I remember that he washed in a bowl in the courtyard, and that we watched him from the cellar window . . .

That German . . . was young and lonely, well brought up, and aware that his world was collapsing. I knew that somehow he was courting my mother and that she teased him, to hide the anger in her heart. At least he allowed her to go upstairs to the telephone. And in the course of that visit, an episode took place that really should have been in a film.

One day, my mother played a trick on him. She left out a large diamond ring in a box bearing the mark of a French jeweller. The ring was a fake made from so-called 'Czech glass'. Only the box was from Paris.

When we lived upstairs, I remember hunting pigeons. After scattering something on the windowsill, we would fasten a string onto the outside of the window. When the string was disturbed, the window would shut. The pigeon would flap around the room, and I don't know what happened next. But soon there was 'chicken broth' . . . I knew that it wasn't chicken.

I also remember a night when the Germans caught Allied planes in their searchlights and their artillery hit their target. My mother ordered us to pray for the pilots. We prayed loudly in the courtyard with our heads turned up towards heaven.

Evacuations of civilians went on all the time. Once we were hurried along on foot in a huge column. But we managed to escape [somewhere on Novogrodek Street]. Without a moment's thought, my mother jumped with two people over a hospital fence. It did us little good. The hospital was under the control of brutalized Ukrainians, who had already lost their homeland. The Germans had carried out executions among them, and as a result they flaunted their cruelty. I remember women with stomachs cut open. My mother forbade me to watch. The drunken soldiers had been practising Caesarean sections with bayonets in the maternity ward.

When I was ill with food-poisoning, my mother cooked me some barley on the candle. She also had some cosmetics with which she could pretend to have tuberculosis. It worried the Ukrainians. She made herself up to look frightening, with black beaten eyes . . .

We were twice put up against a wall for execution, and twice reprieved. I didn't understand that this was supposed to be the end of us; but I do remember the clamminess of my mother's hands.

After that, my mother was taken to be a human shield, to protect a German division from insurgent snipers. Before leaving, she wrote my name on my skin with an indelible pencil in case she did not return. She told me never to wash it off. She took with her nearly forty kilos of clothing, even though it was summer . . .

Then we were taken in a hurry to the railway station . . . On the way, I stumbled on a dead body and fell onto a dead man. My mother thought that it would leave a lasting trauma . . . Two other events stuck in my mind. First of all, a dog was howling on the upper balcony of a burning house. It could not see the fire. We watched as the flames reached the balcony and the dog was burned. Secondly, near the railway station, our march was interrupted by galloping dray-horses. The Germans had bombed the brewery stables with incendiaries, and the horses were charging around in convulsions. Many years later, when I saw the burning giraffes of Salvador Dali, I recognized the same famous image from my childhood.[1]

Krzysztof Zanussi

Allied commanders in Italy and on the Piazza Venezia in Rome, on the very spot where five years earlier Mussolini had declared: '*La Polonia è liquidata.*' The citation ended with the words: 'The outstanding leadership and tactical ability displayed by Gen. Anders were primary contributions to the success of Allied Forces in the Italian campaign. FRANKLIN D ROOSEVELT.'[101]

Anders's meeting with King George VI had taken place earlier at Perugia. For security reasons, the King had been disguised as 'Gen. Collingwood':

> After the parade and the march-past there was a visit to Gen. Alexander's Field HQ and in the evening a dinner at Gen. Leese's Eighth Army HQ. The band of the II Polish Army Corps played during dinner, and the King expressed a particular liking for the song . . . *'And if I have to be born again, then let it only be in* [Lvuv] . . .' We all sang, and the King hummed. The music and words (spelled phonetically) of this song were later conveyed . . . to the King as a souvenir of that evening.[102]

One wonders whether the King knew where Lvuv was, or that the Soviet Army was about to annex it on the very next day. The men of the 5th (Border) Division, who had stormed Cassino and who largely came from Lvuv, would henceforth have no homes to return to.

Anders's opinion about the Warsaw Rising matched that of the Commander-in-Chief. He was not opposed in principle. But he was more than sceptical about the practicalities. As a former prisoner of the NKVD, he didn't trust the Russians, and doubted if the Premier's policy of seeking sensible, Western-backed compromise would bring results. As a soldier, he saw that the Home Army was on its own, and shared the Commander-in-Chief's fears about their vulnerability. In his memoirs he quoted a telegram sent by the Commander-in-Chief from Italy to London: 'the experiment of coming into the open in Poland and of co-operation with the Red Army would be a failure.'[103]

The Battle for the Gothic Line, which ended on 2 September when the Poles captured Cattolica near Rimini, had demanded a tenacious advance across lofty ridges and through the densely wooded ravines of the eastern Apennines. It had cost the 2nd Corps 2,150 men. Just before it was concluded, Anders had received a visit from Winston Churchill in person:

> PM CHURCHILL: Do you remember, General, the last time that we met and talked in Cairo? [on 22 August 1942, when they had discussed the situation of the Poles in Russia]
>
> GEN. ANDERS: I do remember, of course.
>
> CHURCHILL: You were right at that time.[104]
>
> After that he asked: 'What is the state of your soldiers' morale in view of the events they witness at present?'
>
> Gen. Anders answered that the morale of the troops was excellent, that each soldier . . . was perfectly aware . . . that the first task and obligation was the destruction of Germany . . . but that they were most

anxious at the same time about the future destiny of Poland, and about all that was happening in Warsaw.

Prime Minister Churchill said that he also was fully aware of these facts, but when, with President Roosevelt, he had approached Stalin for assistance to the Warsaw fighters, they had received no answer at all to their first request, and a negative reply to their second . . . 'We were not ready for any action in Warsaw, and now we are trying to do our best to give assistance from the air.'

Prime Minister Churchill also stressed the fact that the Russians were barely 30 kilometres [eighteen miles] from Warsaw, and there could be no obstacle in the way of their giving assistance, whereas the British must fly 780 miles [1,255km] from their bases in Italy.

Then Mr Churchill mentioned that he did not think we were satisfied with his speech last winter.

GENERAL ANDERS: 'We still have a grudge against you, Prime Minister.'

PRIME MINISTER CHURCHILL: 'In concluding the treaty of alliance with Poland, Great Britain has never guaranteed her frontiers. She . . . undertook the obligations for the existence of Poland as a free, independent, sovereign and great state, . . . free from any alien interference. I can assure you, General, that we have not changed our point of view; Poland will not exist but she must be a champion of Europe. You must trust us; we will keep our pledges. But you must not rigidly insist on the maintenance of your eastern boundaries. You will get territories in the west much better than the Pripet marshes . . .'

GENERAL ANDERS: 'History tells us that some corrections of frontiers occur after each war . . . But we will never consent to the Bolsheviks, even during the war, taking as much territory as they wish . . .'

PRIME MINISTER CHURCHILL: 'Obviously these matters can be settled at a peace conference.' (Turning to the General and touching him with his hand): 'You will be present at the conference. You must trust us. Great Britain entered this war in defence of the principle of your independence, and I can assure you that we will never desert you.'

GENERAL ANDERS: 'Our soldiers have never for one moment lost faith in Great Britain. They know that first of all Germany must be beaten, and they are ready to carry out any task for this end . . . But . . . we are convinced that all Stalin's announcements that he wants a free and strong Poland are lies and impostures . . . The Russians entering Poland are arresting and deporting our wives and children to Russia as they did in 1939. They disarm the soldiers of our Home Army, shoot our officers, and imprison members of our Civil Administration, destroying those who have been fighting the Germans without interruption since 1939. Our wives and children are in Warsaw, but we prefer that they should perish there rather than live under the Bolsheviks. We all prefer to perish fighting rather than to live cringing.'

PRIME MINISTER CHURCHILL (deeply moved): 'You should trust Great Britain, who will never abandon you – never. I know the Germans and Russians are destroying your best elements, particularly the intellectuals. I deeply sympathise with you . . .'

GENERAL ANDERS: 'Russia was preparing for war for twenty years . . . immediately after the war she will resume this policy, while you will not keep 6,000,000 men under arms and 70,000 aircraft in the air.'

PRIME MINISTER CHURCHILL: 'We have a treaty with Russia for twenty years.' (After a short pause): 'It may be that this will not last. But I believe that the situation in Russia has changed, and the men who hold power at present will not keep it to the same degree after the end of the war . . . Hence all your apprehensions are superfluous, especially as you must trust Great Britain and the United States, who will never desert you . . . And it is necessary to realise that the potentialities of Great Britain and the United States are unlimited . . . We used only two-fifths of our forces for the powerful blow which we struck in invading Europe, scoring successes which far outweighed all Soviet contributions to the war . . .' (Changing the subject of a conversation): [The Commander-in-Chief] is considered to continue Beck's policy. [The Premier] is a good man, is he not?'

GENERAL ANDERS: 'I do not know him well. I consider that he might talk with Stalin, but he had no right to speak with traitors, that is, with the "Union of Polish Patriots" in Moscow . . .'

PRIME MINISTER CHURCHILL (having observed that the meeting was being photographed): 'If Stalin sees this photograph . . . General, he will be furious. But I consent that you may publish this photograph. Let Stalin be angry. But I do insist that you send me a copy. Stalin dislikes you – he says you are a wicked man.'

Gen. Anders, returning to the question of the 'Committee of Patriots', observed that Stalin had Governments ready for all the countries he would like to put under Communist rule. Then he added jokingly: 'I am sure that he already has a man ready to take your place, Mr Churchill.'

PRIME MINISTER CHURCHILL (laughing): 'The same as the Germans had one.

> But they did not have the chance.' . . . (He repeats once more): 'I and my friend President Roosevelt, who will again be elected President, will never abandon Poland. Put your trust in us.'
>
> . . .

GENERAL ANDERS: 'We are soldiers, and for this reason we are well able to distinguish between politics and truth.'

PRIME MINISTER CHURCHILL (smiling): 'Oh yes, I see you are also a good politician.'

GENERAL ANDERS: 'We were taught to be so in Russia.'[105]

Gen. Anders recalled this conversation somewhat ironically. 'I was fully aware of the difficult circumstances with which he [Churchill] had to deal . . . [But] Polish soldiers were then fighting in Warsaw, in Normandy and in Italy, and Polish sailors and airmen were playing their part. For what was the Polish soldier shedding his blood?'[106] [**PRAYER**, p. 349]

Churchill and Anders do not appear to have discussed the rights and wrongs of the Rising at any great length. But a private letter written by Anders at that same juncture leaves no doubt that he must be counted among the Rising's most unrelenting critics:

> I was completely shocked by the outbreak of the Rising in Warsaw. I regard it as the greatest misfortune in our present situation. It didn't have the slightest chance of success, and exposed all parts of the country still under German occupation to new and appalling repressions . . . No one who is not dishonest or blind could have had the least illusion that everything which has happened was always going to happen; i.e. not only that the Soviets will refuse to help our beloved, heroic Warsaw, but also that they will watch with the greatest pleasure as our nation's blood is drained to the last drop.
>
> Like all my colleagues in the 2nd Corps, I was always of the opinion, at the time when the Germans were collapsing and the Bolsheviks were coming in and destroying the best of our people, just as they did in 1939, that the Rising had no sense, that it was even a crime. . . .
>
> Of course, no words can express our pride and wonder at the heroism of our Home Army and of the capital's population. We are with them with every beat of our hearts . . . We are hurt to the quick by our helplessness . . . All our own battles, from Monte Cassino onwards, strike us as puny in comparison to the battle in Warsaw.[107]

PRAYER

A group of religious youngsters put faith in the power of prayer

When I crossed to the other side of Jerusalem Avenue, I ran into a trio of my female friends: Marysha O. and her two friends from 'Eight', Lily W. and Jane M. Whilst preparing for the Rising, [they] had raised the idea of an 'Action for God' and a few of them had organized a 'prayer point' in the convent chapel in Vola. When Vola fell, it was a miracle that they avoided the notorious 'Kaminski Brigade', and after a few adventures, they made it to the City Centre. That's when we met.

The church 'on Moniushko Street' now became their 'prayer point'. They wanted to inspire the whole of Warsaw to pray. 'If it is ordained that we die', they said, 'let it be with clean hearts, in a state of grace.' The 26th of August, the Feast of the Black Madonna, was set as a particular date for prayer. They ran from street to street, fearless in the face of bombs and bullets, putting up posters, recruiting helpers, and above all inspiring priests to action. They sometimes had to 'winkle out' the more fearful of God's servants from their hiding places, and encourage them to carry out their duties . . .

The 'Day of the Black Madonna' really became an almost universal act of faith in the Warsaw Rising. It was supported by the Home Army Command, and thousands of people came to receive the sacraments. Since the churches had largely been reduced to rubble, Holy Mass was celebrated in courtyards, in cellars, and on the battle line. Christ in the Eucharist was among his people . . . I myself succeeded in leading a priest to our unit's redoubt. After that, with cleansed souls, we calmly awaited an uncertain future . . .

I have often been asked if I was afraid during the Rising. Of course, when bombs were exploding all around and bullets whistled past me, I naturally felt fear. I hid behind the wall, pulled my head down, or went to the shelter. Nonetheless, I was dominated by a strange conviction, that with God's protection I would come out alive.

One day I went to visit Marysha and her girls at the 'prayer point' by the church 'on Moniushko Street'. We had barely met when Marysha interrupted the conversation and bade me farewell. She had heard explosions and wanted to get to the shelter quickly. I expressed surprise that she had such little faith in God's protection. She replied, 'Yes, I am afraid, but I am glad that I can feel with the whole population what we are all going through.'

Marysha went to the shelter, whilst I knelt before the Holy Sacrament in the chapel to pray. Hearing a plane overhead, I experienced an awful paroxysm of fear, which I had never known before . . . Then I understood that my peace of mind was not due to my fortitude but to the mercy of God, which he had withdrawn for a moment to turn me to jelly. In my view, therefore, the Rising was not just a story of battle and destruction, but also a 'History of the Soul'.[1]

A. Janicki

Anders did not publicize his opinion at the time. The irony was that he, together with the Commander-in-Chief, topped the list of 'anti-Soviet' culprits who were widely believed to have planned and promoted the Rising.

By the turn of September, the Soviet authorities were running out of excuses for not helping Warsaw. The momentum of Rokossovsky's armies was carrying them slowly but inexorably into the Capital's eastern outskirts. The Ukrainian Front, by driving into the Balkans, had drawn off German reserves, and had rendered it unlikely that the Warsaw district could be defended in depth. The Soviet Air Force was becoming as dominant in the skies as the Soviet artillery was on the ground. Soviet diplomats were increasingly subjected to requests, questions, and insinuations. Stalin no longer had a plausible argument for prevaricating.

Moscow was also required to react to unexpected events in Slovakia, which for the previous five years had been a satellite of Nazi Germany. At the end of August, a revolt took place among the professional Slovakian military, who resented German domination and who appealed to the advancing Soviets for support. As in Warsaw, the insurgency proved premature. Spontaneous partisan outbreaks gave warning of the danger, and pushed the chief conspirators into challenging the influx of German reinforcements in disadvantageous conditions. At the time, the 4th Ukrainian Front, 480km (300 miles) to the south of Warsaw, was separated from Slovakia by the high and heavily defended passes of the Carpathian Mountains. Nonetheless, Moscow gave the order to attack at all costs. Throughout September and into October, the Soviet Army battled ferociously to break into Slovakia. In that one sector, particularly at the Dukla Pass, they were prepared to lose four times as many men as they did on the approaches to Warsaw. One may assume that helping Slovakia was judged to be in the Soviet interest.

Early in September, Polish Communist circles somewhat changed their tune. They were still bellowing about the 'traitors' and 'criminal leaders' of the Rising. But as from 1 September, they again released several messages to the effect that the First Polish Army was marching to Warsaw's rescue. Such was the sense of Order Nr. 13 from the Commander of the LWP. It was repeated by Radio Lublin. A speech of the Committee's Chairman sought to gain effect by talking of 'our 200,000 brethren' murdered in Warsaw. The number stuck. [**BRIEFE**, p. 352]

Realists might have been more impressed by some of the practical measures which the Lublin Committee took at this time. On 31 August, for example, it passed a decree 'for the punishment of fascist-Hitlerite criminals . . . and of Traitors of the Polish Nation.'[108] Published some weeks later but put into immediate effect, this draconian decree made provision for special penal courts and for the punishment not just of offenders, but equally of their aiders and abettors. It listed a huge range of punishments, from the death sentence to imprisonment, hard labour, confiscation, and loss of civil rights. Most shamefully, since it made no attempt to define treason, it placed all the Committee's political opponents in the category of potential traitors. Other organs were leaving no margin of doubt over who was to be targeted. On 4 September, the Committee's main newspaper issued an article entitled 'We warn you', which contained the chilling sentences: 'He who opposes the Polish Camp (i.e. the Lublin Committee) is the same as a member of the Nazi Camp. No third camp exists.' In other words, since an earlier decree had declared all conspiratorial organizations to be illegal, all members of the Home Army, including those fighting the Nazis, were deemed to be Nazi supporters. Here was a fine example of Applied Dialectics. (See Appendix 24.)

Nonetheless, one can observe a certain divergence within the Communist ranks. Whilst the Moscow media was busy arguing that sending aid to Warsaw was pointless, the Lublin press was again saying 'Warsaw is going to be liberated', appealing for 'all able people' to join the rescue. In the course of a polemic directed at Gen. Boor, the same Lublin paper admitted that the Rising had broken out on 1 August after all, i.e. in the period when Lublin had pretended that nothing was happening. The head of the People's Army was told to send patrols into the outskirts of right-bank Warsaw 'to save what is worth saving'. These statements may be interpreted in the light of the prospect, which would have been known in Lublin, that Gen. Boor was really preparing to capitulate.

The Lublin Committee's apparent change of heart towards the Rising

BRIEFE

A nineteen-year-old German lieutenant, who had fought on both the Eastern Front and in Normandy, writes home

From a letter to his parents, 7 September '44

. . . They've bandaged my other eye now; I have shrapnel wounds on the left side of my head, but only shallow ones. Everything's returning to normal. The previous wound has healed now . . .

There was a strange repetition, which everyone considers a bad omen: our own soldiers were killed (first time six of them, second time two) and a few wounded by our own weapons. The enemy fired at us, detonating a thousand kilos of explosives just three metres from my vehicle. I don't consider myself at fault. But it makes no difference. If you bring bad luck you'll be stigmatized, as if you really were guilty. It's a curse. You can see it in everyone's faces. After the explosion, I was lying for hours, blinded, among the groaning wounded. Now I'm safe and calm. I believe that ill fortune and responsibility educate a man . . .

From a letter to his parents, 16 September '44

. . . After I was wounded for the second time I stopped fighting. A colleague of mine, who was very keen, replaced me. I'm quite pleased about the arrangement because I'd had enough. But I seem to have been too pleased with myself . . . I'm the commander of a base and deal with everyday company matters. Fifty per cent of my work involves furnishing flats for our officers. My boss is an interior decorator and he's very demanding. I really enjoy changing things round. I'm on my fourth flat now. From half-ruined houses we take the best stuff: sculptures, sofas, rugs, etc. – soon it will all go up in flames. Everything is being smashed to pieces. We pick our way through utensils, rubbish, broken china, and dirt. Horrifying and unimaginable desolation. That's the propagators of European culture for you. Let them steal! . . .

We live near a power station. I often get to see beautiful well-built flats with elegant furniture. In Hungary too I was most impressed. It seems that small, mainly Slavonic countries are in the lead when it comes to aesthetic taste. Could it be a sign of great times to come for them? The Germans can't compete, and neither can dusty old France – I'm leaving Russia out of the picture. How long will it last? . . .

From a letter to his fiancée, 28/29 September '44:

. . . I have the strongest and most passionate desire that the war should not carry on in its present direction, leaving aside the prospect of the unpredictable 'wonder weapons' or whatever. In Warsaw you can see the real face of this war – terrible than in our own country. I've got used to the sight of male corpses – they a part of everyday life; but not to the remains of women's bodies, where a life of love and innocence once grew, or when I see the bodies of children, all of whom I consider innocent whatever their mother tongue and all of whom I love in these horrendous times . . . – I know you will say I must not write about it . . .

In a long letter to my father I mentioned a girl who was much talked about in our unit. I never saw her, but I heard a lot about her, and because I held some vivid memory of certain scenes and their background, I could easily call it the most beautiful experience ('beautiful' is dubious, I should say 'deep experience'): it was during the seizure of a bank. Bombers, anti-aircraft cannon, mortars, and explosive gases had been used to capture this particular building. When the line of machine guns drew close to the basement, most of the civilians surrendered. They came out, faces covered in dust, mute from fear. They crawled out whimpering, with cannons firing over them. Yet this girl stood there erect, with a calm and serious expression, shaking her head slightly in disbelief at this mad activity . . . She stood there proudly amidst the flames, insane but in one piece . . .[1]

P. Stolten

---

caused waves in the Home Army ranks. On 7 September, one group of AK officers formally asked Gen. Boor to contact the leaders of the Committee's Army. On the 9th, Monter himself expressed the view that joining up the Lubliners was preferable to capitulation. Boor judged these requests completely unacceptable.

At this juncture, with capitulation still in the air, Boor was tormented by reports that the Soviet Army was edging ever closer to the eastern suburbs. So he prepared the necessary instructions for his subordinates. The Soviets were to be treated with caution. The commanders of the Berling Army were to be treated likewise, but the rank and file were to be warmly greeted as compatriots. No concessions were to be made to the Lublin Committee. As from the 11th, capitulation talks were to be suspended.

On 12 September, a communiqué from the front announced that German defences had indeed been penetrated, and the satellite town of Rembertov captured. The next night, two female couriers from the Communist People's Army successfully swam the Vistula, and personally pleaded with Marshal Rokossovsky for help. The Lublin press repeated the story, and promised that 'Help will be provided'. Soviet aircraft reappeared in the skies over the city. That same day, the Soviet 143rd Infantry Division reached the right bank of the Vistula. Soviet soldiers and Varsovian insurgents caught sight of each other for the very first time.

British readers who take pride in the 'Retreat from Mons' or the 'Miracle of Dunkirk' should have no difficulty in grasping the significance of the Home Army's Evacuation of Warsaw's Old Town or the fighting withdrawal from the Riverside. They were operations that wrenched survival from impending annihilation.

The decision to evacuate the Old Town had been taken during the night of 25/26 August after seven days of constant bombardments and massed attacks. The armed defenders had been reduced from 8,000 to 1,500. The first stage was to bring out the AK Command and Government authorities through a previously unused sewer, which started only 200 metres (650 feet) from the German positions and passed directly underneath them. The second stage was to mount a flurry of local counter-attacks to divert the Germans and to cover the exodus of the Home Army's main detachments. The third stage was to extract the rearguard Parasol Battalion. Each stage was executed on successive nights from 31 August to 2 September.

The departure of Underground officialdom was achieved without serious loss. Their entry, one by one, into the manhole at the corner of Long Street was not discovered. Their passage was led by *kanalarki* or specialist girl 'sewer guides'. It consisted of crouching and wading for two hours through a chest-high stream of heavy noxious sludge. Their orders were to grip the person in front, and to keep on moving, even if someone sank. Their arrival in the City Centre was greeted like a victory.

Before leaving, Gen. Boor took one last look at the shattered and shadowy outlines of the Old Town which he would never see again. 'Six hundred years of history lay in those ruins',[109] he remarked. He then turned to the officer commanding the rearguard, Col. 'Vachnov':

> Calm as usual, [the officer] spoke in clipped, whispered tones. He understood perfectly what his task entailed – to fight to the last for the remnants of the Old Town, and thereby to enable other districts to hold on until relief arrived. I knew that . . . he would observe his duty to the end. At 1 o'clock in the morning, he took us to the manhole.[110]

The next night, some 300 soldiers of the AL left the Old Town without warning and in the opposite direction. Their HQ had received a direct hit, which killed all their senior officers. Their departure caused lasting controversy.

The diversionary attacks, which persisted for five days, served their purpose well. Von dem Bach again called on the Ninth Army for reinforcements. Intense fighting flowed back and forth in Stalingrad-style through the ruins of the State Paper Factory. At the time, thousands of unseen men and women were edging their way out in the sewers. They even managed to evacuate all the staff and patients out of a major insurgent hospital, who would not otherwise have survived. When the hospital roof had been marked by a red cross, it had been immediately dive-bombed. [**KATYN**, p. 356]

The concluding exodus of the rearguard was less deadly than expected. One group, dressed from head to toe in SS uniforms, walked out on the surface through the Saxon Square, mimicking the actions of a German night patrol. The very last party, under Col. 'Aurochs', ran to the manhole at 8 a.m. on the 2nd, seen off by a burst of machine-gun fire. They duly emerged in the City Centre to pose for a photograph.

The worst of all tragedies was encountered by the 35,000 civilians and 7,000 unmovable wounded who were left behind. As soon as the SS arrived, a selection was ordered, as on the ramp at Birkenau. Those judged incapable of work – the old, sick, and wounded – were promptly shot. The healthy were formed up for immediate transportation to concentration camps, mainly to Mauthausen or to Sachsenhausen. A German tank drove over the tomb of the Unknown Soldier, and pulverized it. The Sigismund Column was felled by a single vandal shot, and left where it lay.

The fall of the Old Town was followed almost immediately by a sustained German assault on the Riverside district. The aim was to deprive the insurgents of the prospect of a junction with the Soviet Army, of whose imminent approach the Germans were all too well aware. The house-to-house battles moved inexorably southwards over two weeks, until all that remained for the Home Army was one small patch of land. The civilian population had fled to the City Centre, causing intense overcrowding. The group of Col. Aurochs, who was wounded, were again in the thick of it.

KATYN

A family from Volhynia whose father had disappeared in Russia in 1939 move to Warsaw for safety

In March 1944, seeing the atrocities inflicted on the Poles by Ukrainians, my mother decided to leave [Hrubieshov] Volhynia and to take her whole family to her uncle's in Warsaw. Stanislas R. was an optician, and had a practice on New World Street. That's where we stayed before the Rising.

[In August], we survived a bombardment which brought down a seven-storey building opposite ours, trapping us in the cellar. We escaped by knocking down the wall to the neighbouring cellar.

When the Germans took the Old Town, our whole family was rounded up as civilians who had aided the insurgents. This was on 6 September 1944. We were herded into the small park by Vauxhall Street, and lined up against the fence to be shot . . . At the last minute a messenger came with fresh orders. They took us to the building that is now the Army Museum. We walked down the street, and the drunken SS men on the pavements stuck out their legs and laughed, shouting obscenities . . . We watched the bombardment of insurgent positions by low-flying aircraft.

A few hours later they marched us off [by way of the Kościuszko Embankment along Cooper Street, where they looted the jewellers' shops. In front of our very eyes they shot a group of Jewish insurgents discovered in the rubble near the Cracow Faubourg. We walked [along Elector, Cool, and Vola Streets] until we reached the big church in Vola, where they made the first segregation. They separated the women and the elderly from the men and children above fourteen years old. My brother and I managed to stay with Mother, Grandma, and Aunt Marysha. [Cheslav L.], the husband of my mother's sister, took his life in his hands by coming back to our side. Then they took us to the Western Station. We walked in the middle of the road to avoid the heat of the burning buildings, though even the tarmac was hot . . . Many fainted with the effort. A slow electric train was waiting to take us to the camp which had been set up in the railway repair yards at Prushkov.

After three days sitting amidst filth and starvation in hall number 7 we were told that anyone who wanted could board a train. We decided to risk it, knowing very well that the destination might be either Auschwitz or slave labour in the Reich. After a twenty-four-hour journey, however, it turned out that they were setting the passengers at liberty in the town of Opochno. There we were warmly greeted by the roadside as heroes from Warsaw. We were offered bread and fruit, which created a tremendous impression after the hunger we had experienced. We then headed for the village of

[Vola Opochynska], imagining that it would be easier to survive in the countryside. In return for digging potatoes we found a place on an estate, we were fed and cared for. My brother and I, already weakened by hunger, caught dysentery. Grandma, who looked after us, caught it herself . . .

We finally made it to Cracow on 6 October 1944. We arrived there just before curfew, and got into a tram designated 'for Germans only', because at that hour Poles were not allowed to move around freely. At the entrance to Smolensk Street we ran into a German police patrol. The chief turned out to be Austrian, and on checking our documents he too treated us as heroes from Warsaw and personally escorted us safely home. A few days later my mother went off to fetch Grandma and Auntie. Sadly Grandma was so ill with dysentery that she died on reaching Cracow on 10 November 1944.

My mother spent years awaiting my father's return. Searches carried out during and after the war were to no avail. She always believed that Daddy would come back and she lived in hope. But she never discovered what became of him. She died on 7 August 1978, not knowing of the murder and burial of the Starobielsko camp prisoners.[1]

Roman Sulimir

German artillery was firing heavy shells from elevated positions on the Vistula scarp. But the defenders could still not be dislodged. They could now hear the guns that were disputing nearby Praga. The time eventually came when they again saw soldiers in Soviet-style uniforms on the opposite bank. Late in the evening of 14 September, three Home Army swimmers crossed the river under cover of darkness. They discovered that the newcomers were Poles.

Capitulation talks were in progress throughout early September, and for two weeks the insurgents were under intense pressure to surrender. There was no prospect of relief. The suffering of the wounded and of civilians was indescribable. The Western airlift was faltering. Ammunition was running out. Soviet propaganda was relentlessly hostile. Rokossovsky's long-awaited offensive was eternally at hand, but never quite realized.

By mid-September, the Home Army negotiators had obtained most of what they had hoped for. They had won combatant status, and a promise of no reprisals. Ignoring Gen. Rohr's ultimatum, they sought instead to cement further guarantees and clarifications. They were on the very brink of signing. But when the Soviet Army definitely appeared, and after it the Berling Army, the spirit of resistance revived. The capitulation talks collapsed.

Junction

Rokossovsky's occupation of Praga in mid-September finally put an end to the long-drawn-out uncertainties on the central sector of the Vistula Front. All major German positions east of the Vistula had been overrun. The Soviet Army had taken control of a crucial springboard for further advances. At the strategic level, it now held all the ground which could serve as the base for pincer movements north and south of Warsaw and could open the way for a major breakthrough. At the local level, it appeared to hold the German garrison in Warsaw at its mercy.

The overall balance of forces in the sector undoubtedly stood in the Soviets' favour. Rokossovky's setback in the previous month had been fully overcome.

The German Ninth Army's log of 16 September assessed the prospects very gloomily:

> Today, a new phase of the Warsaw–Modlin sector is beginning. Reconnaissance indicates that the First Polish Army will exploit the [continued existence of] the Rising and will force the Vistula to establish a [new] bridgehead in northern Warsaw. Simultaneously, the 47th [Soviet] Army Group will try to break the southern wing of the IV SS Panzer Group, and, by a second crossing of the Vistula, will reach the Kampinos Forest, where close to 8,000 insurgents are still operating. This would threaten the rear of the Ninth Army, and penetrate our frontline in the Vistula–Narev triangle. It would also pose a grave danger for East Prussia, since a pathway towards Danzig would be opened . . .[111]

With Marshal Rokossovsky's assent, therefore, Gen. Berling issued an order on 16 September 1944. Units of the 1st Battalion, 9th Infantry Regiment of the First Polish Army were to force the Vistula and to link up with the insurgents. Here was the order which Gen. Boor had expected six weeks earlier.

Crossing the Vistula under fire was no easy feat. Though some cover was provided by a belated artillery barrage, by Soviet aeroplanes, and by a smokescreen, the men had to crouch and crawl across wide, exposed sandbanks, wade into a shoulder-high stream or lie on crude pontoons, slowly drifting into the line of enemy machine-guns. They were led by a Soviet officer, and they were met on the western bank in the district of Cherniakov by two Home Army officers, Maj. 'Whip' and Capt. 'Butterfly'. The long-awaited junction had been made. 120 out of the 150 men in the leading company were lost. [**FRAGMENTS**, p. 360]

In theory, the link-up between the insurgents in west-bank Warsaw and the Soviet forces on the east bank should have been turned into a winning combination. The insurgents still controlled their three extensive enclaves, in the north, in the City Centre, and in the south; and Berling was expected to deliver the arms, ammunition, food, and manpower which had been so sadly lacking. The main Soviet force, which now lined the Vistula, threatened to encircle the German garrison on all sides, and hence to deter the commitment of further reserves. In practice, the task of resupplying the Rising proved almost unsurmountable. The same factors which had prevented the Germans from dislodging the insurgents now prevented the reinforced insurgents from dislodging the Germans. Nothing short of a full-scale Soviet offensive was going to produce a decisive result. From the insurgents' viewpoint, of course, the hope was that the limited landing by Berling's men would be the prelude to something much greater. Everyone in central Warsaw knew that the largest army in the world was now less than a quarter of a mile away. Everything was going to depend on the decisions of the next two weeks.

Concerted, not to say fevered, attempts were made by the Home Army Command to establish reliable communications with Rokossovsky's headquarters. Gen. Boor assumed, whatever Stalin's ultimate intentions might be, that Rokossovsky would wish to work with him in the local operational theatre. After all, Soviet aircraft were now regularly dropping supplies – usually without parachutes – and the Soviet artillery had opened up over the river against German positions in the Citadel and the Danzig Station. To this end, therefore, Monter was ordered to organize a party of seven men, who were not only to visit Rokossovsky in person, but were to take radio equipment with them, to ensure a permanent link. The group was led by Lt. 'Poppy', a 'dark and silent one' who was Monter's chief of radio communications, and included the Soviet officer Kalugin, a representative of the People's Army, Lt. 'King', and four other AK officers. It took them three days to travel from the city centre to Praga, first moving through the sewers from the city to Mokotov and eventually crossing the Vistula under cover of darkness on the night of 18/19

FRAGMENTS

The mind of a seven-year-old boy stores images that have lasted a lifetime

Our tenement house, [202] on Cherniakov Street, had been under constant fire, mainly from the grounds of the YMCA building, from the very start of the Rising. Sitting in the cellar and listening to the gunfire, we children were pleased 'when it finished' because we would find a mass of bullets and shells outside to play with.

The first insurgent unit had appeared in our courtyard early on. There were a dozen or so young men and a girl who acted as a sniper on the roof. Was there just one girl? I no longer remember, although I can still see them exactly standing in the middle of the courtyard . . .

The Rising created a collection of short images in my head, sometimes static pictures, sometimes frames that are partially obliterated, others distorted perhaps by the 'memory screen' of the brain. Some of the images are silent, others have sound. I remember the dramatic warning cry of 'Ukrainians!', for example, which signified a greater danger than that posed by the Germans. Just as in a thriller film, danger came up the stairs with an invisible face. Leaning against the banister on the stairway, I would then look at the arm of the retreating uniform. Fortunately it was always someone from the Home Army (AK) unit. (I only heard about the existence of a People's Army (AL) after the end of the Rising.)

The Germans fired from mine-throwers we called 'bellowing cows'. The name came from the six 'bellows' before every series of explosions, as six mines were cranked into position. The cranking was as loud as the explosions. I will never forget that sound until the end of my days. After the cranking there was nothing one could do. If one heard the explosion, it meant that one had not been killed.

A shell from the Big Bertha cannon destroyed the fourth-storey annexe of our house. I will never forget it, because it caused the first death that I had ever witnessed. My uncle sank right on top of me. 'Uncle, what are you doing?' I asked, thinking it was a joke. But he was no longer alive. Was it Big Bertha? Almost certainly. No planes could be heard at the time. And I had a good ear for differentiating the various death-dealing sounds.

When we fled the Riverside district for the City Centre on 10 September, the weather had been very good. But the one-kilometre trek from Riverside to Three Crosses Square took up a day, and halfway down Moon Street a couple of bullets whistled past my ear. We resorted first to sheltering in courtyards, and then to following a trench all the way along Cherniakov Street [to Ludna]. We went underground under Hospital Street, entered a small building on Conflict Street, and worked our way through the ruins of some warehouses. After that, an extremely dangerous stretch of shrubbery that was under fire awaited us, before we reached safety in the grocery store on the far side on the path to Three Crosses Square and Crane Street. In the City Centre we moved mainly through cellars. I was accompanied by a strange fear of being buried alive for two whole months . . . The final destination was 39 Basket Street, near Constitution Square.

The tenants of our new lodging said that the pile of rubble in the courtyard concealed the remains of an anti-aircraft post knocked out in 1939 . . . The same pile of rubble served as a hunting-ground for my grandfather who, with help of a homemade catapult, repeatedly tried to bag a pigeon for me. The food situation was very bad. There was only barley, and in ever-dwindling quantities. My grandfather would walk to Lvuv Street with two water buckets fitted with cross-shaped covers to stop the water swilling out. My teddy bear was another important item because the remnants of my family's fortune was sewn inside him in the form of 'piglets', or gold five-rouble coins. Apart from him, the only things which I managed to salvage after the Rising were a drinking glass and a half-burned copy of *Dr Dolittle*.

Throughout my life I have avoided the subject of the Rising. I avoided reminiscences, I did not even go to see André W.'s film *Kanal* ('Sewer').[1]

Jacek Fedorowicz

September. On reaching Rokossovsky's HQ, they ran straight into trouble. The NKVD had found a German propaganda leaflet, purporting to emanate from the Home Army and urging the Varsovians to fight against Bolshevism.

On 17 September, Boor tried another tack. He sent a telegram to Rokossovsky via London and Moscow, giving precise instructions on how to reactivate the municipal telephone cable under the Vistula:

> The cable runs from French Street to Paderewski Park. The junction box is situated 2 metres from the corner of Washington Avenue on the park side. Other boxes can be found 49, 68, and 69 metres from the first one. Three cables are bonded together in a triangular formation. We use the thick, upper cable. To operate a field tele-

phone, you have to link up all 24 strands of the cable and connect both earth wires. Once contact is made transfer to a double line, because of phone-tapping. Your station is ['Lomzha']; ours is [Rashin]. We are listening for your call-up sign from 18/9, 20.00 hours.[112]

Apart from passing on this correspondence, Barnes Lodge was involved in the delicate task of listening in to Soviet radio traffic from Praga and of breaking Soviet military ciphers. They appear to have succeeded. According to a former operator, this was the probable source of the news that the Soviets intended to establish a second bridgehead in the northern suburb of Marymont.[113]

The Marymont bridgehead, like its counterpart 8km (five miles) to the south at Cherniakov, turned out to have been organized by the Berling Army. It was greatly facilitated by the successful exchange of two liaison missions – one, a joint AK and AL venture, which crossed the river at the second attempt, and another in the opposite direction undertaken by a Soviet telegrapher called Vurdel, who parachuted into the Home Army Command centre in Jolibord. This toehold on the western bank, first established on the night of the 17/18th, received an advance party of seventy-eight men from an artillery observation group. It was expanded on the two following nights by 506 soldiers of the 2nd Battalion, 6th Infantry Regiment. Their misfortune was to have landed in a spot that was surrounded by German strongpoints and which was some small distance away from the insurgent positions. But their expectations were high. In the eyes of everyone involved, they were to be the forerunners of much stronger forces to follow.[114]

Like all armies, the Home Army had its political warfare department forming part of the Bureau of Information and Propaganda (BIP). It was subject to the Supreme Commander AK. One may express surprise that such an outfit could function at all in the conditions of the Warsaw Rising. One is compelled to express admiration and amazement not only that it functioned with particular brilliance, but also that it kept going without interruption from beginning to end. The phenomenon can only be explained by the fact that insurrectionary Warsaw formed a close-knit, dynamic community driven no less by cultural than by military energies. The insurgents were fighting to save their way of life.

The press of insurrectionary Warsaw can be studied in great depth on the basis of an unusual five-volume collection, *A Survey of the Home Press in the Period of the Warsaw Rising*, which was assembled by the Ministry of Internal Affairs of the exiled Government in London and which was published for internal circulation only in April 1945. One can only wonder how such an enormous pile of material was smuggled out of Nazi-occupied Europe in the middle of the war. Apart from a full run of the official Home Army *Information Bulletin*, it contains extracts from the socialist *Worker, Warsaw Fights, Insurgent News*, and *Polish Commonwealth*.

Everyday news was dominated by detailed accounts of the fighting, but it contained innumerable curiosities. At one point, for instance, the *Bulletin* announced that the insurgents had been joined by five deserters of Polish descent from the Wehrmacht and by two ex-Soviet soldiers. The latter were wearing a red star alongside the white eagle on their caps. There was also a platoon of deaf-and-dumb soldiers; twenty-one boys and two girls, under their officer 'Yo-Yo'.[115]

Two other features, however, stand out. One was a remarkable awareness of events in the outside world. The other was a passion for culture, and particularly for poetry. [**FELDWEBEL**, p. 364]

News of the outside world was relayed by radio, and was rapidly redistributed. The bombing of Auschwitz by the RAF, for instance, was known within a day. So, too, were the capitulations of Finland and Belgium. Broadcasts from Radio Moscow were tested by comparison with broadcasts from the BBC. Exploits of the Home Army both in the Nazi and Soviet zones aroused special interest. The progress of the Anglo-Americans through the Low Countries and towards the Rhine were followed on a daily basis. The Allied Conference in Quebec was covered in detail. Indeed, it was harder to find out what was happening in Praga than in Canada. Expressions of support and sympathy from foreign statesmen were especially welcome.

The cultural life of insurgent Warsaw was enriched by radio, film, theatre, photography, graphics, art, and literature. Each deserves a volume in itself. Recitations, concerts, and plays were staged at the Palladium Cinema. Evening shows in the open air of an Indian summer were well suited to the needs of amateur troupes. A performance of the drama *Warszawianka* was being prepared in Mokotov until the leading actors were killed by a 'bellowing cow'.[116]

The outpouring of poetry was obviously connected to the heightened emotions of a community facing annihilation. Dozens of poets sprang up spontaneously. Their verses circulated in the underground press or just on

FELDWEBEL

Wounded in three places, and paralysed, a soldier of the K-Div. awaits his fate

There was a tiny glimmer of hope. Hitherto, we had been liable to be shot on sight as armed civilians. But as from 1 September, as *combatants*, we were entitled to be treated in accordance with the Geneva Convention . . .

After our soldiers' departure we were alone and all was reasonably quiet for several hours. Suddenly, the peace was broken by ear-splitting shouts accompanied upstairs by the loud clatter of steel heel-caps, rifle shots, and screams of the wounded being murdered next door. '*Raus*, all those capable out . . . out . . .'

A German soldier appeared in the door of our cellar. He noticed Irka and the other nurse who – against orders – both stayed with us, and still blocking the door with his ample figure he motioned to the girls to stay put and his short '*Schon fertig*, all done,' stopped the others from bursting in. It was only after the war that Irka told me she had discovered his surname: it was *Freitag*, Man Friday.

Time passed: one hour, perhaps two. Then another German rushed into our cellar, a big fellow, a *Feldwebel*. He stood there in the semi-darkness until he noticed me. He was slow on the uptake. He sized me up. Wounded, still breathing, eyes open. *This must be a mistake! Then his eyes rested on my marching boots.* He grabbed my leg. '*Deutsche Schuhe!*' he screamed, drew his gun, and aimed it at my head. But before he pulled the trigger, he noticed another casualty hiding in the darkness. His attention was distracted: '*Zweite Bandit*, another bandit!' he shouted.

Fortunately for me, he was not methodical enough to finish one job before starting another. The third occupant of our cellar, a much older man, spoke fluent German and said, 'Rubbish, we are all civilians.' This proved too much. A cow speaking with a human voice could not have impressed him more. 'Are you German?' he asked, with amazement written all over his bloated face.

'No, but I speak German,' said our man.

The *Feldwebel* recovered his composure. He stretched out his arm: 'Your papers.' Burhardt had documents. We had none.

'You have a German name,' said the Feldwebel with a simile of a smile. A polite discussion followed on the origins of the Burhardt family, the time of their arrival in Poland, etc., etc. Moreover, Mr Burhardt's civilian trousers, with a hole at the site of his wound, seemed to confirm his non-combatant status. (In fact he had just managed to get rid of his army trousers.) In short, we were saved.

We stayed in the cellar for three days. The *Feldwebel* and his men kept visiting us. Their unit was a *Strafkompanie*, or penal company . . . The *Feldwebel* himself, my would-be assassin, was a Rhinelander, the son of a hotelier. Our only common language was French, which, being a frontiersman, he knew better than I. He didn't dare to write to his parents that he was fighting in Warsaw. He had hit his lieutenant when he had found him in bed with his French fiancée, and was sent first to the Russian front and then to the penal unit in Warsaw. Among our German visitors was a Silesian, Romanovski, who spoke Polish. He was in the army's bad books, I presume, because of his suspect origin.

Unwashed for days, I was not conscious of my own smell, but I could feel the stubble on my chin. The next German 'visitor' might shoot me just for my dirty face. And so I asked one of the soldiers to shave me. He applied himself to the task with gusto. I had to persuade him not to leave me a little goatee. And how full of sympathy he was! He was practically shedding tears, because his razor blade was blunt and he hated the thought of hurting me. This was the same man who the day before had been shooting the wounded, when ordered to do so by an officer.

Another German, somewhat embarrassed, returned to our cellar to collect a bunch of grenades he had left behind. Gentlemen that we were, we returned his lost property to him. Yet another, slightly tipsy, sat on my pallet and said, '*Schade, schade ich bin nicht Pole, ich wäre auch Partisan*, pity, pity I am not a Pole, but I too would have been a partisan.'

Naturally, I protested vigorously: 'I am a civilian . . .' He patted me on the shoulder and left.[1]

Stanisław Likiernik

---

handwritten scraps of paper. The favourite style was that of Tyrtulian martial songs. The leading names were Yashinski and Ubish, but none outdistanced the reputation of 'Christophe', who was killed on the fourth day:

> O lord of the Apocalypse! Lord of the World's End!
> Put a voice in our mouths, and punishment in our hand.[117]

By the end of September, the *Bulletin* was starting to publish academic analyses of the course of the Rising. Various opinions were held about the timing of the outbreak, but 'the military passivity of the [Eastern] Front as it approached the Vistula had been something totally unthinkable.'[118]

The German military had always believed that the Home Army was holding out in Warsaw in order to assist the Soviet advance. They now assumed that Soviet strategists would exploit the continued existence of the Rising to link up with the insurgents. For Berlin, the problem was to divine the significance of Warsaw in the wider picture.

As the summer of '44 wore on into the autumn, the contours of Germany's deteriorating predicament became ever more apparent. The Grand Alliance was set on total conquest or unconditional surrender. The Reich was starting to be racked simultaneously from West and East. Yet the rack was far from symmetrical. The Western Allies, though dominant in the air war, had not matched the Soviet performance on the ground. The Soviet Army was more than holding its own against the 2 million men the Wehrmacht had pitted against it. The British and Americans were making relatively slow progress against the 1 million Germans deployed in north-west Europe and Italy. What is more, the Soviets were advancing along a much more extensive chain of fronts. They were closing on 'the lair of the Fascist Beast', as they called Berlin, from three directions at once – from the Baltic coast, from the Danube valley, and, if the roadblock at Warsaw were removed, from the Vistula. For the German High Command, headed by the *Führer*, the critical issue was to calculate where the final assault would be launched and hence where the dwindling defences should be positioned. Looking east from the windows of the Chancellery in Berlin, and knowing how close the Vistula was, it was not hard to conclude that Warsaw of all places should not be surrendered.

In the immediate future, therefore, it was essential for them to liquidate the Rising. So long as the city had been separated from the front, containing the insurgents was sufficient. But now they had to be finished off. Aerial reconnaissance on the 15th and 16th identified a large Soviet armoured column moving up towards Praga. This was taken to be the strike force which Rokossovsky would employ to exploit the junction which he had achieved.[119] From the German viewpoint, the time available looked terribly short. If every effort was not made to dislodge the two new bridgeheads within a couple of days or so, von Vormann could be in danger of losing control of the entire sector.

The Germans did not fail to notice that the Soviets as well as the British were now supplying the insurgents from the air. Like Boor, they could only have guessed what lay behind this change of tack. But the best guess would have suggested that the Allies had settled some political differences, and hence that a major Soviet attack was in the offing.

Initial attempts to dislodge the bridgeheads, however, did not produce much effect. An attack on Jolibord by the 25th Panzer Division on the morning of the 17th was repulsed with over 300 casualties. The officer reported: 'No result. Concrete buildings, high-rise houses infested with snipers, anti-tank fire from the flank and on the riverfront. Our forces exhausted after their heavy losses.'[120] In the south, Gen. Rohr called for reinforcements, and the Dirlewanger Brigade was joined by the 146th Panzer Grenadier Regiment.

Governor-General Frank took no part in these deliberations. Indeed, he had not set foot in Warsaw since September 1943. But a year later, in the middle of the Rising, he was still pondering 'reforms' that would make his fiefdom work more smoothly. Talking with his officials, he was adamant that the Underground as a whole should not be tarred with the same brush as the 'adventurers in Warsaw' and that some form of Polish autonomy was still a viable goal. Once the Rising was crushed, he said, he was going to submit proposals to Hitler for finding a rapprochement with Polish circles. If the proposals were refused, he would not be held responsible for the consequences.[121]

Nonetheless, the Rising in Warsaw was a wretched nuisance for him. Sometime after his last visit to Warsaw, he had written in his diary: 'In this country, we have one point from which every evil emanates. That point is Warsaw. If we didn't have Warsaw in the General Government, we wouldn't have four-fifths of the difficulties with which we must contend.'[122] Thanks to the Rising, those 'difficulties' had increased greatly. Looking through the windows of his grand office in the Royal Castle in Cracow, and surveying the peaceful scene below, he can only have felt doubly confirmed in his earlier bitter judgement.

The Polish Government could not have viewed the Berling Army's arrival before Warsaw with much equanimity. Of course, like everyone devoted to the Polish cause, they rejoiced at the chance that the Rising might be rescued. Yet they could hardly have welcomed the political implications. If the rescue succeeded, the credit would be taken by Berling and by his Soviet-backed associates in the Lublin Committee. If the rescue failed, the Rising would probably go down to defeat; and the Government's influence in Warsaw would come to an end. Either way, the Government's stock was falling fast. [**GRAVES**, p. 368]

The Commander-in-Chief remained in daily radio contact with Gen. Boor and with several other Home Army stations, notably the Kampinos

GRAVES

An insurgent soldier realizes that fighting is not necessarily the hardest part

At some point our unit passed a half-demolished house. An older man emerged from the gate and pointing his hand at the rubble said bitterly: 'Look at what you have done!' . . .

We passed him without a word. What was there to say? . . . He was not the only one who felt that way, and we had heard similar complaints more than once. We went on in confusion, as if we suddenly felt guilty . . . For us, it was a question of dearly held 'ideals', for him, it was his house. In general, the psychological situation was easier for the insurgent soldiers participating in battle than for the civilians who were sheltering in dark cellars and constantly expecting the next bomb to hit them . . .

The majority of the capital's population was practically starving, especially those who had been driven from their houses in panic. The army showed more diligence supplying its own ranks, even though many soldiers went hungry. It never really resolved the problem of providing distribution points for the population at large.

This does not mean, however, that the mass of the population merely awaited their fate. No! Whoever was fit, cooperated actively with the fighters. They transported weapons, organized dressing points and hospitals, and dug passages, tunnels, and barricades. Some directed traffic, others rescued the buried, they extinguished fires, and, at the risk of their own lives, dragged out victims from burning houses.

Worst off were the little children. They were terrified, often extremely hungry, and unable to understand why such awful things were happening. I felt so bad for those little ones . . . But with the older children, it was different. Many teenagers joined the Rising. They often served as messengers, carrying weapons, reports, orders, and the press with enthusiasm. Many of them fell . . . They did not always realize the dangers, and had a greater tendency than us older ones to perform dashing deeds.

People died, individually, in crowds, sometimes in whole families, from machine-gun bullets, from artillery shells, from bombing, or from diseases for which there was no medicine. My school friend Olgierd S., a medical student, died in this last way. He had rescued a boy with diphtheria, and became infected himself. There was nothing to save him. His death was no less heroic than from a bullet on the barricade.

Burials took place wherever it was possible – in squares, in gardens, in parks, wherever in the 'concrete jungle' of a great city there were oases of green grass. The most frequent gravesites were, quite simply, in the ruins of destroyed buildings.

One day, in a small square, I saw six completely naked bodies, which someone had mercifully covered with newspapers. Had some human hyenas stolen their clothing, or had they been humiliated and shot by the Germans? – I do not know. Among those murdered, I recognized the naked body of a younger friend from school, a mild and peaceful chap with a kind smile. I was already accustomed to the sight of dead bodies, but here was someone whom I used to bump into every day. Apart from being killed, he had been abused, the victim of human ignominy. I could not shake off the disgust for a long time.

My friend was laid to rest in a communal grave in the square. I searched around for a blanket, or something that could be used as a shroud . . . there was nothing. Over his grave a small cross of sticks was left and a piece of cardboard with his name: 'Farewell, companion! May God clothe you in his merciful light!'[1]

A. Janicki

Group outside Warsaw. Orders, information, and advice were exchanged. Discussions took place on the attempts to contact Rokossovsky and on Soviet activity in the air. But little could now be done to improve either the stalled diplomatic situation or the battles on the ground. Between 15 and 18 September, a Polish official made three visits to the Soviet Embassy in London. He wished to hand over some letters. One was a copy of Boor's telegram requesting radio communication with Rokossovsky. The next was the National Council's latest appeal to Churchill, Roosevelt, and Stalin. The last was the transcript of Boor's instructions about reactivating the telephone cable in Warsaw. On his first visit, the Secretary of the Embassy accepted the note without comment. But on the second visit, the porter absolutely refused to take receipt of anything. Attempts to get through by telephone resulted in answers stating that no responsible official was present. On the third visit, on the 18th, he managed to get inside the Embassy and to make his way into the Secretary's office. When he pulled the letters from his pocket, he was cut short with the words: 'The Polish Government are no doubt aware that between my Government and them no diplomatic relations exist.'[123] Three days had been wasted. In Warsaw's terms, three days were equivalent to 6,000 deaths.

A major topic of concern turned on varying assessments of Soviet intentions in Poland, and of the Home Army's stance towards the advancing Soviets. Boor kept the Commander-in-Chief well up to date on these matters. On 17 September, he reported that the Soviets were not tolerating any activity by dependants of the exiled Government, whether east or west of the 'Curzon Line'. They were 'liquidating' the Home Army wherever possible. They did not seem in any hurry to declare a Provisional Government, and probably would not do so before taking Warsaw. Boor foresaw the possibility that he would have to decree the Home Army's disbandment. Two days later, he relayed the eye-witness report of an AK soldier who had been arrested by the NKVD and had later escaped from the Berling Army. The witness said that the NKVD put a gun to prisoners' heads to extract the names of officers and the location of arms, and that they had opened two new detention camps. He also said that of 5,000 men conscripted for the army in one town east of Warsaw, only 1,000 showed up and all ran away on the road to the station. All the staff posts in Berling's Army, he said, were held by Russians. In a long reply, the Commander-in-Chief advised the authorities in Warsaw on their conduct in the event of the Soviets capturing the city. They should attempt to negotiate with the Soviets on secondary matters, whilst waiting for the pressure which would undoubtedly be exerted by Britain and the USA.[124]

None of these vital matters was reflected in the British media. Indeed, the longer the Rising persisted, the less was written about it. A lone voice of protest was raised in the House of Commons. 'The contrast between the publicity given to the activities of the *Maquis* in France, and the silence about our Polish allies in Warsaw,' Guy Lloyd noted ironically, 'hits you between the eyes.' The director of the Polish Section of the BBC agreed. The issue surrounding the absence of Soviet assistance to the Rising, he admitted, was 'significantly toned down'. 'Less was said than was known . . . so as not to disturb the need for Allied unity.'[125]

Beyond that, the prime source of tension was the widening political gulf which was dividing the Polish community in London into rival factions. The dominant faction led by the Premier was intent on staying loyal to the Anglo-American alliance and on doggedly pursuing the recommended course of compromise with the Soviets. The opposite faction led by the Commander-in-Chief held that the Premier had made too many concessions both to the Anglo-Americans and to Moscow. If the truth were known, both factions were losing the means to influence events significantly. The Premier's 'moderates' were unable to persuade Churchill and Roosevelt to force the initiative and to engineer a genuine compromise with Stalin. The 'hardliners' were unable to convince the Anglo-Americans of the need for a hard line. Few were conscious of the hidden causes of their impotence. They were trying to play a game without quite knowing what the unwritten rules were or whether they had been changed.

The split was underlined by the visit to London from 17 to 22 September of Gen. Anders. Anders knew Russia like no one else. During the First World War, he had been a cavalry officer in the Tsarist Army. In 1939–41, he had been a prisoner of the NKVD in the Lubyanka; and for two years after that, as commander of the Polish army in the USSR, he had fought his corner daily with the highest officials of Stalin's regime. His opinions, which were thought to be unacceptably 'anti-Soviet' by the British establishment, were based on hard experience. Unlike most British or American officials and advisers, he knew exactly what he was talking about. And as a soldier he didn't mince words. Before leaving Italy, via Algiers, he held a frank discussion with Britain's Political Adviser at Allied Headquarters, Harold Macmillan.

In London, Anders talked to all the leading figures in the Polish camp from the President downwards, and in Churchill's absence to the Deputy PM, to the Foreign Minister, Eden, and to the British Ambassador to Poland, O'Malley. All the British told him that the Commander-in-Chief should be dismissed (as the Soviets had long demanded).

On 22 September, Anders met Premier Mick, who he judged to have little experience of politics and who had 'adapted his policy to the passing needs of the British and Americans'. He thought that 'the integrity of our territory and the sovereignty of our state [were] being violated.' And he said so. Above all, he believed that the quarrel with the Commander-in-Chief was diverting attention from the Warsaw Rising.

At the end of the talk, Anders asked the Premier what was the meaning of his next proposed journey to Moscow. The Premier answered that it was necessary 'in order to preserve the very life of the nation':

> I then said that in my opinion it would be all right for him to go to Moscow, but not in his capacity of Prime Minister, as, if he did, he might easily find himself in the very cell [which] I had occupied in the Lubyanka. We were well acquainted with Soviet methods, by which he would be eventually compelled to state that all his life he had been nothing but a German agent . . . Our conversation led to no understanding between us . . .[126]

As soon as Anders left, the Polish Cabinet formally asked the President to remove the Commander-in-Chief from office. The President procrastinated.

Awaiting his fate, the Commander-in-Chief did one of the few things left to him that was not controversial. He ordered that the most senior of the Polish bomber squadrons under British command be renamed. Henceforth, No. 301 was to be known as No. 301, 'The Defenders of Warsaw'.[127]

After weeks of unrelieved frustration over Warsaw, London and Washington could take little satisfaction from the latest developments. Many officials felt sympathy for their Polish allies, and a duty to help. At the same time, they were painfully aware both of their own limitations and of the impunity with which Soviet ambitions were being pursued. Above all, since the defeat of Nazi Germany remained an absolute priority, they knew that an open rift with Stalin could not be risked. So they see-sawed between resignation and rage. [**SAXONS**, p. 373]

Churchill returned from Quebec inevitably impressed by the major world issues that were now being decided, and equally by the requirement to keep all minor issues from intervening. He was probably most impressed by the unequalled power of the Americans and, hence, by his own subordination to them. Given Roosevelt's coolness on the Polish Question, he was not prepared to stir it up too vigorously. His concern for Britain's predicament was tinged with alarm:

> As the autumn drew on, everything in Eastern Europe became more intense ... Communism raised its head behind the thundering Russian battlefront ... The fate of Poland and Greece [in particular] struck us keenly. For Poland we had entered the war ... Both their Governments had taken refuge in London, and we felt ourselves responsible for their restoration, if that was what their peoples really wished. In the main, these feelings were shared by the United States, but they were very slow in realising the upsurge of Communist influence, which ... followed the onward march of the armies directed from the Kremlin.[128]

The British Prime Minister's sombre mood was confirmed by the extensive correspondence which he pursued in the last two weeks of September with the South African leader, Field Marshal Smuts, who had attended Dumbarton Oaks, and had well understood the Western dilemma about dealing with Stalin:

> The crisis arising from the deadlock with Russia in World Organisation talks fills me with deep concern ... The Soviet attitude struck me at first as absurd.... But second thoughts have inclined the other

SAXONS

An officer of the 73rd Hanoverian Regiment outlines his service during the Rising

After the defeat of Army Group Centre in the middle of July, my division (the Lower Saxon 19th Panzer Division) was sent by train from southern Holland to a base in the Karvitse region near Elk. Before all units were gathered, we were ordered to march in a south-westerly direction to set up a bridgehead to the east of Praga [around Rembertov and Okuniev]. Yet after the arrival of the last transports from Holland, my regiment was once again despatched by rail . . . to Warsaw's Danzig Station. This was August 1st. We were supposed to travel on by road to . . . the other side of the Vistula. But just as we were detraining, a motorcycle messenger arrived with the request that 'an officer from our transport report immediately to headquarters'. I didn't know Warsaw . . . so together with my driver I followed the motorcyclist . . . It was about 17.00 hours. On the second floor I was connected by telephone with an officer from AOK 9, who ordered me not to take my men east across the Vistula but to make our way south-east towards the Varka River, because the Russians had set up a bridgehead there. During this long conversation I could hear the sounds of rifle fire. A bullet came through the window, at which point I took the phone under the desk and carried on talking there.

Our return to Danzig Station was a dramatic affair conducted in almost empty streets. The detraining had been completed, but we had to search the houses adjoining the station because shots were being fired. We took nine prisoners, of whom two were women. They were in civilian dress with red-and-white armbands. Not knowing what we were supposed to do, we released them before moving off. We suffered no casualties on our journey through the city, which we made with the sole aid of a 1:300,000 scale map.

It was an entirely different story for the remainder of our division, which on 3 August was supposed to reach the Varka from the other side of the Vistula, via Praga . . . They suffered heavy losses. As the armoured column of the third company passed by the main station in Warsaw, it came under such intense fire that it could not continue, and its commander decided to reverse and seize the station instead. He and his soldiers remained there for close on two months. His column only rejoined the [rest of us] on 2 October.

Over the next weeks the battles centred on the region to the north of Warsaw [between the Bug, Narev, and Vistula], and on the Varka, which has gone down in military history as the 'Magnushev Bridgehead'. They also found us in Praga, from which on the night of 13/14 September we had to retreat across the Vistula and blow up its bridges. There were immediate attempts by the Polish-Soviet First Army to force a way across the river . . .

On 20 September our regiment was advanced once again to the western bank of the Vistula, facing east. The right flank began at the Citadel. It was an extremely awkward front line, and no one could put their head above the parapet. Either Russian heavy weapons opened up from across the river, or else we would be picked off by Polish insurgent snipers in [Jolibord].

From this position, on the evening of 28 September the 2nd Panzer Battalion of the 73rd Regiment, together with other elements of the division previously located in Mokotov, was finally called upon to suppress the Rising. The attack on [Jolibord] began the next morning. My company, reinforced by a unit of sappers with flamethrowers and three squads of stormtroopers, were to attack some houses up Pototska Street, which is very wide and affords no shelter. For hours we could make no headway and we took thirty-two casualties. In the afternoon we were pulled back. Later, on 30 September, we were engaged to close off a gap in the south-western corner, [and stayed there] right up to the capitulation.

Incidentally, we didn't know the names of our Polish adversaries, who were well disguised by their aliases. When General ['Boor'] met my divisional commander, Lieutenant General Källner, after the capitulation, both stood proudly to attention. As cavalrymen, they knew each other from prewar fencing competitions. [Boor] said to Källner, 'If I'd known, sir, that you were on the other side I'd have surrendered a lot sooner.' He didn't know that 19th Panzer had only spent five days fighting in the city.[1]

> way . . . [the Soviet attitude] is correctly interpreted as one which involves the honour and standing of Russia among her allies. She questions whether she is treated as an equal, or whether she is still a pariah and an outcast. A misunderstanding here, . . . by touching Russian *amour propre* and inducing an inferiority complex may poison European relations with far-reaching results.[129]

Smuts touched on almost every related subject, except Warsaw.

Churchill was acutely mindful that Stalin had been absent at Quebec, and that an effort must now be made to reassure him of the solidarity of the 'Big Three'. He accordingly made plans to fly to Moscow in person; and a date was fixed for the second week of October. He certainly intended to use the occasion to hold frank discussions with Stalin about Poland. But in the meantime, he felt that little more could be done. The

The Enemy in View

right: Home Army marksman

below: Locating German positions

Insurgent Leaders

Gen. 'Boor', Commander of the AK

Gen. 'Monter', Commander of the Rising

Gen. 'Gregory', Chief-of-Staff

Courier 'Novak'

German Military Chiefs

SS-Ostubaf. Oskar Dirlewanger

SS-Brig.Fhr. Mieczyslaw Kaminski

SS-Ogruf. Erich von dem Bach

SS-Gruf. Heinz Reinefarth

Insurgent Barricades

Waiting for the next attack

Action stations

Home Army Fighters

No uniform uniform

A lull in the fighting

Examining supplies

On the Attack

above: Perfect conditions for guerrilla warfare

left: Fighting in the Holy Cross Church

German Counter-measures

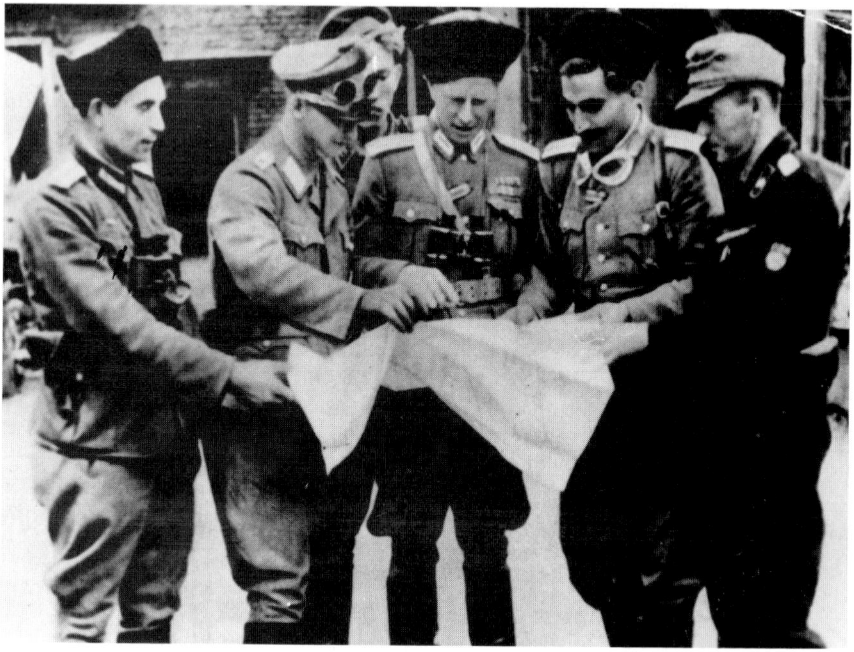

Kaminski confers with Cossack officers

A Wehrmacht officer gives orders

Armoured personnel carrier fires a rocket-propelled grenade

below: A *StuG* German assault gun

Insurgent Successes

above: Captured armoured personnel carrier

right: Captured Panther tank

left: Captured German soldier

below: Captured German staff car

Agonies of Battle

Casualty being tended

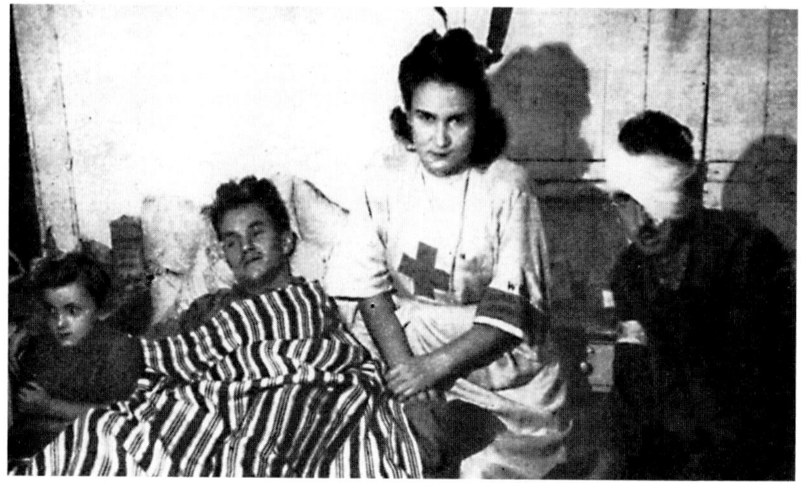

Insurgent hospital

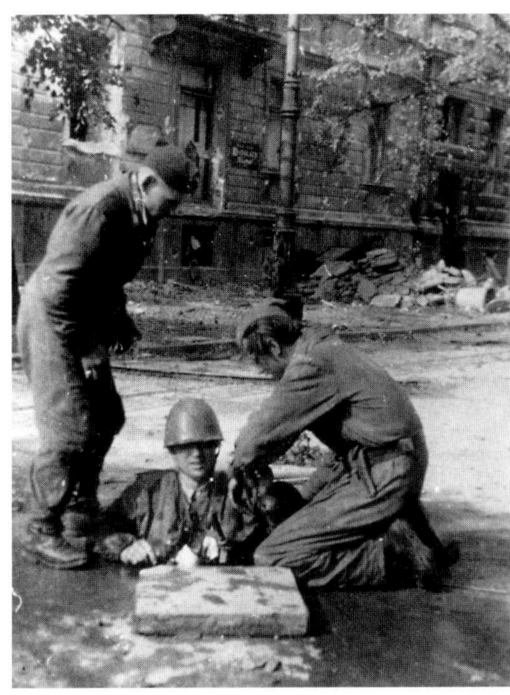

Emerging from the sewers

below: Soldier's funeral

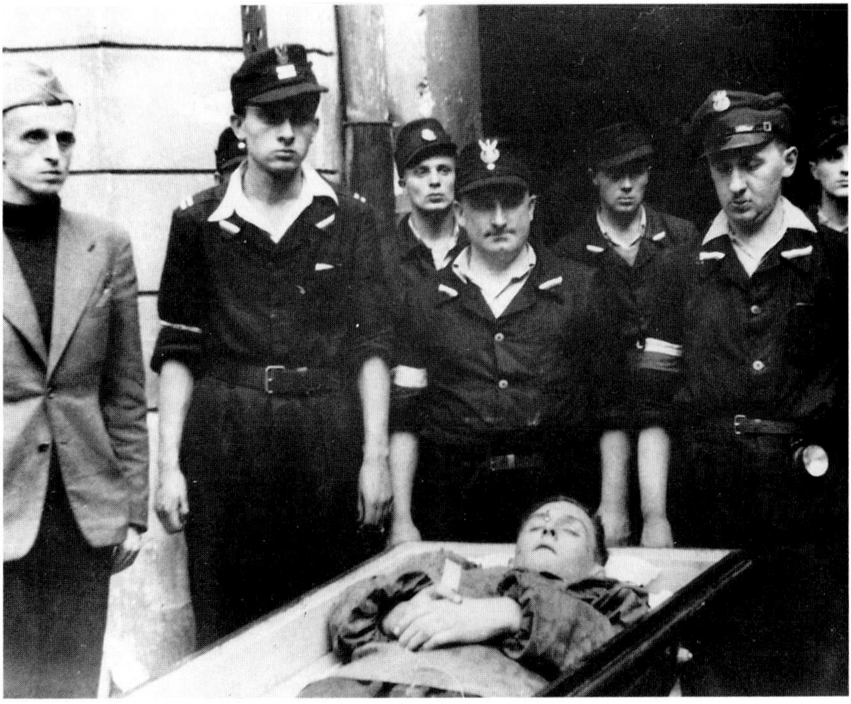

Life Goes On

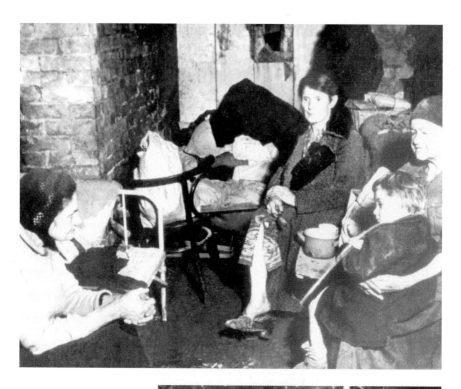

above: Sheltering in the cellars

right: Delivering letters

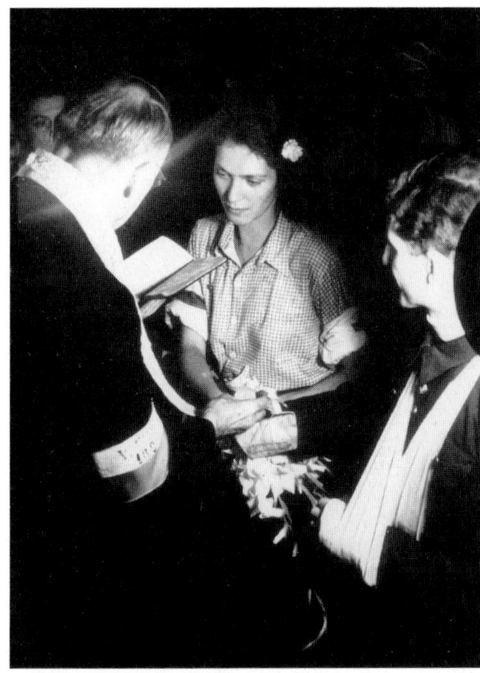

Marrying one's sweetheart

below: Attending underground Mass

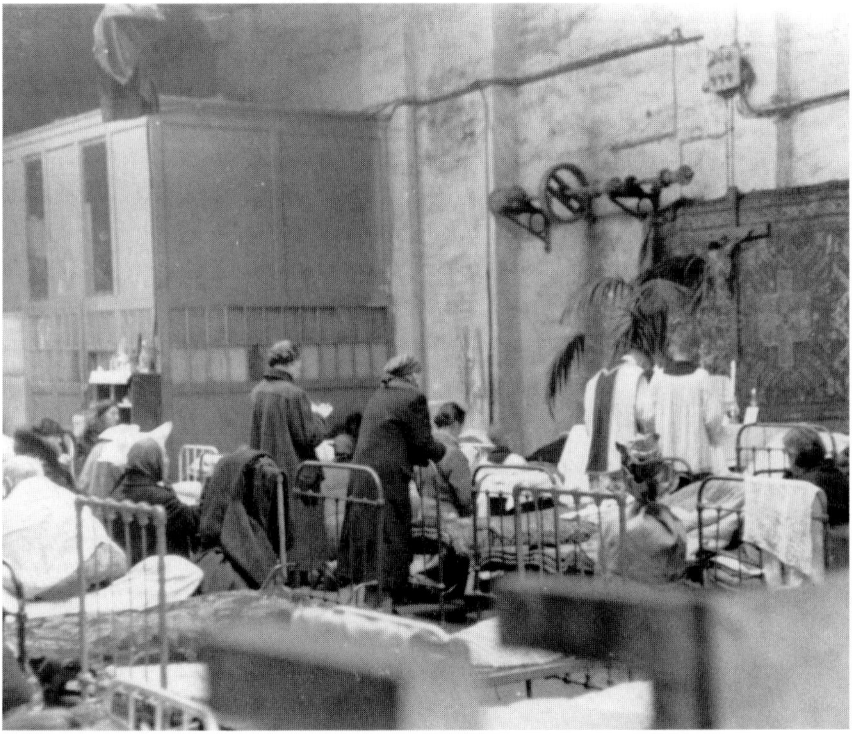

Everyday Chores

Collecting horsemeat

Cooking dinner

Waiting for a message

Repairing the telephone lines

Jewish Insurgents

Saved from Nazi captivity

Rescued by the Zoshka Battalion at Goose Farm

Germany's Central Asian Auxiliaries

Turkmen reinforcements

Home Army Posters

'One bullet, one German'

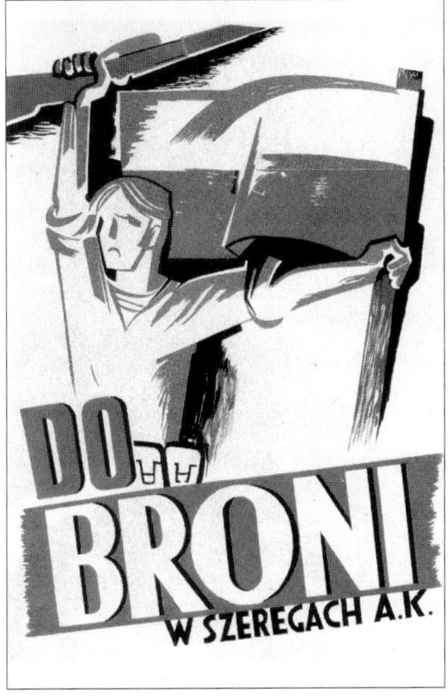

'To Arms in the AK ranks'

Propaganda

Coalition: 'We are not alone'

Catholic

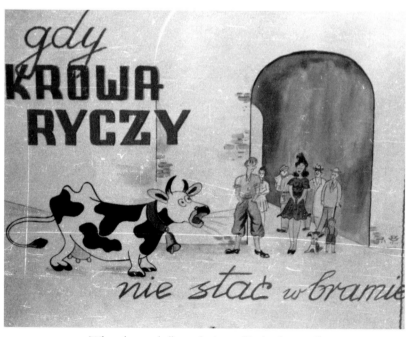

'When the cow bellows, don't stand in the doorway!'

Greetings

from the Communist Army: 'The Giant and the expectorated dwarf of reaction'

below: from the Parasol Battalion, Stalag VIIA, Murnau (Bavaria), Easter 1945

A Halifax on the tarmac at Brindisi

A Liberator over the Adriatic

above: USAAF Flying Fortress at Poltava, Ukraine, 'Frantic mission'

left: A successful drop in the Old Town

International Politics

15 August 1944, Premier 'Mick' (left) returns from Moscow – empty-handed

Roosevelt and Churchill: sixty days to save Warsaw

J. M. Keynes (centre) at Bretton Woods, August 1944: no Poles present

Western leaders at Quebec, September 1944: *not* discussing Warsaw

Devastation

Vola in the wake of Dirlewanger

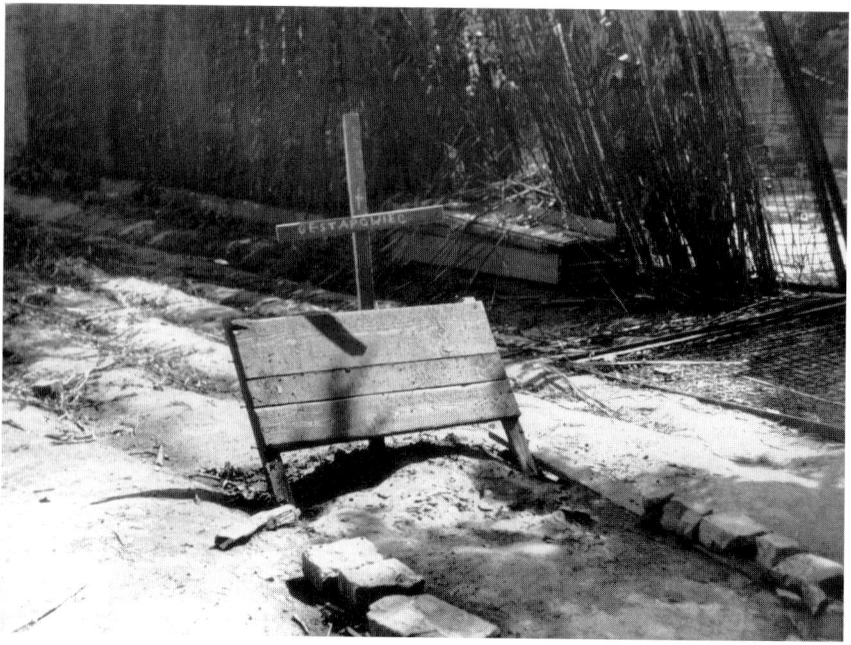

Grave of a Gestapo agent

Burying the dead

Walking home

The Entry of Berling's Army, September 1944

above: Welcome in Praga

right: 'There'll be a Poland'

Crossing the Vistula

Berling's soldiers in captivity

Terminal Affairs

Countess Tarnovska (Polish Red Cross) in truce talks

Blindfolding the negotiators

Ozarov, 2 October: signing the capitulation

Von dem Bach receives General 'Boor' in surrender: 5 October 1944

Last March of the Home Army

Stolze Polen! (Proud Poles!)

Members of the Women's Auxiliary Service

British Foreign Office had posted the Polish Premier's compromise plan to Moscow on 30 August. No reply had been received; and no one in the Foreign Office was making waves to get one.

In this state of suspense, Churchill rose in the House of Commons to make an interim statement on Poland. His speech was a prime example of wishful thinking:

> Territorial changes in the frontiers of Poland there will have to be. Russia has a right to our support in this matter . . . All the more do I trust that the Soviet Government will make it possible for us to act unitedly with them in the solution of the Polish problem, and that we shall not witness the unhappy spectacle of rival Governments in Poland, one recognised by the Soviet Union and the other firmly adhered to by the Western powers. I have fervent hopes that [Premier Mick], the worthy successor of Gen. Sikorski, a man firmly desirous of friendly understanding and settlement with Russia, and his colleagues, may shortly resume those important conversations at Moscow which were interrupted some months ago. It is my firm hope, and also my belief, that a good arrangement will be achieved.[130]

The one success in Anglo-American policy, which now occurred, concerned the long-postponed USAAF overflights to Warsaw. Yet the reaction of the US Administration, having scored this one success, was to drop all further initiatives. When the President's economic adviser, Oscar Cox, suggested that Mayor LaGuardia of New York be asked to provide aid for rebuilding Warsaw, the State Department squashed the suggestion. 'I wonder', argued Charles Bohlen, 'if it would be advisable to single out Warsaw for special treatment when other cities such as Rotterdam, Belgrade, Caen, Stalingrad etc have suffered as much if not more.'[131] More tellingly, Roosevelt made all further aid to Warsaw dependent on Soviet cooperation. 'Whether or not additional operations will be undertaken', he told Harriman, 'is dependent on the date of relief of Warsaw and [on] assistance given by the Soviets in the meantime.'[132] In the meantime, the President was receiving negative views on the situation in Warsaw coming straight from the Kremlin. 'The insurgents are still fighting, but were causing more trouble than support.' 'There are groups in four different isolated parts of the city, who are engaged in attempting to defend themselves without offensive ability.' 'The insurgents are intermingled with the Germans', presumably hindering a Soviet assault. Harriman even told the President: 'Stalin showed understanding and concern for the Poles in Warsaw, and none of his previous vindictiveness.' No less that ten days after the capture of Praga, he reported that it would be 'possible to judge the situation more clearly after Praga had been taken.'[133]

The 1st (Polish) Independent Parachute Brigade was stationed at Stamford in Lincolnshire. Formed in 1943 from Polish servicemen already serving in Britain, it had received a standard dedicated to Warsaw, and its officers had assumed that the eventual liberation of Warsaw from the air was its principal raison d'être. In August 1944, the son of its commanding officer was fighting in the ranks of the Home Army in Warsaw. 'Stan' was the man who led the attack on the German storehouse which gave the AK its German helmets.

When training was completed in the spring of 1944, the brigade was put, by agreement, at the disposal of the British Chiefs of Staff. But it wasn't sent to Normandy. And when the Warsaw Rising broke out, expectations arose, especially among the rank and file, that Warsaw would be its imminent destination. The British authorities explained both to Gen. Boor and the Poles in London that the facilities for transporting the brigade to Poland simply did not exist (which was true). So people in the know were resigned to an alternative assignment.

Even so, the lack of action was unbearable. And on 13 August many men from the brigade had refused to eat breakfast as a prelude to a hunger strike. Their OC wrote to the Commander-in-Chief.

> I report the spontaneous reaction of [my] units to the lack of Allied assistance for Warsaw . . . The soldiers' conduct is within the bounds of good conduct . . . I share their attitude . . . The whole brigade is touched most deeply by the fact that it is not being used for the one task for which it was formed. The fighting spirit of the men will necessarily be affected . . .[134]

In mid-September the 1st (Polish) Independent Parachute Brigade learned that it was going to be sent to participate in Operation Market Garden – Montgomery's ill-conceived attempt to seize the Rhine crossing at Arnhem. It was a bitter blow, which might have caused a mutiny. But it didn't. The Poles stayed loyal. They jumped at Arnhem in the second wave after the British 1st Airborne Division had found that the target area was surrounded by two SS Panzer divisions. Only 2,000 out of 10,000 parachutists escaped the disaster.

Oddly enough, in the same week that the brigade entered the fray at Arnhem, Warsaw's besieged population saw a vast Allied air fleet passing overhead. Tens of thousands of desperate people thought that 'their paras' had finally arrived. [**AIRDROP**, p. 378]

On 18 September 1944, a huge fleet of Flying Fortresses of the US 8th Army Air Force flew from Britain to supply Warsaw, and continued on to the Soviet base at Poltava. It was the first and last time that Western supplies reached Warsaw on this route. A later TASS report described the shuttle flight as 'one of the largest ever to land in Russia.' When the Flying Fortresses passed over Warsaw around 2 p.m., they certainly created a grand spectacle. They were accompanied by sixty fighter escorts. The sky was a perfect blue. The planes were in wide-spaced formation, flying at a great height 'as if on parade'. The silver fuselages glinted in the sun. The engines left multistranded spirals of white vapour trails. A rhythmic roar shook the buildings far below, punctuated by the popping of AA guns. Suddenly, the sky was filled with a mass of multicoloured parachutes, slowly descending, swaying in the breeze. On either side of the barricades, German troops and insurgents watched in amazement. The American report was optimistic:

> Three combat wings (110 B-17s) dispatched to drop supplies at Warsaw. Three a/c returned early. All formations dropped on Primary [target] visually. Approximately 1284 containers dropped with fair to excellent results. 105 a/c landed at Russian bases. Flak: moderate. E/A Opposition: nil. Claims: nil. Losses: 2 B-17s, cause unknown.[135]

In reality, over 80 per cent of the 1,284 containers fell into German-controlled districts. There were no parachutists. And there were no more Frantic missions to Warsaw.

Meanwhile, the RAF flights from Italy continued. They had been grounded in early September by bad weather and by tests on a new bombsight that would be effective from a much higher altitude. Twenty aircraft were ready to take off from Amendola and Brindisi on 10 September:

> A sense of duty kept the Polish crews going. They were an extraordinary collection of men of all types and ages . . . One flyer who came

AIRDROP

The USAAF provide a grand spectacle

On 18 September something extraordinary happened; a large American air flotilla, the first we had seen since the fighting started, appeared overhead. The Flying Fortresses, over 100 planes, were flying at a very high altitude and were thus out of reach of the intense anti-aircraft fire. The countless specks which appeared behind them turned out to be parachutes. Ignoring the danger, people were coming out of the cellars and climbing the heaps of rubble to get a better view of the spectacle in the sky. Their faces beaming with hope and joy, they were embracing one another and crying with relief. As the multicoloured parachutes came closer, somebody shouted, 'Our commandoes are landing!' – but unfortunately he was wrong, they were supplies. Having dropped their cargo, the planes landed on the other side of the River Vistula, on Soviet-controlled territory. Since by now only a small part of the city remained under our control, three-quarters of the eighty tons of supplies dropped from such a great height fell into German hands. Had the help come a few weeks earlier, the outcome of the Rising might have been very different. Now it was too late.

Our daily paper, the *Warsaw Courier*, wrote: 'Stalin had planned the total destruction of Warsaw a long time ago. A vibrant city with a long democratic tradition would have been a source of constant irritation in his vast totalitarian empire. Only when he saw Warsaw almost razed to the ground did Stalin decide to throw a few sackfuls of food to the dying few, an empty gesture designed to deceive world opinion.'

In his memoirs, General Boor colourfully presents the progress of this drop:

> We had awaited the American air expedition with growing impatience. It had been announced and then retracted so many times because of unfavourable atmospheric conditions. At last during the night of 17th and 18th September the BBC announced that the expedition was imminent. We waited tensely for the morning broadcast. If it ended with the song 'Just Another Mazurka', the expedition was going to take off. If 'The March of the Infantrymen' was played out, we would meet with delay yet again.
>
> This time, however, 'Just Another Mazurka' ended the broadcast and a radio message arrived immediately afterwards, informing us that we should expect the expedition between 11 and midday.
>
> It was a sunny day with good weather. A clear sky.
>
> Of course, the inhabitants of Warsaw knew nothing of the imminent help,

so the sight of American aircraft flying overhead, appearing unexpectedly over the city, provoked indescribable joy. The bombers flew extremely high, leaving behind them a trail of white specks. They were parachutes.

The Germans opened a barrage of anti-aircraft fire, which, however, did not reach the machines.

Warsaw lived through moments of indescribable enthusiasm. Everyone except the ill and the injured poured out of the cellars. They deserted their basements, and teemed into streets and courtyards. They assumed from the start that this was the arrival of the Parachute Brigade. A soldier standing not far from me observed the sky through binoculars. Suddenly he shouted loudly:

'Oh my God, the Germans are shooting them all!'

One of the officers tried to calm him down, explaining that they were not parachutists, but only containers with arms and supplies.

'But I can see their legs waving in the air clearly through the binoculars,' the soldier insisted.

No doubt, the Germans were under the same erroneous impression, because they alerted their units.[1]

A German sentry watches the same event

Today, in our command post, we were treated to a scene that most of us have only witnessed in the newsreels. Around 13.55 a fleet of American and British planes appear, at a height of around 1,000 metres, parading at first in twos and threes. There must be about fifty to sixty of them (I get to forty-four and then lose count). There is a mass of them up there, as when a huge flock of birds takes to the wing. Then we realize that something is falling from the planes, it seems directly above us. Parachutes are opening! The alarm is raised and a clatter of gunfire begins. Some claim to have seen men, limbs and hands. So, it's a paratrooper landing at last, like the one in the west? Most unlikely here. The 'chutes descend, and I see black ones, green, yellow, and white . . . Oh, they are supply pods!

. . . Inside the others is German ammunition. Oh, how decent they are. The Americans are bringing the supplies that we left in our haste in the west, and they are delivering it to us in Warsaw, by plane![2]

H. Stechbarth

> from Balkan Airforce HQ was RAF Air Commodore [Raiski]. . . . [He] had fought against the Bolsheviks as a young pilot in 1919[–20]. Now he was on the same flight as a Group, who had been deputy commander of the Polish Bomber Brigade in September 1939. They all shared the hazards of the Warsaw flights with a former airline pilot, an assistant professor of psychology from Warsaw University, a high school teacher, an Argentinian and a Canadian of Polish origin. One inexperienced navigator . . . was briefed for his first trip to Warsaw, neatly packed his few belongings, wrote a letter to his parents in Poland, drafted a will, took off, and never returned. One gunner on a Polish Liberator had been released from a maximum security prison at the outbreak of the war. On a homeward flight over the Balkans, he leaned out of a gun turret entrance, joking with the rest of the crew, and inadvertently touched the traversing switch. The turret swung round and broke his neck.[136]

Air Marshal Slessor received orders that flights to Warsaw must not stop. So on 21/22 September, a mixed group of RAF and SAAF tried once more. This time, exceptionally, they all returned safely to base. But the cloud cover over Warsaw was so thick that the pilots could not find their targets. No confirmation of success was received. Then the dead-moon period set in. Flying was off. Slessor did not receive replacement aircraft.

The loss of an aircraft was always a dramatic event. In the last couple of months, the Varsovians had seen several crashes. One Liberator came down in the City Centre, killing the Canadian crew. Another came down in the lake in the Paderewski Park in Praga. The sole survivor was taken prisoner by the Soviets.

Yet the aircrews' lonely ordeals were something which only they themselves could witness:

> Capt. Erich Endler [SAAF] had used more fuel than his inexperienced crew had allowed for. He had made his drop, and was already over the northern border of Yugoslavia before he was aware of his dangerously low fuel level . . . There was no hope of putting a big aircraft down in the dark safely. There was nothing to do but to bail out, and the pilot gave the order. The co-pilot, Lt. Chapman and RAF Pilot Officer Crook jumped, landed safely, and fell into enemy hands. From the ground, they saw their aircraft, its engine dying, rapidly lose height and crash into the towering crags of the Alps.[137]

Air force losses are calculated in various ways. But one calculation reckoned that 306 planes departed from Britain or Italy for Warsaw, and that forty-one were lost: two US, seventeen Polish, and twenty-two RAF and SAAF. Losses totalled 13.3 per cent. Losses on the run from Italy to Warsaw reached 31 out of 186 aircraft, or 16.7 per cent. This compares with the raid on Nuremberg on 30/31 March 1944, which is sometimes claimed to have been the RAF's 'darkest hour', where losses totalled 11.8 per cent.[138]

For well over a month, Soviet intentions with regard to the Rising had been widely interpreted unfavourably. Churchill himself had called them 'strange and sinister'. Even the Americans had noticed. Pro-Soviet observers would certainly have said that the earlier confusion had been overcome, that serious measures were now in progress, and that the Soviet Union would have much to gain if the Germans were driven from Warsaw and a major foothold established.

Even so, in the present, deficient state of documentation, it is impossible to say for certain whether the Kremlin's apparent change of heart in mid-September was genuine or merely cosmetic. But, given the blatant obstructionism which had prevailed during the preceding weeks, it behoves the Soviet apologists to produce some hard evidence.

On the question of the Frantic missions, for instance, the USAAF were definitely counting to keep the shuttle flights to Warsaw in operation. But after the flight of 18 September, they had to wait on Soviet clearance which did not materialize until the 30th. In other words, when the fate of the Rising hung on a thread, it took Moscow eleven or twelve days to react to the American request. This looks like deliberate stalling. Bad weather prevented the flight on 30 September. But the very next day the Soviets changed their line yet again. The Americans were told at ESCOM that no further flights were necessary, because 'the Warsaw partisans have been evacuated'.[139] This information, as provided by the Soviets on 1 October, was false. They seemed to have returned to their old tactic of 'Rising! What Rising?' [**SISTERS**, p. 382]

The crossings of the Vistula by Berling's Army were surrounded by similar suspicions of half-hearted Soviet support and confused instructions. One cannot accept the argument that Berling took the decision on his own initiative. The Soviet system simply did not permit commanders to act without the prior approval both of their military superiors and of their

SISTERS

A medical orderly decides to rescue the wounded regardless of the consequences

Lt. 'Felix''s unit was guarding an outpost on Duck Street in the so-called 'Alcazar' district. After an unsuccessful foray, three seriously wounded soldiers had been left out in the open. The brother of one of the soldiers and a nurse called 'Bashka' went to collect them. But they too were wounded by German fire and were lying with others on the battlefield. My friend Sophie and I were then summoned, and we made it to the outpost. But there was a problem. 'Felix' thought that we nurses should retrieve the wounded, whilst his deputy 'Igor' said that we had no chance. In the end Felix decided that we must choose, that he would issue neither order nor recommendation.

Sophie and I were determined to go. First, we crawled over a small brick wall, in front of which logs had been stacked as a shield. But beyond that there was nothing but grass. So we crept along on our stomachs, very slowly, pushing our medical kits in front of us. We were fired on all the time, but not hit. With perhaps a dozen metres to go, we heard a girl's voice: 'Keep still, for God's sake! Don't move!'

We stopped in the grass and lay immobile, completely flat. After a time the Germans ceased firing. They probably thought that if we were not moving, we were dead. We lay there for hours. Our mission could not restart until evening, when intensive firing from our own side could cover our movements. Only then were we able to extricate the wounded and to retreat from that no-man's-land.[1]

A nun, 'Sister Teresa', is also kept busy

We looked at the stretchers with dread. The half-charred figures of small children lay there with black, swollen, suppurating faces. It turned out that the Germans, having captured a street, were driving people into mined shelters or were shutting them in cellars, into which they hurled grenades. Some of their victims stayed alive under the rubble for days, until they were found by a patrol, and brought to the hospital.

Soon there were no beds left. We packed the wounded side by side on pallets both in the corridor and the hall. Sheets and blankets were lacking . . . The weather was sweltering. An unbearable stuffiness reigned and we feared an epidemic. We were invaded by insects . . . We were all on the edge of death . . .

On Sundays all the lightly injured, the hospital staff, and the whole 'Mokotov

Square army' walked in line to the chapel of the Sisters of St Elizabeth, where Father Z. celebrated Mass. Father Z. went about in a flying suit and beret, just like the boys. He dug ditches like the boys. There was something very moving about the sight of a chapel filled with young people, listening intently to his fiery sermon . . .

The food situation was deteriorating. Even black bread was meagrely rationed Our hearts ached at the thought that the sick, and particularly the boys, were hungry, at a time when they needed intensive care. We carried dinner for the sick from the main building through a huge clearing in the wall dividing the villa from the hospital garden. But ever more frequently we had to wait a long time for the firing to calm down . . .[2]

---

political minders. Equally, one cannot accept the view that Rokossovsky stood aloof and let Berling go ahead at his own risk. After all, the crossings were supported by Soviet artillery, by Soviet sappers, and – if the Soviet-sourced statistics are not exaggerated – by no less than 2,776 air strikes. Yet the most important fact remains unchallenged. Rokossovsky did not attempt to use any Soviet combat troops; and the First Byelorussian Front did not alter the essential defensive stance which it had been ordered to assume in late August. For whatever reason, the Kremlin did not approve a general offensive in the Vistula sector, even though a general offensive was the only way of breaking the German grip.

Behind the scenes, a furious row was raging between Berling and the Lublin Committee. Even though the Committee had issued yet another public manifesto about the imminent liberation of Warsaw, they were privately incensed by Berling's apparent lack of consultation with them. It is anyone's guess what really caused the row. According to one suggestion, the Committee feared that Berling was plotting to seize Warsaw for himself and, in conjunction with Boor, to exclude them from power.[140] At all events, Berling was sufficiently disturbed to take the desperate step of denouncing the Committee as Trotskyists and demanding a personal audience with Stalin (which was not granted).

As usual, Soviet policy must be judged, among other things, by the activities of the NKVD and *Smyersh*. For as soon as Rokossovsky entered Praga, Gen. Serov and his special regiments moved in to start up the usual purging of the rear areas. Ex-Soviet archivists are still peculiarly reluctant to produce documents on this subject. But there is no reason to think that the NKVD behaved differently in the Warsaw district than in other neighbouring areas, for which documents have been released; and eye-witness accounts from people who were on the receiving end are not hard to find. The NKVD had been rounding up 'illegals' ever since the Red Army crossed the Polish frontier in January, and since July they had specific orders to target members of the Home Army. In September, they were emboldened by the decree from the Lublin Committee which gave their repressions a pseudo-legal justification. Wherever they went, mass arrests, interrogations, deportations, and shootings ensued. In their eyes, the men and women of the Home Army were not to be viewed as allies or even as partners in the fight against Fascism. In the mass of NKVD reports, captured insurgents were classified as anything from 'White Poles' and 'fascist rebels' to common 'bandits' or 'persons carrying unlicensed weapons'.

Few historians have cared to describe the shocking state of affairs that prevailed in the Warsaw district in the last two weeks of September. In the centre of the city, on the perimeters of three shrinking enclaves still controlled by the Home Army, fierce fighting with German forces persisted day by day, as the lot of the surviving civilians went from very bad to terminal. In the western suburbs, long controlled by the German authorities, civilians were being evacuated, suspected insurgents were being shot, men and women were being shipped out either to concentration camps or to forced labour in the Reich. In one part of the eastern suburbs, on the right-bank foreshore, the men of the Berling Army together with some Soviet logistical units were risking their lives, and dying in their droves, to relieve the Rising. In other parts of the eastern suburbs, especially in the sprawling streets and estates of Praga, the NKVD was engaged in operations virtually identical to those in which the SS was engaged only two or three kilometres away. Nazi and Soviet repressions were proceeding simultaneously, in one and the same city. The methods of these simultaneous violations were essentially the same. Ever since 1944, the more courageous sort of historians have repeatedly stated that the Soviets watched passively as the Germans destroyed Warsaw and its inhabitants. This is not an adequate description of the scene.

In the third week of September, a series of meetings took place in Praga between Maj. 'André', the commander of the hidden remnants of the Home Army's District VI, and the front-line Soviet units. These meetings would be a crucial test of Soviet intentions, and in particular of the optimistic proposition that Warsaw would be treated more generously than cities further to the east.

Maj. André was understandably cautious. He had been told that his counterpart in the nearby town, having guided the Soviet spearheads into the town, had promptly been arrested. So when going out to meet the oncoming Soviet soldiers, he concealed his identity. Having hidden behind a wall as the last German troops retreated, he caught sight of a Soviet infantryman carrying a radio-telephone, and waved to him. '*U vas akovtsy yest?*' was the Russian's very first question: 'Do you have any Home Army people here?' A noncommittal reply was followed by: 'Because I'd happily finish those SOBs off!' This one soldier's opinion is not necessarily conclusive. But it strongly suggests that the political department had instructed the men to treat the Home Army as enemies.[141] Some of André's subordinates had better luck with the soldiers of the 1st Division of the Berling Army, whom they led to the Vistula shore.

Already on 14 September, Berling's deputy, a Pole from Polesie with a similar career to Rokossovsky's, was appointed Commandant of Praga. His first decree was to ban all underground organizations, including the Home Army. One of André's colleagues, Maj. 'Louis', immediately reported to him that the Home Army's intentions were neither to recognize the ban nor to permit its men to join Berling.

On 18 September, however, André decided that he should respond to a summons to meet the Commandant in person. He set off in the company of his medical chief and his chief intelligence officer. Walking along Market Street, he was accosted by a man dressed in a Polish uniform. 'I know that you are the Home Army's district commander,' the stranger said, 'and that you are heading for a conference with the Commandant. But before doing that, you have first to register with me.' In response to the question, 'And why should I register with you?', the answer came: 'Because I am the Director of the Security Office in Praga: my name is "Light".'[142] Light was working for Gen. Serov. André did not oblige, but noticed that he was being shadowed. [**ANGER**, p. 386]

It turned out that the point of the meeting with the Commandant was to agree the text of an appeal for all AK soldiers to join the Berling Army. André agreed a text, which he signed. But he did not recognize the text which was published the following week in Lublin and which stated that *all* the AK soldiers of District VI (Praga) had already joined.[143]

André spent two days with Gen. Berling in talks at a villa some miles to the east of Praga. Berling offered him a commission as second-in-command of the 4th Infantry Division. André would have preferred to form a separate infantry regiment consisting exclusively of AK men. No

ANGER

In the later weeks of fighting, the mood of some civilians turns ugly

5 September, Tuesday. The Germans are storming, burning, and murdering, and there's no resistance from our side, because there can't be any. There are no units here, no aeroplanes, no grenadiers. What can you do with bare hands? Many people have left Warsaw. Yesterday's communiqué gave 100,000 as the number of those detained in Prushkov, where they are suffering from hunger and destitution. It's also hard to get about, because of the risk of death or internment, and because of the certainty that . . . your compatriots will loot your own home.

Today, when strength is running out, the mood is changing, and attitudes towards the Rising are changing, too. Almost everybody has lost the will. Almost everybody is asking the same questions: how could it have happened like this, and what for? It's clear it has taken place without agreement between the Allied governments and the Soviet government. Our Premier [Mick] in his speech on 1 September declared that the London government takes responsibility. But what comfort can this declaration bring to those who are dying in the cellars? The fact is that the Allies are giving us no help because they cannot. What next? The Bolsheviks have been standing outside Warsaw for five weeks. There has been no sound of a larger battle, and the only possible conclusion is that they don't want to advance . . . But in that case it would have been better not to have begun the Rising until these matters were sorted out, instead of consigning the city to destruction, to massacre – because this *is* a massacre. It seems to me now that there's no way out. The Rising has lost its strength to drive the Germans out. We can only suppose either that the Bolsheviks will come to an agreement or change their behaviour, or that the Germans will retreat westwards of their own accord. But who knows if a result will come about?

Meanwhile, we are literally dying from hunger, filth, exhaustion, and bombardment. We haven't slept for weeks . . . For lunch today we had boiled potatoes and tomatoes, but apparently daytime cooking is going to be banned, so that smoke doesn't give us away to the planes. Even the insurgents have lost their dream. Three times I have had to take shelter in their bunkers. They give me to understand that they had envisaged the action quite differently, and that they have little hope left.

9 September, Saturday. Yesterday's communiqué [from London] was completely empty. The article that followed was full of declarations about having to 'hold out', with no word about the Bolsheviks' intentions. Nothing much can be made of the reference to Stalin rejecting a proposed agreement between the London government and the Committee for National Unity. A few days ago that agreement was supposedly signed and sealed . . . That's why it's so hard for us . . . What are they telling us to wait for? . . . All these protestations of sympathy, all these 'hearts beating with yours', and 'thoughts going out to you', merely elicit contempt . . . coming as they do from people who for the last six weeks have been eating, drinking, and sleeping in clean sheets . . .[1]

Our struggle is only a fragment in the life of humanity. In whose name is it being pursued? Is it for power, as our increasing doubts suggest? Is it for Ideas? A Revolt against Oppression? A Fight for Freedom? Or something else entirely? How is one to explain the fact that . . . on Long Street . . . amongst those driven forward as human shields in front of German tanks was Father T. That priest was a keen anti-Semite and saw Hitler as the founder of the struggle against international Jewry. He may have given the appearance of spiritual closeness [to us] but in reality he was distant, opposed, and alien. Yet at the end, half dead and bleeding from his wounds . . . he has found a place in Polish sympathies . . .[2]

---

decision was reached. André then announced in writing that he was going to cross the river to consult his superiors in Warsaw. Instead, he took off in the opposite direction, and went into hiding in one of the nearby villages. Almost two months would pass before Light found him.

Others were less fortunate. André heard from Berling that the communications group sent by Monter had landed and that they were being investigated by the counter-intelligence department. After eight days' agonizing delay, 'Poppy' and his radio were sent to the First Army's Communications Department, and for the rest of the month was in daily contact with Monter, but to no great effect. He then made his way to his mother's house, where he was arrested by the NKVD. By early October, he was on his way to the Gulag.[144] Most of his companions were drafted into the Berling Army, before they too fell foul of the NKVD. Capt. Kalugin was shot.[145]

Since the Soviets felt no confidence in the insurgents sent to meet them, they determined to send a mission of their own to find out about the insurgents. On the night of 21/22 September, Capt. Ivan Andreievitch Kolos was dropped into the City Centre by parachute. He was accompanied by a radio operator. Unfortunately, his orders were to make for the HQ of the People's Army (AL) and not for Gen. Boor. Still worse, his operator had injured himself when he hit a balcony on the way down, and his radio set may also have been damaged. Nonetheless, with some delay, the two Russians reached their destination and set to work. Their orders were to locate the main German positions in Warsaw, to discover the whereabouts of British intelligence, and to establish the intentions of the Rising's leadership. Despite the obvious urgency, they had no authority to negotiate.

To put it mildly, Kolos was poorly prepared. When he reached AL headquarters, he was surprised to find that the People's Army had practically no soldiers. He explained this to himself by concluding that the main body of the People's Army must have been cut off elsewhere in the city. (There was, in fact, no main body.) When introduced to the commander of the combined AL, KB, and PAL[146] forces, Col. S., he imagined that he was talking to Gen. S., the Commander-in-Chief, who was in London. When introduced to a Capt. 'Coracle', who spoke fluent Russian and who presented himself as Gen. Boor's adjutant, he was not to know that the only two Home Army officers to use the pseudonym Coracle were long since dead.

The messages sent back by Kolos to his superiors betray his disorientation:

> We landed at the right spot. The German forces in Warsaw are commanded by Gen. von dem Bach. He has two *panzer* divisions, and three motorised divisions at his disposal. The German artillery positions are located in Map quadrant 16. I am pursuing my mission according to plan. Oleg[147]

If von dem Bach had ever been given five whole divisions, he would have been totally amazed.

> The English Intelligence Centre is located in the region of [Cool Street], and has been there for some time. Its main task is to neutralise our [Soviet] activities. I shall continue to research this object.[148]

If British intelligence had ever possessed a centre in insurgent Warsaw, MI6 would have been very interested to learn more.

During an interview filmed fifty years later, Kolos described his preparation for the mission. The NKVD had given him papers with a Polish-sounding name – Kolosovski – and had told him that if he fell into the hands of the Home Army he would be shot. Far from preparing him to assist an Allied force in distress, they had given him the unmistakable impression that he was entering enemy territory. No wonder he was totally at sea. He was taken to see the Home Army command on two occasions, on the 21st and on the 22nd; and he later reported meeting Boor. He would also complain about the 'English intelligence agents' whom he perceived to be milling around in Boor's entourage. His only substantive question was to ask the Rising's leaders how, in their view, the Soviet Army could best capture Warsaw. Monter and Bear Cub responded with the outline of a pincer movement to north and south, which, completely unknown to them, was uncannily similar to the plan which Rokossovsky and Zhukov had submitted to Stalin on 8 August. Since at the time, Berling's limited operations were already disintegrating, the question was more than a trifle surreal. [**AMAZON**, p. 390]

The net result of all this was diplomatic disarray. When the British and American Ambassadors visited Stalin yet again on 23 September, pleading once more for help for the Rising, all purposes were crossed. Stalin, presumably, had not yet received any coherent information from Warsaw via Kolos and the NKVD. If he had, he would have been highly embarrassed. He had been belittling the insurgents for nearly two months, saying that they were incapable of serious resistance, and now his own man on the spot was reporting that they had been holding their own against five German divisions. He would also have learned, if he did not already know, that the Communist forces in Warsaw were not very impressive and were not in charge. So when the ambassadors enquired whether Gen. Boor's messages to Marshal Rokossovsky had been passed on, he began to bluster. 'No one can find this General Boor', he replied unhelpfully. 'We don't know where he is. He must have departed from Warsaw.' This was a new variant of an old syndrome: 'General! What general?' One is tempted to talk of wilful ignorance or bad faith or both. But behind it stood an appalling failure of political and military intelligence.

For the time being, a detailed analysis of Stalin's thoughts about the Warsaw Rising remains beyond the historian's reach. It is not possible to judge, for example, whether his decision to shun the insurgents in mid-August was absolute and final, or whether it was open to modification. One could argue that he was using the Rising as a bargaining chip and that in late September he was still waiting for movement on the key political issues – namely the frontier and the composition of the post-war

AMAZON

A woman soldier passes a day on the edge of the Cherniakov Bridgehead

The 'Watch 49' Group and its command were stationed at 2 Circle Street. The command post was in a solid triangular building with high-roofed cellars and basements. The stairs to the top floor were fixed on the outside.

On the afternoon of 16 September, the Germans forced their way into the courtyard and threw grenades down the basement staircase. I saw the face of the German who threw it as well as the rolling grenade, which unfortunately could not be caught. It exploded and we were injured. I took it in the shins, but not as badly as those somewhat further away. Some people panicked. Major 'Vitold', the commander of Watch 49, gave the order that our building was a stronghold and that no one was to leave or enter without a pass.

The Germans were trying their best to get inside the building, and they eventually succeeded. At four in the afternoon, the picture was that we were holding out in the basement, the attic, and the stairwells. From the attic we directed our fire against Vilanov Street and particularly against the co-operative depot, through which the Germans had reached the bank of the Vistula. Our building had caught fire, which helped us to conceal ourselves.

We then noticed that the Germans were hammering. In fact, I was in the area with 'Little John' when the hammering became significantly louder. They were blowing an opening into our part of the building with a mine. Thanks to Little John's alertness – he stuck the barrel of his machine gun into the opening and fired – the Germans did not get in on that occasion.

However, they did not give up. At five o'clock, they put a Goliath at the corner of Circle and Vilanov Streets . . . If the cable could be cut, the Goliath would not explode. But this time it came very close and demolished the building's streetside corner, which was occupied by a light machine gun and its crew of Berlingers. A terrible crush ensued as the surviving Berlingers withdrew through the basement corridor. Thereupon, cadet officer 'Leslie' headed with me in the opposite direction through the crush. From then on, our communication with the rest of our people on Circle Street passed through the gap that the Goliath had made.

Major Vitold had a plan to break through to the Vistula. But we were already extremely tired, hungry, and, since the nights were drawing in, freezing. We were living off what the Russians dropped us, that is, tins of Spam saturated with fat and American crackers, still with American labels. Everything was full of sand, as if having been offloaded from the Russian planes without parachutes The cans were dented and smashed. But at least we had them.

The whole time, we were under bombardment. The German artillery was firing from the Parliament district, whilst from the other side the Soviet artillery, which was firing towards the Parliament, often fell short and hit us.

We calculated that we had to hold the bridgehead and the Vistula crossing at all costs. We were counting on the ability either of the Berlingers or of the Soviets to come across in force. Once they had done that, we would be able to sally forth and join up again with the City Centre.[1]

Halina A.

Government – which he had expected to be settled long since. If so, one would be arguing from guesswork.[149]

All that can be said with certainty is that there had still been no movement on the key Polish–Soviet issues and that there was still no hint of the Kremlin changing its stance. The Polish Communists were ever more hostile. On 30 September, the Chairman of the Lublin Committee held a press conference in Moscow. 'General Boor', he said, 'is a war criminal. If he fell into our hands, we would put him on trial.'[150]

A valuable source of information regarding Soviet attitudes lies in a group of intelligence reports sent from Praga to Moscow in late September. Three reports entitled 'The Position in Warsaw' were written on 15, 22, and 25 September. Their author, a member of the War Council of the First Byelorussian Front, was Lt.Gen. T. Telegin. Their recipient was the Chief of the Red Army's Political Directorate, Col.Gen. Comrade A. S. Shcherbakov, who forwarded them to Stalin.[151]

The military sections of the reports describe the layout of the insurgent strongholds, the battles of the 1st (Polish) Army on the Cherniakov bridgehead, the evacuation of the bridgehead, and the sorties flown by the Soviet air force. As always, they are meticulous in their lists of types and numbers of weapons and units involved; and they do not conceal the fact that the Home Army provided the principal insurgent force fighting alongside Berling's men.

The political sections of the report, in contrast, make no attempt to present an accurate or objective picture. Telegin's informants are either members of the People's Army or Home Army prisoners under interrogation; and they are not given to saying anything about the Rising's leadership that is vaguely complimentary. The only two political groupings mentioned are the 'Londoners' and the 'supporters of Lublin'. In analysing insurgent opinions regarding the prospects of surrender, three groups are mentioned – an unnamed company of capitulationists; the Londoners, who wish to fight on; and the People's Army, whose views are not defined. Gen. Boor is obviously up to no good. He burdens the People's Army with the most dangerous assignments, and he gives no help to those that cross the river. A nineteen-year-old prisoner is quoted as saying that the Home Army was supposed to clear out the Germans from Warsaw and, after that, from Poland as a whole; but since these expectations were obviously false, 'discontent' and 'desertion' were rife. In a vicious comment about Radoslav, Telegin tells his superiors that the senior AK commander on the bridgehead first fired on the Polish Army then went over to the Germans. He also passes on what he takes to be the Home Army view, namely that the Soviet Army is feeble and 'that England alone can liberate Poland'.[152]

As one would expect, Telegin was intensely interested in the mission of the American Flying Fortresses. He watched them closely, and calculated that of the 1,000 containers dropped, 21 reached the insurgents, 19 fell into the Soviet lines, and 960 were collected by the Germans. In one case, where the parachute and its load landed 40km (twenty-five miles) east of Warsaw, he made a precise inventory of the contents:

> a mine thrower with 20 mines; 2 machine-guns with ammunition, 10 automatic rifles + 3 revolvers with ammunition, 4 grenades, a string of 'Bickford' fuses, and a large food package containing 100 cans of preserves and 6 boxes of biscuits, hard-tack and chocolate. (The weapons were damaged on landing)[153]

The really interesting thing though, was Telegin's conclusion. He did not tell Moscow that the Americans were hopeless bunglers or that their mission had gone disastrously wrong. He told Moscow baldly that 'the English and American airforce is not aiding the insurgents, it is supplying the Germans'.[154] When evaluating bourgeois capitalists and imperialists, the Soviet reflex was to impugn their motives in the worst possible way and to draw themselves towards an assessment that bore no relation to reality.

Telegin's third report carried an interesting quotation purportedly taken from the Home Army's *Bulletin* nr. 43 of 18 September. An article in the *Bulletin* had apparently been explaining to its readers what the Berling Army actually was:

> For the last two days, soldiers of the so-called First Polish Army are in Warsaw, and are taking part in the battles for its liberation. This army has been organized by the Soviet Government in cooperation with the Polish Committee of National Liberation, and has grown out of the 1st (Polish) Kościuszko Division formed eighteen months ago. At the head of the division stands Col.Gen. Berling, the former Chief-of-Staff of the Home Army in the city of Cracow, whose assignment was arranged by Marshal Stalin himself . . .[155]

Readers of the *Information Bulletin* of 18 September would have looked for this article in vain, since in reality, the quotation came from another newspaper, the *Information Communiqué* nr. 43, which was printed by the BIP of the Home Army's Mokotov District. Still more to the point, only the first two sentences of the quotation bore any resemblance to the original. The parts of the article which Telegin omitted expressed views which he presumably did not wish to pass on:

> . . . there is no difference between Polish soldiers . . . Whatever reservations we may have about the politics of the Polish forces in Russia, we see in each soldier of Berling's Army above all a comrade-in-arms, a colleague and a brother . . . [Even if one wanted] one could not organize two separate armies of the Republic where each fighting man feels himself to be the brother of all the others . . . The Vistula will never be the frontier between two Polands.[156]

In short, Telegin's quote was a worthless collage of fact and fiction. What exactly he was doing is hard to fathom. But he was not collecting hard or objective intelligence. [**FOREST**, p. 394]

Of course, one has to wonder whether Stalin ever saw one hundredth part of the mountains of paper that were addressed to him. But even if he did see these reports, it is difficult to imagine what possible use he could have made of them. For he had created a vast informational machine, which produced such an indigestible *macédoine* of fantasies, falsehood, and occasional facts that it was quite incapable of rendering a recognizable picture of outside reality. No one who read Telegin-style summaries could conceivably have been moved to recommend active support for 'the Londoners'. For which reason, the last paragraph of the last page of

FOREST

A boy refugee from the East follows events from the shelter of the forest

We had left our small town – Pinsk – and had gone to the countryside near Warsaw, because Mother said that my father would be there. Father had escaped from imprisonment in 1939 and was teaching in a village school . . . We set off after Mother, who was still a young woman, sold the entire contents of our house and hired a cart. We found him quite by accident, driving through a village [called Sherakov], where my mother called to a man walking along the road. It was Father.

From then on we lived together in a poky little hut without lighting or water. We went to sleep at nightfall, because we had no candles. I was constantly searching for food – a crust, a carrot, anything. Father once announced in class, 'Every child who comes to school tomorrow must bring a potato.' . . . The next day half the class was missing . . .

Nearby, close to a settlement called Palmiry, there was a clearing in the forest where the SS carried out executions. The salvoes deafened us day and night. They transported the condemned in closed, dark green vehicles, behind which the execution squad rode in a lorry. It was part of the ritual that the soldiers in the squad always wore long coats belted at the waist. The village children would follow in the roadside bushes . . . I felt as if frozen ants were crawling all over me . . . After the shooting, the column would return to Warsaw, the SS men smoking and chatting.

The partisans would come at night. Their faces appeared from nowhere, pressed against the glass of the window. Sitting at the table, I observed that they were always preoccupied with the same thought; that they could be killed at any moment . . .

One autumn night, when they came, it was raining. My father had gone into hiding. They spoke to Mother in whispers. We had to dress quickly and leave. A roundup was taking place. Whole villages were being taken to concentration camps.

We escaped to a prearranged hiding place in Warsaw. It was the first time I had seen a tram, multi-storeyed houses, or rows of shops. Why we returned to the countryside, I don't know. We went to a different village across the Vistula. All I remember is sitting at the side of a wooden cart and listening to the warm sand of the bridleway spilling through the spokes of the wheels.[1]

Throughout the war, my dream was for a pair of shoes. In the forest I went barefoot, and the skin on my feet was as hard as leather. I dreamt of solid, hobnailed shoes that would make a ringing sound on the pavement. The fashion, though, was for high knee-boots, a symbol of masculinity . . .

In 1944, I became an altar boy. My parish priest became a chaplain at a field hospital. Rows of camouflaged tents stood hidden in the pine forest. During the Warsaw Rising . . . there was feverish hustle and bustle. The guns of the front thundered nearby and we saw the smoke. Ambulances arrived at great speed. They carried the wounded, often unconscious, and unloaded them chaotically, often on top of each other. The exhausted stretcher-bearers would lay them out on the grass like so many sacks of grain (except that the sacks were leaking blood). Then they took a plastic hose and showered them with a strong jet of cold water. Any who showed signs of life were taken to the tent which contained the operating theatre. Every day, on the ground outside that tent, lay a heap of freshly amputated arms and legs.

The casualties who showed no signs of movement were taken to a huge grave at the back of the hospital. That's where I stood for hours, beside the priest, who held a breviary and an aspergillum. Together, we recited the prayers for the dead and the dying. We pronounced 'Amen' dozens of times a day . . .

At some point, all fell quiet. The nurses and the tents disappeared. The front and the hospital had moved on. Nothing remained except the crosses in the forest.

Ryszard Kapuściński

Telegin's report of 25 September was underlined by someone in Moscow in thick pencil:

> Please give instructions on the following question. To what extent, in the coming days, is it a necessity to render assistance to the insurgents with arms, ammunition, and food-stuffs. The position of the insurgents is really acute, and they cannot reckon on any aid from anyone other than the Red Army. In order to supply the aid within maximum limits, it is necessary for the Front to release 500 tons of B-70 aviation fuel and 2,000 freight parachutes and to transport ex-enemy weapons from our central stores including rifles, machine-guns, and rocket-launchers . . .[157]

According to Communist sources, the Soviet capture of Praga was an isolated exception to the general order which had put the First Byelorussian Front into a defensive stance; and the first crossing of the Vistula by elements of Gen. Berling's First Army on the night of 15/16 September was undertaken 'on the march', that is, by sheer momentum and without pausing to make preparations.[158] Without doubt, conditions in the resultant bridgehead were insupportable. Schmidt's force was bearing down on the attackers from the north, Dirlewanger's from the west, and Rohr's from the south. The insurgents' southernmost stronghold shrank alarmingly. On the 16th it had measured several square kilometres. By the 20th, it measured barely one-tenth of the size. In due course, the Home Army soldiers of the Radoslav Group decided to escape westwards to their comrades, whilst Berling ordered his surviving soldiers to pull back across the Vistula. The junction of insurgent forces with professional troops under Soviet command, which had raised such high hopes in mid-September, turned into one of the most crushing defeats of the whole Rising.

The official tally of the dead in the eight-day battle for the Cherniakov Bridgehead was 4,938. This means that Berling must have injected a force of almost divisional strength; and one might have expected him to obtain a more favourable result. After all, in the seventh week of the Rising, this was the very first occasion that the insurgents were joined by professionals enjoying both artillery and aerial support.

What went wrong? Three factors appear to be responsible. Firstly, there was no element of surprise. The Germans had been waiting for weeks for Rokossovsky to send a force into Warsaw; and, having cleared the greater part of the Riverside district in the previous fortnight, they knew exactly where the landings would take place. They had prepared an extensive complex of bunkers and machine-gun nests, which ensured that the attackers would run straight into a gauntlet of heavy fire. Secondly, Berling's troops had no experience of urban warfare. Unlike the Home Army men, who had learned to use every inch of cover, they were completely unfamiliar with the art of street fighting. Trained in the standard Soviet infantry tactics, which called for wave after wave of frontal attacks irrespective of cost, they threw themselves at the fixed German positions, and were mown down like the British infantry at the Somme. Their officers, who were watched over by Soviet-style politicos, would have been unable or unwilling to accept the advice of their Home Army colleagues. So they paid the price. And thirdly, the logistical support provided by the Soviets was manifestly inadequate.

In this last regard, one is faced with an insoluble puzzle. Rokossovsky's staff must necessarily have given clearance for Berling's operation;

they did provide a certain amount of artillery cover, and, by their own account, they were sending up thousands of aerial sorties. So why, at a time when no other major fighting was in progress, did Rokossovsky not put a greater share of his massive resources at Berling's disposal? One simply cannot know. But certainly much more could have been done.

The desperate scenes on the Vistula beaches on 23 September may be likened to the death-laden chaos which would have occurred in Normandy if the German defenders had stood their ground. The panic was appalling. When the very last pontoon was trying to leave the shore under fire, an accompanying nurse expressed her fury at a perfectly healthy soldier, who took a running dive and landed heavily on the pile of groaning wounded. She was told: 'Don't worry, that's our political officer.' The Germans did not take 'commissars' prisoner.[159]

The smaller bridgehead at Marymont had already collapsed, partly because Berling's men had not managed to join up with the Home Army group in neighbouring Jolibord. Only 13 out of 536 were not counted as casualties. In retrospect, the most interesting detail can be found in the account of 'Louis', a political director of the Communist People's Army (AL), who had established radio contact with the right bank and who was fully convinced of the Soviet Army's impending arrival. At the time, he had attributed the Soviets' failure to share details of their plans to 'war secrecy'.[160]

The collapse at Marymont coincided with the surrender of two more important districts in Jolibord and Mokotov. The City Centre alone was left under increasingly close siege.

With the beaches cleared, and the junction foiled, the German Command could finally turn its full attention to the large group of insurgents in the Kampinos Forest. A huge sweep through the forest was launched on 27 September by three battalions from the Hermann Göring Panzer Division and the SS Panzer Divisions *Totenkopf* and *Wiking*, who acted like beaters in a grouse shoot. All the villages which had given the insurgents shelter were burned, all the male villagers shot. It was typical Nazi anti-partisan warfare. A large column of retreating insurgents was caught in a carefully laid triangular trap in the diminishing space between a road and a railway line. Here were the hunters' hides. By dusk on 30 September, the Kampinos Group had ceased to exist.

*

Once both the Vistula beaches and the Kampinos Forest were lost, the long-standing hopes for the Rising to be joined by the Soviet Army were lost with them. Marshal Rokossovsky had still given no sign of his readiness to move. Hence Gen. Boor was obliged to return to the policy which he had been pursuing before the Bridgehead was established. Whilst continuing to defend his rapidly shrinking positions, he would re-start negotiations with the Germans about the terms of surrender. He would leave the door ajar for a last-minute change of mind if, by some miracle, the Soviets sprang into last-minute action. [**SEWER II**, p. 399]

The Nazis, fanatically following the *Führer*'s order to wipe the rebel city from the map, were not going to give up when they had success in view. So the only amelioration could come from Moscow. It was well within Stalin's power to send Rokossovsky in and call Serov off. And it was well within the competence of Western diplomacy to press Stalin harder. But time was running out; and the true situation in Warsaw was still surrounded by a fog of uncertainties. None of the Allied leaders seemed to have a realistic perception of what was happening. Moscow, in whose so-called 'sphere of influence' Warsaw was judged to lie, was particularly poorly informed. *One* thing alone was clear: if Stalin did not intervene very soon, the Rising was doomed.

Already the poets were practising their dirges. One of them, watching in America, observed the universal implications of the tragedy:

> If Warsaw falls, it's not one city that falls,
> Not just the Polish capital in its cellars laid to rest.
> It will be the freedom of all peoples,
> And the truth of all times, betrayed by everyone.[161]

In Warsaw, another poet imagined the last communiqué of Radio Lightning:

> The station of the Home Army in Warsaw
> Sends soldierly greetings for the last time
> To all its brothers in the world
> Who fight for victory – your victory.
>
> We announce the last item of news.
> A fraternal army is one step away.

SEWER II

A leader of the Polish Socialist Movement and of the Underground parliament escapes to the City Centre

We entered the sewer from Krashinski Square, on the corner of Long Street, on the side of the Palace of Justice. We immediately fell into deep water up to my chest. The water rushed by so strongly that we had to hold on to each other. Our group had a rope to hang on to. Even so people often fell and with difficulty were helped up by others. It was extremely difficult for short persons to use this particular route. They had to be hauled along. The darkness was periodically illuminated by the leader's lantern. The water roared and emitted a frightful stench. People who fainted were carried away . . .

We walked under Honey Street. Thanks to the bombardment, the latrine water could not flow properly through the openings, and it was oozing from the roof, threatening to collapse it. There were strong currents which were carrying not just excrement, but thick gravel and hard stones that flayed the skin from one's legs. Things improved somewhat . . . when we reached the crossroads and we could descend to a lower sewer with calmer water.

But then we found ourselves under the Cracow Faubourg, which was patrolled by the Germans, who from time to time were throwing in hand grenades. We had to progress with great care, neither speaking nor splashing. We heard the rumble of German vehicles and artillery immediately above us. Somewhere close to the Holy Cross Church we entered an even lower sewer, about 120cm in height, but full of latrine sludge, which made every step difficult . . . We had to move hunched up, protecting our heads from the ceiling. At last we reached the manhole by Varka Street . . . and we breathed fresh air.[1]

K. Pużak

A Home Army telephonist is tricked into surrender

The Bashta Battalion had long been separated from the rest of the Rising. But just before the collapse it was ordered to evacuate Mokotov and move to the City Centre via the sewers.

Signal Company K, in which I was leader of a section of telephonists, started to pull out on the evening of 26 September using a manhole on Shuster Street. Being wounded, I entered the sewer at the end of the company and was looked after by a nurse. After overcoming many obstacles, including barricades erected by the Germans . . . I became separated from my unit and was forced to go back. Altogether I spent twenty hours in that black, foul-smelling labyrinth, constantly stepping on dead bodies. I met three young men, who were also lost. So we walked together.

After a while we began to see a faint light, and we heard somebody calling, 'Come on, come on, come on.' We climbed out of the sewer only to find that it was not a Pole who was calling, but a German who could speak Polish.

I saw that the soldiers who caught us were from the unit against whom we had been fighting and that the place around the manhole was covered with corpses. I realized what was awaiting me. I was searched, all my jewellery was taken together with the miniature pistol which my friends had called a 'Panzerfaust'. I and my three comrades were ordered to climb onto some raised ground in preparation for execution. At the time, completely drained, I could not have cared less . . .

When a German jeep arrived and an officer stopped the execution, I did not react. I was in a 'trance'. Half dead, I was taken by the same officer in his jeep to a German hospital [in the Rakoviets district]. As I later discovered, all members of the Warsaw Rising had been given combatant status as from 26 September. Hence the German soldier who caught us by calling 'come on' either did not know of the ruling or he simply wanted to take revenge for the two months of shameful fighting.[2]

Danuta W.

A Russian helmet has been sighted.
We close the broadcast with victory acclaimed.

The Home Army's station reports
That this last programme has been transmitted.
'Lightning': Warsaw: Victory:
Fraternal Trumpets, and bloody Curses.[162]

The true irony of the poem lies in the fact that it was written not in late September, but in August.

Finale

The talk of capitulation which had been rife in early September now returned. The stalled negotiations were restarted on the 28th. The Home Army side was eager to determine the precise terms and guarantees which might still be on offer. But they were equally determined to call talks off if a Soviet offensive materialized.

Negotiations took place for three hours. Col. 'Zyndram' stubbornly stood his ground against the blandishments of *SS-Ogruf.* von dem Bach. The latter wrote in his diary: 'May the Good Lord give me the same powers of persuasion which worked so well in Mokotov'.[163]

Monter reported that the morale of the soldiers was excellent, but that serious hunger had set in among the civilians. A second round of negotiations took place on the morning of the 29th, to the background of a decisive Panzer assault on Jolibord. Von dem Bach was pressurizing its opponents with a show of son et lumière. Gen. Boor penned a virtual ultimatum to Rokossovsky, giving him a maximum of three days in which to launch an offensive. On the 30th, a third round of negotiations began to address some of the technical problems of a general capitulation. But nothing was signed.

Meanwhile, fighting continued unabated, day after day. In the last week of September, German forces had assaulted all three remaining insurgent islands with renewed vigour. In Mokotov, the storm group of Gen. Rohr broke up the relative calm which had reigned for some time. It was assisted by a hurricane of artillery shelling, mortar fire, and aerial bombardment. The defenders were driven into a small block of barricaded streets, and on the 26th, in the course of a two-hour truce, some 9,000 civilians left the district. On the 27th, the local commander, Lt.Col. 'Charles', decided to take his main force out to the City Centre via the sewers, leaving only a small rearguard behind to cover the retreat. It was a repeat performance of the brilliantly executed withdrawal from the Old Town three weeks earlier.

The northern district of Jolibord was relentlessly attacked during these same days by the German 46th Panzer Corps. The insurgents' refuge shrank to a handful of small streets near the river which guarded the dangerous escape route to the Soviets on the opposite bank. The AK commander applied for permission to surrender, which was reluctantly given. Only the City Centre was holding out in reasonable order. It sheltered the Home Army HQ on Pius XI Street, but even there, isolated but well-fortified German positions constrained freedom of movement. Neither the Domestic Economic Bank on Jerusalem Avenue nor the Parliament Building on the Vistula scarp were ever cleared of their dogged German defenders. What is more, every time that columns of civilian refugees headed for the City Centre to avoid fighting elsewhere, the SS entrenched in the area around Schuch Avenue would seek to mow them down. Yet again, massacres of innocents in the streets accompanied the growing throng of sick, starving, and wounded in the cellars. The Rising was tottering on the brink.

Human endurance has mental as well as physical dimensions. People can withstand stress and injury more effectively if they are mentally resilient, if they can believe in something larger than themselves. For this reason, religion is particularly relevant to the history of the Rising. It was of the greatest importance to many people living in extremis, and facing daily death. Any description of the Rising which does not include the role of religion in the experiences both of soldiers and civilians is not worth reading. As death in all its forms grew ever more prevalent, the Roman Catholic religion, with its emphasis on redemption and its belief in the afterlife, grew ever more relevant. [**CRUCIFIX**, p. 403]

Religious observance stood at an unusually high level throughout the Rising, among both insurgents and civilians. Priests held regular masses in all parts of the city, often in abbreviated open-air services among the ruins. They were on constant call to administer the last rites, and to conduct improvised funerals. The demand for consecrated weddings rose sharply:

> One should not imagine the Rising simply as an endless chain of combats . . . Obviously, fighting went on all the time. But people are people. They had to take a rest from time to time and think of other things. They thought more about Love, and about the survival of Love, about the desire for Love to be sealed by the sacrament, to have the sign of permanence . . .
>
> Lt. 'Hawk' and a [woman] courier had been 'going out together', as we say, before the Rising. They saw each other a little during breaks from the barricades. But now they insisted on a marriage – in the cathedral, of course. The vicar agreed, and the ceremony took place in the evening when the shelling died down. [One of the witnesses] had been wounded in the leg and couldn't walk. But the other witness . . . carried him into the undamaged sacristy on his back. There we joyously celebrated the union of 'Hawk' and 'Halina'. We embraced them both. [Shortly after,] the twenty-three-year-old couple were buried alive during a Stuka attack.[164]

The Home Army Command was conscious of the link between religious practice and military morale. Monter issued detailed instructions on how front-line soldiers could continue to say their prayers, to recite the

CRUCIFIX

A priest rescues a figure of Christ from the burning cathedral

On 17 September a few missiles land simultaneously on the roof of the presbytery and the chapel of the Literary Archconfraternity. The unpleasant smell of benzene permeates the air. Flames swiftly take hold of the wooden trusses of the roof and reach the interior of the chapel. Someone informs Father Ka., at the insurgents' hospital at 7 Long Street, that both the cathedral and his apartment are on fire.

The priest bursts into the cathedral. The flames are raging in the presbytery. Here the most valuable exhibits of the Archdiocese Museum had been assembled. The priest had been carrying them into the cathedral for a few days, in the hope of saving them. Both sides of the presbytery are on fire: the beautiful stalls of Yan Sobieski's chantry, a masterpiece of Polish wood-carving, are splintered. Figures of the Kings of Poland carved from wood and marble crumble into glowing embers, the bloody flames climb the columns of the altar. Wooden sculptures burn like torches. The heat is so great that the iron doors of the sacristy, themselves works of art, become red and melt, as if made from wax. The air is stifling and hot as a baker's oven. It is harder and harder to breathe. The smoke invades the lungs and stings the eyes. The dome over the Barichka chapel is on fire. Clouds of thick black smoke fill the Gothic naves of the cathedral and the window openings explode.

Father Ka. comes in through the back entrance to the Barichka chapel. There is silence here and not even much smoke. The priest faces a decision: should he take the figure of Christ from the chapel or leave it there? If it stays, it will burn with the whole cathedral. But to take Christ from the altar and remove Him from the cathedral where He has been all these centuries? What should he do? Soon the fire will come through the presbytery window. The dome is collapsing. The sacristan is coming. They confer. Father Ka. goes onto the altar and tries in vain to remove the great cross. He only manages at last to remove the figure of Christ and at the moment when he gives it to the Sacristan a huge part of a burning chandelier falls next to him.

Under fire, the priest carries Christ past the ruins of the Royal Castle through Canon Street to the gates of the Jesuit Fathers' monastery, where many inhabitants of the Old Town are gathering. At the sight of the miraculous figure of Christ they fall to their knees and sobs burst forth from all their hearts.

'Christ, Christ . . . Save us!'

They dismantle the figures. They take off the arms. People fall upon them with their lips, then they take Christ onto their shoulders and carry him through the courtyard, a cellar, a passage, and openings knocked through the walls. The small group grows with every step. At the head, a hunched Father Ka. walks on. Someone intones the hymn, 'Whoever places himself under the care of his Lord'. In the Market Square of the Old Town unexploded shells, splinters, and unburied bodies lie scattered far and wide. The enemy is constantly firing on the Square from the Royal Castle. People flit by momentarily by the walls of the tenement houses on the Barss side of the Market Square. They come out onto 'Crooked Circle' and then onto New Town Street. The crowd of people carrying Christ reaches Old Street, and the chapel of the Sisters of Charity. They place the miraculous Christ on the altar. Maybe it will be safe here?

The cathedral is burning like a torch. Any action to save it is futile . . . [But the fighting goes on.] In the evening the Germans approach, nearing the small tenement house on Canon Street. Helmets can be seen through the smoke. Lieutenant 'Roman' from the Vigry Group puts a ladder up to the grated windows of the cathedral. His arm marks out an arc. Then there is the awful explosion of a petrol bomb. The echo spreads around the naves. The Gothic vaulting which has been under strain since the siege of Warsaw, in September 1939, collapses into the middle of the main nave. Bricks, stones, plaster, and sculptures fall to the ground, spattering monuments and altars and destroying the pulpit . . . Lieutenant Roman is injured. Second Lieutenant 'Crow', the commander of the 1st Platoon of the Bomber Company, a journalist by occupation, takes over . . .[1]

---

rosary, and to confess themselves. On 15 August, the Feast of the Assumption, he reminded his subordinates that ways must be found to celebrate all the major religious festivals.

The destruction of churches, which in the early days of the Rising had provided good cover for snipers from both sides, did not deter crowds of the faithful from congregating for Mass in the ruins. To receive the holy sacrament in such circumstances held heightened significance. Priests noted increased attendance at prayer meetings and devotional classes. Members of the religious orders, especially nuns, took the lead in the growing practice of devoting one's time to assisting the Rising exclusively through prayer.

Warsaw's Roman Catholic clergy were drawn into the affairs of the Rising at many levels. Some of them had been appointed chaplains to particular military units, whose pastoral care became their full-time concern. Many more tended the increased needs of non-combatants, especially in the crowded cellars and underground hospitals. The catechizing of children, for example, never stopped. Nuns of various orders, whether accustomed to working 'in the world' or not, acted as universal sisters of mercy and won widespread praise. Mortality among them was higher than among most categories of civilians. When captured by the SS, they aroused a special fury, which frequently ended in rape or butchery.

Father 'Stefan' was one of the hundreds of Home Army chaplains who gained his position by virtue of where he was at a particular moment. Aged thirty-three, he had only been ordained a short time earlier, and had been transferred just before the war to the woodland parish of Laski on Warsaw's northern perimeter. Laski was (and is) a very special place. It is the seat of a religious community that arose from the vision of a more modern and more open brand of Catholicism, which on the one hand is devoted to a practical, compassionate Christianity and on the other to rigorous theological and philosophical debate. It patronized a pioneering institute for the education and social integration of the blind; and it quickly became the resort of artists, intellectuals, and radical Catholics. But in 1944, by chance, it happened to find itself in the area of operations of the Home Army's Kampinos Group. So Father Stefan became a Kampinos chaplain. If he weren't so tall and slim, one might have described him as a latter-day Friar Tuck, ministering to Robin Hood's band 'under the greenwood tree'. As God willed, Father Stefan came through the ordeal unscathed.

The religious orders made a very special contribution to the Rising. Male and female, closed and secular, they had formed an essential part of the community for centuries, and with very few exceptions they stayed. They were joined in their prayers by crowds of lay people and insurgents. The deep cellars and crypts of their ancient cloisters served as hospitals and bomb-shelters. The monks and nuns threw themselves into social work as never before.

The Convent of the Benedictine Sisters of the Perpetual Adoration of the Holy Sacrament, for example, found itself in the front line from the first week of the Rising, when a delegation from the Home Army begged the prioress to admit them and to let them man the walls. Situated on the edge of the New Town, the convent occupied a strategic location, and the prioress lifted the ban on male visitors, which had stood since the foundation of the convent in 1678. On 6 August, the doors were opened to accommodate a mass of refugees from Vola. Under the bombs and the crumbling masonry, the sisters cooked, and served, and tended, and nursed, and prayed. In an act of collective sacrifice, they offered their lives to God, with the plea that their gift be joined with compassion for the homeland. One of them formulated the prayer, 'That Poland, when it resurrects, may be neither white, nor red, but Christlike.' Then the day came when the Germans set an ultimatum: either the sisters evacuate the convent by 3 p.m. or see it destroyed. The prioress turned to the Home Army command, which was lodged in the nearby Church of St Mary the Virgin, and asked for their advice. The response stated that 'the sight of nuns and clergy leaving their posts would be a terrible blow for the soldiers'. So the sisters did not leave. [**VANDALS**, p. 407]

Evening prayers began, as always, with the words: 'In the shadow of Thy wings, O Lord, protect us.' 'Bless this House,' the prayer continued, 'may Thy blessing be with us forever.' 'Greetings, Queen of Heaven,' the antiphon started, 'turn thy gracious eyes towards us, and help us to see God.' The whine of aircraft engines overhead stopped. The sisters huddled around the tabernacle. A long, lingering moment of peace and silence followed. A thousand people did not dare to breathe.

The vault of the church collapsed in one thunderous explosion. Hundreds of tons of massive stones, bricks, tiles, and cement rained down. A whirlwind of flying glass – of beautiful coloured death-dealing glass. A cloud of dense smothering dust. Blinding light above from the open roof. Darkness below, as the church floor caved in. Shrieks. Moans. Shouts. The first coherent voice, that of an officer: 'Easy goes, ladies and gentlemen, that was only a pillar falling.' All evening and all night, rescue teams dug to save the living. Dantean scenes like the worst of earthquakes. A much-diminished convent choir was singing to encourage them. At dawn, a handful of nuns, including the convent's chronicler, filed out. Lines of insurgents saluted. And the German guns reopened fire.[165]

For obvious reasons, every part of the German war machine was pleased by the prospect of capitulation in Warsaw. But different Germans had different motives. *SS-Ogruf.* von dem Bach and his men, for example, undoubtedly looked forward to the end with feelings of utter relief. They were still losing about 150 dead every day and, until recently, had been making painfully slow progress. Their combat effectiveness was assessed by the Ninth Army Command in late September as 'declining'. The Wehrmacht, in contrast, was longing for the day when it could finally consolidate the defences along the whole western bank of the Vistula and build fortifications to oppose all Soviet attempts to storm across the river. It was for this reason that the Ninth Army had lent von dem Bach the services of the crack 19th Panzer Division.

VANDALS

The University Librarian, who did not quit his post, watches German vandals

It was terrible watching the vandals at work. The beautiful furniture of the Chetvertinski Palace was prised apart with crowbars and thrown out of the windows onto the street below, where it was used as barricade material. Paintings torn from the walls met a similar fate, as did magnificent sets of glass and porcelain. An antique Chinese gilded screen was cut up and used as curtains. *OLt.* Schmidt oversaw this operation. The librarians made continual protests against the vandalism – to no avail. From the first moment the pictures came under threat, it was made very clear to us that there was no point trying to take anything to the university library.

'If these bandits', they went on, 'persist in attacking us, we will defend ourselves from these barricades. Then we'll set fire to these buildings and move to the library, then we'll burn down the library . . . The whole of Warsaw will be destroyed whether or not they attack . . .'

This happened at the end of the first week of September. The gang of criminals who had carried out the hospital massacre in Vola was sent in to the university for a few days. The officer in charge of the on-site garrison that day, despite the availability of other empty buildings, placed them in the library. Two hours later the offices and reading-rooms, and even parts of the storerooms, were unrecognizable. Tables had been smashed up, papers from drawers and cupboards were strewn about the floor. In the offices, stacks of books awaiting cataloguing had been taken to make window barricades for the defence of the whole building. The criminals tore up other books and defecated on the pages. Engravings and atlases taken from display cases on the ground floor received the same treatment. It began to look like some thieves' magic ritual . . . Within a few days the administrative and reading-room section of the library had been turned into a giant cesspit . . .

On 10 September an SS man turned up and declared that the next day he would be coming 'on the Führer's instructions' to take away the best items from the collections.

The books were loaded into crates lined at the librarians' request with waxed paper. The crates, labelled 'W-1', were nailed shut. This is how all the old publications from room 28, together with most of the Tolochanov collection housed there, were packed and taken away. In all, four lorries took away about 200 crates, in other words about 5,000 volumes.[1]

Only the Nazis, however, took real delight at the thought of Warsaw's fall. In late 1944, they already suspected that the war could not be won even by the *Führer*'s 'wonder weapons'. Equally, they had no reason to suppose that a compromise peace could be arranged, or, if it did, that they would escape retribution. In effect, they were doomed. But, before they went down in flames, they could still complete several of the plans that were closest to their hearts. They could still kill off the remaining 'subhumans' who were within their reach; and they could kill off this accursed capital on the Vistula that had repeatedly defied them. Warsaw was the central city of the *Lebensraum* which they had set out to Germanize. Germanization had not gone too well. But wiping out the Varsovians would represent a lasting achievement, the subject of savage joy.

Certainly, the top authorities of the Reich were assuming that the Rising was virtually over. On 30 September, Hitler awarded high decorations to three leading commanders in Warsaw. Von dem Bach and Oskar Dirlewanger received the Knight's Cross of the Iron Cross. *SS-Gruf.* Reinefarth was singled out, as the 608th German soldier so rewarded, to receive the superior Oak Leaves to the Knight's Cross of the Iron Cross. In one of its rare communiqués from Warsaw, Radio Berlin made a report that sounded like the Rising's obituary as well as an unintended tribute to the insurgents. 'It is a grim and merciless struggle,' the correspondent said, 'which surpasses the imagination of even the most hardened German stormtroopers. The soldiers of the Underground movement are blinded by fanaticism and fight like madmen. If German sappers had not brought in every single weapon in their arsenal, the contest would be hopeless.'[166] For Radio Berlin to talk publicly of 'soldiers of the underground movement' was a distinct novelty.

It is significant that von dem Bach drew up detailed plans for the general evacuation of Warsaw on 30 September, without waiting for an agreement with the Home Army to be signed.[167] The German Command was confident not just that the end was nigh, but that the end could be accelerated.

Von dem Bach, newly decorated, sent a special report to Himmler:

> Reichsführer! Today the 19th Panzer Division, strengthened by two regiments from von dem Bach's corps, captured four-fifths of Jolibord. As a result of my talks with General [Boor], the Polish commander of Jolibord surrendered at 19.40. Prisoners 800, killed 1,000, evacuated civilians 15,000.

Von dem Bach, at last, was pleased with himself.

The Polish Government in London stood to lose most. If Warsaw fell, it was their capital which would be lost; it was their Underground army which would be decimated; it was their political enemies who would steal their inheritance; and it would be their reputation that would be ruined. It would be they, 'the reckless, foolish authors of the fiasco', who would be blamed. [**WITNESS**, p. 410]

The fate of the Commander-in-Chief had hung in the balance throughout September. On the 30th, after days of dithering, the President curtly informed the Commander-in-Chief of his dismissal. Simultaneously, and without warning, he appointed Gen. Boor as the replacement. In a radio telegram to Boor, he apologized for the lack of consultation. 'I believe that the time will come', he wrote, 'when Providence will permit you to execute your duties.'[168] This was asking much of Providence. One can only assume that the President preferred to have no active Commander-in-Chief other than a nominee of the faction who had forced out his friend. For Boor had no chance in the foreseeable future of assuming his post. If the Rising collapsed, he was going to be taken prisoner by the Germans. If the Rising didn't collapse, it could only be saved by the Soviets, who were hardly going to give him a free hand: that is, if they chose not to throw him to the Polish Communists, who were demanding to put him on trial.

In a farewell letter to his soldiers, the departing Commander-in-Chief praised his successor. 'The heroic Gen. Boor,' he wrote, 'the long-term Commander of the Home Army, has won the deepest respect in every soldier's heart, through his superhuman actions. May Warsaw's bloody ordeal move the conscience of the world, and inspire the triumph of law and justice.'[169] The British press on Sunday, 1 October, expressed the widespread view and pious hope that the Commander-in-Chief's removal would facilitate an improvement in Polish–Soviet relations.

Also on 30 September, the Premier addressed a final appeal to Moscow:

> To Marshal Stalin – Moscow
>
> Your Excellency,
>
> After sixty days of relentless fighting against the common enemy, the defenders of Warsaw have reached the limits of human endurance . . . At this extreme hour of need, I appeal to you,

WITNESS

Three witnesses provide conflicting accounts of the fate of Jews in the Warsaw Rising

I know that Jews played a large role in the Warsaw Rising. In our company in the Old Town there were a dozen or so people (Jews) of semitic appearance, but no one paid this any attention. There was not one incident when someone was victimized or badly treated. As for me and my friend Adam R., our commander knew of our origins.

The following episode is typical. On 7 August 1944, at the start of the Rising, Captain K. chose Adam R. and me as the most reliable and trustworthy people to escort the delegation from the London government on an important mission from the Old Town to the centre.

Another incident illustrates the relationship between the Home Army command and Jews in our unit. One day, it was decreed that document checks and personal searches would be carried out on anyone moving between the Old Town and other neighbourhoods. During one of these checks, a Walther revolver was found on a Jewish man, the type used before the Rising exclusively by members of the Gestapo and Kripo. He had a pass book from the Jewish Fighting Organization (ŻOB). This organization, with a strength of a dozen or so people (the rest were survivors from the Warsaw Ghetto), fought at the side of a larger insurgent group. In the beginning, the [Underground] gendarmerie did not believe him. When our commander found out, he summoned me to him and after verifying ŻOB's existence, he intervened to release the man. After that his weapon was returned and he was issued with a pass entitling him to move freely within the Old Town.[1]

Efraim K.

Ignatius B., a director of Phillips in Lodz, his wife Esther, eleven-year-old daughter Noemi, his sister, and her daughter hid with others in the few weeks before the [Rising] in a bunker at 4 Straight Street. In the third or fourth week of the Uprising a few insurgents came into the bunker and ordered the six men there to accompany them to Headquarters. They led them only as far as the gateway and the insurgents' lieutenant told them, 'Gentlemen, you are Jews, waiting for the Bolsheviks. The Bolsheviks will come but you will not see them,' and he gave his people the order to shoot all six of them. The bodies were thrown into a shallow grave, hollowed out by a missile close to the house. Then they went into the bunker and shot the remaining women on the spot.

Abram, brother of the murdered Ignatius, usually stayed with the family in the bunker, but by chance had gone out. When he went down into the cellar and heard murmuring, he retreated and hid. He reported a blow-by-blow account of the events, but then discovered that insurgents from the Valiant Group had carried out the murders.

In liberated Warsaw, Abram B. recovered the remains of his family and buried them in the Jewish cemetery in Warsaw on Trench Street.[2]

[2 September]

The Germans were telling people to surrender, and encouraged by fear we raised the white flag. Women and children were immediately segregated, and of the rest, six of us were sent to Krashinski Square. On the way, I noticed a group of six priests and twenty Jews talking in Yiddish and Hungarian. The insurgents expressed pride and admiration for the Jews' activities during the Rising. Those Jews freed from the Ghetto (probably from Goose Farm) were completely indifferent as to whether they lived or died.

After working on Krashinski Square, from where I had seen the Germans shoot their way into the insurgents' hospital at 7 Long Street, we were marched up to Leshno Street. In the exit of the former gateway of the Ghetto, a Gestapo officer stopped us. Nineteen Jewish insurgents were led in ranks into the courtyard of 89 Iron Street, where the Gestapo officer put a bullet in each of their heads. After this shooting, another group of twenty-two Jews was led in, including an old woman of nearly seventy. The Nazi thug shot her. I noticed no signs of resistance either among the unarmed Jews, or the unarmed Poles. In the afternoon, we were marched towards Vola. As I passed 89 Iron Street, I saw clouds of smoke where the bodies of the forty-one murdered Jewish insurgents were burning.[3]

Stefan S.

> Marshal, to issue orders for immediate operations that would relieve the garrison of Warsaw and result in the liberation of the capital. Gen. [Boor] has addressed the same appeal to Marshal Rokossovsky.[170]

Westminster and Washington watched the agony of the Rising with sorrow and bewilderment. The people with inside information may have known what part the Western powers had played in the tragedy. But the majority were simply baffled by their First Ally's bad luck. As Churchill's deputy, Clement Attlee, had remonstrated, when appealed to by a delegation of desperate Polish socialists: 'What more could we have done?'

British and American experts in political warfare knew one thing that could be done. With skilful management, the damage could be limited. For the duration of the war solidarity with the Soviet Union had to be maintained at all costs. So, in the organs under official control, the action or inaction of the Soviets was not to be discussed. The Poles should be praised for their courage. Their leaders were to be blamed for their irresponsibility. [**SWIMMER**, p. 413]

His Majesty's Government, however, did not escape completely unscathed. On 26 September, Churchill faced a couple of questions in the House of Commons about the meagre assistance to the Rising, and he provided the stock answer. He paid tribute 'to the heroism and tenacity of the Polish Home Army', before pleading that everything possible had been done. He drew special attention to the operation of the US Flying Fortresses which had taken place in the previous week.

The House was evidently not satisfied. On the following day, the Foreign Secretary faced a much more hostile and damaging barrage of questions: And he was reduced to wriggling like a snake with its tail in a trap:

MAJ-GEN. SIR ALFRED KNOX (C) asked . . . what reason was given by the Government of the USSR for their refusal of permission for RAF planes to land in Soviet territory after dropping munitions and supplies for the patriot forces in Warsaw.

THE SECRETARY OF STATE FOR FOREIGN AFFAIRS (MR EDEN) There has never been any question of aircraft of the Royal Air Force undertaking such shuttle flights to bases in Soviet territory . . .

SIR A. KNOX: Is it not a fact that by repeated broadcasts from Moscow the Soviet Government urged the Underground Army to rise . . . and that by September 14, six weeks later, they had still not given permission for Allied aircraft to land . . . and that, therefore, they rendered the position of the Polish forces tragic?

SIR JOHN WARDLAW-MILNE (C): May I urge my Rt. Hon. Friend . . . to make the [Prime Minister's] statement yesterday very widely public, because there is a very erroneous impression in this country about what has been done by our Forces?

MR EDEN: I think that there is very good cause for my hon. Friend's supplementary . . . I think that I can also say that H.M.G. did everything in their power to bring about unity and understanding in this matter between our Allies.

SWIMMER

A soldier of the Zoshka Battalion, trapped on the Cherniakov Bridgehead, swims the Vistula

A hopeless situation. The heavily injured are strewn around in basements. Indeed no one is doing anything for them. There are no bandages, there is no medicine, there is nowhere even to put them . . . Starvation, lack of water . . . From early morning, the Germans are letting fly storm after storm, wanting to liquidate this already microscopic bridgehead . . .

The radiotelegraphic operator, just before the batteries had run out at noon, received news from the headquarters of the First Army. Under cover of fierce artillery fire, rowing boats would arrive and take us away from this hell in the evening. Only that these hours drag on so painfully slowly . . .

At last darkness is falling . . . Crawling, we reach the very bank of the Vistula, via Solec Street. There are only guard outposts. We gather by the half-sunken boat, the *Fairytale.* This is where the rowing boats are to arrive. Up to now barely three have arrived, and one of them was only a kayak . . . There is no hope that more will arrive. On the *Fairytale* an incredible throng mills around. Captain 'George' tries to establish some order . . .

The Germans realized that we had left Vilanov Street, but the noise coming from the *Fairytale* told them the right direction to fire . . .

Again someone approaches George. It is 'Vitold' with Major L. L. wants to send a messenger to the other side of the Vistula, to report our tragic situation to the headquarters of the First Army, and to ask them to send a rowing boat at any price. The messenger had to be able to swim across the river. The chances of success are minimal. At least three people should attempt the swim, so at least one might make it . . .

George expressed his agreement. But who will swim?

Vitold made up his mind. He also suggested me and 'Kurp' . . .

We arm ourselves with carbines and grenades and, bending down low to the ground, we move without a sound along the very banks, right alongside the stream. We do not know where the German outposts are. We are moving extremely cautiously. Along the way we pass a whole pile of corpses. They were daredevils, who had tried to swim the Vistula before us.

Here we jump, or rather slip into the water . . . Vitold first, me second, and Kurp last. The current of the Vistula pulled me away violently . . . I drew back my injured hand sharply, wrenched off the sling, and began to part the water strongly and rhythmically. I overcame the strongest current . . . I raise my head – I look for my companions. I cannot see them.

I call: 'Stefan! Vitold!'

Kurp gives a sign of life. We swim towards each other. He has been shot in the leg. We shout, 'Vitold.' No sign of him. Maybe he drowned.

Whistling bullets hit the water. I dive . . . Slowly, metre by metre, we distance ourselves from burning Warsaw. We are approaching the middle of the Vistula, there is supposed to be a sandbank . . .

At last I can feel the sand. The water comes up to my chest, but we squat down, so that only our heads are visible. The sky is hellishly bright from searchlights and rockets. The sound of gunfire resounds in all directions, illuminating the depths of the sea. Kurp and I hold hands. In that way, it is easier for us to walk against the current . . . The water gets deeper and deeper. The sandbank breaks off. We start to swim again, straight towards the bank . . .

All of a sudden something explodes . . . The Germans have dropped a fire barrier of grenades on the Praga bank . . . I am losing hope . . . But I can already touch the ground with my feet. Holding each other up, we flounder ahead. At last, the hard, dry bank. We are safe . . .[1]

Stanisław Krupa

SIR A. KNOX: Is it not a fact that the Soviet Government refused to give permission until September 14?

MR EDEN: My hon. and gallant Friend is asking me why one of our Allies did not give assistance to another of our Allies . . . but I would prefer to give consideration to my reply.

At that point, the temperature of the debate rose perceptibly:

SIR A. KNOX: . . . Is [the Secretary of State] aware that members of the Polish Underground Army, who, under orders from the Polish Government, have co-operated with Soviet forces in the liberation of their country, have been arrested and deported by the Soviet authorities . . .?

MR EDEN: Yes, Sir. My attention has been drawn to the reports to which [you] refer, and I have brought them to the notice of the Soviet Government. The latter have now informed me that they do not consider that these reports give a true picture of events . . . [The Secretary of State did not disclose that his attention had been drawn to the matter on 29 July, eight full weeks earlier.]

SIR A. KNOX: Is it not true that several individuals have been arrested and deported because they refused to take the oath of allegiance to the so-called Committee of Liberation?

MR EDEN: As I have said, as soon as these reports were brought to my notice, I brought them to the notice of the Soviet Government, as I thought it my duty to do . . .

EARL WINTERTON (C): Is it not a fact that my Rt. Hon Friend cannot be responsible for differences of opinion between our Allies . . .

MR MCGOVERN (I.L.P.) Does the Rt. Hon. Gentleman think that there is anything to be gained by covering up the fact that an Ally of ours is both shooting and deporting Nationalists and Socialists in Poland?

MR EDEN: . . . I must tell the House that not only are these affairs of delicacy between Allies, but also that there is some difficulty in establishing the facts . . .

Despite a number of interventions that sought to get Eden off the hook, the questioning grew 'warmer and warmer':

COMMANDER SIR ARCHIBALD SOUTHBY (C): While it is true that these are matters of delicacy, are not matters concerning our responsibility to our ally, Poland, also matters of principle?

MR EDEN: Yes, Sir, and our responsibility has been fully, and I might add gallantly, discharged.

MR ASTOR (C): Are there not liaison officers on the spot, from whom the Government gets information?

MR EDEN: We have been supplied with information from Warsaw; but perhaps my hon. Friend will put that question down.

As Eden well knew, Britain had not a single liaison or intelligence officer in Warsaw. But he was using the conventional appeal to national security to avoid a direct answer. Churchill was sitting alongside in silence.

COMMANDER BOWER: . . . Would the Prime Minister make a full statement on the matter?

THE DEPUTY PRIME MINISTER (MR ATTLEE) (LAB): I would refer [you] to the statement which was made yesterday . . .

COMMANDER BOWER: . . . The public have heard a great deal of rumour, very few facts and an absolute spate of extremely tendentious Communist propaganda . . .

MR ATTLEE: I cannot agree . . .

MR GALLACHER (COMM.): Is it not the case that, instead of a campaign of

Communist propaganda, we heard a tendentious campaign of anti-Communist propaganda?

COMMANDER BOWER (C) asked the Minister of Information to what extent restriction of publication of reports on the Polish Rising in early August was imposed . . . either by prohibition or request.

PARLIAMENTARY SECRETARY TO THE MINISTRY OF INFORMATION, MR THURTLE: No restriction was imposed nor any request to this effect made by the Ministry of Information.

COMMANDER BOWER: Are we then to assume that by some peculiar feat of telepathy almost the entire press of this country held up this extremely important information for several days?

MR THURTLE: . . . We have nothing at all to do with it . . .

MR PETHERICK (C): Has the Ministry of Information made no such representations to any of the Service Departments?

MR THURTLE: I am unable to speak for the Service Departments.[171]

On 2 October, Churchill received the Polish Premier in person, to hear the news that Warsaw was about to surrender. He would later be presented with a translation of the Homeland Council's final appeal:

> This is the stark truth. We were treated worse than Hitler's satellites, worse than Italy, Romania, Finland. May God, who is just, pass judgement on the terrible injustice visited on the Polish nation, and may He punish accordingly all those who are guilty.
>
> Your heroes are the soldiers whose only weapons against tanks were revolvers and bottles of petrol . . . Your heroes are the women who tended the wounded, cooked in bombed-out cellars . . . and comforted the dying. Your heroes are the children who went on playing in the ruins . . .
>
> Immortal is the nation that can muster such universal heroism. For those who have died have conquered, and those who live will fight, will conquer and will bear witness again that POLAND HAS NOT PERISHED YET, SO LONG AS WE STILL LIVE.[172]

'These words', wrote Churchill in his memoirs, 'are indelible'.

In Washington, US officials were informed that the Frantic flight scheduled for 2 October had been 'disapproved' by the local Soviet ESCOM. 'Disapproved' presumably meant approved and then cancelled. The reason given by the Soviets was said to be that 'the Warsaw partisans have been evacuated.'[173] Since it derived from the previous day, if not earlier, it was not true. As researchers in the Polish files in the Roosevelt Library may discover, little on Poland follows until 1945.

Commentaries on Soviet conduct in the last week of September 1944 do not concentrate on the Vistula front. To the north, Cherniakovsky's armies had almost overrun the Baltic States and were poised to overrun East Prussia and thereby to invade the Reich. To the south, Tolbukhin was deep into Hungary and approaching Budapest. In Slovakia, the battles were still raging. But on the Vistula, most sectors were eerily quiet. The Soviet bridgehead at Magnushev still held, but had not been enlarged. The pressure on the fortress at Modlin at the junction of the Vistula and Narev had been kept up; but had not been pushed to a conclusion. The line of the mid-Vistula had been fully occupied; but it had stayed static. To observers watching these developments in the West, it was becoming obvious that Stalin had already taken a strategic decision to give priority to occupying Eastern Europe and to postpone the march on Berlin.

Yet the aims of Stalin's deeply ambiguous intentions with regard to Poland remained obscure. The Soviet armies had occupied a belt of land to the east of Warsaw representing perhaps one quarter of the territory which Moscow was prepared to recognize as Polish. But they had not attempted to go further. The Lublin Committee had been given considerable legal, administrative, and military functions. But it had not been raised to the formal status of a Government-in-waiting. It was all very perplexing. Moscow had made no secret of its view that the future of Poland was vital to Soviet security, indeed that Poland was more important than any of the other countries east of Germany. Yet little progress was being made compared to, say, Romania, where a Soviet-backed multi-party Government had already been installed, or Bulgaria, where similar developments were in hand. One could have been forgiven for wondering what exactly Stalin was waiting for. The answer, almost certainly, since Poland was a Western ally, was Western acquiescence.

The local deadlock in the environs of Warsaw reflected this waiting game. Rokossovsky did not reply to Boor's final plea either favourably or unfavourably. Stalin did not respond to the Premier's last letter. Three scenarios are conceivable. One of them suggests that Stalin had decided in mid-August to let the Rising be crushed and that he was now sitting back and watching his plan come to fruition. The second suggests a lesser degree of devilish cunning, where, having permitted a limited measure of aid to the

Rising, he was now perplexed by Berling's defeat. The third suggests that the Rising had posed Moscow with too many uncertainties for a coherent policy to emerge. Scenario 1 implies a conspiracy. Scenarios 2 and 3 imply a long series of mix-ups. Historians, deprived of documentation, may take their pick. All one can say is that Stalin was no stranger to foul conspiracies, and that the sealed and secretive Soviet system was tailor-made for mix-ups. There could have been a lethal combination of both. The main point remains: Rokossovsky did not move, even when he could have done.

Following the insurgents' surrender in Jolibord, a small group of about fifty people connected with the People's Army refused to give up. On the evening of the 30th, having summoned Soviet artillery cover, they made a rush for the river. Almost half of them were felled by German fire. The rest managed to reach the far shore. Among them was Comrade K., who had a prominent career in front of him. [**LOGISTICS**, p. 419]

Capt. Kolos also made ready to recross the Vistula and to report to Rokossovsky. He buried his radio, but took some documents with him. According to his own account, the documents were proof that Boor was in treasonable contact with the German command and was preparing to hand over Warsaw to the Nazis. Kolos had evidently got wind of the unconcluded capitulation talks, and had put the worst possible interpretation on them. In this, he was following normal Soviet practice. On 1 October, with the help of AL guides, he found his way through the sewers to the riverfront, and successfully reached the opposite shore. He was greeted by Rokossovsky with the award of the Red Banner. On the following evening, by a pre-arranged signal, he informed his comrades in the People's Army that he had arrived safely. Those flashing lights in the dark were the last sign of human contact from the Soviet side.

Marshal Georgii Zhukov, Stalin's military deputy, arrived on the Vistula sector 'at the end of September'. He had spent the previous month in Bulgaria, and had now been sent to weigh up the situation before Warsaw. His arrival was in itself an indication of uncertainties in the Soviet Command at a juncture when the Cherniakov Bridgehead had been abandoned but the insurgents had not capitulated. 'At the beginning of October' – persumably on the 1st or 2nd – he visited the Soviet Forty-Seventh Army, which was taking heavy casualties in its attempts to cross the River Narev to the north of Warsaw. And he ordered it to assume defensive positions. He was immediately ordered to fly to Moscow the very next day, and to take Rokossovsky with him.

As later described by Zhukov, the ensuing military conference in the

LOGISTICS

A professional historian and insurgent examines one of the enduring puzzles of the Rising

One of the things that still evokes the deepest admiration and amazement is the question of how the insurgents managed to arm and supply themselves. Initially Monter had counted on the possibility of waging battle for two or three days, partly because there were insufficient weapons and ammunition. Yet the battle was protracted for sixty-three days.

It is worth citing statistics from a description that emerged in a POW camp, penned by two officers of the Home Army Headquarters Bureau for Information . . . in the face of other details, published by Adam B. Commander Monter, on the day prior to the outbreak of the Uprising, in the city of Warsaw and the surrounding area, had at his command in the region of 45,000 soldiers; perhaps there were even a few more, up to 50,000. Of these armed men, 600 platoons were led to fight on the left bank of the Vistula, including around 41,000 people of whom certainly only 100 platoons were fully armed. The People's Army (AL) provided him with another 4 battalions of 800 people. The Security Corps (KB) provided the Home Army with a few less – around 600.

. . .

Home Army numbers could undoubtedly be increased many fold by the Rising mobilization, mainly volunteers; however, the problem of arming them arose, a problem with no solution in the political-military conditions of the Home Army. Arms came from four sources. The first was weapons hidden in 1939; in general deceptive, which consisted of a minimal amount of equipment that was still fit to use in war. The second source was supplies dropped for the Home Army by the English from their bases in Italy and England; the drops were valuable as regards quality but even so yielded little. The third source was captured German weapons. Finally the fourth source – the production of the Underground's own workshops.

The state of armament on 1 August can be reconstructed, but with great difficulty. As a rough figure, I would say that Monter had about 7 heavy machine guns, 60 assault rifles, 20 anti-tank guns, 1,000 guns, 300 sub-machine guns (30 per cent of them were home-made, Lightning and Sten), around 25,000 grenades, 95 per cent of which were home-made, and – more or less – around 1,750 pistols. Apart from the Warsaw Region Headquarters' depot, there was a reserve of weapons at the disposal of the Headquarters. On the day before the Rising broke out, it supplied Commander Monter with 100 sub-machine guns and ammunition.

Our homemade flame-throwers also turned out to be quite effective – during the Uprising over 100 were produced . . . Street fighting and fighting against tanks required the mass production of petrol bombs – over 100,000 were produced. The grenade became an equally aggressive defence, especially those produced by the Underground. It had at its disposal a certain reserve of explosive materials, mainly easily transportable English plastic explosives.

The provision of ammunition was the weakest link in the weapons-supply chain. On the second day of the Rising, Monter counted on using it up within the next forty-eight hours if the current intensity of battle raged on. If the Rising were to last, however, another sixty days, the ammunition base would not have been drops (which fell mainly towards the end of the action), but captures from the enemy. The most significant were in the Cedergren building (telephone switchboard), the Post Office building, and among the reserves, of particular divisions and soldiers. These had not been declared to the underground, but were jealously guarded. They were concealed, for the purpose of settling accounts, mainly with the Germans.

During the battle in Warsaw and its surroundings, the insurgents captured a great deal – 4 tanks, 2 armoured vehicles, 1 75mm field gun, 12 mine throwers, 4 light anti-tank guns, over 200 Panzerfausts [anti-tank weapons], 16 heavy machine guns, 86 assault rifles, 155 sub-machine guns, 596 repeater rifles and ammunition for particular weapons, but of a limited nature. The insurgents supplemented their weapons with homemade ones and from drops. In the City Centre 36 tonnes were collected, 16 tonnes from an American drop – mostly anti-tank weapons, sub-machine guns, somewhat heavy weapons.

From 13 September Soviet drops began, every night; they delivered about 150 tonnes. However, there was still not enough. Weapons, whatever their quality, were expensive. Because the riflemen were exceedingly good shots, the Germans suffered twice as many killed as injured, whereas in the normal course of battle it is the other way round. For this reason, the German side thought that there were great reserves of ammunition in the City Centre. The fact is, in addition to all the other factors, the glaring lack of ammunition provided yet another reason for capitulation.[1]

Alexander Gieysztor

Kremlin, on either 2 or 3 October, revealed 'a dispute'. The two marshals, hot-foot from the Vistula, were confronted by 'a restless Stalin' and by a suspicious Molotov:

MOLOTOV: Comrade Zhukov, you are proposing that the offensive be stopped now when the defeated enemy is unable to stand up to our pressure. Is that sensible?

ZHUKOV: We are suffeirng unjustifiably heavy losses.

STALIN, to Rokossovsky: Do you share Zhukov's opinion?

ROKOSSOVSKY: Yes.

STALIN: But what if we support 47 Army with aviation and reinforce it with artillery and armour? Will it be able to reach the Vistula between Modlin and Warsaw?

ROKOSSOVSKY: It is hard to say, Comrade Stalin . . .

STALIN, to Zhukov: And what do you think?

ZHUKOV My opinion is that this offensive will yield us nothing but casualties.[174]

Thereon, the marshals were abrupty dismissed whilst the decision was made. After twenty minutes, Stalin announced that the offensive would be called off. Next day, he replaced Rokossovsky with Zhukov as commander of the First Byelorussian Front.

If Zhukov's unverified account is to be believed, no mention was made at this meeting of the Rising, which in all probability was still in progress. One presumes that the Soviet leaders no longer rated it an important factor. But it is impossible to say for sure.

Soviet authors are not strong on the unvarnished truth. Zhukov assigns only a few sentences to 'an uprising in the city', whose outcome he blames exclusively on the failings of General Boor. He even suggests (most unfairly) that the withdrawal of Berling's troops from the Cherniakov Bridgehead (which he calls 'the Warsaw Embankment') was due to Boor making 'no attempt to contact them.' Most telling is the fact that Zhukov's *Memoirs* are completely silent about the critical period between the last week of July, when he watched the two crossings of the Vistula south of Warsaw, and the last week of August, when he left for Bulgaria.

Much, therefore, remains obscure. One can see that Stalin held his marshals on a very tight rein. Yet one can't learn the motives and reasonings behind key moves. A historical note may not be irrelevant. Of course, 'the Battle for Warsaw' in 1944 was not a repeat performance of the 'the Battle of Warsaw' of 1920. But there were numerous parallels. In late July 1944, Stalin had insisted that Zhukov secure Lvuv before moving on to the Vistula. This was one of the manoeuvres which Stalin himself had failed to attempt twenty-four years before. The repulse of Rokossovsky's armies at the gates of Warsaw in early August was not unlike the repulse of the two Soviet armies, which had once approached the city from the east in exactly the same sector. And the Forty-Seventh Army's offensive to the north of Warsaw in late September, which Stalin and Molotov were obviously keen to pursue once the Rising was out of the way, also had a precedent. It was following exactly the same line that Tukhachevsky took in 1920 immediately prior to his calamitous defeat. The two elements which Stalin might have been looking for in 1944, by analogy to his earlier experience, but which were *not* present, could have been further sources of unease. One was an Interallied Military Mission that would have been pulling strings from behind the scene. The other was a hidden counter-force, like that of Piłsudski's, which might strike without warning. To Stalin's suspicious mind, the best policy in such circumstances was one of caution.

On the right bank of the Vistula, Lt.Gen. Telegin was still watching. His report of 3 October summarized the events of the previous week. He assumed that the insurgents were going to capitulate. Prisoners were coming in thick and fast; but he was still at pains to establish the balance in numbers and influence between the AK and the AL. Having talked with several AK officers, he was also trying to examine their claims that their meetings with their Soviet counterparts, and their attempts to agree on cooperation, went back to 14 July. But he sturdily maintained that the Home Army's political 'agitation' had pointed to the intention of fighting the Soviets, not the Germans. Their slogan, he said, was 'Germany is defeated. The Bolshevik – a stronger foe – remains.'[175]

Soviet political reports of the high Stalinist period were evidently written in accordance with formulas for which historians of the Warsaw Rising have not yet discovered the key. It may be, given the terrible purges of the late 1930s, that the authors were so petrified by the deadly consequences of expressing honest opinions, that they deliberately resorted to writing nonsense. It is more likely that they were constrained to operate within rigid political and ideological conventions, and that all individual or divergent comments had to be cloaked in phrases and devices whose purpose remains largely unintelligible to the uninitiated. What on earth was Comrade Telegin doing, one might ask, when he told Moscow that Gen. Berling had once been in the Home Army and that his commission had been arranged by Stalin? At one level, he was talking patent claptrap, even if he had mistaken the Home Army for the pre-war Polish Army. Yet at another level, simply by associating Berling with the great Stalin, he was doing Berling a huge favour; and by throwing the Home Army into the package, he could have been hinting that the AK was not too bad either. In the context of Berling's dispute with the Polish Communists, it does begin to look less idiotic. In the meantime, one may be sure that nothing written by Telegin or Serov was conducive to a more magnanimous stance towards the outside world. Nothing they said would have speeded a compromise with Premier Mick. International negotiations were not within their remit.

In the best of times, it is no simple matter first to arrange the separation of two bitterly bloodied armies and then to negotiate an orderly surrender. To do so in the middle of a ruined city full of desperate civilians, and in conditions where one party had been committing mass atrocities for months, required supreme nerve and judgement. *SS-Ogruf.* von dem Bach seemed to assume that the Home Army negotiators would simply click their heels and accept his dictates. They did nothing of the sort. They might well have submitted to exhaustion, to the apparent hopelessness of their plight, to the strains of bilingual exchanges or to the hostile environment of von dem Bach's headquarters. Instead they performed as resolutely at the bargaining table as on the barricades.

The start of proceedings was necessarily ragged. In two or three places, AK commanders had been forced into a local truce or surrender, which Monter was then obliged to disavow. And the first round of general talks, on 29 September, got nowhere. Von dem Bach chose to present his terms in the form of an ultimatum. If they weren't taken up immediately, he blustered, the city would be annihilated together with everyone in it. Since he had been failing to do this for weeks, he cut no ice. [**CEASEFIRE**, p. 424]

That evening, a decisive meeting of the Home Army Command was convened in the wrecked General Telephone building on Pius XI Street. The chief negotiator, Lt.Col. Zyndram, reported on his earlier exchanges with von dem Bach. Gen. Monter summarized the state of his troops with maximum optimism – 'morale exemplary', 'defensive positions good', 'ammunition and weapons generally satisfactory, sufficient for several days' intensive fighting', 'food supplies critical'. He foresaw that his soldiers would only lose heart if the civilian population were evacuated without them.

There followed a powerful speech from the Chief Government Delegate, offering the opposite opinion:

CEASEFIRE

A soldier of the Parasol Battalion is surprised by the silence of the ceasefire

2 October. The square in front of the Polytechnic is empty and quiet. I spent several hours watching the site from our vantage points: on the right, the main entrance to the Polytechnic, and straight ahead the hospital buildings occupied by the Germans. Further away, a small chapel where before the Rising candles used to be lit. On our side barricaded houses.

This peace is deceptive. Next to the Polytechnic and the hospital, the Germans have grouped machine guns in bunkers that keep the square in cross-fire. But now it is quiet. Strange things are taking place. On the German side a group of officers enters the square with a white flag. On our side, a group of people come forward with a white rug attached to a stick: a mixture of officers and civilians. They walk across the square with the Germans and disappear round the corner . . .

3 October. The ceasefire has been agreed for sure. We have the details. It has been officially confirmed that we are Allied soldiers. We shall leave with our guns and banners. We are to be solely under the Wehrmacht's control; prisoners of war according to the Geneva Convention. Unbelievable . . .

Weird atmosphere in our unit. The remains of the food supplies were handed out for a decent meal. The unit's cash has been distributed. I've ended up with 1,500 zloties. We were also promised some American dollars, but it never happened. The guns are the major problem. We have to hand them to the Germans. I can't contemplate saying goodbye to my Sten. I imagined the end would be different . . .

I talk to my colleagues about it . . . If we surrender without the guns they will think we have hidden them and might persecute us. One of my colleagues has a completely different view: those who are caught with guns are going to be shot dead. Eventually I buried my Sten with its magazine in a basement. And one of my colleagues presented me with an old pre-war gun with no lock.

We have to get ready for our march into captivity. I attach a small potato sack to my nice leather braces as a makeshift rucksack. It previously held hand grenades. It's not easy to find a blanket but I managed to get a warm sweater, and I bought a decent overcoat with my 1,500 zloties. Most importantly I have my silver spoon. You never know when some soup will come a soldier's way . . .[1]

Preparing to join the evacuees, General Boor's adjutant meets people already thinking of the future

Everyone was preparing to leave. They were going into the unknown. [But] walking through the ruins, I met a colleague, Stanislas D., who was a town planner by profession. 'Call on me tomorrow,' he said, 'I have something for you.'

Next day, I went to his house, and found another planner there, Casimir M. I saw how the two of them were already thinking of the city's restoration. Casimir, on a large sheet of paper, was sketching out the residential district of Muranov to be built on the ruins of the Ghetto. And Stan handed me a draft of *Outlines of a Programme for Warsaw's Reconstruction*, which he had knocked out on a surviving typewriter. I was surprised by the precision of his formulations, and by his unbreakable belief. The draft had been composed amidst the smouldering rubble of destruction. He gave it me, because he did not know for whom he had written it, but thought it might be useful. I remember thinking – how good to be a planner.[2]

> Further fighting has no sense. It's madness. Politically, we have achieved a great deal. Yet, since we have not received the assistance expected, we should save what is most dear to us, namely, the biological substance of the nation. This is all the more important because the whole cultural and scientific elite of society is concentrated in Warsaw. We won't be able to salvage much from the fabric of the capital, which as Gen. von dem Bach assures us, will become the scene of battles between the Germans and the Soviets. So we should aim to save our people at least. I am in favour of ending the struggle.[176]

The phrase 'the biological substance of the nation' passed into legend.

Summing up, Gen. Boor concluded that negotiations should resume, especially on civilian issues, but that no final commitment should be made. (Shortly afterwards, the large AK group in the Kampinos Forest surrendered unilaterally. On the 30th, the northern enclave followed suit.) Yet, from the purely military point of view, much remained that could be defended. A quarter of the Home Army's personnel was still active. They could be counted on to obey orders to the last. The principal insurgent enclave, in the City Centre, though much diminished, was still 2 or 3 miles square. Even if the German attacks were redoubled, and German progress were accelerated, the last insurgent strongpoints were not going to be reduced in a couple of days or even a couple of weeks.

One such strongpoint was typical of scores of others. Set up in mid-August by Capt. 'Roman', the hero of the battle for the east–west throughfare, it occupied the former post-office building in a corner of the main station. For six weeks, it had defied all German attempts to storm it. It was only going to be knocked out if and when a special task-force armed with heavy equipment, explosives, and flame-throwers could find the time to give it their undivided attention.

The resumption of talks took place in two stages. First, one group of negotiators arranged a truce that came into effect after the 1st. During this meeting, a witness reported how Gen. Källner, the commander of the 19th Panzer Division, had 'barked as only a Prussian can bark'.[177] Finally, at 8 a.m. on the 2nd, the Home Army's main delegation under Col. 'Anthony' headed off to the crucial confrontation with their German counterparts. Bargaining lasted all day. Von dem Bach started a long monologue, describing himself as 'an incurable optimist' for judging the Poles capable of making a realistic agreement. He was more convincing when he announced that no assistance could be expected from Rokossovsky. The Germans were most concerned to prevent the insurgents from going back on any arrangement agreed. They demanded immediate disarmament, demolition of barricades, and destruction of ammunition. They would not budge on their demand for the complete removal of the entire population.

Col. Anthony's team, in contrast, were most concerned to close all the loopholes whereby the German side might evade their obligations. So, point by point, hour by hour, the text was hammered out. Anthony insisted, for example, that if all civilians were to leave, they must be properly cared for and not be subject to any form of collective punishment. He also held out until the right of combatant status, which was being offered to the Home Army, had been extended to all insurgent formations, including the AL, the PAL, and the NSZ. In short, the capitulation agreement was to exclude all Nazi-style discrimination. It was finally signed at 2 a.m. on 3 October – in the early hours of the sixty-fourth day of the insurgency.

Even before the capitulation was signed, Gen. Boor had made his dispositions. He sent his last report by radio to London. He then addressed his subordinate commanders throughout the country:

1. In Warsaw, further battles have no chance of success. I have decided to end them. The terms of capitulation guarantee combat-

ant status for the soldiers and humane treatment for the civilian population. I myself must enter captivity together with my soldiers.

2. As my successor in conspiratorial work, I appoint citizen Bear Cub.

3. Operation Tempest should now be limited to a minimum, the main effort being directed to the self-defence of the people.

4. I thank all soldiers of the Home Army for their toil, effort and fraternity for the good of the cause. I am confident that all Home Army troops will fulfil their soldierly duty to the end, faithful to the standard of the Polish Republic. I believe that by generous sacrifice of blood, we shall win through to victory and to the freedom of the homeland.[178]

The last shot of the Rising was fired in the evening of 2 October. German sources recorded it at 20.00 hours Berlin Time. The Home Army, which had been running since 1939 on pre-war Warsaw Time, put it at 19.00 hours. Nothing introduced by the Nazi occupation, not even the clocks, was regarded as valid.

Many tears were shed, and many bitter lines composed, on the news of Warsaw's fall. 'The fate of the world', ran one such line, 'has been written in the fate of one city.'[179] [**VERSES**, p. 428]

Almost all accounts of the Rising say that it lasted for sixty-three days. Historians conventionally count the period from the outbreak on 1 August to the final shot on 2 October.

Yet the story did not end there. Though firing had stopped, several organs of the insurrectionary authorities continued to function. On 3 October, the Homeland Council of Ministers published its final appeal *To the Polish Nation*. It bitterly denounced the lack of effective aid from abroad. Parallel statements were issued by Gen. Boor, by the Warsaw Command of the AK, and by the Chaplain of the Warsaw District. A German transmitter, masquerading as the AK's Radio Lightning, sowed confusion in a broadcast which proposed that the Home Army's biggest mistake was to have put their trust in the Soviets. 'The Home Army entered agreements with those Asiatics quite unnecessarily,' it declared. There had been no such agreements. On 4 October, Gen. Monter issued his orders to the Special Battalion, which was to stay behind to keep order during the evacuation. Radio Lightning made its final broadcast; and the last issue of

VERSES

The Rising inspires a fulsome flood of verses and poetry

Warsaw! We shall join you again,
Marching in when the present bloody glare
Gives way to a golden sunset
And our battles are ended
. . . .
The rumble of tanks and the blast of shells
Will silently yield to words of joy
As we, the soldiers of Fort Mokotov,
Conclude our final fight. 9.8.44[1]

Why does London keep playing that mournful dirge
When we at last enjoy a long-awaited holiday?
Girls are fighting here alongside the boys;
Children fight: as the blood flows joyfully.
Hello! Warsaw calling! Heart of Poland here!
Please cut that funereal song from your programme.
We have spirit enough for you and for ourselves;
We ask for no applause: only for ammunition![2]

I know that Warsaw will sometime reawake.
I know that Warsaw, so completely destroyed
That birds no longer wheel above the ruins,
Has not perished. She is just cruelly wounded,
Lost in thought, in a terrible, deathless stubbornness.[3]

We shall not rise again, but you will not die.
The song will carry you away, the legend preserve you.
You will float into history, O Home Army,
In a storm of praise.[4]

What could you have thought, women of Warsaw –
Mother, wife, daughter, sister, and shield of a German tank?
That the barricade is very close:
That it hides your son or husband:

That it's dark before your eyes and slippery underfoot:
That one moment of great pain
Will redeem an ocean of guilt:
That it will buy freedom with blood
Sealed with the sign of the cross.

. . . .

For they ordered us to shoot,
Since we have very little strength left after five years
And only a drop of water and a crust of bread
Though much hope remains
And with that hope a corner of heaven.
For freedom is near after those five years.
They say that it's right here, just across the river,
That help has been promised.

. . . .

Even so, those women perished,
And every stone bleeds from their wounds.[5]

Between the shell which hit your forehead
And the flash that blinded your pale poet's eyes,
How many eras did you survive?
(You knew, you were a God-bearer)
Did you meet your mother's hand or smile
Or perhaps the shadow of the woods by the Narev?
How long it lasts, how long it hurts
That short moment when the world is impoverished!
How harshly the screech of the strings
Cuts into the hearts of those poor people.[6]

Armless invalids of the age!
We lived through the terrors of war and peace.
Deformed spirits, we crawl on our crutches,
And time tips salt into the wounds,
Causing them to bleed constantly
With fresh sorrow.[7]

the *Information Bulletin*, nr. 102, appeared. 'The battle is finished', it wrote. 'From the blood that has been shed, from the common toil and misery, from the pains of our bodies and souls, a new Poland will arise – free, strong, and great.' On Thursday 5 October, the order to leave was then given to the Home Army's 36th and 72nd Infantry Regiments, together with the staffs of the AK Command, of the Warsaw District, and of the Warsaw Corps. Gen. Monter took the salute at a farewell parade amid the towering ruins. Sixty-six days had passed since 'L-Hour' on 'V-Day'. 'L' had stood for Liberation. There was no Liberation.

PART THREE

After the Rising

CHAPTER VI

VAE VICTIS: WOE TO THE DEFEATED, 1944–45

THE CAPITULATION OF WARSAW was a vast and terrible event performed in a surreal setting. In the western half of the city, largely ruined, a residual community of half a million people were being forced to surrender themselves to Nazi captivity, whilst in the eastern half, the largest army in the world pretended not to be there. In all other sectors of the Eastern Front, the Germans and Soviets were still engaged in a savage war, where the Soviets held the distinct advantage. But, here, on the Vistula, the two armies were acting in silent, unwritten connivance. They were divided only by a broad but shallow and eminently fordable river, low in water in the summer heat, more of a demarcation line than a major obstacle. New Yorkers might grasp the enormity of the scene if told that Manhattan was being emptied by the Nazis of its entire population, whilst the Soviet Army stood watching from the other end of a derelict Brooklyn Bridge. Londoners would have grasped what was happening if told that everyone was being systematically deported from districts north of the Thames, whilst across the river in Battersea, Lambeth, and Southwark nothing moved, no one intervened. No shot was fired; no help was offered; no word of sympathy was expressed.

The Capitulation Treaty had been hammered out by German and Home Army negotiators in day-long, tortuous discussions on 2 October. Though it could not mask the horrendous disaster that was unfolding, the final text was far more favourable to the insurgents than they could have earlier expected. On paper at least, it guaranteed that the Varsovians would be decently treated. The Germans recognized that Home Army soldiers were legitimate combatants and that henceforth both they and their auxiliary units would be dealt with, like other captives from Western armies, as POWs protected by the terms of the Geneva Convention of 1929. This was a step which the Nazis had consistently refused to apply to Soviet prisoners, and which the Soviet Army was never to take with respect to prisoners in its own care. The Germans had tried to exempt Communists from the Treaty, to extend the capitulation to all AK units outside Warsaw, and to split the civilians from the military. They failed on all three scores. But they were absolutely unmoveable in their determination to clear the capital of its inhabitants. In the end, they conceded that civilians would not be charged with previous offences against German regulations and that civilian evacuation would not begin until the withdrawal of the Home Army had been safely completed. Common measures were to be taken for the orderly dismantling of barricades and the maintenance of policing. The terms caused considerable elation. At last, they showed the insurgents a measure of respect, thereby ensuring acceptance. But they could not conceal the prospect that Warsaw itself was doomed.

Not surprisingly, the capitulation talks had sparked some fierce exchanges. A German staff officer complained that six parleyers sent with white flags to arrange the truce had all been killed. An AK major, who had been parachuted into Poland by SOE, vented his anger on Gen. von dem Bach in person. 'You, the nation which gave Goethe and Schiller to the world,' he said, 'have tried through terror to take the rights of freedom and existence from us.' Von dem Bach responded, 'This is war.'[1] The Nazis did not believe that established international norms applied to them.

Nonetheless, the final product displayed considerable attention to detail. Home Army soldiers, who wore no regular uniform, were to be accepted as lawful combatants if they possessed red-and-white armbands or White Eagle badges. Personal documents made out on the basis of pseudonyms were also to be accepted on condition that prisoners revealed their full identity on surrender. Women soldiers were to be given the option either of going to separate POW camps for females or of accepting civilian status. All Polish POWs were to be guarded and transported by members of the German Wehrmacht, and not by personnel of other formations or nationalities. One thing could not be guaranteed. No one could say whether an agreement signed in good faith by representatives of the Wehrmacht would later be honoured by the SS and the Gestapo.

The evacuation, when it began on 3 October, made a brave sight. Home Army units formed up four or six abreast, and marched off in long columns to the pre-arranged entry points to the German lines. They marched proudly, with grim faces but with heads held high. They had done their duty, and more; and they were the ones whom Providence had chosen to survive. They were all wearing their red-and-white brassards and their White Eagle badges for the very last time. The men had their weapons shouldered – anything from captured *Panzerfausts* to Sten guns, rifles, and revolvers. The women were carrying their first-aid kits, postbags, and radio equipment. They were nearly all overpoweringly, sensationally, young. Having reached the German lines at Filter Street, Napoleon Square, or Vola Street, they passed groups of German soldiers and officials, who watched in silent amazement or took photos. Having deposited their arms at agreed sites, they entered streets that were lined with curious onlookers. In some places, they saw men and women fall to their knees in a gesture which in Catholic Poland is generally reserved to honour the dead. Their columns moved off in a constant stream through the daylight hours of 3, 4, and 5 October. In all, 11,668 soldiers surrendered in this way, including some two thousand uncounted women. [**ADMIRATION**, p. 481]

As the evacuation proceeded, members of the Underground awaiting their turn to leave performed the last rites. In some instances, when officers broke the news of the Capitulation to their men, soldiers turned their guns on themselves. But most acquiesced calmly in a decision that had been long foreseen. On Tuesday 3 October, the Home Council of Ministers published its final declaration, which echoed the Commander-in-Chief's statement of 1 September:

> We received no effective support . . . We have been treated worse than Hitler's allies in Romania, Italy, and Finland . . . [Our] Rising is going under at a time when our armies abroad are helping to liberate France, Belgium, and Holland. We restrain ourselves from passing judgement on this tragedy. But may the God of Justice pronounce a verdict on the terrible wrong which the Polish nation has encountered, and may He punish the perpetrators.[2]

The Home Army Commander issued his last order, thanking both the soldiers and the civilians who had supported them. 'We all remain soldiers and citizens of independent Poland,' he concluded, 'believing in the ultimate victory of our rightful cause, believing in our beloved country.'[3] After the last broadcast by Radio Lightning, the precious transmitter was smashed with a sledgehammer.[4]

The last to leave were members of AK's High Command. The GOC (General Officer Commanding) of the Warsaw District, Gen. Monter, took the salute at a final march-past of the 78th Infantry Regiment. Gen. Boor, dressed in a civilian coat and trilby hat, joined five generals as they walked to surrender, to be driven away in German staff cars. Most of them would never see their native country again.

Once the military evacuation was nearing completion, the appearance of the civilians, the sick, and the wounded made an equally moving but more sombre sight. Two vast streams of humanity, each several hundred thousand strong, wound their weary way towards the two German transit camps. Dirty, exhausted, starving and bewildered, they had 15 to 20km (nine to twelve miles) to walk without assistance. Women clutched babies and children. Men carried the aged and infirm on their backs. Faltering helpers supported faltering dependants. Emaciated, blinded, bleeding, bandaged, or limping, the walking wounded clung to each other. Improvised carts and shaky stretchers bent under the weight of the immobile, the paralysed, and the dying. Hour after hour, day after day, this mass of suffering humanity shuffled slowly forward under the watchful guns of the German guards. Some, who took a back route or simply wandered off, were able to escape. Others, who broke away, were hunted down. Most of them had no thought but to keep going till they reached their uncertain destination. They were leaving countless killed and loved ones behind. These were the scenes which critics of the Rising would find hardest to forgive. [**EXODUS**, p. 476]

Exactly as planned, the anonymous mass of civilians provided excellent cover for the Home Army's reserve command, whose members had been held back for this eventuality. Undetected by the watching Germans, Gen. Bear Cub and his deputy Nile got clean away, heading for south-west Poland, where they were to establish the new resistance HQ. Together with other civilian leaders, the Chief Delegate, Sable, passed unnoticed through the transit camp on false papers, and was duly released on grounds of age. Contrary to appearances, the great Polish conspiracy had not yet been crushed.

Certainly in the first phase, the Germans were as good as their word. There was no recurrence after the Rising of the atrocious massacres which had occurred during it. There was no attempt to weed out Jews or other 'undesirables'; and, generally speaking, evacuees at the transit camps were not beaten, or starved, or otherwise abused. Many thousands contrived to evade the net or were summarily released. The great majority of Home Army prisoners were sent, as agreed, to regular POW camps run by the Wehrmacht. At Murnau (Bavaria), Sandbostel (Saxony), or Woldenberg (Brandenburg), they joined their comrades from 1939, and like other POWs from Western countries were treated tolerably well. Women POWs, as agreed, were sent to separate camps, notably to Erfurt (Thüringen) or to Oberlangen on the Dutch frontier, or were simply given their freedom.

Even so, as time wore on and the sheer crush of numbers diminished, the more unsavoury parts of the Nazi machine reasserted themselves.

When the final reckoning was made, it was found that well over 100,000 Varsovians had been sent as slave-labourers to the Reich, in contravention of the Capitulation agreement, and that several tens of thousands had been sent to SS concentration camps, including Ravensbrück, Auschwitz, and Mauthausen.

As expected, the *Führer*'s reaction to the fall of Warsaw was one of elation but also of merciless revenge. The demolition of west-bank Warsaw proceeded methodically for more than three months. Despite a critical military situation, in which every last soldier of any age was being impressed into service for the defence of the Reich, thousands of German troops were employed in the ruins of Warsaw, fulfilling the *Führer*'s orders for its total razing. Some of the units were brought in daily from billets in the countryside; others camped out in the eerie wasteland, huddling round their braziers as the nights grew ever colder. *Brandkommandos* or 'fire squads' attacked the empty, desolate, and largely roofless houses with flame-throwers. Demolition teams used dynamite and heavy equipment to bring down the larger buildings and monuments. Gangs of impressed peasants collected scrap metal and other usable building materials, and carted them off. The operation proceeded without a break, day by day, street by street, district by district. The Soviets watched impassively, making no move. If the work was undertaken energetically, there was a good chance that it could be completed before the next Soviet offensive.

Lt.Gen. Telegin stayed in his post in Praga until mid-October, and probably longer. His reports of 5, 6, and 10 October provide a post-mortem on the Rising as seen through Soviet or pro-Soviet eyes. Capt. 'Oleg' was debriefed, and explained that the Rising was launched 'to capture Warsaw before it was captured by the Red Army', and to hand it over to the exiled London Government. Telegin's grasp of basic facts was rudimentary in the extreme. He questioned whether Gen. Boor was ever in Warsaw, and stated that the identity of the Delegate and other political leaders sent by London could not be established. Yet he did not hesitate to repeat the wildest gossip. For example, he charged the Home Army's Security Corps with murdering all the Ukrainians, Jews, and Soviet POWs in the city. 'You shot us at Katyn,' he reported an insurgent officer as saying, 'so now we are going to shoot you.'[5]

Telegin's description of the Capitulation derived from two members of the People's Army Security Corps.[6] His description of civilian attitudes to the Rising derived from a left-wing journalist who had worked for the *Democrat*, and who was at pains to stress that his circle (unlike others) had promoted 'the idea of friendship between Poland, the USA, Britain, and the USSR.' The outbreak of the Rising was received with enthusiasm, he reported, but the mood soon changed, especially after the failure of the Premier's talks in Moscow. The Home Army leadership discriminated against the AL and the PAL, fomented lies against the Lublin Committee, and by the end had earned 'the hatred of the Nation'.[7]

Comrade Telegin had been collecting information in Warsaw for a month or more. Judging by his reports, he did not once interview an informant connected with the Home Army, and he did not once tell Moscow about the views and motives of the dominant insurgent force. Fair-minded reporting was not part of his brief.

In the interval when Warsaw was being obliterated, the small provincial city of Lublin served as the focus for reviving Polish life. It must have been a strange place to be. The town was full of Soviets and of Polish soldiers, who had marched out of Russia. Many of them had terrible stories to tell, not only of the fighting but also of Soviet camps and prisons. It was equally the centre for a ruling political committee which was made up of almost completely unknown politicians, many with false names, which was packed with Russians pretending to be Poles, and which was subordinated to droves of agents, informers, and secret policemen. On 7 October the Committee announced the creation of the Citizens' Militia, a new-style police force that was subordinated to the security organs (UBP). A flood of decrees followed, especially on judicial and criminal matters, confirming that the Committee had every intention of overthrowing the established laws of the Republic. On 3 January 1945, in his capacity as Chairman of the National Homeland Council, Citizen Bierut, a member of the Politburo of the Communist Party, publicly stated with breathtaking gall: 'I am not associated with any party.'[8]

The propaganda of the Lublin Committee in this period was absolutely merciless. Not content with denouncing Boor as a traitor, the Home Army as a whole was presented as a Nazi agency. Boor was the friend and drinking-partner of von dem Bach. The Home Army was full of fascists, 'native Hitlerites', and *Volksdeutsch*, an element of an imaginary

'AK–NSZ–Gestapo network'. The Commander-in-Chief was Hitler's puppet. And these 'reactionaries' were stirring up civil strife against the rule of law.[9]

At the same time many aspects of ordinary life were being restarted after a five-year break. The German occupiers had been cleared out, and all the public talk was about 'the victory over Fascism'. In education, for example, schools and universities which had done no teaching since 1939 opened their doors again to pupils and students. Lublin's *Liceum* No. 1, which had been founded in 1580 but had been used until recently as a German military hospital, took in its cohorts of boys and girls on 1 September 1944. It did this when the Rising was still raging less than a hundred miles away. The Catholic University of Lublin, which had not been allowed to function during the war, reopened for the new school year on 1 October – again, while the Rising was still in progress. On 23 October, a completely new institution of higher learning, the Marie Curie University (UMCS), received its founding statute. Refugees were flooding in. Jewish people reappeared. Fortunate families were being reunited. The smart grasped new opportunities. The unobservant could have been forgiven for imagining that things were returning to normal.

In London, meanwhile, the British press was seeking to come to terms with the Capitulation in Warsaw. Some editors continued to take a cautious line, praising the insurgents' bravery whilst waiting for a clarification of political aspects. Yet a surprising number, from different points of the spectrum, were shocked into making bold statements of opinion from which, throughout the Rising, they had long refrained. They were particularly offended by the denunciations of Gen. Boor that were pouring from the Communist camp. On 6 October, for example, the *Spectator* commented on 'the completely outrageous and the apparently mendacious declarations of the head of the completely negligible Lublin Committee' and 'their despicable strictures on the man who has been fighting in Warsaw with the courage and tenacity of the defenders of Stalingrad.' *The Economist* followed suit next day. After noting that 'the conciliatory steps' of the exiled Government had, to 'everybody's surprise', received 'an unworthy and obstructive reply', it rounded on the Lublin Committee:

> Various members of the Soviet-sponsored Committee of Liberation chose . . . to launch a vituperative attack upon the Polish Government

> and upon . . . the Commander of the Rising in Warsaw . . . The General was branded a criminal . . . The leaders of the Committee have apparently taken no notice of the joint British and American statement, in which both Allied Governments recognise Gen. [Boor's] Army as a combatant force protected by the Allies. Does the Soviet Government endorse these threats?

The same day, the journal *Time and Tide* pointed to the Lublin Committee as the source of all the trouble. 'This Committee', it wrote, '. . . has no legitimate authority and is unsupported by any considerable section of the Polish people.'

Once again, however, it was George Orwell's voice in *Tribune* which pronounced the most damning verdict:

> No, the 'Lublin Regime' is not a victory for socialism [in Poland]. It is the reduction of Poland to a vassal state . . . Woe to those in a vassal state who want to maintain their independent views and policies . . . If they happen to lead a heroic rising that embarrasses the protégés of the great 'Protecting' power, they will be stigmatised as 'criminals' and threatened with punishment . . . Please do not ask us to show enthusiasm for such policies . . .[10]

During the sixty-six days when the Warsaw Rising was in progress, the fighting on all other fronts of the Second World War was developing very strongly in favour of the Grand Alliance. On the Western Front in Europe, the British and Americans had liberated both France and Belgium. They had not crossed the Rhine; but they were closing on the heart of the Reich from the Netherlands, the Rhineland, and Alsace. On the Eastern Front, the Soviets had taken over both Romania and Bulgaria. They had not moved on from the Vistula; but they were closing on both Belgrade and Budapest and were threatening to break into the Reich both from the Baltics and from the Balkans. In the Far East, the Americans had cleared the Japanese from much of the South Pacific, and by landing on Okinawa were about to lay siege to the home islands of the Rising Sun. The time had come for the Grand Alliance to finalize thoughts about the post-war order.

For this reason, Winston Churchill travelled to Moscow to talk in person with Stalin at a conference that opened on 9 October and was appropriately code-named Tolstoy. He had failed to persuade Roosevelt to accompany him. The top item on his agenda was the future of Eastern Europe as a whole. But he also wanted to press Stalin for help in the final attack on Japan; and he was eager to reach agreement on Poland. For this last purpose, he invited Premier Mick to fly out and join the party.

The Soviet advance into the Balkans had ruined Churchill's earlier plans for the region. Ever since the disastrous Dardanelles Campaign in the First World War, which in part had been his brainchild, he was fascinated by the idea of striking at Germany and Austria through 'the soft underbelly of Europe'. Three decades later, he was still playing with it. For a time, for example, he was obsessed with the largely mythical 'Ljubljana Gap', which was supposed to be 'the keyhole to Vienna's back door' and which would offer a brilliant finale to the Italian Campaign. But by October '44, all these schemes had been outflanked. The western armies of Gen. Alexander were several hundred kilometres short of Ljubljana whilst Marshal Tolbukhin's forces were already entering the Danube Gap on the historic pathway to Vienna. So Churchill was flying in on a damage-limitation exercise. The most he could hope for was a share for the Western Allies in the post-war Balkan arrangements, and, if he was lucky, a dominant share in the one country which interested him most – Greece. Hence, at a critical moment during his meeting with Stalin, he pulled a battered old brown envelope from his inside pocket, and scribbled the following table on the back:

	Russia	Others
Romania	90%	10%
Greece	10%	90%
Yugoslavia	50%	50%
Hungary	50%	50%
Bulgaria	75%	25%

The percentages referred to proportions of intended involvement. Stalin puffed on his pipe, and in a gesture which some took to mean assent, he placed a blue pencilled tick on Churchill's 'naughty document'.[11]

Apart from confirming Churchill's preoccupation with Greece, the Percentages Agreement was significant for saying nothing about Poland. The country whose fate was most in the news at that juncture did not rate a mention. Yet the omission was unavoidable since so many vital issues had remained in suspension. In the fourth year of the Grand Alliance, no consensus had been reached about the precise implications of 'spheres of influence', about Poland's post-war Government, about Poland's Underground army, or about Poland's eastern frontier. This is where the Polish Premier intended to participate.

It is not true that nothing was said about the Warsaw Rising during these discussions. Stalin was aware of Churchill's bruised feelings, and at one point he made a gesture which could have been mistaken for an apology. He was keen to explain why Soviet forces had not responded to Churchill's pleas and had not moved to Warsaw's rescue. He now told Churchill that Rokossovsky had suffered a major reverse on the Vistula sector during August, and that the extent of the reverse had to be kept secret at the time for operational reasons. He did not try to explain why a temporary setback on the ground could have justified his own decision to obstruct British and American assistance to Warsaw coming by air.

The discussions about Poland began on 13 October, barely ten days after Warsaw's capitulation. They provided one of the most heart-breaking moments of modern diplomacy. The Polish Premier entered the meeting with Stalin and Molotov fully aware of the weakness of his position and of his adversaries' implacable demands for the 'Peace Boundary' of 1939, now called the Curzon Line. But, with Western help, he still hoped to reach some sort of a compromise, and he started the talks in good faith. For the first time, he was attended by British and American diplomats, and he had been specifically assured in advance by Eden that his plan of 30 August was 'endorsed' by Churchill. In fact, he had been lured onto a stage with an open trapdoor, whose existence he may not even have suspected. At the crucial moment, when he started to explain his position on frontiers, Molotov rudely interrupted him and told everyone that Churchill and Roosevelt had agreed to the Curzon Line the previous year. The Soviets could not understand why the Poles were continuing to quibble:

> 'But this was settled at Teheran,' [Molotov] barked. He looked from Churchill to Harriman, who were silent . . . And then he added: 'If your memory fails you, let me recall the facts. We all agreed at Teheran that the Curzon Line must divide Poland . . . President Roosevelt agreed to this solution and strongly endorsed the line. And then we agreed . . . not to issue any public declaration about our agreement.'
>
> Shocked, and remembering the earnest assurances which he had personally received from Roosevelt at the White House, [Premier Mick] looked at Churchill and Harriman, silently begging them to

> call these damnable deals a lie. Harriman looked down at the rug. Churchill looked straight [ahead]. 'I confirm this', he said quietly.[12]

The Polish Premier had been well and truly conned, not so much by the Soviets, who had been brutally direct, but by the Western allies. There was nothing for him to do, but to keep his dignity and to announce that he was returning to London to consult his Cabinet.

Churchill, too, felt deceived. He had regarded his earlier talk with Stalin about the Curzon Line as a proposal not as a firm agreement. Hence his enormous efforts over the year since Teheran to push the exiled Government into a compromise. He now found not only that the ground had been cut from under him by Roosevelt, but also that his American colleague had not even bothered to tell him. It turned out that in a separate private meeting at Teheran, the American President had coolly assured the Soviet dictator that Churchill's proposal would pose no problems. So Molotov, though not entirely accurate, had *not* been lying. It was an object lesson in the relative weight of the British and American leaders and in Roosevelt's devastatingly casual habits.

If the fate of several million people had not hung in the balance from the underhand dealings now revealed, the discussions at Moscow might well be regarded as a simple farce. One such moment was reached in the plenary session, when Bierut, on behalf of the Lublin Committee, managed to keep a straight face in a presentation of grotesque obsequiousness. 'It is the will of the Polish people', he said, 'that [Lvuv] shall belong to Russia'; and no one from the Western side of the table protested. Another moment occurred in private, when Churchill flew into a mad rage over the attitude of Premier Mick, whom he had just admitted deceiving. The rage was that of a man found out:

> You are no Government if you are incapable of taking a decision. You are callous people who want to wreck Europe . . . You have no sense of responsibility . . . You do not care about Europe's future . . . You only have your own miserable selfish interests in mind . . . It is a criminal attempt on your part to wreck agreement between the Allies by your 'Liberum Veto'. It is cowardice . . .[13]

The really exquisite moment, however, came when Eden, who had brought Premier Mick to Moscow under false pretences, suddenly suffered a comical *crise de conscience*. Eden's anguish was observed by a British diplomat serving in the Moscow Embassy:

> Eden himself became emotionally involved in the question of [Lvuv]. He felt it would be wrong if the British Government were to give way to the Russian demand for this ancient Polish town. He seemed unhappy and uneasy. [That] evening, he came back late to the Embassy after a long session with Molotov and the others. He seemed exhausted and depressed as he came into the Ambassador's room, where one or two of us sat talking over the day's events . . . He strode up and down the room for a while . . . Suddenly he stopped: 'If I give way over [Lvuv]', he said, 'shall I go down in the history books as an appeaser?' He did not wait for an answer. First he put the question to the Ambassador, and moved on. Then he came to my colleague, and put it again and moved on. Then he put it to me . . . Perhaps he didn't want an answer. It was clear to me that he was plagued almost beyond endurance to make what he regarded as an unreasonable and unjust concession.[14]

Eden's belated soul-searching, and Churchill's rage, were undignified symptoms of their impotence. Both British statesmen had fallen into a pit of their own making; and they did not enjoy it.

Stalin's intransigence on the frontier issue is usually explained in terms of his unbending personality and his territorial ambitions. This may be so. But archival documents show that he was under pressure from a quarter which was hidden from the British delegation. In the middle of the Moscow Talks, Beria sent Stalin the copy of a report which stated that elements of the Polish population of western Byelorussia were resisting 'repatriation' to Poland because Premier Mick's Government was thought to be holding out against acceptance of the Curzon Line.[15] The implications of this document are fascinating. For one thing, the NKVD had pre-empted any diplomatic settlement, and, in October 1944, was already engaged in a programme of population exchange. For another, if the programme was already in motion, it was almost impossible for it to be reversed and already too late for any minor modifications of the Curzon Line to be relevant. It is evident, in fact, that Stalin must have taken a decision, earlier in the year, to start demographic engineering as soon as the Red Army occupied the Borders. If so, he must have been genuinely convinced about the final settlement of the frontiers at Teheran; and he must have been genuinely appalled in October to find the whole process being questioned. One cannot say how he might have reacted to Premier Mick's propositions if they had been put to him under Churchill's patronage in the first part of 1944. But one can say with confidence that by October, Churchill, Eden, and Premier Mick had well and truly missed the boat.

For Premier Mick, who had risked so much and worked so hard for a compromise, the Moscow meeting came close to a political knock-out. The 'optimist faction' in the exiled Government was discredited. They had not been able to deliver. So the 'cynics' took the upper hand. After the Premier's return from Moscow, his Cabinet collapsed. On 24 November he resigned his post in favour of the socialist leader Thomas, who had been flown to England four months earlier with Salamander. Henceforth, he could only pursue the path of compromise in his personal and party capacity.

Premier Mick fell from power six weeks after the Capitulation in Warsaw. His fall was the inevitable consequence of the failed strategy that he had pursued throughout his tenure of office – namely, of relying on the Western Allies to help restore a working relationship with the Soviet Union. His successors, headed by Thomas, did not share Mick's uncritical trust of Roosevelt and Churchill, nor his determination to do business with the Communists on the Communists' terms. In the light of history, one can say, in an abstract sense, that they were perfectly right. Yet, in the realm of practical politics, they were dangerously isolated. Like Mick's group, they were very largely dependent on the British, who – whether they liked it or not – were not in sympathy with their views. And, on their own, they had few means of influencing international developments. Above all, they had reached office at a most inopportune moment. A year or eighteen months earlier, before the Rising, before Teheran, before Stalin's entry into Poland, their realism might have had an effect. As it was, they arrived on the scene virtually as liquidators, seeing out the terminal phase of a failing firm.

In the eyes of its Communist opponents, and of all too many Westerners, the new Cabinet was made up of a gang of anti-Soviet extremists. It was nothing of the sort. The hard line was coming from Moscow and Lublin, not from London. The gang was made up of genuine democrats, patriots, and social reformers, who were hoping against hope that something could still be salvaged of the independence of their country. Yet the weakness of their position was manifest. They were beholden to the Western powers, who were no longer prepared to protect or even to consult them. At the same time, by refusing to bow to Soviet dictates, they were cutting themselves off from the international process that was now heading for the decisive conference at Yalta.

Thanks to the impasse, several pressing issues were allowed to fester. Nothing was done, for example, to help establish a modus vivendi between the exiled Government and the Lublin Committee, which the USSR could now promote without heed or hindrance. On 31 December, in anticipation of the Yalta Conference, Moscow unilaterally recognized the Committee as 'the Provisional Government'. Nor was anything done to regulate the status of the Home Army within the Allied camp. After the Warsaw Rising, well over 200,000 AK soldiers remained in the field, and continued to harass the Germans. They answered to the replacement Command under Gen. Bear Cub which had successfully extricated itself from Warsaw and which had set up a new secret HQ. Yet their predicament was rapidly becoming untenable. They were the long-standing formal allies of the Western powers; they were now accepted as legal combatants both by the West and by Germans: but they continued to be treated by the Soviets as common 'bandits'. One can only wonder what Western intelligence knew of all this. If Western analysts didn't know, they were incompetent. If they did know, they could only have been overruled by their political superiors, who must thereby take responsibility for the torrent of deaths and blighted lives which ensued.

Soon after the 'Tolstoy' talks in Moscow, the Soviet Army scored another sensational success. On 21 October, elements of the Second Byelorussian Front broke into East Prussia from Lithuania. They had finally seized a patch of the Third Reich, thereby raising headlines across the world. Although their advance was repulsed, they stayed long enough to create still more headlines of a particularly repulsive sort. At the village of Nemmersdorf they committed numerous rapes and atrocities. Goebbels sought to exploit the incident and to strengthen German resolve by sending in a camera team and publishing pictures of the women of Nemmersdorf who had been stripped, raped, and crucified upside-down on barn doors. He achieved the opposite of what was intended. Most of the inhabitants of Germany's eastern provinces determined that if and when the Soviet Army returned they would flee.

Throughout 1944, the exiled Government had been pressing their British patrons to join them in sending fact-finding and liaison missions to the home country. They had not made much headway. It was devilishly difficult in London to find out what was really happening. The Soviets and their numerous mouthpieces were saying one thing, and the exiled Government and its agencies were saying the opposite. Fortunately, Poland still had enough friends in high places who thought it worthwhile to seek out the truth. The result, highly belated, was a mission that was given the code-name of Freston.

The Freston story had begun while the Warsaw Rising was still in progress, or even before. Deeply frustrated by the negative stance of the Foreign Office in general and in particular of Anthony Eden, who had repeatedly blocked the scheme since Premier Mick's proposal in February, the leaders of SOE decided to make preparations on their own initiative. Their earliest approaches to prospective personnel were made in July. But their progress was painfully slow. They were encouraged by Churchill, who on 4 September made the comment 'Why not?', but were again set back by a meeting on the 19th with Foreign Office representatives, who were still maintaining that the mission required Soviet approval. That same week, with the Warsaw Rising at its most critical phase, Col. Perkins' file reveals a scribbled note, probably from Churchill's office, saying 'Mission granted, further papers unnecessary'.[16] The obstructions had lasted for seven months.

The difference of opinion between SOE and the FO, as aired in the meeting of 19 September, deserves closer examination. The SOE spokesman, Col. Keswick, had come armed with a letter from a Home Army commander urging the despatch of British and American officers 'to prevent the Russians from liquidating our COs and disarming our units.' In this light, the FO's insistence on prior Soviet approval for the mission looks decidedly perverse. The presence of 'C', the nameless head of MI6, had no visible effect, though it is not inconceivable that 'C' subsequently set the wheels in motion and inspired the mysterious note of permission which SOE received some days later.[17]

Freston was to consist of six members, each identified by a three-letter personal code:

Lt.Col. 'Bill' Hudson (SOE)	GIN	Mission Commander
Maj. Peter Solly-Flood (MI6)	MUR	Deputy Commander
Maj. Alun Morgan (SOE)	NAG	
Maj. Peter Kemp	RUM	
Capt. Anthony Currie	CUR	
Capt. P. Galbraith	DON	(Royal Corps of Signals)

These men were thought to be exceptionally experienced. Hudson had been in Yugoslavia, the first British officer to find Tito. Morgan had been in charge of Operation Torment. Kemp had fought in the Spanish Civil War. And Solly-Flood, a diplomat turned intelligence officer, had been added at the suggestion of the Embassy in Moscow. Currie, nicknamed 'the Prof', was actually a Pole who spoke fluent German; Galbraith was a dour Scot. They were to carry 300 gold dollars and £1,000 in notes, and they were to be paid £1 per day danger money. They each carried a grotesquely inaccurate identity card, marked in makeshift Russian, and took off from Hurn airport near Bournemouth on 13 October – the day that Premier Mick was being diplomatically mugged in Moscow. When they landed at Monopoli near Bari, no one was expecting them.

No less than ten weeks of further waiting followed. Their pathfinder agent, Grp.Capt. 'Rudko', whose task was to prepare the landing zone, had already left wearing a gold hat – 'quite the best dressed agent we ever sent into the field.' The weather, both in the sky and in the Foreign Office, was less impressive. Two flights were aborted; and Eden twice tried to intervene and stop the mission in protest against the formation of the new 'Anti-Soviet' Government in London. Eventually they took off on the afternoon of Boxing Day, 26 December, and landed successfully, but with some hard knocks, in a frozen field in the countryside, near the village of 'Ducks' Mud', east of Chenstohova.

On arrival, the Freston team spoke with a Soviet partisan officer – probably Capt. Fedorov – who had been parachuted like them behind German lines, and who announced that local relations with the Home Army were good. They also met three British ex-POWs, who had escaped from Lamsdorf and who were serving with the Polish Underground. Billeted on the country estate of 'Madam R.', they spent a boisterous New Year's party to the accompaniment of vodka, canapés, patriotic songs, wild shots fired through the ceiling, and shouts of 'Down with the Curzon Line' and 'To hell with the Lublin Committee'.

On 3 January 1945 the mission travelled by horse-drawn sleigh to visit Gen. Bear Cub in his secret retreat. Grp.Capt. 'Rudko' was there. Bear Cub presented the Britons with a detailed résumé of German forces in the region and with his views on the Soviets, 'who were more concerned with politics than with defeating the enemy quickly'. He had no objection to communism in principle, only to Russian domination. The British and the Americans, he thought, would soon be obliged to halt further Soviet aggression.

At another meeting, Col. Hudson proposed a toast to 'Churchill, Roosevelt, [Mick] and Stalin':

> The mention of Stalin's name brought cries of 'NO' and howls of protest from all those assembled . . . Hudson was visibly shocked, indeed the reaction came as a surprise to all members of the Freston team except Tony Currie . . . With his knowledge of Polish History, he knew the record . . . Not for the first time Currie said 'I told you so.'[18]

The district was saturated with German troops, German officials, and German settlers. Cossack cavalry under German command were foraging in the villages. Fiesler Storch reconnaissance planes flew over twice a day. Local peasants were losing their homes to make way for the *Volksdeutsch*. On one day, the Freston team's Home Army bodyguard had to fight off a patrol of four German tanks, losing a man. On another occasion, in the middle of a forest, they walked straight into a group of some 200 *Waffen-SS* men, who were hiding from the advancing Soviets and whose 'energies were totally spent'.

Col. Hudson had always known that the mission was likely to end as soon as the Soviet allies appeared. His orders on this point were simple. He was to present himself directly to the Soviet CO and impress on him that the Soviet High Command was aware of his presence, and to request immediate transport to the British Embassy. As foreseen, the expected encounter duly occurred, but at a moment on 15 January, when members of the team happened to be in two different places.

Mur and Cur were riding in a peasant cart when they met a huge Soviet column rumbling slowly westwards. They reached their destination only to find it overrun with 'Soviet Mongolian troops' belonging to a tank brigade. 'These are British officers', their companion said, 'They have been fighting with the Underground and are our allies and friends':

> The Mongols . . . replied by saying: 'Roosevelt good, Churchill good, Stalin good, Hitler bad' . . . Eventually [Mur and Cur] were bundled into a jeep and driven through the intense cold to a cottage a mile or so away . . . Sitting at a table was a Lt.Gen. of about 45 years of age and a Col. of the NKVD. [Mur] saluted and presented [their] documents . . . The General was polite, and said that he had received no information about them . . . In the meantime, the Col. had been examining the documents. Suddenly, he asked them why they had

> been spying on the Red Army. He continued that, in his opinion, Allied soldiers would not be found living with bandits, collaborators, war criminals and enemies . . . Mur told him that, as a British officer, he resented being called a liar. . . . . . Following some disparaging remarks by the Col. about the Polish Home Army, [the two] were removed from the room. They were shortly re-admitted to be told that they were under arrest . . .[19]

Hudson and the rest of the team were taken to the same cottage the following day:

> The table was now covered by a tattered map . . . A staff officer was marking the map in coloured pencils as he took reports from an American-made field telephone. . . . The Lt.Gen. returned Hudson's salute and indicated that they sit down. A little while later in walked a short thick-set man with a flabby face and wearing the greatcoat of a Maj.Gen. He ignored Hudson's salute and sat at the table staring at him . . .
>
> Hudson explained: they were part of a British Mission working with the Poles against the Germans, and the authorities in Moscow had been informed . . . He offered to show them the identity documents, but the Gen. refused to look at them, saying that they could easily have been forged by the Germans. The Gen. then started to ask Hudson what was the name of his organization, what was the name of [his controller] in London, who were their Polish contacts and what frequencies their radios worked on. Hudson refused to answer, saying that he was not authorized to do so . . . The Gen. paid no attention, and said instead that they hand over their weapons. Hudson [again] refused, and reminded the Gen. . . . of the general principles of courtesy between allies . . .

The whole team was then driven under guard to the farm where they had been staying. The farmer told them that all his livestock had been confiscated, and that his farm-workers had been formed into a committee to run the estate. Inside the farmhouse, 'the Russian troops . . . stole anything they could and smashed the furniture, and befouled every part of the building with their excreta . . .' In the evening, the farmer's wife, 'a grey-haired old lady . . . sat at the piano playing Chopin. She played the Revolutionary Study, op. 10 written after the Russians' defeat in the Rising of 1831 . . .'.[20]

> Also in the building were some 40 refugees, mainly from Warsaw. They were able to provide the team with first-hand knowledge of the uprising, as well as of more recent engagements . . . In Radomsko, the Gestapo HQ was wiped out to a man. The Germans resisted in [Chenstohova] for long enough to enable Fischer, the ex-Governor of Warsaw, and his staff to escape.[21]

In due course, the Freston team were thrown unceremoniously into a lice-ridden cell in the jail at Chenstohova, only recently liberated from the Gestapo. A powerful bulb shone day and night in the centre of the ceiling. There were no toilet facilities. Meals consisted of rye-bread and of watery gruel served in a filthy bucket. At the first 'feeding', Hudson kicked the bucket over. Guards peered through a slot in the door, offering remarks such as: 'Allies, how are you?'

Hudson and his colleagues were saved after three weeks through the efforts of the British Embassy in Moscow. SOE had sounded the alarm when the Freston radio fell silent. On 11 February, a Dakota was sent to pick them up. After four flights and an overnight railway journey from Kiev, they reached Moscow on the 17th. Embassy staff told them that the Yalta Conference had taken place during their imprisonment. The one and only British Military Mission to Poland had been unable to make a single report before the 'Polish Question' had been settled.

The Freston group waited a further three weeks for Soviet exit visas. The members of the mission flew out from Moscow on 16 March, reaching London after five days, via Baku, Teheran, Cairo, and Gibraltar. 'George', the mission's Home Army guide, stayed on as a guest in the British Embassy until September, when he left as the personal companion of the Ambassador.

One last detail deserves mention. Before leaving Moscow, the Freston team were talked to by 'the senior British officer' in the Embassy. He impressed on them that they were 'not to tell the real story to anybody, and were to maintain that they had been liberated by the Red Army from a prisoner-of-war camp in Eastern Germany.'[22]

The 'real story' did not emerge for several years. When it did, Maj. Mur spoke his mind. The mission 'was in every respect a complete failure.'[23]

The Freston Mission was SOE's last dealing with Poland. It provided some sobering reflections. Gen. Gubbins was appalled at Britain's failure to help its Polish allies. 'Of course, they'll simply be dropped overboard,' he commented about this time to Sue Ryder, 'We expect to squeeze as much as we can out of them, and then we'll drop them.'[24]

At the time of the Warsaw Rising, Western leaders had been advised that the war in Europe could be concluded by Christmas. By October, however, this advice was seen to be evidently misplaced. There were two reasons. The British and Americans were making lamentably slow progress in the West; and the Soviets, instead of driving for Berlin, had preferred to invade the Balkans.

Nonetheless, Allied determination to destroy the German Reich did not waver. As the autumn of 1944 progressed, the stranglehold was tightened. The German frontiers had been breached. The British and Americans were into the Rhineland. The Soviets were in East Prussia. The day of reckoning was in sight.

In the last months of 1944, therefore, the action was everywhere except in the Vistula sector. For the time being, the Wehrmacht held on to the ruins of Warsaw. The Soviet Army made no move. This meant that the Lublin Committee had to rest content with its control over the provinces immediately to the east of the Vistula. The NKVD was given time to process the population of the same rear areas.

Though few outsiders were aware, the NKVD was already pushing ahead with its programme of population exchanges. Byelorussians, Lithuanians, and Ukrainians from the west of the River Bug/Curzon Line were being expelled to the USSR. Poles from the east of the Curzon Line were being concentrated in collecting centres and were waiting for transport to the new Poland. The Lublin Committee had provided a legal framework for these operations by signing agreements in the Ukrainian SSR, the Byelorussian SSR, and the Lithuanian SSR in September. (From the standpoint of international law, it had no right to do so.)[25]

In December 1944, Gen. de Gaulle paid an official visit to Stalin in Moscow. Knowing his interest in Poland – the two men had both fought in the war in 1920 – Stalin tried to persuade the Gen. to recognize the Lublin Committee in return for his own recognition. De Gaulle declined.

In that same period, the Soviet *Stavka* started to draw up its masterplan for the decisive blow against Berlin. Stalin's choice was for a campaign launched in the central sector of the Eastern Front and led by Marshal Zhukov. The central sector offered the most direct route to the heart of the Reich; it was made more attractive by the trans-Vistula bridgeheads, which had resisted all attempts to dislodge them; and it had been freed from the political complications of the Warsaw Rising. Zhukov was preferred to Rokossovsky, who, much to his own annoyance, was directed in November to an assignment of secondary importance on the Baltic coast. A massive superiority of 10:1 in men and material was gradually built up on the bridgeheads. The launch date was set for 12 January 1945. If all went well, the ruins of Warsaw would be occupied within the first few hours.

The implications of the planned offensive were threefold. Firstly, the Soviet Army would control the whole of Poland in the space of two to three weeks, giving it a springboard for the terminal assault on Berlin. Secondly, the next meeting of the Big Three scheduled for Yalta in the Crimea would take place at a juncture when the Soviets were in a stronger position than that of the Western Allies. Thirdly, nowhere in Poland could hope to provide an easy hiding-place from the all-avenging power of the NKVD.

In the first months of 1945 – that is, in the last months of the War in Europe – events moved much as the Soviet planners would have wished. Zhukov's January offensive carried all before it. The German defences were overwhelmed. Scores of armoured columns surged across the Polish plain, crossing Poland's pre-war western frontier in late January and reaching the Oder in early February. Zhukov's armies were due to conquer Berlin single-handed, without Western help. The snowbound ruins of Warsaw fell to the Soviets on 17 January with hardly a shot being fired. At Yalta, Churchill was the weakest of the 'Big Three', and Roosevelt was dying and allegedly depressed. They called on Stalin almost as petitioners. They desperately needed his cooperation for the showdown against Japan; and they had very little more to offer to guarantee victory over Germany. So they acquiesced in his takeover of Eastern Europe with barely a whimper. Whilst not withdrawing recognition of the Polish Government in London, and continuing to benefit from the services and sacrifices of the Polish forces in the West, they raised no objections either to the installation of the so-called Provisional Government in Warsaw or to the depredations of the NKVD in their First Ally's homeland.

Each of these events directly affected the fortunes of the survivors of the Home Army, the Secret State, and the Warsaw Rising. Zhukov's January offensive, for example, provoked the formal dissolution of the Home Army. Watching from his hideout in western Poland, Gen. Bear Cub realized that the game was up. The AK had justified its existence for five years as part of the Allied fight against Germany. But if the leading Allies no longer supported them, and if the Germans were to be driven out by the Soviets, there was little sense in fighting on. What is more, if the AK were still to be on a war footing when the NKVD took hold, there was going to be a pointless bloodbath. So, on 19 January, only a fortnight after meeting the Freston mission, Bear Cub issued his final order:

> Soldiers of the Home Armed Forces!
>
> The rapid progress of the Soviet offensive may lead to the occupation by the Soviet Army within a short space of time. This is not the victory of the just cause for which we have fought since 1939 . . . We do not want to fight the Soviets, but we will never accept life in anything than a free, independent Polish state espousing the creed of social justice . . .
>
> Soldiers of the Home Army! I give you my last order. Carry on working and acting with the aim of regaining full independence of the country. In this, each of you must be his own commander . . . I hereby release you from your oath of allegiance and declare the Home Army to be dissolved.
>
> On behalf of the service, I thank you for your sacrifice to date. I deeply believe that our Holy Cause will prevail and that we shall meet in a truly free and democratic Poland.
>
> Long live a free, 'Independent and prosperous Poland.'
>
> Place of Stay Bear Cub
> 19 January 1945 Maj.Gen.[26]

Thereafter, the insurgents belonged to no recognized collective. They were on their own.

One of the more exotic figures who was serving in the Kieltse district at the time of the Home Army's disbandment was Sat-Okh, or 'Long-Feather', a.k.a. Stanislaw S. (1922–2003), pseudonym 'Cossak' (Kozak). Half Pole, half Native American, he was the son of Tall Eagle, a Shawnee chieftain from the Yukon Territory, and of a Polish woman who had fled from Tsarist exile in Siberia and had crossed the Bering Straits with a party of Polish refugees. A Canadian citizen, he had been trapped in Poland by the outbreak of war, whilst visiting his mother's relatives. His adventures read like a film scenario. They included service as an Underground scout, capture and arrest, imprisonment and torture in the Gestapo jail at Radom, escape from a transport to Auschwitz, multiple wounds, and further service in the AK 'Spruce' Group (Jodło). Like many of his comrades, Sat-

Okh would end his wartime service in the claws of the Communist security police.[27]

The Soviet Occupation of Warsaw's ruins took place as soon as the Germans withdrew and a pontoon bridge could be thrown across the Vistula. Headed by NKVD units, soldiers of the Polish People's Army (LWP) entered the empty snowbound streets to be greeted by small groups of survivors who had somehow kept alive in the cellars. One of the early tasks was to put up propaganda posters denouncing the 'coughed-up dwarfs of Reaction' to be seen by all subsequent returnees. Here was an unmistakable signal that all former insurgents belonged to a condemned species.

Sure enough, Gen. Serov was there on the spot very promptly, writing to Beria about the extent of the destruction in Warsaw and making provisions for the return of the inhabitants. Notwithstanding the desolation, he was taking no chances.

> With a view to introducing proper order in Warsaw, we have done the following:
>
> 1. Operational-Chekist groups have been organized for the filtration of all inhabitants wishing to cross into Praga.
> 2. Operational groups are at work, consisting of our own Chekists and of employees of the Polish Ministry of Security, and aiming to expose and capture the leadership of the AK, the NSZ, and other underground political parties.
> 3. In order to ensure the success of the above operations, the 2nd NKVD Border Regiment and 2nd Battalion of 38th Regiment have been deployed in Warsaw and have already set to work.
>
> I. SEROV.[28]

To mark the Soviet Army's entry into Warsaw, Moscow Radio broadcast the Manifesto of the Provisional Government together with a version of the city's recent history:

> 'While the Polish Forces were shedding their blood in the battle for Praga,' [Boor] 'was organizing the bloody rising, and having forced the population to undertake a hopeless rising against the Germans, he gave himself up to the enemy and assisted [them] in arresting the greatest patriots. While the Polish Army was fighting for the liberation of Warsaw, members of the Home Army and the National

> Armed Forces were murdering and assisting the Germans in the forcible evacuation of entire towns and villages. Brothers! We wish to assure you that we shall deal with those traitors of the Nation as they deserve! . . .'[29]

Attentive listeners may have noticed that 'the Polish Army' was now identified exclusively with the formations under Soviet command, that the blame had spread from Boor's leadership to the Home Army as a whole, and that the Home Army was linked to the NSZ. No substantiation whatsoever was offered for the charges of murder and collaboration.

The Polish clauses of the Yalta Agreement were largely dictated by Soviet demands. Poland's eastern frontier was fixed on the Soviet interpretation of the Curzon Line, with no concessions to Polish claims whatsoever. The Provisional Government set up by the Soviets was to stay in being and to form the basis of a post-war Government of National Unity. Elections were to be held, and a limited number of ministers from London admitted, but on terms dictated by the Soviets' clients. This meant, in effect, that the democratic Polish Government would never return, and that all its former adherents would be suspect. Within weeks, Churchill was telling Roosevelt that he feared they had put their names to 'a fraudulent manifesto'.

Many weeks passed in Warsaw whilst the gruesome task proceeded of reburying and, where possible, identifying corpses. But a symbolic end to the task was marked on 25 March by a solemn state funeral that was awarded to the leaders of the People's Army killed in the Old Town. Broadcast on radio and attended by 'representatives of the Allied nations', it was the occasion for political speeches, notably by 'Citizen Bierut' and by C.-in-C. Rola-Z.:

> BIERUT: Citizens! We are looking now on four simple coffins, but we know that around us are thousands of graves . . . This heap of rubble is hiding the uncounted graves of those who fell at their posts in the fight for Warsaw. We are standing by the graves of those who led the fights when it appeared that the fighting could not be avoided. This fight, and the tragedy which resulted from it, was not necessary for Poland . . . The Warsaw Rising was instigated by the folly and lust for power of those to whom the fate of the nation was of no importance . . . The greatest crime the world has ever seen . . . was instigated by reactionary politicians under conditions which condemned it to failure in advance . . .

Earth was scattered on the coffins. Salvoes were fired. Wreaths were laid.

> ROLA-Z.: . . . The people of Warsaw hated the invader with a sacred hate . . . A clique of bankrupt politicians living as émigrés used this hatred to promote their political ends . . . In their fight, the People's Army took a leading part. Its heroic exploits were ignored by London propaganda, but it is now quite clear that they bore the brunt of the fighting . . . It is only when comparing it to the titanic efforts of the People's Army that the miserable and shameful part of the Homeland Army became evident. The Homeland Army wasted the blood of our best sons while the People's Militia . . . and the People's Army leaders remained close to the nation to the end . . . Farewell, Comrades in Arms! May the soil of Warsaw, which you defended so beautifully, lie upon you . . . Hail to you, O Heroes![30]

Also in March, the diligence of the NKVD brought about the capture of Bear Cub and fifteen other Underground leaders. They were trapped by a stratagem of the meanest sort. Once their new 'place of stay' had been located, Bear Cub and Sable received a written invitation to meet the local Soviet commander, who promised them a safe conduct and a flight to London for consultations. 'Mutual trust and understanding', the letter said, 'will permit us to solve important problems and to prevent them from becoming acute.'[31] Yet when they appeared on 27 March, they were unceremoniously arrested, interrogated, flown to Moscow, and cast into the Lubyanka Prison. As far as the outside world was concerned, the 'Sixteen' had simply disappeared.

Apart from Gen. Bear Cub and Chief Delegate Sable, the arrestees included the Chairman of the Council of National Unity, three ministers, nine leaders of democratic parties, and their interpreter. Almost all these men had lived through the Rising in Warsaw. With the sole exception of the Underground leaders of the Socialist Party (PPS), who had steadfastly refused to participate in the proposed parley, they constituted the entire democratic leadership of the country. Their removal meant that democratic hopes had been decapitated, even before the war had ended. Their whereabouts became the subject of intensive international enquiries. It remained unconfirmed for five weeks. On 4 May 1945, at the opening of the United Nations conference in San Francisco, Anthony Eden asked Molotov for a response to his enquiries. He was casually told that 'the Sixteen' were awaiting trial in Moscow because they had been conducting hostile operations against the Soviet Army.[32] Eden did not protest.

On 21 April, the Provisional Government signed a twenty-year Pact of Friendship, Mutual Assistance, and Cooperation with the Soviet Union. It was in no position to sign anything but a totally one-sided scheme for Soviet political, economic, and cultural domination. It guaranteed the Oder–Neisse frontier, before the Western allies had even discussed the issue; and in security, military, and political matters, it perpetuated Soviet control over Poland's internal affairs. This treaty made nonsense of the Western contention that the post-war order would be settled by inter-Allied agreement. Also, long before it was formed, it ensured that the 'Government of National Unity', as foreseen by Yalta, was going to be a cipher.

By the end of the war in May 1945, therefore, it was absolutely clear who the winners and losers of the Warsaw Rising were. The exiled Polish Government and its Home Army were the principal losers. They had taken a gamble, which had not worked. The former had lost its military arm and its main political base; and the latter had lost its guiding political authority.

Indirectly, the Western powers had lost their reputation for ethical politics and fair dealing. They had guaranteed Poland's independence and had seen it crushed. They had expended much rhetoric about the 'War for Freedom and Democracy' but in this case they had not stood up for their principles. Poland's reliance on Churchill and Roosevelt had proved worthless.

In the short term, Germany was among the winners. The threat posed by the Warsaw Rising to the Wehrmacht had been overcome; the Vistula sector had held firm for five months, in which the defence of the Reich could have been marshalled; and the Nazis had the satisfaction of so completely destroying Warsaw that they thought they had achieved another 'final solution'.

Yet the outright winners were Stalin, the Soviet Union, and Stalin's Communist clients. Before the Rising, it still seemed possible, or even likely, that Stalin would have been obliged to strike a deal with the exiled Government and with the wartime Resistance movement. After the Rising, it was more than likely that no such deal would be necessary. The cream of Poland's patriotic and democratic youth, who in normal circumstances would have taken over at the end of the war, had been eliminated. Stalin's puppets could now assume power in their stead with no regard to popular opinion or to democratic niceties. They set up a dictatorship which lasted for forty-six years.

*

Once the Rising was over, the generals and armies which had fought in and around Warsaw were ordered elsewhere. Von dem Bąch, for example, who had gained a reputation for ruthlessness, subseqently commanded two SS Army Corps in the desperate defence of the line of the River Oder, east of Berlin. Gen. Vormann, commander of the Ninth Army, who wrote daily reports on the Rising between August and October, was appointed nominal commander of the fabled 'Alpine Redoubt', where the Nazi leadership was expected to make its last stand. Gen. Reinefarth was appointed Commander of Fortress Küstrin on the Oder, but his unauthorized breakout prior to the Soviet conquest caused him to be arrested on Hitler's orders. Gen. Stahel, meanwhile, was made Commander of Bucharest on the eve of that city's surrender. He entered Soviet captivity and died in the Gulag in 1955. Dirlewanger and his brigade, in contrast, were transferred to Slovakia, before moving on to their bloody 'last stand' on the Oder in February 1945. The remnants of the RONA Brigade were transferred to the Vlassov Army and saw action in Bohemia. At the end of the war, they were handed over to the Soviets for retribution. The elements of the Cossack Brigade, who had fought in Warsaw, ended the war in the British zone of Austria. There, amid indescribable scenes of mass suicide, they, too, were forcibly handed over to Beria's bounty hunters.

On the Soviet side, Rokossovsky, feeling demoted, took charge of the Front to the north of his preceding command, and ploughed on into the Reich. In parallel to Zhukov and Konev, he took Danzig, smashed the Pomeranian Wall, drove through Stettin, and approached Berlin from the north-east. The 1st and 2nd (Polish) Armies stayed with the First Byelorussian Front, and participated in the main battle for Berlin. Soldiers of the 1st (Polish) Army, which had been the sole formation under Soviet command to assist the Rising, ended up at the Brandenburg Gate. Long before they arrived in Germany, their commander, Gen. Berling, who had quarrelled with the Lublin Committee, was sent off to honourable exile in a military training school in Russia, and did not return to Warsaw, and not without great difficulty, until 1946.

The 2nd Guards Tank Army, whose alleged sighting on 31 July on the outskirts of Praga had sparked the Rising, drove all the way. Gen. Gorbatov, who had been one of Rokossovsky's chief subordinates on the approach to the Vistula, finished the war as the Soviet Commandant of Berlin.[33]

*

A valuable perspective on Poland's plight as the war drew to a close can be found in the *Osobaya Papka* or 'Special File' which was presented to Stalin by the NKVD.[34] In 1944–45, the great Dictator was deluged by reports on a vast range of internal subjects from mass hunger in Central Asia or oil production in Iran to the deportation of the Chechen and Kalmyk nations. So long as the war lasted, he was obviously most concerned with military matters, including the regular hunt behind Soviet lines for enemy infiltrators. Poland was by no means top of his agenda. In August to September 1944, for example, at the time of the Warsaw Rising, he seems to have been most worried by the activities of the nationalist Underground in Ukraine. There were half a dozen countries where 'anti-Soviet elements' were being eliminated.

Yet in 1945 Stalin clearly paid closer attention to Polish affairs. In January, he received a personal report from Serov on the situation in Warsaw and he even found time to discuss whether a pre-war senator should be admitted to the Provisional Government. He wanted to hear from Beria how the May Day parades had been organized in various Polish towns. Above all, he took care to supervise 'preparations' for the show trial of the sixteen Underground leaders which was to demonstrate his ultimate political triumph.

For decades after 1945, historians could learn very little about the Moscow Trial except from the highly propagandistic publications that were issued by the Soviet Government at the time[35] and the reports of Western journalists who were admitted into the courtroom. Since the collapse of the USSR, however, documents have been released from the Russian archives revealing the lengthy process of investigation which preceded the trial. These documents fall into two sections – those which refer to the initial examination of 'the Sixteen' following their entrapment in Poland, and those relating to the lengthy preparations for the trial conducted in the Lubyanka in Moscow. These reveal as much about the mindset of the NKVD investigators as about the alleged crimes of the prisoners.

The preliminary interrogation of the 'Sixteen' Underground leaders consisted of endless, repetitive questioning about the history, organization, and functions of the Secret State and of all its constituent organs, both civilian and military. It is probably true that the NKVD investigators were trying to trap their prisoners into contradictions and inconsistencies and to elicit confessions of 'anti-Soviet activities'. But what emerges most strongly is that the Soviet officials were woefully unfamiliar with the subject, and could not easily comprehend the simplest facts about the Polish Resistance movement. They really could not grasp, or admit to grasping, how anyone could be genuinely 'anti-Nazi' and yet non-Soviet.

One of the most interesting and extensive files is devoted to the initial examination of Maj.Gen. Bear Cub. For eight days in early April, his captors sat him down and required him to compose a deposition on a long list of subjects in his own words. The resultant document, which runs to seventy-five printed pages, was translated into Russian, typed up, and forwarded to the higher levels, in the first instance to Beria and to Merkulov. It starts with a description of preparations for Bear Cub's flight with SOE in April 1944 and ends with his assessment of the current situation.[36] (See Appendix 31.)

Bear Cub's approach to his task was perfectly open and straightforward. In describing the Commander-in-Chief's instructions prior to his flight to Poland, he listed: 1.) to continue the fight with the Germans to the end, and 2.) to explore the possibilities of restoring diplomatic relations with the USSR. But he mentioned the Commander's prediction that Poland would be turned into the 17th Republic of the USSR.[37] On the question of the 'English Military Mission', he made a full exposé of Col. Hudson's intentions as he understood them. These included permission to talk not only with the Home Army, but also with the AL and the NSZ. By way of conclusion, Bear Cub expressed the view that good, neighbourly relations with the Soviet Union were for Poland 'a matter of life and death.'

A succinct account of the Warsaw Rising, written under pressure by one of the Rising's key planners, only six months after the Capitulation, is clearly a source of considerable importance. If it had not been buried in the Moscow archives for sixty years, it could have had a significant influence on all the subsequent debates. Bear Cub wrote with military precision. He discussed the Decision; the Course of the Battle; Attempts to link up with the Soviet Army; and the Capitulation. The whole discourse occupied only fourteen printed pages.

According to Bear Cub, there had been nine reasons for launching the Battle for Warsaw, and four arguments against it. Reason No. 1, surprisingly perhaps, was 'to seize Warsaw before the arrival of the Soviet Army.' It was justified by the need to establish state power and to welcome the Soviet Armies in the role of host. After that, he listed:

2. to show the whole world our determination to fight the Germans:
3. to resolve the Polish–Soviet conflict by fighting together against Germany:

4. to avenge five years of German repression:
5. by paralysing German forces to facilitate the Soviet encirclement of the city:
6. to obstruct the stabilization of the front along the line of the Vistula:
7. to block the Germans' intention of taking 100,000 men for building work:
8. to prevent the collapse in military and civilian morale which would have occurred if we had done nothing:
9. to take control of the struggle which, without our leadership, would have broken out spontaneously and chaotically

The military and political leaders in Warsaw held divided opinions. But Bear Cub, Gregory, and Monter had all been in favour, and they carried the day. 'The commanders and soldiers who fought for Warsaw for sixty-three days', he believed, 'were fulfilling their simple duty to the nation.' There was no word of regret. On the contrary: if the Rising had not been launched, 'future generations of the Polish nation, and other states and nations, would have to judge us cowards, whose courage failed them at the decisive moment.'[38]

Bear Cub's account of how he persuaded Boor after the Capitulation to let him lead the next stage of the Underground struggle fits well with his principled opinions. 'The battle with Germany', he claimed to have said, 'does not finish with the fall of Warsaw.' Boor had opposed him before the Rising and was opposing him after it. But he ceded the argument on both occasions. And he formally transferred his plenipotentiary powers to him. 'That same night, I took my leave and left the Staff, not saying a word to anyone, just as Boor had demanded.'[39]

What Bear Cub's captors made of all this the file does not record. They noted down his comments, and passed them on. But even they must surely have sensed a remarkable human being. For they would never break him. Bear Cub at bay was the ultimate *chevalier sans peur et sans reproche*, 'a true knight without fear or stain'.

In May 1945, British intelligence finally caught up with RAF Sgt. John Ward – the only British serviceman to have been present in Warsaw during the Rising, and the author of numerous radioed reports, several of which had been published in *The Times*. He was carefully debriefed, and an extensive report was written of his adventures.[40]

Ward, though an amateur in the world of intelligence, had all the qualifications of a first-rate agent. Aged twenty-six, he was fit, energetic, and, as shown by his repeated escapes, extremely daring. He was a fluent German speaker, and a trained wireless operator. His time as a POW in Germany had lasted from 10 May 1940 to 20 April 1941. It was mainly spent in a camp near Lissa where he was employed as an interpreter. He twice absconded, the second time successfully.

His time in the Polish Underground, after seven days on the run, began in the town of Sheradz, where he went to confession in a local Catholic church and was duly put in contact with members of the ZWZ. By May, he was in Warsaw and was put to work making transcripts of BBC broadcasts. He acquired a duplicator, and produced an English-language news-sheet called *Echo*.

The Warsaw Rising broke out shortly after he had recovered from a bullet in the thigh, received during a skirmish with the Gestapo. Another wound followed during the fighting in Mokotov. But it did not obstruct his work as a reporter and radio operator for the Home Army's Office for Information and Propaganda.

Ward escaped from Warsaw on 4 October in the company of two Red Cross nurses. They evaded the Germans, but were robbed by a couple of Ukrainian deserters. They were heading south, where Gen. Boor had told him that he could pick up a clandestine RAF flight. The strategy did not work. And for two months Ward shared the ordeals and deprivations of the 17th AK Division, which was operating in the vicinity of Chenstohova. He endured several firefights against the Germans, and a clash with an AL unit, in which he was again robbed. After the arrival of the Soviets on 20 January, he was interrogated for several hours by the NKVD but was not detained.

Ward's next move was to double back to the Warsaw District, and, with the help of former AK colleagues, to make contact with London by radio. It worked at the second attempt, and he learned that SOE was looking both for him, and still more desperately, for the Freston Mission, which had not been heard of for three weeks. London then ordered him to present himself to the Soviets, assuring him that Moscow had been informed of his whereabouts. His compatriots, ever trustful of their Soviet allies, seemed to think that he would be helped to track down Col.

Hudson's party. But if the NKVD had been told where he was, he had little choice. On 5 March, he took the electric train in the direction of the city, no doubt gaped at the ruins, and, with great reluctance, reported to the authorities.

Ward's British interrogation says little about his interrogations by the NKVD, except that they were rather lengthy. In fact, he was kept for two months. He did not have to track down the Freston Group, who in the meantime had shown up in Moscow. He was eventually sent by rail to catch a British ship in Odessa, whence he sailed on 16 May on the *Duchess of Bedford*, bound for Malta. From Valetta, he was flown to England by the RAF, arriving on the 20th, almost exactly five years to the day since he had taken off in his ill-fated Fairey Battle.

John Ward is an important figure in the history of the Warsaw Rising. He was a lonely symbol of the Anglo-Polish alliance on which the Rising had been predicated. Like Col. Hudson, he wrote a glowing account of the Home Army and its feats. These accounts were filed seven months after the Capitulation of the Rising and four months after the disbanding of the Home Army. By that time, they possessed nothing more than purely historical value.

The Trial of the Sixteen, which took place in Moscow between 18 and 21 June 1945, was a key event in revealing the direction in which Soviet policy was moving. It confirmed both the incorrigible bad faith of the Communists and their determination to crush all political opponents. An archetypal show trial, replete with absurd accusations, brainwashed defendants, and suborned witnesses, it had nothing to do with real offences. It was staged to show that the Soviets were all-powerful, that 'Soviet justice' could perpetrate the most blatant injustices with impunity, and that the Western powers were impotent to prevent it. Indeed the performance was so orchestrated that the British and Americans were persuaded to connive in the public scourging of their former comrades-in-arms. For on two points, the libretto of Stalin's pre-war show trials was not followed. Official Western observers were present; and the Soviet procurators made no demands for the death sentence. One is fully entitled to wonder whether these two features were not in some way connected.[41]

Independent historians who have studied the Moscow Trial of the Sixteen have stressed a variety of its more scandalous aspects. The legalists stress the fact that the application of the Soviet Penal Code to foreign defendants who had committed no offence in the USSR and who had been kidnapped in their own country was totally invalid in international law. The politically-minded stress the coincidence of the trial with negotiations for the formation of a Polish Government of National Unity, which were proceeding in the same city and at the same time. This coincidence ensured that delegates to the negotiations who were not connected with the Soviet or Communist interests could be intimidated, and could be persuaded to make concessions which they might otherwise not have contemplated. The British and American diplomats, including Dr George Bolsover, who observed proceedings from the gallery but did nothing more than file a confidential report, were participating in the ritual humiliation of the principles by which the Allied coalition had once been inspired.[42]

The British political elite were still so spellbound by Stalin that few cared to notice what was actually happening. In the weeks preceding the Trial, when questions had been asked about the fate of the Sixteen, the House of Commons had reverberated to opinions such as 'the Poles are preparing the Third World War' or 'the Poles and the Russians are as bad as each other' or another which revealed that the Foreign Office quite liked the Provisional Government in Warsaw because of its apparent commitment to agrarian reform. The London edition of *Soviet News*, which on 25 May announced preparations for the Trial, contained a vituperative attack on Gen. Boor and other 'dirty adventurers' who had 'bravely surrendered to the Germans'. On 12 June, the Foreign Office had to respond to a British soldier from the 51st (Highland) Division, who had been a POW in a German camp and who had written a letter to confirm 'the appalling behaviour of the Russians in Poland'. Lord Dunglass, then a rising official, wrote in the letter's margin for his secretary's guidance: 'Could you devise some harmless stalling answer?'[43]

The proceedings of the trial, which was held in the same grandiose Hall of the Trades Union that had housed the pre-war show trials, produced few surprises. A well-known purge judge, Col.Gen. V.V. Ulrich, presided. The prosecutors sat at baize-topped tables. Huge chandeliers cast a brilliant light. The fixed bayonets of the guards glinted. Newsreel cameras whirred. All but one of the sixteen defendants were visibly cowed. Not waiting for a verdict, the headlines of the Soviet press announced 'Polish fascist Bandits disguised as Democrats', 'Destroy German Fascist Agents' and 'Hitler's Executors!'

Day 1 began with the indictments. The defendants were identified as members of the 'Home Army', an 'illegal organization'. They had been caught in possession of 'illegal radio transmitters'. They had slanderously described liberation by the Soviet Army as 'a new occupation'. They had disbanded the Home Army as 'a cover for further activities'. They had been engaged in 'terroristic diversions' and 'espionage' in the rear of the Soviet Army. They had prepared 'a plan for a military coalition and aggression . . . with Germany against the USSR.' All the defendants except one pleaded guilty. Former Home Army witnesses supported the charges.

Day 2 was given over to cross-examinations. It had its moments. The defendants, for example, did not always grasp the Soviet terminology. When a lawyer was going on about 'Western Byelorussia' and 'Western Lithuania', someone asked, 'Do you mean Poland?' And the judge let it pass. Or again, the defendants would not accept the court's assumptions about the Home Army's alleged passivity or its supposed collaboration with the Germans. 'The Commander-in-Chief', said Bear Cub bravely, 'specifically ordered the Home Army to fight the Germans to the end.' But one of the defendants finally did agree to the proposition that the Home Army had been hostile to the USSR.

Day 3 was largely taken up with defence statements, especially with that of Bear Cub. The court was told that Bear Cub's one defence witness had unfortunately been delayed by bad weather (in June). But it did not stop Bear Cub from presenting what must be the most courageous speech in the whole wretched history of Stalinist mis-trials. 'The Home Army was an organization of the Polish nation,' he maintained to the ill-concealed displeasure of the judge; 'therefore the accusations of the court are directed against the whole Polish people.' The exiled Government in London was 'lawful'. Contrary to the court's assertions, he was neither a landowner, nor a servant of the *Sanacja* regime. He was 'the son of a peasant' and 'an opponent of the *Sanacja*'. 'The Warsaw Rising', he insisted, 'was *not* a political adventure.' It was 'necessary' and 'heroic'. Finally, he said, 'Yes to Polish–Soviet friendship', but 'No, to enslavement'.

Closure came in the early hours. The defence lawyers begged for leniency. The defendants were 'dupes'. The prosecutors stuck to the script and agreed. Three of the accused should be acquitted. The others should be given mild sentences. The judge acquiesced. By Soviet standards, the verdicts were indeed indulgent. Bear Cub received ten years' hard labour; Sable received eight years'. The three ministers were each given five years'. Seven of the party leaders were handed down short terms of eighteen, twelve, eight, six, or four months'. The other three and the interpreter were released. The Soviet press resounded to paeans of praise for the boundless humanity of Soviet justice.[44]

Three days later, Stalin hosted a reception at the Kremlin. His guests were the Polish delegates who had just agreed on the composition of the Government of National Unity. They were due to assume office within the week. The leading lights of the former Lublin Committee were there. So, too, was the former Premier Mick – the only senior member of the former exiled Government to participate in the exercise. So, too, were the British and US Ambassadors. As they ate their caviar and drank their *Shampanskoye*, Bear Cub, Sable, and eleven other convicts were starting their prison terms.

With some delay, the British diplomatic machine reviewed the Trial of the Sixteen, and pronounced its own assessment. The leading analysis was provided by HM Ambassador to Moscow, Sir Archibald Clark Kerr, who composed a long paper that was circulated to the British Cabinet. As befitted a 'mandarin', Clark Kerr's opinion was beautifully balanced. On the one hand, he warmly approved of 'the courage, dignity and honesty of the Poles' who 'plainly were not fascist reactionaries or landlords but good democrats and patriots.' He specially praised the 'courage and tenacity' of Bear Cub. On the other hand, he made no attempt to question the totally unproved contention that the accused had been guilty of 'anti-Soviet activities'. The purpose of the Trial had been twofold: to discredit the exiled Government in London and to destroy all potential opposition to the incoming Government in Warsaw. Clark Kerr's final remarks were exquisite. Since it did not foster reconciliation, the Trial was 'a failure', an example 'of bad Russian psychology'. Yet it was redeemed by the lenient sentences. 'The Trial was a blunder', the Ambassador concluded, 'but not a crime'.[45]

The last word on this prime exhibit of British cynicism was appended when it went the rounds of the FO departments. A minute of supreme smugness was added by an official who, fortunately, omitted to sign it:

> It was, I think, essential that the Poles be shown once and for all that . . . the idea of a Polish–German orientation should be killed outright, in fact the Russians should exercise their strength brutally. That they have now exercised it with moderation is a remarkable evidence of their (occasional) susceptibility to outside opinion.[46]

If proof were needed that Bear Cub and other authors of the Warsaw Rising were wrong to place their trust in their British allies, this is it. There was no such thing as 'a Polish–German orientation'. Equally, there was no sense of obligation to Bear Cub, whom the British had originally flown in. He was destined to die in Soviet captivity, in mysterious circumstances, in December 1946.

At the time of the Moscow Trial, the exiled Government published an eighty-seven-page booklet in English entitled *Poland during the First Half of 1945*. It was a masterpiece of erudition and compassion, and opened with an idea from Eurypides: 'Events cast their shadows before them.' The shadows of forecoming events, it said, are lying gloomily over almost half of Europe.[47]

The author of the booklet, alas, remained anonymous. Indeed, it could well have been a collective work. At all events, it was written in polished, faultless English; and its judgements and descriptions were supported by an amazing array of quotations: from the classics of Marxism-Leninism, from the decrees of the Lublin Committee and Provisional Government, from radio transcripts, from the press at home and abroad, and from eye-witness accounts. Despite the self-evident political stance, one could not hope for a better summary.

Several passages referred to the Warsaw Rising and to the Home Army. One of them laid out the correspondence between the Lublin Committee and the American Labor leader, Norman Thomas. Rebuffing the 'fraternal greetings', Thomas's reply left no room for doubt about his feelings:

> The Rising of the Warsaw workers in the summer of 1944 has been recognised as one of the finest pages in the history of struggles for freedom. Russia's betrayal of this struggle is one of the most shameless and most tragic episodes of this war.

Another passage, in the chapter on 'Libellous Propaganda', described a broadcast made by Lublin Radio in April 1945 on the second anniversary of the Ghetto Rising. Listeners to the broadcast learned that the Home Army had not fought against the Germans but alongside them:

> The insurgents [i.e. the Ghetto fighters] had against them the German air force, the SS, German tanks, Polish hooligans, Polish reactionaries, and indeed the Home Army itself. We shall do everything in our power to overcome these bandits [and] criminals of the Home Army.[48]

The poisonous smear of labelling the Home Army as 'anti-Semitic reactionaries' was already being spread.

A substantial section exposed the propaganda campaign aimed at discrediting Britain and America, and at undermining wartime loyalties. The essay closed with a statement of faith in the long-term future. 'Once again the Polish community [has taken] up the slogan "We shall survive",' it declared, 'in the unshaken belief that the day will finally dawn when freedom will cease to be "a bourgeois dream" (Lenin) and will become a joyful reality.'[49]

On 12 June 1945, the last Foreign Minister of the exiled Government sent a copy to Sir Owen O'Malley at the Foreign Office. The reaction was not enthusiastic – 'an excellent little essay' but 'useless to expect the Prime Minister to read it.'[50]

At first sight, the fate of the Warsaw insurgents has all the appearances of an impossibly complicated subject. Certainly, within a couple of years of the Capitulation, survivors of the Rising were found on every continent of the globe. Yet the causes of this remarkable diaspora become much more readily intelligible if one asks when, where, and by whom each category of survivors was captured. To this end, one has to remember that in 1944–45, Poland was divided into a German and a Soviet zone of occupation, that ex-insurgents were unwelcome in both zones, and that the dividing line between the two zones was constantly moving westwards. Hence survivors picked up in the Warsaw district before 17 January 1945 would have been taken by the Gestapo, whilst those captured there at a later date would have been taken by the NKVD. One must also remember that the Third Reich collapsed in May 1945, thereby releasing all surviving captives in Germany to a variety of destinations. The Soviet Union and the Soviet Bloc, in contrast, did not collapse for forty-five years.

The nature of the treatment varied according to time and place. During the Rising itself, when neither Nazis nor Soviets regarded the Home Army as a legitimate combatant force, captured insurgents were in the greatest danger of being shot out of hand. In the period between the Capitulation and the end of the war, the Germans generally sent all their prisoners into formal captivity. The Soviets, in contrast, were given to weeding out officers from rank and file. The former, if not shot, were most likely to be shipped off to the Gulag or to re-education centres.

The latter were often drafted for immediate military duty. After the war, when the Nazi regime no longer existed, the Soviets and their minions continued as before. But now they had all the leisure they needed for political investigations, lengthy torture, secret or show trials, and judicial murder. In this situation, they occasionally succeeded in persuading their captives to change sides and to join in the persecution of their erstwhile comrades.

The real complications may be discerned from the fact that ex-insurgents could easily fall into two or more of the above categories. Those who had stayed in German captivity until May 1945, for example, usually had the choice either of staying abroad or of returning to Poland. If they returned, they were immediately liable to be rearrested by the NKVD and were frequently deported. So it was perfectly possible for men to serve time both in a Nazi camp and then in a Soviet camp. By the same token, insurgents who were drafted into the Soviet-run Polish armies could easily fall foul of their political commissars and find themselves in short order on the road not to Berlin but to Siberia. Similarly, as happened to one of the most famous ex-insurgents, time in the Gulag could turn out to be the prelude to re-arrest by the Communist security organs in Poland and to a second, terrible sentence. The permutations were legion. It is not beyond the bounds of realism to imagine people who saw the inside of the Paviak before 1944, and the inside of a Nazi concentration camp afterwards, before progressing to the Gulag in the late 1940s and to a Polish Communist prison in the early 1950s. In some history books, this is called the period of Liberation.

During the Rising Warsaw was completely cut off. Up to 12 September 1944, it was surrounded by German forces on all sides. From 13 September to 3 October, the Germans continued to control the left bank of the Vistula, whilst the Soviets moved up to the right bank. Military cordons filtered all movement on the city outskirts. Escape was extremely difficult, but not impossible – especially for civilians who chose to test sectors guarded by friendly Hungarian troops. Otherwise, escapers had to take their life in their hands. [**IRKA II**, p. 473]

In the early days of the Rising, the Germans made no special provision for Varsovians who wanted to leave. They relied on a number of catchment centres which received individuals caught by the cordon and which were used as the first stage on the way to the main transit camp. But at the end of August they relented. Regular announcements were

IRKA II

The young widow of a Home Army soldier, living outside Warsaw, waits for news of her husband

On 23 August I had given birth to a son. The doctor from the nearest town did not make it, so my aunt delivered the baby. He had a lot of hair on his head – and everyone remarked on his unusual resemblance to his father. Many years later, friends of my husband, meeting my son on the street, stopped him, asking, 'Are you by any chance André F.'s son?'

At the time [in August and September], dozens of people had come to my uncle's place, expecting to stay. All day we heard the thunder of gunfire, the ominous noise of bombers overhead and even the distant detonations caused by bombs, which we clearly differentiated from the gunshots. In the evening we watched with fear as the sky heated up from ever greater fires. It soon seemed that the whole of Warsaw was burning. However, I believed that the man closest to me was alive.

Throughout the next three months I waited for his return. A camp had been set up, a few kilometres away in Prushkov, where new transports of Warsaw's inhabitants had been constantly arriving. We went there every day, searching for people and for news of those who had survived and those who had perished. No one told me that André was dead – although often, when I joined a group of people in conversation, they suddenly fell silent. Later I understood that they had been talking about it but that no one had been brave enough to tell me. Everyone had guessed long ago what that sudden silence might mean, but I continued to believe that my husband was still alive . . .

Three months after leaving the camp at Prushkov, my parents-in-law found themselves in Grodzisk. They determined to take me to their house, so that I would discover the truth from their own lips. André was one of four brothers, so they really loved me, as the first 'daughter'. I will not forget my father-in-law's words, which may seem grandiloquent, but I know that he only wanted to tell me exactly what he felt. He put his arms around me and said quietly, 'We should both be proud – your husband, and my son, died for our country.'

[He had been killed on the second day of the Rising.]

During the Warsaw Rising three men from André's family had been killed – André, his sixteen-year-old brother, and a cousin. My father-in-law was the owner of an estate in the Kuyavy region, which had been theirs for several generations. The family was of German origin. It is worth pointing out that when the Germans arrived in 1939, they offered to give my father-in-law *Reichsdeutsch* papers. And he would have been free to leave. Refusal could be punished by arrest, yet he chose to escape immediately, and to hide with his whole family in Warsaw.[1]

---

made about protected evacuations. Times and meeting-points were designated, even though most Varsovians ignored them.

Prisoners of war posed a major problem. At first, the Germans gave it no thought. Since they massacred perhaps 50,000 civilians in the first week, one need not reflect too long on how they dealt with the 'bandits' who had caused this mess in the first place. But attitudes changed as the Rising wore on. The German Command knew that the insurgents were holding a considerable number of German prisoners, also that the Western powers had belatedly publicized the Home Army's combatant status. So in the later stages, the number of instances increased where German soldiers refrained from killing captured insurgents outright.

On the opposite side of the Vistula, the Soviet authorities had priorities of their own. They were not officially at war with the insurgents, but granted them no more respect than the Germans did. There is ample evidence to show firstly that any insurgent who crossed the Vistula to the Soviet lines was promptly arrested, and secondly that after 13 September the NKVD was conducting a systematic round-up in Praga.

The tasks faced by the NKVD after arriving in Poland can be gauged from the stream of reports sent to Beria by Gen. Serov, and by Beria to Stalin.[51] Having completed the liquidation of Home Army units east of the Bug, the Soviets may well have been labouring under the illusion created by the misinformation supplied earlier. If so, they would have been quickly disabused. They would have found that the People's Army was not even the most influential branch of the socialist movement, let alone of the Underground as a whole; that the great majority of workers and peasants supported the Home Army; and that the Home Army, which was actively fighting the Germans, was the only Underground formation that really counted. They must have been deeply disappointed by the inability of the Lublin Committee to act as an efficient or reliable partner; and they can only have been bewildered to find in August that the Warsaw Rising had brought the AL and the AK together. Their first practical measure was to call for a special NKVD battalion to guard the Soviet diplomatic building in Lublin.[52] Before long they were calling for a general increase of NKVD troops.[53]

In August and September 1944, the NKVD was working through a considerable backlog in its efforts to filter the population of the occupied areas. Beria only reported on 3 August on the completion of disarmament operations in Lithuania, and on 16 September from Novogrodek in Byelorussia. His letter to Stalin on the latter occasion concluded: 'Military-Chekist operations for the liquidation of bandit-insurgent formations are continuing.'[54] In NKVD jargon, 'liquidation' was, to put it mildly, ambiguous, but orders dating from 20 July indicate the established procedures:

1. Permit representatives of the Berling Army to enter the collecting centres for AK prisoners with a view to recruiting suitable NCOs and privates.
2. NCOs and privates who earlier expressed a willingness to serve in the Berling Army should be drafted . . . for use in auxiliary units of the Soviet Army.
3. AK staff officers with operational significance should be transferred to the relevant organs either of the NKVD-NKGB or of *Smyersh* counter-intelligence.
4. Remaining AK officers should be sent to NKVD camps since otherwise they would occupy themselves by forming Polish underground operations.[55]

At this juncture, the main catchment centre was on the upper Bug. The principal destination of officers transported to Russia was Ostashkov near Kalinin, a notorious NKVD camp in a disbanded monastery on Lake Seliger, which had figured earlier in the Katyn story.

It is in this context that one can make soundings about NKVD conduct in Praga, which the Soviet Army occupied when the Rising was still in progress. There can be no doubt that Serov was there, and that the usual apparatus of filtration and repression was put into place. Arrests and deportations certainly occurred. The only query concerns their scale. Since fighting persisted until the end of the month, it is possible that Serov kept a relatively low profile until this particular 'rear area' stabilized.

Nonetheless, there can equally be no doubt that numerous insurgents managed to cross to the Soviet side in the dying days of the Rising, and that they received something short of a warm welcome. Abundant evidence exists to suggest that Soviet practice was to arrest everyone and anyone, wounded or not, who came to them from across the river, and to leave it to their prisoners to prove their innocence. [**EXODUS**, p. 476]

EXODUS

Civilians leave Warsaw filled with various degrees of despair and determination

'*Raus! Alle Männer raus!*' they shout ever more violently.

On the way to the Western Station a crowd blackening into a large seething mass moves slowly, weighed down with packages clutched in complete silence. Expressionless, it does not let the watching Germans see the tragedy unfolding inside every one of us.

The guards spaced out along the length of the street do not sneer, but watch with interest and even admiration. Warsaw has set a new record, beating the length of Stalingrad's resistance by a few days, even though the odds had been more heavily stacked against us. We are rather proud of that.

We walk past burnt-out houses. On the pavements, the charred bodies of people and animals tell a tragic tale. As we walk through this city of vampires our consciousness is gradually permeated by the pompous tones of Chopin's funeral march. Someone passing us whistles it through gritted teeth.[1]

2 October, Monday

The whole of Mokotov had been captured and every last one of the inhabitants expelled onto the Mokotov Fields. It was a beautiful day and people walked with bundles on their backs and suitcases in their hands. The sick were carried by the healthy, children by their mothers, all dazed, lamenting their fates. The German soldiers were not bad to us, transporting the old and the sick, giving us apples and sweets. The Ukrainians, however, were awful, stopping people and robbing them.

At last we reached the Race Course, where twelve barracks had been set up. We settled down on the bare ground, and on benches, but there was not enough room. Some lighted bonfires, which had to be put out at dusk, because of the air raids. So they paced up and down so as not to freeze. In the daytime the Germans brought black coffee and bread, and soup in the evenings, but we ate nothing because we had no utensils and no one wanted to lend us any.

At last trains consisting of cattle wagons arrived for the journey to Prushkov, which was rumoured to be a model camp run by the International Red Cross. There would be care for the elderly, children, and the injured, and food and clothes. But people fought to get onto the train, so the Germans waded in with rifle butts. It was impossible to sit down. There were few benches and no free places. The carriage was closed from the outside and we travelled for three hours. People were wailing, unable to see to their toilet needs; and they stood in urine and excrement.

We arrived on a beautiful September afternoon. After a two-month break, we caught sight of baskets of fruit, white bread, and of people walking about freely.[2]

'We knew that the first stage was the transit camp at Prushkov, near Warsaw, whither we were to be transported by rail. As we were passing through Tvorki station we heard some encouraging words and I jumped from the train with my mother. Well, I was pushed. We hid ourselves in the local psychiatric hospital. I remember it most intensely. (I later made two films in that hospital, *Illumination* and then *Wherever It Is*.) The director during and after the war was Dr K., and I had to hide under the bed whenever he came into the ward with Germans. My mother was disguised as a patient and all around there were more false patients than real ones. For a child the real patients were frightening. From Tvorki we went to a farm and lived there until the day when my father, who had been in Cracow, found us through the Red Cross. We managed to reach him before Christmas. In Cracow, I saw the Germans leave and the Russians arrive.'[3]

Krzysztof Zanussi

An insurgent soldier prepares to surrender

We left Warsaw disarmed, but with heads held high, at regulation pace, four abreast. We passed a group of German officers, who looked with interest at this insurgent army, which they had not been able to get the better of for sixty-three days: a force, which had destroyed a significant number of their tanks, and inflicted heavy losses, but which now marched bravely past, as if victorious. I heard one of them saying loudly to his men '*Stolze Polen*' (Proud Poles).

We neither looked nor felt defeated. It was deeply enshrined in our minds that we had done something great, despite the eventual capitulation. I did not predict that it would be fourteen years before I saw Warsaw again, and that the city would not be really free even then. The civilian population also left Warsaw in a disciplined manner, with high personal self-esteem and national pride.[4]

A. Janicki

Even so, in a few cases, Home Army personnel went over to the NKVD as an act of deliberate choice. A few of them may well have done so in the hope of saving their skins. But some had more serious purposes in mind. Louise Z., for example, a nineteen-year-old courier, was sent by her superiors to infiltrate the NKVD ranks and to send back information on their activities and intentions. She had crossed the river in early September, when the bridges were still open, and had gone to stay with her family in one of the suburban villages near Praga. After a few days, the Soviets duly arrived and she walked into the nearest NKVD post and asked for a job. The ploy was successful. The NKVD were happy to employ a harmless local girl who knew the neighbourhood and spoke Polish. They thought nothing of the fact that she appeared to have a boyfriend who rode up on his bicycle every other day for a spot of canoodling. Thus began an assignment that was to prove harder to terminate than to initiate.

After the Rising, the central sector of the Eastern Front on the Vistula remained static until 12 January 1945, when Zhukov's winter offensive raced across Poland. Before 12 January, therefore, districts west of the Vistula remained largely in German hands. After 17 January, almost the whole of Poland was in the Soviet grip.

The huge contingent of Varsovians who were not taken into permanent captivity, or somehow escaped, were left to their own devices. They were homeless, often penniless, and often with sick or under-age dependants. Those who could, made for the homes of friends or relatives, if possible in the mountains or in the far south, as far from the front as they could go. Many headed for the country villages, where there were hopes of food and shelter. Others crowded into the small suburban towns to the west of Warsaw, where reception centres were improvised and where they filled the schools and parish halls. At a stroke, all Varsovians who weren't prisoners were refugees.

Military POWs from the Warsaw Rising who surrendered to the Germans at the Capitulation, were sent to a variety of *Stalags* and *Oflags* scattered round the Reich. They were not investigated by the Gestapo, and received a modicum of food, shelter, and warmth. In fact, they were in just about the safest place to be. Other Varsovians were struggling to survive either as forced labourers or in the concentration camps. Naturally, conditions varied. But generally speaking they were correct. POWs held in Sandbostel, for instance, recalled endless roll-calls, watery turnip soup, the delights of the *Latrinekommando*, and the constant cold caused by living through the winter in the tatters of summer clothes. But they also received Red Cross parcels, participated in educational courses, and even traded on the black market with the locals.[56]

As Germany's labour shortage intensified, the camp authorities were increasingly tempted to bend the rules and to lease out their prisoners for agricultural or industrial work. In some instances, the prisoners were content to be kept occupied. In others, they were callously exploited. But they were not in the defenceless position of that of their compatriots who had fallen into the hands of the SS.

In the last months of the war, as the Reich was pincered from east and west, Polish POWs waited anxiously to see which of the Allied armies would reach them first. It could make all the difference between liberation and renewed captivity. Officers held at *Oflag* VIIA at Murnau in Bavaria, for example, were confident that they would be saved by the Americans, who duly arrived in April 1945. Soldiers held in camps in northern Germany were freed by the British. But the inmates of camps in Germany's eastern provinces, such as Lamsdorf or Sagan in Silesia, were freed by the Soviet Army. For them, a straight jump awaited them from the Nazi frying pan into the Soviet fire.

It has to be argued, therefore, that the civilian evacuees from Warsaw had a harder ride than the POWs. The largest single contingent, variously estimated at anything from 30,000 to 60,000, was sent to Breslau, the capital of Silesia, which was beyond the range of Allied bombing and which in 1943–44 had been the recipient of several heavy industrial enterprises transferred from the Ruhr. The vast *Berthawerk*, for example, which had been built in the nearby town of Markstädt by Krupps of Essen, manufactured heavy artillery. The FAMO works produced rolling stock, and other establishments produced V2 engines, artillery fuses, and tanks. All of them were desperately short of labour. The shortage was being filled partly by work brigades from the local concentration camp at Gross Rosen and partly by foreign workers. Conditions were oppressive.

> Life for the top class of forced labourers seemed relatively benign . . . Shelter, food and pay (though very poor) was guaranteed. Yet the list of prohibitions was endless:
>
> We were obliged to wear an armband marked P, and we were not allowed to ride on the trams, to enter a church, theatre, restaurant, opera or circus or even to visit the zoo or botanical garden. We could not participate in any sports, speak Polish in the street, listen to the radio or read the press. We were not even free to sit on park benches, which were marked with the words: FÜR POLEN

> UND JUDEN SITZEN VERBOTEN. We were not permitted to study or to get married . . .
>
> Any transgression of these rules was treated as a 'breach of contract' and risked immediate investigation by the Gestapo.
>
> Life for the lowest class – slave workers – meant a daily confrontation with death. Nothing except maltreatment was guaranteed.[57]

In January 1945, after Hitler ordered that Breslau be turned into a fortress to be defended to the last man, the Gauleiter expelled the great majority of German civilians but insisted that workers engaged in war production should stay. As a result, some 200–300,000 foreigners were forced to endure the ensuing Soviet siege, which lasted for nearly five months. Not a few men and women who had survived the hell on earth during the Rising were killed by the hell on earth of the Siege of Breslau.[58]

Nor did the entry of the Soviet Army herald anything resembling rapid relief. Mass looting, gang rapes, and licensed mayhem were the order of the day. Liberated Breslau, soon to become Wrocław, looked very much like liberated Warsaw – an ocean of rubble inhabited by a horde of desperate, damaged, grieving people.

Given Germany's acute want of manpower, it is not at first clear why in October 1944 so many Varsovians should have been condemned to the concentration camps. They were not, in the main, Jews, and they were not, in the main, active insurgents. But the fact remains, tens of thousands of Varsovians were dispatched to Auschwitz and to other such hellholes.

One may presume that insurgents and civilians from Warsaw found themselves in Nazi concentration camps through one of two sets of circumstances. In the first place, some insurgent soldiers, who were captured before the October capitulation, especially after the fall of the Old Town, were shipped off to the camps as a form of punishment. They were supposed to count themselves lucky for this privilege, since most of their captured comrades, including the wounded, had been summarily shot. In the second place, roughly 12–15,000 Varsovians were packed off after the Capitulation either to Mauthausen-Gusen or to Ravensbrück, apparently for no other reason than that the SS wanted their share of free labour. [**ADMIRATION**, p. 481]

A well-known novelist and poet, Thaddeus B., was among a group of several hundred sent to Auschwitz in August 1944. A member of an AK unit, he was trapped by accident in a street round-up in Warsaw, and

ADMIRATION

A young German officer risks severe punishment by writing to his parents and sending them an honest opinion about the Capitulation

from a letter to his father, 5 October 1944

. . . The Capitulation was undoubtedly one of the most extraordinary things you can imagine. The reality of it puts all drama, all tragedy into the shade. They came out with fully deserved honours after true heroism in battle. In truth they fought better than we did. What we can learn from it is the following: 1) that nothing sensible can come from this kind of subjugation of an entire nation. Sad but true! 2) we don't have a monopoly on fortitude, spirit, patriotism, and sacrifice (we can't take the Poles' credit away from them). 3) that a city can defend itself for months on end, with much heavier losses on the attacker's side . . . and much can be learned from this by a neutral observer. 4) that although a fighting spirit and a pure and courageous approach can achieve a great deal, in the end this spirit will always succumb to material advantage.

Can history ever be just? Not here. However strong the idea of nationhood, the fact of power will always overwhelm it . . .

from a letter to his mother, 16 October 1944

. . . The '*Wochenschau*' (newsreel) is filmed here where I am and I saw at first-hand the drama of the Polish capitulation. Let's not deceive ourselves: Warsaw fell thanks to our heavy weaponry and not to the courage of certain units, however well they fought. Our losses amounted to about half those of the September campaign (incidentally, what would have happened without our unit, of which no mention was made? If it hadn't been for us, not a single soldier could have mounted an attack). Warsaw was a well of human passion – weaknesses, aspirations, bestiality, and madness. This unprecedented and many-sided war has revealed unplumbed depths of humanity and bestiality. Nothing from the realms of poetry, reality, or soldierly lore can touch it. In spite of everything, the most heroic fighting, given the conditions, was done by the bandits themselves. And if London, which ruled on everything down to the last detail, had not ordered the capitulation, we would have found ourselves with a tough nut to chew for a lot longer. Much more blood would have flowed. The insurgents deserved to be treated like soldiers. The Poles had nothing left to hope for, after the loss of their statehood and all their means of defence. I myself wouldn't like to live under German administration. They led off General [Boor] in a column of cars, and some colonel presented his army's declaration of surrender. Then they marched by in step, four abreast, avoiding the tear-stained and pain-ridden faces of the women, dressed wherever possible in remnants of Wehrmacht or party uniform, with their weapons ready to be surrendered. All done without a sign of despair, heads held high with national pride. Exemplary![1]

P. Stolten

---

spent nine months in Auschwitz-Birkenau. His experiences were reflected in a number of searing post-war novels, including *Dzień na Harmenzach* (1946) and *This way for the gas, ladies and gentlemen* (1976). Thaddeus B. belonged to the small number of former insurgents, who, having tasted the worst of fascism, was to be converted to the ideals of communism. But his work is mainly preoccupied with the problem of human suffering. Ultimately he could not take the strain. Like his fellow inmate, Primo Levi, he survived Auschwitz only to commit suicide six years later.[59]

Vatslava L. had been a Home Army cook during the Rising. She was transported to Auschwitz in October 1944, since she was regarded as a recidivist, who had been discharged from KZ *Warschau* on condition of her good conduct. She was the widow of an army officer who was taken prisoner by the Soviets in 1939, and whom she attempted to visit by walking in the winter snows of 1939–40 from Warsaw to Kozielsk in western Russia. (She was to learn that her husband had been murdered at Katyn.) Handed over by the NKVD to the SS during the currency of the Nazi–Soviet Pact, she passed two years in the Goose Street camp within KZ *Warschau* before her conditional release. Her brief service in the Home Army, therefore, formed but a brief interval between one concentration camp and the next. She survived the rigours both of Auschwitz and of the 'Death March' to the Hanover District which was carried out in the first weeks of 1945, but in Bergen-Belsen she caught typhus, and expired a mere ten days before the arrival of its British liberators. In all probability, she was buried alive in a ditch with other sufferers and killed with quicklime. This woman was totally innocent. She paid with untold anguish for the love of her family and her country. Nothing could be more painfully symbolic than the lot of her son who lost his father through the savagery of the Soviets and his mother through the savagery of the Nazis.[60]

The group of some 5,000 Varsovians sent to Mauthausen-Gusen in Austria entered what many regarded as the lowest ring of the KZ system. This was a place which could not formally be classed like Treblinka or

Sobibor as a death camp: its clients, who were put to work in the granite quarries, were subjected to the cruellest of treatments and enjoyed no such luxury as a rapid death. Mixed in with Jews and Soviet prisoners, the Varsovians were held in the open throughout the winter of 1944–45, suffering a horrendous depletion rate. Only a handful lived to tell the tale.[61] [**POW**, p. 486]

The group that wound up in Ravensbrück seem to have been the victims of a particularly cynical trick. They formed part of the female civilians from Warsaw who had volunteered for labour in the Reich. They had entered the cattle wagons expecting to be set to work on German farms or German factories. But when the doors were thrown open at the end of their journey, they were already inside the one part of the Reich that they had hoped to avoid.[62]

Meanwhile, back in the ruins of Warsaw in late 1944, the Germans were finding that they were not entirely alone. From time to time, especially at night, their patrols would hear voices, or catch sight of a furtive figure scurrying among the rubble. They lobbed speculative grenades into cellars, and dropped poison into wells; and on several occasions, after setting an ambush, they shot one or two of the 'vermin' dead. But the phenomenon was on a much larger scale than they could have imagined. For a group of men and women had decided not to trust German promises but instead to dig in and to hold out until the Germans departed. Numbering 2,000 to 3,000 and later known as 'Robinson Crusoes', they were predominantly Jewish, and in large part had belonged to the Home Army's medical services. Helped by their departing comrades, they stockpiled canned food, bottled water, candles, and medicines; they fitted air tubes and peep-holes to their well-concealed bunkers; and in some instances they were physically bricked in from the outside before the rest of their units marched off to surrender. They had expected to lie low for a few weeks. But the weeks passed. The *Brandkommandos* toiled above and around them. Explosions and shuddering falls of masonry marked the progress of demolition. Searing heat alternated with acrid smoke, then the ever colder nights were followed by ever colder and ever darker days. Notches scratched on the walls recorded the movement of the calendar. As the year drew to a close, entrances were eased open, and night-time forage parties ventured forth looking for water and for information. If they returned, they reported little of interest: Germans bivouacking round a camp-fire: non-German footprints in the snow: the grandeur of a star-lit winter sky: an eerie silence: and no signs of Soviet soldiers anywhere.

Ladislas S. (1911–1999) was especially deserving of the label of 'Robinson Crusoe', for he had chosen to be marooned in isolation. He was a Pole of Jewish descent who had worked before the war for Radio Warsaw as a well-known songwriter, pianist, and bandleader. He had lived through both Risings in Warsaw, and had seen enough not to trust the Nazis. So he lived on his own like a sparrow in ruined attics, learning to crawl along roofs and gutters and above all to stay out of sight and earshot. His great find on an upper floor was a shell-shattered bathroom in which the bath was still filled with uncontaminated water. Yet, as the frosts set in, traversing the rooftops became ever more perilous. And the day arrived when he was sighted. Having accidentally driven a long wooden splinter into his finger, through carelessly climbing through a burnt-out doorway, he was busy contemplating the wounded hand, when he heard steps on the stairs:

> I rushed towards the entry to the attic, but this time I was too slow. I was standing face to face with a German soldier, whose none too intelligent face was framed by his helmet and his gun. He was no less shaken by our unexpected encounter than I was. He asked me in broken Polish what I was doing . . . then, pointing the barrel of his gun straight at me, he ordered me to accompany him. I made as if to comply, then told him that he would have my death on his conscience and that, if he left me alone, I would give him half a litre of pure alcohol. He accepted the deal quite eagerly, saying only that he would be back and that I would have to give him more. As soon as it was done, I climbed into the attic and pulled up the ladder behind me, and closed the trap-door. Within quarter of an hour, [the soldier] came back in the company of a sergeant and several others.
>
> Hearing their steps, I crawled out of the attic onto a strip of the steep but undamaged roof. I lay there spread-eagled, holding myself in place by standing on the overhanging gutter. If the gutter had buckled or given way, I would have slipped . . . and fallen five floors to the street below. But the gutter held . . . and my life was saved once again. The Germans searched the whole building, piling up tables and chairs, and finally came up to my attic. But it did not occur to them to look on the roof . . . They left empty-handed, cursing and calling me names . . .[63]

By December, ice and driving snow rendered Warsaw's ruins ever more inhospitable, and the fugitive had to scavenge for food even further from his base. One day, he had just found some food cans in an abandoned larder, and again was totally absorbed:

> I never heard anything until a voice right behind me said, 'What on earth are you doing here?'
>
> A tall, elegant German officer was leaning against the kitchen dresser, his arms crossed over his chest.
>
> 'What are you doing here?' he repeated. 'Don't you know the staff of the Warsaw fortress commando unit is moving into this building any time now?'
>
> I slumped on the chair by the larder door. With the certainty of a sleepwalker, I suddenly felt that my strength would fail me if I tried to escape this new trap. I sat there groaning and gazing dully at the officer. It was some time before I stammered, with difficulty, 'Do what you like to me. I'm not moving from here.'
>
> 'I've no intention of doing anything to you!' The officer shrugged his shoulders. 'What do you do for a living?'
>
> 'I'm a pianist.'
>
> He looked at me more closely, and with obvious suspicion . . .
>
> 'Come with me, will you?'
>
> We went into the next room, which had obviously been the dining room, and then into the room beyond it, where a piano stood by the wall. The officer pointed to the instrument.
>
> 'Play something!'
>
> Hadn't it occurred to him that the sound of a piano would instantly attract all the SS men in the vicinity?
>
> When I placed my fingers on the keyboard they shook. So this time, for a change, I had to buy my life by playing the piano! I hadn't practised for two and a half years, my fingers were stiff and covered with a thick layer of dirt, and I had not cut my nails since the fire in the building where I was hiding. Moreover, the piano was in a room without any window panes, so its action was swollen by the damp and resisted the pressure of the keys.
>
> I played Chopin's Nocturne in C sharp minor. The glassy, tinkling sound of the untuned strings rang through the empty flat and the stairway, floated through the ruins of the villa on the other side of the street and returned as a muted, melancholy echo. When I had finished, the silence seemed even gloomier and more eerie than

POW

A POW, who was to become a priest and a headmaster, tastes the good life of 'English' prisoners

We marched from Ozharov to the 'Cable Factory'. From there we travelled in sealed goods wagons. We cut a large hole in the floor of the wagon with my bayonet for our hygienic needs. We ripped up the trapdoor boards at the end of the wagon. Escape looked possible . . . The train moved off, but in the cab of the next wagon was a guard with a Schmeisser. Game over.

For two days we got nothing to eat or drink. We were thrown off at Lamsdorf, near Opole, in German Silesia. The Germans threw themselves at us in fours, yelling, like vultures and, attacking us.

Starving and exhausted, we marched sloppily for around ten kilometres . . . We could already see the gates and the barbed-wire of the camp when suddenly two German fighter planes collided overhead and struck the earth.

'A good omen,' someone said.

The Germans wanted to shove us immediately into the barracks, from which they had just driven the Bolshevik POWs . . . But our commander declared that a Polish officer would not enter such filthiness; they were to clean the barracks and generally treat us well. They were surprised at these pretensions of Poland being a great state. They rang General von dem Bach in Warsaw, who replied, 'Yes, treat them as if they were English'. . . .

Our POW group was looked after by a sergeant, who we named 'Dud Daddy'. 'If we hadn't been ordered to treat you like the English,' he declared honestly, 'I would have given you a hiding . . . You killed my son in the Rising, and when I was in Warsaw you twice took my weapons . . .'

We had no idea of how POW life looked in a 'normal' officers' camp. It turned out that it was a rich life. In our honour, the local orchestra gave an excellent classical music concert. In the camp theatre, *The Marriage of Figaro* was performed. There were many university professors, engineers, teachers, and academics in detention. Throughout the last five years, they had passed their knowledge on. Some people even obtained academic degrees. We also acquainted ourselves with the full repertoire of Underground songs, that were sung during the Rising and by the Partisans:

'Hey, we met in the last battle . . .'
'Hey, lads, with fixed bayonets!' . . .

And on a lighter note:

'Every lad wants to be wounded, for nurses are fine ladies,
When a bullet gives you a scratch, will the lady give you a kiss . . .'

The chaplain, Father Ki., immediately bowled me over with his direct approach and sense of humour. We Home Army types did not meet with the approval of all the officers of 1939, [who had been in the camp for five years]. Father Ki. defended us, saying 'Considering all that they suffered during five years of occupation, they are fantastic.' . . . Unfortunately, Father Ki. was shortly discovered to have been part of a conspiracy, and was sent to Dachau. . . .

At last the day of freedom arrives: 29 April 1945. We know that liberation will come soon, because the sounds of battle are extremely close. German soldiers were already hanging up white flags on the gates, the guards came down from their watch-towers. Expectation, tension. . . .

A unit of the SS had stopped outside the town of Murnau. Officers were arriving at our gates in two cars. They did not see in time that tanks were approaching from the other side. Suddenly the tanks appeared. Instead of surrendering the Germans began to shoot. The tanks replied with cannon fire. The SS officers were killed.

Unfortunately, at the same moment, Lt. M. died from a ricochet. Five years of detention, and now that . . . One of the tanks ripped straight through the barbed wire. A hatch in the turret opened and an American soldier appeared. He waved and said quaintly in old-fashioned Polish, 'How fare ye, yeomen?' He was greeted with a shout of joy. They had sent us American Poles! . . .[1]

A. Janicki

Lamsdorf: a Jewish insurgent has other worries

Another ritual we were subjected to on our arrival [at the camp] was the so-called delousing in the common shower room. It was a waste of time, as the straw in our mattresses provided an excellent breeding ground for lice and we soon became adept at the technique of catching and squashing them between two thumbnails.

Once again, the mark of my Jewishness gave me some anxious moments. In the first few days I still worried that somebody might notice it in the shower room and give me away. But nobody bothered. Our guards did not care whether anyone was a Jew, nor did my companions. In captivity, for the first time in five years, I felt safe under the protection of the Geneva Convention.[2]

J. Lando

before. A cat mewed in a street somewhere. I heard a shot down below outside the building – a harsh, loud German noise.

The officer looked at me in silence. After a while he sighed, and muttered, 'All the same, you shouldn't stay here. I'll take you out of the city, to a village. You'll be safer there.'

I shook my head. 'I can't leave this place,' I said firmly.

Only now did he seem to understand my real reason for hiding among the ruins. He started nervously.

'You're Jewish?' he asked.

'Yes.'

He had been standing with his arms crossed over his chest; he now unfolded them and sat down in the armchair by the piano, as if this discovery called for lengthy reflection.

'Yes, well,' he murmured, 'in that case I see you really can't leave.' ...[64]

The 'Pianist' had met one of the few human beings who were both willing and able to help him. Three days later, the officer returned with loaves of bread and jam. Before he left for good, he brought more food, an eiderdown, and an overcoat, and the invaluable news that the Soviet Army would be advancing at any time. The officer was destined to die in Siberian captivity. The fugitive was destined to live, and to play Chopin once again on Polish radio.

To the east of Warsaw, the NKVD continued to trawl for insurgents and for other 'illegals'. ('Illegal' referred to anyone not specifically licensed by them.) Early in October 1944, they received strong reinforcements. But the reinforcements arrived at the time immediately after the Capitulation, when the pool of fugitive insurgents was drying up. So they concentrated on other things – on tracking down Home Army 'safe-houses', on eliminating radio stations that were still communicating with London, and on keeping an eye on the Catholic clergy, whom they regarded as uniformly subversive. In this latter regard, Serov wired Beria on 13 November seeking approval for a general round-up of the clergy. It wasn't approved.[65]

Faced by the mass of statistics regarding the arrest of Home Army soldiers, 'bandits', 'illegals', 'fascists', and 'bandit-insurrectionaries', historians cannot always distinguish Varsovian insurgents from the rest. But time and time again, when named insurgents, especially officers, are known to have been in the Soviet zone after the Rising, it turns out that one way or another they found their way into the care of the NKVD. Such was the fate of Capt. 'Nora', Boor's radio operator, of Maj. André, the AK Commander of Praga, and no doubt of many others. Maj. André was among the luckier ones. Arrested by Lt. Light at his mother's house on 27 November, he was given a death sentence, subsequently commuted to ten years, but was successfully sprung from jail in June 1945. A hundred or so of his comrades in Praga were less fortunate. Arrested in December 1944 for circulating an illegal news-sheet called *Alarm*, they were packed off to a camp at Stalinogorsk in the Urals.[66]

The NKVD records of the period reveal an extraordinary attention to detail. For Serov's men did not simply root out undesirables. They collected facts on anyone and anything that would throw light on the attitudes and activities of the communities which they were processing: and literally tons of evidence was forwarded to Moscow. When they captured a Home Army radio station in Lublin, for example, they also captured its archive and all its correspondence with the exiled Government in London. Even they must have been amused to find a summary of Anthony Eden's speech to the House of Commons of 27 September and of his view that no arrests were taking place. They also found a report from the station operator telling London what local conditions were really like:

> Telegram, nr. 303, from 28/X
>
> 1. Mass arrests of Home Army soldiers and also of civilians faithful to the London Government have intensified since 10 October, with the simultaneous seizure of landowners, teachers, doctors and educated people. The Militia and the NKVD are pacifying villages which oppose the Lublin Committee. Public and secret shootings of Home Army soldiers are the order of the day. In the towns, round-ups take place in the evenings . . . The prisons and concentration camps are overflowing. When intoxicated, Soviet officers talk openly about shooting Poles . . .[67]

Such was life in the districts adjoining Warsaw within a month of the Capitulation.

As the NKVD took in their latest wave of prisoners, others could be considered for release. In December 1944, for instance, Stalin told Beria that 'Comrade Bierut' should be allowed to see the full roll-call of the NKVD's Polish prisoners and that he could submit a shortlist of names for special amnesty. Bierut duly submitted twenty-three names of 'Poles and Polish Jews'. They were all pre-war Communists who had been languishing in the Gulag since the purge of 1937–38.[68]

One individual, who fell into the hands of the NKVD on 12 November 1944, proved to be of exceptional interest. A Varsovian by education and an army officer by profession, Boleslas P. – alias 'Sablevski' – had served in 1939 in a tank unit commanded by Arrow, and in 1943–44 had commanded a battalion which operated in western Byelorussia. In July '44, he had disbanded his unit in order to facilitate their infiltration into Warsaw. But surrounded by the Red Army, he had not managed to reach the Rising and had gone to earth in a village only ten miles north-east of the capital. Both his brother and his first wife were AK soldiers killed in the Rising.[69] The really interesting thing about him, however, was his pre-war membership of the illegal fascistic offshoot of the nationalist movement and his reputation as the ideologist of an extreme right-wing faction of radical Catholics, who admired Gen. Franco and who favoured a strong-arm totalitarian regime. In short, he was the sort of politician whom the Communists badly needed. They shared his contempt for Western-style democracy, and welcomed his readiness to defy the traditions and authority of the Roman Catholic hierarchy. And they soon realized that he could be very useful in their designs for splitting the Church. As a result, Sablevski was given special treatment. Taken by the NKVD for interrogation at the Royal Castle in Lublin, he was subsequently handed over to the Polish Secret Police, and held by them in the Mokotov Prison amid the Warsaw ruins. In due course, as the President of the Catholic PAX movement, he would emerge as one of the Communists' key collaborators. By the lights of Western political science, he was a figure that was not compatible with Communism. But in the light of Soviet practice, he was entirely acceptable.

What exactly ensued during Sablevski's imprisonment by the NKVD and the UB has been the subject of much speculation. But one may assume that he was made a tempting offer that he could only have refused on pain of death: '[Sablevski] was a figure larger than life . . ., a fanatic who [threw] himself in full frenzy into the extremist politics which [overwhelmed] Europe and ravaged the lives of its inhabitants like a medieval bubonic plague.'[70]

The openings for opportunists like Sablevski were made by the gaps left by the decimated generation of the Rising. But he paid dearly. His brother was killed in the first days of the Rising. His first wife, courier

'Halina', a Protestant, was shot dead on 14 August, when carrying an order from the AK Command. His second wife was a colleague of his first wife from the Radoslav Grouping. His first son, who had survived the Rising as an infant, despite his mother's death, was cruelly murdered in 1957 by avengers who fled to Israel.

A new stage of intensive work began for the NKVD with Zhukov's January offensive. Warsaw fell almost immediately into Soviet hands, followed rapidly by all the villages, towns and cities west of the Vistula. [**GHOST TOWN**, p. 492]

At one small town near Warsaw, the NKVD were given an unusual mission which reveals much about their trade. A popular author, Ferdinand O., who enjoyed international acclaim and whose Mongolian travelogue *Beasts, Men and Gods* (1922) had been translated into many languages, was on their blacklist. Among other offences, he had written a less than reverential semi-fictional biography of Lenin. When they came to arrest him in mid-January 1945, they were told that he had died only a few days earlier. So for good measure, they exhumed his body to make sure that he was dead.[71] False burials were widespread: Home Army men on the run were adopting the disgraceful practice of erecting gravestones to themselves. The NKVD was no doubt tired of hearing 'Sorry, he was killed in the Rising.' [**SIBERIA**, p. 495]

The next big group of ex-insurgents to fall into NKVD hands were the 'Robinson Crusoes', who came out of hiding as soon as the Soviet Army moved into the ruins of Warsaw on 17 January. Many of their fellow stowaways had not managed to hold out. In the following days and weeks, when every inch of the ruins was thoroughly searched, scores of hideouts were found inhabited only by the dead. They had perished from cold or hunger or despair, frequently shot through the head with their own last bullet. But many hundreds, if not thousands, of gaunt and ghostly individuals were able to emerge, and in scenes of extreme emotion to greet their liberators. As usual, they were warmly greeted by the common soldiers. But as soon as the NKVD arrived the climate of their reception changed abruptly. It made no difference that they were the heroic survivors of the sixty-three-day battle against the Germans or that many of them were Jews. In the eyes of the NKVD, they were illegals who had been living on the enemy side of the front and who, having failed to die, were potential collaborators. Without exception, they were hauled in for questioning.

GHOST TOWN

A young woman, a double agent working for the Home Army, enters Warsaw in the company of the NKVD on the first full day of the Capital's liberation

For me, the most tragic experience of all was entering Warsaw. I saw a wilderness, terrifying sights . . .

I was almost the very first person to go in, on the first or second day, before the civilian population was allowed to cross the pontoon bridge. I walked across that bridge with all those Soviet officials and various others. I think I may have been the first . . . I know that I had to get permission beforehand, and that I went in the company of my 'colleagues' from the NKVD. All the top leaders went – Colonel Shkurin, Petrov, and two others from another unit. The procession was a large one; but there wasn't a single Pole among them. I'd have remembered if I had seen a Polish uniform. They wanted to cross [the river] like conquerors . . .

The bridge, which was built on pontoons, swayed as we walked over it. Terrible sights, such as I'd never seen before. It seemed as if the world had fallen apart.

One started from Diamond Street, an image of destruction, picking a path through the rubble. Sometimes one had to scramble up to the height of the first floors, and then to clamber down. The figure of Christ was lying there, beside an overturned cross, as if He had again fallen under its weight.

The smell of dust and smoke was wafting around, mixed with the stench of corpses . . . Hardly anyone was to be seen, except for those who had stayed on [after the Rising] and who now came out of their hideouts, terrible shadowy figures. I could not approach them, or talk to them. I just walked like a robot in the direction of Skolimov Street, until I lost my way, surrounded by ruins. I met someone who said that everyone in the house [nearby] had been shot . . . I didn't cry; I just sat there. It quickly grew dark; and I realized that there was no point whatsoever in looking for anything. There was not much point either in asking those few people with their bundles: they didn't react.

But I asked someone after Skolimov Street. The most important thing was for me to find out what had happened there. People were weeping, kneeling, and praying beside the mass of improvised graves. Some of the crosses had notes pinned to them on a scrap of paper or cloth. But the writing had faded, or had been washed away [by the snow and rain].

I spent the night with an old woman on Diamond Street. I must have told her that I was with the army, because she was very suspicious and took me in very reluctantly. At least she allowed me to stay, and gave me something hot to drink . . .

I asked her about the Rising . . . I could not forgive myself for not having been there . . . I asked her how it had been. But she said nothing.

I returned to Praga, completely broken. They [the NKVD] immediately jumped on me, demanding to know if I'd met any Home Army types, if any conspiratorial cell was still operating. I snapped back at them: 'What do you think? Could any conspirators have survived in those ruins?' . . . When they saw how depressed I was, they started talking politics. 'Look, girl,' they said, 'see what the AK has done – so much destruction, so much death.'[1]

Ludwika Z.

One of the larger companies of 'Robinsons' consisted of some thirty men and women who had immured themselves in a complex of cellars in the City Centre between Slippery and Hay Streets. Led by Dr Henry Beck and his wife Yadviga, they included a Polish army officer, a dentist called Dr Schindler, an AK nurse and her underground journalist friend, and two Greek Jews liberated by the AK from the Goose Street Camp, together with the Fisher, Goldberg, Sobelsohn, and Goldfarb families. They kept a dog called Bunker, who never barked. When their water ran out, they had succeeded in digging an effective well that was 9m (thirty feet) deep. Their first outside reconnaissance had taken place on 18 November, when they joined up with a fugitive Soviet officer called 'Vania'. Their liberation came suddenly, when Dr Schindler returned from a patrol with the news: 'The Bolsheviks are here!'[72]

Another group of some twenty Robinsons survived in a cellar at 26 Golden Street. Their leader, an AK officer known as 'Selim', had arranged that his fiancée, Eva, would leave Warsaw at the Capitulation and that she would return to release them. When Eva duly returned 107 days later, she found to her horror that 26 Golden Street had been taken over by a unit of the NKVD. So she told them everything. The NKVD men thereupon descended to the cellar, knocked down the dividing wall, and saw eighteen half-living creatures emerge on all fours through the resultant hole. They shot two people, who could not make it, and promptly took the rest under armed guard to a special investigation villa in Jolibord. Selim contrived to escape from the villa, married Eva, and at the first opportunity emigrated to Venezuela, where (one presumes) they lived happily ever after.

The 'Pianist's' liberation almost proved fatal:

The Germans had withdrawn without a fight . . . I ran downstairs, put my head out of the front door of the abandoned building, and looked out into the [Independence] Boulevard. It was a grey, misty morning. To my left, not far away, stood a woman soldier in a uniform that was difficult to identify at that distance. A woman with a bundle on her back was approaching from my right. When she came closer I ventured to speak to her:

'Hello. Excuse me . . .' I called in a muted voice, beckoning her over.

She stared at me, dropped her bundle and took to her heels with a shriek of, 'A German!' Immediately the guard turned, saw me, aimed and fired her machine pistol. The bullets hit the wall and sent plaster flaking down on me. Without thinking, I rushed up the stairs and took refuge in the attic . . . I heard soldiers calling to each other as they went down into the cellars, and then the sound of shots and exploding hand grenades.

This time my situation was absurd. I was going to be shot by Polish soldiers in liberated Warsaw, on the very verge of freedom . . .

I began slowly coming down the stairs, shouting as loud as I could, 'Don't shoot! I'm Polish!'

Very soon I heard swift footsteps climbing the stairs. The figure of a young officer in Polish uniform, with the eagle on his cap, came into view beyond the banisters. He pointed a pistol at me and shouted, 'Hands up!'

I repeated my cry of, 'Don't shoot! I'm Polish!'

The lieutenant went red with fury. 'Then why in God's name don't you come down?' he roared. 'And what are you doing in a German overcoat?'

However, I could not go with them just like that. First, I had to keep a promise I had made myself that I would kiss the first Pole I met after the end of Nazi rule. Fulfilling my vow proved far from easy. The lieutenant resisted my suggestion for a long time . . . Not until I had finally kissed him did he produce a small mirror and hold it up to my face, saying with a smile, 'There, now you can see what a good patriot I am!'[73]

A considerable number of insurgents from Warsaw found their way into the 1st and 2nd Polish Armies from the autumn of 1944 onwards. Even more Home Army men had been trapped by the Soviet cordon on

SIBERIA

A Home Army courier evades the Germans but not the NKVD

Before the end of the Rising, I was ordered to leave Warsaw, so as not to fall into German hands. After burning my promotion to second lieutenant, I was transported from the Hospital of the Infant Jesus to Prushkov, hiding among the elderly. Then I reached my uncle and grandmother's place, to show that I was still alive, scrub up, do my washing, get warmer clothes, sleep, and eat as much as I could. In Gerardov, I received a bicycle. My direct superior, Captain J., arrived once in a while with orders.

On Sunday 11 February 1945, a day off from my work for the Underground, I cycled to Alexandrov. There I met seventeen-year-old Fela, and we rode back together. In the dark, by the market square at Viskitki, we were forced by the cobblestones to dismount. Suddenly the strong lights of torches were directed at us. It was a group of Russian soldiers demanding documents. I handed mine over, they looked over them, gave them back, and let me leave. Fela had no documents, so they took us both. I whispered to Fela, 'Remember, we do not know each other.' I, after all, was the one that was heavily implicated, not her.

This regiment was marching to Berlin on foot, between twenty and thirty kilometres daily. We were taken in 'lifts'. In the evenings and at night an investigating magistrate interrogated me. After a month and a half, Fela was taken home and I was passed on to another department. The new investigating magistrate's assistant beat me in the face, twisted my arms behind my back and stretched them above my head. He threw me on the floor and jumped on me, breaking my ribs, and he arranged for me to stand at attention for several days without food or drink, with a light bulb right next to my eyes. On the fifth day (Easter Saturday), I pretended to faint. They stopped torturing me. In Mezeritz the military court sentenced me to eight years' hard labour in educational camps, and I was stripped of my citizen's rights for three years. It was 9 May 1945.

I was then taken with thirteen women, mainly Russian, to a jail in Brest. After a few months we were transported to Orsha Prison, and then after a while to Gusino Camp, near Smolensk. Here and in the next two camps we repaired part of the Moscow–Berlin highway. Then for fourteen extremely frozen days we travelled in cattle wagons to a camp at Nuzdzialsk. I worked in the forest felling trees, pruning them and arranging them in two-metre piles. At night it was another eight kilometres to load the wood onto the trains.

After a while, to the envy of the Russian women, I was chosen to work in the kitchen. There were one and half thousand slaves in the camp, but only three workers. We worked forty hours with eight hours' sleep and no break. After three months, it was unbearable. I was taken to the fifth and last camp – at a State Collective Farm called 'Sielanka' (in Russian it meant a 'village woman' and in Polish 'idyll'), near Solikamsk [in the Komi Republic]. After a three-month stay in the camp hospital, I resembled a zombie. At night I mended men's clothing and by day I worked. I spent the most time on day shifts as a pig-tender, rising to the rank of chief pig-tender. In the end I was taken to the dairy. Here the Russian women showed me respect because I was working 'in the manger'. I made butter and cheese, which were taken to be sold in the city. The work lasted twenty hours with four hours' sleep.

Suddenly, there was a telephone call and a letter from Moscow: I was ordered to stop work and to prepare to leave. Two days later, I was taken to a transit camp in Solikamsk, and waited for news of my fate for over a month. At last, on 8 September 1948, I was loaded into a railway prison wagon and a month-long journey began, stopping at a variety of prisons. I was in Kazan, where my great-great-grandmother had died in 1863, and in Molotov, where I met a group of Polish women from Lvuv, who had been taken into captivity in 1944. They left us in Biala Podlaska. Here they wanted to clothe us so that we did not reveal our prison stripes. I was given a train ticket to Warsaw and 200 *zloties*. I had arrived back in Komorov before the middle of November. I discovered where I should look for my parents. Only then did I know for certain that my older sister and three brothers had really fallen during the Rising.

And so I spent forty-four months in the hands of the Russians, or three years and eight months.

Maria Getka

---

their way to assist the Rising. Many of these men continued to give trouble. As hardened veterans, they were very welcome to the fledgeling Communist-run forces. On the other hand, as self-reliant and independent-minded individuals, proud of their patriotic sacrifices during the Rising, they were exactly the sort of recruits which irked the political department. Yet cannon-fodder was badly needed. And more of them came forward in January and February '45, after Poland was fully occupied and the AK had been disbanded. So the problem grew, until it came to a head in the spring, when the Battle for Berlin was already underway. To the NKVD's horror, it was discovered not only that their Polish charges were in possession of 'illegal' radio transmitters but also that they were using them to communicate with their compatriots who were fighting under British command in Italy and the Netherlands. The alarm was sounded. Wildly exaggerated reports were sent back to Moscow, warning of a dastardly plot which would bring a million-strong army of Polish exiles, led by Gen. Anders, marching through Germany to contest Soviet domination. The reaction was true to form: arrest all suspects![74] So yet another contingent of innocents wended their way to the pit of misfortune. If they were lucky, such prisoners were sent to one of the milder NKVD camps, where the chances of survival for fit young men were moderate. If they were unlucky, they were drafted into a Soviet penal battalion, which was used among other things for clearing minefields with nothing more sophisticated than human feet.[75] [**FIRESTORM**, p. 499]

The principal NKVD collecting centres for political prisoners from Warsaw at this time were located at two separate sites at Rembertov, 10km (six miles) to the east of Praga. Throughout that freezing winter, prisoners were frequently held in the open, without shelter, in a compound surrounded by barbed wire. It was a preliminary to the 'softening-up process'. According to reports, when locals enquired about the suffering prisoners who were clearly visible from a nearby road, they were told that the compound contained *Volksdeutsche* and Nazis. From January, further centres were prepared in Warsaw itself, notably, as reported by locals, in the deserted grounds of the former KZ-*Warschau*.

A man who passed through Rembertov described the conditions. They were not to be compared to the relative luxury at Sandbostel or Murnau:

> The camp ... had been organized on the terrain of a former armaments factory. NKVD units manned both the guard and the administration. In March 1945, the majority of the prisoners were Poles who had been arrested and brought in from various parts of the country. Apart from them, there were German POWs, Volksdeutsche, ex-Soviet POWs released from captivity in Germany, Soviet civilians, Vlassovites, Russian émigrés from the time of the Revolution, and a few Jews ...
>
> Crush-Stink-Lice: and organizational chaos. Overcrowded, two-tiered bunks would collapse, causing injuries and even fatalities ... The numerous attempts at escape ended in volleys of gunfire and collective punishments. In short, not very pleasant ...
>
> The lavatory was but one of many torments ... It was designed for a few dozen people, but was supposed to be used by several thousands, many suffering from dysentery. Huge queues formed. Figures would squat all round this inaccessible building day and night,

> and the Soviet Guard would amuse themselves by shooting at them. More casualties ensued. (Every morning, the corpses would be carried along the ranks at roll-call for the purposes of identification) . . .[76]

Conditions on the trains which carried many of the prisoners into the Soviet Union were no better. The passengers were packed into bare, locked cattle-trucks, with one small window covered with a grating. The train consisted of fifty or sixty such wagons which were guarded by riflemen riding in raised pill-boxes. Rations were handed out on average once every two days. They were made up of a chunk of bread and a slice of salted fish for each person, and a bucket of water for each wagon. Hot meals were served up only once or twice a month. A longer stop was fixed for a couple of days in a siding near Moscow, where a disinfection station was located. The prisoners stripped naked. Their clothes passed through a steam chamber, while they washed their bodies from a tap. They were then shaved above and below by women wielding cut-throat razors. The journey from Warsaw to the first camps in the Urals took four to five weeks. At journey's end, the mortuary wagons at the back of the train would be emptied of their cargo. In a transport of 2,000 prisoners, 300 to 400 could expect to arrive as corpses.[77]

It is evident that some captured insurgents found their way directly into the depths of the Gulag at a very early date. Some of them must have been transported from Warsaw, or most probably from Praga, before or immediately after the Capitulation. One such report was made by a Catholic priest who was condemned to a sentence in the great concentration camp complex at Vorkuta in northern Russia six years after the war. When he arrived in the camp, he was surprised to find a group of some 250 former insurgents from Warsaw, all young men and women, some of them still wearing the tattered remnants of their grey scout uniforms. He was even more surprised when a man from the group offered him the whole of his daily food ration. 'We are all dying,' the youngster explained, 'but you must live in order to return and to tell the world.'[78]

So long as the war against Germany lasted, the Soviet authorities had little time or inclination to sift carefully or to classify the millions whom they captured in their westward drive. The NKVD was faced with vast tides of German prisoners, of Soviet 'repatriants', and of the civilian deportees whom they cleared at random from the rear areas. Their practice was to ship off the captives en masse and to ask questions afterwards. They could not pay any special attention to the 'bandit-insurgents' of the

FIRESTORM

An ex-insurgent, imprisoned in Stalag IVB in Saxony, is taken on a work party to an unknown city

10–12 February [1945]. We are getting off at a suburb where the guards, typically for Germans, are shouting, jabbering, and prodding us. Our job is to dig trenches. There are hundreds of German civilians, including women, digging alongside us. I have no intention of helping the Germans, so I'm looking for a chance to escape. I don't look like a prisoner of war in my grey overcoat.

It is clear that we are in the remote suburbs of [a large city], connected to the centre by an electric train line. I need money to buy a ticket so I sell a packet of American cigarettes. On Monday I leave my group under the pretext of having to go to the toilet, and I don't come back. At the station I go to the ticket office and say: '*Wo ist Bahnhof, bitte.*' It worked!

For two hours I wander around and fail to locate the main station. Near a park, I can see some subways marked '*Luftschutzkeller*'. I guess they must be air-raid shelters. It's getting dark, I'm cold and tired, so I go downstairs where an entirely empty room is lit by low-voltage bulbs. I sit on a bench, eat a rusk, and fall asleep.

I wake up from powerful bomb explosions that feel like an earthquake, and the wail of sirens. Soon afterwards I am surrounded by a crowd of terrified Germans who fill up the shelter fast. The Germans are shaking with fear as much as I am. The planes come in waves. The bombs drop for hours. The lights in the shelter flicker and then go out. A heavy German hand drops on my shoulder.

Wer bist du? – the man next to me asks, shining a torch in my face.

Ich bin ein Kriegsgefangener – I answer hopelessly.

Polnische? – he asks.

How does this German sod know?

Jawohl! – I say.

Also Raus! Du Polnische schweine! Raus! Clear off!

Before I reach the exit I feel the fists of the excited mob on my body. The women hit the hardest.

God, I think to myself, Germans know how to hate – even when they are facing death themselves.

It's still night but the skies are lit by fires and exploding bombs. I don't want to risk a confrontation, so I cross the street and hurry towards the park. I find a ditch where I lie down flat, next to a big tree.

God! – I pray. – You didn't want me to die in Warsaw, where I could have been buried under rubble in the Old Town. Please don't let me die here, on German soil so packed with hatred.

Tuesday, 13 February. Just after midnight. Endless explosions and the roar of aeroplanes. I bury my face in the dry autumn leaves and block my ears. A plane flies above and scatters orange pellets. They look like Christmas-tree decorations but they explode with devilish fire, burning everything – walls, concrete, asphalt and . . . men. People are running out of the shelters, like human torches, screaming with horror. And so their lives end, lives full of hatred. But there are children in the shelters too . . . Choking with emotion I tell myself that's the price to be paid for the Rising and the lives of innocent Polish children. No! No! No! A hundred times no. Enough hatred!

I feel an urgent need to leave this city which no longer exists. I wander around, aimlessly. The railway station has gone because [the city] has gone, too. Rubble everywhere. Just like the Old Town in Warsaw not so very long ago.[1]

L. Halko

Home Army, who were one of the smaller categories and who, despite predictions, were not openly resisting. In any case, once the back of the Home Army had been broken by the Warsaw Rising, the policy was to build up the security organs of the emerging Communist regime in Poland and, if possible, to leave the local problems to them.

It was typical of the rough-and-ready methods of those days that the NKVD did not always know whom they had arrested. All Home Army soldiers used pseudonyms and false identity papers. Forged *kennkarte*, which had routinely fooled the Germans who had supposedly issued them, were not going to be questioned by officials who had recently arrived from Russia and who, in some cases, could barely read the Latin alphabet. Hence, on 7 March 1945, no one gave a second thought to an incident in the little town of Milanovek near Warsaw, when an NKVD agent stopped a middle-aged man in a random search and found that he was carrying a roll of American dollars concealed in a packet of coffee. The possession of foreign currency, especially dollars, was a criminal offence in Soviet eyes. So the offender was automatically classed as a *spekulant* or 'speculator'. He volunteered no information about himself, though he had the papers of a railway worker. Without more ado, he was arrested, sent to Rembertov, and thence conveyed to Russia, where he was sentenced to two and a half years' hard labour. He served out his time in several camps in the Urals and in the district of Kazan. In this way, throughout the years when

Poland was being annexed by the Communists, no one knew what had happened to the second-in-command of the Home Army, Bear Cub's deputy. His whereabouts were known neither to the NKVD, nor to his comrades in the Home Army, nor to the British, who had first sent him to Poland. Gen. Nile had simply evaporated.

Three days before the end of the war, on 5 May 1945, the NKVD arrested Janina Fieldorf, the wife of General Nile. (Unbeknown to them, her husband was already a prisoner in Russia.) As she remembered it, her Russian interrogator lost his temper when discussing the Warsaw Rising and let slip some revealing remarks:

> 'And what were you Poles thinking?' the Russian asked rhetorically. 'Did you think that you were going to take control of Warsaw on your own and then start fighting our Soviet forces? And do you know what Stalin told our commanders, who had stopped before Warsaw? [Stalin said] "Don't move an inch. Wait while the Germans kill as many Poles as possible, and there'll be less work for us to do." '[79]

Of course, a third-hand report of this sort is no real evidence for what Stalin may or may not have said nine months earlier. But it does indicate something about prevailing attitudes in the NKVD.

After the war, many striking differences between Soviet and Western attitudes became immediately apparent. Winston Churchill had expressed his own views about steadfastness in conflict, defiance in defeat and magnanimity in victory. But magnanimity played no part in Stalin's philosophy. Indeed, he insisted on treating his own people as suspects and the entire world beyond the new Soviet borders as a nest of 'anti-Soviet' spies and vipers. All manner of groups and individuals who had found themselves outside Soviet control during the war were rounded up. Democratic formations, like Poland's Home Army, were not just excluded from public life. They were slated for destruction.

In Poland, the formation of an Internal Security Corps (KBW) in May 1945 was an important sign of the times. The KBW was no mere armed gendarmerie on the French model. It was a fully fledged, elite military force on the lines of the NKVD's 'special regiments'. It was highly trained, highly mobile, heavily armed, and entirely separate from the regular armed services. It posed a special challenge for the remnants of the Underground. Working alongside the People's Militia under the Ministry of Public Security, it gave warning that all non-conformers and resisters were to be treated to a mailed fist. The one benefit lay in the prospect that the NKVD's own special troops could be gradually withdrawn.

The victory over Germany in May 1945, and the establishment in Poland of the Government of National Unity in June, obviously brought relief for many, and opportunities for some. But for those whom the new regime regarded as mortal enemies, the war had *not* ended. On the contrary, it was soon transformed into open and vicious internal warfare. Since the Soviets and their Polish clients continued to harass and persecute their democratic opponents, showing no readiness for reconciliation, the most determined democrats were driven to review their earlier inclination to wait and see. They were increasingly convinced that the decision to disband the Home Army had been a mistake. If they were going to be wiped out for doing nothing, they had little to lose by returning to the conspiratorial resistance which had sustained them against the Nazis for the previous six years.

Such were the circumstances which led in June 1945 to the formation of the secret Freedom and Independence Organization (WiN) which in all but name was the Home Army, mark II. Like another of its predecessors called NIE ('No'), which Gen. Nile had tried to launch in 1944 in the Soviet-occupied zone, it was pitted against the growing power of the Soviet-run regime; and its enemies were quick to put it in a negative light by denouncing it as 'reactionary' and 'anti-Soviet'. But its aims were positive enough. They were to preserve the groups and individuals which were devoted to the ideals of democracy and patriotism. This time, however, all outside support was denied. The Western powers, which had once helped and encouraged the Home Army, were not prepared to support WiN, even verbally. And a war-weary society that was mourning millions did not have the stomach for another fight. The result was a lonely struggle of small isolated cells and armed groups who faced the combined powers of the NKVD, the KBW, and the UB in a very unequal conflict. It goes without saying that veterans of the Warsaw Rising joined WiN in considerable numbers. But not all veterans favoured the policy of open confrontation; and WiN was only one of several similar underground bodies. The unequal battle lasted from the summer of 1945 to the summer of 1947 and beyond. It was an essential background to the renewed wave of political repressions which occurred in those same years.

*

In Germany, meanwhile, all Allied prisoners were being freed. Much depended on who freed them, but for the Poles, there were three basic choices. Military prisoners, including Home Army soldiers, could head for Polish forces stationed in the West. In practice, this meant travelling either to northern Italy, where the Anders Army was based at Rimini, or to Matchkovo, which was the zone of occupation in northern Germany occupied by Maj.Gen. M.'s division.[80] The second choice was to move into one of the numerous Displaced Persons camps which the Allied Control Commission was now opening. The third and riskiest choice was to try to return home – if one still had a home to return to. British and American officials were under orders to recommend this last course of action. They were not always aware that 'Liberation' in the east did not have the same connotations as Liberation in the west. Nor did they seem to realize, having approved the annexation of the eastern half of Poland by the Soviets, that half of the Polish refugees, by 'going home' would not be going to Poland.

No POW or camp survivor ever forgot the moment of liberation. For the inmates of KZ Sachsenhausen near Berlin, it came on 22 April with the arrival of the 2nd (Polish) Army. Adam S., a member of the Polish Socialist Party (PSP), had been captured in Warsaw's Old Town on 2 September, and had found himself inside Sachsenhausen within twenty-four hours. Thanks to a leg wound, he was still lying in the camp sick-bay seven months later when he heard a cheery Polish voice. 'I'm Shenkevich', the young soldier announced; 'Well, not Shenkevich exactly, but Blumstein.' It turned out that the two men had lived on the same street in the Riverside. 'Good Street no longer exists,' said Adam S. 'My family no longer exists,' replied Blumstein.

The main advantage of being freed by the Soviets rather than by the British or Americans lay in the fact that it tended to happen early. Indeed, the Soviet Army was reaching POW camps in Silesia and Pomerania in January 1945. A prisoner thus freed from Stalag IIC at Woldenburg was able to rejoin Bear Cub in the Underground shortly after the AK was disbanded. In due course, Bear Cub made him his deputy, just as Boor had invested Bear Cub. When Bear Cub failed to return from his meeting with the Soviets, 'Chairman' automatically assumed command. [**FUGITIVE**, p. 505]

One particularly joyous moment, however, has to be recorded. Stalag VIC at Oberlangen was situated in north-west Germany very close to the Dutch frontier; and it was the principal POW camp for the female soldiers of the Home Army. Its 1,500 inmates consisted mainly of former nurses, couriers, and other women auxiliaries from the Warsaw Rising. On 12 April, word spread that 'the English Army', as they called it, would be arriving at any minute. The story is best told by one of the soldiers of that 'English Army' driving along in his jeep at the back of an armoured column:

> We covered the ground very quickly. In the totally flat and treeless countryside a camp appeared with its watchtowers and its barbed-wire fence . . . Everyone drove up to the main gate, but I turned off some 200 metres to the side. My [driver] leapt out of the jeep, and ran right up to the wire, Sten gun in hand . . .
>
> The historic shout of one of our soldiers can't sum it up. *O rety, ile tu bab*, 'Oh cripes! What a crowd of birds!' He was right. There was a huge crush of women. And how well they looked. After four years of looking at pale and skinny Scots girls, we thought every one of these women was a picture of health and beauty. The intense joy of liberation made them all look absolutely marvellous. It was impossible to believe in the cold and hunger which, in reality, had ravaged that penal camp – for that is what it was.[81]

What a coincidence! The women soldiers from the Warsaw Rising had been liberated by the men of Gen. M.'s division. It was equally a coincidence on that same day that the women's former commander, Bear Cub, was about to complete his deposition for the NKVD.

For ex-insurgents who decided to join the 2nd Corps of Gen. Anders in Italy, the prospects were highly exhilarating. Having experienced both the horrors of the Rising and the boredom of the prison camps, the journey across the Alps in the spring or early summer of 1945 must have aroused deep feelings of joy and relief. For, as they climbed the Brenner or the St Gotthard Pass in the back of the British army trucks sent to collect them, surrounded by magnificent snow and sunshine, they were leaving their wartime woes behind. And they knew that as soldiers of Gen. Boor they were driving to the warmest of welcomes.

Life in German Displaced Persons camps was not so rosy: but most participants were able to resign themselves to temporary discomforts in the hope of better fortunes to follow. Most of them hoped either to join the European Voluntary Worker scheme or to emigrate to North America, Australia, or South Africa. The time of waiting could be distressing. Living conditions were primitive. US quotas did not provide for sick or disabled candidates. Local German officials were often appointed as supervisors.

FUGITIVE

A fugitive POW, who spent the last weeks of the war among Czech partisans in Bohemia, finds the way to freedom on an ex-German motorcycle

6 May 1945

The peace in our ravine was interrupted by Thomas' hysterical shriek.

'Americans! The end of the war! . . .' We drive into a wide valley, where units of General Patton's 3rd Army are pitching camp. The news is fantastic! Hitler is dead, and in Italy they have strung Mussolini's corpse up by the legs . . .

8 May

The behaviour of the American soldiers does not inspire trust. In the afternoon they fired coloured rockets over the valley. Later their colonel climbs onto a tank and begins to shout something. His soldiers shout even louder! Worse! They begin to shoot! But no, they are celebrating victory! If so, me too! I get out my pistol, load it and fire it into the air – once: a habit from the Rising . . .

19 May: on the road in Saxony

My greatest desire is a glass of water. A grey old man opens the door.

'*Wasser, bitte schön,*' I say. The old man invites me inside and points to a bucket. I drink two large mugfuls. Everywhere there are visible traces of former luxury and of terrible destruction. I get out a packet of American coffee from my rucksack.

'Coffee?' I ask. '*Ich bin Polnische Kriegsgefangener.*'

'*Ach ja?* I speak a little Polish,' he says. 'I once lectured in Cracow.'

We heat up some American tinned food and he adds potatoes. A feast fit for a king. We eat on beautiful Meissen porcelain, with silver cutlery, sitting on broken armchairs. [My host] begins to chat. He is a widower; his son died at Leningrad; and his daughter fell into the hands of the Bolsheviks.

I sympathize, but I cannot stop myself from commenting on Nazi barbarity. 'You Germans also carried out monstrous crimes!' I said. 'Now the whole world knows about the crematoria in Auschwitz, and many other concentration camps, where Germans murdered millions . . .'

'Yes, you are right, and what is worse, Goebbels, the choirmaster of deception, is dead, but thousands of his pupils survive and at some point will shift responsibility to others . . .'

At the interzonal border

The border runs through the suburbs of Chemnitz. In front of it are the Russians, and the Americans beyond. The Russians are playing cards. The Russian officer reads my document, and points to the border. I let out my breath and [wheel] the motorcycle under the barrier. I feel a gun barrel in my stomach! The American soldier is looking at me with deep suspicion! I show him my permit from the [Czech] hospital. He edges it out of my hand with the barrel of his gun and then treads on it with his boot . . . The Soviet officer laughs. 'American culture!' he says . . .

Sunday 20 May

I sleep tucked in a German duvet next to a Russian. A piercing shriek from the next room wakes me. I see Soviet soldiers struggling with two women, whose clothes are in tatters. No one hears the hysterical cries. A queue forms, ready to rape the mother and daughter. I feel sick . . .

I wash in a mug of water and go to my motorcycle. I must get away at any price! I ask the Russians for a few litres of petrol. They agree, but they all want to have a go. Not one of them knows how to ride. The Americans laugh and lift up the barrier. One of the Soviet soldiers managed to drive a dozen metres, but the engine cuts out. I run over, pretending to help him, and thereby cross the border. I start the motor, sit on the seat, and start going. I drive in a small circle near to the Americans then drive off in zigzags at top speed. No one shoots . . .[1]

L. Halko

And Soviet officials were permitted to visit the camps looking for people whom they alone regarded as Soviet citizens. On those occasions, anyone who felt threatened – including those born in eastern Poland or even in Warsaw before 1914 – tended to take to the woods.

Refugees, deportees, and ex-prisoners returned to Poland in 1945 for any number of reasons. But they did so at their own peril. Most wanted nothing more than to be reunited with their families and loved ones. Some wanted to recover property or businesses. Some thought to test the conditions of the new regime. Others returned with the clear intention of contesting the regime with every means at their disposal. Such were Vitold P., 'Roman,' the hero of Auschwitz I, and his partner, Barbara, who had both fought in the Rising in the ranks of the AK.[82] Both spent a couple of idyllic months with the Second Corps in Italy before following the call of duty.

All returnees faced manifest dangers. If they presented themselves at the ports or at official frontier crossing points, they had to run the gauntlet of security officials who were trained to look on anyone who had been abroad as contaminated. They had to undergo pedantic screening which aimed to uncover false identities and which, in the case of ex-insurgents, could trigger peremptory arrest. If, on the other hand, they attempted to enter the country illegally, usually via one of the mountain tracks leading from Czechoslovakia, they stood to be caught in the net without a question being asked. As many an old conspirator was learning, it was not so easy to fool policemen of one's own nationality as it had been to fool the Germans. For ex-insurgents, lying low and avoiding recognition was now becoming as hard as standing up to fight.

Britain was slow to celebrate victory in the Second World War. VE-Day, which celebrated victory in Europe, took place on 8–9 May 1945. But Britain was still at war with Japan. VJ-Day took place on 15 August, on the day of the Japanese surrender. And after that there was no special appetite for more junketing. V-Day or 'Victory Day', with its grand parade, was postponed until 8 June 1946. All, or almost all, of Britain's wartime allies were invited to participate.

An embarrassing problem arose, however, with regard to Poland. It appears that an official invitation was sent to the Government in Warsaw, before someone noticed that the Warsaw regime had not been Britain's wartime ally. The embarrassment was increased by the fact that the former exiled Government of Poland, now the Government-in-Exile, had lost its formal recognition shortly after VE-Day. It had been permitted to remain in London, but it was not entitled (in British eyes) to represent Poland on official occasions and it was no longer legally responsible for the Polish Armed Forces which were still in Britain and which were in the process of demobilization.

The faux pas was not corrected until the very eve of the parade, when HMG realized that the Warsaw Government was not going to send any representatives. In consequence, a last-minute invitation was sent by Foreign Minister Bevin directly to the Chief of Staff of the Polish Army, General Kopański, who was still in post in London, and other invitations were sent to the chiefs of the Polish Air Force and the Polish Navy, and to individual generals. The belated invitations were courteously declined.[83]

As a result, the Victory Parade in London passed off without the participation of any units, colour parties, or representives from Poland.

None of the Polish soldiers who fought at Narvik, at Tobruk, in the Battle of the Atlantic, at Monte Cassino, in Normandy, or at Arnhem were present. No one showed up to honour the Polish section of SOE, the Home Army, or the 'Dark and the Silent', who had been among the most faithful of allies. No doubt there were Britons who assumed that the Poles were playing true to form and causing the usual trouble. (The only Polish servicemen and servicewomen to join the parade were a sprinkling of the fliers and ground crew who attended in their capacity as members of the various RAF formations into which they had formerly been integrated.)

In Warsaw, the anniversary of VE-Day was duly celebrated. So, too, was the anniversary of the supposed founding of the Lublin Committee on 22 July, which had been raised to the status of a 'National Day'. But the regime run by Messrs Bierut, Berman, and 'Vyeslav' Gomulka was not going to show its face in the nest of capitalism and imperialism in London. What is more, they would see that on every 1 August in Warsaw for the foreseeable future, every anniversary of the Warsaw Rising would be meticulously passed over in grim silence.

Fortunate nations can celebrate their victories as a matter of course, without inhibitions. But the men and women who stayed loyal to the aims of Poland were not in such a happy position. They had no real victory to celebrate. As a soldier who had been serving in 1944 as a radio operator in Barnes Lodge remembers, VE-Day and V-Day were staged for those, like the British, whose only aim was to win the war against Nazi Germany. They were not for others for whom the struggle against Germany had been but a step to a more important goal. 'The overwhelming majority of Polish soldiers in the West,' the former radio-man was to recall, 'were not fighting simply for the destruction of Nazi Germany, but rather, and above all, for the restoration of their country's independence. We felt it very strongly. For us, the war had ended in catastrophe. Personally, if I had been ordered to take part in the Parade, I would have done everything in my power to avoid it. Because for me, it would have been the "Parade of Defeat".'[84]

These sentiments may be contrasted with the glowing words that had been uttered five and six years before. 'On the day of victory,' a British minister had said in 1940, 'Poland, as the first nation to stand up to Hitler, while others have been grovelling on their bellies, should ride in the van of the victory march.'[85]

CHAPTER VII

STALINIST REPRESSION, 1945–56

IT HAS BEEN SAID THAT public discourse in post-war Poland was governed by two taboos. One laid down that no one was permitted to speak badly of the Soviet Union. The other laid down that no one could speak well of the Warsaw Rising. Certainly, by the time a full-blown Stalinist regime had been established in 1948, all freedom of speech had been crushed, and all favourable mention of the wartime alliance with the Western powers was anathema. The word now was that the Soviet Union had won the war against fascism single-handed; that democracy was to be identified with something called 'the dictatorship of the proletariat'; and that the ruling party could do no wrong. Anyone who dared to praise pre-war independence, or to revere those who fought during the Rising to recover it, was judged to be talking dangerous, seditious nonsense. Even in private, people talked with caution. Police informers were everywhere. Children were taught in Soviet-style schools where denouncing their friends and parents was pronounced an admirable thing to do.

Nonetheless, despite its self-proclaimed hostility to the West, Stalinism was not destined to receive the opprobrium in Western eyes that was directed against Fascism. Even at the height of the Cold War, when the Soviet Union became an imminent enemy, Western opinion about the Second World War stayed set in its former ways. It did not respond as much to the known facts as to the one-sided nature of Western experience. In accordance with the facile scheme which appealed no less to the puritanical Manichaeism of the Anglo-Saxons than to the Marxist dialectics of Soviet ideology, Fascism was irredeemably evil. Communism, in contrast, though it obviously had its defects, was a doughty foe of fascism and hence, at least in part, admirable. Holocaust-deniers or minimizers were to be driven from civilized society. But leading academics, who often adhered to the Communist movement throughout Stalin's time and beyond, and who consistently denied Stalin's mass crimes, were thought perfectly respectable. It was not until 1948 that the British Government thought fit to bar Communists from the civil service and the security organs.

Of course, Stalinism had a twenty-year career in the USSR before it ever reached Poland. Having removed the Old Bolsheviks from power in the 1920s, it began to apply Lenin's principles in a systematic manner in the 1930s, culminating in a reign of state terror that has no equal in European history. During the war, it was permitted a few tactical modifications to assist the war effort. But it returned to its old dogmatic path as soon as victory was assured. It survived the death of the Great Leader in March 1953, by which time it was armed with nuclear weapons and had been spread from the Soviet Union to most of Eastern Europe, to China, North Korea, and Vietnam, and, a few years later, to Cuba. It did not begin to retreat until Khrushchev's 'Secret Speech' in 1956, and was never completely eliminated as long as the Soviet Union lasted.

Conventional analysis dates the introduction of Stalinism into Poland from December 1948, when the Polish United Workers' Party and the so-called 'One Party State' were inaugurated. Yet there is much conviction in the argument which holds that Stalinism arrived with the first Soviet unit to set foot on Polish soil in 1944. For Poland was not like neighbouring Czechoslovakia where the legitimate Government returned from abroad only to be removed by a Communist coup when the time was ripe. Poland was in Soviet and Stalinist hands from the start. The key feature lay in the fact that the Stalinists, lacking all spontaneous support, needed several years to organize their cadres and to eliminate the opposition. For this reason, three distinct periods can be identified. The period of improvisation and of so-called 'civil war' lasted from 1944 to 1947. The period of Stalinist consolidation covered the years 1947–54. The period of limited Stalinist retreat began in 1954 and ended in 1956.

The 'civil war' of 1944–47 saw the infant Communist establishment pitted against an array of political opponents who could not possibly have been defeated without the active intervention of Soviet forces. In the political sphere, the democratic opposition centred on the former Premier of the Government in London, who was leader of the country's largest party, the Peasant Movement (PSL) and who was the only politician of substance to join the post-war regime. In the military sphere, three groups proved most active: the WiN group, which was closely linked to former AK circles; the NSZ, which had survived in the Underground intact; and the Ukrainian UPA, which operated in the mountains of the south-east.

Many of the people who participated on the democratic side strongly objected to the 'civil war' label. Although they often found themselves pitted against Polish soldiers and policemen, they regarded their adversaries as Soviet puppets; and they saw the conflict as an extension of the international campaign against Poland that had begun in 1939. They saw themselves as the continuators of the independence movement. One can only sympathize with the predicament of those democratic underdogs, who had been totally cast adrift by their erstwhile Western allies and who had been driven to carry on an unequal and uncoordinated rearguard action against overwhelming odds. There may have been 40–50,000 Underground fighters in the field. Ranged against them were several hundred thousand professional soldiers, internal security troops, militarized police, and Communist reserve militia, officially designated as 'volunteer' regiments. Crucially, behind all these local units, stood the almost limitless reserves of the NKVD and Soviet Army. There were no pitched battles – only repeated raids and ambushes from one side and elaborate dragnet sweeps from the other. According to official figures, the Communist security forces lost 18,000 men. Losses among their Underground opponents are impossible to estimate.

The political programme of the new regime, which accompanied the 'civil war', was inspired by a vicious mixture of fraud and force. As some of the regime's luminaries would eventually admit, they could not possibly have allowed a margin of free politics, because they would have lost the reins of power immediately. So they tried to maintain a facade of democratic reconstruction, whilst relying on crude coercion. The 'free and unfettered elections' that had been promised by the Yalta Agreement never took place. Instead, in July 1946, a spurious referendum was staged, whose results were fixed beforehand. The general election of January 1947, which was predictably won by the Government bloc, was another victory for 'the department of party mathematics'. It was followed by the suppression or forcible merger of all the remaining opposition parties, whose membership was attacked by a sustained campaign of beatings, disappearances, unexplained killings, and judicial murders. Fifty death sentences per month were announced in the *People's Voice*, rising to a hundred per month after the election. The game was up by the end of 1947, when the Underground ceased to resist and when the former Premier Mick was forced to flee for his life. There can only be one verdict: the political birthright of the generation which had fought and bled during the Warsaw Rising was systematically usurped.[1]

The so-called 'One Party State', which emerged in December 1948, cannot be properly described in the conventional language of Western political science. Indeed, 'One Party State' is a rather inadequate starting-point from which to launch an accurate account of the essentials. For the outward forms were less important than the inner motors. One may list the Marxist-derived socio-economic schemes which included central command planning, five-year plans, collectivized agriculture, and the cult of heavy industry. One can emphasize the Leninist-inspired political features including so-called 'democratic centralism', the duplicated organs of party and state, the absolute principle of obedience to the party, the cult of the Great Leader, the ubiquitous vigilance of the not-so-secret political police, the grotesque proliferation of concentration camps, and the routine application of state terror. And one would be right to emphasize the aspirations of the party to total social control over every aspect of welfare, employment, education, and culture. Yet these descriptive lists do not reach the heart of the matter.

The key to Stalinism, as to many other forms of totalitarian regimes, lies in the ethos of a secular religion which taught its adherents both to believe its precepts and to condemn all non-believers. For Stalinism was a special form of sectarian cult, which possessed its infallible leader, its dogmas, its rituals, its superstitions, and its Great Satan. On the political scale, it stood as far from pluralistic, tolerant, utilitarian democracy as one can get. Its hell was the outside world, where its norms could not be enforced. Either through fear or through faith, its followers simply could not envisage compromise.

One of the best introductions to Stalinism, therefore, was written by a political left-winger, who had initially been drawn towards Marxism but who, having seen the Soviet system from the inside, wrote the most devastating critique ever penned. A writer and poet, who had disagreed with the Warsaw Rising and had fled as soon as it started, briefly served the post-war regime before fleeing for good to the USA. He likened Stalinism in Poland to the 'Art of Ketman' as performed under the oriental despotism of the Shah in feudal Persia:

> Ketman was the art of double-think, of dissimulating and of deceit – the profession of an army of toadies and lick-spittles who pandered to the whims of 'Him' with limitless flattery and cynicism, simply to promote their careers or to save their skins. According to the Comte de Gobineau, who first described the Persian Court to the world at large, 'there were no true Moslems in Persia.' According to the author, 'there were very few true Communists in Poland.[2]

The closed, mystical nature of the world of communism was confirmed by a member of the inner circle, a Varsovian, who stayed loyal to the movement throughout the Stalinist period despite serving seven years in the Gulag and losing a brother in the pre-war purges. His perseverance may be explained by the fact that he also lost his parents in Treblinka:

> For the Party . . . is a word that replaces all known concepts and expressions; it is an absolute, an abstraction. It is always right; it is our honour, our happiness, our life's goal. And if you ask any Communist about its infallibility, . . . he will say: the Party didn't commit mistakes; people committed mistakes. The leadership, abusing our trust, committed mistakes . . .[3]

The inner circle of the post-war political elite, who took all major decisions and who passed on instructions from Moscow, did not exceed perhaps half a dozen individuals. In the early years they were headed by the General Secretary of the PPR, Comrade 'Vyeslav' G., and by Bierut, the Chairman of the KRN, who posed for the time being as a 'non-party man'. The former was the only one who, though a loyal Communist, held a modicum of independent views and who did not owe his position directly to Moscow. After his removal in 1948, the circle was reduced to a 'Troika' of three – Bierut, now both General Secretary of the United Workers' Party and President of State, Jacob Berman, the Security Chief, and Hilary Minc, the economic supremo. These men, 'Muscovites' to a fault, held all the reins of power. They controlled all other party functionaries through the rules of party obedience. They controlled all non-party ministers and officials through the party-run nomenklatura system which oversaw all appointments, high and low. So long as they maintained Stalin's confidence, they were untouchable. Unlike the mass of their subjects they lived in style – with access to luxurious, party-owned villas, to well-stocked shops reserved for the party, to limousines, to servants, and to the supreme symbol of power – the *vyerskhuvka* telephone, a dedicated, direct line to the Kremlin.

In November 1949, the 'Troika' was joined by none other than Marshal Rokossovsky, the Soviet commander who had halted his armies within view of the Warsaw Rising five years earlier. The Marshal, who was a Soviet citizen, was now appointed Poland's Minister of Defence in a move to re-subordinate the Polish military establishment to its Soviet superiors. His appointment, accompanied by an army of Soviet advisers, was occasioned by the creation of NATO and by Stalin's fears about Poland's reliability in the looming international conflict.

Two or three times a year, Bierut and Berman would travel together to Moscow for a personal meeting with Stalin. They usually met him either late at night or in the early morning. Stalin used these meetings to test and to humiliate his henchmen. Once, Berman had to dance with Molotov whilst Stalin wound the gramophone. He learned that Molotov's wife was being held in the Gulag – 'just in case'. On another occasion, Stalin pressed Bierut to say whom he liked better, Berman or Minc. 'It was like a child being asked whether he loved Daddy or Mummy.' Bierut passed the test, replying that he liked both of them equally.

On one such occasion Bierut received a rude shock about the realities of his position. Years after the purge of the KPP in 1938, he was still trying to discover the fate of numerous pre-war comrades, who had disappeared without trace. And he had dared to ask Stalin about it face to face. Stalin went through the same routine that he had laid on for Gen. Sikorski in 1941 when asked about the whereabouts of the thousands of missing Polish officers subsequently unearthed at Katyn. He called in Beria and spoke sharply to him. 'Where are they?' he would enquire; 'I told you to look for them. Why haven't you found them?' Beria did not see the funny side. Leaving the room in Bierut's company, he warned him off in no uncertain terms. 'Why are you fucking around with Iosif Vissarionovich?' he began. 'You fuck off and leave him alone. That's my advice to you, or you'll regret it!' An open warning from a monster who by that time had already killed millions was not to be ignored.[4]

'Poland's Stalin', who was viewed at home as an all-powerful dictator, was a mere mouse to be played with in the presence of the real Stalin. Yet such is life among gangsters. The big fry beat the lesser fry; and the lesser fry beat the small fry. Many of the inner circle had done time in the Gulag or in Soviet prisons. One member of Bierut's Politburo had been so badly tortured in the USSR that, unusually, he couldn't even mention it. Another had reputedly broken his own arm to avoid signing a confession that would have ended his life. Eventually, when many of the grisly facts were made public, all denied having any knowledge of them.

When Stalin died on 5 March 1953, millions wept. One may think that they wept because the 'Great Leader' had been loved and admired. But that would be an unjustified generalization. Certainly, he was widely admired in the Soviet Union as the victorious war leader, who had made Russia great again. He was loved by those who had taken his cult at face value. But for tens of millions, especially in the satellite states, he had never been remotely loved or admired. They saw him simply as a bloody tyrant. But they wept as well – from shock, from relief, from disbelief, from the realization that everyone else was weeping. Having been told that Stalin was immortal, or having lost hope for an end to the nightmare, commissar and schoolchild, veteran or victim, they all felt the wave of shock and emptiness.

Yet Stalinism did not die with the death of Stalin. The system which he had created over thirty years did not possess any mechanisms for change or reform. In Moscow, a collective leadership emerged, which for its own safety killed Beria, but which was otherwise committed to keeping the system intact. In Warsaw, Bierut was unchallenged and unchallengeable. The United Workers' Party continued to rule supreme. The security apparatus continued to function as before.

The 'Thaw', as it was called, began imperceptibly. It was first noticed in Poland when compulsory collectivization was quietly abandoned in 1954. It was gathering pace in 1955, when public criticism of the regime was first aired by party members. In this regard, the publication of a *Poem for Adults* by Adam W. contained some really shocking lines.

> They ran to us shouting
> 'Under socialism
> A cut finger does not hurt'
> But they felt pain.
> They lost faith.[5]

By the time that the hated Ministry of Security was removed in the same year (if only to be replaced by something rather similar) the prospect for more fundamental reform was in the air.

The denouement came in March 1956 with Khrushchev's 'Secret Speech'. At a meeting of the Soviet Party Congress, one of Stalin's most notorious henchmen announced that Stalin had been a criminal, guilty of crimes against the party. (Khrushchev said nothing about Stalin's crimes against ordinary people.) Bierut had travelled to Moscow to attend the Congress. He returned in a coffin, having suffered a heart attack in uncertain circumstances. Things would not be the same again. It was nearly eleven years after the end of the war, nearly twelve years since the start of the Rising.

*

Life restarted in post-war Warsaw in a setting that resembled Hiroshima. The evacuation of the inhabitants had been almost total. The physical destruction, which in the principal, left-bank districts of the city was almost complete, exceeded the devastation of Dresden. Yet the determination to restore the city as the country's capital was virtually unanimous. For a couple of years, many Government institutions had to be located elsewhere, notably in Lodz, simply for lack of accommodation. But the intention was clear from the start: *Varsovia revivenda est*.

Many post-war observers commented on the shocking, ghostly nature of the ruins. Yet the most terrible of the ghosts which stalked the shattered streets and walked the broken walls was 'the Rising' itself. It was the cause of the city's disaster. Yet in the climate of the new, post-war order, it was all but unmentionable.

The rebuilding of Warsaw after 1945 was a grand act of national defiance which stated in bricks and mortar that the late *Führer*'s will would not prevail. In practical terms, it didn't make sense. Since Poland had lost over half of its territory, Warsaw now stood on the extreme eastern periphery. Urban planners would have preferred to prepare a purpose-built capital on the lines of Canberra or Brasília somewhere nearer the centre. But the political and emotional arguments were overwhelming. Warsaw could not be left to die. The size of the task was horrendous. Some 80km^2 (thirty square miles) had to be cleared of rubble and corpses before construction could even begin. Eight or ten years would be needed before even small districts, especially the Old City, could be fully restored. Fifty years would pass before the Royal Castle rose again to its former glory. The irony was: the people who ordered the rebuilding were the very ones who had benefited most from the destruction. They took great care to conceal what had actually happened. Everything was blamed on 'the fascists'.

For obvious reasons, qualified city planners were in great demand in post-war Warsaw; and it was almost inevitable that ex-insurgents would figure among them. One such specialist was Capt. 'Agaton', a 'dark and silent', who had been parachuted in by SOE in March 1942 and who subsequently fought in the Rising in the AK's 'Fist' Battalion. After the Capitulation, he served as Gen. Boor's adjutant. But on arrival in England, he made straight for Liverpool University and a course in urban planning. On graduation, he returned to Poland without delay; and, despite his political connections, he was allowed to work in the Warsaw Planning Office undisturbed. He was one of the very few ex-insurgents who

Dead City

A wilderness of ruins

Mountains of rubble

Civilian Exodus

Preparations to leave

The long walk

A column of sick and elderly

Transit Camp, Prushkov

Destinations

A member of the master race reluctantly accepts a sub-human bandit as a POW

Home Army women at Stalag XIB, Fallingbostel

Auschwitz-Birkenau

Vorkuta

Endgame

Stalin and Churchill: no meeting until October 1944

Soviet Liberation: the official truth

17 January 1945: the Communist-run Army enters the ruins

Churchill and Roosevelt arrive at Yalta: too late

Post-war Trials

Moscow: trial of Poland's democratic leaders

Nuremberg: Warsaw not on the agenda

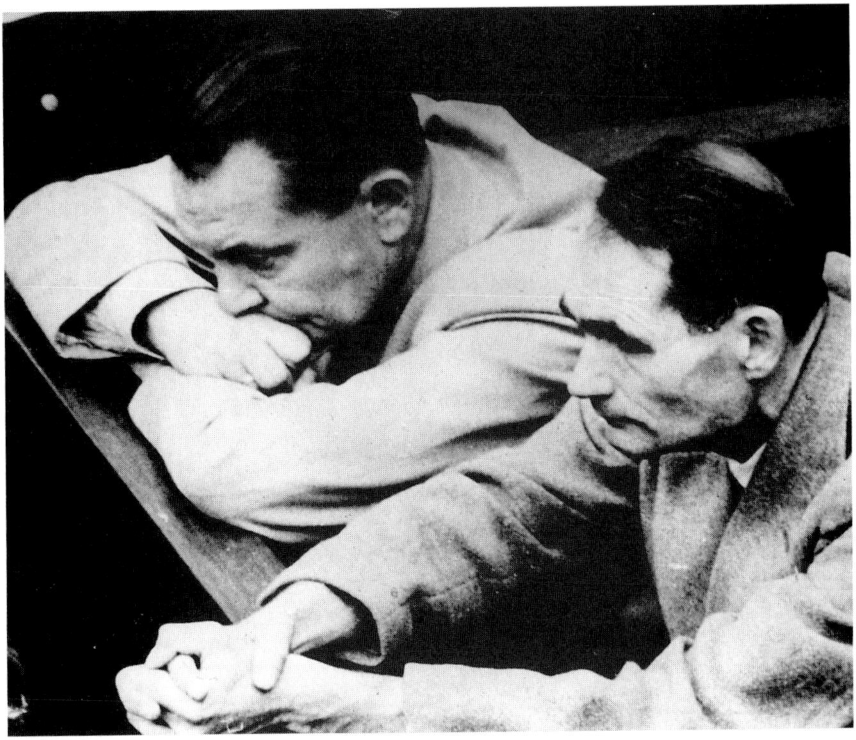

Göring in the dock, with Hess: 'Victors' Justice'

Trial of Captain Piletski, pseudonym 'Roman,' March 1948

Varsovian Destinies

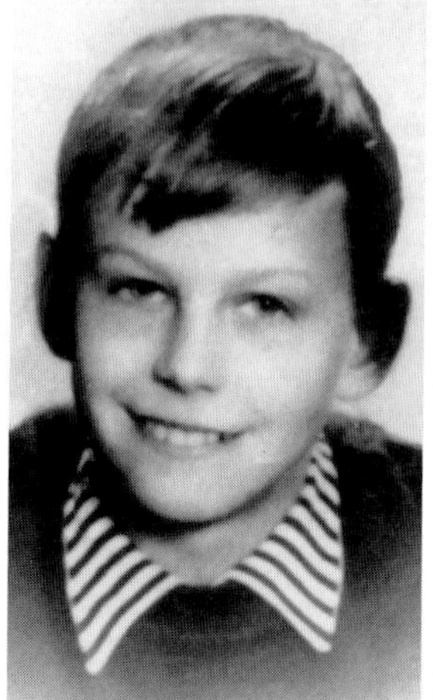

Tadek, died in battle (aged eleven)

'Bear Cub', died in the Lubyanka, 1946

'Roman', shot 1948

'Wolf' died in Mokotov Jail, 1949

Kontrym, shot 1953

'Nile', hanged 1953

'Teofil' of Zhegota: sentenced to death

Szpilman, 'The Pianist', survivor

'Ludwig', Comrade Kliszko

Father 'Stefan', future cardinal and Primate

Images True and False

Home Army 'Anchor' badges: P.W. = *Polska Walczy* ('Poland is Fighting')

German *Warschau* campaign badge

Soviet medal, 'Liberation of Warsaw'

People's Poland medal,
'Warsaw 1939–45'

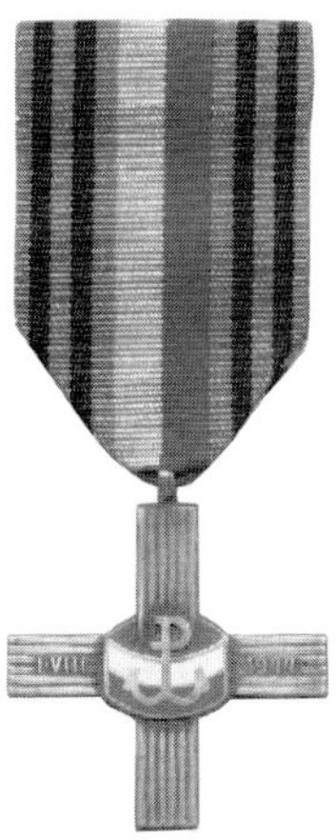

Warsaw Rising medal
(Warsaw, 1981)

Victory Parade, London, 1946: no Polish representatives

Delayed Respects

Chancellor Brandt's *Warschauer Kniefall*, December 1970, when no monument to the Warsaw Rising existed

RAF graves from 1944: British War Cemetery, Cracow

above: 'The Little Insurgent': recovery of 'Antek' 's body, August 1944

above right: Monument, 1981

right: Warsaw Rising Monument, 1989

below: 1 August 2002: the annual candlelight vigil, Warsaw Military Cemetery

Aftermath

Warsaw, September 1944

General 'Boor' in exile, London, 1956

participated both in the battle for the capital in 1944 and in the subsequent campaign of reconstruction.

The priorities in Warsaw's reconstruction said much about the new ruling elite. The restoration of the Old City, which was undertaken in loving detail at a time of great austerity, was shrewdly designed to establish the patriotic credentials of the post-war order. And the provision of high-quality, stone-built, and spacious living quarters for official families was a standard feature of Soviet-style capitals from Moscow to Bucharest or East Berlin. But it contrasted sharply with the cramped and shoddy accommodation provided with much greater delay for the working class in low-grade multi-storeyed concrete blocks. The massive Joseph Stalin Palace of Culture and Arts, which rose in the vicinity of the Central Station and on the site of some of the heaviest fighting in 1944, was designed to dominate the skyline. Nominally a gift from the USSR, it was more than paid for from the grotesquely unfair trade terms which the Soviet Government had imposed. Polish coal, for example, was sold to the USSR at 5 per cent of its international market value. The Palace of Culture was a blatant piece of architectural oppression. It was a secular replacement for the Tsar's gift of the Russian Orthodox Cathedral which had dominated the city's skyline before 1914 and which the Varsovians had dared to demolish.

So, despite appearances, this was not really an attempt to restore the old Warsaw. It was a new capital, run by new people with completely new priorities and with no intention of letting the old spirit revive. Thanks to the strict control of residence permits, preference was given to dependants of the regime; and political undesirables, like the surviving families of ex-insurgents, could easily be prevented from returning and from reclaiming the ruins of their old homes. The social policy of the Communist regime was systematically exclusive.

Post-war policy on historical monuments followed similar political priorities. Some of the pre-war landmarks were duly replaced. The Sigismund Column was raised again above the Cracow Faubourg. The Chopin Statue reappeared in 1946 in the Lazhenki Park, having been rescued from a German scrapyard. It still bore the magnificent quotation from Poland's national bard:

> Fire may consume the colourful relics of the past
> And thieves may plunder the prizes of the sword.
> But the melody will survive intact.[6]

There was a grandiose Soviet War Memorial to the fallen of 1945, replete with oversize figures and T34 tanks, which dominated the modern freeway leading to the airport. In Praga, there was a memorial to Polish–Soviet brotherhood-in-arms, which, thanks to memories of the Rising, came to be known as 'the Four Sleepers'. Yet many other items were strangely absent. There was no Polish War Memorial to the fallen of 1939. When the Tomb of the Unknown Soldier was restored, most of the original inscriptions were removed. There was no reference to the Battle of Warsaw 1920, though battle honours from the International Brigades of the Spanish Civil War were inserted. A fine monument to the Heroes of the Ghetto was unveiled in Muranov in 1947. But no public monument whatsoever was allowed to the memory of the Warsaw Rising.

This last omission was enforced for nearly half a century, and had far-reaching consequences. There had been two risings in wartime Warsaw, one in 1943 and a much larger one in 1944, yet only one of the two could be publicly commemorated. Right from the beginning, therefore, the world was systematically schooled in the false belief that the Ghetto Rising and the Warsaw Rising were one and the same thing. Misinformation was officially promoted.

A similarly perfidious strategy was followed with regard to the numerous commemorative tablets which appeared on almost every street-corner in post-war Warsaw. The favoured formulas announced such things as 'HERE THE FASCIST OCCUPANTS SHOT 119 CITIZENS' or 'ON THIS SPOT, 50 MEMBERS OF THE RESISTANCE MOVEMENT WERE KILLED BY BESTIAL HITLERITE FORCES'. Nowhere was any information given about exactly what had occurred. One could name the enemy but not the patriots. Terms such as 'Home Army' or 'Warsaw Rising' were entirely absent.

One must also mention the National War Memorial which was erected in those same years in Byelorussia at a village called Khatyn. Byelorussia had probably suffered a greater percentage of civilian casualties during the war than any other country in Europe, so it definitely deserved a fine monument. But it did not deserve the disgraceful trick that was played by the Soviet propagandists. Khatyn, near Minsk, was one of hundreds of villages which had been razed to the ground during the Germans' anti-partisan campaigns. Indeed, its buildings were burned and its inhabitants slaughtered by none other than the Dirlewanger Brigade, which distinguished itself in a similar style in Warsaw. Yet its chief attribute as a memorial site lay in the fact that its name could be easily confused with that of Katyn, near Smolensk. Hence, exactly as the Risings of 1943 and

1944 were conflated into one mythical event, so Khatyn was deliberately conflated with Katyn. For decades, busloads of tourists and schoolchildren would be cynically driven to Khatyn, to pay homage to the victims 'barbarously murdered by the fascist invaders'.

Contemporary history did not figure in the cultural schemes of the new regime. Indeed, the combination of increasingly rigid censorship and of plans to reconstruct the historical profession along Marxist lines meant that in the early post-war years very little history was published at all. When new school textbooks appeared in the late 1940s, they had nothing to say about controversial wartime issues. The Academy of Sciences did not launch its plan to prepare an official History of Poland until 1951, and the volume dealing with the Second World War and the formation of the PRL was destined never to appear in nearly fifty years of communism. In this situation, meaningful comment about the war years could only be found by reading between the lines of the official media, by risking punishment through importing foreign publications, or by scanning literary and artistic works for hidden allegories and oblique references.

Comments on the Warsaw Rising in post-war history textbooks were few and far between. Whenever the Rising was mentioned it was condemned in crude terms:

> The Polish reactionaries, grouped round the so-called 'Polish Government in London', saw that they were losing. The talks which their representatives held with the Lublin Committee in Moscow failed. Determined to do anything to prevent the formation of People's Poland, they issued a criminal order to the leadership of the Home Army: to launch a Rising in Warsaw.
>
> The people appointed as leaders of the Rising . . . were associated with the Gestapo and with the forces of occupation. Their intention was to seize control of Warsaw at all costs, and to prevent the creation of a democratic Government.
>
> The population of Warsaw had long been waiting for the chance of fighting the Nazis . . . The great majority of inhabitants rose heroically to the struggle . . . The People's Army, though not informed of the decision, also took part . . . No one knew that the reactionary leadership of the AK had pushed the patriotic masses into a hopeless battle.
>
> The First Byelorussian Front and the Polish Army tried to help

> the insurgents. Units of the 1st Polish Army twice crossed to the other bank, only to be destroyed by the Germans.
>
> The Rising ended in catastrophe. It consumed tens of thousands of victims . . . The Hero-City burned . . . The treacherous leaders of the AK surrendered to the Nazis, taking Count [Boor] with them with full honours, supposedly into 'captivity'.[7]

This unusually fulsome account dated from 1951. In Communist eyes, of course, the Home Army's plan was to divert history from its predetermined direction.

The official media was unwavering in its mendacity. And all inconvenient facts were suppressed. Poland had been defeated in 1939 through the treachery of its fascist, militarist, and capitalist rulers and through their ridiculous alliance with the West. The War had been won by the Soviet Union. The Resistance movement had been run by Communists. The 'People's Power' was entirely legitimate and fully supported by the people. The so-called Government in London was a lackey of the anti-Soviet Western powers and was trying to provoke the Third World War. None of which explained why so many wartime resisters were now being tried for alleged wartime crimes.

The Polish community abroad was subject to endless attacks, and 'the émigré' became a stock figure of 'social realist' literature. The attacks began promptly in 1945 when the party line was laid down by George B. and when suitable books, like Stefan L.'s *Twilight of London*, were written to order. The writer Stefan A. made that theme a speciality. One volume, *Targovitsa lies over the Atlantic* (1952), dealt with the period 1938–52, whilst *Passengers of the Dead Visa* (1954) dealt with émigré affairs in 1952–54:

> [Targovitsa] signifies all the traitors, renegades, turncoats, and cheats, who, in pursuit of their own narrow class interests, have rejected their homeland and have entered the service of foreign imperialists in Britain, America, and West Germany. Driven by hatred against their homeland they have hatched the foulest plots, only to fall beneath the level of circus clowns . . .[8]

In reality, 'Targovitsa' was the label given long ago in the late eighteenth century to a group of traitorous émigrés who had planned the Second Partition of Poland in St Petersburg. But now, as Orwell had noticed in 1944, Russia was the one place where Poles could not be émigrés.

No amount of propaganda, however, could cover up the human and material traces of the Rising which were in evidence at every hand. 'Children of the ruins' who grew up in post-war Warsaw knew more than the Communist educators might have wished:

> My father had fought with 'Bashta' in [Mokotov], commanding a small team and then a platoon. He was seriously wounded by a dum-dum bullet on the very first day, during the successful attack on the Race Course . . .
>
> My brother and I were fascinated by two pistols, one of them a Parabellum, which Father had possessed during the Rising. Apart from that, we were told a great deal about the partisans, about lads who would go straight from a dance to some shoot-out, sometimes their last: about betrayals and verdicts, and about the Rising itself. Ten years after the war, on the quiet street in [Jolibord] where my parents found a place to live, we were still finding helmets, bayonets, and bullets. One day my brother found a mortar bomb and started banging it against the pavement. Fortunately, my father saw it . . .
>
> At our primary school, a bearded gent from the People's Army would come and tell us about his comrades' bravery, and stick pins into the Home Army, as various schoolbooks did. But we just laughed . . .[9]

Fifty years later, Lech K. would be elected President of Warsaw.

Cinema was a mass medium close to Communist hearts. But its purely propagandist purposes were sometimes defeated. A budding film director, André W., for example, sought to screen the adaptation of a novel that had portrayed the dilemmas of post-war youth. The novel *Ashes and Diamonds* (1948), by George A., had pleased the authorities, because it implied that violence had been generated by the democratic side.[10] The film, which was not made until 1958, in contrast, was far more ambiguous, and considerably more sympathetic to the ex-Home Army characters. Another of his films, *Sewer* (1957), was the very first portrayal of the Rising on screen. It was passed by the censors probably because it depicted the searing tragedy of the insurgents, and by implication the futility of their sacrifice. Yet the film's effect did not match the censors' expectations. The scene which everyone remembered was the one where a group of desperate survivors, wading through the effluent, reach an exit grille on the bank of the Vistula, and gaze in dying frustration at the far side of the river. No one watching the film could fail to realize who had been occupying the right bank of the Vistula in September 1944 or what they had done.

Nothing was more desirable, however, than the embodiment of the Warsaw Rising into a fully documented and carefully reasoned historical account. To this end, two separate teams of historians set to work shortly after the war. One of them was organized by Adam B., 'Pepi', a veteran of the Home Army who had served in the 1930s in the Army's Historical Bureau, had edited an insurgent journal, *Barykady*, and had been commissioned by Gen. Bear Cub to collect materials. The other was directed by George K., a former Home Army officer who had co-authored the original plan a for a general Rising and who, being trapped outside Warsaw in August 1944, had joined the Berling Army. He was appointed director of the People's Army Historical Section.[11] Of the two teams, the former made the most progress. Eagerly supported by veterans, it founded an Institute of National Memory, assembled an impressive archive, and sent a large body of documents to the Nuremberg Tribunal. What is more, its organizers believed that they enjoyed official approval. They had only revealed themselves to the authorities during one of the post-war 'amnesties' on the express undertaking that they would be allowed to continue with work. Yet it was all to no avail. In 1948, George K., falsely charged with conspiracy in the 'Generals' Case', was arrested, tortured, and sentenced to life imprisonment. In 1949, the Institute of National Memory was cut down in similar fashion. Its entire archive was confiscated on the pretext that the papers were needed for the trial of Pepi's wife, a war invalid from the Zoshka Battalion. She was sentenced to seven years in jail, having been charged with 'collecting documents with a view to glorifying the Home Army and to smearing the People's Guard'.

With history in a straitjacket, historical discussions on sensitive subjects had somehow to find another outlet, and they often found their way, in varying disguises, into literature. The Warsaw Rising was able to figure, for example, in several works of post-war fiction. Of course, the censors kept a tight rein on the content. But they did not pull the shutters down completely, so long as the overall impression of the Rising was negative. One novel, *Man Never Dies* (1951), was penned by an author, Casimir B., who had duly confessed his fault. 'I loved the heroism of the soldiers', he wrote, 'and I closed my eyes to the stupidity of their leaders'.[12] Another novel of that year, *Generations* by Bogdan C., passed through the filter because its insurgent heroes disliked their 'masters from London' and were longing to join up with the Red Army. In this way, the novelist was able to present other elements, such as the solid support for the Rising amongst Warsaw's working class, which would otherwise have been suppressed. (Communists always put greater store on love for the Soviet Union than on love for the working class.)[13]

Throughout those years, no insult was too nasty for it to be withheld if it was aimed at Generals Boor or Anders. One writer started a novel with the sentence 'Count "Boor" was terrified by the consequences of his crime, frightened like a rat by the smoke of the burned city and by the sight of cunningly spilled blood.' Another wrote that he longed for the day when 'Boor' would become a joke; 'in the meantime, I hate him.' A third, who called the Government-in-Exile 'a litter of werewolves', claimed that Anders had built concentration camps in Palestine and Italy to prevent his soldiers from returning home.[14]

Most interesting, however, was the heated debate which took place soon after the war on the arcane subject of the 'Conradian ethos'. To the uninitiated, Joseph Conrad may not seem to have much in common with the Warsaw Rising. Yet to those familiar with inter-war intellectual trends, the connection was obvious. Conrad, the Polish seaman turned master of the English language, was one of the most popular and most translated authors of the day. The morality which he promoted of self-reliance, dignity, and integrity under pressure was highly attractive to the educated youth of independent Poland. His ideal of 'being true to oneself' was their ideal too. It was not for nothing that the 'Class of 1920', which formed the most typical cohort of the insurgents, has been called 'Conrad's children'. And it was no accident that the post-war Communist regime viciously attacked the legacy of a generation which revered an émigré.

The offensive was mounted by a young Marxist critic, Yan Ko., who later mended his ways and became a distinguished Shakespeare scholar. It was clever, arrogant, and totally unforgiving. 'Conrad supports the sort of heroism which leads nowhere,' wrote Yan Ko., 'heroism which justifies nothing, heroism which has no higher purpose than itself.' Conrad's heroes, he claimed, were marked by 'internal pride and spiritual self-destruction.' Their actions 'are always individual . . . devoid of social justification, of a moral code based on collective welfare, and of a desire to improve conditions.' 'Tragically,' they maintain 'blind obedience to the great *armatorom* of this world.' Lest there be any doubt about the target, Yan Ko. referred directly to recent events. 'We ourselves witnessed', he wrote, 'how, in the long years of German Occupation, people who fought for freedom were called traitors . . . how in the name of honour and loyalty, it all ended up with the self-immolation of Warsaw.' In the language of 1945 'people who fought for freedom' referred exclusively to Communists and their friends.

The defence of Conrad – and by implication of the Home Army – was bravely and calmly undertaken by a well-known writer, Maria D. She rejected the idea that Conrad's heroes were self-obsessed or servants of foreigners, stating instead that they were inspired by universal values. 'We have to be moral beings irrespective of sanctions, obligations, rewards or punishments,' she wrote, 'but simply from a sense of responsibility towards our own fate and that of others.' In conclusion, she ensured that her comments would not be mistaken for abstractions:

> Today's world has seen all the bounds of human decency breached and the authority of all beliefs, doctrines and dogmas broken. It stands, in fact, before the test of the Conradian ethos. We are not in a position yet to say whether it will pass the test. But we can say with absolute certainty that things will be better if the world does not dismiss Conrad's approach completely.[15]

One has to wonder how many outsiders, had they encountered this rarefied literary argument, would really have grasped its meaning.

For the time being, the most interested party to the debate, the ex-insurgents themselves, had no voice. But many years later, when they could speak out, they were more than ready to recognize their debt to Joseph Conrad:

> We urgently needed some firm substantiation for the only thing that illuminated our risky road, that is a justification for the undefined but imperative feeling that *tak trzeba*, 'There's no other way'. Joseph Conrad, who like us was both a sceptic and a romantic, supplied many of us with that substantiation more effectively than anyone else. Conrad was deeply convinced of the pointlessness of all expectation concerning final truth, and hence saw the sense of life in the preservation of feelings of human dignity. This for him provided the highest trace of truth and divinity which we are capable of recognizing in ourselves and defining. Fighting as we often were in isolation and confusion, cast on the resources of our own consciences, we accepted this attitude spontaneously. For the times demanded that we meet suffering without illusion and that our loyalty be a prize in itself . . .[16]

Such were the intellectualizations. Most insurgents were content with the simple conviction that 'there was no other way'.

In the years that followed 1945, London was a city of austerity and anxiety. It was the capital of a country that was virtually bankrupt, and of an empire that was visibly disintegrating. Londoners recovered pre-war standards of living very slowly. They faced food rationing, housing shortages, and unemployment. If they thought about problems abroad, they thought of the places where British troops were still coming under fire – in Trieste, in Greece, in Palestine and in India. With very few exceptions, they were not thinking much about Poland. Their First Ally had slipped almost completely from the active political agenda.

Yet the Polish Question was still present. The exiled Government, which had now become the Government-in-Exile, had taken up residence in Eaton Square. Despite the departure of many individuals, the Polish community in Britain was actually growing. Indeed, when the Anders Army and its dependants arrived in 1946, a Polish Resettlement Corps had to be formed to manage the influx and to prepare them for absorption into civilian life. The Poles and their troubles had not gone away.

The Polish Embassy in Portland Place was taken over by diplomats from Warsaw as soon as the Government of National Unity gained diplomatic recognition on 27 July 1945. On that day Count R., Ambassador to St James since 1934, was obliged to leave, relinquish his post, surrender his credentials, and be replaced by a Communist nominee. He would not set foot in the building again for forty-five years. The Warsaw regime's mission then arrived in force. Their tasks were to obfuscate what was really happening in Poland, to mount surveillance on the exiled community, and, by hook or by crook, to persuade as many as possible to go home. The new Ambassador, who did not last long, was Henry S., a pre-war industrialist who had been Minister of Trade in Sikorski's Government.

Gen. Boor, who reached London in May 1945, did not seek to shine in the Government-in-Exile. He held on to his position as Commander-in-Chief for little more than a year, then resigned in favour of Gen. Anders. He accepted one or two token ministries, including the Ministry of Sea Transport, and served for a time as Prime Minister, but was not interested in the notorious political feuding of his compatriots. He is remembered as a quiet, polite, and extremely modest man. His main concerns centred on his young family, and on the Home Army Association, of which he was president. His memoirs were published in 1951. His visits to the USA, where he was well received, brought much satisfaction. But he sought no profit for himself. When presented in New York in 1946 with a cheque for $12,000, he kept $300 for a deposit on a small terraced house, and gave away the rest to his soldiers' association.[17]

Intensified espionage was one of the central features of the intensifying Cold War, and London was one of the spies' favourite playgrounds. It was a game at which the Soviets excelled, not least because they had successfully penetrated the higher reaches of British Intelligence. The 1940s, both during and after the War, was the decade when the 'Cambridge Five' – of Philby, Burgess, Maclean, Blunt, and Cairncross – were shopping state secrets to Moscow with impunity. London also became a destination of skulduggery through the continuing presence of the Polish Government-in-Exile, which had no reason to be reconciled to the post-war order and which, rightly or wrongly, was suspected in some quarters of pressing for a showdown with Stalin. The Warsaw regime was bound to send a strong team of security and intelligence officers to help the Soviet resident in London keep tabs on their exiled compatriots.

One of the unsolved mysteries of that era relates to the intelligence archives of the exiled Government, which were handed over to the British Foreign Office at the end of the war. Both the Home Army and the General Staff had maintained extensive networks of agents both in the Third Reich and in the USSR, and, at the onset of the Cold War, the records must have been of prime value. Some of the records were burned in the yard of St Paul's School in London, where the II Bureau was based, but the rest were duly handed over to the British as the unspoken price of allowing the Government-in-Exile to stay. Forty-five years later, a liberated Polish Government requested the return of its archive, only to be told that the files had been 'inadvertently destroyed'. Most specialists thought the explanation ingenuous.[18]

The work of the Warsaw mission specially targeted the émigré military circles, among them the former Commander-in-Chief, Gen. Boor, and, when he arrived with his troops from Italy, Gen. Anders. Yet it was one of the ironies faced by a now divided nation that many of the watchers had once been colleagues or subordinates of the watched.

Marcel R. came to London at a slightly later date. He was a regular officer of the Ministry of Security, seconded, as cover, to the Consulate General. He must have known much about the Warsaw Rising, for in

1943–44 he was sheltered in the right-bank Warsaw home of the Catholic couple to whom he owed his life. In London, Marcel R. was one of several intelligence agents working out of the Consulate. He had a spacious flat, a large American car, and lots of time to go to concerts and the theatre. He was to remember Furtwängler and Laurence Olivier. He wrote a report on the British re-education centre for top-class German prisoners at Wilton House, and made light of his work collecting information on his compatriots. In due course, he came under suspicion as a 'cosmopolitan', returned to Warsaw, and resigned. 'I myself had no contact with the Poles in London,' he commented.[19]

In 1945–46, 'Salamander', duly recovered, was still active in London in Polish affairs. Through his personal acquaintance with Stafford Cripps, now Chancellor of the Exchequer, he obtained a huge grant of £5 million for reconstruction work in Poland. He made three trips to Warsaw to distribute the largesse, which came mainly in the form of military trucks, pontoon bridges, road-making equipment, boots, and balaclavas, all purchased at discount prices from British Army surplus stores. The regime's officials were ready enough to accept the gift. But they incensed Salamander by refusing to acknowledge it publicly. They did not want Britain to be cast in the light of a friendly power. On his final trip, in 1946, Salamander was further incensed to find that his faithful assistant 'Celt', who had carried him aboard the rescue plane two years earlier, had been 'detained'. He was eventually able to secure Celt's release in inimitable style, by placing a direct call to Molotov in Moscow.

Salamander, however, had many other irons in the fire; and, as his Polish interests faded, his pan-European interests bloomed. During the war, he had established close links with a number of politicians, such as Paul-Henri Spaak, who were active in other exiled Governments and who subsequently formed the core of the future European movement. Salamander not only joined them, he set about coordinating their schemes; and he seems to have acted as a key go-between with powerful interests in the USA, which sought to guide the European movement onto its own tracks. He was one of the organizers of the Hague Congress of 1948. And in 1953, he co-opted Prince Bernhard of the Netherlands and founded the so-called 'Bilderberg Group'. In this role, in the eyes of the 'anti-globalizers', he became the unrecognized genius who set up the secretive society of power-brokers who have ruled the world ever since.[20]

Initially, the Warsaw regime had hoped that the Polish military in Britain would be repatriated en masse. When this step was ruled out, and

HMG refused to envisage anything other than 'voluntary and individual repatriation', Gen. Mo. returned to Warsaw, and his underlings were left to report on the formation of the Polish Resettlement Corps and on the toings and froings of the émigrés. Yet the British authorities remained largely unsympathetic. In 1946, the Foreign Minister Ernest Bevin issued a circular addressed in Polish to all Polish citizens urging them 'to go home to Poland'. He was still not fully aware that the majority of those who stayed had homes in Poland's former eastern provinces, which were now (with full British acquiescence) occupied by the USSR. Despite their war service, Polish officers who declined either to join the Polish Resettlement Corps or to be repatriated were forcibly interned as 'recalcitrants'.[21]

The Warsaw regime was eager to lay its hands on Nazi war criminals, and the Foreign Office records contain seventeen files headed 'War criminals wanted by Poland'. Each file lists thousands of names of suspects, victims, and witnesses.[22] Unfortunately, Communist ideas of who was a Nazi and who was a Nazi sympathizer or collaborator were often rather fanciful. Nonetheless, several suicides occurred among German prisoners who felt that they would be sent to Warsaw. The Polish Mission in London would undoubtedly have known of the semi-secret interrogation centre at 8 Kensington Palace Gardens, known as the London Cage. According to the account of the cage's director, all available tactics were used – which presumably included physical violence. All the interrogators were fluent German-speakers, many of them German Jews. Cells were bugged; stooges were placed among prisoners who pretended to be from the same town in Germany; and in really stubborn cases, a man dressed as a KGB officer sat in on interrogations demanding extradition to the USSR.[23] These proceedings may be seen with a certain irony.

The Warsaw regime was also specially keen to learn the inside story about the Warsaw Rising from the leading participants now in London. The task was coordinated by a security officer who knew many of the ex-insurgents from his days as a POW in Germany. He interviewed most of the big names in person, assuring them of total discretion before conveying the text of their conversations to his masters. In due course, his report was published in Warsaw. In good Marxist fashion, his analysis was predicated on a dialectical split between the 'irresponsible adventurists' led by Monter and the advocates of caution. His main witnesses were Monter and Tabor. Revealingly, the former told him that at the time of the Rising's outbreak: 'The problems of cooperation with the Red Army, of the despatch of the Parachute Brigade, and of supplies both for the insurgents and for civilians had all been settled in London beforehand.'[24] One wonders who was kidding whom.

By far the biggest coup achieved in those years centred on the departure for Warsaw of a key group of officers led by Gen. Tabor. This complicated affair can only be understood by reference to several other matters, belonging to the murkiest passages of émigré politics. Suffice it to say that Tabor had surrounded himself with a small secret group of like-minded officers soon after the collapse of the Warsaw Rising, and that their activities gradually alienated them from the rest of the military and political leadership of the Government-in-Exile. Tabor, however, did not resign as Premier Mick did. On the contrary, he kept his post, and his commission, whilst privately pursuing Mick's goal of an accommodation with the Warsaw regime. Yet he did not participate openly in Mick's campaign. Nor did he join the five generals who in 1945 openly declared their intention of returning to Poland. Whatever Tabor's purposes were, they were extremely well concealed. They involved the collection of large amounts of money, gold bullion, and houses. And they increasingly attracted the suspicions of his compatriots, both in London and in Warsaw. When, with much delay, the authorities in Warsaw eventually condemned the 'Tabor organization', few people were inclined to believe in the organization's existence.

Tabor's 'unofficial' activities spanned 1944 to 1949. They began in autumn 1944, when the dismissal of the Commander-in-Chief and the resignation of Premier Mick radically changed the external predicament and the internal make-up of Polish London. In this period, many wartime structures, including the VI Bureau, were in a state of disintegration. Tabor and his associates were able to take control not only of some financial bodies, such as the Polish Self-Help Foundation, but also the 'Hel' network of couriers and foreign liaison stations. Their 'Committee of Three' seems to have invested some money in houses – notably 11, 13, and 15 Cornwall Gardens SW7, whose cellars served as a strong room where safes containing gold bars and cash could be stored. Their stock gradually fell with the Government-in-Exile, not least when Gen. Anders arrested one of their associates, who committed suicide. Their contacts with the Warsaw regime, and with the regime's agents in the West, intensified correspondingly. Whether, by transferring assets to Poland, they were simply following Salamander's example and assisting in the country's reconstruction, or were engaged in something more sinister, is difficult to judge. (Who is to say whether a consignment of beagles was designed to restock Warsaw's decimated pet population or to present the militia with trained police dogs?) At all events, though clearly at odds with Premier Thomas and the Government-in-Exile, they were not merely biding their time. In 1947 they accepted consular passports from the regime. Tabor paid extended visits to Warsaw in 1947 and 1948. And in October 1949 he went there permanently. It did not do him much good.

Specialists in émigré affairs have unearthed much information about Tabor's dubious dealings. But the point of most general interest concerns the dilemma of people from the Soviet bloc who held left-wing opinions but who nonetheless wanted to maintain a modicum of independence for themselves and their country. Different sorts of left-wingers reacted in different ways. Premier Thomas, for example, had impeccable socialist credentials, but he was convinced that the Popular Front-type of solution would not work in countries where the Communist minority was backed by an all-powerful army and police. Tabor and his associates, in contrast, seem to have held unusually positive views about Stalin's benevolence and, hence, to have overrated the prospects for Stalin's tolerance of 'national Communists' like Comrade Gomulka. In pursuing this line, they involved themselves in large measures both of deception and self-deception. In the end, they found themselves out of step not only with former colleagues in London, but also with the 'comrades' back home. For this, they paid a heavy price.

At the same time, one cannot fail to notice that Tabor's political views coincided with those of many Britons with whom he would have come into contact. He was certainly very well viewed by the Foreign Office, who, by the same token, virtually boycotted the exiled Government in its final phase under Premier Thomas. Whether or not he was drawn into active cooperation with the British special services is another matter. What *is* known is that Kim Philby's supposedly anti-Soviet department of MI6 made much use of Polish agents and that a distressingly large proportion of them were quickly eliminated by Communist counter-intelligence. Gen. Tabor's decision to depart for Poland permanently, even when the political trends there were not moving in his preferred direction, can perhaps be explained by the fact that the Government-in-Exile was belatedly investigating his many irregularities. The net was closing.

There remains the intriguing puzzle of Tabor's private manipulation of radio communications with Poland, both during and after the war. According to the OC at Barnes Lodge, unauthorized messages were both sent and received. In 1944, they were probably linking him with someone to the east of the Vistula. If so, his correspondents have not been identified.

Since Poland was closed both to serious history-writing and to free debate, information about the Warsaw Rising could only circulate freely in the outside, Western world; and this was the decade when everyone was writing their war memoirs. The Rising was still fresh in the minds of the various Western leaders who had been involved, and it was the prime topic of controversy among those former insurgents who were trying to establish themselves abroad. London remained the principal centre for discussion. But from 1947, the *Kultura* Literary Institute began its sterling work in Paris, publishing both the influential monthly *Kultura* and, with some greater delay, the *Historical Notebooks*. And in 1951, the US-funded Radio Free Europe began broadcasting from Munich. The long-term director of RFE's Polish section was none other than the legendary 'Courier from Warsaw', Novak, who had made his last trip to Poland on the very eve of the Rising. The information battle had begun in earnest.

Winston Churchill was the only one of the 'Big Three' to write his war memoirs, which were immensely influential in the English-speaking world. Like all politicians, he did not indulge in much self-criticism. But no one could have been more acutely aware than he of the Varsovian tragedy:

> The struggle in Warsaw had lasted more than sixty days. Of the 40,000 men and women of the Polish Underground Army, about 15,000 fell . . . The suppression of the revolt cost the German Army 10,000 killed, 7,000 missing and 9,000 wounded. The proportions attest to the hand-to-hand nature of the fighting.
>
> When the Russians entered the city three months later, they found nothing but the shattered streets and the unburied dead. Such was their liberation of Poland, where they now rule. But this cannot be the end of the story.[25]

Former war correspondents who had served at the front were well placed to publish the earliest surveys of the war as a whole. Chester Wilmot, for example, who had accompanied the British and American armies on the Continent, wrote his best-selling *Struggle for Europe* in 1952. He had not been to Warsaw, so his account of the Rising was based on the most readily available opinions and press reports. It was contained in a single paragraph and was suitably sceptical:

> Supply difficulties and the arrival of German reinforcements ... prevented the Russians from breaking into Warsaw and joining forces with the Polish Underground, which had risen in revolt at the start of August. In their eagerness to gain control of the capital before the entry of the Red Army, the Poles had risen prematurely. But it is hardly likely that the Russians would have allowed themselves to be halted at the gates of the city if the insurrection had been raised by the Polish Communists and not by [the] Home Army, which was hostile to Communism and to the Soviet Union. In the circumstances, Stalin may well have been content to hand his military opponents the task of wiping out his political enemies.[26]

Alexander Werth, who had reported for the *Guardian* and the *Sunday Times* from the Eastern Front, possessed much more first-hand information. He was no more privy to the key decisions than anyone was, but he had seen the Warsaw tragedy develop at close quarters. In his *Russia at War* (1964), he challenged the findings of the official Soviet History in detail, and he reached conclusions that have stood the test of time:

> It might, of course, be argued that if the Russians had wished to capture Warsaw *at any price* ... they might conceivably have captured it. But this would have upset their other military plans ...
>
> There is no question but that the Warsaw rising was a last desperate attempt to free Poland's capital from the retreating Nazis and at the same time to prevent the Lublin administration from establishing itself ...
>
> Once more in Poland's history this valiant struggle for independence was defeated by the overriding, although conflicting, great-power interests of other states. Still, with Moscow determined ... to control the future destinies of Poland, [Boor] would have been eliminated one way or another, just as they managed a few years later to rid themselves of [ex-Premier Mick].[27]

Since the only Briton present in Warsaw in 1944 did not write his memoirs, there were no British eye-witness accounts of the Rising to be read. But the next best thing, certainly in emotional terms, was penned in

1951 by Maj. Mur in his memoir of the Freston Mission. His tone was contrite:

> I had learned in a few months what I might never have learned in a lifetime ... I was no pilgrim when I went to Poland, because a pilgrim has belief and I had none. The Poles gave me belief. I believe implicitly in the freedom of the true Polish nation. With the spirit that has sustained them for centuries of adversity, the hymn of the Polish exiles cannot be an idle dream. Unless the whole civilised world is enslaved, they must surely return in due time to a Poland that is their own.[28]

On the Polish side, two memoirs were particularly significant. Gen. Boor's *The Secret Army* was published in English in 1951. Directed at a readership that was not familiar with Polish affairs, it sought to set down the facts in a brusque and soldierly fashion. A preview was published in *Reader's Digest* under the title of 'The Unconquerables'. The Rising occupied only part of the story, and elicited no apologies. Boor's stance was very similar to that of Bear Cub. He and his soldiers had simply been fulfilling their patriotic duty. They viewed the Rising as just one chapter in a struggle that started in September 1939.[29] Another memoir, in contrast, which appeared in 1954, served as an introduction to the politics and workings of the Underground State. One of the chapters was devoted to the Rising.[30]

In 1946, the Government-in-Exile set up a Historical Commission whose task was to research, document, and publicize all aspects of the war in Poland. The commission was joined shortly after by the Polish Underground Studies Trust in Ealing, an independent foundation, whose labours were specifically directed to the records of clandestine operations. These two organizations were to stay hard at work for the rest of the century.

Since history in 'People's Poland' was shackled, the first works specifically devoted to the Warsaw Rising could only be published abroad. André P.'s *Warsaw Rising* (1945) heads the list. It was solidly based on documents from the wartime Government's archives, and was informed by a firm commitment to the cause of Polish freedom which the insurgents had shared. Necessarily short, it rebutted the usual criticisms that had filled the press, and was far superior to many much larger volumes that followed.

Another short but well-informed study appeared in Canada on the tenth anniversary of the Rising. Subtitled *The First Conflict of the Cold War*, it was inspired by the emotions provoked by the international tensions of the mid-1950s, and consequently it concentrated in large measure on a very negative assessment of Soviet policy. It concluded with 'Warsaw's Warning to the World':

> There are already many more ruins in the world, numerous other nations have also lost their freedom, and peace is still far from being achieved. Let the tragic experience of Warsaw be a warning about the real objects of Soviet policy to all countries which are still free.[31]

Whilst the Varsovians rebuilt their city, and the Government-in-Exile dug in for a long sojourn in London, many of the ex-insurgents sought to create a new life for themselves wherever they could find it. The majority of them were young, tough, and glad to be alive. But they were also on the loose in a variety of foreign countries. Having lost the chance of an education during the war, they mostly lacked qualifications; they were not usually proficient in foreign languages; and they were separated from their friends and families. They had survived the Rising and the POW camps. And they now faced a challenge of a totally different kind. They needed to study; they needed companionship; and they needed the prospect of somewhere permanent to live and work. Their search would take them, quite literally, to all ends of the earth. Generally speaking, their experiences proved to be much more profitable than those of their older compatriots.

Like other displaced persons and refugees, few Varsovians cast adrift in 1945 thought initially of permanent emigration. On the contrary, there was to begin with a strong feeling that the chaotic arrangements which prevailed at the war's end would somehow be sorted out and improved. After all, Warsaw, though wrecked, was still in Poland. The so-called Government of National Unity was still only 'provisional'. Elections were due. The United Nations was still to assemble. The post-war Peace Conference had not been officially abandoned. So the obvious policy was to wait and see: and while waiting, to study for a diploma, to earn some money, to learn a language, to marry, or even to see the world.

Britain, where the largest concentration of Poles resided, offered the best chances for a quick post-war education. Two centres in particular offered courses for Polish ex-servicemen. One of them, at the University of Edinburgh, trained a distinguished contingent of medical doctors and engineers. The other, the Polish University College attached to the

University of London, specialized in faculties of medicine, chemistry, mathematics, and engineering. But there were many other possibilities. The Catholic University of Louvain in Belgium, for instance, was a mecca for would-be Polish students in the immediate post-war years. So, too, was Dublin. [**BRITAIN**, p. 538]

By 1948–49, when most of the ex-service students were beginning to graduate, conditions in Poland were even less favourable for returnees than previously. The Iron Curtain had solidified. The People's Republic was looking ever more antagonistic. The Cold War was setting in. So permanent emigration grew into an ever more attractive option.

Several assisted emigration schemes were operating in the late 1940s and early 1950s, and would-be emigrants were faced with a choice of destinations. In all cases, however, applicants with professional skills or established technical experience were preferred, so it was beneficial to postpone one's application until the best qualifications had been obtained. The Varsovians, who in the main had higher academic aptitudes than the average soldier or refugee, were the most likely to enter higher learning and the most likely to stay in it longer. This meant that often they were not ready to contemplate emigration until five, six, or seven years after the war.

The USA was the most attractive destination. It was a vast country with a long immigrant tradition that could absorb large numbers of 'tired and weary' from the Old Continent. It possessed several large Polish communities, in cities like Chicago, Detroit, Buffalo, or Cleveland (Ohio), where there were good opportunities for employment. Above all, it was a country virtually untouched by war – a half-continent of apparently unlimited promise and prosperity where one could forget the horrors of Warsaw completely. [**USA**, p. 539]

Canada offered many of America's attractions with fewer of its drawbacks. Being British, it accepted British qualifications more readily; and it was entering a phase of dynamic expansion. But the Canadian 'Polonia' was not so developed; and the size of the population and hence the sum total of employment opportunities was much less. [**CANADA**, p. 546]

Australia beckoned from the other side of the world. It was hot, huge, and hungry for immigrants. But in the immediate post-war period, it had many of the characteristics of a remote, colonial backwater; and it did not possess the open, multicultural, and outward-looking society that has since grown up there. Poles, like other European emigrants of that era, such as

BRITAIN

A survivor of the Rising, who had joined the 2nd Corps in Italy, takes his first steps in another foreign country

We are crossing the English Channel. We can see the white cliffs of Dover, vertically dropping into the sea. Soon we will land . . . It is 11 August 1946. Two years have passed since we began the Rising . . . We did not see much of London, only in transit from St Pancras to Paddington, and west to Beaconsfield. From there we travelled straight through the forests to Hodgemore Camp, where the Carpathian Division command was to be stationed. . . .

Penn Wood Camp

We protect the camp from an invasion of English squatters. There is a housing crisis and the English look upon us with disdain. They have already forgotten the role the Poles played in the Battle of Britain and our war effort on their side. They do not understand why we do not return to 'free' Poland. There is also a lot of unemployment and Poles are fierce competition as cheap labour and extremely hard workers.

South Wood

I turn twenty-six today. I do not feel weighted down by it, but all the same, it is a significant chunk of time and what have I achieved up to now? . . . Lt. B. arrived and relieved me of command . . . Under his strong hand, the camp took on a different appearance . . . and he spoke so understandingly to the soldiers, raising their spirits and explaining the current difficulties, whereas I . . . complained along with them.

I received my first letter today, from my friends and family, after nineteen months . . . They had returned to Warsaw. I felt deep joy and gratitude towards God for protecting them, but it renewed my longing for them. I left their lives two years ago and life had carried on without me . . .

Sudbury

And yet another move, to a camp near Sudbury in Suffolk. I came here as an English teacher. My English is weak, but I was ordered to do it . . . I found out that the corps was to be disbanded. A mass of soldiers, non-commissioned officers, and even officers were signing up to go home. It was no great surprise. There was little likelihood of war, their families were waiting. Anyone who did not bear too heavy a debt to Poland's new authorities could risk it.

It was the first time I had been in a local Catholic church in England. The atmosphere was much more rigid than in Poland or Italy. Awful Latin with an English accent and pronunciation, and they passed the plate around three times. The soldiers got their coppers ready, but by the second and third collections they had got rid of them, so they had to put more valuable coinage in. The priest beamed with admiration at Polish generosity . . . (the following Sunday he probably changed his mind: there were not as many pieces of silver on the plate). Some soldiers were late and by accident ended up at the Anglican church . . . As a result an Anglican minister arrived at the camp wanting to make contact with the *Polish Protestants.* He was reluctant to believe me when I told him there were none.

Witley Camp

In my letters from Poland there was not even the slightest suggestion of my possible return. It was then that I truly realized the real danger for my relatives. For a while correspondence was not even sent in my name, but I became 'Auntie Klimcia'. It was funny to read letters from my mum or sister addressed to 'Darling Auntie'.

Sitting in a meadow chatting to Jules P., I happened to catch sight of English workers laying a telephone cable from post to post with long, frequent tea breaks. What they managed to do in a week, I could have done in two days, even with such tea breaks . . .

And then there was an officers' party. There were practically no Polish girls, just English girls. One, extremely fat, was the 'sweet-heart' of one of our officers. When we teased him about his taste, he replied, 'Look on and be jealous, so much there and all of it mine.' I had already danced with a few two-metre-tall dry English girls, but still there was no Ela . . .

I arrived in London on 15 January 1947. I moved to a new flat with Lt. Z., a communications officer, who had been in Murnau. His whole family had been lost in the bombing of Lodz. He had no one to return to. I found an inexpensive room for two people near the hospice (it turned out to be extremely cold). We were fed at the hospice. Horse and whale meat featured frequently on the menu, because they were the cheapest and could be obtained without ration cards. On Sunday, we had lunch at 'Lyons', lacking in taste, but nourishing.[1]

Greeks, Yugoslavs, and Italians, fitted well into the official 'White Australia' policy. But they did not always fit so well into some of the narrow-minded Anglocentric and late Imperial communities into which they were expected to integrate. There was a ready welcome for physical labourers in the outback or in some of the major Government projects like the Snowy River Scheme. But there were far fewer openings for a sophisticated

Varsovian who was hoping to encounter the (idealized) delights of pre-war Warsaw in Sydney or Melbourne. Above all, Australia and New Zealand in the pre-jet age were off the map, separated from the 'Old World' by a sea journey of nine or ten weeks. They were good places for forgetting. Emigrants who took ship in Britain on an assisted passage rarely expected to see the shores of Europe again. [**AUSTRALIA**, p. 551]

One should not imagine, therefore, that such people set off for these distant continents without very mixed feelings. They could not know in advance what really awaited them, and in most cases they had no desire to separate themselves forever from their home country and their native culture. Yet they were driven by necessity – by the need for work, the need to provide for growing families, the need for stability. These basics were not in ready supply for uprooted people in war-damaged Europe.

Beyond and above economic necessity, however, another factor was at work, perhaps the decisive one. It reflected the political captivity of their home country. In any other political circumstances, almost all exiled Varsovians would have returned home en masse; and they would have flung themselves into the task of reconstruction, no matter how harsh the deprivations might have been. But they were not going to devote their energies for the benefit of foreign masters, whose ideology and practices they deplored. So, despite the risks and the anxieties, they stayed abroad; and they bore all the adversities with fortitude, because they had chosen to do so of their own free will. Many years later, when asked about their life decision, they would generally answer with disarming frankness and absolute clarity: 'Our country was not free.' 'There was no place for us there.' 'Members of othe Home Army were persecuted, imprisoned, sent to Siberia, or brutally murdered.' 'We sincerely hoped . . . that we would again be called to fight for free Poland.'[32]

Of course, for many émigrés of the older generation the decision about changing continents never arose. As often as not, they could neither go home nor think of moving on. So they stayed where they were – usually in London or Glasgow or in one of the other centres of Polish concentration. If they were officers, they were automatically in a cast of undesirables in 'People's' Poland'. If they were big names, like Boor or Anders, they were probably on a list of 'traitors', sentenced in absentia. If they were middle-aged they had limited capacity to study or to 'nostrify' their qualifications, or to earn anything other than a pittance in the most menial of jobs. Apart from anything else, the Varsovians amongst them were victims of an especially mean decision of the British Ministry of

USA

Mary R., a widow from Rocky River (Ohio), recalls her late husband's path to a scientific career

Voychek R. was born in Warsaw in 1921, the son of a professor at the Higher College of Agriculture, and his wife Maria. In 1939 he completed studies at the Adam Mitskevich School in Warsaw and went on to gain some community work experience. When the Rising broke out he joined a conspiratorial unit, nr. 1147, also known as 'Girder's Company'. The Rising was an important experience for him because despite the trail of victims it left among his comrades and civilians, it symbolized his own and his generation's wish to fight the enemy openly. They had called his unit 'Girder's' to commemorate its commander, who lost his life in the City Centre on the second day of the fighting. The unit was not allocated to the front line, its role was to support Major Vola, a divisional chief based in the north of the City Centre. When two subsequent commanders were wounded Voychek, who was also injured but not seriously, took over in September. Eventually he became a prisoner of war, together with the 28th Division of the AK, in Bergen-Belsen, Gross Born, and Sandbostel. Later on he was demobilized in Calais and sent to Belgium to study. In 1947 he graduated from the University of Louvain. After he had received his PhD he emigrated to the United States.

From 1961, he worked for many years as a scientist for NASA. He gained international acclaim for his extensive and valuable theses and numerous discoveries. He wrote a book, *Imperceptible Worlds*. Among his formal achievements were dissertations on liquid hydrogen axial-flow pumps and the explanation of certain functions in axial-flow compressors and the stability of rocket engines. Apart from analytical research and writing, he also did contract work for Aerojet and Rockedyne in California and other established companies. In 1971 he received a doctorate in applied mathematics from his alma mater in Louvain.

He was the first to develop a complete mathematical model, scientifically tested, for the course of sound waves in a bent conduit. In six further papers he explained the basic manifestations of the movements of sound waves in mildly and severely bent conduits having smooth and sound-dampening walls. He was frequently quoted in the Scientific Citation Index and NASA recognized his scientific discoveries that among others included the formulation of a new, undefined integral – to be found today in all the mathematical tables – by presenting him with numerous awards.

For many years Voychek was an active member of the Regional Group of the AK. For twelve years he was the Chairman of the Collective Regional Group of the AK in the United States, which represented the AK combatants dispersed in America.[1]

Pensions, which paid a modest emolument to ex-servicemen who had fought under British command in the West, but which absolutely refused to pay a penny to ex-members of the Home Army. Both the British and Americans had gone to considerable lengths to publicize the fact that the Home Army's ranks were Allied soldiers entitled to combatant status. The Third Reich was reluctantly obliged to observe the fact. But the two bodies which consistently refused to observe it were the NKVD and the British Ministry of Pensions.

As a result, several of the most distinguished émigrés were reduced to a life of near penury. They survived through the charity of their less pinched compatriots, through the solidarity of their community, through the ministration of the Polish Catholic Mission, in some cases through the help of British friends and sympathizers. But most often they survived through their own resourcefulness and ingenuity. There were generals who worked as waiters. There were judges and professors who toiled in the dirtiest departments of the Cherry Blossom Boot Polish factory or the National Coal Board. Not to put too fine a point on it, there were war heroes who had to knuckle down and work the night shift in the least promising branches of trade and industry. Most of them did so without complaints, though, no doubt, behind the scenes, they produced more than their share of buskers, con-men and the mentally ill – the last group faithfully tended in the Polish Wing of the Mabledon Hospital by the late Marshal's daughter, Dr Vanda P. Their flagship company was the 'Silver Brigade', a group of high-ranking Polish officers who cleaned the silverware at the Ritz Hotel in London's Piccadilly. Gen. Boor, who was fifty years old when he reached England, lived out his last two decades quietly with his family in a drab London suburb largely supported by his wife's curtain-making.

Many of the leaders of the Warsaw Rising were to be found in the Polish circles of post-war London. Gen. Anders long presided. Apart from Boor, Gregory, and Heller, many others could be regularly observed at the tables of the Polish Hearth on Exhibition Road, or in the various clubs of the Ex-Combatants' Association. But two groups of names which had been prominent in 1944 were missing: those who, in spite of everything, had returned to Warsaw, and those who evidently felt ill at ease among their former comrades and had departed elsewhere. Premier Mick, when he escaped from Poland in 1947, took up residence in the USA, not in Britain. The former Commander-in-Chief lived in Montreal. Gen. Monter chose Washington, DC. [**CAVIAHUE**, p. 557]

One specific milieu in London was heavily coloured by its links with the Warsaw Rising. The Polish Section of the BBC had performed doughtily during the war; and afterwards it acted as a natural magnet for all those who had gained a passion for broadcasting in the Underground. Novak, Yan. K-P, Thaddeus Kania, and Zbig B. were all ex-insurgents and all were BBC employees in the immediate post-war years.

In 1951, when the US Congress decided to provide funding for a radio station directed to the countries of the Soviet bloc, the Polish Section of the BBC inevitably supplied much of the talent for the Polish Section for Radio Free Europe in Munich. Novak was appointed director, and began a career which no amount of Soviet jamming could hold back, and which gave him in all probability the best-known and the best-loved voice in Poland.

Novak's career had many highlights. But none surpassed the day in 1954 when his office in Munich was enlivened by the most exciting of post-war defectors. The newcomer, who had fled from the East via the U-Bahn in Berlin, had more inside knowledge about the workings of the Communist system in general and of 'People's Poland' in particular than almost anyone else at liberty. Until then, he had been director in Warsaw of the X Department of the Security Bureau, the man charged with keeping the secret police files on the top Communist leadership. The torrent of facts which he was due to reveal in a long series of interviews struck a deadly blow at the regime, not least in the eyes of its loyal, but unthinking, supporters. His name was Joseph Light. He was the dubious policeman who in September 1944 had run the Security Office in Praga. For the ex-insurgents and their ex-enemies, the world was coming full circle.[33]

In Western countries, the Nuremberg trials are generally considered to have brought a fitting end to the Second World War. Although Hitler and Himmler had both escaped justice through suicide, a substantial group of leading Nazis were put into the dock, were tried under the rule of law, were found guilty of horrific crimes after the presentation of damning evidence, and were deservedly punished. Twelve were sentenced to death by hanging: seven served terms of imprisonment varying from ten years to life; and three walked free.

So far, so good. The enduring weakness of the Nuremberg trials derived from the fact that they had not been constituted by an impartial or independent judicial authority. They were set up by a self-appointed selection of the victorious Allied powers, whose representatives decided the procedures, the appointment of judges and counsel, the charges, the limits on the defendants' rights, and indirectly the verdicts and sentences. As a result, they were not, and could never have prepared, a fair and open-minded examination of all the war crimes and crimes against humanity that were committed during the Second World War. At one point, *Reichsmarshall* Göring complained about 'Victors' Justice'. He was echoed unintentionally by the Chief Prosecutor, Sir Geoffrey Lawrence QC, who silenced all talk about Allied conduct during the war: 'We are here to judge major war criminals,' he reminded the court, 'not to try the conduct of the Allied powers.' When assessing the trials, therefore, one must weigh what was achieved against what was excluded.[34] [**MEXICO**, p. 561]

The Warsaw Rising, for example, would normally have been a prime topic for examination at Nuremberg. The razing of the capital city of an Allied power, the deliberate mass murder of 50–60,000 civilians, the negligent killing of perhaps 100,000 more through indiscriminate shelling and bombing, and the failure to apply the Geneva Conventions to Allied soldiers and prisoners, all provided the clearest of grounds for prosecution. Yet even the most superficial enquiry into the events of August to October 1944 would inevitably have raised questions about Soviet actions and would probably have become a raw bone of contention between the Soviet and the Western powers. So the Warsaw Rising never appeared on the Nuremberg agenda.

The point was not completely lost at the time. Several protests were lodged. A doughty Scottish writer, for instance, who had already published a dozen pamphlets about Poland, returned to the fray in 1945, when Allied intentions were becoming more apparent:

> 'The betrayal and abandonment of Warsaw,' he wrote, 'is the single greatest crime that has been committed in the present war, and it is surely ironical that those who perpetrated this and other outrages upon the Polish people are now assiduously engaged in compiling a list of war criminals whom they intend to bring to justice.'[35]

Searching the Nuremberg transcripts, it soon becomes evident that the ordeal of Warsaw could only be mentioned in peripheral circumstances and rarely as a main item of discussion. Under examination, former Governor-General Frank demonstrated a sound understanding of the circumstances behind the Rising.

> [The] revolt broke out when the Soviet Russian Army had advanced to within about 30 kilometers [eighteen miles] of Warsaw on the eastern bank of the Vistula. It was a sort of combined operation; and, as it seems to me, also a national Polish action, as the Poles at the last moment wanted to carry out the liberation of their capital themselves and did not want to owe it to the Soviet Russians. They probably were thinking of how, in Paris, at the last moment the Resistance movement, even before the Allies had approached, had accomplished the liberation of the city.[36]

Most telling was the scene at Nuremberg on 7 November 1946 when the man who had crushed the Warsaw Rising, *SS-Ogruf.* Erich von dem Bach, made his entrance into the court. He was not a defendant, but a witness for the prosecution. One might have thought that the Soviets in particular would have insisted on trying the Nazi brute who, as the *Bevollmächtiger für den Bandenkampf in Osten* (Commander of Anti-partisan warfare in the East), had also been responsible for numberless atrocities against Soviet civilians including Khatyn. But they did not. They had their reasons. They had no wish to give him the chance to compare his own methods with those of his Soviet adversaries. So they much preferred, one presumes, to turn him against his fellow Nazis.

Von dem Bach had evidently agonized over how to *play* Nuremberg, but he decided to cast himself in a favourable light and to pin responsibility on Himmler, the Wehrmacht, and the Army High Command. Despite his fearsome reputation, he was undoubtedly useful to the prosecutors, and he was described by the American attorney Francis Biddle, with extraordinary latitude, as 'a mild and rather serious accountant.'[37]

Von dem Bach's testimony was a damning indictment of the Wehrmacht. 'The commanders in chief with whom I collaborated,' he declared, 'Field Marshals von Weichs, von Küchler, Bock, [and] Kluge, Col.Gen. Reinhard, and Gen. Kitzinger, were as well aware as I was of the purposes and methods of antipartisan warfare.' This promoted Göring's famous outburst – 'That dirty treacherous swine! . . . the dirty son of a bitch! He was the bloodiest murderer in the whole goddamned set up! The dirty filthy *schweinhund*, selling his soul to save his stinking neck!'[38] The exchanges between defence lawyers and von dem Bach grew heated and frequently outran the simultaneous translators. When he finally left the stand, and walked past the dock, Göring barked at him: '*Schweinhund Verräter!!*' Von dem Bach stopped dead, flushed, and then continued to his

CANADA

During the Warsaw Rising I was a messenger and, when needed, a nurse in Major 'Horn''s grouping, in the 'Boar' Battalion. They fought in the Old Town, in one of the most difficult areas of insurgent Warsaw. I had many duties, one of which during the bombing was to carry canisters of petrol from Vola. After the fall of the Old Town I went through the city sewers to the City Centre, where I served in the battalion command until capitulation. I left Warsaw in the ranks of the Home Army. I did not make it into captivity. Before we reached Ozharov I escaped along the way, hiding myself in a wheat field.

In January 1952, during one of the meetings held at Vavel Castle in Cracow, we were arrested. After a trial before the Voievodeship (County) Military Court, I was sentenced to four years in prison, which was later extended to eight years for membership of the Home Army. I did time in the Montelupi Jail in Cracow, in Graudenz, and in Fordon, where I finished my prison sentence, freed conditionally after three and a half years on the strength of an amnesty. My state of health, combined with political conspiracy in the People's Poland, meant it was impossible for me to work in education.

In the Underground I had met Stanislas S., my fiancé, whom the Germans had imprisoned in the Paviak, and then three days before the Rising had taken to the concentration camp at Dachau. He died on 8 May 1945, that is the day that war ended. His cousin Stan K. proposed marriage to me. He was living in Toronto in Canada. I got married by proxy. Three years passed before the authorities of the PRL decided to let me leave Poland, on conditional release from prison.

When I left Poland, as the wife of a Canadian citizen, I reassured my remaining family that I was leaving for good but not for ever. My husband greeted me with an enormous bunch of red and white roses. My standard of living, however, turned out to be rather more modest than I had imagined. Although my husband had graduated from university in Switzerland, he was employed in a workshop repairing antiques. We lived in a small room in an attic, and I had brought a porcelain dinner-service for twenty-four and a mass of books. We travelled to our wedding by tram.

Slowly, I settled into the difficult life of a Polish emigrant in Canada. After my husband's death I tried to return to Poland, but all my friends there advised me against it. A single mother with a disabled child had a very low earning capacity. I got married again, to a soldier of the 2nd Corps, who had come through service in Africa and had fought at Monte Cassino. I undertook work in the community with Home Army Soldiers, the Association of Polish Combatants, and the Union of the Eastern

Territories. With my husband I established a foundation whose main aim was to contest the lies about Polish history propagated by the PRL. Now its focus is promoting works by Polish writers, academics, and artists.[1]

Nelli T–S.

---

seat. Göring was docked his tobacco ration and exercise privileges. After that, no prosecution witness was required to file past the accused.

Even so, there is a persistent rumour that von dem Bach supplied Göring with the cyanide pill which the *Reichsmarschall* used to kill himself. According to his own account, von dem Bach was in the habit of always greeting Göring at Nuremberg in an exaggerated and affected manner. The guards were used to the spectacle, and apparently suspected nothing when the two finally shook hands transferring the cyanide ampoule in the process. Suspicions were confirmed when von dem Bach surrendered a second ampoule for inspection, which was duly shown to be identical with the one found in Göring's mouth.[39]

After the Nuremberg trials, von dem Bach was held in prison awaiting extradition to Poland. But the extradition never happened. Instead, he travelled to Warsaw in the winter of 1946–47 in order to appear again as a prosecution witness. The defendant on this occasion was his former colleague, Dr Ludwig Fischer, the wartime Governor of Warsaw. Von dem Bach's immunity says everything about Soviet attitudes. Though he had publicly confessed to mass murder and had openly declared himself 'an absolute Hitler man', he was never formally accused.

In the final reckoning, relatively few of the Nazi murder-mongers who had operated in Warsaw met with the retribution that they had earned. *SS-Gruf.* Reinefarth, for example, escaped scot-free. After leaving Warsaw, he was appointed commander of the Fortress of Küstrin on the Oder. But in the chaos of the German collapse in March 1945 he was arrested for leaving his post. This incident no doubt helped his later claim to have been an anti-Nazi Resistance fighter. All attempts to have him extradited to Poland were vetoed by the Americans to whom he had surrendered and for whom he had acted as an adviser on Soviet military methods. So he was free to pursue a political career in West Germany. He never stood trial, and publicly denied that he had ever been a member of the SS.

Nonetheless, a few Nazis did meet their deserved end. *SS-Ostubaf.* Oskar Dirlewanger was one of them. After Warsaw, he had taken his brigade to Slovakia and Hungary, and to the Oder front where he was wounded. Recuperating at Altshausen in Bavaria, he was eventually captured by French Occupation forces, recognized by Polish POWs, and beaten so hard that he died of a fractured skull. Rough Justice.

Some of the Nazis who had operated in Poland were returned there to face trial. Rudolf Hoess, the former Commandant of Auschwitz, was one of them. He was hanged at the scene of his crimes in April 1947. Ludwig Fischer, the Governor of Warsaw, was another. His trial ended in the death sentence. His successor, Jürgen Stroop, SS Chief in Warsaw during 1943, who had supervised the liquidation of the Ghetto, was hanged in Warsaw in September 1951. The last man to hold that infamous office, Paul Geibel, committed suicide in his Polish prison cell in the 1960s.

In comparison to their numbers during the war, however, and the unprecedented scale of their crimes, relatively few prominent Nazis were made to face justice from a Polish dock. And, when they were, they sometimes escaped very lightly. In March 1951, for instance, a Warsaw court tried Rudolf Dengel, who had been Mayor of Warsaw throughout the Occupation. He was charged with planning to destroy the capital and with reducing food rations to starvation levels. He was sentenced to fifteen years. He was treated by the Communist authorities with greater leniency than they treated the majority of the capital's defenders. An observer from the British Embassy described the trial as 'a piece of political theatre'. 'Every opportunity was used to contrast the peaceful aims of People's Poland and the GDR with the bestial policies of the Third Reich and (by implication) of the western "Imperialists"'.[40]

Security was a Soviet and a Communist obsession. All outsiders were treated with malicious distrust. All insiders were handstrapped by police and bureaucratic controls. Even officers of the security services could land in their own camps and prisons for minor misdemeanours or misfortunes.

Western analysts have often attributed this mania to the fact that the USSR had been brutally invaded by the Third Reich. They were only repeating what Soviet officials had taught them to say. The explanation does not hold water. For the Soviets had been no less obsessed with security before the German invasion than after it. In any case, they had invaded their neighbours rather more often than they had been invaded themselves. Deep-seated paranoia was a central feature of the Soviet mindset; and it was a necessary adjunct to the reign of terror that had been rising and falling ever since the Bolsheviks seized power. It had flourished during the Civil War of 1918–21, had reached unprecedented intensity during the purges of the late 1930s, and had merely been reactivated in full measure in the post-war years. It was bequeathed with relish to each of the satellite states. [**IRKA III**, p. 564]

The machinery for post-war repression in 'People's' Poland' was considerably more systematic than anything operating during the wartime Soviet takeover. It was the joint creation of the Soviet NKVD and of the new Polish Security Ministry working in tandem. It aimed to bring the entire population under police control and hence to eliminate all forms of unlicensed activity. Among other things, its techniques included carefully targeted nocturnal police sweeps, in which every single inhabitant of a given locality would be reviewed in the middle of the night, and checked for the accuracy of their papers and the suitability of their political connections. Mass arrests and recurrent interrogations became routine, as did the use of torture. Trials were usually held in secret. Defendants were often unaware both of the nature of the charges and of the laws on which the charges were supposedly based. Independent defence lawyers did not exist. Lengthy sentences of hard labour and of solitary confinement were handed out for imaginary or apparently trivial offences. Death sentences for purely political dissent were frequent. Veterans of the Home Army were treated to the same official hostility that was meted out to Nazis. Post-war prison life was designed not just to chastise but also to humiliate. 'Politicals', such as the Home Army veterans, were either held in solitary confinement or mixed in with the most dangerous categories of common criminals, who were encouraged to taunt and abuse them.[41] [**IRKA IV**, p. 569]

Deportation to the Soviet Union remained a common option. It is no accident that several of the earliest insider's accounts of the Gulag were written by Poles, especially by members of the Home Army:

> 'The forest grew sparser as we travelled on, and the trees more stunted. Then there were only low bushes and finally the emptiness of the tundra . . . Everywhere there was snow, metres of it. Everything gradually turned white as far as the eye could see . . . We reached Vorkuta . . . on the thirty-third day . . .
>
> The doors opened and we were given bread, and some sugar to make up for the past few days when there had been no food. Through the open door [of the railway wagon] I could see some huts and camp watch-towers . . . We began to move again . . . After

several hours of travelling past coalmines, camps and watch-towers, we reached an encampment built entirely of wood and filled with [electric] lights . . .

Outside, two lines of guards stood with their guns trained on us. Other guards watched from a distance. We were told to line up in ranks of four . . . The transport chief handed our confidential files to the NKVD colonel responsible for our reception: "Here are the documents for wagon nr.13." The colonel gave us a sharp look, and asked: "Did you get your food ration today?"; "Yes, but not yesterday", some of us replied.

"I asked about today . . . Listen to me . . . This is not a forest of the kind where you roamed with your bands. There are no towns or villages to offer you protection. This is a holding-camp whence you will be sent to coalmines and building sites. Through diligent work . . . you may be able to make up for your crimes against our government and our people. But you must prove that you have repented. Our government is just, like our system. Forget any dreams you may have had. Justice and law are here. Understood?" '[42]

Poland's Ministry of Public Security (MBP) was created in 1944 under NKVD guidance as a completely separate body from the Ministry of Internal Affairs (MSW). Under the pre-war dispensation the Interior Ministry had run all police and security matters, but ex-Premier Mick made the bad mistake of making control of internal affairs a precondition of his joining the Government. On arrival, he found that he had gained control of traffic control and dog-licences, but not of state security.

From start to finish, the Security Ministry was headed by Col. Stanislas R., a pre-war Communist who had spent the war in the Red Army and who in 1944 had run the security office of the Lublin Committee. His two deputies, Roman R. and Mechislav M., were trained in the USSR to hold foreign loyalties. The operational departments were run by a gallery of ill-starred rogues. The Investigative Department, directed by Yatsek R., a former NKVD agent, was responsible for preparing charges against 'enemies of the people'. The Social Department, which initially covered cultural, youth and church affairs, was directed by the notorious Julia 'Luna' B., whose speciality was working between the sheets in order to recruit intellectual collaborators. The Department of Party Vigilance was directed by another degenerate, Anatole F., who held the party elite in fear. It was his deputy, 'Light', who eventually spoiled the game for

AUSTRALIA

Many ex-insurgents, still lingering in DP camps or in dead-end jobs in Western Europe, decide to sail away 'Down Under'

Australia was looking attractive, offering government-sponsored jobs for two years. Films were shown. There was one showing cattle being driven . . . I was not interested in cattle but something caught my eye. The power poles carrying electrical wires . . . looked so primitive – half-rotten wood leaning one way or another. In Warsaw or German towns that sort of wiring had long since been underground. Electricians were obviously going to be in demand in Australia.

We embarked sometime in late November 1950 onto the *Anna Salen.* The trip lasted thirty-five days. The boat arrived in Perth to take on provisions, then sailed for Melbourne to disembark. When we were halfway there, the boat suddenly turned around back to Perth (Fremantle). We had to make the quota for 1950; and the ship could not make Melbourne by the last day of 1950. We arrived back in Fremantle on 31 December 1950 at 22.00 hrs. However, I did not step down on the fifth continent until 1 January 1951, 00.15 hrs! The wharf was dark, sparingly lit by electric bulbs, all hanging from old leaning power poles.

Here we were, at last earning money, at a start of a real new life. I was never unemployed. I had only three jobs in Australia – four months in a stone quarry, twenty years in an electronics factory, then twenty years in a physics laboratory at a university, all of them most enjoyable times! I long forgave the old leaning power posts for misleading me.

PS I am retired and live with my wife in a large house in a Sydney suburb. My street is nice, except for the ugly old leaning power poles. I love them now![1]

In 1950, the Korean War broke out. My colleagues were called up into the forces. Since we had a one-year-old son, and baby food was disappearing from the shops, I decided it was time to leave [France].

We travelled to Paris to talk to the Australian consul . . . Mr Rice, who turned out to be a liar. He told us we would live in 'motel-style' accommodation and reassured me that I would be able to work in my profession as a textile engineer, saying, 'We have the best wool in the world, and it all needs turning into cloth.'

We found ourselves in Australia, in the Bonegil Camp, in tin shacks, eating mutton stew and working on a two-year contract of physical work. When I produced my [professional] diploma, the official said, 'Oh good, you can fix the car!' At the end of the contract, my French qualifications were not recognized, and I had to start a correspondence course in English . . .

In the 1950s Australians were suspicious of us, and many thought that we had been sent out from Europe for some sort of criminal offence . . .[2]

We sailed for Australia on 20 May 1952 on the *Oronsay*. During the five-week voyage, we fed the apes in Gibraltar, haggled in the bazaar at Port Said, and swam in the sea with elephants in Ceylon . . . We landed in Sydney at the end of June, and that same evening we were loaded onto the Coonamble mail train. Our worldly possessions consisted of two cases, a sack containing a sewing machine, and £15 in sterling.

We travelled to the little town of Dubbo, where I was given work digging artesian wells. There were only jobs in the steelworks, mines, or on building projects in the semi-desert outback of New South Wales. A Polish couple rented us their veranda, where we lived for the next two years. We then bought a building plot on the outskirts. Despite having no diploma, I got work as a draughtsman. I could manage because my father had been a surveyor and my brother a civil engineer, so I was used to plans, measuring, and theodolites.[3]

In the Rising, my pseudonym was 'Bullet'. I frequently acted as deputy commander of the volunteer 'Attack Company'. No one knew that I was only seventeen . . .

In 1964, sponsored by fellow Poles, I, my wife, and my daughter arrived in Adelaide. We landed on 29 December. It was a huge country full of freedom and wide open spaces. The weather, after [Britain], was marvellous. And a large Polish community helped us find our feet. I got a job in a factory, and by taking out a loan, we were able to buy a house. I felt myself needed, no longer a 'bloody foreigner'. A year later we took out Australian citizenship. I was made a departmental manager, and stayed there until retirement as a war veteran in 1987 at the age of sixty.

In Australia, as in Britain, I always took part in the work of Polish organizations, especially among ex-combatants.[4]

---

everyone. The best informed man in Poland on the foibles and vices of the party leadership, he defected to the West in 1953. Col. Stanislas R. was arrested, Feigin dismissed. In 1955, the ministry itself was disbanded.[43]

The training, development, and operations of the MBP were subordinated to the Soviet authorities from beginning to end. On 20 March 1945, Gen. Serov himself, the commander of the NKVD's special regiments, was appointed an adviser to the Ministry. As one historian remarked, 'advisers do not come much higher than Commissar of State Security of the Second

Rank'.[44] The appointment could only have been more prestigious if Beria himself had moved from Moscow to Warsaw. No less revealing is the fact that once the war had ended Beria stationed the largest concentration of repressive force not in Germany but in Poland. Moscow judged ten NKVD security regiments sufficient for defeated Germany, whilst fifteen regiments under Gen. Selivanovsky were allocated to 'victorious' Poland. Selivanovsky was appointed 'counsellor' at the MBP. 'This perhaps was the best indication of the truth behind Stalin's assertion at Yalta that the Soviet Union was interested in "the creation of a mighty, free and independent Poland".'[45]

Soviet advisers, and the units which accompanied them, stayed in Poland in large numbers for years. They were locally known as 'POPs' – both a word which means 'Orthodox Priest' and an acronym for 'Persons Pretending to be Poles'. Throughout this time, Gen. Serov, who used the pseudonym 'Ivanov', was effectively in charge. After the so-called 'civil war' the number of advisers decreased, but the vigilance remained. Soviet officers could be found at every level. After Rokossovsky's arrival in 1949, their presence swelled once more, though they were now more noticeable in the military than in the internal security sphere.

The activities of the Security Ministry bore little resemblance to those of legal states. Arrests, for example, generally took the form of shock raids. They took place in the street in broad daylight or through the dreaded knock on the door in the middle of the night. They often descended on social gatherings, such as parties or weddings, so that whole droves of captives could be put into custody and sifted.

Imprisonment on open-ended remand was a dire punishment in itself. Political prisoners from the Home Army or the democratic parties were habitually cast into cells with Nazis or with known recidivists. Awaiting interrogation themselves, they had routinely to tend the battered bodies and maltreated minds of cellmates whose turn had come first.

The purpose of interrogation was less to establish the truth than to extract confession on pre-arranged accusation. The distinction between suspect and accused was ignored, and prisoners were rapidly disarmed and disorientated by their truly Kafka-esque surroundings. Crude physical torture was often more bearable than the various techniques of sensory deprivation which the NKVD had perfected. One of the inner circle, who had witnessed these methods, spoke of 'the Asiatic cruelty'.[46] Prisoners who were not intended to appear in court could be thrashed to a pulp. But those whose outward appearance had to be safeguarded could be treated to more refined torments. Interrogations were customarily done at night under bright lights. The interrogated were prevented from sleeping properly during the day, often by being forced to stand in flooded cellars where they could neither sit nor lie and where their sodden feet would swell. Women would be sexually assaulted or humiliated. Men were beaten on the kidneys where the pain was excruciating but the damage invisible. All could be starved, dehydrated, poisoned, drugged, electrocuted, needled, singed, racked, dazed by ultrasound, bloated by forced drinking, or psychologically broken by false promises. In the end, once the required confessions and undertakings had been obtained, the human wreck could be rendered presentable if necessary by a few solid meals, hot showers, and a comfortable bed. Individual experiences varied. But persons who had the misfortune to experience both Nazi and Stalinist captivity were apt to consider the latter the more dreadful.

This last topic deserves intensive research. Survivors report a marked difference in the psychological environment. The SS made no secret of the fact that they regarded their victims as mere animals who had no right to live. They were cruel and ruthless in the extreme; but at least they made their prisoners' predicament abundantly plain. The NKVD and its disciples, in contrast, specialized in psychological disorientation. They were seeking to rid the world not of inferior blood, but of polluted minds. As a result, they devoted more time to their prey, endlessly asking them questions, alternately promising them relief or threatening them with pain. Within a relatively short time, they were confident of reducing the majority to a state of cowed, quivering confusion with no hope of a quick death. Particularly relevant is the incidence of prisoners who were held for years for the purposes of interrogation but were never brought to trial.

Stalinist trials had little to do with justice. In essence, they were rituals whose course was determined in advance and where the outcome was frequently murder. Verdicts were often handed to the judges by party officials before the court had convened. Prominent cases were determined by discussions in the Politburo. Charges were wrapped up in impenetrable ideological drivel. Prosecutors were assured of results. Defence lawyers were considered a disposable luxury. If appointed, they were nominated by the same authorities that appointed the judges. Witnesses were thoroughly rehearsed, often after being tortured in parallel to the accused. They would normally be convicts hoping to gain reprieve for a convincing performance. Inconvenient evidence was simply ignored. Judges were judged by their superiors on subservience not on judicial competence. Lenient sentences were unusual: commutations were rare.

Thousands upon thousands of lesser figures were judicially processed *in camera*. They were fortunate to receive a perfunctory hearing. They had no means of demanding a lawyer's presence or of persuading the lawyer, if present, to contest the charges. They usually settled for writing a plea for mercy. Sackloads of such pleas have been found in the archives – unopened.

Sentences followed a tariff that did not appear to conform to the gravity of named offences. In the Soviet system, they included a wide range of punishments starting with administrative exile or internment under a milder penal regime. In Poland, they consisted largely of incarceration with or without solitary confinement, or with or without hard labour. Terms of punishment were routinely harsh. Five, ten, or fifteen years were run-of-the-mill. Death sentences, by shooting or hanging, were common, and were far less frequently commuted for political convicts than for others. But analyses of the major trials reveal no discernible policy or pattern. The condemned lived or died at random or at the whim of Comrade Bierut and his underlings.

One last distinction, however, is necessary. The judicial and security strictures of 'People's Poland' were divided into separate civilian and military sectors. The Security Ministry, though supposedly concerned with non-military affairs, frequently directed its cases, after interrogation, to military courts. The Ministry of National Defence operated its own parallel system. The innocuously named Chief Bureau of Information was the resort of the special military services, which included security, intelligence and counter-intelligence branches. It possessed its own interrogators, its own prisons, its own procurators and its own courts. It was particularly zealous in rooting out ex-insurgents, because, where convenient, as former members of the Home Army, ex-insurgents could be claimed by the military as distinct from the civilian sphere.

Most of these horrors were hidden from public view, and were only revealed many decades later. All media were strictly censored; and no critical reporting was permissible. The press reported some trials and verdicts, but it could not criticize them. So, after 1947–48, the democratic opposition lay low or went into hiding; and many oppositionists were confirmed in thinking how right their instincts to oppose had been. For, as many ex-insurgents knew in their hearts, lost causes are not necessarily wrong.

One of the most penetrating insights into the realities of political relationships during and after the Second World War was written by a survivor of the Warsaw Rising, who spent eleven years in Communist jails after 1945. Lt. 'Badger' was a graduate of the *Institut des Hautes Écoles Internationales* in Paris, and had worked for the Home Army's BIP. During the Rising had edited the *Insurgent News*. Arrested in August 1945, he was subjected to two trials – one in 1946, when he was given ten years, and another in 1952, when he was sentenced to death. Yet the most peculiar experience of his imprisonment began one day in March 1949, when he was pushed into a cell in Block XI at Mokotov Jail. There were already two prisoners inside. One of them said, 'We're the so-called war criminals, Germans.' The other said, 'My name is Stroop, with two o's, Christian name Jürgen. Rank of lieutenant general. *Enchanté, Monsieur.*' Here was Communist theory being put into practice. Fascist and democratic prisoners were both 'anti-Communist'. Therefore, they were equally guilty. The SS man and the Home Army soldier may conceivably have fought each other. But *objectively*, as the Marxists might say, they had been collaborating. Therefore, they deserved to rot in the same cell.

Badger decided to benefit from the opportunity. For 255 days, he had limitless time and leisure to interview his cellmates at length and to examine the mind of a totally unrepentant and unreconstructed Nazi. He asked endless questions and memorized the replies. For Stroop had been SS and Police Chief of Athens and Warsaw and was the liquidator of the Warsaw Ghetto. 'He officially received double rations'. 'He was carefully dressed in a well-tailored deep wine-red jacket, white cravat, . . . fawn trousers and beautifully polished brown shoes.'[47]

Stroop was eager to relate his adventures, especially in the Ghetto:

> The fighting was so intense that day that my troops were beginning to falter. I decided the time had come to burn every house still standing . . . The Jews dashed through the flames like devils, appearing in windows or on balconies, sometimes teetering on ledges. Some shot at us; others sang what might have been psalms, or chanted in unison *'Hitler Kaputt'* or 'Death to the Germans', or 'Long live Poland'.

CAVIAHUE

The former commander of the Zoshka Battalion makes a new life in the New World

Capt. 'George' sailed for Buenos Aires in July 1948. Three years earlier, after release from German imprisonment, he had joined the Polish Parachute Brigade in Britain. And in 1946, at the head of a relief mission to Poland, he had succeeded in bringing out his wife and children, who had passed the war in Cracow. But the travails of post-war Europe were not for him. A graduate of Warsaw Polytechnic and a qualified civil engineer/architect, he possessed readily exportable skills. So he headed for happier climes.

In Argentina, however, the captain's family ran into the troubles fomented by the regime of General Perón. Buenos Aires was a city of political turmoil, strikes, and street-fights. So they started a further stage in their long journey to the West. They travelled 1,300 kilometres to the end of the railway line in the province of Neuquen, and then into the foothills of the Andes. They eventually settled in the wilderness, by the lake of Quillen below the high Cordilleras, in the former kingdom of Araucania, in the land of the Mapuche Indians. It was the native home of the *Araucaria araucana*, the 'monkey puzzle tree'. They built their own house, like the Swiss family Robinson. They hunted for food, as Capt. George had once hunted for Germans in the Old Town. They lived with the Indians, and learned their ways. They only moved to the city of Zapata in 1961, when their children were in urgent need of schooling.

Like many Polish exiles, in the mould of Malinowski, Przewalski, or Bronisław Pilsudski, Capt. George turned to anthropology. A founding member of the Araucanian Society, he made numerous studies and collections of the language, lore, and natural religion of the Mapuche Nation and of associated tribes. These 'People of the Earth' had resisted both the Incas and the Spaniards before coming under the unrequested rule of Chile and Argentina. They are one of Latin America's many indigenous peoples fighting for survival and recognition. Like the Varsovians under German and Soviet rule, they simply wanted control of their own destiny.

Yet, as a scout and an engineer, Capt. George sought above all to create something permanent. Working for the provincial Energy Department, he planned and helped build the new mountain resort of Caviahue, nearly 2,000 metres high at the foot of a volcano. By the time that he retired in 1983, he had seen the settlement grow into a year-round health and ski station, powered by its own hydro-electrical system, graced by hotels and lakeside promenades, and serviced by a tourist airport. A refugee from the 'city of destruction' had left the most constructive of marks on the map of his adoptive continent.[1]

> It was total pandemonium. Flames. Smoke. Showers of sparks mixed with dust. The stench of scorched flesh. Explosions which almost drowned out the shrieks of the 'parachutists' . . .
>
> 'What do you mean by parachutists?' [Badger] enquired.
>
> 'That's what my SS men called the Jews, Jewesses, and children who leaped from the windows of the houses that had been ignited below . . . the fun sometimes lasted all night.'
>
> Stroop, highly excited, mimed a duck shooter hunting his prey. Striding around the cell pointing an imaginary shotgun, he shouted, '*Paf, paf, paf, paf* . . .'
>
> A glance [at our faces] caused Stroop's cheeks to lose their glow. With a shrug he turned to the window and began humming the Horst Wessel song.[48]

Stroop took a keen interest in all aspects of the Polish resistance, confirming that in his last job, where he had been ordered to coordinate a German resistance organization against the advancing Americans, he had tried to imitate Polish methods:

> 'Herr Mocharski,' he said, 'don't you agree that the Poles are the world's best schemers? It's in their blood!'
>
> 'History has forced us to become a nation of plotters,' I admitted.

Stroop did no soul-searching. He had seen his utopia, and regretted nothing but its passing:

> 'We should have started the liquidation programme sooner,' he said emphatically. 'As I learned in the Warsaw Ghetto, a contaminated forest must be uprooted and burned to the ground. Heinrich Himmler knew this, of course. If only we could have convinced all Germany in 1933 of the need for racial and spiritual purity. . . . the Reich would have been impervious.'[49]

Stroop's reflections were expressed without any inhibitions. He thought quite literally that 'German history is the most beautiful in the world.' Then he moved on. 'Good-bye, Herr Mocharski. See you soon at St Peter's Gate.'[50]

The NKVD removed tens of thousands of people from circulation. Serov's successors, Lt.Gen. N. Selivanovsky and Minister S. Kruglov, wrote report after report about the elimination of this group or that group, about the numbers of people and weapons seized, about the sum total of Poles held in various parts of the NKVD's underworld. Not until October 1946 did Moscow feel sufficiently confident to reduce the number of its internal ministry troops.

Of course, the profile of ex-insurgents gradually decreased within the tides of the repressed. In the course of 1945, the specific category of 'bandit-insurrectionary' fades away. But there undoubtedly were significant groups of ex-insurgents within the various categories of 'fascists', 'illegals', 'bandits', 'members of NIE', 'members of AK', and 'members of WiN' whose arrest was recorded.

Among the published documents, some of the most interesting relate to the manifest failings of the security services in the immediate post-war period. On 11 October 1945, for example, Adviser Selivanovsky writes to Beria to tell him that 'the organs of public security in Poland are littered to a high degree with traitors, members of Underground organizations, bribe-takers, marauders and other criminal elements.' In the previous three months, 333 security officers had been arrested, and 365 relieved of their posts:

> The criminal element, which has penetrated the security organs, exploits its position in the service: by forming anti-state groups within the organs . . .: by giving information to the Underground and other active bands . . .: by cooperating with the bandits in attacks on the militia and on prisons: by issuing death threats against security agents: by selling agency reports for bribes, by destroying interrogation reports, by releasing prisoners: and by engaging in robberies and muggings.
>
> The Minister, together with our instructors, has taken steps to recruit a better sort of agent and to improve their material benefits. Bierut has been informed.[51]

Obviously, there were problems.

In July 1947, Minister Kruglov reported to Molotov on hunger strikes among two groups of Polish prisoners in Russia – in camp nr. 454 at Ryazan and in camp nr. 27 at Krasnogorsk.[52] The camps were classed as having a 'light regime', the former held 5 generals, 894 other Home Army soldiers, and 567 Home Army 'supporters'. The latter was a special camp for Polish aristocrats, its prisoners possessing an array of titles as princes, barons, and counts. In both cases, the strikes had been largely provoked by uncertainties concerning the date of return. And in each case, the leader of the action had links to the Warsaw Rising. Gen. 'Arrow', otherwise Ludwik Bittner (wrongly identified by the Russians as Winter), had been appointed by the Home Army to liaise with the Peasant Battalions and had been arrested by the NKVD on 14 August 1944 as he prepared to assist the Rising. Prince Yanush R. had been arrested by the Gestapo in the first week of August, following the outbreak of the Rising, and taken to Berlin. Returning to his estate near Warsaw in October, he was promptly whisked off to Moscow by the NKVD. He was consigned to the camp by Beria in person, for refusing to compose an appropriate statement about the situation in Poland. Both men went home at the end of 1947. For the rest of his life, Prince R. lived in a two-room flat in Mokotov.

Among the unpublished files, there are vast quantities of relevant documents that were to remain unseen and unread to the end of the century. But some curious items have surfaced, especially from 1945. The NKVD made great efforts, for example, to check up on the progress of every single political party or grouping, including the Communist Workers' Party (PPR). An acid report from Lt.Gen. Selivanovsky tells Beria that the PPR's membership figures are much inflated. They were claiming to have 45,000 members in the Warsaw District, whereas only 14,000 had registered.[53]

Much time was also devoted to the Jewish issue. An extensive, undated report from late 1945 reviews the overall situation. It starts, somewhat tendentiously, with the statement: 'Throughout the entire course of history, the existence in Poland of hostile attitudes towards the Jews has been a permanent phenomenon.'[54] After reviewing the revival of Jewish parties and organizations of post-war Poland, it summarizes the distribution of Jews in the various branches of the Government service:

> In the Ministry of Public Security, Jews constitute 18.7% of the employees. Jews occupy 50% of directorial posts.
>
> In the 1st Department of this Ministry, 27% of the employees are Jewish: 7 persons have directorial duties.
>
> In the Personnel Department (Special Inspectorate), there is 33.3% of Jews, all holding responsible positions. In the Health Department, the figure is 49.1%: in the Finances – 29%.
>
> In the central apparatus of press control, Jews constitute up to 50%, in the branch at Radom – 82.3%.[55]

'Such a situation', it concludes, 'is provoking the acute discontent of Poles.'[56] In reality, the presence of such a large Jewish contingent in

MEXICO

An ex-insurgent from Warsaw debates the Rising with a Soviet diplomat

I have lived in Mexico for almost half a century. In all that time, I haven't met anybody who, on finding out about my involvement in the Rising and the AK, didn't show an interest in one of the bloodiest battles of World War II. I regularly attended the extremely interesting lectures and monthly discussions at the Asociación Histórica de Militaria (Military Historical Association). In 1986, when Poland featured prominently in the Mexican press due to 'Solidarity', they asked me – as a member of the Mexican Group of the AK – to talk about the Rising but 'without touching on the political aspects'. I accepted the invitation enthusiastically, and suggested giving a talk at a meeting on 6 August, a few days after the anniversary . . .

I had no idea that diplomats from the American and Soviet Embassies were going to attend. Just as I was preparing for my presentation, the Soviet military attaché came up to me and said: 'I'm sure you'll talk from a very different point of view to that held by the General Staff of the Red Army. I'd like to offer to you General Sergei Shtemenko's book as a gift.'

For an hour and a half I lectured on the military situation before and after the Rising, the heroism of the AK soldiers and ordinary people, the bravery of the Polish and Allied air forces, as well as the lack of strategic and tactical help. I mentioned the reluctance of the Soviets to assist the Rising and Moscow's ban on the landing of Allied aircraft . . . I also mentioned the Polish division that had successfully crossed the river, proving that the river could be crossed and that the Russians had no intention of doing so. When I finished, I was applauded generously.

The second half of the meeting consisted of a discussion, in which many questions were raised. Towards the end the Soviet attaché asked me: 'Don't you think that if the Poles had not been divided and had not had two governments, Warsaw would have been spared?' I took this as an invitation to talk about political and historical issues. First of all, I made it clear that *there were not two governments.* In London we had a legal government recognized both by the Poles and by the rest of the world. The 'Committee' founded by the Soviet authorities in Moscow could not claim any right to represent Polish citizens. I pointed out how united the Polish nation had been during the uprisings of the nineteenth century, during the battle for independence in 1920 against the Bolsheviks, and during the whole Second World War. I added that I greatly admired the Polish forces abroad and the AK for their loyalty to the Allies. I then explained that the Polish people were sympathetic to the view of the government in exile, which had affirmed, contrary to the Kremlin's propaganda, that the Polish officers at Katyn had been victims of the Russians and not the Germans. Finally I said that the Polish people's support for 'Solidarity' proved that they could unite against any enemy. I turned to the Soviet attaché and said, 'I hope that now you have the facts, you will admit that I am right . . .!' All eyes were on the diplomat. After a few seconds, the Russian became very red in the face. Finally he said: 'From your point of view you are right.'

A few years passed. Poland contributed to the fall of the Communist bloc and of the Berlin Wall. I finally got round to reading the 'dissertation' by General Shtemenko. It contained nothing but lies about the Rising. I imagine that such lies can only be told by someone who has either a hammer and sickle or a swastika on their coat of arms.

Every year on Memorial Day I am invited to the American cemetery in Mexico. On one of those occasions I again bumped into my 'friend', the same Soviet diplomat. Dressed in Russian naval uniform, he came towards me, introduced himself as a financial attaché, and asked if I remembered him. I said I remembered him well and added: 'Will you agree with me now about Poland's unity and about the Rising?' Quite unexpectedly he said: 'Yes. In the past we had no access to the truth. Now things have changed, and I agree with you entirely.'[1]

J. Skoryna

Berman's notorious organization would not have aroused the same level of suspicion if the Communist authorities had not routinely denied employing any Jews whatsoever.

The first anniversary of the Warsaw Rising was seen by the UB with some reason as an occasion for vigilance. On the eve of the anniversary, four members of the 'Warsaw Organization of the Home Army' were picked up by security officers. Two had been trying to board a plane for Cracow, carrying two pistols and 150 copies of 'anti-Governmental' and 'anti-Soviet' leaflets. One of them, George Z., was a former employee of the Security Ministry in the city of Stettin. That same night, posters were pasted on street walls around the city carrying slogans such as 'DOWN WITH THE OCCUPIERS', 'LONG LIVE [PREMIER MICK]', 'DOWN WITH [BIERUT]', 'POLAND WILL WIN', and 'WE ARE FIGHTING'.[57] Investigations showed that the '*Bandgruppa*' had been operating since January. It was commanded by a certain André, and was divided into two sections – Warsaw (west) and Warsaw (east). It was supposedly engaged in robberies and terrorist acts against the security organs and party members. On 24

July it had robbed a bank of 200,000 *zloties*. The report finished ominously: 'Measures are being extended to capture the remaining members of the Underground.'[58]

For many years after the war, no studies could be made of the murderous repressions which had overwhelmed the democratic opposition in Poland. Official sources passed over the events in silence. Foreign observers had few means of verifying the many rumours. Once Poland disappeared behind the Iron Curtain, Western public opinion lost interest. Two periods were distinguished. The first, which ran from 1944 to the end of the 'civil war' in 1947, was characterized by a very large number of victims who were eliminated systematically, but often in a summary, almost casual manner. The second, from 1948 to 1955/56, was characterized by a diminishing number of victims, who were finished off by the more formalized procedures of extended trials and judicial shows. Survivors of the Warsaw Rising figured prominently among the victims of both periods.

During the so-called 'civil war', the tactics of the Communist forces concentrated on destroying the infrastructure of Underground support by arresting suspected sympathizers and burning down their houses. They also made use of a series of 'amnesties' which promised their adversaries safe passage if they surrendered and laid down their arms within a given period. Many fighters were enticed out of the woods in this way, only to find that the amnesty was not what it seemed. As often as not, it was a prelude to rearrest. Recurrent arrest and retrial of the same defendant was a feature of the process.

Col. Wolf, the Home Army commander from Lithuania, for instance, was arrested on three separate occasions. Having escaped from a Soviet penal camp at Vologda, he returned home to Vilno in 1947 only to be rearrested there by the NKVD. 'Repatriated' to Poland, he was formally arrested by agents of the Security Office on 3 July. He survived four years of interrogation in the Mokotov Jail in Warsaw, without trial, before dying in the prison hospital in 1951.

Throughout the 'civil war' and beyond, therefore, oppositionists of one sort or another were brought to trial, sentenced, and removed from circulation. The culmination of this phase was reached in January 1947 when a major trial of the leadership of WiN was staged. The main defendant was Bear Cub's deputy and successor, 'the Chairman', who had

IRKA III

The widow of an insurgent falls victim to false charges of espionage

Three years passed [after my husband's death in the Rising]. I was constantly on the move, a single mother contending with all manner of difficulties to support my two children. Thanks to my knowledge of languages, I managed to obtain a job in the visa department of the US Embassy. This was the cause of my later arrest in the largely fabricated case against Polish pilots who had served in the RAF . . .

As it subsequently transpired, the chief defendant in the case, Ladislas Sl., an acquaintance of ours, was almost certainly engaged in foreign intelligence. He was eventually executed. All the others, after years of cruel interrogation, were condemned to sentences from ten years to life, only being rehabilitated during the 'thaw' after Stalin's death. They included many ex-RAF personnel [such as Skalski, Novicki, and Radomski] . . . We were victims of a system that was not interested in genuine offences, only in sowing terror.

My arrest occurred when I was caught in a so-called 'cauldron' set by the police in Ladislas Sl.'s flat. Security agents picked up everyone who called there over a period of some four weeks . . . When they found that I was employed by the American Embassy, they set up another 'cauldron' in my own flat; and I was immediately taken to the Ministry of Security to be interrogated by Col. Yatsek R. in person. 'It's hardly surprising', he declared, 'to see a landowner's daughter working for the Americans and befriending a spy. But it would be a shame if a good-looking young woman should rot in prison for ten years and her children be put in an orphanage. I propose, therefore, that you be sent home by limousine without delay: but on one condition, that you visit our ministry from time to time to talk about matters which concern us.' When he received no agreement, he sent me to the cells, saying, 'A pity, but it's your choice.'

I survived two years of interrogation without signing any false statements. There was only one military judge at my secret trial, and two bored assistants, but no defence lawyer. Two former RAF pilots were called as witnesses against me, although they had already dissociated themselves from their accusations, extracted by torture. Even so, just as the Colonel had promised, I was given ten years, 'for abetting espionage'.

I spent the first three weeks in an isolation cell, where someone had written the entire Morse code on the wall. I learned it by heart. For the next seven years, in various prisons, I acted as a regular telegraphist tapping out messages to neighbouring cells. This system of communication was so widespread that we knew the names and sentences of virtually all the prisoners . . . For three months, I 'talked' for hours every day with the commander of WiN, who was waiting to be executed . . .

The methods applied to prisoners who refused to confess followed a well-known pattern. For six months, I had a 'stool pigeon' placed in my cell, and was endlessly grilled about my experiences under the Gestapo in the Paviak in 1941 . . .

In time, all the successive stages of interrogation were imposed on me. 'Intensive interrogation' in my case lasted for eighteen months . . . I became so exhausted, I had to be revived by a series of injections administered by a German prisoner-doctor. I was given six weeks of so-called *stójki* or 'standings', with only two one-night breaks, kept at attention on my feet throughout the night after day-long questionings.

By way of conclusion, three colonels beat me unconscious with belts before leaving me naked on a cold and filthy cement floor, deprived of access to a toilet . . . I saved myself from being raped by a specially nasty warder by protesting I had VD. I then had to listen to the terrified screams of a woman in a neighbouring cell, who paid the price for my escape.

But those were just the physical tortures. For two years and a half, I received no word from my parents, spoke to no lawyer, and heard nothing of my children, who were four and five when I left them . . .[1]

---

been the most prominent figure in the ex-AK Underground after Bear Cub's death.

The regime struck another chilling blow in March 1948 when it caught up with Capt. Roman, an ex-insurgent and sometime soldier of the Anders Army, who has rightly been dubbed 'the bravest of the brave'. There can be little doubt that Capt. Roman was collecting intelligence for the Government-in-Exile and that he had returned to Poland with the full expectation, if caught, of being treated as a traitor and a spy. He was tried and executed in the Mokotov Jail. 'As a paid agent of Gen. Anders' Intelligence Service,' the court declared, 'he organized a spy network on Polish territory, collecting information and sending it abroad,' thereby 'betraying state secrets.'[59] This was not too remarkable. Far more extraordinary were Seraphim's earlier adventures.

Roman, aka Seraphim, real name Vitold Pilecki, was a Pole from the east, born on the shores of Lake Ladoga and educated in Lithuania. A pre-war cavalry officer, he was active in Underground conspiracy in Warsaw from 1939 onwards. (During the Rising, he commanded the company from 'Valiant II' which, almost alone, closed the east–west boulevard to German traffic for the first two weeks of August in the area which came to be known as 'Pilecki's Redoubt'.) But his place in history had been secured earlier, in September 1940, when he succeeded in getting himself arrested by the Gestapo in order to see the inside of Auschwitz for himself. (His camp number was 4859.) Having set up the first Resistance cell inside the camp, he contrived to escape in April 1943, and wrote the first authoritative report of conditions there. His anti-fascist exploits earned him no mercy from the Communists. He has no known grave.[60]

A second trial, which began in October 1948, is usually known by the acronym START. In effect, it represented an act of collective repression directed against the Home Army's former internal police unit. The prosecutors argued that the unit had been used for purely political purposes and, in particular, for killing Communists, Soviet partisans, and Jews. The chief defendant was none other than the legendary Maj. Kontrym, the 'Samogitian'. After the war, he had been in Bergen-Belsen and in the 1st (Polish) Armoured Division. He, too, was shown no mercy, and was shot in January 1953 having been tormented for over four years.[61]

Confronted with overpowering odds, therefore, many ex-insurgents and other Home Army people decided to disappear into hiding. Some built semi-permanent hideaways in barns or forest huts, much as fugitive Jews had done during the Nazi occupation. Others took off for the 'Recovered Territories' in western Poland, where they hoped to find anonymity among the flood of post-war refugees and 'repatriants'. The Security Office was very well aware of the ruse. A major sweep codenamed 'Action X' netted many thousands in 1948 in Lower Silesia, including a large group of Wolf's followers from distant Lithuania.[62]

Incongruously, therefore, the city prison of Vrotslav witnessed the last moments of not a few ex-Warsaw insurgents. L.Cpl. 'Griffin', for example, had a rich biography. A boy scout brought up in Warsaw, the son of a professional footballer, he had fought in the Rising in the Kampinos Group. Liberated in 1945 by the Americans from Stalag XIB, he promptly joined the US forces and served for several months in a tank battalion of the US Third Army. Ending the war in Czechoslovakia, he returned to Poland and joined WiN. His way out, when the pursuit heated up, was to join the People's Army (LWP). His luck finally folded in August 1950. Charged with 'anti-state agitation', 'espionage', and the creation of a (non-existent) WiN cell, he was shot in the prison yard on 30 August 1951, aged almost twenty-five.[63]

Yet another group decided that the best policy was to seek protection within the Communist apparatus. A number of ex-Home Army personnel figured after the war in the company of shady lawyers and policemen employed by 'People's Poland'. Such was Judge Yan H. and a senior military procurator, Maj. Cheslav L., whose legal practice continued in Warsaw untouched for forty years. The latter were eventually taken into custody at the start of the twenty-first century during enquiries into the death of Maj. Kontrym.[64]

Though the precedent for show trials of Polish democrats had been set in Moscow in June 1945, the home-grown stage of the phenomenon did not really start for some years. But, as Stalinism progressed into ever more irrational and purely terroristic realms, the machinery of repression widened its sights, targeting all and sundry, consuming the loyal servants of the state as well as its opponents. Once the formal dictatorship of the United Workers' Party came into force after 1948, no one could feel safe. True to type, the new wave of terror began with the finger of accusation pointing at the regime's own ranks. The first in a run of major trials of serving army officers began in May 1948. Known as the 'Z-L Case', it was directed against sixty soldiers from the towns of Zamost and Lublin, where the percentage of pre-war officers was unusually high.

One of the horrendous relics of this particular trial is a report dated 22 July 1948, written by a Soviet adviser who was working in the capacity of an investigator at the Chief Information Bureau. The report was filed to explain the demise of an obdurate prisoner, and it describes in detail the various methods which were unsuccessfully applied in order to extract a confession. The adviser was called Sergei Malkovskii. The prisoner who died was Lt.Col. Z., chief of staff of the 3rd Infantry Division.[65]

Malkovskii described interrogation as a duel. The investigating officer was aiming to extract a confession – in this case of association with WiN. The prisoner was trying to avoid confessing. But that was not how he put it. The officer, he said, 'is fighting for his country, and its independence, and for democratic freedoms'. But the other, 'the criminal', 'is fighting for the opposite aims, and is only concerned for his own person, perhaps for his life.' There were three degrees of interrogation. At the first, the prisoner was simply questioned intensively. At the second, the interrogators applied 'the conveyor belt', where relays of officers kept up a non-stop barrage of questions and insinuations, if necessary for weeks on end. At the third, 'interrogation of the third degree' was used as a euphemism for physical torture that would continue until the duel was either won or lost.

According to Malkovskii's report, Lt.Col. Z. never wavered. He held out for a month under stage one, followed by ten days of the conveyor belt. Guided by the instructions of Anatole F., he was then subjected to the 'third degree' in the form of 'combined treatment', where one policeman posed the question and a second beat his heels and feet. This routine began on 13 July, but at two the next morning Malkovskii was woken in his bed to be told that the prisoner had fallen from the table on to the floor. Medical advice was called for. An injection was administered, but five days later, the prisoner was suffering from a high fever and a left leg that had turned completely black and was still not fit to resume. He died on the 'National Day' of 'People's Poland', whilst the leaders of the regime were presiding at a grand parade. He had won the duel.

The case of Chairman 'Basil' came to court in November 1948. It was occasioned by the fact that the Communist Party was merging with the remnants of the broken Socialist Party, and hence that the genuine leaders of the Socialists had to be eliminated. Basil had seen the inside of Tsarist jails for his beliefs. He had been the Chairman of the Underground inter-party council; he was one of the Moscow 'Sixteen'; and he was a survivor of the Warsaw Rising. He was sentenced to ten years. He committed suicide in jail barely a year later.[66]

And so it went on: year after year, trial after trial, death after death: all behind the facade of a self-proclaimed progressive regime and of post-war reconstruction. Nothing encouraged the tale to be told. No one in the Soviet bloc was able to tell. Few in the West, even at the height of the Cold War, were interested. Repetitive accounts of secret torture and concealed killing became tedious. 'After all', as someone commented about Stalin's crimes, 'the killing was so boring.'[67]

The 'Zoshka Case' started on Christmas Eve 1948 with the arrest of 'Anode', a student of architecture who four years earlier had fought in the Zoshka Battalion. Within a month, Anode was dead. But it was the aftermath which marked a new stage in the escalation of repression. In one single night in February 1949, up to 5,000 people were arrested, all of them, like Anode, connected in some way with the scouting movement. They were much too numerous to be put on trial. The regime was moving into the realm of mass social terror.[68]

In 1948–49, the 'Zhegota Case' resulted in the secret trial and imprisonment of all the leading survivors of the Underground's Council for Aid

IRKA IV

Imprisoned on false charges, a young mother faces the prospect of ten years in solitary confinement

Immediately after being sentenced, I was transferred to the so-called '*ogólniak*' or 'general prison' on Rakoviets Street. About a hundred women, politicals and criminals, were crammed into a large cell designed for twenty. I was depressed by the knowledge that I had no chance of an amnesty, yet cheered by access to things that had been banned during the period of my interrogation. We eagerly devoured the news from the Communist newspaper [*Trybuna Ludu*] and, on the principle of 'know your enemy', read any book available, including works by Marx, Engels, and Lenin. We also had the rare opportunity to meet very distinguished women from the wartime and post-war Underground, including the wives of leading figures from the AK, WiN, UPA, and PSL.

After six months, I was taken to Fordon Jail, [on the lower Vistula] to underground cell number 13. This is where 'the most dangerous enemies of the Polish Republic' were held. None of us enjoyed the right to work in the prison laundry or on the potato-peeling squad. So once every couple of weeks when a warder called for volunteers to scrub the kitchen and lavatory floors, it was a huge attraction . . .

The regulations allowed a daily fifteen-minute walk round the prison courtyard. We had to walk in Indian file, in silence. We were allowed one book per month from the prison library. Every morning, we received half a litre of black coffee and a chunk of black bread; and a bowl of soup twice a day . . . Three times a year, on New Year's Day, May Day, and 22 July, we enjoyed a special feast of meat rissoles and cabbage or fish and salad.

My mother struggled to get permission for a visit, which would not be behind a grille. She came with my children, already aged seven and eight, and we met in a small room after a wait of several hours. I sat them on my knee in turn. They sang me songs and told me stories. When we were ordered to say 'goodbye', I lost sight of them as the warder tugged me away. My daughter Magdalena cried in the train all the way back to Warsaw.

Thanks to Mother's efforts, the children were placed in an orphanage run by the Sisters of St Elizabeth. She took them home to her one-room flat every weekend, where she constantly told them of my love for them and of the possibility of remission. Their father had been killed in the Rising and their mother was a convict!

After two years in Fordon, we were woken up in the middle of the night, and we were driven off in an open lorry to an unknown destination. God forbid, not to the

Soviet Union. In two hours, we arrived at an isolation centre. On arrival, the governor told us that we were there because of the 'solidarity of the enemies of People's Poland'. (Solidarity, in that era, was a pioneering concept.) . . . All visits and correspondence were stopped. We were issued with small pieces of toilet paper, to prevent us reading the news on the scraps of newspaper that were issued elsewhere . . .

As best I could, I defended myself against mental breakdown. I walked for hours back and forth across my 3m x 2.5m cell, and at night, when the warders weren't watching, I did gymnastic exercises. I composed a children's book in verse about a family of rabbits, and learned it by heart. I also set myself various intellectual problems, such as the basis of free will. In due course, I was mortified to find that I had come to the same conclusion as Engels.

Several prisoners committed suicide. So we were put three to a cell. One of my companions was mentally disturbed and talked to no one. The other was a religious fanatic, preoccupied with her rosary until three in the afternoon; and then she would start recounting her rich history of erotic adventures . . .

One day, we heard church bells ringing and sirens blaring. Two months later we learned that Stalin had died . . . That event was to lead to the release of almost all political prisoners like me . . .

I have always regarded those seven years in prison as my 'first university'. They taught me how to think . . . I also met some wonderful people of various nationalities and religions: Czechs, Ukrainians, Germans, Catholic nuns, Jews, Communists . . . I especially remember a Jewish woman, Anka G., a believing Communist, whose husband had taken his life. We learned that a person's capacity for nobility, heroism, and compassion has nothing to do with ethnicity, religion, or education . . .

I was finally rehabilitated by the Supreme Court in March 1955.[1]

Irena Bellert

---

to the Jews. In other words, at the height of the campaign against 'cosmopolitanism', the security services took care to eliminate a group of heroic and dedicated Catholics, who were publicly identified as active opponents of the Holocaust. The Communist regime systematically repressed, and besmirched, a body, whose humanitarian and anti-Nazi credentials were impeccable. In Communist eyes, it was intolerable to leave highly regarded Catholic Resistance heroes at liberty.

The best-known member of Zhegota, 'Teofil', had worked during the Rising as a journalist of the Bureau of Information and Propaganda. He now spent eight years under sentence of death. Released in 1954, he was one of the few to see the triumph of his lifetime's ideals. Highly decorated by the State of Israel, he was imprisoned for a second time in 1981–83 as a Solidarity activist. But he emerged to become one of the prominent personalities of the Third Republic – Ambassador to Vienna and Berlin, and in 1997–2001 Foreign Minister. An unstoppable optimist and raconteur, he was still going strong at the start of the new millennium.[69]

Jacob Berman's attitude to Zhegota is instructive. Although his own brother, Adolf, had belonged to the organization, he said that he had never heard of it until long afterwards, and he regarded it as an exception in Polish society as a whole, which in his view was 'very anti-Semitic'. This comment dating from 1982 drew an understandable reprimand from his Solidarity interviewer:

> [Mr Berman]! [Your] security services, where all or nearly all the directors were Jewish, arrested Poles because they had saved Jews during the [Nazi] occupation, and you say that Poles are anti-Semites. That's not nice.[70]

Collective slander was a Stalinist speciality.

In August 1949, a Polish link opened up to the grand international 'Field Case'. Earlier in the year, the American philanthropist and Communist sympathizer, Noel Field, had disappeared on landing at Warsaw airport. (Unknown to the outside world, he had been taken into custody by the ever diligent Light.) The ramifications of the affair gradually became apparent first when he was mentioned in Budapest in September as a source of information in the trial against the Party Secretary, Laszlo Rajk, and then in November when his friend and colleague, Alger Hiss, was found guilty of spying for the Soviet Union in New York. In an extraordinary web of suspicion and intrigue, Stalin's campaign against the alleged 'Zionist Conspiracy Centre' in the Communist movement had become intertwined with Senator Joe McCarthy's campaign against alleged Communist infiltrators in the USA. Field and his family were implicated in both ends of the plot.

Many brows started to furrow when Moscow ordered the immediate arrest of all party members who had ever been in contact with Noel Field. Berman's own secretary, Anna D., figured on the wanted list: and he did not hesitate to hand her over. It emerged that the lady had served in the Warsaw Rising in the ranks of the People's Army, and that after her time in a German POW camp she had made her way to Switzerland where Noel Field was running a Unitarian Centre for Refugees. In

Stalinist eyes, she was patently guilty as not charged. She spent five years behind bars, left prison in 1954, emigrated to Sweden in 1968, and died in Israel in 1974.

Forty years after the event, Berman claimed that he had no option but to arrest Anna D. He had received a directive, he said, from Stalin himself. After all, there were many fingers pointed in his direction as a possible 'Zionist conspirator'. 'I became the perfect candidate for a [Polish] Slansky,' he explained.[71] In fact, he stayed perfectly loyal and reliable to the last.

By way of a diversion, it is not without relevance to note what Noel Field had been doing at the time of the Warsaw Rising. He was formally employed by the American OSS; but together with Alger Hiss and others he was at Bretton Woods, working on the United Nations project. Indeed, it was Alger Hiss who drafted the UN Charter. Owing to the scepticism of the British, this group of UN planners, which included some of Roosevelt's closest advisers, worked in close liaison with a team of Soviet experts. When the critical phase of the Rising arrived in the summer of 1944, and Churchill was urging Roosevelt to lean on Stalin hard, it is not difficult to imagine what their advice would have been.

On 31 July 1951, yet another trial began in Warsaw. Ninety-three army officers were charged with various degrees of treachery and of collaboration. It developed into a long series of sub-trials which lasted for three years. The great majority of the defendants were former members of the pre-war officer corps. The chief defendant was Gen. Tabor. At the final count, three of the defendants died during interrogation: thirty-eight were condemned to death, and twenty were executed. It was a foul and bloody story that was carefully timed to open so that the first reports would make the headlines on the morning of the Rising's seventh anniversary. On 1 August 1951, before any charges had even been discussed, the Communist press was loading the defendants with epithets such as 'a pack of bandits', 'the filthy progeny of crime', and 'Pilsudski's dwarfs'.[72]

Tabor, who had been well viewed during the war by Allied leaders for his advocacy of close cooperation with the Soviets, had finally fallen foul of his erstwhile friends.[73] Needless to say, his Titoist opinions – if that's what they were – were anathema to Stalin, for whom Tito had become public enemy number one. On 13 August 1951, he was lucky to be handed nothing more than a life sentence. He served five years.

Several men in the 'Officers' Case' had close connections to the Warsaw Rising. One brigadier general, 'Boguslav', a graduate of the *École Supérieure de Guerre* in France, had signed the Capitulation on 2 October

1944. He, too, received a life sentence. An infantry officer, 'Radoslav', sometime commander of the Home Army's K-Div., was another sentenced to life, though soon released. The last man to be executed had fought among the victors of Monte Cassino.[74]

In some respects, the purge of the Polish People's Army after 1948 resembled Stalin's attack on his own (Soviet) Red Army after 1936. Very few officers who had served in the Home Army came through unscathed. Yet exceptions did occur. Gen. 'Krystynek' had left Warsaw in the entourage of Gen. Boor, and had returned in December 1945. He was untouched. Lt.Col. 'Iron' returned from London in 1947, but was left alone and was able to publish his memoirs.[75] Suspicions inevitably arose that some sort of price must have been paid.

As the 'Officers' Case' was drawing to a close, the last senior insurgent to stay at large was reaching the end of his own lonely struggle. In later years, the case of Gen. Nile was to become a cause célèbre. It was marked by extreme vindictiveness even by the standards of Stalinist justice. Its details provide eloquent testimony to the procedures of judicial murder. They are contained in the 123 pages of the file for case 'no. 417/50 versus Fieldorf, Emil August . . .'[76] They undoubtedly reflect the treatment which would have awaited Nile's superiors, such as Anders and Boor who had been condemned *in absentia*, but who had evaded the Communist net. [**BOOR**, p. 572]

Emil August Fieldorf (1895–1953) – pseudonym Nile, alias 'Valenty' – had successfully returned from the Soviet Gulag without detection. But he was caught because in applying for registration as a former military officer he had entrusted his true identity to his former regimental commander from 1939. He was not to know that this man, though employed by the Forestry Commission, had gone over to the Communists. He was bundled into a car on the street in Lodz, and driven post-haste to Warsaw. The order for his further detention was signed on 21 November 1950 by Lt.Col. Helena W. from the office of the Supreme Military Prosecutor.[77] It cited Article 86.2 of the Military Penal Code: 'Whoever attempts to change the political system of the Polish State by the use of force is liable to five years' imprisonment at least or to death.'[78] It contained the most disgraceful catalogue of pseudo-accusations that one could invent. No one would ever show that Nile had used force except against the Nazis.

Most of Nile's twenty-four intensive interrogations took place in Warsaw's Mokotov Jail. He never succumbed; and after the final interrogation by the Deputy Prosecutor-General, Benjamin W., he pleaded not

'BOOR'

One of General Boor's sons, who survived the Rising as a two-year-old child in a German-held section of Warsaw, recounts the family's fortunes

When asked why he hadn't forewarned his heavily pregnant wife, Irena [née Lemazan-Salins], to leave before the Rising, my father replied that there were countless other pregnant women in Warsaw and there was no way that he could abuse his position for his wife's benefit. My mother wrote in her unpublished memoirs: 'Neither of us even considered the possibility of my fleeing the capital when so many others had to stay. My husband came round early on 1 August, and I tried to get in enough condensed milk to last young Adam for six to seven days. The Rising was imminent. The Home Army had about six days' supplies in hand, which was the time they anticipated before Russian forces would arrive. My husband told me that he would greet the Russians as the host of his sovereign country. Both of us were under no illusions that he might land in a Soviet jail. Other members of the Resistance would stay underground.'

The Rising caught me and my mother living behind enemy lines on Marshal Foch Street in the Polytechnic district. (My mother, officially, was 'Janina Marynovska', and I had been registered as the son of a man who later turned out to be a bachelor!) Due to her condition, my mother was unable both to flee and to carry me. Miraculously, we survived the random executions of civilians, and finished up in September in the transit camp at Prushkov. Discharged, we headed for nearby friends. But shortly afterwards, my mother gave birth to my brother George in the most primitive conditions, alone in a derelict shack with no medical assistance. The child was born with Down's syndrome. He was extremely weak and ill, and due to the absence of medicines, my mother decided to travel to Cracow. He went on to live to the age of forty-nine, a valued and cherished member of the family.

Following the Rising, my father passed through several POW camps, including Colditz. He was appointed Commander-in-Chief of the Polish Armed Forces. He reached London in the spring of 1945 . . .

Meanwhile, the Soviet Army had occupied the whole country, and the NKVD were actively searching for my mother, who was hiding in a country village outside Cracow, drawing charcoal portraits in exchange for food. Against all advice, she decided to escape via Czechoslovakia, and made an audacious dash across the frontier, talking her way past NKVD checkpoints and using my own bawling as a diversion. The British Military Attaché in Pilsen then arranged for a volunteer pilot to fly out to a local field and to pick us up. A picture of us appeared in the London *Evening Standard* with the by-line 'British pilot flies the family of General [Boor] to England'. (In 1994, I was invited to meet that pilot, by then the seventy-year-old Johnny Jordan, over tea.)

In actual fact, we had not been able to cross the Channel. The British government had put an embargo on our entry to Britain. So we stayed in Brussels until Éamon de Valéra heard of our plight and the family was invited to Ireland. Only then did the British let us in! We were in London by Christmas 1945 and lived at first in Barons Court. The next summer we went on holiday to Banff in Scotland, where my father's former cavalry regiment [the 9th Uhlans] was stationed. We later moved to Wembley, and I attended school at St Benedict's in Ealing . . .

My father never talked about the Rising at home. It wasn't a topic of family conversation. But from my earliest days I never had any doubts about its validity or about its callous betrayal by the Soviets. I never had to be explicitly told. My father always accepted total responsibility for his decision to launch the Rising, and the tragic losses certainly weighed heavily on him. But it was something which he had considered unavoidable if Poland was to have had any chance of freedom. A dedicated patriot, soldier, and horseman, he had planned to retire and run the family estate when events overtook him. He had a strong sense of duty but little personal ambition. A thoroughly modest man, he possessed an excellent sense of humour and was interested in many sports. As far as I know, he only once rode a horse in England. He loved watching football and tennis. He was truly an officer and a gentleman. But to me he was just a father.[1]

Adam Komorowski

---

guilty to all charges. In his capacity as commander of the Home Army's K-Div. organization, he declared, 'he had never ordered his subordinates to liquidate or penetrate Soviet, People's Guard' or People's Army partisan units, as he had been busy just fighting the Germans and their collaborators.'[79]

Nile's trial *in camera* occupied eight hours at the Warsaw Provincial Court on 16 April 1952. The presiding judge, a woman, had been appointed by the security services. So, too, had the defence lawyer. Prosecutor W. demanded the death sentence under Article 1 of the decree of 31 August 1944 'concerning the punishment of Hitlerite–Fascist criminals.' The verdict was negative. The sentence was to be death by hanging. It stripped the convict of all public rights and of his entire property. A plea for mercy from the condemned man's wife was rejected. 'Convict Fieldorf does not deserve mercy.'[80]

The appeals procedure lasted from May 1952 to February 1953. The Supreme Court upheld the verdict. The party leader, Bierut, declined to recommend clemency; and the Council of State refused a pardon. According to the judges' opinion, 'the convict manifested an intensification of criminal will . . . there is no possibility of re-socialization.' Since by that time he was unable to stand, he listened to his fate lying on a stretcher.[81] He was executed by hanging at Mokotov Jail on 24 February 1953. The hangman used a length of common string. Since the bodies of convicts were buried in unmarked mass graves, the exact location of his burial remains unknown.

Some details of the case were no less disturbing than the bare fact that an innocent man had been killed by judicial murder. Everything points to an interpretation which holds that the prosecutors and their minions would not have been satisfied by liquidating a political opponent:

> It was not just a matter of taking a man's life. It was an act of desecration and defilement against a whole organization, a wilful attempt to break people's pride in belonging to it, and a desire to deprive the defendant of all personal dignity . . . In the case of Gen. Nile, one observes an identity parade of a long list of policemen, lawyers and prosecutors who were responsible, between them, for the murders of hundreds, if not thousands . . .[82]

Thirty years later, when Berman was interviewed about Nile, he feigned ignorance:

[INTERVIEWER]: Was that how Nile died?

BERMAN: I don't recall the case.

[INTERVIEWER]: Curious . . . None of you gentlemen seems to know the name, although the man was a national hero. He was the head of the Home Army's Directorate of Subversion K-Div. First the NKVD arrested him under a false name and sent him to Siberia and then the Polish security services arrested him when he got back.

BERMAN: If he belonged to the Home Army leadership, his case certainly can't have been dealt with on a low level. Still, it must have passed me by.[83]

In September 1953, six months after Stalin's death, the regime signalled a new stage in its programme of repressions by arresting Cardinal Stefan W., the Primate of Poland.[84] It was a step which even the Nazis had hesitated to take. Moreover, in the old Polish tradition, the Primate was taken to be the *interrex*, the supreme political authority, whenever the country had lost its legitimate ruler. So the Communists knew that they were risking popular fury. The Primate was incarcerated in a remote monastery in the south, and held incommunicado. The problem, of course, was that the Roman Catholic hierarchy took their orders from the Vatican. They formed part of an international organization which lay beyond Moscow's control. So if the orders could not be stopped, the people who received them had to be locked up.

The Cardinal's virtues were many. His reputation was built on the fact that he had been a humble Home Army chaplain during the Warsaw Rising. He was a shepherd who would never leave his flock. Unbeknown to him, however, the security services would never leave him. Long after his death, when the archives of the Security Ministry were opened, it was found that daily reports on the imprisoned Primate were filed by agent 'Little Bird', the codename of Sister Maria-Leonia G. This Franciscan nun had been positioned by her controllers to watch over the prisoner's every movement. On the tenth anniversary of the Rising, she filed her copy as usual:

> 31.7.[1954]. The evening was rather gloomy. We remembered the Rising. The Primate asked me to hum the 'Warsaw Melody' because he couldn't recall the words. Together with the Chaplain we then sang the 'March of [Mokotov]'. The Primate grew very sad, thinking again of the Rising. I, too, had many painful memories from that time.
>
> 1 August. In the morning, the Primate prayed for the fallen of the Rising. Perhaps he is in a black mood not merely because of the Rising, but because of his approaching birthday and the anniversary of his ordination . . .[85]

When the Primate was finally freed, Sister Maria-Leonia asked him to release her from her vows.

In retrospect, however, one can see that the Stalinists were forging the rod that would break their own backs. The head of anger was gathering in the ruling Party as well as in the nation as a whole. By a curious act of symmetry they had placed under house-arrest, but not eliminated, both the leading Polish Communist, Comrade Gomulka, and the most respected national leader, Cardinal Stefan W. Unwittingly they had prepared the ground for the grand solution of 1956, when Stalinism collapsed. Both the Comrade and the Cardinal re-emerged to forge the historic compromise that kept the People's Republic intact for the next thirty-four years.

CHAPTER VIII

ECHOES OF THE RISING, 1956–2000

1956 WAS A MAJOR WATERSHED for Eastern Europe. It was the year of Khrushchev's 'Secret Speech', which confirmed 'the Thaw'; and it was also the year of the Hungarian Rising, which was suppressed by Soviet tanks and which set strict limits on the relaxation of the Communist dictatorships. Poland escaped Hungary's fate by a whisker. The Party leadership, which had chosen Comrade 'Vyeslav' as their General Secretary without prior Soviet approval, mobilized the army in readiness to resist Soviet intervention; and Khrushchev, no doubt with the Warsaw Rising in mind, backed off. Comrade Gomulka, who was neither a liberal nor a democrat, nonetheless embarked on his 'Polish Road to Socialism' with a significant degree of popular support. By making concessions to the Church, the private farmers, and the cultural elite, he put an end to the nightmare of Stalinism, and gave the Communist regime a new breath of life that was not finally extinguished for more than thirty years.

The Constitution of the People's Republic had been passed by the Legislative Assembly on 22 July 1952. It was carefully timed to remind everyone of the Lublin Committee and of the Soviet takeover of 1944. It had little practical significance, since the state was subjected, according to Leninist principles of 'Democratic Centralism', to the overriding dictatorship of the Communist Party. Indeed, such were the political certainties of the Stalinist era, that the Constitution of 1952 completely omitted the two most important rules of the system, namely the unbreakable 'alliance' with the Soviet Union and the 'leading role' of the Party. When, on Brezhnev's insistence, amendments to the Constitution were introduced in 1975–76 to embody these rules in law, open dissent was expressed.

From 1956 onwards, however, the ideological, social, and economic capital of the regime was steadily declining. Of course, the decline did not follow a simple path; and thanks to the Soviet alliance and to the Party's grip on the instruments of coercion, it seemed for a long time that the regime could never be effectively challenged. Yet in retrospect, one can see very closely that the foundations of Communist power were inexorably eroding. Under the leadership of the Cardinal-Primate, and later of his understudy, the Archbishop of Cracow, who in 1978 was elected Pope, the authority of the Church rose as that of the discredited politicians fell. Despite the pressures of intense industrialization, the workers in whose interests the People's Republic was supposed to be organized grew ever more disaffected. In 1980–81 they founded the Solidarity Movement, which was temporarily suppressed by a military coup but which eventually supplanted the regime. Meanwhile, the balance of power within the intellectual and cultural elite tipped. Whereas in the 1950s no dissident intellectuals had been free to operate, a clear majority of educated people, whether openly or in secret, sympathized with the opposition by the 1980s. Soviet communism and its various clones and imitations formed one of the few major political systems in modern European history which died on its feet from natural, internal causes.

Throughout those decades, attitudes to the Warsaw Rising formed an accurate barometer for the declining health of People's Poland and the increasing vigour of the opposition. After all, the Rising had been the key event whereby the post-war Soviet-backed and Communist-run establishment had come to power. One can identify three main periods. In the late 1950s and 60s, though the criminal tendencies of the Rising's instigators continued to define the official scenario, it became acceptable to praise the heroism both of the common people and of the insurgents. In the 1970s and 80s, though it was still only permissible to publish critical accounts of the Rising, it was increasingly possible to describe 'the London camp' and its followers including the Home Army, and to engage in reasoned discussion. In the 1990s, as during the brief Solidarity interlude of 1980–81, all sides of the argument could be put with equal force; and many 'blank spots' in the existing factual information were filled. Each of the decennial anniversaries – 1964, 1974, 1984, and 1994 – acted as the spur for publications, conferences, reunions, and memorials.

The Roman Catholic Primate of Poland was one of the two central figures of the 1956 settlement. He possessed the popular authority which the ruling Party lacked; and by reaching a public understanding with Comrade Gomulka, he ensured that the People's Republic enjoyed a generation of relative stability. In essence, the settlement between Church and state adopted a strategy of mutual restraint. The Party would stop undermining the liberties of the Church so long as the Church did not call the legitimacy of the Party-State into question. The Party Secretary agreed to the deal because, as a Marxist, he believed that the hold of the Church on an industrializing and modernizing society was bound to wane. The

Primate agreed, confident in the belief that a Church free from political interference could actually strengthen its hold. He was proved right. For twenty-five years, he carefully nourished the religious and cultural life of the nation, teaching them that the battle of minds was more effective than battles on the streets. He quickly became the supreme moral authority in the country, attracting a degree of affection and admiration to which no party leader could ever aspire. So long as he lived, he wielded unparalleled influence. His was the archetypal positivist line – not to fight with sticks and stones, but to preserve and strengthen the essential spirit and sinews of the nation.

For the Primate's biographers, there is no small problem in reconciling this triumphant positivist strategy of his later years with the fact that in 1944 he had served as a Home Army chaplain (Father 'Stefan') tending to the spiritual needs of the Kampinos Group. Suffice it to say that the problem revolves around means and methods, not around goals. A man of profound faith like the Primate took the same uncompromising intellectual and moral stance towards communism that he had earlier taken against fascism. He was not going to compromise on fundamentals. On the other hand, he was not the militant sort of priest who packed a pistol under his soutane. He became involved with the Home Army more by chance than by design. As the parish priest of Laski, a village in a beautiful woodland setting on the northern perimeter of Warsaw, he had taken charge of a religious community which had developed a particularly open-minded and non-judgemental brand of Catholicism. But his parish happened to lie in a district where clashes between the Home Army and the Germans were a daily occurrence. His duty was neither to condemn nor to praise the actions of the insurgents, but to care for their spiritual needs. He undertook it without hesitation. Whether he approved of the armed struggle is open to question. But he could not have failed to witness its terrible consequences. What is certain is that after the war he decided that the overwhelming force of totalitarianism had to be contested by different means. He lived to see the Solidarity movement, and one can say without fear of contradiction that Solidarity's brand of non-violent opposition was close to his own convictions. Indeed, Solidarity, which owed much to memories of the Rising, but which was destined to humble communism without a shot being fired, was very much the product of his inspiring and unyielding leadership.

*

The first signs of 'the Thaw' were already visible in Poland before the crisis of October 1956 erupted. The policy of forcible collectivization had been abandoned in 1953–54. The much-feared Ministry of Public Security was dismantled in 1955 and replaced by a Ministry of the Interior that took the reorganized security services under its wing. Mokotov Jail was closed, and turned into the headquarters of Polish Radio. Comrade Gomulka, the leader of the 'national Communists', was already starting to influence the party line before Bierut's last journey to Moscow. Most importantly, the great majority of political prisoners were released. As often as not, they were formally exculpated of the false charges brought by Stalinist courts and rehabilitated with full civil rights.

'Rehabilitation', however, fell far short of restitution. It usually consisted of a piece of paper which stated that the judgement had been invalid, and that, in consequence, the sentence imposed was now terminated. There was nothing approaching an apology; compensation was rarely paid to the victims; and the guilty judges and procurators were not usually put on trial.

In some sensitive cases the process of judicial review lasted for years. In the case of Nile, the review began with a hearing on 28 February 1957, when the chief witness withdrew all his evidence. The Supreme Court then overruled both of Nile's sentences, and asked the Provincial Court to reconsider the case as a whole. On 4 July 1958, the prosecutor abandoned the case 'due to the absence of evidence of the defendant's guilt'.[1] This step was equivalent to instating a verdict of 'not proven'. At a further hearing in July 1960, Nile's widow, exceptionally, was granted the sum of 50,400 *zloties* by the Ministry of Justice for the 'improper judgement'. The money was used to erect a symbolic gravestone in Warsaw's military cemetery.

None of the officials who had caused Nile's death was severely punished. The judge continued to practise. The military prosecutor who laid the false charges, transferred to the reserve, continued to lecture thereafter at the Law Department of Warsaw University. In 1968, among people persecuted by the Communist regime, she emigrated to the United Kingdom, where she obtained British nationality.[2]

In the period after 1956, therefore, a great burden was partly lifted. Former Home Army people were still viewed with suspicion by the Communist authorities, and were obliged to exercise discretion about their past. But they were no longer actively persecuted and many were able to find a niche where they could lead a relatively normal existence for the first time in nearly twenty years.

Contrary to widespread impressions, the number of ex-insurgents who joined the Communist Establishment, especially after 1956, was not insignificant. A few, either through blackmail, opportunism or desperation may have joined during the Stalinist years. But the influx grew when the Stalinist nightmare passed and the People's Republic was thought to be safely in place for the foreseeable future. One such recruit was Casimir K., sometime soldier of the AK Vigry Battalion, and an ambitious post-war journalist. He found common cause with the Communists through his atheist views; and he earned the label of a 'janissary of socialism'. He never denied his Home Army connections, publishing a history of his battalion in 1971. After editing several newspapers he came into prominence in the 1970s as a Minister of State and director of the Office of Religious Denominations. This body was the Communists' watchdog on the Roman Catholic Church; and its director's function was to shadow, and if possible to diminish the influence of, the Primate. He was seriously worried in 1974 when the Archbishop of Cracow declared that 'Catholics do not want to be treated as second-class citizens'. He put on a brave face. 'Just as I am obliged to smile in my duties as a state minister,' he confessed, 'so will I as a Communist fight religion and the Church . . . If we cannot annihilate the Church, we should at least prevent it from doing damage.' But he did not fail, as ex-insurgent to ex-insurgent, to mark the Primate's seventy-fifth birthday with a gift of flowers. His position became untenable in October 1978 when one of his two key charges was elected Pope. According to a later report, the news was so unbelievable that he rang Moscow, not Rome, for confirmation. The reply was positive.[3]

Col. Radoslav made his peace with the Communists by a different route. Nile's deputy in K-Div., and a very prominent commander in the Rising, he escaped a Communist death cell by signing an agreement with his captors. He then made a career as chairman of a housing cooperative. But his real service to the regime lay in the field of veterans' affairs, where, in contrast to most of his comrades, he did not shun the so-called Association of Fighters for Freedom and Democracy (ZBoWiD) and rose to its top echelon. The Association was one of the Commu nists' vehicles for appropriating the memory of the Second World War to themselves; and it had nothing in common with Freedom and Democracy as once understood by the Home Army (or the rest of the world). His reward was a host of medals; and promotion to the rank of major general.[4]

History and its manipulation were always prime concerns of Communist Governments – after all, so-called 'historical materialism' was the cornerstone of their philosophy. Yet in the world of Marxist-Leninism, Marxist precepts invariably took second place to the iron rules of Leninism, which insisted that absolute priority be given to the interests of the ruling Party. In this regard, no amount of sophistry could conceal the events of 1944. It was not in the Party's interests that children should learn how the people of Warsaw had stayed loyal to the 'bourgeois Government' in London, nor how the great fraternal army of the Soviet Union had mysteriously ceased its advance. So despite the relaxations of 1956, many aspects about the Rising continued to be taboo. In nearly forty years of its researches the Communist-run Academy of Sciences (PAN) could never agree on the content of the volume covering the war years in its official *History of Poland*.[5] Party historians who were licensed to write about the war had a strange habit of running out of ink when they reached 1943.[6]

Nonetheless, the breathing space supplied by the 'Polish October' facilitated the publication of important studies suppressed in the preceding period. Both of the historical teams whose work had been wrecked by the Stalinist regime regrouped and managed to find their way into print.

The study of the Warsaw Rising by Pepi, which saw the light of day in 1957, carried the subtitle 'A survey of military operations' and was clearly seeking to avoid political controversy:

> I know that I shall not satisfy the advocates of the legend created by some *ad maioram gloriam suam*, also that I shall not convince people of ill will . . . [Yet] the shadows only serve to highlight the unparalleled dedication, spiritual values, and love of freedom of a generation which raised the national characteristics of the Poles onto the highest level.[7]

Such public praise of the Rising had not been previously heard. 'The extraordinary stamina of the defenders', Pepi concluded, was partly due to 'the in-born bravura of the Poles' and to their deep hatred of the Germans. 'But it was also bound up with an ungrounded belief in the miracle of victory.'[8] What he could not say was that the Home Army had not counted on a miracle, but on practical assistance from the Soviets.

The authors of school textbooks did not have an easy task. Faced with readers who possessed alternative sources of information at home, they must often have longed for the time not long gone when the Rising had been unmentionable. In retrospect, it is fascinating to see how the hard line imposed in the 1950s was successively softened and supplemented. In the 1960s, the censors were apt to present the People's Army not only as the chief heroes of the Rising but also as one of the chief victims. In the 1970s, the Home Army and its leaders became mentionable, but only as the unhealthy forces of reaction that had caused a terrible setback to the onward march of socialism. At least, they had ceased to be portrayed as traitors and Nazi collaborators. Still, descriptions of the Warsaw Rising published after 1956 continued to omit some of the most crucial details:

> On 1 August 1944, the population of Warsaw took to arms and threw themselves into yet another heroic but tragic struggle. The Germans hurriedly strengthened the line of the front along the Vistula, and halted the Red Army's offensive near Warsaw.
>
> The insurrectionary units fought with indescribable bravery . . . Our youth fought in the front ranks. People died under the bombs . . . and under the masonry of falling houses.
>
> The hopeless struggle lasted until October. Almost 200,000 persons perished. Warsaw's streets were transformed into cemeteries and heaps of rubble. Those who were left alive were ordered to leave the city immediately. Anyone whom the Hitlerites caught was carried off to the camps. The city was burned down.[9]

Few statements here were obviously untrue, but pupils would not have known who the 'insurrectionary units' were, whose orders they followed, or how long the Red Army's offensive was delayed. The most important piece of information was contained in the phrase which indicated that the battling youth of the Rising was 'ours'.

The military establishment eventually dropped its former vindictiveness towards people with insurgent connections. In 1972, for example, the Minister of National Defence funded an important change to the symbolic grave of Gen. Nile. An imposing gravestone was added, correctly stating the General's dates, his rank, and his commissions – including 'Chief of the K-Div., AK Supreme Command'. Two other pieces of information appeared:

HE DIED A TRAGIC DEATH
POSTHUMOUSLY REHABILITATED[10]

In those same decades, most of the serious historical study of the Rising was conducted abroad, mainly in Britain. The Historical Commission of the Government-in-Exile and the Underground Study Trust pressed forward with their labours, and in time, several scholarly syntheses were produced. Two rival trends emerged – the condemnatory and the laudatory. The former was best encapsulated in the work of Dr Yan C., the latter in that of Professor Janush Z.[11] Both authors had served as boy soldiers during the Rising, both had seen terrifying things, and both had established themselves as professional scholars. But each had reacted in opposite directions. The one felt betrayed by the ineptitude of the London Government and its subordinates. The other felt proud of his comrades' stand against the Nazis, and was duly dismayed by the conduct of the Allied Powers. In consequence, two diametrically opposed interpretations were produced from the same sources and by the same academic methods.[12] Dr C.'s work concentrated on the politics and the diplomacy, offering no coherent picture of the struggle, and picking out every conceivable fault in the leadership's decisions. It conveniently glossed over the key factor of Soviet policy on the grounds that insufficient documentation was available for scholarly scrutiny. It was duly translated, and published in People's Poland. Professor Z.'s work, in contrast, concentrated on the heroics and on the Home Army's lonely fight both with the Wehrmacht and, on the political front, with its Allies. It spent much space condemning the condemners. It was never published in People's Poland.

Dr C. concluded:

> Thus the insurrection and its aftermath helped rather than frustrated the Communist assumption of power in Poland. The defeat had, to a certain extent, been brought about by the political and military ineptitude of the pro-London leaders, particularly by their inability to come to terms with Stalin as Churchill had advised. Such a rapprochement would have been very costly to Poland, but in the second half of 1944, it was the only realistic course to adopt.[13]

This statement begs more questions than it answers.

Professor Z. concluded:

> If Warsaw had not fought, the unsympathetic would have said that Poles did not deserve their freedom, that they had assented to or abetted Nazi tyranny, and that they had been unwilling to fight for the common cause. The Poles fought, and the unsympathetic say that they fought alone because they refused to 'co-operate' with the Soviet Union. This is simply misinformation ... The tragedy of Poland was not only that her enemies destroyed Warsaw, but also that her friends did not fully understand what was taking place and why.

Two names stand out, however, for their refusal to bend either to undue defeatism or to excessive glorification. 'Kite' was a pre-war socialist who had headed the Home Army's Propaganda Section. His pithy, penetrating account of the Rising, regrettably not translated into English, has not been surpassed:

> The Warsaw Rising revealed the political and moral unity of the nation ... Warsaw became an armed camp in which the whole population fought and lived like a single family, sacrificing everything to the recovery of freedom. This great moral-political success is further proof of the dynamism, vitality, and maturity on which we will build together our better future.[14]

Dr Joseph G. (b. 1913) was a Home Army intelligence officer during the war, and a prolific historical author after it.[15] He was not present during the Warsaw Rising, having been denounced by an informer, and transported to Auschwitz. But his Irish wife, Eileen, had lived through the Rising, where she had worked as a nurse. They were reunited in London in 1945. Dr G.'s account of the Rising is not uncritical.[16] But he judged it a 'historical necessity'.[17]

Fictional literature proved to be the best vehicle for examining contemporary events. The regime, though no longer paranoid, was still insecure. The censors were omnipotent. And the boundary between the permissible and the impermissible was opaque. In any case, readers often preferred hints, winks, allegories, and allusions to cruel facts.

Of course, much of the literature produced during the Rising remained on the Index. There was no chance that readers in the People's Republic would be allowed to contemplate lines such as:

> They stand silent beyond the Vistula
> Those scum from beyond the Volga[18]

Or those addressed to Berling's Army:

> For Poland's the same as Freedom. No other Poland exists.[19]

Even after 1956, if the censors could stop it, no one was going to hear the words of 'The Scarlet Plague' – the disease 'that will save us all from the Black Death'.[20] The sheer quantity of works that were banned needs to be set alongside the mere trickle of books about the Warsaw Rising that somehow slipped the net.

Zbig. H. (1924–99) became the leading poet of post-war Poland. He occasionally claimed to have participated in the Warsaw Rising, though critics suggest otherwise. Nonetheless there can be no doubt that his verse of 1956 about 'The Fall of Troy' was not really about Troy:

> O Troy, O Troy!
> The archaeologist
> Runs ashes through his fingers
> And a fire greater than in the *Iliad*
> Spreads onto the seven-stringed lyre.
>
> Too few lyre strings.
> One needs a choir
> For such a sea of laments
> For such mountains of sobbing
> And the rain of stones.
>
> How might one extricate the human beings
> From those ruins?[21]

It was not clear at the end of the war whether the poet 'Christophe' was alive or dead. In fact, he had been buried in the ruins of the City Hall on 4 August, on the day he died. But his family did not know his fate; and numerous false sightings had been reported. It was only at the very end of 1946 that his grave was exhumed. By then, fragments of his poems were circulating, and critical notices were being posted. The collected works were finally published in 1961, and were soon accompanied by an authoritative study from the great Cracovian literary critic, Casimir W.[22] Christophe emerged by general consent as the authentic voice of the lost generation. Casimir W.'s assessment of his poetry resonated with admiration. He was equally certain of Christophe's prowess as a wordsmith and of his crucial role as a continuation of the romantic strand in national literature. In conclusion, he quoted one of his Cracovian colleagues: 'We belong to a nation whose fate is to shoot at the enemy with diamonds.'[23]

In the meantime, the legend of the poet who had died on the fourth day of the Rising grew into a major literary phenomenon. It did not develop simply because a brilliant writer was cut down in the flower of his youth, but because it was the apotheosis of a much older tradition in which revolutionary poets were supposed to die tragically, but had rarely managed to do so. Polish history was filled with failed insurrections and with insurrectionary poets who had called their compatriots to battle. But very few of those poets had lived up to expectations and perished in the accepted manner. The national bard, Adam M., for example, whose writings greatly influenced the Risings of 1830 and 1863, had fought in defence of the Roman Republic but never in his native land. But now, with a century's delay, Christophe could be Poland's Byron, or Poland's Petőfi. Many of his lines were eerily prophetic:

> How good you did not live to see the day
> When they will raise a monument to heroes like you
> And your murderers will place flowers on your tomb.[24]

For obvious reasons, there is always a limit to the amount of heroics which the reading public can take. Hence two works published around 1970 turned to the experiences of the civilian population during the Rising. Both explored the appalling consequences for people who were in no sense responsible for their suffering.

Maria D. was an established writer of social novels long before she was caught in Warsaw by the Occupation and the Rising. She was not an active insurgent, but she came to the defence of the Home Army in the post-war Conrad debate; and in the depths of the Stalinist nightmare, with no hope of early publication, she set to work on a fastidious description of the months spent in a single cellar. The result was a long chapter in her *Adventures of a Thinking Person* (1972), which finally saw the light of day eighteen years after completion and five years after her death:

Tell me, Joe . . . How will this hell end? And tell me, was it all a mistake?

No, it wasn't a mistake – he said firmly. *If somebody saw his mother drowning, and dived in to rescue her, even if he had no chance, and would probably drown himself, that wouldn't have been a mistake, would it?*

The defeated always have to pay, whispered Joanna. Then shaking herself she suddenly said – *We have lost, and yet I don't regret it . . . There were moments of such wonderful hope and excitement . . . And it is so good to have suffered so much, and to have survived. When it is finished, there'll be such a blessed sense of peace . . .*

Tom was silent, and slowly pressed the scrap of tobacco into the holder.

Only, we have to realize that this is rock bottom, that we can't fall any further.

Then, carefully striking a match split into two, he answered himself.

But this might not be rock bottom yet.[25]

In 1952, such a passage would have been unpublishable: and in 1972 it was still seriously subversive.

Miron B. (1922–83), though thirty years younger than Maria D., was another Varsovian resident who had taken virtually no part in the fighting. Throughout his career he was preoccupied with the inner life of 'the private person'. He was only interested in the outside world in so far as it impinged on his thoughts and emotions. As a result, his *Memoir of the Warsaw Rising* (1967) bore no resemblance whatsoever to what other people were writing. The language imitated the everyday speech of ordinary citizens, full of repetitions, clichés, poor grammar, and awkward formulations. The content appeared to be utterly banal, recording all the minute details and casual observations which others judged insignificant:

How long did we sit there? A long time, but not till the morning. At the half-light, it began to quieten down. Quick. It has stopped. We fled. A handful of tools. Whatever – pick it up. Quick. What else, I don't remember. Only that it was very quick. Cobblestones. That must be the sky. August. Something under my arm: a spade. Church St. A corner, next to a barricade . . . here . . . quiet – only a couple, him and her – insurgents, boy and girl – they're sitting at the side of the barricade. On duty. They're chatting. As if nothing else was happening, or was supposed to happen. Only it is warm. They're sitting. The barricade, the side of a piece of furniture. And a chat. I also remember that I was happy, that I was returning.

Morning – straightaway: sun, heat, smoke, aeroplanes, bombing, burning. I suddenly recall. If someone wants to imagine the three destructions of the Warsaw – in September 1939, in the Ghetto from 19 April to around 20 May, and in the Warsaw Rising – all of them took place in the same sunshine, the same heatwaves, the same burnings and bombings. The heat, the sun, and the blue sky, mingled with fires, smoke, crashes, and crumblings, hard to believe but they added something exotic, an extra tripling in the head.

Those were the days, when every hour, or every half-hour, something collapsed around us, nearer, further, higher, lower, but always crumbling. Every now and then, newcomers would enter our shelter. Still covered in plaster dust, with bundles, or without bundles, or with nothing or with children, with families, on their own. They walked in. They rushed in. All were accepted. . . .

Good morning! Can we. . . .

Yes, do come in. Of course. Where've you come from? There's room here. Please . . .[26]

Historical monuments, and the manipulation thereof, were a Communist speciality. Every town and village in the Soviet Bloc had its memorial to the Soviet Army. Portraits of the Communist pantheon – Marx, Engels, Lenin, and Stalin – were brought out on any pretext; and pictures of the current General Secretary of the ruling Party hung in all public places. At the same time, all inconvenient traces of the former times were scrupulously removed. Hence in People's Poland, long-dead figures such as Copernicus or Chopin were widely honoured in order to bolster the Party's patriotic credentials, but persons connected with either the pre-war *Sanacja* regime or the Government-in-Exile were routinely cast into oblivion. The main Censorship Office kept a register of names that could be praised, names that could be mentioned for the purposes of condemnation, and names that could not be mentioned even to be condemned.[27]

Thanks to its turbulent history, Poland has a highly developed funereal culture. Graveyards are constantly filled with flowers. Candles flicker beside the graves. On All Souls' Day, families congregate to pay their respects. Yet Stalinism had even invaded the cemeteries. The very first memorial to the Rising was raised in late 1956 in Warsaw's military cemetery to members of the Grey Ranks. Others gradually followed. Plaques and tablets began to appear in churches, not least in the rebuilt St John's Cathedral. The limits of official tolerance were strict. Henceforth, the memory of the Warsaw Rising was to be tolerated in silence on consecrated ground; but elsewhere, or in public, not at all.

Memorials relating to the Second World War therefore caused very complicated contortions. The Communists regarded 'the anti-fascist struggle' of 1939–45 as their principal raison d'être, yet they were unwilling to admit that the great mass of Polish anti-fascists were equally opposed to communism. So very little, apart from the Soviet Army, could be commemorated. The soldiers of 1939, who fought the Wehrmacht in defence of the pre-war Republic, were still not judged worthy of remembrance. The soldiers, sailors, and airmen who fought shoulder to shoulder with the British and Americans were treated as pariahs. And the men and women of the Home Army might as well have never existed. For more than forty years, the Communist regime consistently refused to erect a suitable monument to the Warsaw Rising. The only memorials permitted were raised either to abstractions, to obscure Communist activists, to unnamed civilian victims, or to the Heroes of the Ghetto.

The fact that the Ghetto Rising had been commemorated properly, whilst the Warsaw Rising was *not*, fostered deep confusion. The belated wave of interest in the Holocaust which arose from the 1960s on magnified the false impression that the one and only rising in wartime Warsaw had occurred in the Ghetto. For decades, foreign visitors went to see the fine monument to the Ghetto Fighters, designed by Rapaport and erected straight after the war. But they could not be shown the far more numerous sights connected with the events of 1944. Official guides were ordered to pass over the Warsaw Rising in silence, or if pressed, to bad-mouth its leaders as criminal 'anti-Communist' adventurers. There was no central point or symbolic object in Warsaw on which the memory of the Rising could focus. As a result, when the then German Chancellor, Willy Brandt, visited Warsaw in December 1970 to pay his nation's penance, there was still only one suitable monument before which he could kneel.

The largest single project for a major war monument in the 1960s and 70s was that of the 'Warsaw Nike' – a female personification of 'Victory'. Inspired by the Communist concept of the triumphant war against fascism, it was completely unrelated to the Capital's own wartime experiences.

Chancellor Brandt travelled to Warsaw to sign a German–Polish Treaty, a central building block in the Federal Republic's new *Ostpolitik*.

He arrived on the morning of 7 December 1970. He went first to the Tomb of the Unknown Soldier, writing in the visitor's book: 'In memory of the dead of the Second World War, and the victims of violence and betrayal, in the hope of an enduring peace and of solidarity between the nations of Europe.' He then moved on to the Ghetto Memorial, and, in a gesture as spontaneous as it was unforgettable, fell to his knees before the world's cameras. 'I did not plan it,' he said afterwards, 'and I'm not ashamed of it':

> My gesture was intelligible to those willing to understand it . . . The tears in the eyes of my delegation were a tribute to the dead. As one reporter put it – then he knelt, he who has no need to, on behalf of all who ought to kneel, but don't, because they dare not, or cannot, or cannot venture to do so. That was what it was: an attempt through the expression of fellow-feeling, to build a bridge to the history of our nation and its victims.[28]

Willy Brandt's *Warschauer Kniefall* provoked worldwide comment, both positive and negative. An opinion poll showed that 41 per cent of Germans judged the gesture 'appropriate', whilst 49 per cent though it 'exaggerated'.[29] The British Ambassador in Bonn noted: 'The picture of a Chancellor with an irreproachable record of opposition to the Nazis kneeling at the Jewish Ghetto Memorial was widely publicised and made a profound impression, though it was not universally endorsed.'[30]

While the world's press welcomed Brandt's act, the majority of foreign commentators did not notice a distressing omission. In the enthusiasm of the moment, it was sufficient for most observers to realize that a German leader had finally admitted his nation's guilt. Yet any serious examination of Chancellor Brandt's *Ostpolitik* would confirm that his main aim in Warsaw had been to promote the cause of Polish–German reconciliation. To that end, it was desirable that he paid his respects to all the victims of all Germany's wartime crimes. During his stay in Warsaw, one might have expected him to salute both of the city's two great acts of resistance. But he signally failed to do so. No one breathed a word about the Warsaw Rising. The inscriptions on the Tomb of the Unknown Soldier did not include a single line about the Home Army or about 1944. The ex-insurgent veterans were not represented. They had been killed in their thousands by the Nazis in far greater numbers than the Ghetto Fighters. They had fought and died for their capital. They had been persecuted, tortured, and judicially murdered by the Stalinists. And now, in the moment of reconciliation, they were officially sidelined.

In the fresh political environment after 1956, the paths of the former insurgents began to diverge. A few, who were well hidden under false identities, continued to deny their past. Some were again able to emigrate. Others followed apolitical careers. A few chose to throw in their lot with the reformed regime.

The ex-insurgents who made their peace with the regime found various ways of doing so. Casimir Mo., 'Badger', for example, the man who had served time with Jürgen Stroop, joined the Democratic Movement (SD), a Communist client party, which enjoyed a small margin of autonomy.[31] Most of the military officers with AK connections, like Gen. Tabor, now returned to their commissions and stayed there until retirement.

Many of the most scrupulous ex-insurgents, however, sought careers and occupations which involved the minimum of official approval. Ladislav B., 'Teofil' (b. 1922), for example, started work in 1957 in the Catholic weekly *Tygodnik Powszechny*, which, like him, had been put out of circulation in the preceding period.[32] In 1963, he was awarded the title of 'Righteous Among Nations' by the Yad Vashem Institute in Jerusalem, which thereby recognized his service with the Zhegota organization. He was one of the first of thousands of Poles who were similarly recognized and who would form the largest national contingent to receive the honour. In 1972, he was appointed General Secretary of the Polish section of PEN Club International, and in 1973 Lecturer in Modern History at the Catholic University of Lublin. In the history department he joined his comrade from 1944, Professor George Kl. (b.19), 'Peterkin' of the Bashta Battalion, who was well on the way to becoming a prominent medievalist.[33]

'Paul' (1890–1970) was a Home Army veteran, but not a Warsaw insurgent. He was a Polish writer from Lithuania, had worked with 'Cat' M. under the German occupation and had fought with 'Lupashka''s army. After the war, under the pen-name of 'Jasienica', he wrote a number of colourful and highly readable history books, which made him the best-loved historian in the country. In March 1968, Comrade Gomulka named him as a hostile conspirator. He knew that he was being watched. 'My home is not my castle,' he remarked, shortly before he died, 'indeed, I am not even master of the drawers in my desk.' The tale took a surprising twist when his security file was opened in the 1990s. The file was crammed with hundreds of informers' reports. By far the most assiduous and longest-serving informer was a woman who had been a long-standing confidante and who, in 1969, had become his wife. Still more shocking, she was an AK veteran who had fought in the Warsaw Rising. Her marriage had taken place with the Security Office's approval. Her missives were usually penned in the toilet. Her last report on him was written during his funeral.[34]

In which regard, the extent of official controls over people's lives, even during the 'Thaw', may be gauged from the fact that the State Censorship Office insisted on editing every single printed word, including funeral notices. (The same was true for birth announcements, wedding invitations, party invitations, and business cards.) In practice, therefore, all funeral notices, which were customarily posted outside the churches, were required to adhere to official norms. With luck, the dead person might be described as 'soldier', or 'member of the Resistance movement', or, at some risk, as 'a patriot of 1944'. But in the 60s and 70s, 'insurgent' and 'AK' and the AK's anchor symbol stayed firmly beyond the pale.

Alexander 'Borodich' G., yet another professional historian, had a relatively smooth ride.[35] During the Rising, he had directed the Home Army's Bureau of Information and Propaganda, but having worked during the war in the secret campaign to preserve samples of the fabric of destroyed monuments, he was indispensable to post-war reconstruction. A medievalist of special distinction, and a scholar with wide international contacts, he was able to promote an independent academic career with unusual success.

Of course, ex-insurgents with more practical professions – engineers, medics, scientists, or musicians – were less likely to fall foul of the authorities on ideological grounds. In the first post-war decade, as 'enemies of the people' they were largely barred from studying, and many were thrown back into menial jobs. But they were often able to catch up after 1956, and in due course to shine in their chosen field. The composer Vitold L. (b. 1913), for instance, who in 1944 had been an underground entertainer, was prevented before 1956 from publicizing the dense atonal counterpoint for which his style would become famous. Indeed, his First Symphony (1948) was performed only once before being banned. But, with his *Travermusik* (1958), he returned to experimentation. His *Jeux Vénitiens* (1961) adopted 'controlled aleotoricism' which gave the players a certain latitude in producing new sounds of their own. From then on, he was well established as one of Europe's top talents.[36] His success ran somewhat ahead of André Pan. (1914–91), with whom he had played in Warsaw's wartime cafes, but who succeeded in 1954 in emigrating to Britain.[37]

Adam B., in contrast, sometime member of the Watch 49 Battalion, studied medicine, and rose in due course to be a neurosurgeon. At one of the first occasions in the 1960s when veterans from abroad were first allowed to attend the unofficial celebrations in Warsaw, he met Yan B., a fellow ex-insurgent who had trained in the USA and who now worked like him as a neurosurgeon. From then on, to the end of the century and beyond, the two Home Army men who had turned to saving lives in the surgical theatre because their own lives had been spared could regularly be seen together at all the Rising's anniversaries.[38]

Many ex-insurgents prospered abroad in a great many fields. It may well be that the trauma of their youth created an inner strength and a determination to live the rest of their life to the full. At all events, once they had found their feet and their métier, they often rose to the highest reaches of their calling, which, by rights, should have been theirs in Warsaw.

In Britain, where the hierarchy of Polish exiles was firmly occupied by the older generation, the Varsovians rarely figured prominently in communal organizations. But they made their mark in a great variety of walks of life. L.Cpl. 'Jagiello' reappears as a senior don and political philosopher at Oxford University. His colleague from Bashta, Cpl. 'Julius', in contrast, joined the throng in the BBC, whilst devoting much time and passion to his vocation as a poet. Courier 'Hanka', who in September 1944 had been spared when an SS man chose not to pull the trigger as she emerged from the sewers, lived to survive three husbands, to be a grandmother and great-grandmother, and to edit a short history of the battalion.[39]

In the USA, Wenceslas duly rose to become a successful lawyer and a professor of law at several US universities, including Indiana, Notre Dame, and Detroit. In 1944, he had been a special duties officer of the AK's 'Harnas' Battalion and editor of the underground *Warsaw National News*. Both his sisters served in the Warsaw Rising.[40]

Zbysek. M., 'Ed', who lost a leg in the Rising, did not allow his handicap to obstruct a career as a director of a Californian engineering firm. Born in Zakopane, he became a world champion in legless skiing. On 31 July 1944, he had been sitting on a rooftop in Praga, making notes on the redeployment of the Hermann Göring Panzer Division. He made his escape through the sewers on crutches, the stump of his leg protected by oilskins.[41]

The Varsovians are present in Canada in force. A retired Professor of Semantics at McGill, who lost her first husband on the first day of the Rising, spent nine years after the war in solitary confinement in a Communist jail, having earlier been held in the Paviak by the Gestapo. Her son, born during the Rising, is now a businessman in New York. Her daughter is a senior stewardess for Delta Airlines based in Florida. Her neighbour in Rawdon, Quebec was another insurgent from the Parasol Group.[42]

In Australia, there is no shortage of people with links to the Rising. A distinguished retired professor of sociology at ANU Canberra is one of the 'fathers of multicultural Australia'. A graduate of LSE, in August 1944, as a second lieutenant in the Parachute Brigade, he was the chief briefing officer for RAF crews flying out of Brindisi for Warsaw.[43] Cpl. 'White', who was wounded fighting in the 'Thunder' Battalion, emigrated to Australia in 1949, having obtained a technical diploma, and became the owner of a refrigeration firm at Lakemba, NSW. Maria G. (born 1917), known during the Rising as 'Maria Kovalska', had been an AK courier.[44] She lost three brothers and a sister. After the Soviet capture of Warsaw in early 1945, she was captured by the Soviet Army, and subsequently spending 'only forty-four months' in the Arctic camps. A teacher by training, she emigrated to Australia in 1958 to join her brother. She married and settled in Melbourne. 'We used to talk about returning home,' she wrote, 'but not to Communist Poland.'[45]

Wherever one meets these Varsovian victims – in Ealing, in Manhattan, in Toronto, or in Sydney – one easily receives the impression of dynamic, intelligent people who have integrated well into their host communities. Though they have been able to visit Poland without serious hindrance since the 1960s, they have put down new roots. They have beautiful homes. They have families who are considerably less Polish than they are. They are happy to know that their beloved Warsaw, like them, has been given a second lease of life, that the Communists who took away their birthright, have finally dropped down 'the manhole of history'.

Yet, on one point, Varsovians around the world do have a grievance. Time and again, if one asks, one hears the same sad responses: that their neighbours know nothing about the Warsaw Rising, that their children have nothing exciting to read about it, that there is no disinterested person to tell the next generation what 1944 was all about. 'Our neighbours here have virtually no knowledge of the Warsaw Rising,' writes a lady living near Manchester. 'The cause lies in the shortage of literature on the subject in English, and too little mention of it in the media.'[46] Or again, 'Young Australians, like young Poles, don't take much interest in history. I've met many Australians who make no distinction between the Ghetto Rising and the Warsaw Rising. One has to explain very calmly that the former was in 1943 and the latter in 1944.'[47]

By the end of the 1970s, the Communist regime was entering a deepening crisis. Its politicians were discredited; its economic strategy had failed; its standing among the working class was in free-fall. A series of strikes over food prices and living conditions was helping to swell an ever-more insistent chorus about the ruling party's lack of legitimacy. By general consent, the visit of Pope John Paul II in June 1979 acted as a catalyst, which turned discontent into a much more focused body of opposition. The Polish Pope was the godfather of Solidarity.

The Pope's visit did not lack allusions, and even open references, to the Warsaw Rising. In the course of his long homily on Victory Square in Warsaw on 2 June 1979, he returned to the topic repeatedly:

> If it be right that the history of a nation has to be understood through each and every person in that nation, then simultaneously there is no way of understanding individuals other than through their national community. . . . There is no way of understanding this nation, whose past has been both so wonderful and so fearfully difficult, without Christ. There is no way of understanding this city of Warsaw, Poland's capital, which in 1944 undertook an unequal battle against the invader, abandoned by its powerful allies, if one fails to remember that Christ the Redeemer, with his cross on the [Cracow Faubourg], lay under those same ruins . . .[48]

In that same homily, he remembered the 'hundreds of thousands who perished in the Warsaw Ghetto', 'the people who lived with us and amongst us.'

Addressing the state authorities in the Belvedere Palace, he returned to the wartime theme:

> For us, the word 'Homeland' possesses a conceptual and emotional meaning that, it would appear, is unknown to other nations . . . who

> have never experienced such losses, such dangers and such injustices. The war ended thirty-five years ago . . . However, we cannot forget the experience of war and occupation. We cannot forget the Polish men and women, the victims, who paid with their lives. We cannot forget the heroism of the Polish soldier who fought on all the world's fronts 'For our freedom and yours'.
>
> We relate with respect and gratitude to all those who extended us their assistance. And we think with bitterness of all those occasions when we were let down.[49]

No one in the audience needed reminding who had tried to help them, and who had let them down.

Finally, speaking in St John's Cathedral, the Pope turned to the very Varsovian theme of resurrection:

> Warsaw's Cathedral of St John the Baptist was almost totally destroyed during the Rising. The building in which we now find ourselves at present is completely new. It is a fitting symbol of the new Polish and Catholic life of which it is the heart. It is a sign of the Christ who once said, 'Destroy this temple, and in three days, I will raise it up.'[50]

The wave of pride and self-confidence which followed had incalculable effects. Poland would never be the same again.

During the sixteen months between August 1980 and December 1981, when the Solidarity movement functioned openly, Poland enjoyed the first period of free speech in the whole Soviet bloc. *Glasnost* came into being without the name of *glasnost*. Though the official censorship still controlled a broad range of publications and activities, no action was taken against people who gave a voice in public to 'inappropriate opinions'. History was near the top of the list of subjects in which free debate flourished. The most popular subjects included the Polish–Soviet War of 1919–20, the Katyn Massacres, the Government-in-Exile, and the Warsaw Rising.

The supporters of Solidarity had many close links with the Warsaw Rising. Though most of them were far too young to remember much before 1956, and though they resolutely chose the path of non-violence, they saw themselves as the true heirs of the Home Army. They rejected the AK's methods of fighting the enemy with guns and grenades. But they regarded the struggle as one and the same. It was a struggle against totalitarian rule, against an inhuman ideology, and against foreign domination.

What is more, the ranks of Solidarity contained a formidable company of dissident historians. The younger leaders belonged to the generation who knew that the Rising was one of the great 'blank spots' of their parents' lives. It was absolutely natural, therefore, that works related to the Rising should have poured out of Solidarity's unofficial presses. One such product, written under a pseudonym, was typical of the period. It had three main objectives – to defend the Rising's leaders against the more absurd changes of treason and criminal intent, to raise the issue of Soviet inaction, and to revive the moral standing of the insurgents. It indulged in some fundamental assertions:

> Both legally and practically, the Home Army was an integral part of the armed forces of the state, part of the Polish Army subordinated to the legitimate authorities of the Republic . . . [But it] was more than a military organization; it was the core of the national Resistance movement with a well-defined ideological profile . . .
>
> The tragic end to the Rising is well known. The leaders had not reckoned at all with the possibility that the Soviet Army might not enter the capital in the course of the battle. Yet, on the personal intervention of Stalin, the Red Army halted before restricting its activities in the Warsaw sector, passively observing the destruction of the Polish Capital and the ruin of the Polish Underground State . . .
>
> Some time ago, [a commentator] said that the Warsaw Rising was a political mistake, a military nonsense, and a psychological necessity. Today, I am inclined to paraphrase the comment as follows: The Warsaw Rising was inadequately prepared and faultily directed; it was a political gamble of the highest order. Psychologically, however, it could hardly have been avoided.[51]

Equally important for the historical record were a number of extensive interviews and investigations, conceived or conducted in 1980–81, which drew the veil from issues relevant to the Rising and which helped to illuminate many of the subsequent distortions. One of these was a long conversation with Mark E., a sometime Bundist and leader of the Ghetto Uprising, whose views exposed many of the misconceptions about wartime Polish–Jewish relations.[52] A second was a series of interviews with a selection of surviving Stalinists, like Berman, whose unreconstructed opinions spoke with unmatched authenticity about the Communist takeover and the murderous post-war repressions.[53] Forty years on, Berman made no apologies about the Communists' totally undemocratic practices; he was still maintaining that the suppression of the Warsaw Rising had been a beneficial milestone in the onward march of progress.

In the brief Solidarity interlude, the ex-insurgents gained a definite success in the realm of historical memorials. Still frustrated in their hopes for an official monument to the Rising, they nonetheless persuaded the authorities to permit the erection of a statue to the 'Boy Soldier' or the 'Little Insurgent'. Funded by public subscriptions organized by the Scouting Association, the diminutive statue was placed beside the medieval walls of the Old City and quickly became a popular landmark. It depicts a tiny lad with curly locks, swamped by an outsize helmet, but proudly gripping his Sten gun. It was inspired by the true story of the thirteen-year-old Cpl. 'Antek', who was killed nearby in combat on 8 August 1944.

Another success in the painful field of remembering was gained in the mid-1980s through the construction of the so-called 'Observer' monument on the eastern bank of the Vistula facing Cherniakov. Dedicated to Berling's First Army, which suffered thousands of casualties in the attempt to cross the river in September 1944, it portrays a giant soldier trying to reach out to the insurgents on the western bank. Since, like Berling, his feet are cased in concrete the soldier can do no more than 'observe' the scene of the Rising. Gen. Jaruzelski, who in 1944 had been a young officer of the line in the First Army, had been among 'the observers'. But he and his fellow *Berlingowcy* were denied their monument for forty years, just as the Home Army were. He only succeeded when, after 1981, he became Poland's unchallenged dictator.

The day after martial law was declared in Poland on 13 December 1981, a survey of Polish history was published in Oxford. *God's Playground* had a winning title, and the good fortune to reach the market at the point when the demand for knowledge about Poland peaked. Moreover, it was the first prominent study to challenge the Communist version of modern Polish history in a systematic and non-nationalist way. A review in *The New York Times* called it '*the* book about Poland'. Another, totally dishonest, which appeared in Warsaw, praised it fulsomely only to conclude that 'the author's talent inexplicably deserted him when he reached the twentieth century'. The treatment of the Warsaw Rising in *God's Playground* did not exploit any new sources and did not express any strong opinions. Whilst feeling uneasy about the reigning criticisms of the Rising, the author at least felt confident enough to add some words of admiration.[54]

Even so, the months of free speech in 1980–81 had broken the official taboos about the Rising, and the Communist authorities were never able to return to their previous line, even when Solidarity was suppressed and martial law introduced. The years of Gen. Jaruzelski's military–party dictatorship, therefore, were marked by two features relevant to the evolving Rising story. On the one hand, the uncontrollable *samizdat* operation of the Solidarity Underground made up the backlog on previously untranslated foreign publications. On the other, official historians and textbook writers were forced to make ever-greater concessions. Schoolchildren were allowed to learn more than ever before. A textbook from 1982, for example, gave an astonishingly frank account of the composition of the insurgents:

> The units of the Warsaw District of the Home Army formed the core of the heroic insurgent ranks. Units of the People's Army also subordinated themselves to the Rising's leadership – and one of them from the League of Youthful Struggle ... covered itself in glory during the defence of the Old Town. Two battalions from the 'Grey Ranks', Zoshka and Parasol, were particularly famed for their heroism ...[55]

Inclusivity was on the march.

Yet there were limits beyond which the Communist establishment was still unwilling to go. In August 1984, they refused to patronize the fortieth anniversary of the Rising; though they did not interfere with the huge crowds that gathered spontaneously at the City's military cemetery. And they again resisted demands for a proper Rising monument.

However, once Jaruzelski had taken the unprecedented step of ordering the prosecution of security officers who had murdered a pro-Solidarity Catholic priest,[56] it was increasingly difficult for the military–party leadership to ignore public opinion on other issues. With Gorbachev's Moscow moving itself into the era of *Glasnost*, determined citizens increasingly took unlicensed initiatives. An independent committee formed to design and construct a monument to the Rising, and to fund it by public subscription, refused to give up. This time, instead of arresting the organizers, the authorities tried to infiltrate the Committee and thereby to influence its decisions. But they failed. In 1989, a colossal, impressive monument was finally unveiled on the edge of Warsaw's Old Town, next to the manhole cover through which the district's defenders had once escaped to safety. It had taken forty-five long years to achieve. There could have been no better signal to announce that the Communist regime was on its last legs and was losing the will to defend the fictions on which it had been built.

The monument to the Warsaw Rising was not to everyone's taste. It was grandiose, sensationalist, almost exhibitionist. One of its two groups of extra-life-size figures is frozen in combat. The other, which represents a wounded man, a nurse, and a chaplain heading for the sewers, is more suitably reflective. Designed in tandem by a sculptor and an architect, it dominates a corner of the Old Town, long since rebuilt. And yet, in a very real sense, its gigantism is appropriate. For the Rising hung over the capital for forty years like a giant unseen ghost. Henceforth, and quite properly, the ghostly giants of 1944 are anything but invisible.

In the meantime, public events in honour of the Warsaw Rising could only be held abroad. The fortieth anniversary, which passed in near silence in official Warsaw, was marked in Washington by a meeting at the White House addressed by President Reagan:

> This month, we commemorate a desperate battle of the Second World War, an heroic attempt by free Poles to liberate their country from the heel of Nazi occupation, and to protect it from post-war foreign domination . . .
>
> Today we honor three individuals, heroes of the Polish Home Army, never given their due after the Allied victory. It's my great honor to present the Legion of Merit to the families or representatives of these men: to Stefan 'Arrow', who was executed by the Gestapo; to the son of Gen. 'Boor', the leader of the Warsaw Uprising, who later died in near poverty in exile in London; and finally to Gen. 'Bear Cub', who was lured into a trap and died under suspicious circumstances in Moscow . . . These brave men and the courageous individuals who fought under their command represent the best of the human spirit . . .
>
> If there's a lesson to be learned from the history books, it is that Poland may be beaten down but it's never defeated . . .[57]

Some would say that this speech shows 'the great Communicator' at his best. Political opponents would say that Ronald Reagan never missed an opportunity to bang an 'anti-Soviet' drum. But such politicking misses the point. The Home Army was neither 'right-wing' nor 'left-wing'. It contained representatives from all points on the democratic spectrum; it was both 'anti-Nazi' and 'anti-Soviet', as all true democrats were bound to be. As leader of the Free World, President Reagan had a simple duty to recognize wartime allies who cherished the values the USA so readily proclaims. The only thing wrong with the speech is that it was forty years overdue.

The collapse of the People's Republic, which was completed by the democratic presidential election in December 1990, initiated freedoms previously unknown to the majority of citizens. Among many other changes, it led to the abolition of the censorship. For the surviving ex-insurgents, it had momentous consequences. For the very first time since the Rising, they were able to talk, to publish, to organize, and to commemorate exactly as they pleased.

As in 1955–56, the regime had begun to crack before it collapsed. One sign of its weakness could be observed in the tack of the censorship towards much greater leniency. Another sign was seen in the willingness of the judicial system to re-open the unsatisfactory reviews of Stalinist trials that had been undertaken in the late 1950s and early 60s. At the end of one such review, dated 7 March 1989, the Procurator-General of the People's Republic entered a decision changing the formula which had been used in 1958 to justify the abandonment of the case against Gen. Nile. The new formula stated unequivocally that the said person 'was not guilty of the acts of which he was accused'.[58] It had far-reaching consequences. A memorial tablet to him was unveiled on 1 September 1989 at the spot where he had been arrested in Lodz in 1950. Another tablet was unveiled on 11 November 1989 by the Lord Mayor of Cracow on the house where Nile had been born. Full recognition of Poland's war heroes was no longer confined to the churches and cemeteries.

A major change came with the emergence of unrestricted media. Prior to 1990, the state authorities had given up long ago on trying to control private conversations. But they had still kept a tight rein on radio, television, and the press. After 1990, most controls were cast aside, and for a time the Rising became one of the many passionate topics of popular debate. Any number of interviews, articles, and investigative programmes were produced in which, at last, the ex-insurgents could have their say. A variety of opinions were expressed. The Home Army voices did not have it all their own way. They had to contend with entrenched opinions; and indeed, on several key issues, they did not present a united front. But bit by bit, the facts about 1944 surfaced; and the public at large found itself in a position to take an informed view.

The rush of publications about the Rising in the 1990s covered many categories. There were numerous memoirs by ex-insurgents who had now entered retirement age, detailed logs of the battle trail of particular units, and excellent studies of barricade design or insurgent security services. Simultaneously, a number of authors and editors moved into topics that had been out of bounds in People's Poland. German policy in 1944, for example, was illuminated by collections of translated military documents and by serious document-based studies. Soviet policy, too, was opened up, though with more mediocre results. Most importantly, perhaps, initiatives were taken to collate existing information and to present it to the public in accessible forms. A day-by-day chronicle of the Rising, for example, which was first prepared as a series of radio programmes enjoyed wide acclaim. The trend was expanded with great energy by a series of historical compendia, chronicles, anthologies, biographical dictionaries, and encyclopedias. The process could not have been trouble free. Different researchers belonging to different traditions were using different sources. Great offence was caused, for instance, when the *Great Encyclopaedia of the Warsaw Rising* listed the Home Army's Crag-Crusher Regiment and Oaza Battalion as units of the Polish People's Army.[59]

At long last, however, Polish schoolchildren were completely free to learn about the deeds of their grandfathers without official interference. But freedom brought its own problems. For half a century, the textbooks had suffered from sterile conformity, ideological interpretations, and factual selectivity. They now suffered from a profusion of diverse emphases. Teachers who had been trained in an authoritative system that provided all the answers suffered from a lack of authoritative sources. Everyone was obliged to learn or relearn. Generally speaking, though, the nostrums of the former Communist regime collapsed before the tidal wave of information. And a new generation of open-minded authors replaced the closed state pedagogical industry of previous times. A sceptical approach to history was encouraged; and criticisms emerged not only of the Soviet Union but also of the Western Powers.[60]

Historical scholars in Western countries continued to disgorge enormous quantities of work on the Second World War, but they showed little interest in reviewing the Warsaw Rising. A much-praised American synthesis of the war contained an extensive passage on the Rising, expounding a curious mixture of outdated and risky new judgements:

> The Polish Government-in-exile was itself frequently divided internally, but practically none of its members was prepared to agree to the territorial demands of the Soviet Union. The other Soviet demand . . . was for a major change in the personnel of the Polish Cabinet . . . The issues were complicated in 1944 by two further factors. This was an election year in the United States, and President Roosevelt was hesitant to take steps which would alienate the Polish American voters . . .[61] The other and more important element was the functioning of the Polish underground army . . . The advancing Soviet units utilized the assistance of the AK . . . until an area was firmly under Red Army control and then arrested and either shot or deported them.
>
> These issues all came to a head in late July 1944 as the Red Army approached Warsaw . . . even as [Premier Mick] flew to Moscow to confer with Stalin. Expecting to overrun the Polish capital quickly, Soviet radio on July 29 called on the public in the city to rise against the Germans. The British Government had made it clear to the Poles that they could [not] carry out extensive air operations . . . On July 31, the Polish commander in the city ordered an uprising for the next day.
>
> General [Boor] [had], decided that it was better to take a chance than to stand aside, and it is clear that the bulk of his associates agreed. What is not so clear is why this reversal from previous AK strategy was made with very little preparation. When the rising took place as ordered on August 1, the insurgents were unable to seize many key locations, and the Germans rallied their forces. No one has explained why the Polish underground learned nothing from the uprising in the Warsaw ghetto the year before; for those who have studied the 1944 uprising, as for the civilians in the rest of Warsaw at the time, that event might as well have taken place on another planet . . .
>
> For weeks, the Soviet Union refused either to send aid itself or to facilitate the sending of aid by the British and American air forces. The latter did send some supplies by air drops from Britain and Italy, but these operations were . . . more effective for morale than supply purposes . . .

> In early October the remaining AK forces surrendered, and the Germans levelled to the ground most of what was left standing of Warsaw.
>
> Now that the regimes of Poland and the former Soviet Union have publicly admitted Soviet responsibility for the Katyn massacre, the line on the events of 1944 may also change . . .[62]

On either side of the Fiftieth Anniversary, various academic symposia were organized. The time had come for conflicting interpretations to joust and to be subjected to cross-examination. The exercise was a healthy one. For too long, the followers of the rival condemnatory and justificatory camps had sulked in their separate tents, and had not been required to confront their critics. Finally, in August 1996, a pioneering Polish–German symposium on the Rising was held in the Masurian lakeland. The participants included staff and students from Polish and German universities, an array of international speakers, and a group of eye-witnesses who had been on one or other side of the barricades in 1944. A Russian speaker from the Military Academy in Moscow had been a Soviet intelligence officer in August 1944. The badly needed internationalization of the subject had begun in earnest.[63]

Some of the more practical obstacles to removing institutional equality, however, proved harder to overcome. An Act of Nullity, in 1991, removed all the politically based legislation of 1944–56 from the statute book. And in 1992, the Ex-Combatants Act gave equal rights to all veterans. But these measures proved insufficient. In the veterans' case, for example, 'ex-combatant' was not satisfactorily defined. No less than eighteen registered associations now catered to the ex-insurgents' interests. Yet the larger and older ex-combatants' organizations, whilst obliged to accept Home Army personnel, were unwilling to offload some of their more unsavoury categories of membership. Under Communist management, all branches of the military in People's Poland, including military prosecutors and former members of the organs of repression, had enjoyed an honourable place; and no opposition had been offered to the fiction that Communist Party officials were ipso facto 'fighters for peace' and hence eligible for ex-combatants' benefits. Under their chosen strategy of 'drawing a line' against recriminations over the past, the democratic Governments of the 1990s failed to address many a running sore; and the problems continued to rankle.

Particular difficulties arose with regard to honours and medals.

Although the Communists' Order of Grunwald had been terminated in 1992, some circles in post-Communist Poland continued to regard it as the equivalent of the much older Order *Virtuti Militari* founded by the last king of Poland in 1792. Home Army veterans who had been awarded the VM were less than happy to find themselves in the same honourable category as former recipients of the Grunwald Cross who included, among others, Bierut, Berling, Bulganin, Rokossovsky, and L. Brezhnev.[64]

Anticipating the forthcoming Fiftieth Anniversary of the Rising, several documentary films were produced, and greatly benefited from the discussions and revelations of the early 1990s. A production from the state television service, presented several witnesses never seen before in Poland. One was a former German officer, who wept in front of the camera unashamedly. A second was the sole survivor of a British aircrew who had crashed in Praga. A third was none other than Ivan Kolos, alive and well in Moscow.[65]

Another film from the same era presented a biography of Gen. Boor. It did not emphasize the Rising. Instead it concentrated on sequences in his life which best illustrated his personality. It showed him in the old Habsburg army. It showed the happiest decade of his life when he was commander of a cavalry regiment in the idyllic setting of the eastern Borders, dreaming of retirement to the garden of his beautiful old manor house. It showed him with his equestrian team at the Berlin Olympics. And it showed him with his family at their modest suburban house in London. All in all, it was a sympathetic portrait of an attractive man. It was a revelation for Polish viewers who had only heard of Boor as a 'criminal', an 'incompetent', and an 'émigré adventurer with blood on his hands'.[66]

The Fiftieth Anniversary of the Rising was celebrated on 1 August 1994. It was patronized by President Lech Wałęsa, and was supported by all branches of the newly liberated, democratic state, not least by the army. Invitations were sent to the presidents of Poland's immediate neighbours, and to representatives of members of the wartime coalition. It was a great occasion for pomp, parades, speeches, and memories. But it did not pass off painlessly. The President of the Russian Federation did not attend; and the President of the German Federal Republic committed a most embarrassing gaffe. He graciously agreed to attend, but he did so in a letter which revealed that his advisers had imagined the occasion to be the fiftieth anniversary of the Uprising in the Ghetto. 'Fifty years ago', President Wałęsa declared:

> the insurgents of Warsaw took to arms . . . Freedom came out against slavery. The flame of the Rising remained in people's hearts and souls. It was passed on by the baton of the generations . . . The spirit [of the Rising] proved indestructible and immortal. Soldiers of the Rising. You did not fight in vain.[67]

No one had voiced such a ringing affirmation of the Rising in half a century.

President Herzog struck a matching tone of homage and remorse:

> The First of August 1944 is for ever the unblemished symbol of the Polish people's will to fight for freedom and human dignity . . . It became the embodiment of Fighting Poland which never submitted to humiliation, to lawlessness and to the threat of extermination . . .
>
> Today, I bow my head before the fighters of the Warsaw Rising, as before all the victims of war. And I beg forgiveness for that which was perpetrated by Germans against each and every one of you.[68]

In a separate ceremony four days later, a memorial tablet was unveiled to the liberation of the Goose Farm Camp by the Zoshka Battalion on 5 August 1944. After explaining that the Goose Farm had been a death camp, not just a concentration camp, the former commander of Zoshka's Panzer Platoon, Capt. 'Vatsek' took the stand. Born of a Polish family in St Petersburg in 1915, Vatsek at twenty-nine had been older than many of his insurgent comrades. Now, at nearly eighty, he was a resident of Geneva, a retired executive of the United Nations and a veteran of countless Third World development projects:

> On 27 July, the Germans decided to evacuate the Goose Farm Camp to Dachau. More than 400 inmates, incapable of marching, were shot . . . A column of about 4,000 Jews was marched off, but disappeared without trace.
>
> And now the Zoshka Battalion was standing in front of this camp. They remembered the Scouting Statute, which says that a scout is a friend to every other human being and a brother to every other scout. We all wanted to attack immediately . . . And, since we had captured a couple of tanks, the situation was rather better than in the previous days. So four of us went back to Radoslav to ask for

> permission. Radoslav was a cautious man and shared the view that the fortified positions should not be attacked frontally. But he agreed on condition that the attacking force be small in number and be composed entirely of volunteers . . .
>
> We carried it off by surprise. Our tank was a great success, because the Germans [in the camp] had no anti-tank weapons. After the main gateway was destroyed Felek's platoon moved in . . .
>
> But, ladies and gentlemen, I wish to talk about something else, about the meaning of this ceremony. Because it is all about that scouting principle, about people being friends to others . . . I live in the wider world. I've been to Bosnia; I've seen the cruelties of the Tutsi and Hutu in Ruanda; and everyone asks me where this bestiality comes from. So I say that every man and woman is born with kernels of good and evil. If we wish to nourish the kernel of good, it is a long and hard road. But it leads to interest in others, to friendship, to trust and in the end, by Christ's teaching, to love for one's neighbour . . .
>
> Let us remember that anti-Semitism is a sickness of half-intelligent people who are underdeveloped spiritually. It is the same with anti-Polonism on the Jewish side. We must struggle on all sides that people be brothers to other people. Such is the meaning of this tablet, and of this ceremony.[69]

President Herzog, of course, had not been alone in confusing the Warsaw Rising with the Ghetto. Much of the Western media made the same mistake. So, too, did the advisers of the British Prime Minister. The *Guardian*, NBC News, and Reuters all told the world a false story. The *Euronews* Channel reportedly announced the fiftieth anniversary of a rising in the Ghetto that had lasted for sixty-three days and had ended with the deaths of 200,000 Jews. At a later date, when Queen Elizabeth II visited Warsaw, her advisers requested a trip connected with the Warsaw Rising only to cancel it on realizing that they had something else in mind.

Perhaps one should not be too harsh, therefore, on those who persist in conveying the same misinformation. The conflation of the Warsaw Rising with the Uprising in the Ghetto had become an established piece of contemporary mythology. In 2001, a US television channel screened a four-hour miniseries called *Uprising*, which was completely devoted to perpetuating the myth.[70] In 2002, Roman Polanski's otherwise excellent and award-winning film *The Pianist* so telescoped the events of the two risings that almost all reviewers assumed the story to be exclusively about the Ghetto and the Ghetto's aftermath.[71]

A major task was also incomplete in persuading Poland's neighbours that the story of the Warsaw Rising contained something valuable for them. By the end of the century, the Germans had largely forgotten such opinions about the Rising that the older generation might have had. But, judging by a long article in the respected Moscow journal *Nash Sovryemennik*, Russian opinions were still firmly stuck in their ancient mind-set. As part of a tirade entitled 'The Polish Nobility and Us', its chief editor launched into a denunciation of the Poles and their alleged imperialism going back to the occupation of the Kremlin in 1612:

> The anti-Russian spirit of the *Szlachta* ['nobility'] was revived by the Risings, which were forced on Polish society 'from the top'. The Warsaw Rising was its last echo. [In 1944], the curdled residue of the Polish nobility, having deserted to distant England, tried to return to power in Warsaw over the dead bodies of Russian soldiers. Fortunately, Stalin deciphered their intentions and blocked them.[72]

This opinion dates not from 1952 or 1652, but from 2002. One could only hope that it was not typical. The awareness of Stalin's crimes in Russia was much lower than the awareness of Hitler's crimes in Germany. Indeed, a German memorial to the Warsaw Rising was already in preparation. A model of the project, created by Fee Fleck, was unveiled in November 1999 in Mainz, in the foyer of the *Landtag* of Rheinland-Pfalz.[73]

Nonetheless, throughout the shifting evaluations of the Rising over half a century and more, one man's opinions did not change. In 2000, the former Teofil – sometime inmate of Auschwitz, member of Zhegota, and soldier of the AK – was foreign minister of his country: and he was still expressing the same views that he had expressed all along: the Rising was 'unavoidable'; 'We had no choice', and 'I'd do the same again':

> I see the Warsaw Rising in the historical perspective as just one stage on the long, hard road which the Poles had followed since the eighteenth century. That road had led them from Kościuszko's Rising and the [Napoleonic] Legions . . . to the defence of the Vistula in 1920. I see it as one of the many occasions when the Poles said 'No' to successive occupiers, partitioners and usurpers who sought to limit or to abolish our nation's sovereign existence.[74]

Or again

> Today, Polish and foreign historians are still divided over the wisdom of launching the Warsaw Uprising . . . One should bear in mind, however, that the decision to fight was the last sovereign decision [which] the Polish authorities made . . . and that soon afterwards, the Poles were denied the right to decide about their own future for the next 45 years.[75]

By the turn of the millennium, the great majority of surviving ex-insurgents were aged between seventy and eighty. The urge to see the Rising properly commemorated in their lifetime, therefore, was strong. The fiftieth anniversary had provided a crucial stimulus, but it was no less important to make further provision for permanent exhibitions and for memorials to local events and to particular units. Several separate monuments were raised in Mokotov, for example, to the memory of the Bashta Battalion. No less significant than the presence of such landmarks were the precise, genuinely informative tablets that accompanied them:

> TO THE INSURGENTS OF [MOKOTOV] / SOLDIERS OF THE HOME ARMY / FROM THE BASHTA REGIMENT / AND OF OTHER UNITS / FROM THE FIFTH DISTRICT / AND TO THE TENTH DIVISION OF [MATTHEW RATAJ] / WHO FOUGHT IN THE DAYS / FROM 1 AUGUST TO 27 SEPTEMBER 1944.[76]

Even ten years earlier, such an inscription had been unthinkable.

By now, former taboo themes had lost their spell; and it was possible to think of memorials to the victims of communism to match those to the victims of fascism. The largest of these, depicting the dreaded cattle wagons on a mangled railway track, was raised in 1995 to the vast tides of innocent people deported to Siberia. It was located to the north of the Old Town not far from another monument to the former *Umschlagsplatz*, whence other trains took other human cargos to other destinations. But for many ex-insurgents, a much less demonstrative assembly on a bleak suburban site was specially moving. It consisted of a tall, simple cross, four or five granite boulders strewn by the wayside, and a twisted remnant of prison bars. It is the Monument to the Victims of the Stalinist Terror, and it stands on the place to which were brought the unidentified bodies of executed political prisoners:

Traveller!
Lower your head; hold your step awhile.
Every grain of this earth is soaked with martyrs' blood.
This is [Sluzheviets], this is our Thermopylae.
Here lie those who chose to fight to the very end.
No funeral way conducted us to this spot.
No one received a wreath or a salvo of honour:
Just a quick shot in the neck in [Mokotov] Jail
And a pony cart to carry us to this forsaken ground.
We marched with [Wolf] . . . with Her name on our lips,
To conquer or to die, to the walls of the Old Town
To Narvik, to Tobruk and to Monte Cassino,
Only to end our soldiers' journey in this sand.[77]

Half a century's backlog could not be made good in a day. Every company from 1944 demanded its tablet. Every Underground workshop deserved its marker. Every ill-starred plate from the 1940s and 1950s would preferably be replaced. As always, the womenfolk were the least demanding. But finally, on the fifty-eighth anniversary of the Rising, in 2002, they received their memorial like everyone else. The statue to the 'Girl Couriers' of the AK, was unveiled in a small town near Warsaw. It was a fitting tribute to all those thousands of 'Evas', 'Halinas', 'Sophies', 'Maryshas', and 'Magdas' without whom the Rising could not even have been started.

After the political fall of Wałęsa, and a number of years when Polish politics was dominated by the ex-Communists, the Government returned to more open support for the Rising and its memories. In 2000, ceremonies were held in Warsaw under the patronage of the Prime Minister, the last president of the former Government-in-Exile, and the ex-insurgent Foreign Minister, 'Teofil'. On 31 July, a meeting was held at the Gloria Victis Monument in the Military Cemetery; and at L-hour on 1 August a Mass was celebrated before the Rising Monument in the presence of the Papal Nuncio. The homily was delivered by the Cardinal-Archbishop of Vrotslav:

> Today, the anniversary of the Warsaw Rising, is historically beautiful: and not only beautiful but very important. For when L-hour struck, Varsovians rushed to armed conflict, most properly, in the cause of national freedom.[78]

The only thing missing was a permanent museum to the Warsaw Rising in Warsaw.

There remains the question of the 'lost generation'. Little doubt surrounds the contention that in normal circumstances the class of youngsters decimated by the Warsaw Rising would have emerged as the core of the post-war elite. They were the best educated, the best motivated, and the most dedicated element in the population of the country's capital. No peaceful ending to the war could possibly have held them back. As it happened, their birthright was taken over by a counter-class of opportunists, time-servers, and political sectarians who owed their first allegiance to a foreign power and who maintained their monopoly for nearly half a century. So the query arises whether, when communism collapsed, the 'lost generation' might not have recovered the reins of power. The answer, alas, must be in the negative. For too many lives had been lost; too many personalities had been broken; too many years had been squandered. The Third Republic, which emerged in 1990, was not a simple reversion to the Second Republic of 1939. It could only be run by a diverse range of people who, all in their different ways, were the products of the intervening half-century. Like many of the other crimes of Hitler and Stalin, the effects of the Warsaw Rising were largely irreversible. The damaged and discriminated could not be suitably compensated. The elderly could not be restored to their youth. The dead could not be resurrected. The hope was for one thing alone: that the Rising be properly remembered.

The Class of '44 in Poland was exceptional in many respects. Its members were the sons and daughters of patriotic families who had reaped the benefits of their country's independence only a quarter of a century before the Rising. They were kids who had something very valuable to lose, something larger than themselves, something for which they did not hesitate to fight. They were rightly convinced that their fledgeling republic, for all its faults, was infinitely preferable to the totalitarian regimes in Germany and Russia that threatened them from either side. Like the British generation of Rupert Brooke, Wilfred Owen, and Edith Cavell, who were cut down in 1914–18, they were exceptionally motivated, exceptionally dedicated, exceptionally unselfish. Their country has not seen their like before or since.

Nearly sixty years had passed since Warsaw rose and fell. The great majority of the survivors were nearing the natural terms of their lives.

The sixtieth anniversary in August 2004 would be the last major occasion when they would be able to pay their respects to their fallen comrades. It was high time that the rest of the world, which sets such rhetorical store on Freedom, should also pay its respects to a matchless generation of men and women, whose devotion to the cause of Freedom had few equals. Old political wrangles should be forgotten. For everyone who values the free world of today owes the Varsovians of 1944 a deep debt of gratitude. They set a worthy example of the old-fashioned values of patriotism, altruism, steadfastness, self-sacrifice, and duty. Like the Spartans of Leonidas at Thermopylae, magnificent in defeat, and like the Ghetto Fighters of 1943, they merit a similar, admiring epitaph:

> Go, passer-by, and tell the world
> That we perished in the cause,
> Faithful to our orders.

Interim Report

By the turn of the twenty-first century, the Warsaw Rising was finally passing into history. The Nazi Reich, which had suppressed it, was long since dead. The Allied Coalition, which had failed to render effective support, had been superseded by new organizations and by fresh political combinations. The Soviet Union, which had stood idly by, had recently died on its feet. The totalitarian ideologies of fascism and communism, against which the insurgents had staked their all, had totally lost their credibility. The soldiers of 1944 had largely passed on. The survivors of the Rising, who in 1944 had been little more than children, were now in the autumn of their lives.

Nonetheless the Warsaw Rising still needs to be considered seriously in any overall assessment of the Second World War in Europe. Britons and Americans both share the tendency to praise the war as an unconditional success, as a wonderful enterprise which ended with the liberation of the world from Evil. They forget that some of their partners in that enterprise did not necessarily enjoy the same sense of a good job well done. In the eastern half of Europe, one foul tyranny was driven out by another; and Liberation was postponed for nearly fifty years. By the yardstick of Freedom and Democracy as proclaimed by the Western powers, this outcome must be judged an abject failure. It tarnishes the overall balance sheet of apparent success. It shows that victory was somewhat limited, that the Western powers were not all-powerful, that evil was not banished. Indeed, Poland's misfortune was not exceptional. It is a sobering thought to realize that in 1944–45 exactly the same number of European countries were subjugated by communism as were reclaimed for democracy.

As viewed from Warsaw and elsewhere, the Second World War can be seen to have been a three-sided struggle, in which the centrepiece was provided by the duel of two totalitarian monsters, fascism and communism, and in which the Western democracies frequently featured as a third party of only moderate importance. Whether one likes it or not, the Soviet Union made the largest military contribution to the defeat of Nazi

Germany. But it was not interested in the least in the ideals of Freedom, Justice, Self-determination, and Democracy that inspired the West. As a result, the Western powers could not fairly claim to have been the all-conquering liberators of their own legends. In reality, they were repeatedly obliged to pander to Stalin's ambitions in order to keep the Coalition intact. But that is not the whole story. For in the process of cosying up to Stalin, many Westerners assumed a strange state of self-deception, a form of near-mesmerization, where principles could be forgotten and loyal friends could be deserted. The smouldering ruins of Warsaw illustrated the consequences.

The Warsaw Rising also played a prominent role in the origins of the Cold War. When Westerners looked back in the 1950s and 60s and asked themselves when relations with the Soviet Union had started to go wrong, they would invariably point to 1944. And when they analysed the events in which Stalin had shown evident malice and Westerners could have employed greater wisdom and resolve, they put Warsaw high on their list. The Rising did not cause the Cold War by itself. But it was a major step in that direction.[1]

The Warsaw Rising has gained a permanent place in military history. It is the archetypal model of urban guerrilla warfare. It shows how the determination of the warriors is the most vital factor in combat, how skill and bravery can hold out against the heaviest weapons, how men and women devoted to their cause can put professional armies to shame.

Equally, the Warsaw Rising stands as a warning against coalitions of convenience. It demonstrated that great powers may have democracy on the tip of their tongues but not always at the top of their priorities. Anyone who joins such a coalition should not expect to be treated as an equal, or to see their interests fully defended. Coalitions are rarely organized for the common benefit of all participants.

Finally, the Warsaw Rising carries a deathless moral message. There are some things in life that are dearer than life itself. Like the heroes of the Ghetto Rising, who had fought the same enemy in the same doomed city only one year earlier, the most devoted insurgents of 1944 faced death willingly – not gladly, but by choice. They could not regret the prospect of death, therefore, but only the circumstances that made it necessary. They would have preferred to win, but would not have been defeated by defeat. They would only have asked that their cause and their sacrifices be not forgotten.

So much is certain. As for the rest, since several parts of the picture remain hidden, historians can only write an interim report.

Gut reactions to the Warsaw Rising are still divided. Stalin described the Rising as 'an escapade' or 'a prank' that was run by 'a gang of criminals', and this quickly became the conventional view within the Soviet Bloc. It contained no hint of compassion, let alone of admiration. So one might not have expected such an opinion to win much currency in the outside world fifty or sixty years later. Yet one can be surprised. Of three senior Oxford dons of Polish descent opining on the subject in 2002, two did not hesitate to characterize the Rising as 'criminal'. One, who had actually served in the Rising as a youngster, was particularly bitter: 'If I had my way,' he said, 'I would have had them lined up against a wall and shot.'[2] He may have been speaking metaphorically.

Other critics give a more pragmatic tone to their judgements. They often quote an elementary principle taken from military manuals: 'If an operation is impossible at the outset, it should not even be attempted.' A number of high-ranking officers, including the then Minister of Defence, had shared this opinion in 1944. According to the Minister, the Rising was an ill-begotten attempt 'at waging war without having political and military authority in the same hands. War is simply not conducted in that way . . . It could never have worked in our terrible conditions.'[3]

There are historians a-plenty to agree. One of the prominent specialists on this subject adds his own voice to the chorus of disapproval. 'The Warsaw Rising was our day of blood and glory,' he writes, 'but it was not capable of becoming our day of victory.' In other words, the Rising was not merely a failure. It was a reckless undertaking, that never had a chance of success. 'Through the overrating of the available forces and the neglect of the requirements of the international situation,' the same historian adds, the Rising was 'a great day of warning.'[4] He goes on to compare the dreadful tragedy of 1944, when the call to arms failed, with the marvellous success of 1989–90 when the Communist regime was overthrown without a shot being fired. People of this persuasion are apt to assume that the case is closed. Not surprisingly, they attract a fair amount of opprobrium, especially from ex-combatants. If they happen to be ex-combatants themselves, they are likely to be accused unceremoniously of 'fouling their own nest'. Feelings are still raw.

Certainly, as almost all historians would agree, grave mistakes were made. The list of miscalculations committed by the instigators of the Rising was a long one. The disunited leaders of the exiled Government in London, for example, gave their subordinates in Warsaw carte blanche over the final order, thereby losing control of developments. The military and political leaders in Warsaw, who launched the final order, undoubtedly erred in some aspects of the timing. The choice of 5 p.m. as 'L-Hour' caused much confusion, and reduced the number of objectives which could be gained in the first surprise attacks. Thanks to the earlier policy of removing weapons from Warsaw, they sent the Home Army into battle amidst a dramatic shortage of weapons. Coordination with the Western Powers was weak, and with the Soviet Union virtually non-existent. On the political front, the Home Army indulged in a serious gamble that didn't pay off. They aimed to take hold of the capital, to protect the civilian population from a possible act of German barbarism, and to take charge of the city prior to the Soviet Army's arrival. Instead, they did not take definitive control: the Germans did not leave; up to 200,000 people lost their lives and the Soviet Army never arrived.

The odd thing is, however, that Polish critics train their accusations almost exclusively on Polish faults. All too often the debate has been reduced to an unseemly barrage of recriminations between rival Polish factions. All too often, it has been forgotten that the insurgents of 1944 were not in the same position as their predecessors of 1794, 1830–31, or 1863, who fought a lone battle against the national enemy. The Home Army fighters were part of an international Allied coalition that was committed to fighting the enemy in unison; and it is the workings of the coalition that need to be examined most closely.

In the circumstances, therefore, it is essential to formulate a number of more precise lines of enquiry, and hence to establish a more equitable division of responsibility. Three questions in particular present themselves. One, given the information available on 31 July, is whether the risk taken by the Rising's authors was reasonable; the second is whether the early mistakes were critical to the Rising's eventual failure; and the third question would be why the various members of the Allied Coalition failed to participate effectively.

On the first point, it is all too easy to blame the Rising's authors for things which they could not possibly have known for certain in advance. In retrospect, for example, it became evident that two key decisions had been separately taken on 28 July without the knowledge of other affected parties. On 28 July, the Soviet *Stavka* ordered Rokossovsky to occupy the whole line of the Vistula by 2 August at the latest. This would seem to indicate that the AK Command were perfectly correct in launching the Rising exactly one day before the Soviet Army's expected arrival. Yet also on 28 July, unbeknown either to the Soviets or to the Poles, the command of the German Army Group Centre decided to commit an unusually large part of its strongest reserves to the Vistula sector. This was the reason why the plans both of Rokossovsky and of the Home Army went awry. It was something which Clausewitz would have called 'the fog of war' and which could not have been easily predicted. What is more it did not cause the Rising to collapse. So it can't be invoked as proof of the Home Army's incompetence or foolhardiness.

Similarly, on the diplomatic front, it was unfortunate for the Home Army that the Rising was launched before the Premier had discussed the matter with Stalin. It would have been much more satisfactory if the attempt to reach a Polish–Soviet agreement had taken place earlier. Yet one cannot pretend that this in itself was the cause of the ensuing impasse. Neither Gen. Boor nor Premier Mick could have foreseen that the diplomatic problems – for which they were not responsible – would have turned into such an insuperable obstacle. After all, they firmly believed that they had the full support of the Western allies, and that Western support would prevent Stalin from cutting up rough. They were perfectly aware that they were taking a risk. But given what Churchill and Roosevelt had assured them, they had good grounds to feel that they were not taking a wild gamble.

For obvious reasons, the massive death-toll among civilians is a specially painful issue. Critics often hold the Rising's leaders personally responsible. However, it is all too easy to be wise after the event. The Rising's leaders were not indifferent to the fate of civilians. But they were also alive to the dangers of doing nothing either if the Germans evacuated the city or turned it into a front-line fortress. The London Blitz would not have occurred if Churchill had not insisted on fighting Germany. But Churchill is rarely blamed for the Blitz.

With regard to the various mistakes and misjudgements which the Home Army Command undoubtedly made, it is essential to identify the precise consequences. And in reality, though serious, the consequences, were not catastrophic. The premature launch, for instance, did not cause the collapse of the Rising, which continued for ten or twenty times longer than originally expected. Thanks to the policy of 'One bullet, one German', the ammunition shortage never led to a halt in the firing. Most importantly, the sum total of Home Army misjudgements did not rule out the key junction between the insurgents and Soviet forces. The junction, though much delayed, did take place. The fact that it was subsequently allowed to wither was not the insurgents' fault.

Everything points to the contention, therefore, that the workings of the Allied Coalition were decisive to the catastrophe. In which case, historians should stop grubbing around in the minutiae of Polish affairs, and should try to examine the broader picture. The Warsaw Rising occupied just one square on a much vaster chessboard. The roots of the tragedy will never be uncovered until the conduct of the major players is examined with the same rigour that has heretofore been reserved for the minor actors. Close attention must be given to the interrelation of the Warsaw Rising with the divergent priorities within the Grand Alliance as a whole.

For a start, historians must also take a critical look at the convention whereby the 'Big Three' arrogated all key discussions to themselves. The convention was just as alive in the 1940s as it had been at the Congress of Vienna or the Congress of Berlin; and it had its advantages. Yet it also had its obligations. One may assume, for example, that if the Big Three were to make all the strategic decisions, they were nonetheless obliged to keep their allies fully informed. Critics of the Rising come out with phrases such as 'disregard for the requirements of the international situation'. But they rarely enquire into what was meant by 'the requirements'. In Communist culture, the prime requirement was deference to the Soviet Union, and hence the unquestioning acceptance by all Moscow's clients of all Moscow's judgements. Democratic culture, in contrast, requires a much higher degree of trust, a much higher level of shared information, and much closer attention to joint consultation and coordination. It may well be that the Varsovians fell foul not only of a clash between these two political cultures within the Grand Alliance, but also of malfunctions within the Western part of the Alliance.

The absence of effective military and political coordination was manifest on all sides throughout the duration of the Rising. The Home Army never found the means to coordinate its moves with the Soviet Army. The exiled Government in London did not coordinate well with the British and Americans. The British and Americans did not manage to coordinate their dealings with Moscow. Indeed, Churchill and Roosevelt did not always coordinate well with each other. And the Soviets usually did not see fit to coordinate their actions with anyone. There is no reason whatsoever why the Poles should take the sole rap for these failings.

Many historians have taken the line that the political underpinning of the Rising had not been properly prepared. 'Without immediate assistance coming from the Western Allies and the Soviet Union,' wrote Professor Karski, 'the uprising never had any chance of success. That assistance had not been secured before orders for the rising were given.'[5] It is a damning accusation, which, on the face of it, looks unassailable. For, as is absolutely undeniable, no cast-iron promise of assistance had been obtained beforehand.

Yet surely, such statements, though correct, do not tell the whole story. One could equally say, with equal documentary proof, that the Allied Powers had been properly informed about a probable Rising in Poland and that they had done nothing either to forbid it or to facilitate it. Indeed, when the Western Chiefs of Staff were briefed in June 1944, they gave a very strong impression of approving the Polish Premier's intentions which they knew to include both a Rising and a plan for coordination with Moscow. For its part, the Soviet Union gave specific orders to its state-controlled media to encourage the Rising to take place. It deliberately led all Varsovians to believe that the Soviet Government would view a Rising favourably. So the failure to secure detailed promises of assistance in advance was not the critical issue. Such promises were desirable, and might well have been secured if the Western Allies had approached the Soviet Union more energetically and in better time. But their absence did not mean that no assistance could ever have been rendered. War is full of surprises. Cockups, confusion, and misunderstandings are commonplace, even in the most distinguished of armies. In coalitions and multinational alliances, they are entirely predictable, not to say tiresomely routine. Yet, given goodwill, they can be rectified.

The critical issue at Warsaw, therefore, is not that misunderstandings over Allied assistance arose. It is that despite two months, when remedial action could have been taken, no inter-Allied consensus was reached. Here historians are swimming in much deeper and murkier waters than the failings of the exiled Polish Government or of the Polish Underground, and they have every right to present a whole series of new questions. Why, for instance, if London and Washington were expecting a Rising to take place, did they not approach Moscow well in advance and obtain the necessary assurances for their isolated Polish ally? Or why, since Moscow clearly anticipated a Rising in the capital of an ally of the Western powers, did the Soviet authorities not attempt either to discuss the matter with Western leaders or even to reach a local agreement? These questions require fuller discussion. But one cardinal conclusion can be made without further ado: the tragedy of the Warsaw Rising cannot be attributed solely to local mistakes.

For five weeks, from late August to early October 1944, Rokossovsky's First Byelorussian Front was close enough to Warsaw not only to render intensive assistance but also, if orders had been given, to effect a rescue. For two weeks at the end of September, a limited force from one of Rokossovsky's five armies was actively engaged. Yet orders for a renewed offensive on the Vistula were not given. In this light, historians should stop repeating the explanations that were given for Soviet inaction in early August, and should concentrate their enquiries on the period when Soviet action was eminently possible. They would then stress the analysis made by the German Ninth Army, which was on the spot and which was expecting Rokossovsky to advance at any moment; and they would soon reach the conclusion that the reasons for Soviet passivity were very largely political.

Given the existence of the coalition, however, the politics of the Rising cannot be reduced to the actions, or inaction, of one single party. One has to analyse the problem in the round, and to observe the interactions of all interested parties. Indeed, one has a duty to examine both what the coalition did and what it failed to do.

The answer on the first score is that the 'Big Three' addressed the Warsaw crisis through a series of totally uncoordinated initiatives and of ill-tempered exchanges. The Western Powers arranged for Premier Mick to go to Moscow, but then left their unsupported client at Stalin's mercy. When that key meeting bore no fruit, they protested against Soviet obstructionism; but they showed no urgency whatsoever in bringing the negotiations back on track. The Western leaders had no coherent strategy for dealing with Stalin, or for easing the path for their Polish ally.[6] On the diplomatic front in particular, they produced no initiative, no common plan on how to proceed, no sign of a willingness to protect their ally from Moscow's manifest malevolence. Though they insisted that Germany recognize the Home Army as a legitimate combatant force, they never once thought of asking the Soviets to do the same.

Ideally, of course, any inter-Allied scheme concerning Poland should have been finalized long before the Rising broke out. Almost nine months had passed between November 1943, when the 'Big Three' first discussed Poland at Teheran, and L-Hour on 1 August 1944. Even so, time had not run out. A further six weeks were available for inter-Allied consultations. Premier Mick returned empty-handed from Moscow in mid-August and the insurgents' capitulation did not occur until October. Given due energy, one might be forgiven for thinking that much might still have been accomplished. In the event, the Polish Premier was not given another chance to visit the Kremlin until 10 October. By that time, the Rising had been crushed: the Home Army was broken: and the dice were loaded far more heavily against an agreed solution. Everything considered, the coalition performed feebly and sluggishly. One is tempted to conclude that the insurgents had fulfilled their duty ten times over; the Allied politicians did not fulfil theirs.

Much can now be said about Soviet policy with certainty. Stalin took an extremely ruthless and unbending stance from the minute that the advance into Poland beckoned in the winter of 1943–44. He set his eyes on half the country's territory and on a radical reconstruction of the Government. He installed a committee of puppets; and he ordered the elimination of all agents and soldiers loyal to the legal authorities. After the outbreak of the Rising, he rejected Rokossovsky's plan for the liberation of Warsaw, obstructed Western efforts to send aid, diverted the main Soviet offensive into the Balkans, and approved only half-hearted and much-belated measures of assistance. Once the central sector of the Vistula Front had recovered from the German counter-attack, he held Rokossovsky back in an essentially defensive mode. One can only describe this attitude as callous.

What is not known, however, is whether Stalin might not have been prepared to be more amenable if faced by a firm Western stand. It turns out that he had reopened unofficial feelers to the exiled Government in London in June and July 1944; and it is not beyond the realms of possibility that he might have reached a deal with Premier Mick in early August, if Mick had been properly briefed and supported. Nor is it inconceivable that he might have relented if Roosevelt had agreed to join Churchill's intended showdown, or if the Western leaders had backed their Polish ally with determination. All one can say is that Stalin's hard line hardened in parallel to the realization that his Western partners did not intend to propose an alternative line of their own. So long as Soviet domination of Poland could be imposed at no cost, Stalin was not going to back off.

One has to remember that the Soviet Union under Stalin had adopted a stance of extreme, formalized hostility towards everything outside its borders or beyond its control. Unless instructed otherwise, all Soviet organizations routinely treated all foreigners, including pro-Communist sympathizers, as suspects or enemies. They routinely arrested and eliminated any Soviet citizens, including prisoners of war, who had been abroad without permission or had been in unauthorized contact with non-Soviet persons. In this state of affairs, which was well known to the USSR's neighbours, there was no possibility whatsoever that the Polish Underground could have reached a modus vivendi with the Soviet Army of its own accord. Equally, the exiled Polish Government, which in 1944 was not recognized by Moscow, could never have reached an agreement with the Soviets without the energetic backing of the Western Allies. No compromise was ever going to be reached on any Polish issue without intervention at the very highest level. In practice, this required a united policy pursued jointly by Roosevelt and Churchill and by the diplomats acting on their behalf. In 1944, no such united policy or joint action had been initiated. So Moscow's hardline stance did not change.

From Stalin's point of view, his Western partners were not just suspiciously ambiguous about Poland; they were extremely dilatory. Time and again, the opportunities for reaching an agreed, inter-Allied position were overtaken by events. For example, it would seem that Molotov told Ambassador Harriman in Moscow as early as 5 July 1944 that the Red Army expected to liberate Warsaw in conjunction with the (Communist) People's Army.[7] This piece of information might have provided an excellent opening for a discussion about the composition of the Polish Underground and the role of the Western-backed Home Army within it. Yet there is nothing to show in the following weeks that the British or the Americans took any steps to clarify the issue. The British in particular did nothing when, with four days to spare, they were officially informed by Count R. that a Rising in Warsaw by the Home Army was imminent. As a result, they passed over the last chance of establishing inter-Allied cohesion prior to the outbreak. More importantly, they despatched the luckless Premier Mick to Moscow to deal with Stalin alone, and on diplomatic ground that was completely unprepared.

Hence, whatever his own undoubted contributions to the crisis, Stalin had reason to feel aggrieved. In early August, he was obliged to take a major strategic decision about the Soviet Army's next offensive in a climate of acute political tension. He was pushed by the Western leaders into negotiating with Premier Mick over matters which he had been led to understand had already been conceded at Teheran. In this light, it is not very surprising that he chose to send his forces into the Balkans and to denounce the 'adventure' in Warsaw. Yet even then, he was not faced by evidence of determination or urgency from London and Washington. He was not pressed to recognize the Home Army as an Allied combatant force, or to give assurances about Soviet conduct towards it. He was not asked to share intelligence about the Rising. He was not asked to receive Premier Mick for a second time, even though the Premier's revised plan was available at the start of September. All he saw was Churchill and Roosevelt giving priority to everything else except Warsaw. In the meantime, events moved on. Reserves were moved away from Rokossovsky's front. The Lublin Committee was issuing its hardline decrees. And the Polish–Soviet exchange of population was put in motion. Every day that passed made it more difficult for Stalin to change his line.

British policy to Poland, in contrast, appears to have been seriously schizophrenic. Churchill, the war leader, showed much more commitment than many of his subordinates. He understood that Britain was indebted to its First Ally, and he did not flinch from ordering the Warsaw Airlift even when the cost in British lives was high. He spotted Stalin's malice at an early stage; and he reached the point when he favoured a showdown with Moscow. The Foreign Office, meanwhile, repeatedly dragged its feet. It was much more impressed than Churchill was by the perceived imperative of not upsetting the Soviets. Indeed, it was close to appeasement. In August 1944, at the very time when Allied policy to Warsaw was hanging in the balance, Foreign Office officials produced an important position paper, recommending the compliant approach of Edward Beneš, the exiled Czechoslovak president, as the model to be followed.[8] One does not have to be reminded of the fate of Beneš. In the last resort, however, Churchill was less deterred by the proposals and the malingering of the Foreign Office than by President Roosevelt.

American policy had its own distinct priorities. Having refrained from entering the war during the Polish Crisis of September 1939, and having no formal treaty with Poland, US leaders felt no special obligations. At the same time, they were pursuing several vital projects where Stalin's cooperation was urgently needed; and in general, they harboured many delusions about 'the Great Leader'. Roosevelt's only serious doubts lay with the reactions of Polish-American voters. Fortunately for him, the Rising broke out more than three full months before the presidential election in November. His key meeting with Polish-American Democrats was not scheduled until October.

Crucially, in the summer of '44, US foreign policy was already preoccupied with grander global concerns. Since the war in Europe was clearly being won – and Gen. George Marshall was predicting that it could be won by Christmas – the best minds in Washington were being turned to the post-war order and to the dominant role which the USA intended to play within it. Three urgent issues had come to the fore: the design of a new worldwide economic and financial system, the preparation of a worldwide political body, and the post-war settlement in the Far East, especially China. Each of these global matters came to a head at the time of the Warsaw Rising. The International Monetary Conference, which gave rise to the World Bank and the IMF, convened at Bretton Woods (New Hampshire) between 1 and 22 July 1944. The Draft Charter for the UN was drawn up at an international meeting on post-war security held at Dumbarton Oaks (Maryland) between 21 August and 29 September 1944. The Octagon Conference, to discuss the Far East, convened at Quebec, 10–16 September. The UN Relief and Rehabilitation Agency (UNRRA) held its founding assembly at Montreal, 18–26 September. None of these key strategic matters was directly related to Poland. Yet they all involved the USSR. It was one of the ironies in the politics of 'the Big Three' that in order to elbow the fading British aside, the USA needed the help of Moscow. More immediately, the US administration was increasingly alarmed by the fact that existing Allied resources would be insufficient to defeat Japan when fighting moved to the Asian mainland. Stalin possessed the only available army in the world which possessed the necessary manpower. So, in the eyes of Washington, Stalin had to be courted; his misdemeanours were to be overlooked. Surrounded as he was by unabashed admirers of the Soviet Union, Roosevelt was never going to change course lightly, to encourage Churchill's intended showdown, or to put his relationship with Moscow at risk. Nor did he possess sufficient time or imagination to consider intervening in some milder manner. Though he held the strongest cards in the diplomatic pack, he preferred to play none of them, and to let the tragedy of Warsaw run its course. Roosevelt's inaction was every bit as detrimental as Stalin's.

Such was the unpromising framework within which the exiled Government was obliged to operate. Here, one must insist that Premier Mick and his ministers be seen for what they were – men of moderation and conciliation. They were not the violent anti-Communist extremists or ultra-nationalists, as portrayed by Soviet propaganda, nor were they the foolish romantics, the tank-charging cavalrymen, of the popular stereotype (and as repeated by Churchill in moments of exasperation). Their 'policy of compromise', which Roosevelt had backed with millions of dollars, always included plans for a national rising, but only in the context of unrelenting war against Nazi Germany, of unstinting loyalty to the West, and of a political deal with the USSR. In the last analysis, Premier Mick performed everything short of political suicide in order to meet his commitments. The same cannot be said about his more powerful partners.

The chemistry of international coalitions is a complex business: and the actions and reactions within them are by no means predictable. Their success or failure depends on the interplay of a long list of well-defined components ranging from personalities and political ideology to shared intelligence, divisions of labour, and practical coordination. The Grand Alliance of 1941–45, which triumphed in its main task, undoubtedly possessed many virtues. The Warsaw Rising revealed that it also suffered from numerous deficiencies.

The personalities of the Grand Alliance were dominated by the remarkable, larger-than-life figures of Roósevelt, Churchill, and Stalin. Yet the unspoken convention whereby the 'Big Three' arrogated all major decisions to themselves put everyone else at a disadvantage. Gen. Sikorski may or may not have possessed the force of character and prestige to overcome this obstacle. But Premier Mick clearly did not. The head of a quarrelsome cabinet, he could not lean too far either to the left or to the right; and he depended to a large degree on his ability to work with Churchill. For this reason, he repeatedly bore Churchill's intermittent rages with fortitude; and he accepted Roosevelt's blandishments at face value. Such was his eagerness to please his patrons, he does not appear to have thought of insisting, for example, that no one in the coalition be permitted, quite openly, to treat his soldiers as 'bandits'. Needless to say, playing away and alone he was no match for Stalin.

From Casablanca onwards, the politics of the Grand Alliance in Europe were reduced to the single-minded purpose of forcing the unconditional surrender of Nazi Germany. Unfortunately, this policy coincided in large measure both with the Soviet-driven ideology of anti-fascism and with the similarly dialectical tendency of the Americans to believe in Manichaean concepts of Good and Evil. The effect was to turn Stalin miraculously into a benevolent Uncle Joe, and to dismiss all who opposed him as trouble-makers. To put it at its crudest, the mass murderer who was leading the fight against the fascist mass murderer ceased to be a villain in the minds of Western officialdom; and the millions he continued to kill during the war became both invisible and unmentionable. Churchill, whose mental map of the world long antedated the Soviet Union, was pretty resistant to this way of thinking, but it infected many influential quarters of Anglo-American opinion. It is hard to quantify. But it has to be one of the major factors in explaining the strange paralysis which overcame the Allied coalition whenever – as in the case of the Warsaw Rising – Stalin needed to be restrained or at least to be talked to. One of the few contemporary voices who described this mental mechanism at work was that of George Orwell. But Orwell's was a voice crying in the wilderness.

The anti-fascist model was certainly responsible for the erroneous assessment of the divisions within the exiled Government in London. In accordance with their dialectical thought processes, the Soviets had long demanded the removal of several leading figures who were said to be 'anti-Soviet', 'reactionary', 'right-wing', 'pro-German', and generally undesirable. When the Rising broke out, it was these same supposedly 'anti-Soviet elements' who were blamed for inciting it. In later Commo-speak, the authors of the Rising were said to be 'national romantics' whilst the 'realists' were those who 'wished to cooperate with the USSR'. Nothing could have been further from the truth.

Nonetheless, the British diplomatic service appears to have accepted the scheme, and huge pressure was exerted to make Premier Mick comply with this 'right thinking' of the day. On 30 July 1944, for example, when the Premier flew into Moscow on the eve of the Rising, the British Ambassador urged him to accept four points: the exclusion from the Polish Government of 'certain elements thought to be reactionary and anti-Soviet'; the acceptance of the Curzon Line as a basis for negotiations; a withdrawal from the suggestion that the killing at Katyn was done by the Russians; and a working arrangement with the Polish Committee of National Liberation. In retrospect, every single one of these points must be judged unjustified. The British Ambassador was not acting as honest broker, let alone as the patron and protector of Britain's 'First Ally'. He was not assisting the Premier's desire to enter into meaningful negotiations and to reach a satisfactory compromise. In effect, he was telling the leader of an Allied nation that he must either swallow Stalin's lies and demands in full or that he was on his own and must take the consequences.[9]

Time and again – before, during, and after the Warsaw Rising – Western officials insisted that Poland, lay within 'the Soviet sphere of influence', and that no activity there could be countenanced without 'the cooperation of the Russians'. On the surface, their insistence looked perfectly sensible, yet in practice the idea can be seen to be hopelessly misguided. For no one seems to have defined precisely where the spheres of influence lay, nor under what terms they were supposed to function. No clear distinction was made between a military 'theatre of operations' where the relevant Allied power was expected to dictate military priorities, and a much more comprehensive 'sphere of influence' where the relevant power would be entitled to control all aspects of political, social, economic, and 'security' policy. No one paid attention to the obvious fact that the concept of spheres of influence might conflict with other equally valid principles, such as the sovereignty of other Allied powers. Lastly, it never seems to have struck British or American officials that it was up to them to try and secure the rights of their Polish ally in Poland or, in the absence of a firm understanding, that the well-known totalitarian practices of the Soviet juggernaut would automatically prevail. As a result, they were constantly taken by surprise. They were deeply shocked when the Soviets denied landing rights to the RAF and the USAAF in Warsaw's hour of need. They were similarly nonplussed when Rokossovsky was halted before Warsaw. Throughout the period of the Rising, they wondered in vain about the 'rumour' that the Soviets were rounding up the Home Army. In short, they simply refused to believe bad news about the Soviet system when it stared them in the face. Mesmerized perhaps by Soviet power, and deeply committed to an ethos of team-play, which the Soviets did not share, they shied away from playing their own powerful cards, fearful of provoking a negative reaction. Hence Stalin's own cynical view of a sphere of influence was installed without protest, and democracy was doomed.

Forty years later, when Churchill's close associates were pondering what had gone wrong at the end of the war, Sir William Deakin pointed to the absence in Anglo-American circles of any concept of how to deal with Stalin. Speaking in Fulton (Missouri) in 1984, at the same location as Churchill's famous 'Iron Curtain' speech, Deakin pointed to Poland as the first casualty of this weakness. 'Poland', he said, 'became a grim test of the Anglo-Soviet alliance as a whole.'[10]

Sir John Slessor, the former deputy commander of Allied air forces in the Mediterranean, who had presided over the catastrophe of the Warsaw

Airlift, held similar views. He rated his involvement in the crisis as 'the worst six weeks of my experience':

> '[The Rising] is a story of the utmost gallantry and self-sacrifice on the part of our air-crews . . ., of deathless heroism on the part of the Polish Underground Army . . ., and of the blackest-hearted, coldest-blooded treachery on the part of the Russians. I am not a naturally vindictive man; but I hope there may some very special hell reserved for the brutes in the Kremlin, who betrayed [Boor]'s men and led to the fruitless sacrifice of [our fliers]. . . . It is generally considered easy to be wise after the event. But the events of Yalta and Potsdam came after the events of August and September 1944; and those of us who took part in those events may be excused if we fail to understand the attitude towards Stalin and the Russians exemplified in the later chapters of Robert Sherwood's book on Harry Hopkins. How, after the fall of Warsaw, any responsible statesman could trust any Russian Communist further than he could kick him, passes the comprehension of ordinary men.'[11]

Western assessments of Soviet practices and intentions were grossly complacent. Neither London nor Washington grasped the absurdity of pressing their Polish ally to reach a settlement with Stalin at a juncture when Stalin's security apparatus was killing and deporting the ally's personnel and when they themselves were accepting all Moscow's assurances at face value. Neither saw the point of intervening. Both the British and the American governments were troubled by the Soviet Army's halt on the Vistula; and both were angered by Soviet obstructions over joint air operations and landing facilities. Yet no one in the upper reaches of government seems to have drawn the obvious conclusions. No one in particular seems to have comprehended the implications of the fact that Allied planes on their way to Warsaw were regularly fired on by Soviet artillery and fighters.[12]

As always, the sequence of events was important. 1944 was a year in which the shape of post-war Europe was still in the earliest stages of realization. Before Yalta, little had been finally decided. There was much to play for. Many key issues awaited a resolution. The crisis in Warsaw preceded the liberation of Paris. At the time, Stalin had not recognized the Lublin Committee as a provisional Government, just as the Western Governments had still not recognized de Gaulle's Free French as the future rulers of France. Indeed, as late as December 1944, when de Gaulle visited Moscow, Stalin attempted to trade Soviet recognition of his group in return for de Gaulle's recognition of the Lublin Committee. All the indications were, that Soviet policy towards Poland in mid-1944 remained fluid. If a concerted Western scheme had been launched at the highest level to reach the desired compromise, it is possible that something might have been achieved. Regrettably, no such scheme was ever produced. No comprehensive compromise was ever floated. The longer a solution was delayed, the stronger Stalin's hand grew. By the time that Roosevelt and Churchill travelled to Crimea in February 1945, all the trumps relating to Poland's future were firmly in Stalin's grip. After Yalta, it was too late to change anything.

The catalogue of shortcomings within the Allied Coalition is so long that it threatens to grow tedious in the telling. Allied intelligence about Warsaw, for example, was lamentable. And each of the major powers was as helpless as that of the others. The British were receiving conflicting information from Polish and from Soviet sources, but made no serious provision to resolve the dilemma. The abortive trip of Salamander wasted months of valuable time, ended in fiasco, and was not followed up. For its part, Soviet intelligence was locked in its ideological straitjacket, and was quite incapable of effective analysis. In the eighth week of the Rising, a lone Soviet agent was still wandering round Warsaw, talking to no one of importance, trying to work out the most elementary facts such as where the insurgent formations were located or who was in charge. American intelligence was no better. US military intelligencers were apparently responsible for passing on the catastrophic misjudgement about the fall of the Old Town which was used by Roosevelt's entourage to reject Churchill's pleas for joint action. In other words, and quite literally, poor Allied intelligence was fatal.

Military and political liaison was negligible. The British had placed scores of officers in Yugoslavia, Albania, and Greece, but none in Poland. The British 'Freston' Mission to the Home Army, first requested in February 1944, did not land until Christmas – by which time the Rising had been crushed. Neither the Americans nor the Soviets bothered to establish a link with the Home Army leadership.

The inconsistences of Western policy were manifold. On several occasions, Churchill and Roosevelt failed to act in concert, with consequences of varying gravity. Yet on one issue – the Curzon Line – their persistent and shifty machinations can only be described as disgraceful. It was bad enough that they kept their discussions at Teheran secret. But their subsequent pretence over many months that Polish–Soviet differences over territory were still open to discussion, was unforgivable. They had misled Stalin, by giving him to believe that his territorial demands had been fully accepted and would not be questioned. But they also misled their own diplomatic services, who continued to work on plans for territorial compromise. And they misled Premier Mick most horribly by urging him to negotiate with Stalin and to make proposals which were almost certain to be rejected. No other issue did so much to undermine trust within the Alliance; and it came to a head in the first week of August 1944, when Stalin's cooperation over Warsaw was most sorely needed. It was not addressed again so long as the Rising lasted.

Interdepartmental friction arose at every turn. In the early years of the war, the British had granted the Polish Government a large measure of autonomy. But by 1944, the cross purposes of the Foreign Office and of SOE over Poland rendered them all but incapable of working together. The worst instance of their incompetence occurred at the most damaging moment, namely on the eve of the Rising when SOE was urging Churchill to adopt active measures which the Foreign Office had independently ruled out. Everything made for confusion and paralysis. It played straight into the hands of the most malevolent pro-Soviet element which was bound to get its way if no effective assistance to Warsaw was mounted. Philby & Co. were not obliged to torpedo a plan. There was no plan to be torpedoed.

Sad to say, Britain's SOE, which was the main Allied agency for liaison with European Resistance movements, virtually abandoned its Polish clients in their hour of need. After priority was given first to Yugoslavia and then to France, the will and the means to help Poland were greatly diminished. (Western planners, if they thought at all, seem to have assumed that the main task of supplying Warsaw would be taken over by the Soviets.) Prior to August 1944, the head of SOE, Gen. Gubbins, had met with one of his Polish colleagues almost every single week. But on 13 August, at the height of the Warsaw emergency, he took off for France; and Gen. Tabor didn't see him again for some three months. He left an operation that was near to collapse. There were no ready plans, few resources, and little equipment. It turned out that barely 10 per cent of the long-range aircraft intended for the 'air-bridge' to Poland had actually been delivered. Due to lapses in communication, no one had passed on details of the changing provisions of the British Chiefs of Staff; and Gen. Boor in Warsaw had been left to the very last moment with the false illusion that both the Polish Parachute Brigade and the Polish squadrons of the RAF could somehow be made available. Everything deteriorated into an improvised scramble. Coordination between Warsaw, London, Washington, and Moscow was so fitful and slow that nothing approaching a common front or a joint response could be concocted.

A still more sinister scenario must be considered. Several commentators have noted that 'an element of fantasy' had entered into SOE's relationship with Poland.[14] According to one of SOE's most senior officer, '[we] were so deeply committed to the Polish cause that we funked facing them with the realities of their situation'.[15] Writing long after the war, Col. Peter Wilkinson admitted that preparations were not competently handled: 'On Gubbins' instructions,' he wrote, 'over the next twelve months I wasted hours in make-believe joint planning with the Polish General Staff, working out the logistics of a full-scale airborne invasion of German-occupied Poland which both they and I knew could not possibly take place.'[16]

If this account is correct, then the British as well as the Poles had been deluding themselves. And no one had cared to inform the Home Army.

The disaster, therefore, was a joint one. Any objective reviewer of these grave failings must judge every single member of the Allied coalition to hold a share of the responsibility. In essence, the tragedy of the Warsaw Rising resulted from a systemic breakdown of the Grand Alliance.

A parable may well be appropriate. A man wades into a river to grapple with a criminal gang. He does so because the criminals have been beating, murdering and humiliating his family for years, and because he belongs to a team that is dedicated to bringing them to justice. What is more, he has been assured by the team leaders that everyone will pull together; and he chooses a moment when 'friends of friends' appear in strength on the far bank and are expected to help. Then, everything goes wrong. The criminals do not flee, but turn to fight. They trap the man, and massacre his relatives. The 'friends of friends' hold back. The man begins to flounder. The team leaders call across the river, and plead with their friends for help. Their calls are confused and half-hearted. Their friends still hold back. Repeated pleas bring no response. Eventually only one would-be rescuer enters the water, and quickly gets into difficulties himself. After a long struggle, the criminals tighten their grip on the man's throat, and push him under. The man drowns. Who is to blame? And who is to be commended?

APPENDICES

List of Appendices

Poland's Historical Commonwealth

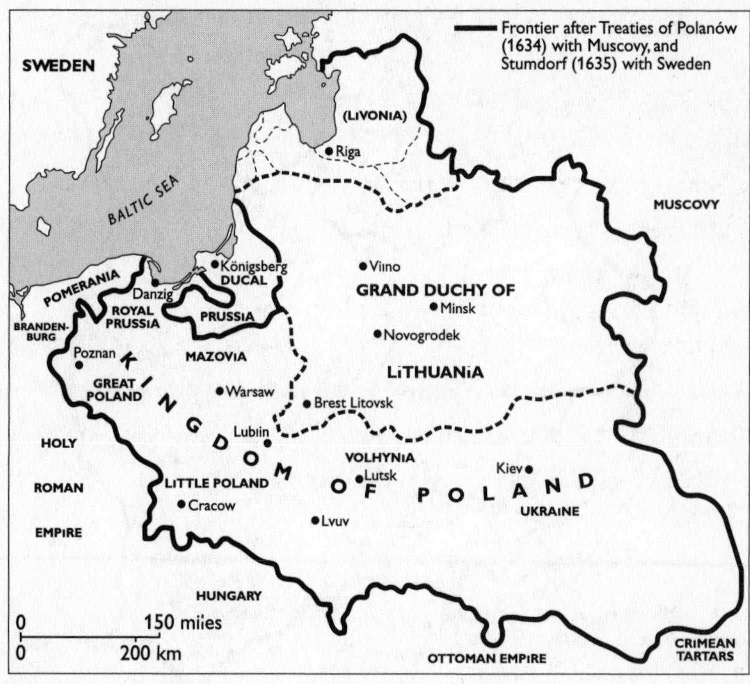

The Polish Republic 1918–1939

W. J. Rose – *Poland* (1939): cover

Nasze Drogi – A Polish view of Poland

OBJAŚNIENIA:
POLSKA W ROKU 1939. OBSZARY R.P. W ROKU 1771.
OBSZARY R.P. W RÓŻNYCH OKRESACH MIĘDZY R. 999 A 1667.

'Warszawianka'
(The Warsaw March of 1831)

Words by Casimir Delavigne Translated by K. Sienkiewicz
Music by Karol Kurpiński

Oto dziś dzień krwi i chwały
Oby dniem wolności był
W tęczę Franków orzeł biały
Patrząc lot swój w niebo wzbił
Słońcem lipca podniecany
Woła na nas z górnych stron:
Powstań Polsko, skrusz kajdany
Dziś twój tryumf, albo zgon!

(Refrain) Hej, kto Polak na bagnety!
Żyj swobodo, Polsko Żyj!
Takim hasłem cnej podnięty
Trąbo nasza wrogom grzmij
Trąbo nasza wrogom grzmij.

Free Europe, 9 March 1945

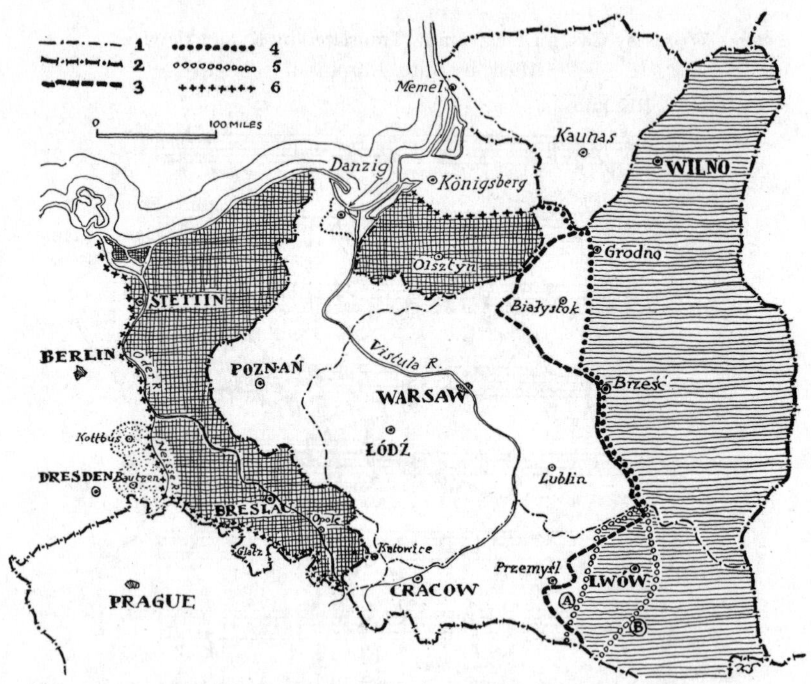

(1) The Russian–German frontier in 1914.

(2) The Polish frontiers in 1938.

(3) The Soviet–German demarcation line fixed by a treaty signed in Moscow on September 28, 1939, by M. Molotov and von Ribbentrop.

(4) Demarcation Line of December 8, 1919. This Line was accepted by the Supreme Council which met in Spa, on July 10, 1920, as a basis for a decision with regard to the Polish–Soviet Armistice. On the following day Lord Curzon sent a proposal for an immediate armistice to Moscow, and the Line which he suggested has since been known by his name.

(5) Two variants of the Demarcation Lines between Poland and Eastern Galicia proposed by the Commission on Polish Affairs at the Peace Conference in June, 1919. The extension of the Curzon Line into Galicia, and especially the adoption of Line A for this purpose, is a violation of the agreement reached in Spa in 1920. (For details see C. SMOGORZEWSKI: About the Curzon Line and Other Lines, pp. 13–14, Free Europe pamphlet No. 7).

(6) The new western frontier of Poland claimed by the 'Polish Provisional Government' of Lublin.

Areas shaded horizontally represent the territories east of the Curzon Line which, according to the decision of the Crimea Conference, Poland is going to lose.

Areas [hatched] are those which, in their entirety or in part, are to be incorporated into Poland.

The dotted area represents the land of the Lusatians, or Wends, where the Slavonic language is spoken to this day.

The German Occupation of Poland 1939–1944

Polish frontier 1939
Nazi–Soviet Frontier 28 Sep 1939
Polish territories annexed to Reich September 1939
Grossdeutschland frontier 1941
Territory annexed by the USSR 1939-41, and divided into German administrative districts 1941-44
Main German concentration camps
(Estonia)
(Latvia)
REICHSKOMMISSARIAT
(Lithuania)
Vilno
OSTLAND
Koenigsberg
Danzig
Stutthoff
EAST PRUSSIA
Suvalki
REICHSGAU
DANZIG
WESTPREUSSEN
Bromberg
BEZIRK BIALYSTOK
ZICHENAU
Treblinka
Poznan
WARTHELAND
Kulm
Warsaw
Lodz
Gross Rosen
Breslau
GENERAL
Sobibor
REICHSKOMMISSARIAT
Lublin
Maidanek
Chenstohova
UPPER SILESIA
GOVERNMENT
Gleiwitz
UKRAINE
Auschwitz-Birkenau
Cracow
Plaszov
Belzec
PROTECTORATE OF BOHEMIA & MORAVIA
1939 – 45
Lvuv
DISTRIKT GALIZIEN
Drohobich
(added to G.G. 1941)
SLOVAKIA
HUNGARY
RUMANIA
0 150 miles
0 200 km

The Warsaw Ghetto 1940–1943

KZ-Warschau

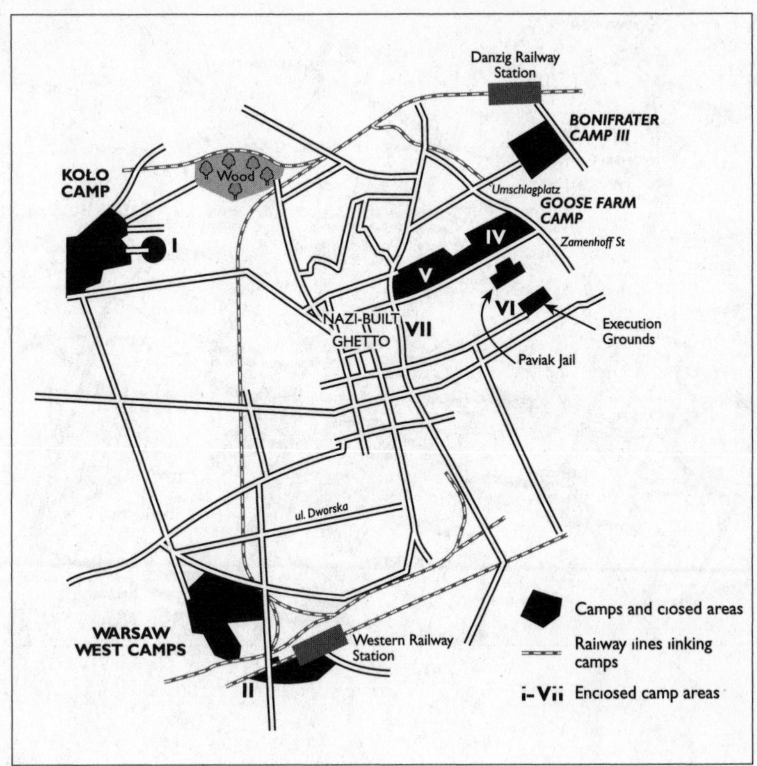

Suggested Layout

Wartime Warsaw

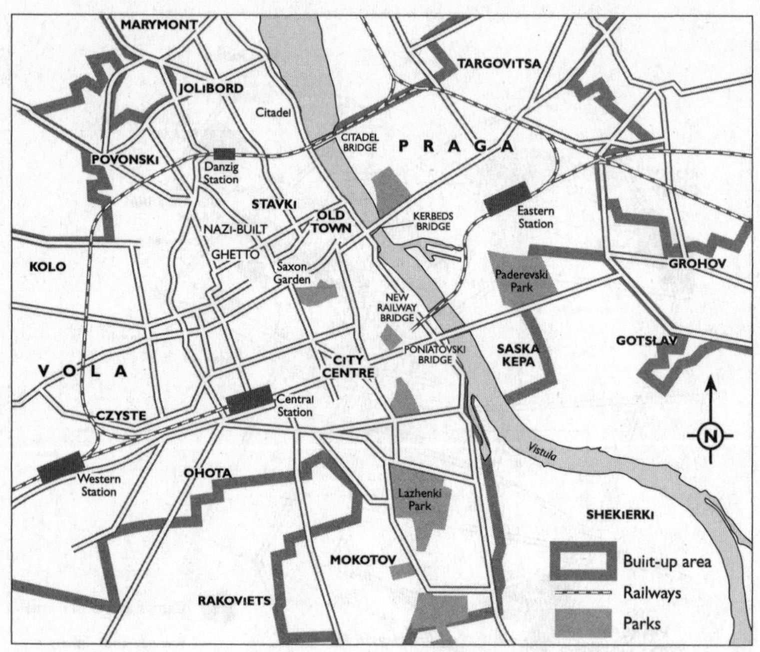

Poland's 'Secret State' (1944)

after Marek Ney-Krwawicz and Andrzej Kunert

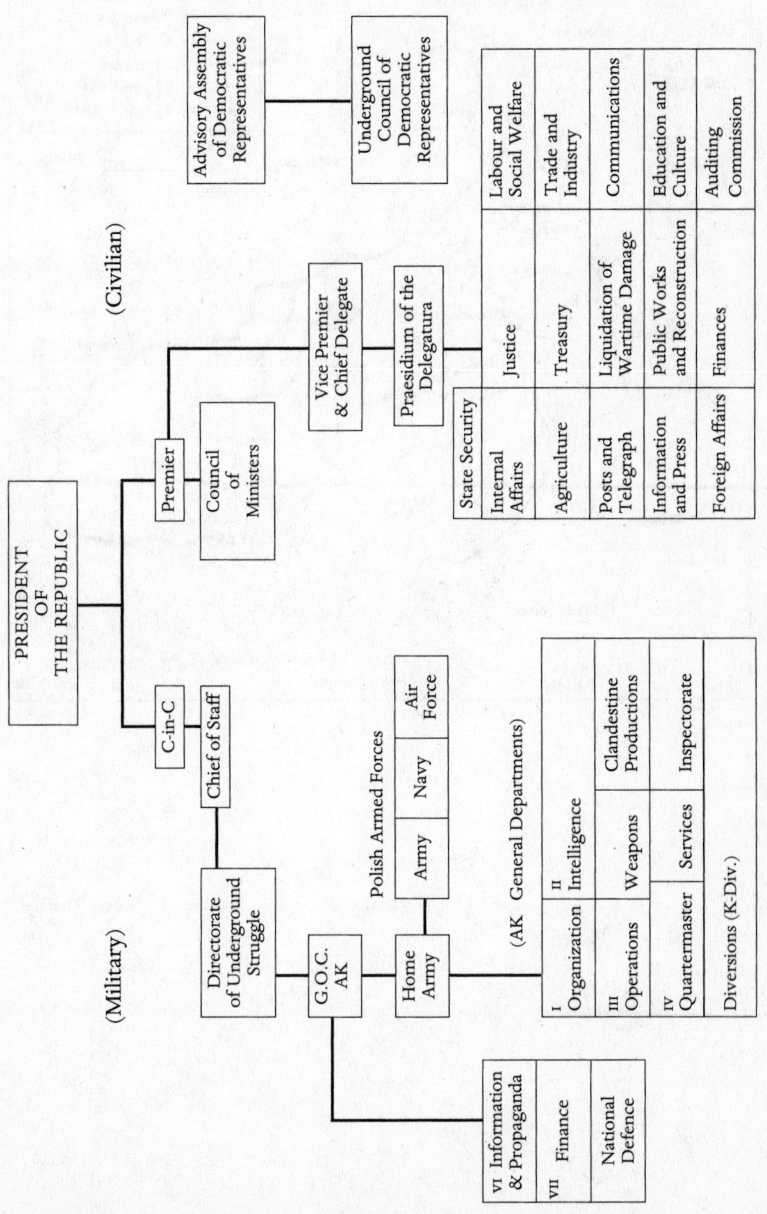

The Eastern Front: from Stalingrad to Warsaw 1942–1944

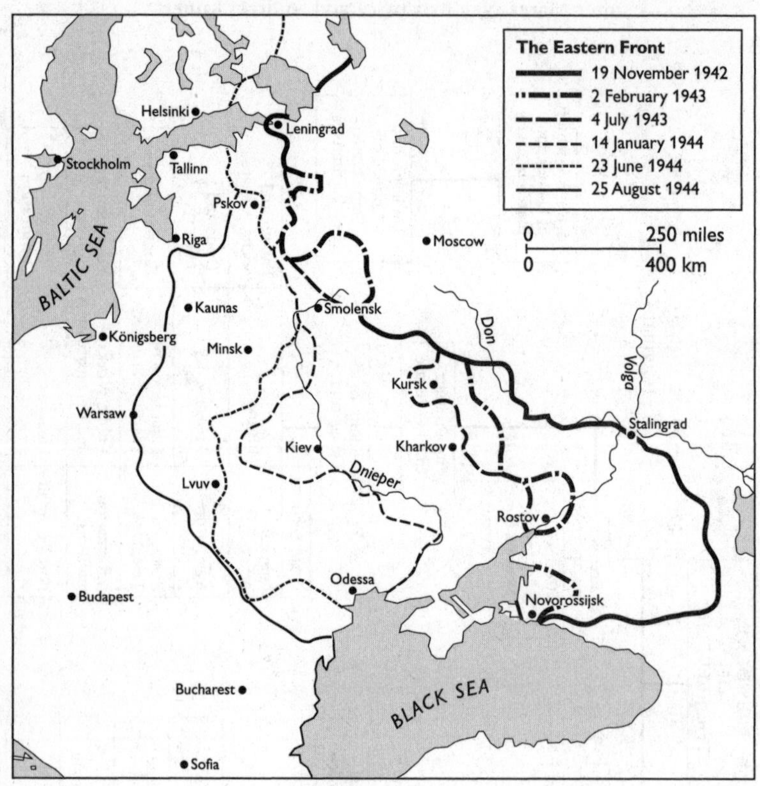

The Soviet View of the Curzon Line

State frontier of the USSR

Curzon Line

from *Izvestia*, January 1944

Poland's Eastern Borders, 1939–1945

0 100 miles
0 150 km
BALTIC
SEA
LITHUANIA
Neman
Königsberg
Gdańsk
(Danzig)
EAST
PRUSSIA
Grodno
Narev
Bialystok
Vistula
Bug
Warsaw
Brest
POLAND
Lodz
Pripet
Pripet
Marshes
Radom
Lublin
Varta
Kieltse
San
Vistula
Cracow
A
Lvuv
GALICIA
B
Dniester
SLOVAKIA
The so-called Curzon Line (1920), with extensions (A & B) into E. Galicia
The 'Peace Boundary' established by the German–Soviet Treaty of Friendship, Co-operation and Demarcation, 28 September 1939
Polish–Soviet frontier 1945-1991
International frontiers, 1 September 1939

Appendix 15

David Low cartoons, 1943–1944

(1)

(2)

(3)

October 1944, *Evening Standard* (London)

(1) Seeking to restore the country's pre-war frontier is labelled 'The Small Nation Mind'.

(2) Although the Soviet Union had invaded Poland in 1939 and not vice-versa, Poles who resisted Soviet demands were dubbed 'irresponsible' for conducting a 'Private War on Russia'.

(3) For daring to point out that the British were not assisting Warsaw with the same loyalty which which the Poles had defended London, the Commander-in-Chief, Gen. Sosnkowski, is characterized as an 'Unhelpful Friend' and an example of 'Political Ineptness'.

Letter from the Foreign Office to Ambassador E. Raczyński with regard to rendering assistance to Warsaw

being the reply of Sir Orme Sargent on 28 July 1944 to questions raised the previous day by Ambassador Raczyński in his conversation with Foreign Secretary Sir Anthony Eden about preparations for the battle for Warsaw . . .[1]

No C 9937/8/G
My dear Ambassador,

You discussed with me this morning the three proposals you had put briefly before the Secretary of State yesterday:

1. that His Majesty's Government should intervene with the Soviet Government to prevent any victimisation of Polish units who have been cooperating in the struggle against the Germans, and
2. that the following measures of assistance might be given to further a rising in Warsaw:
   a) despatch of the Polish parachute brigade in the United Kingdom;
   b) bombing by the Royal Air Force of airfields around Warsaw, and
   c) despatch to Polish airfields of Mustangs and Spitfires now operating with the Royal Air Force.

The Foreign Secretary has instructed me to take up with the Soviet Ambassador the question of the treatment of Polish Underground units by the advancing Soviet forces.

I am afraid that, quite apart from the difficulties of co-ordinating such action with the Soviet Government, whose forces are operating against the Germans in Polish territory, operational considerations alone preclude us from meeting the three requests you made for assisting the rising in Warsaw. It would not be possible to fly the parachute brigade over German territory as far as Warsaw, without risking excessive losses. The despatch of fighter squadrons to airfields in Poland would also be a lengthy and complicated process which could, in any case, only be carried out in agreement with the Soviet Government. It could certainly not be accomplished in time to influence the present battle. As regards bombarding Warsaw airfields, Warsaw is beyond the normal operational range of Royal Air Force bombers and the bombing of airfields would in any case be carried out much more appropriately by bombers operating from Soviet-controlled bases. Insofar as your authorities may have had in mind shuttle-bombing, about which there has been some publicity lately, this is carried out by the American Army Air Force and not by the Royal Air Force. I am afraid, therefore, there is nothing that His Majesty's Government can do in this connexion.

You also mentioned the desire of your Government that the British Broadcasting Corporation should broadcast a warning to the Germans to prevent them killing members of the Polish home army captured by them. I find that the Foreign Office were already in communication with the appropriate British and Polish authorities with a view to arranging a broadcast on these lines. For reasons which have already been explained to your Embassy, it will be necessary to make some changes in the text you proposed, but I think the revised text will meet the object you have in mind.

Yours sincerely,
O.G. Sargent
(for Sir Alexander Cadogan)

28.7.1944

Comment: Taken in isolation, this document appears to be a definitive statement of the British Government's negative stance towards the Warsaw Rising. Whilst revealing that HMG had been officially informed of the imminence of the Rising on 27 July – i.e. four days before the final decision was made – it exudes a degree of detachment and disapproval that is hardly required by the letter's contents. Penned by a relatively junior official on behalf of Eden's deputy, it was signally lacking in the least expression of sympathy for Poland's predicament or of regret for Britain's apparent inability to help. On the one point which touched on the Foreign Office's own competence, it did not agree to press the Ambassador's concerns about the victimization of Home Army units, but merely to raise the question with the Soviet Ambassador – which could have meant anything. Reading this thinly disguised diplomatic brush-off, one would never guess that Ambassador Raczyński's military colleagues were about to receive a favourable hearing the very next day to more extensive requests that would be forwarded to Prime Minister Churchill. One can only conclude that British policy was not so much hostile, as incoherent.

ND.

The Vistula Sector: August 1944

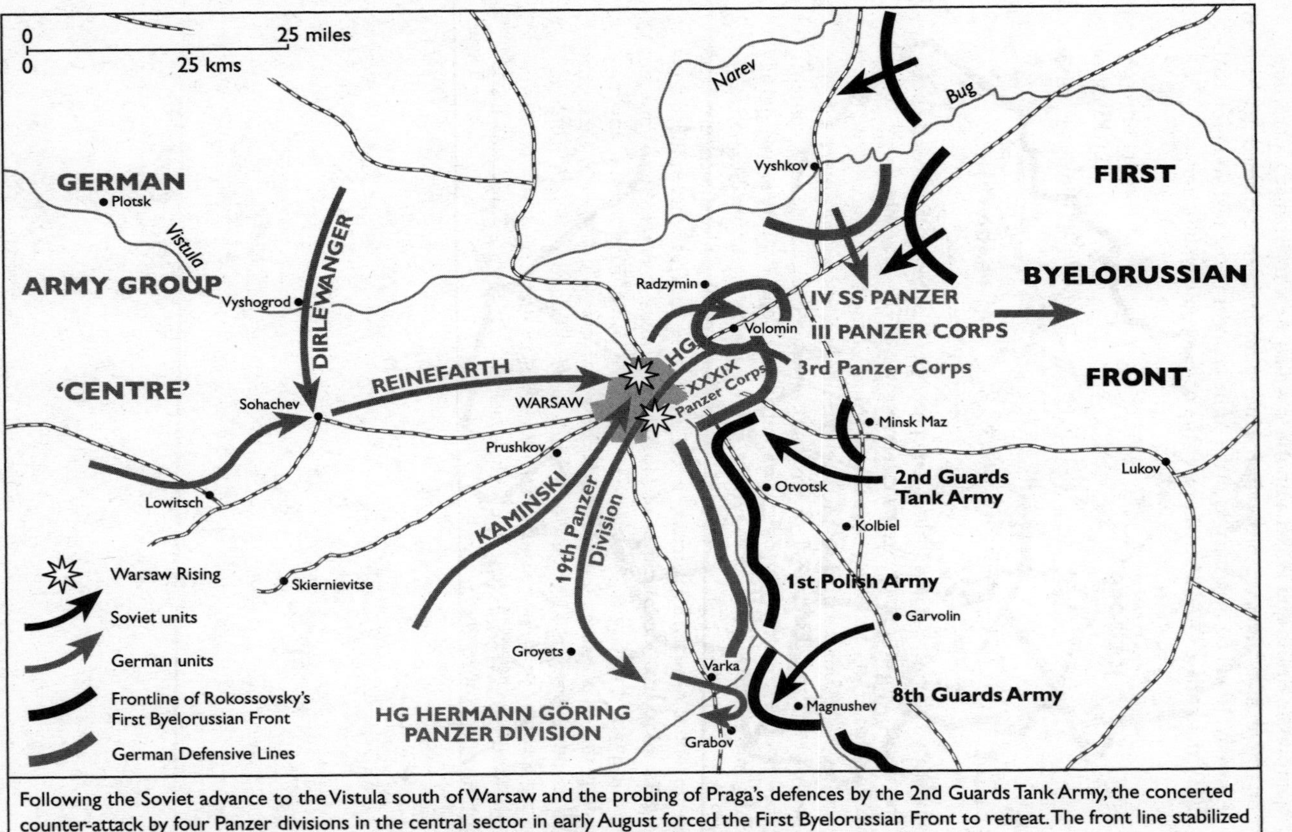

Following the Soviet advance to the Vistula south of Warsaw and the probing of Praga's defences by the 2nd Guards Tank Army, the concerted counter-attack by four Panzer divisions in the central sector in early August forced the First Byelorussian Front to retreat. The front line stabilized in mid-August 40–50 miles to the east. Rokossovsky did not capture Praga until mid-September.

Home Army Districts: Warsaw

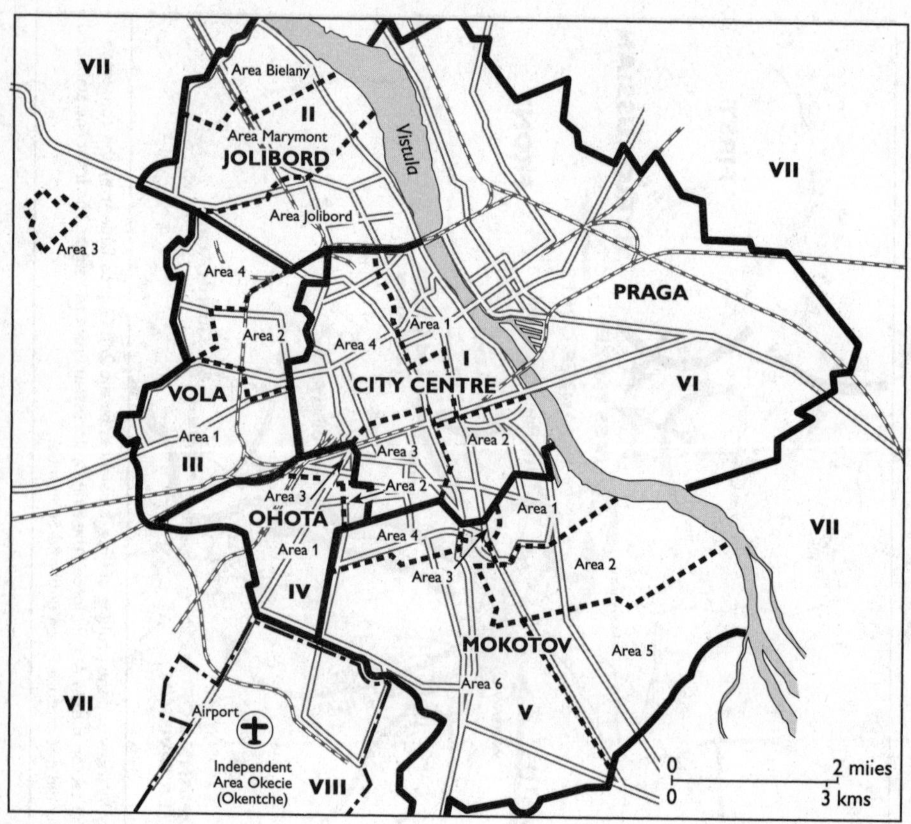

Insurgent Warsaw: Maximum Extent, 5 August 1944

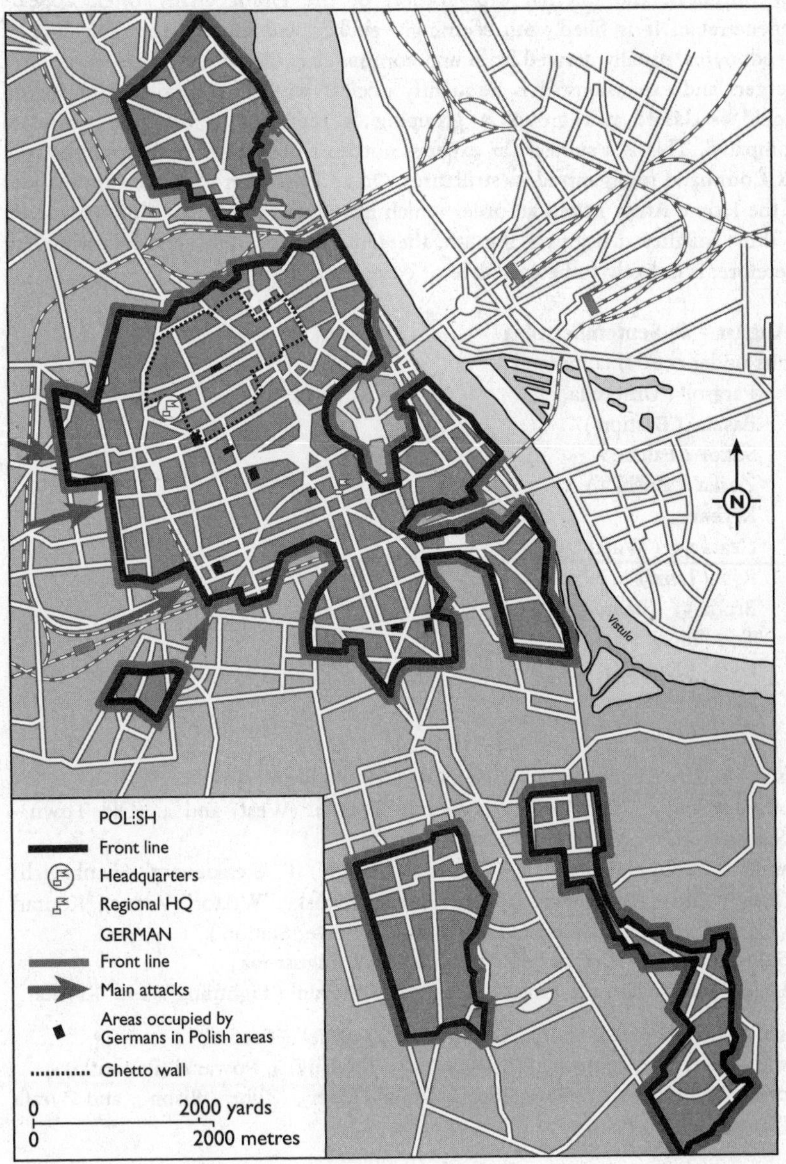

Home Army Units during the Warsaw Rising

For outsiders, the internal organization of the Home Army often appears impenetrable. It is filled with seemingly endless and incomprehensible lists of pseudonyms, usually derived from unit commanders. Equally, because of constant mergers and expansions, it is frequently unclear whether a particular formation should be classed as a 'group', a 'grouping', a 'regiment', a 'battalion', or just a 'company'. This is a subject for experts, not least because in mid-September the AK Command re-organized its structures. On 21 September 1944, the Commander of the Home Army issued an order which introduced a Warsaw Corps made up of three infantry divisions – the 8th, the 10th, and the 28th. The following list, therefore, is unlikely to be complete or completely accurate.

1 August – 20 September 1944

Units under central command

'Parasol' ('Umbrella')
'Baszta' ('Bastion')
'Sokół' ('Falcon')
'Zośka' ('Zoshka')
'Krybar'
'Czata 49' ('Watch 49')
'Ryś' ('Linx')
'Broda 53' ('Beard 53')
'Topolnicki'
'Dysk' ('Discus')
'Miotła' ('Broom')
'Pięść' ('Fist')

District I (City Centre/Śródmieście): OC Col. 'Radwan'
- sub-districts: 1. (Old Town) 2. (South-West) 3. (West) and 4. (Old Town – Stawki)
- units: 'Chrobry ('Valiant') I', 'Chrobry ('Valiant') II', 'Sienkiewicz' (Shenkevich), 'Rum', 'Gurt', 'Bartkiewicz', 'Róg' (Horn), 'Kiliński', 'Wiktor' (Viktor), 'Konrad' ('Conrad'), 'Unia' ('Union'), 'Elektrownia' ('Power Station')
- Sub-district 'City Centre South' formed on 7 August 1944
- Units: 'Sarna' ('Deer'), 'Golski', 'Bogumił', 'Piorun' ('Lightning'), and 'Kryśka'

District II (Żolibórz/Jolibord), OC Lt.Col. 'Żywiciel' ('Feeder')
- sub-districts: 1. (Central) 2. (Marymont) 3. (Bielany) 4. Powązki (Povonski)
- units: 'Żaglowiec' ('Sailing Ship'), 'Żmija' (Viper), 'Żubr' ('Bison'), and Żyrafa' ('Giraffe')

District III (Wola/Vola), OC. Maj. 'Waligóra' ('Crag-Crusher')
- sub-districts: 1. (Czyste) 2. (Koło) 3. (Wawrzyszew)
- units: 'Balbo', 'Hal', 'Wojownik' ('Warrior')

District IV (Ochota/Ohota), OC. Lt.Col. 'Ojciec' (Father)
– sub-districts: 1. (Central) 2. (Żwirki) 3. (West Station)
– units: 'Zych', 'Korczak', 'Gustaw'

District V (Mokotów/Mokotov), Acting OC. Lt.Col. 'Daniel'
– sub-districts: 1, 2, 3, 4, 5, (Sadyba)
– units: 'Baszta' ('Bastion'), 'Wrak' ('Wreck'), 'Monopol' etc.

District VI (Praga), OC. Lt.Col. 'Andrzej' (André)
– 5 sub-districts, all overrun in the first week.

District VII (Greater Warsaw), OC. Lt.Col. 'Kalwin' (Calvin)

District VIII (Okęcie/Okentche), Maj. 'Wysocki'

From 20 September 1944
The Warsaw Corps, AK, OC Brig.Gen. 'Monter'

– 8 Infantry Division (Żoliborz/Jolibord District)
  13 Infantry Regt., 'Kampinos' Group
  21 Infantry Regt., 'Dzieci Warszawy' ('Children of Warsaw'), 'Żaglowiec' ('Sailing Ship') Grouping.
  32 Infantry Regt., 'Żbik' ('Wildcat'), 'Żubr' ('Bison'), and 'Żyrafa' ('Giraffe')

– 10 'Rataj' Infantry Division (Mokotów/Mokotov District)
  28 Infantry Regt.
  30 Infantry Regt.
  31 Infantry Regt.

– 28 'Okrzeja' Infantry Division (City Centre)
  15 Infantry Regt.
  36 Infantry Regt. (Academic Legion)
    – 1 Batt. 'Krybar'
    – 2 Batt. 'Dowgierd'
    – 3 Batt. 'Żmudzin'
  72 Infantry Regt.
    – 1 Batt. 'Golski'
    – 2 Batt.
    – 3 Batt.

German Anti-insurgent Formations in Warsaw as at 20 August 1944 (excluding the German Ninth Army)

Unit **Strength (Officers/Men)**

A – Battle Group 'Rohr'

Defence Section 'D'
1st Regt. of Kaminski Brigade
627th Pioneer Battalion
500th Panzer Pioneer Battalion (part)
80th Flak Regiment (part)
3rd Battalion SS 'Viking' Flak Regiment

90/6161

B – Battle Group 'Reinefarth'

I Attack Group 'Dirlewanger'
SS Regiment 'Dirlewanger'
2nd & 4th Battalion Police Task Force 'Walter'
1st & 2nd Battalion 111th Regiment (Azeri)
4th Heavy Machine Gun Platoon 111th Regiment (Azeri)
80th Flak Regiment (part)
Flame-thrower Battalion 'Kroner' (part)

29/1939

II Attack Group 'Reck'
1 anti-tank platoon
3 panzer-grenadier companies
1 cavalry platoon
1 pioneer platoon (Azeri)
1st & 6th Battalion Police Task Force 'Walter'
1 SS-Heavy Machine-Gun Platoon 'Röntgen'
Police Company 'Warsaw'
Flame-thrower Battalion 'Kroner' (part)

21/1559

III Attack Group 'Schmidt'
608th Security Regiment
Grenadier Battalion 'Benthin'
Police Battalion 'Burkhardt'
2 platoons of 4th Battalion 111th Regiment (Azeri)
Flame-thrower Battalion 'Kroner' (part)
Armoured Train 75

38/1514

IVa Reserves
200th Replacement Assault Gun Detachment
302nd Tank Detachment
Storm Pioneer Regiment 'Herzog'
500th Panzer Pioneer Battalion (remainder)
218th Storm Panzer Company
638th Heavy Artillery Battery
3rd Company of 21st Police Battalion 'Sarnow'
Flame-thrower Battalion 'Kroner' (remainder)

51/1999

IVb 21st Police Battalion 'Sarnow' (remainder)
3rd Battalion Police Task Force 'Walter'
1st Platoon SS-Company 'Röntgen'
4th Cossack Detachment of 57th Security Regiment
572nd Cossack Battalion
69th Cossack Battalion

60/3524

V 501st Panzer Pioneer Battalion
579th Cossack Detachment
580th Russian Cavalry Detachment

Total **289/16,696**

(Source – Hanns von Krannhals, *Der Warschauer Aufstand* (Frankfurt/Main, 1964), pp. 381–3)

Battles for the Magnushev Bridgehead: 9 August–12 September 1944

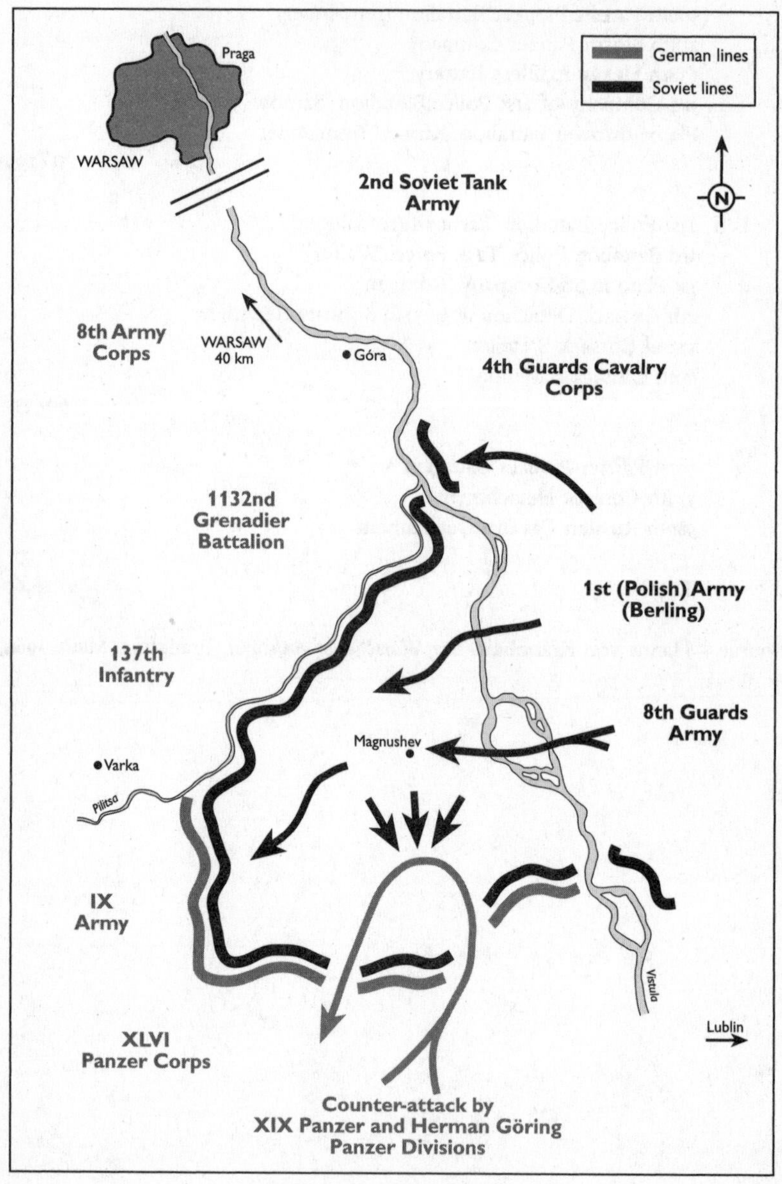

Warsaw Airlift: September 1944

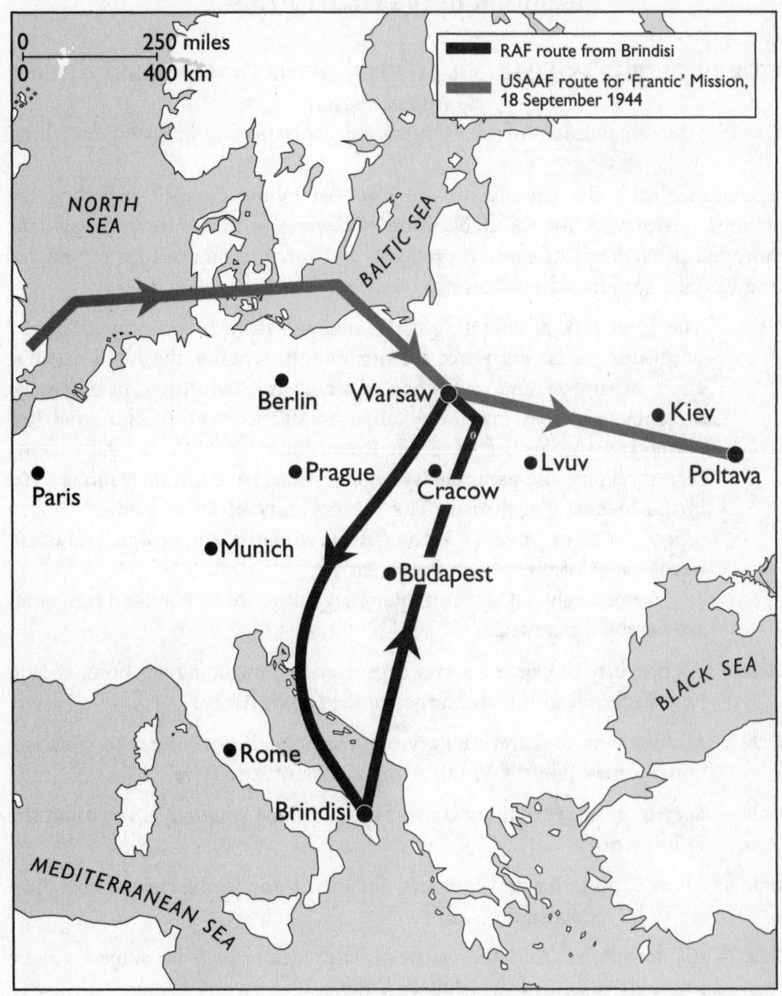

24 August 1944: At the height of the Warsaw Rising, the Communist-controlled Lublin Committee decrees the abolition of the Home Army

DECREE OF THE POLISH COMMITTEE OF NATIONAL LIBERATION
24 August 1944
concerning the disbandment of secret military organizations in liberated territories[1]

In accordance with the decision of the National Home Council regarding the provisional procedures for the publication of decrees with the force of law, the Committee of National Liberation proposes and the Praesidium of the National Home Council confirms the following:

Article 1. The great task of liberating the Homeland from Nazi occupation, and of ensuring a lasting peace for our nation, requires the rapid organization, expansion, and unification of a reborn Polish Army, in order that a complete victory may be obtained in alliance with the fraternal Red Army and the armies of Great Britain and the USA . . . All existing secret military and paramilitary organizations have lost their *raison d'être* in the liberated territories. The present duty of every soldier – every officer, NCO or private – is to offer his strength, knowledge, and talent to the ranks of the reborn Polish Army.

Accordingly, all secret military organizations in liberated territories are hereby disbanded.

Article 2. All property of existing secret organizations, including weapons, should be transferred to the authorities of the Polish Army.

Article 3. All members of secret military organizations, if not subject to conscription . . . may join the Polish Army as volunteers.

Article 4. Service in secret military organizations will be counted as service in the Polish Army.

Article 5. All existing ranks and honours obtained prior to the day of liberation are to be recognized . . .

Article 6. All deviations from the articles of this decree will be subject to the penal provisions of the Military Code.

Article 7. The execution of this decree is hereby placed in the hands of the Director of the Office of National Defence in consultation with the Director of the Office of Public Security (UB).

Article 8. The above decree comes into force on the day of its publication.

Chairman of the KRN	Bolesław Bierut
Chairman of the PKWN	Edward Osóbka-Morawski
Director of the Office of National Defence	Michał Rola-Żymierski (General)

A further decree dated 31 August 1944 listed the punishments, including the death penalty, to be applied to 'fascist-Hitlerite criminals' and 'Traitors of the Polish Nation'. It defined such criminals and traitors as 'anyone acting on behalf of the occupation authorities' and 'anyone acting against persons present in the confines of the Polish State'.[2]

The political context of these decrees may be judged from the sentiments about the Warsaw Rising expressed in an Appeal circulated on 18 August 1944 under the auspices of the Central Committee of the Polish Workers Party (PPR):

> 'A band of ruffians and lackeys from pre-war *Sanacja* and ORN circles is today raising its filthy paw against the Polish Army which is pursuing a heroic and selfless struggle for the freedom of the homeland. A handful of ignorant leaders of the Home Army, acting on the orders of [General] Sosnkowski and in the name of the threadbare political games of the *Sanacja* clique, have pushed the population of Warsaw into battle.'[3]

Insurgent Warsaw: September 1944

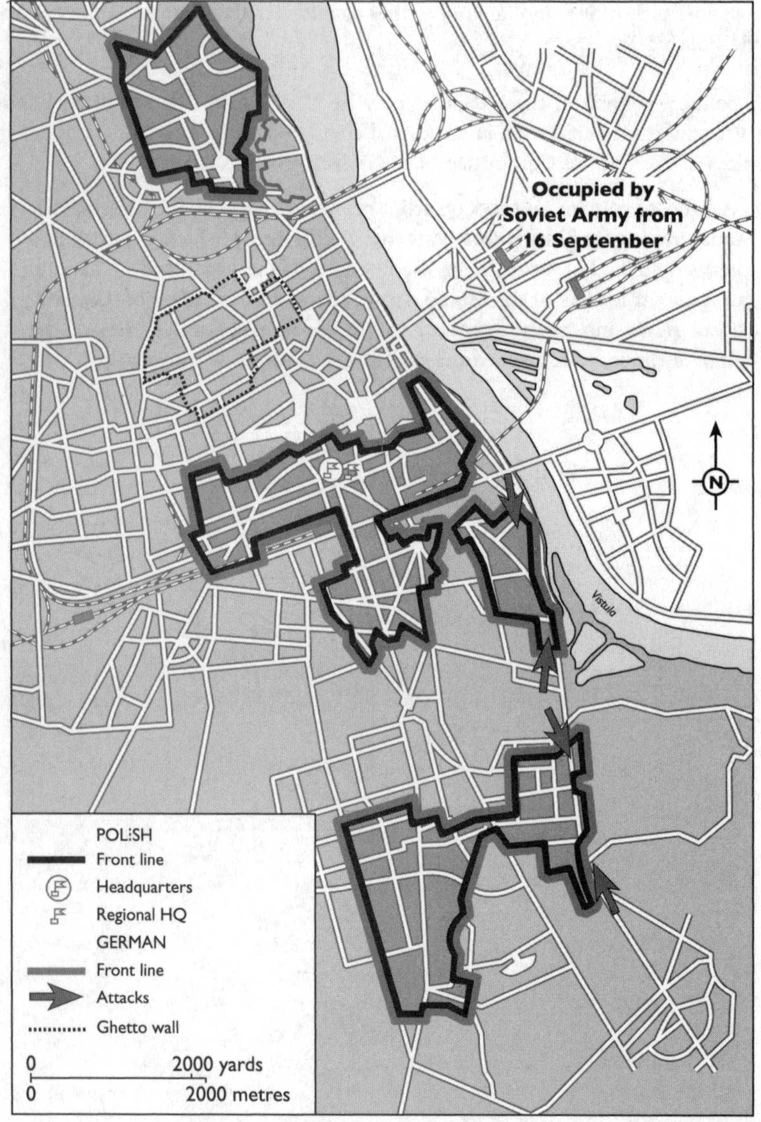

George Orwell
'As I Please' (from *Tribune*, 1 September 1944)

It is not my primary job to discuss the details of contemporary politics, but this week there is something that cries out to be said. Since, it seems, nobody else will do so, I want to protest against the mean and cowardly attitude adopted by the British Press towards the recent rising in Warsaw.

As soon as the news of the rising broke, the *News Chronicle* and kindred papers adopted a markedly disapproving attitude. One was left with the general impression that the Poles deserved to have their bottoms smacked for doing what all the Allied wirelesses had been urging them to do for years past, and that they would not be given and did not deserve to be given any help from outside. A few papers tentatively suggested that arms and supplies might be dropped by the Anglo-Americans, a thousand miles away: no-one, so far as I know, suggested that this might be done by the Russians, perhaps twenty miles away. The *New Statesman*, in its issue of 18 August, even went so far as to doubt whether appreciable help could be given from the air in such circumstances. All or nearly all the papers of the Left were full of blame for the *émigré* London Government which had 'prematurely' ordered its followers to rise when the Red Army was at the gates. This line of thought is adequately set forth in a letter to last week's *Tribune* from Mr G. Barraclough. He makes the following specific charges:

1. The Warsaw rising was 'not a spontaneous popular rising', but was 'begun on orders from the *soi-disant* Polish Government in London'.
2. The order to rise was given 'without consultation with either the British or Soviet Governments', and 'no attempt was made to co-ordinate the rising with Allied action'.
3. The Polish resistance movement is no more united round the London Government than the Greek resistance movement is united round King George of the Hellenes. (This is further emphasised by frequent use of the words *émigré*, *soi-disant*, etc., applied to the London Government.)
4. The London Government precipitated the rising in order to be in possession of Warsaw when the Russians arrived, because in that case 'the bargaining position of the *émigré* Government would be improved'. The London Government, were are told, 'is ready to betray the Polish people's cause to bolster up its own tenure of precarious office', with much more to the same effect.

No shadow of proof is offered for any of these charges, though 1 and 2 are of a kind that could be verified and may well be true. My own guess is that 2 is true and 1 partly true. The third charge makes nonsense of the first two. If the London Government is not accepted by the mass of the people in Warsaw, why should they raise a desperate insurrection on its orders? By blaming Sosnkowski and the rest for the rising, you are automatically assuming that it is to them that the Polish people looks for guidance. This obvious contradiction has been repeated in paper after paper, without, so far as I know, a single person having the honesty to point it out. As for the use of such expressions as *émigré*, it is simply a rhetorical trick. If the London Poles are *émigrés*, so too are the Polish National Committee of Liberation and the 'free' Governments of all the occupied countries. Why does one become an *émigré* by emigrating to London and not by emigrating to Moscow?

Charge No. 4 is morally on a par with the *Osservatore Romano*'s suggestion that the Russians held up their attack on Warsaw in order to get as many Polish resisters as possible killed off. It is the unproved and unprovable assertion of a mere propagandist who has no wish to establish the truth, but is simply out to do as much dirt on his opponent as possible. And all that I have read about this matter in the press – except for some very obscure papers and some remarks in *Tribune*, the *Economist* and the *Evening Standard* – is on the same level as Mr Barraclough's letter.

Now, I know nothing of Polish affairs, and even if I had the power to do so I would not intervene in the struggle between the London Polish Government and the Moscow National Committee of Liberation. What I am concerned with is the attitude of the British intelligentsia, who cannot raise between them one single voice to question what they believe to be Russian policy, no matter what turn it takes, and in this case have had the unheard-of meanness to hint that our bombers ought not to be sent to the aid of our comrades fighting in Warsaw. The enormous majority of left-wingers who swallow the policy put out by the *News Chronicle*, etc., know no more about Poland than I do. All they know is that the Russians object to the London Government and have set up a rival organisation, and so far as they are concerned that settles the matter. If tomorrow Stalin were to drop the Committee of Liberation and recognise the London Government, the whole British intelligentsia would flock after him like a troop of parrots. Their attitude towards Russian foreign policy is not 'Is this policy right or wrong?' but 'This is Russian policy: how can we make it appear right?' And this attitude is defended, if at all, solely on grounds of power.

The Russians are powerful in eastern Europe, we are not: therefore we must not oppose them. This involves the principle, of its nature alien to Socialism, that you must not protest against an evil which you cannot prevent.

I cannot discuss here why it is that the British intelligentsia, with few exceptions, have developed a nationalistic loyalty towards the USSR and are dishonestly uncritical of its policies. In any case, I have discussed it elsewhere. But I would like to close with two considerations which are worth thinking over.

First of all, a message to English left-wing journalists and intellectuals generally: 'Do remember that dishonesty and cowardice always have to be paid for. Don't imagine that for years on end you can make yourself the boot-licking propagandist of the Soviet regime, or any other regime, and then suddenly return to mental decency. Once a whore, always a whore.'

Secondly, a wider consideration. Nothing is more important in the world today than Anglo-Russian friendship and co-operation, and that will not be attained without plain speaking. The best way to come to an agreement with a foreign nation is *not* to refrain from criticising its policies, even to the extent of leaving your own people in the dark about them. At present, so slavish is the attitude of nearly the whole British press that ordinary people have very little idea of what is happening, and may well be committed to policies which they will repudiate in five years' time. In a shadowy sort of way we have been told that the Russian peace terms are a super-Versailles, with partition of Germany, astronomical reparations, and forced labour on a huge scale. These proposals go practically uncriticised, while in much of the left wing press hack writers are even hired to extol them. The result is that the average man has no notion of the enormity of what is proposed. I don't know whether, when the time comes, the Russians will really want to put such terms into operation. My guess is that they won't. But what I do know is that is any such thing were done, the British and probably the Americans would never support it when the passion of war had died down. Any flagrantly unjust peace settlement will simply have the result, as it did last time, of making the British people unreasonably sympathetic with the victims. Anglo-Russian friendship depends upon there being a policy which both countries can agree upon, and this is impossible without free discussion and genuine criticism *now*. There can be no real alliance on the basis of 'Stalin is always right'. The first step towards a real alliance is the dropping of illusions.

Finally, a word to the people who will write me letters about this. May I once again draw attention to the title of this column and remind everyone that the Editors of *Tribune* are not necessarily in agreement with all that I say, but are putting into practice their belief in freedom of speech?

Comment:
Orwell's principled stand is all the more remarkable given the patriotically charged atmosphere of wartime, when serious criticism of Britain's Soviet ally was everywhere inhibited. None of the leading dailies took a similar stand. Apart from the Catholic *Tablet* and various Scottish publications that were influenced by the Polish troops stationed in Scotland, the left-wing *Tribune* was virtually alone in the strength of its concern for Warsaw. On 15 September, it published a letter from the political writer Arthur Koestler, who declared that the Soviet attitude to the Warsaw Rising was 'one of the major infamies of this war which, though committed by different methods, will rank for the future historian on the same ethical level as Lidice.'

(P. M. H. Bell, 'The Warsaw Rising', in *John Bull and the Bear: British public opinion . . . and the Soviet Union, 1941–45* (London, 1990), p. 164.)

Rokossovsky's Occupation of Praga: 10–15 September 1944

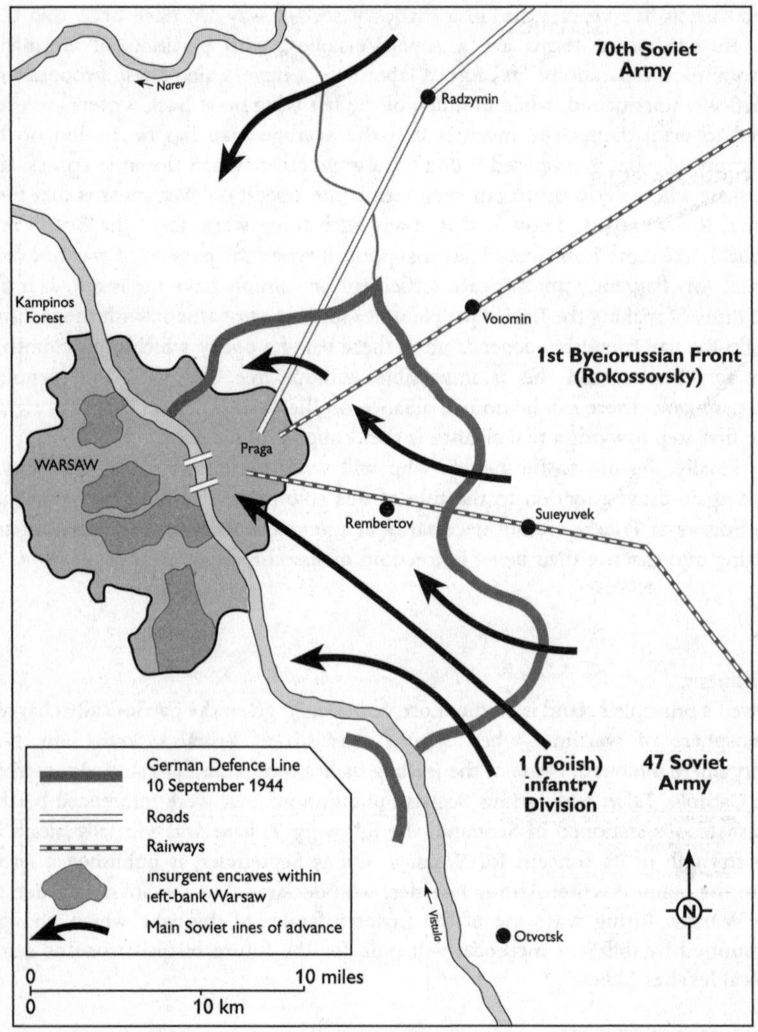

Insurgent Warsaw: Cherniakov Bridgehead, 16–23 September 1944

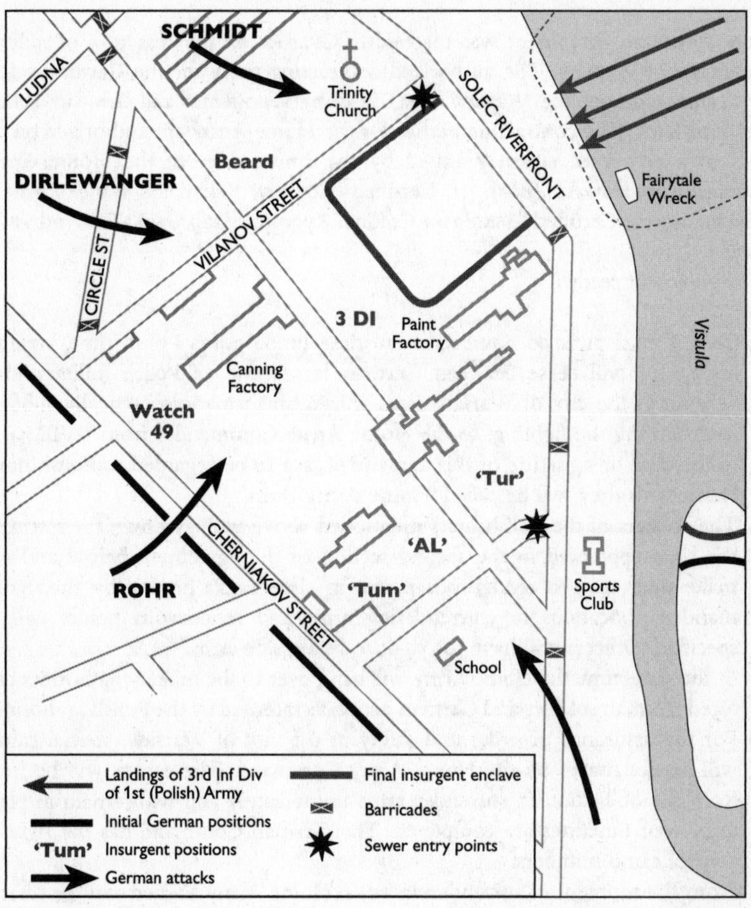

Capitulation Agreement between the German Army and the Home Army[1]

(Translated by Wanda Wyporska)

On 2 X 1944 an agreement was reached in Ożarów on the cessation of military operations in Warsaw. The authorized contracting party for the German side is the Commander of the Warsaw area, *SS-Obergruppenführer und Gen. der Polizei*, von dem Bach. The contracting parties for the Home Army are authorized on the basis of a power of attorney issued by the commander of the Home Army, General Komorowski (Bór): 1) Certified Colonel Kazimierz Iranek-Osmecki (Jarecki), and 2) Certified Lieutenant Colonel Zygmunt Dobrowolski (Zyndram).

The agreement reads:

I.

1) On 2 X 1944 at 20.00 hours German time (21.00 hours Polish time) military operations will cease between German forces and all Polish military units fighting in the city of Warsaw area. All Polish formations tactically subordinated during the fighting, to the Home Army Commander from 1 VIII 44 up to the date of signature of this agreement, are to be regarded as Polish units. Henceforth they will be called 'Home Army Units'.
2) The soldiers of the Polish units mentioned above will lay down their arms at the time appointed in the second section of the agreement below and will make their way to rendezvous points in close ranks headed by their commanders. Locations for surrendering arms and rendezvous points will be specified. Officers will have the right to retain side-arms.
3) At the same time the Home Army will hand over to the military authorities captured German soldiers and German nationals interned by the Polish authorities.
4) For the assurance of order and safety in the city of Warsaw, special camps will be designated by the Home Army Command. The camps will be freed from the obligation to surrender arms immediately and will remain in place until their functions are completed. The German Command has the right to control camp numbers.
5) From the moment of surrendering arms, Home Army soldiers will be treated in accordance with the regulations of the Geneva Convention of 27 VII 1929 concerning the treatment of prisoners-of-war. Home Army soldiers captured in the city of Warsaw during the battle from 1 VIII 1944 will also be subject to the same regulations.
6) The rights of prisoners-of-war will also be assigned to those non-combatants accompanying the Home Army according to article 81 of the Geneva Convention without respect to gender. In particular this concerns female workers at the HQs and in the areas of communications, supplies, aid, information and press services, war correspondents etc.
7) In accordance with the application of the Geneva Convention, officers' ranks issued by the Home Army Command will be recognized. Identity cards with

pseudonyms will be sufficient proof of membership of the Home Army. Real names will be disclosed to the German military authorities. Members of the Home Army who have lost their identity cards will be identified by appointed Home Army commissions. The commissions will be established by the Home Army Command as required. The provision of this article is to be applied to those persons enumerated in article 6.

8) People who in accordance with previous articles are regarded as prisoners-of-war will not be prosecuted for their military or political activities during the battle in Warsaw or in the preceding period, even if they are freed from a prisoner-of-war camp. They will not be prosecuted for the contravention of German legal regulations, in particular for the failure of officers to register, previous escapes from prisoner-of-war camps, illegal visits to Poland etc.
9) No collective responsibility will be born by the civilian population which was in the city of Warsaw during the battle. No one who during the battle was in Warsaw will be prosecuted for carrying out activities within the organization of administrative authorities, justice, security services, public welfare, social and charitable institutions, or for participation in battles and military propaganda. Members of the above-mentioned authorities and organizations will also not be prosecuted for their political activities prior to the Rising.
10) The evacuation of the civilian population of the city of Warsaw requested by the German command will be executed at a time and in a manner which will cause minimal human suffering. They will facilitate the evacuation of items of artistic, cultural and religious value. The German authorities will do their utmost to protect remaining public and private property.

II.

1) As from 7 o'clock German time (8 o'clock Polish time) on 3 X 44, the Home Army Command is obliged to remove its barricades, especially those lying closest to the German lines.
2) The Home Army Command will hand over all German prisoners-of-war, and also where possible German civilian internees, to representatives of the German Armed Forces on 2 X 44, no later than midnight German time (1–3 X Polish time).
3) Should the removal of the barricades not begin on time, the German Command reserves the right to annul this agreement on 3 X 44, beginning at midday German time (13.00 hours Polish time). In that case the annulment will become effective two hours after the delivery of the document voiding the agreement to the Polish lines.
4) The Home Army Command is obliged to leave Warsaw on 4 X 44, in order to surrender weapons, one regiment or possibly 3 battalions leaving from the various divisions. The tanks of these divisions must cross German lines on 4 X 44 at 9 o'clock German time (10 o'clock Polish time).
5) All remaining Home Army units, with the exception of those described in chapter I, page 4 of this agreement, will leave Warsaw to surrender arms on 5 X 44.

6) Home Army units will leave the Polish lines armed but with no ammunition. They will follow the following routes:
   a) from the City Centre South – along Śniadecki Str., 6 August (Schuch Str.) – Dry and Filter Streets.
   b) from the City Centre North – aa) Napoleon Square, Sikorski Avenue (Reich Str.), Grojecka Street (Radomer Str.) bb) (infantry regiment) Grybov, Cool (Eisgruben Str.), and Vola (Litzmannstadt Str.)
7) The following Home Army forces will remain in the city:
   a) to maintain order, 3 infantry companies armed with pistols, sub-machine guns and rifles.
   b) for the protection and transfer of three regimental warehouses of ammunition and equipment, 30 people armed as above.
   c) medical units for the care and transport of the injured and the evacuation of the hospital – disarmed.
8) In agreement with the Chief Medical Officer of the Home Army, the Medical Chief of the German Forces will arrange for the evacuation of injured and ill Home Army soldiers and medical materials. The evacuation of the families of medical personnel will take place in the same way.
9) Home Army soldiers will be identified by red and white armbands or by badges with the Polish eagle, regardless of whether they are uniformed or in civilian clothing.
10) The parties to the agreement affirm that transport, accommodation, guards, and the care of prisoners-of-war remain exclusively under the control of the German Armed Forces (der Deutschen Wehrmacht). The German side guarantees that demands relating to Home Army soldiers will not be entrusted to foreign formations.
11) Women, who, under the terms of chapter 1, point 6 are prisoners-of-war will be placed in camps equivalent to 'oflags' or 'stalags'. The female ranks of sub-commander, commander, senior commander, and inspector will be considered to be officer ranks. At their wish, female prisoners-of-war may be treated in the same way as civilian population of Warsaw.
12) The German military authorities will immediately inform the *Auswärtige Gefangenenhilfe der YMCA* in Sagan about the location and number of those placed in the Home Army soldiers' camps and of persons accompanying them.
13) For technical help in the execution of this agreement *SS-Obergruppenführer und Gen. der Polizei* von dem Bach will have three Polish officers at his disposition.

III.

In the event of contraventions of this agreement the guilty parties will bear full responsibility.

Signatures
Von dem Bach
Iranek, Casimir Colonel
Dobrowolski Lieutenant Colonel

Barricaded Districts of Warsaw

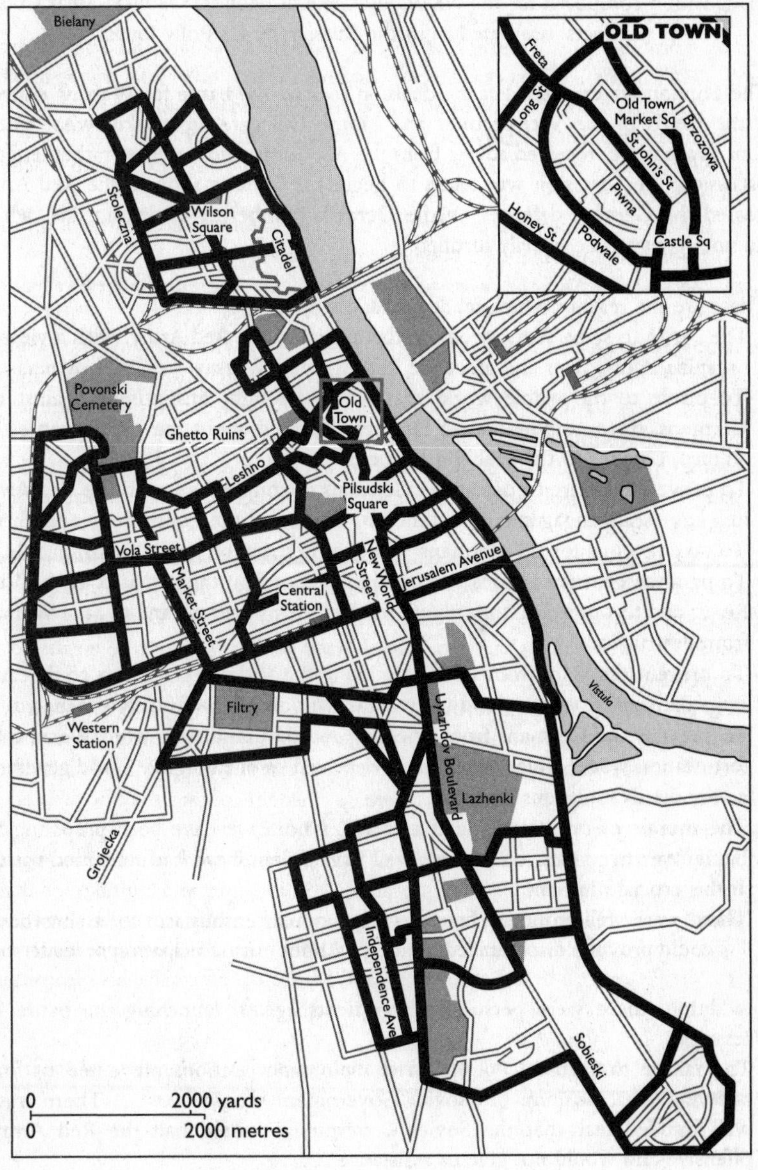

The Warsaw Rising: its causes, course, and capitulation

Deposition composed for the NKVD by General Leopold Okulicki 'Bear Cub'
(Extracts: translated from the Russian by Dr Polly Jones)

'The London government left the decision to start the battle for Warsaw entirely in the hands of the Vice-premier and Home Delegate Iankovskii, who, as the front approached, received advice from the AK Command . . . After rather lengthy discussions, the decision was taken to begin the fight as soon as the Red Army crossed the German defences on the Otvotsk–Rembertov–Radzimin line, which did not appear to be heavily fortified.'

'These are the reasons which made the Battle necessary:

1. The desire to seize Warsaw before the arrival of the Red Army, with a view to organize state power and greet the Red Army as Warsaw's rightful owners.
2. To prove to the whole world that we had fought unstintingly against the Germans, since nothing had so far been reported about our earlier battles (in Vilnius, L'vov, and the Liublino regions).
3. To prove our desire to defeat the Germans in conjunction with the Red Army in a large-scale engagement, and thereby to resolve the Polish–Soviet conflict.
4. To take revenge for the Germans' five-year destruction of the Polish people.
5. To paralyse German actions and communications on the left bank of the Visla River: and through this, to facilitate the Red Army's attack and to save Warsaw from destruction.
6. To prevent the front from stabilizing along the Visla, because this could cause huge damage to Warsaw and to civilians, who might be forcibly evacuated.
7. To prevent the Germans from selecting 100 thousand men from Warsaw for fortification works which would have deprived us of strength . . . and generated a very disadvantageous situation.
8. The morale of our soldiers and civilians, whom we have been preparing for battle over five years, could very well have fallen, if we had remained passive at this crucial moment . . .
9. There were well-grounded fears that the popular enthusiasm for a showdown . . . could provoke disorganized fighting without our participation or leadership.

In addition, there were persuasive arguments *against* launching the battle for Warsaw:

1. The failure to regulate Polish–Soviet diplomatic relations prevented us from knowing what position the Soviet Government would take . . . There was a well-founded fear that the Soviet Government would halt the Red Army's offensive and would not give us assistance . . .
2. The absence of communication with the Red Army command meant that we could not coordinate our actions with them.
3. The fear that the forces stationed in Warsaw were inadequate . . . There were

not enough arms, especially for fighting German tanks, and an absence of artillery, AA equipment, and planes . . . General 'Monter'-Khrustel, the commander of the Rising, announced that he had sufficient resources for only five days' fighting.

4. There were fears about large numbers of civilian casualties and about large-scale damage to the city, especially if the Red Army were to halt its advance.'

Two opinions had formed in the High Command. The first opinion proposed that the rising begin at the moment when the front ranks of the Red Army had crossed into the German bridgehead. The second, more cautious opinion proposed that the rising be launched to coincide with the Red Army's occupation of Praga, the forcing of the Visla, or the encirclement of Warsaw. Despite the huge amount of slanderous propaganda put out by the press of the Provisional Lublin Government, which depicted us as traitors and criminals . . . I admit that I, as a member of the High Command, was the prime initiator and proponent of the first option . . . If anyone has to stand trial, then I should take responsibility for forcing through the decision adopted . . .

Notwithstanding the Provisional Government's arguments, I will continue to maintain that the decision was correct . . . Had they not fought for 63 days in Warsaw, and had not incurred those losses, the Polish people would have emerged from this war with enormous disadvantages for their future independent existence . . . The next generation of Poles, as well as the peoples of other states, would have been right to condemn us as cowards, who lacked courage at the decisive moment.

Within the High Command, General 'Bur' Komarovskii had supported the more cautious option. General 'Gzhegozh'-Pelchinskii supported my view, as did the head of the 2nd department, General 'Geller'-Iranek and the General 'Kutshev' (I do not know his surname). General 'Monter'-Khrustel . . . was convinced that he would be able to seize Warsaw and defend it until the Red Army arrived.

In my opinion, therefore, the failure of the Warsaw Rising must be attributed to political factors rather than to mistakes by the military leadership. If a political mistake was made, the people responsible are the politicians who should have reached a settlement in our relations with the USSR. The commanders and soldiers of the AK, in carrying out the Battle for Warsaw, were only fulfilling their obligations. They could not have acted otherwise.'

B. The progress of the battle

'General fighting began on 1.8.44 at 17:00, although firing had begun earlier in some places. We did not succeed in taking the Germans unawares, because they had been prepared in advance to crush a rising . . . The first attacks only succeeded in taking 20% of the designated objectives. This was a difficult time. The German tanks came out onto the streets and an unplanned battle began . . . Fighting with the tanks went on for another 3–4 days. Our fortifications became stronger, and the soldiers learned how to fight the tanks, using bottles, grenades, handmade flamethrowers and grenade-launchers. The Germans suffered heavier and heavier losses with each passing day (we were able to seize about 10 Tiger tanks in good working order and to use them for our own purposes) ... The supplies and equipment seized from the Germans convinced us that we would be able to continue fighting for a relatively prolonged period.'

'From the first days of fighting, the Germans concentrated their efforts on clearing the roads leading to the Visla bridges ... There were particularly fierce battles round Vol'skaia Street and Erozolimskii Alley. After ten days, the Germans were able to move traffic across the Kerbedz bridge, but they were never able to break through to the Poniatovskii Bridge ... They also broke into Schuh Street, where the Gestapo HQ was located. We were left in total occupation of the City Centre, the Old Town, Zholibodzh and Mokotov.'

'The next phase saw the Germans directing heavy artillery and aerial bombardments onto particular districts ... Their advance on the Old Town began in mid-August and lasted for 20 days ... Every house was fought over. An order found on the body of a dead German battalion commander allowed us to discover that the Germans had directed 12 infantry battalions, masses of artillery, mortars and tanks against this area and had subjected it to a large-scale aerial bombardment. Our remaining forces escaped through the sewers to reach the Zholibodzh district and the City Centre.'

'The Germans then hit the Povisle district and began bombing the city centre's northern perimeter. The defences did not withstand it, through poor leadership and lack of fortifications ... Aerial bombardments spread fire ...'

'Around 10.9.44, the German commander, Von dem Bach, building on these successes, proposed via the Polish Red Cross that negotiations for the surrender of Warsaw should begin. The Germans announced that since England and the USA recognized the Home Army's combatant rights, all AK officers and soldiers would be accepted as prisoners of war in accordance with the Geneva Convention ... General 'Bur'-Komarovskii began these negotiations, at first in order to gain time. But in due course it was discovered that he was taking them seriously. The London government had granted him the authority to resolve the issue. And it took a great effort to break the negotiations off ... But the rumble of Soviet artillery and the appearance of Soviet bombers ... increased our strength for further combat.'

'As the Red Army approached Praga, the Germans made for Cherniakuv, with the objective of taking over the Visla shore and preventing Red Army detachments from joining up with Warsaw. The fighting lasted several days. One of the battalions involved was part of Berling's Polish Army. It was not the least prepared for street-fighting; and, unfortunately, no further reinforcements arrived. Owing to the absence of observers, Soviet artillery support turned out to be insufficient.'

'After the fall of Cherniakov and of Mokotov, the Germans concentrated significant cavalry and armoured tank forces on the approaches to Zholibodzh. As far as I recall, around 30.9.44, the fighting in the Zholibodzh district was stopped by Bur-Komarovskii . . . Negotiations began for a second time with General von dem Bach on 30.9.44 and immediately led to the fall of Zholibodzh, which was in a hopeless position.'

Attempts to establish links with the Red Army

'1. At the beginning of the rising (I do not recall which date), the Red Army captain Kalugin came to see General 'Monter'-Khrustel . . . On the 5th or 6th of August, he transmitted a dispatch addressed to Marshal Stalin via our radio-station. He also assured us that he could contact Marshal Rokossovskii. As proof he showed us a letter from Rokossovskii, which, turned out to be a forgery. Captain Kalugin had been tricked by a blackmailer . . .
2. On 14.8.44, General 'Monter'-Khrustel sent a radiotelegram via London to Marshal Rokossovskii, in which he . . . asked for assistance. As far as I know, he did not receive a reply.
3. Immediately after the Red Army's occupation of Praga, an officer was sent across the Visla with all the information necessary to establish radio communications with Rokossovskii's HQ. Through this, around 20.9.44, we received a radiotelegram from the Marshal, in which he asked us to say how we thought the Red Army's entry into Warsaw should be organized, and how we could co-operate. Our demands and opinions were sent back immediately via radiotelegram, but we received no answer.
4. Independently of the measures taken by us, Marshal Rokossovskii sent in two of his own officers by parachute. Their radio-station was damaged by the jump, but we quickly managed to fix it. One of these officers was soon killed, and the other recrossed the Visla.
5. Seeing our forces were suffering from a near-complete absence of provisions, on 26 or 27 September, we sent another telegram to Marshal Rokossovskii, indicating that we could only hold out until 30.9.44. This radiotelegram also received no reply.'

'Relations between the Kraiovaia Army (Home Army) and the Liudova Army and the PPR (Polish Workers Party) were in my opinion good, despite the fact that the Liudova army (AL) and the Korpus Bespechenstva (KB) were extremely weak. (They constituted about 5% of those fighting.) The Polish Liudova Army (PAL) did not post a single platoon.

The accusations directed against the Kraiovia Army of fascism and of crushing elements subject to the provisional Liublino government does not correspond to reality. On the contrary, we did everything possible to save these elements from German repressions.'

C. The surrender of Warsaw

'The reasons for the capitulation, which was decided on by Government Delegate Iankovskii during the night of 30.9.44, were:

1. The absolute absence of food provisions. There were already incidents when soldiers had tried to take food from civilians by force . . .
2. The near-total absence of water. Disturbances were started to occur round the sources of water . . .
3. The curtailment of the Red Army's advance. After the fall of Mokotov and Zholibodzh, the situation had become all but hopeless.
4. We had been unable to organize a voluntary evacuation of civilians.'

'Reasons for the imprisonment of large numbers of officers, who were necessary for further fighting with the Germans:
1. Fatigue from having worked in secret for five years . . .
2. The fear that the Germans would easily catch everyone after the capitulation.
3. The conviction that Germany would soon fall and that, as a consequence, it would be possible to break through to the Polish Army abroad and together with them to return to Poland.
4. Fear of the Soviet authorities. It was well known that arrests had been carried out in Vilnius, Lvov and Liublino provinces.
5. An incorrect understanding of the idea of honour in fulfilling the conditions of surrender agreed with the Germans.'

'Over 12,000 officers and soldiers were taken prisoner . . . A much smaller number, I guess around 3–5 thousand, went into hiding with the civilian population. Each did as his conscience dictated.

During the night of the 30.9.44, I asked 'Bur'-Komarovskii for his ideas on the continuation of fighting with the Germans and on its leadership. I told him I was not tired, and that I was ready. After a prolonged discussion, he agreed with me, transferring all his powers to me and informing London. That same night, I said farewell to him and left HQ, without speaking to anyone else.'

'The further leadership of the Home Army

Given the conditions imposed by Bur-Komarovskii, I could not take anyone from HQ with me. On 3.10.44, I left Warsaw in the company of a woman and a child and two other officers whom I had met on the street . . . I ended up in the camp at Prushkov. On 4.10.44, we were loaded onto wagons and taken in the direction of Krakow where we were going to be sorted . . . As we passed Kyeltsy, I jumped from the wagon and with the help of a doctor of my acquaintance, who worked in the children's hospital, I contacted the chief of the staff of the Keltsy region, Lt.Col. 'Eliton' (I don't know his surname). I then sent a radiogram to London . . . requesting that an order be issued for regional commanders to obey me. After several days, I received an answer from General Kopanskii stating that the matter had been attended to . . .'

April 1945

GARF, Moscow. No file number supplied.

Polish People's Republic 1945–1989 showing 'Recovered Territories'

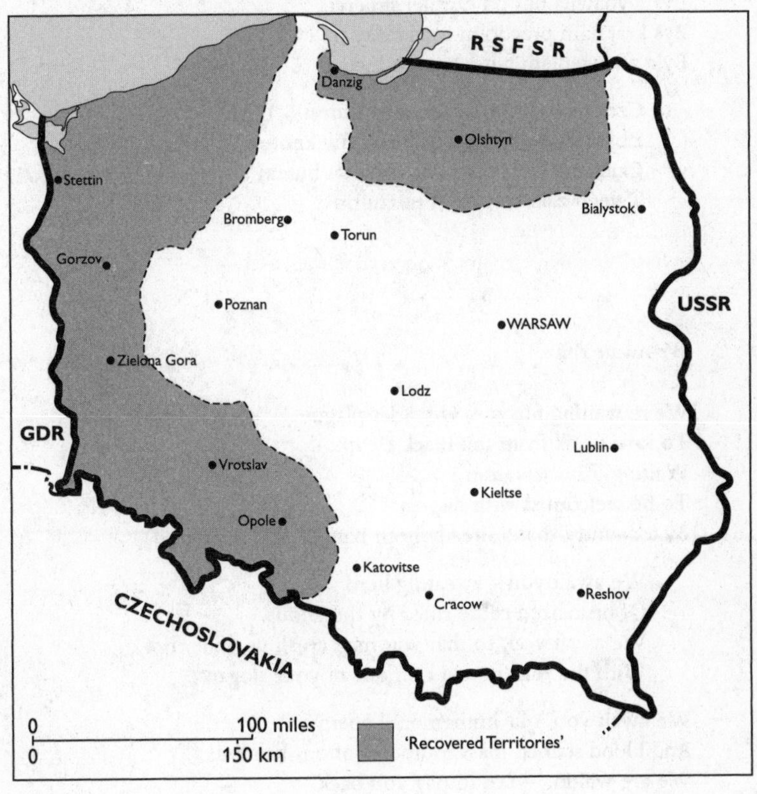

'Czekamy Ciebie'

Czekamy ciebie czerwona zarazo
Byś wybawiła nas od czarnej śmierci,
Byś kraj nam przedtym rozdarłszy na ćwierci
Była zbawieniem witanym z odrazą

Czekamy ciebie – ty potęgo tłumu
Zbydlęcałego pod twych rządów knutem
Czekamy ciebie byś nas zgniotła butem
Twego zalewu i haseł poszumu.

.....

We Await You

We're waiting for you, O scarlet plague
To save us all from the Black Death:
Waiting for a salvation
To be welcomed with disgust
By a country that's already been hanged and quartered.

We await you – sweating herd
Of brutalized cattle ruled by the knout.
We await you, so that you may crush us underfoot
With the torrent and clamour of your slogans.

We await you, our immemorial enemy
And blood-stained mass murderer of our brothers.
We are waiting – not to pay you back
But to greet you with bread and salt at our ruined threshold.

If only you knew – O hated saviour
How we wish you'd perish
How we shake your hand from impotence,
Seeking aid from a criminal.

If only you knew how much it hurts,
For us, the children of a free and sacred country
To fix the shackles of your cursed mercy
That reeks of the yoke of ancient slavery.

If only you knew, O hangman of our forebears
And grim legend of Siberian jails
How everyone here will curse your kindness –
And all of us Slavs, all your kin.

Your victorious scarlet army
Has stopped beneath Warsaw's fiery clouds
And like a vulture with a carcass sates itself
On a handful of madmen, who are dying on the ruins.

We await you, not for us soldiers
Or for our thousands of wounded.
But because there are children here, and nursing mothers
And disease is spreading through their cellars.

. . . .

We are waiting whilst you delay and delay.
We know very well that you fear us.
That you'd prefer us to be killed.
So you are waiting, too, – for our extermination.

. . . .

Yet no illusions. From our graves
A new, triumphant Poland will be born.
And it won't be you, O scarlet tyrant
O depraved power, that rules the land.

Joe from Parasol
(Józef Szczepański)
'Ziutek'

(translated by Norman Davies)

'My Pierwsza Brygada'

'Legiony to – żołnierska buta;
Legiony to – ofiarny stos;
Legiony to – żebracka nuta;
Legiony to – straceńców los,
My Pierwsza Brygada,
Strzelecka Gromada,
Na Stos, rzuciliśmy,
Swój życia los,
Na stos, na stos.'

'The Legions stand for a soldier's pride.
The Legions stand for a martyr's fate.
The Legions stand for a beggar's song.
The Legions stand for a desperado's death.
We are the First Brigade.
A regiment of rapid fire.
We've put our lives at stake.
We've willed our fate.
We've cast ourselves on the pyre.'

The hymn of Pilsudski's Legions, 1914–17
Quoted in Norman Davies, *Heart of Europe*
(Oxford, 2001), p. 211.

Guide to Modified Names Used in the Text

This list summarizes the modified forms of names that are used in the text, together with the Polish originals. It is in no sense comprehensive either as a guide to the pseudonyms circulating during the Warsaw Rising – of which there were c. 50,000 – or as a gazeteer to wartime Warsaw. Those seeking more comprehensive information are directed to the indices of Andrzej Kunert's three-volume *Słownik biograficzny konspiracji Warszawskiej 1939–44* (Warsaw, 1991) and Władysław Bartoszewski's *Dni walczący stolicy* (Warsaw, 1984). This list consists of five parts: I Pseudonyms, II Military Formations and Networks, III Personal Names, IV Geographical Names, and V Comparative Tables of Ranks.

(Compiled by Wanda Wyporska)

I Pseudonyms

In the text	Original	Name
Agaton	Agaton	Stanisław Jankowski, Capt.
Alder	Olszyna	Tadeusz Wiwatowski
Anchor	Kotwica	Maciej Kalenkiewicz
André	Andrzej	Antoni Żurowski, Maj.
André	Andrzej	Józef Rybicki, Capt.
Anode	Anoda	Jan Rodowicz
Anthony		see Heller
Arrow	Grot	Stefan Rowecki, Gen.
Aurochs	Tur	Stefan Tomków, Col.
Axe	Topór	Tadeusz Gajcy, Cadet Officer
Badger	Borsuk	see Maurycy
Bashka	Baśka	Barbara Matysówna
Bashka	Baśka	Barbara Szerle
Basil	Bazyli	Kazimierz Pużak
Bear Cub	Niedźwiadek	Leopold Okulicki, Gen.
Black Vitold	Witold Czarny	Witold Morawski, Lt.
Boguslav	Bogusławski	Franciszek Herman, Lt.Col.
Boor	Bór, Lawina	Tadeusz Komorowski, Gen.
Borodich	Borodzicz	Aleksander Gieysztor, Prof.
Bullet	Kula	
Butterfly	Motyl	Zbigniew Ścibor-Rylski, Capt.
Calvin	Kalwin	
Cat	Cat	Stanisław Mackiewicz
Celt	Celt	Tadeusz Chciuk
Chairman	Prezes	Jan Rzepecki
Charles	Karol	Henryk Petryka, Sgt.
Charles	Karol	Józef Rokicki, Lt.Col.

In the text	Original	Name
Christopher	Krzysztof	Krzysztof Kamil Baczyński
Coracle	Korab	
Crag-Crusher	Waligóra	
Crow	Korwin	Edward Matuszyński, Krukowski, Weloński
Daniel	Daniel	Stanisław Kamiński, Lt.Col.
Danuta		Krystyna Krahelska
Ed	Ed	Zbigniew Edward Mróz
Ela	Ela	Elżbieta Ostrowska
Elephant	Słoń	Jerzy Szaniawski
Falcon	Sokół	Władyslaw Olszowski, Capt.
Father	Ojciec	
Feeder	Żywiciel	Mieczysław Roman Niedzielski
Felix	Szczęsny	Michał Panasik, Lt.
Flash	Błysk	
Flight	Lot	Bronisław Pietraszewicz, Cpl.
Forester	Leśnik	Jan Szypowski, Lt.Col.
George	Jerzy	Ryszard Białous, Capt.
George	Jerzy	Szymon Zaremba
Girder	Rygiel	Kazimierz Pogorzelski, Lt.
Godziemba	Godziemba	Kazimierz Sosnkowski, Gen.: C-in-C
Gregory	Grzegorz	Tadeusz Pełczyński, Gen.
Griffin	Gryf	
Hammer	Młotek	Wacław Chojna
Hanka	Hanka	Danuta Wiśniowiecka-Wardle, née Frydrych
Hard Tommy	Twardy Tomasz	Leszek Kowalewski
Hawk	Jastrzębiec	
Heller	Heller	Kazimierz Iranek-Osmecki, Col.
Hubal	Hubal	Henryk Dobrzański, Maj.
Iron	Iron	Felicjan Majorkiewicz, Lt.Col.
Julius	Juliusz	Bolesław Taborski, Cpl.
Karski	Jan Karski	Jan Kozielewski
King	Król	
Kite	Kania	Tadeusz Żenczykowski
Krystynek	Krystynek	Tadeusz Kossakowski, Gen.
Laundry	Pralnia	
Leliva	Leliwa	Henryk Roycewicz, Capt.
Leslie	Leszek	Leszek Wójcicki, Cadet Officer
Light	Światło	Józef Fleischfarb, Lt.
Lightning	Błyskawica	
Little John	Mały	Janusz Stolarski
Louis	Ludwik	Zenon Kliszko

In the text	Original	Name
Maria Kovalska	Maria Kowalska	Maria Gatęska
Mark	Marek S	Zdzisław Sierpiński
Marten	Kuna	Aleksander Strzałkowski
Maslavski	Masławski	
Maurice	Maurycy	Kazimierz Moczarski, Lt. 'Rafał', 'Borsuk', 'Stern'
Mick		Stanisław Mikołajczyk, Premier
Monter	Monter	Antoni Chruściel, Gen.
Nile	Nil	Emil Fieldorf, Maj. Gen.
Nora	Nora	see Poppy
Novak	Jan Nowak	Zdzisław Jeziorański
Oliva	Oliwa	Jan Wojciech Kiwerski
Paul	Paweł (Jasienica)	Lech Beynar
Pepi	Pepi	Adam Borkiewicz, Col.
Peterkin	Piotruś	Jerzy Kłoczowski, Prof.
Plough	Pług	Adam Borys, Maj.
Poplar	Topola	
Poppy	Mak	Czesław Pieniak, Lt.
Power	Moc	
Radoslav	Radosław	Jan Mazurkiewicz, Col.
Radvan	Radwan	Edward Pfeiffer, Col.
Rake	Grabie	Jan Józef Lipski
Raven	Kruk	Tadeusz Kruk-Strzelecki
Roar	Ryk	
Roman	Roman	Witold Pilecki, Capt.
Sable	Soból	J. S. Jankowski, Chief Delegate
Sablevski	Sablewski	Bolesław Piasecki
Sadovski	Sadowski	Stanisław Edward Grodzki
Salamander	Salamandra	Józef Retinger
Shenkevich	Sienkiewicz	Olgierd Ostakiewicz-Rudnicki
Stag	Jeleń	Władysław Nowakowski, Maj.
Stan	Stasinek	Stanisław Sosabowski
Stefan, Father		Stefan Wyszyński, Father
Tabor	Tabor	Stanisław Tatar, Gen.
Teofil	Teofil	Władysław Bartoszewski
Thomas	Tomasz	Tomasz Arciszewski, Premier
Thunderbolt	Piorun	Franciszek Malik, Capt.
Tiger	Tygrys	Tadeusz Kroński, Prof.
Tony Flamethrower	Antek Rozpylacz	Antoni Godlewski, Cpl.
Vachnov	Wachnowski	Karol Ziemski, Col.
Vatsek	Wacek	Wacław Micuta, Capt.
Virski	Wirski	
Vitold	Witold	Kazimierz Nowacki, Capt.

In the text	Original	Name
Vitold	Witold	Tadeusz Runge, Maj.
Vola	Wola	Bernard Romanowski, Maj.
Vyeslav	Wiesław	Władysław Gomułka
Whip	Bat	
White	Biały	
Wildcat	Żbik	
Wolf	Wilk	Aleksander Krzyżanowski, Col.
Worm	Robak	Tadeusz Pełczyński, Gen. 'Gregory'
Yagiello	Jagiełło	Zbigniew Pełczyński, L/Cpl
Yan K.	Jan K.	see Karski
Yanka	Janka	
Yo-Yo	Jo-Jo	
Yur	Jur	Jerzy Lerski
Zo	Zo	Elżbieta Zawacka
Zyndram	Zyndram	Zygmunt Dobrowolski, Lt.Col.

II Military Formations and Networks

In the text	Original
Anchor	Kotwica
Arcadius	Arkadiusz
Beard 53	Broda 53
Boar	Dzik
Brooke	Ruczaj
Broom	Miotła
College A	Kolegium A
Columbus	Kolumb
Crag-Crusher	Waligóra
Cyprus	Cypr
Discus	Dysk
Fist	Pięść
Forester	Leśnik
Horn	Róg
K-Div.	Kedyw
Kilinski	Kiliński
Laundry	Pralnia
Lightning	Piorun
Pawn	Pionek
Pawnshop	Lombard
Pegasus	Pegaz
Radoslav	Radosław
Shenkevich	Sienkiewicz

In the text	Original
Stag	Jeleń
Valiant I/II	Chrobry I/II
Vigry	Wigry
Watch 49	Czata 49
Zhegota	Żegota

III Personal names
(ranks and titles precede initials, first names and surnames)

Abraham G.	Abraham Gancwajch
Abram B.	Abram Bursztyn
Adam B.	Adam Borkiewicz
Adam M.	Adam Mickiewicz
Adam R.	Adam Rotrubin
Adam S.	Adam Szczypiorski
Adam W.	Adam Ważyk
Air Commodore R.	Ludomił Rajski
Alex T.	Olek Tyrawski
Anatole F.	Anatol Fejgin
André F.	Andrzej Findeisen
André P.	Andrzej Pomian
André Pan.	Andrzej Panufnik
André W.	Andrzej Wajda
Anka G.	Anka Getsów
Anna D.	Anna Duracz
Antony S.	Antoni Słonimski
Arthur G.	Artur Goldfeder
Barbara D.	Barbara Drapczyńska
Benjamin W.	Benjamin Wajsblech
Bogdan C.	Bogdan Czeszko
Boleslas B.	Bolesław Bierut
Boleslas P.	Bolesław Piasecki
Capt. K.	Kalinowski
Capt. M.	Wacław Micuta
Capt. P	Antoni Pośpieszalski
Cardinal W., Father 'Stefan'	Stefan Wyszyński, Cardinal
Casimir B.	Kazimierz Brandys
Casimir K.	Kazimierz Kąkol
Casimir M.	Kazimierz Marczewski
Casimir Mo.	Kazimierz Moczarski
Casimir Pużak, 'Basil'	Kazimierz Pużak
Casimir W.	Prof. Kazimierz Wyka

In the text	Original
Cheslav L.	Czesław Łapicki, Maj.
Chief of Staff Gen. Ko.	Stanisław Kopański
Christine P.	Krystyna Paderewska
Christopher K. B. 'Christophe'	Krzysztof Kamil Baczyński, 'Krzysztof'
C.-in-C., Gen. Casimir S.	Kazimierz Sosnkowski 'Godziemba'
C.-in-C. Rola-Z.	Michał Rola-Żymierski
Col. A.	Col. Iranek-Osmecki, 'Heller', 'Iranek'
Col. K.	Aleksander Krzyżanowski
Col. M.	Leon Mitkiewicz
Col. R.	Stanisław Radkiewicz
Col. S.	Julian Skokowski
Comrade K., 'Louis',	Zenon Kliszko
Count R.	Hrabia Edward Raczyński
Dr Adam B.	Adam Bielawski, Dr
Dr K.	Stefan Kaczorowski, Dr
Dr Max	Zbigniew Dworak, Dr
Dr P.	Ryszard Petzel, Dr
Dr Yan C.	Jan Ciechanowski, Dr
Emanuel R.	Emanuel Ringelblum
Emilia P.	Emilia Plater
Father K.	Kisiel
Father Ka.	Wacław Karłowicz
Father Ki.	Tadeusz Kirschke
Father Ko.	Kosibowicz
Father L.	Lubiński
Father M.	Madaliński
Father R.	Rosiak
Father S.	Sawicki
Father Stefan	Father Stefan Wyszyński
Father T.	Trzeciak
Father W.	Wiacek
Father Wi.	Henryk Wilczyński
Father Wr.	Wróblewski
Father Z.	Jan Zieja
Ferdinand O.	Ferdynand Antoni Ossendowski
Gaston P.	Gaston Palewski
Gen. M.	Stanisław Maczek
Gen. Mo.	Izydor Modelski
George A.	Jerzy Andrzejewski
George B.	Jerzy Borejsza (Goldberg)
George K.	Jerzy Kirchmayer
George Kl. 'Peterkin'	Prof. Jerzy Kłoczowski 'Piotruś'
George Z., Lt.	Jerzy Zubrzycki

In the text	Original
Helena W., Lt. Col.	Helena Wolińska (Brus)
Henry S.	Henryk Strasburger
Herr Mocharski	Kazimierz Moczarski
Hilary M.	Hilary Minc
Ignatius B.	Ignacy Bursztyn
Igo S.	Igo Sym
Jacob B.	Jakub Berman
Jane M.	Janeczka Michalska
Joseph G., Dr	Józef Garliński, Dr
Joseph Pilsudski	Józef Piłsudski
Joseph R.	Józef Retinger
Joseph W.	Józef Wybicki
Josephine K.	Józefa Kęszycka
Jules P.	Julek Piątkowska
Julia 'Luna' B.	Julia Brystygier
Julian B.	Julian Biodrowski
Julian T.	Julian Tuwim
Ladislas B. 'Teofil'	Władysław Bartoszewski
Ladislas S.	Władysław Szpilman
Ladislas S.-G.	Władysław Gizbert-Studnicki
Ladislas Sl.	Władysław Śliwiński
Lech K.	Lech Kaczyński
Lily W.	Lilia Wantowska
Louis K.	Ludwik Kalkstein
Louise Z.	Ludwika Zacharasiewicz
Lt. Z.	Janusz Zapolski
Lt. Za	Zaborowski
Lt. Col. Z.	Lucjan Załęski
Luke C.	Łukasz Ciepliński
Lupashka	Łupaszka
Madame R.	Rubachova
Maj. La.	Stanisław Łatyszonek
Marcel R.	Marcel Ranicki, Reich, Reich-Ranicki
Maria D.	Maria Dąbrowska
Mark E.	Marek Edelman
Marysha A.	Marysia Ajzenstatt
Marysha O.	Marysia Okońska
Matthew Ratay	Mateusz Rataj
Mechislav Kaminski	Mieczysław Kamiński
Mechislav M. 'Mietek'	Mieczysław Moczar
Miron B.	Miron Białoszewski
Mordechai A.	Mordechai Anielewicz
Novicki	Stanisław Nowicki

In the text	Original
Olgierd S.	Olgierd Skirgiełło
Paul J.	Paweł Jasienica (Lech Beynar)
Prince R.	Janusz Radziwiłł
Prof. H.	Marceli Handelsman, Prof.
Prof. Janush Z.	Janusz Zawodny, Prof.
Prof. K.	Jan Kossakowski, Prof.
Prof. L.	Edward Loth, Lt. Col. Prof.
Prof. Yan B.	Jan Bełza
Richard	Ryszard
Roman D.	Roman Dmowski
Roman M.	Roman Mularczyk (Bratny)
Roman R.	Roman Romkowski (Grynszpan)
Romanovski	Romanowski
Sigismund Berling	Zygmunt Berling, Gen.
Sister Maria-Leonia G.	Maria-Leonia Graczyk
Sophie K.	Zofia Kojro
Stan K.	Stanisław Krysiak
Stanislas D.	Stanisław Dziewulski
Stanislas G.	Stanisław Grabski
Stanislas M.	Stanisław Mikołajczyk
Stanislas N.	Stanisław Nowak
Stanislas R., Col.	Stanisław Radkiewicz, Col.
Stanislas So.	Stanisław Sokołowski
Stanislas Z.	Stanisław Zieleniewski
Stefan A.	Stefan Arski
Stefan L.	Stefan Litauer
Stefan S.	Stefan Starzyński
Thaddeus B.	Tadeusz Borowski
Thaddeus R.	Tadeusz Romer
Ubish 'Vik'	Mieczysław Ubysz, 'Wik'
Vanda P.	Wanda Piłsudska
Vanda W.	Wanda Wasilewska
Vatslava L.	Wacława Lutoborska
Vera G.	Vera Gran
Vitold L.	Witold Lutosławski
Vladimir D.	Włodzimierz Denkowski
Voychek R.	Wojciech Rostafiński
Wenceslas	Prof. Wieńczysław Wagner
Yadviga	Jadwiga
Yagiello	Jagiełło
Yagiellonian dynasty	Dynastia Jagiellonów
Yan D.	Jan Dangel
Yan H., Judge	Jan Hryćkowiak

In the text	Original
Yan K.	Jan Kozielewski, see 'Karski'
Yan K.P.	Jan Krok-Paszkowski
Yan Ko.	Jan Kott
Yan M.	Jan Malinowski
Yanek	Janek
Yanka	Janka
Yanush K., Dr	Janusz Korczak, Dr
Yashiński	Zbigniew Jasiński
Yatsek R.	Jacek Różański (Goldberg)
Zbig. B.	Zbigniew Błażyński
Zbig. H.	Zbigniew Herbert
Zbig. M. 'Ed'	Zbigniew Edward Mróz
Zoshka	Zośka

IV Geographical Names

Alexandrov	Aleksandrów
Augustov	Augustów
Bagatelle Street	Ulica Bagatela
Bank Square	Plac Bankowy
Barichka Chapel	Kaplica Baryczków
Basket Street	Ulica Koszykowa
Belzec	Bełżec
Biala Podlaska	Biała Podlaska
Bialovyezha	Białowieża
Bialystok	Białystok
Biebra, River	Biebrza
Bogushkov	Boguszków
Bohnia	Bochnia
Bonifrater Street	Ulica Bonifraterska
Borislav	Borysław
Brest-Litovsk	Brześć-Litewski
Bright Street	Ulica Jasna
Bromberg	Bydgoszcz
Canon Street	Ulica Kanonia
Castle Square	Plac Zamkowy
Chenstohova	Częstochowa
Cherniakov	Czerniaków
Cherniakov Street	Ulica Czerniakowska
Chetvertinski Palace	Pałac Czetwertyńskich
Chopin Street	Ulica Chopina
Circle Street	Ulica Okrąg

In the text	Original
Citadel	Cytadela
City Centre	Śródmieście
Commodity Street	Ulica Towarowa
Conflict Street	Ulica Rozbrat
Constitution Square	Plac Konstytucji
Cool Street	Ulica Chłodna
Cooper Street	Ulica Bednarska
Cracow Fauborg	Krakowskie Przedmieście
Crane Street	Ulica Żurawia
Crooked Circle Street	Krzywe Koło
Crossroads Square	Plac Na Rozdrożu
Dakovski Café	Dakowski
Danzig	Gdańsk
Danzig Station	Dworzec Gdański
Dean Street	Ulica Dziekania
Diamond Street	Ulica Karowa
Dombrova	Dąbrowa
Domestic Economic Bank	Bank Krajowy Gospodarczy
Drohobich	Drohobycz
Duck Street	Ulica Kacza
Duck's Mud	Kacze Błoto
Elector Street	Ulica Elektoralna
Filter Street	Ulica Filtrowa
Flora Street	Ulica Flory
French Street	Ulica Francuska
Garvolin	Garwolin
Gerardov	Żyrardów
Golashevo	Gołaszewo
Golden Street	Ulica Złota
Good Street	Ulica Dobra
Goose Farm	Gęsiówka
Goose Street	Ulica Gęsia
Gorzov	Gorzów
Gotslav	Gocław
Grabov	Grabów
Great Poland	Wielkopolska
Grohov	Grochów
Grojecka	Grójec
Graudenz	Grudziądz
Grünberg	Zielona Góra
Grybov	Grzybów
Hay Street	Ulica Sienna
Helm	Chełm

In the text	Original
Herb Street	Ulica Zielna
Holy Cross Mountains	Góry Świętokrzyskie
Honey Street	Ulica Miodowa
Hospital of St Stanislas Kostka	Szpital Świętego Stanisława Kostki
Hospital Street	Ulica Szpitalna
Hrubieshov	Hrubieszów
Independence Boulevard	Aleje Niepodległości
Inovrotslav	Inowrocław
Iron Gate Square	Plac Żelaznej Bramy
Iron Street	Ulica Żelazna
Jerusalem Avenue	Aleje Jerozolimskie
Jolibord	Żoliborz
Kabaty Woods	Lasy Kabackie
Karvitse	Karwice
Katovitse	Katowice
Katyn	Katyń
Kerbeds Bridge	Most Kierbedzia
Khatyn	Chatyń
Kieltse	Kielce
Kilinski Square	Plac Kilińskiego
Kingdom of Poland	Korona
Kolbiel	Kołbiel
Komorov	Komorów
Kościuszko Embankment	Wybrzeże Kościuszkowskie
Krashinski Square	Plac Krasińskich
Kuyavy	Kujawy
Laski	Laski
Lazhenki	Łazienki
Leshno Street	Ulica Leszno
Little Poland	Małopolska
Lodz	Łódź
Lomzha	Łomża
Long Street	Ulica Długa
Low Street	Ulica Niska
Ludna Street	Ulica Ludna
Lukov	Łuków
Lutsk	Łuck
Lvuv	Lwów, L'viv, Lvov, Lemberg
Lvuv Street	Ulica Lwowska
Magnushev	Magnuszew
Marian Street	Ulica Mariańska
Market Street	Ulica Targowa
Marshal Foch Street	Ulica Focha

In the text	Original
Marshal Street	Ulica Marszałkowska
Matchkovo	Maczkowo
Mazovia	Mazowsze
Milanovek	Milanówek
Mirov Hall	Hala Mirowska
Mitskevich Street	Ulica Mickiewicza
Mnishev	Mniszew
Mokotov	Mokotów
Mokotov Fields	Pole Mokotowskie
Mokotov Square	Plac Mokotowski
Moniushko Street	Ulica Moniuszki
Moon Street	Ulica Księżycowa
Muranov	Muranów
Napoleon Square	Plac Napoleona
Narev, River	Narew
Narutovich Square	Plac Narutowicza
Natolin Street	Ulica Natolińska
Neisse, River	Nysa
New Town	Nowe Miasto
New Town Street	Ulica Nowomiejska
New World Street	Nowy Świat
Novogrodek	Nowogródek
Oder, River	Odra
Ohota	Ochota
Okentche	Okęcie
Okuniev	Okuniew
Old Street	Ulica Stara
Old Town	Stare Miasto, Starówka
Old Town Square	Rynek Starego Miasta
Olshtyn	Olsztyn
Opochno	Opoczno
Otvotsk	Otwock
Ozharov	Ożarów
Paviak Jail	Pawiak
Peacock Street	Ulica Pawia
Pilitsa, River	Pilica
Pilsudski Square	Plac Piłsudskiego
Pius XI Street	Ulica Piusa
Plaszov	Płaszów, Plaschau
Pleasant Street	Ulica Miła
Plotsk	Płock
Pomerania	Pomorze
Poniatovski Bridge	Most Poniatowskiego

In the text	Original
Pototska Street	Ulica Potocka
Povonski	Powązki
Poznan	Poznań
Prushkov	Pruszków
Pulavy Street	Ulica Puławska
Pulko	Pólko
Rakoviets	Rakowiec
Rakoviets Street	Ulica Rakowiecka
Rashin	Raszyn
Raven Street	Ulica Krucza
Rembertov	Rembertów
Reshov	Rzeszów
Riverside District	Powiśle
Royal Castle	Zamek Królewski
Ruvno	Równo
St John's Cathedral	Katedra Świętego Jana
St John Street	Ulica Świętojańska
Saxon Garden	Ogród Saski
Saxon Square	Plac Saski
Scarishev Park	Park Skaryszewski
Schuch Avenue	Aleja Szucha
Shekierki	Siekierki
Sheltse	Sielce
Sheradz	Sieradz
Sherakov	Sieraków
Shieltse	Siedlce
Shmilovitse	Śmiłowice
Shuster Street	Ulica Szustra
Sigismund Column	Kolumna Zygmunta
Silesia	Śląsk
Skiernievitse	Skierniewice
Skolimov Street	Ulica Skolimowska
Slippery Street	Ulica Śliska
Sluzhev	Służew
Sluzheviets	Służewiec
Smolensk Street	Ulica Smoleńska
Sobibor	Sobibór
Sohachev-Vlohy	Sochaczew-Włochy
Solec Street	Ulica Solec
Stanislavov	Stanisławów
Starch Street	Ulica Krochmalna
Stavki	Stawki
Steel Street	Ulica Stalowa

In the text	Original
Stettin	Szczecin
Straight Street	Ulica Prosta
Suleyuvek	Sulejówek
Suvalki	Suwałki
Targovitsa	Targowica
Three Crosses Square	Plac Trzech Krzyży
Tlomat Street	Ulica Tłomackie
Tlomatska Synagogue	Synagoga Tłomacka
Tolochanov	Tołoczanów
Torun	Toruń (Thorn)
Trench Street	Ulica Okopowa
Truskav	Truskaw
Tvorki	Tworki
Tyniets Street	Ulica Tyniecka
Uyazhdov Boulevard	Aleje Ujazdowskie
Varka	Warka
Varka Street	Ulica Warecka
Varta, River	Warta
Vauxhall Street	Ulica Foksal
Vavel	Wawel
Vaver district	Wawer
Vilanov Street	Ulica Wilanowska
Vilno	Wilno, Vilnius
Viskitki	Wiskitki
Vistula, River	Wisła
Vola	Wola
Vola Opochynska	Wola Opoczyńska
Vola Street	Ulica Wolska
Volhynia	Wołyń
Volomin	Wołomin
Vrotslav	Wrocław (Breslau)
Vyshkov	Wyszków
Vyshogrod	Wyszogród
Washington Avenue	Aleje Waszyngtona
West Station	Dworzec Zachodni
Wilson Square	Plac Wilsona
Yedvabne	Jedwabne
Zamenhoff Street	Ulica Zamenhoffa
Zamost	Zamość

IV Comparative Table of Ranks

Waffen-SS/SS	Abbr.	Wehrmacht	Abbr.	British Army	Abbr.
SS-Oberstgruppenführer	SS-Obstgruf	Generalfeldmarschall	GFM	Field-Marshal	F-M
SS-Obergruppenführer	SS-Ogruf	Generaloberst	Gen.Oberst		
		General der Infantrie etc.	Gen.Inf	General	Gen.
SS-Gruppenführer	SS-Gruf	Generalleutnant	Gen.Lt.	Lieutenant-General	Lt.Gen.
SS-Brigadeführer	SS-Brig.Fhr	Generalmajor	Gen.Maj	Major-General	Maj.Gen.
SS-Oberführer	SS-Obfhr	–	–	Brigadier	Brig.
SS-Standartenführer	SS-Staf	Oberst	Obst.	Colonel	Col.
SS-Obersturmbannführer	SS-Ostubaf	Oberstleutnant	OtL	Lieutenant-Colonel	Lt.Col.
SS-Sturmbannführer	SS-Stbf	Major	Maj.	Major	Maj.
SS-Hauptsturmführer	SS-Hstuf	Hauptmann	Hptm.	Captain	Capt.
SS-Obersturmführer	SS-Ostuf	Oberleutnant	OLt	Lieutenant	Lt.
SS-Untersturmführer	SS-Ustuf	Leutnant	Lt.	2nd Lieutenant	2Lt.
SS-Oberscharführer	SS-Oscha	Feldwebel	Fw	Warrant Officer	W.O.
SS-Unterscharführer	SS-Uscharf	Unteroffizier	Uffz.	Sergeant	Sgt.
SS-Rottenführer	SS-Rttf	Obergefreiter	Ogefr	Corporal	Cpl.
SS-Sturmmann	SS-Strm	Gefreiter	Gefr.	Lance Corporal	L.Cpl.
SS-Grenadier	SS-Gren	Grenadier (etc.)	Gren.	Private (etc.)	Pvt.

(There are a number of SS and other German ranks for which there is no British equivalent, but this is broadly correct for comparative purposes.)

Source – Terrence Booth, *WWII German Military Symbols and Abbreviations 1943–5* (London, 2001).

List of Capsules

Notes

The following abbreviations are used for frequently recurring positions:

AKD: Studium Polski Podziemnej, *Armia Krajowa w Dokumentach, 1939–45*, Tom IV (London, 1977). **DWS:** Władysław Bartoszewski, *Dni Walczącej Stolicy: Kronika Powstania Warszawskiego* (Warsaw, 1984). **GARF:** State Archive of the Russian Federation (Moscow). **HIA:** Hoover Institution Archive (Stanford., Ca). **PRO:** Public Record Office (London). **PSZ:** Polish Institute, Polskie Siły Zbrojne (London). **RGVA:** Russian State Military Archives. Andrzej K. Kunert (ed.), *Rzeczpospolita Walcząca: Powstanie Warszawskie, 1944: Kalendarium* (Warsaw, 1994) **Sbkw:** A. K. Kunert (ed.), *Słownik biograficzny konspiracji warszawskiej, 1939–44*, 3 vols (Warsaw, 1987–91). **SPP:** Studium Polski Podziemnej (London). **TNA:** The National Archives, formed in April 2003 from the Public Record Office and the Historical Manuscripts Commission. **ZH:** *Zeszyty Historyczne* (Paris).

Foreword pp. ix–xvi

• **1.** As an introductory English bibliography, the Oxford Libraries Information System (OLIS) under 'Warsaw Rising' may be accessed at <http://library.ox.ac.uk>. • **2.** The latest generation of source books on the Rising, almost all in Polish, include Andrzej K. Kunert (ed.), *Rzeczpospolita Walcząca: Powstanie Warszawskie, 1944: Kalendarium* (Warsaw, 1994) (RW): idem, *Słownik biograficzny konspiracji Warszawskiej, 1939–44* (Warsaw, 1987–91), 3 vols: and *Encyklopedia Powstania Warszawskiego*, vol. 3 (Warsaw, 1997). W. Bartoszewski, *Dni Walczącej Stolicy: Kronika Powstania Warszawskiego* (Warsaw, 1984) is a mine of information. A conference collection, Z. Mańkowski and J. Święch (eds), *Powstanie Warszawskie w historiografii i literaturze, 1944–94* (Lublin, 1996), contains specially valuable surveys of recent historiography and literature. • **3.** Norman Davies, *Heart of Europe: a short history of Poland* (Oxford, 1984), revised edition, 2002. • **4.** Norman Davies, *Europe: a history* (Oxford, 1996, New York, 1997), • **5.** Quoted in Krzysztof Gluchowski, 'Dickens and Poland' in *The Dickensian*, no. 456, vol. 98, part 1, Spring, 2002, p. 48. • **6.** See 'How God invented Polish' at <www.cartoonstock.com ref.sb0779>.

350/XXX/999 TO8 DE1 pp. 1–13

• **1.** Barnes Lodge, Ruckler's Lane, between King's Langley and Hemel Hempstead (Herts). Acknowledgement is due for many intimate details in this section to Mr Zbigniew S. Siemaszko, who served at Barnes Lodge in 1944. • **2.** See Gerhard Weinberg, *A World at Arms: a global history of World War Two* (Cambridge, 1994), pp. 667ff: 'The Assault on Germany from all sides'. • **3.** Zbigniew S. Siemaszko, 'Łączność Radiowa Sztabu Naczelnego Wodza w przededniu Powstania Warszawskiego', *ZH* (Paris), August, 1964, pp. 64–116. • **4.** Jan Karski, *The Great Powers and Poland, 1919–45* (Lanham, MD, 1985), Part two, 1939–45, pp. 385–624. • **5.** Zbigniew S. Siemaszko, correspondence with the author, 28 August 2002, 28 December 2002. • **6.** Józef Garliński, *Intercept: the Enigma war* (London, 1981): see also F. W. Winterbotham, *The Ultra Secret* (London, 1974): J. Cairncross, *The Enigma Spy* (London, 1997). • **7.** I. C. B. Dear (ed.), *Oxford Companion to the Second World War* (Oxford, 1995), p. 849. • **8.** Zbigniew S. Siemaszko, letter 28 August 2002. • **9.** Max Hastings, *Overlord: D-Day and the Battle for Normandy* (London, 1984). • **10.** Siemaszko, op. cit., p. 78. • **11.** See D. Stafford, *Britain and European Resistance, 1940–45* (London, 1980). • **12.** C. MacDonald, *The Killing of SS-Obergruppenführer Reinhard Heydrich* (London, 1989). • **13.** See Denis Mack Smith, *Italy and its Monarchy* (New Haven, 1989), pp. 329ff. • **14.** Siemaszko, op. cit., p. 113. • **15.** Ibid. • **16.** Reconstructed Morse text, JUŻ WALCZYMY. FLAGA BIAŁO-CZERWONA POWIEWA NAD WARSZAWĄ (after Siemaszko, op. cit., p. 153). • **17.** Ibid. • **18.** Ibid., p. 89. PSZ III, p. 665. • **19.** S. Kopański, *Wspomnienia wojenne, 1939–46* (London, 1961), p. 323. • **20.** A. Pomian, 'Military Messages', *The Warsaw Rising: a Selection of Documents* (London, 1945), p. 1.

Chapter 1: The Allied Coalition pp. 17–70

• **1.** See Stanisław Maczek, *Od podwody do czołga* (London, 1984), p. 146. • **2.** Norman Davies, *Heart of Europe: a short history of Poland* (Oxford, 2001). • **3.** A. J. P. Taylor, *Beaverbrook* (London, 1972), p. 363. • **4.** Simon Newman, *The British Guarantee of Poland 1939* (Oxford, 1976). • **5.** W. Jędrzejewicz, *Poland in the British Parliament, 1939–45* (New York, 1946), vol. 1, p. 26. • **6.** Ibid., passim. • **7.** Beaverbrook to R. H. Mummy, 21 March 1939, in Taylor, op. cit., p. 391. • **8.** Ibid., p. 394. • **9.** Ibid., p. 395. • **10.** See <http://news.bbc.co.uk/1/hi/special-report/1999/08/99/world_war_ii/430071.stm>. • **11.** S. Grzelak, *Dziennik Sowieckiej Agresji, 1939* (Warsaw, 2000), pp. 38–9; also Nicholas Bethell, *The War Hitler Won* (London, 1972); and Adam Zamoyski, *The Forgotten Few: the Polish Air Force in the Second World War* (London, 1995). • **12.** Count Edward Raczyński (1891–1992), see his *In*

Allied London (London, 1962). • **13.** When Raczyński officially informed the Foreign Office on 18 September about the Soviet Union's aggression against Poland, he was immediately told that 'the Anglo-Polish alliance concerns Germany, not Russia'. The National Archives (TNA): PRO (Public Records Office) COPY FO 371 23103/18. • **14.** Tadeusz Bór-Komorowski (1895–1966): see his *The Secret Army* (London, 1950); Tadeusz Pełczyński (1892–1985), see his *Na swięto żołnierza* (London, 1950); Antoni Chruściel, 'Monter' (1895–1960); Leopold Okulicki, 'Bear Cub' (1898–1946); Emil Fieldorf, 'Nil' (1895–1953): see Maria Fieldorf, *Generał 'Nil': August Emil Fieldorf: fakty, dokumenty, relacje* (Warsaw, 1993). • **15.** D. Carlton, *Anthony Eden: a Biography* (London, 1981), p. 246. • **16.** Józef Garliński, *Poland in the Second World War, 1939–45* (London, 1985), pp. 92–3. • **17.** Zamoyski, op. cit., p. 96. • **18.** Ibid., p. 97. • **19.** See 350/XXX/999 TO8 DE1, note 6 above. • **20.** *Documents on Polish–Soviet Relations*, Sikorski Institute (London, 1961), vol. I. The military potential of the Red Army was thought to be low, as it was in 1939. Prior to the September Campaign, the Polish Army was judged by Anglo-French specialists to be a better partner. See Julian Jackson, *The Fall of France, 1940* (London, 2003). • **21.** Keith Sword, *Deportation and Exile: Poles in the Soviet Union 1939–48* (London, 1996); Jan T. Gross, *Revolution from Abroad* (Princeton, 1988); Irena G. and Jan T. Gross, *War through Children's Eyes: the Soviet Occupation of Poland and the Deportations, 1939–41* (Stanford, 1981). • **22.** Frank Roberts, 21 March 1942, The National Archives (TNA): PRO (Public Record Office) COPY FO 31081/2428. Quoted by V. Rothwell, *Britain and the Cold War* (London, 1982), p. 153. • **23.** Anthony Beevor, *Stalingrad* (London, 1998). • **24.** See M. Harz, *Bibliografia zbrodni katyńskiej, 1943–93* (Warsaw, 1993). • **25.** See Keith Sword (ed.), *Sikorski, Soldier and Statesman: a collection of essays* (London, 1990). The puzzle of the accident at Gibraltar remains unsolved. • **26.** Stanisław Mikołajczyk (1901–66), see A. Paczkowski, *Klęska realisty* (Warsaw, 1991); Kazimierz Sosnkowski (1885–1969), see Maria Pestkowska, *Kazimierz Sosnkowski* (Wrocław, 1995). • **27.** See R. Steel, *Walter Lippmann and the American Century* (London, 1980). • **28.** Arthur Bliss Lane, though confirmed in September 1944, delayed his journey to Europe to July 1945, when he made straight for Soviet-run Warsaw. See his *I Saw Poland Betrayed* (Minneapolis, 1948). • **29.** SPP, 6. 3–3, 1 July 1944. • **30.** Philip Bell, *John Bull and the Bear: British public opinion, foreign policy and the Soviet Union, 1941–45* (London, 1990). • **31.** 2 August 1944, in Carlton, op. cit., pp. 239–41. • **32.** William Mackenzie, *The Secret History of SOE* (London, 2000), Part I 'Origins', pp. 3–71. • **33.** Tadeusz Romer (1894–1978); Stanisław Kopański (1895–1976), see his *Wspomnienie Wojenne, 1939–45* (London, 1972). • **34.** Alan J. Foster, in *New Dictionary of National Biography* (Oxford, 2000), pp. 154ff; see also Peter Wilkinson, *Gubbins and SOE* (London, 1993) and *Foreign Fields* (London, 1997); O. O'Malley, *The Phantom Caravan* (London, 1954). • **35.** General Stanisław Tatar, 'Tabor', see Zbigniew S. Siemaszko, *Działalność Generała Tatar* (London, 1999). • **36.** J. Pomian, *J. H. Retinger: Memoirs of an Eminence Grise* (Sussex, 1972). • **37.** Stephen Dorrill, *MI6: Fifty Years of Special Operations* (London, 2000). • **38.** Zbigniew S. Siemaszko, 'Retinger w Polsce w 44 roku', *ZH, XII*, 1967, pp. 56–115. • **39.** Dixon, 15 February, quoted by V. Rothwell, op. cit. • **40.** W. F. Reddaway (ed.), *The Cambridge History of Poland* (Cambridge, 1941, 1950), 2 vols; W. R. Morfill, *Poland* (Oxford, 1893): see also Roman Dyboski, *Poland* (London, 1933). • **41.** W. J. Rose, *Poland* (Harmondsworth, 1939), p. 243. • **42.** Polish Ministry of Information, *The Black Book of Poland* (London, 1942). • **43.** Republic of Poland, *The German Occupation of Poland* (London, 1942). • **44.** E.g. Victor Cazalet, *With Sikorski to Russia* (London, 1942), and others. • **45.** Apart from official Government publications, a Polish Information Committee was very active in New York. Titles included *Poland Fights* (1941–46), *Polish Facts and Figures* (1944–45), and *Poland of Tomorrow*. • **46.** R. Addinsell, *The Warsaw Concerto*: Dangerous Moonlight (1941). Directed by Brian Desmond Hurst. Released in the USA in 1945 with the unfortunate title of *Suicide Squad*. • **47.** E. Raczyński, *W Sojuszniczym Londynie* (London, 1997), p. 433. • **48.** Ibid., p. 432. • **49.** *Poland's Eastern Frontier*, The National Archives (TNA): PRO COPY FO 404/30, C1482/1551/55 (19 November 1943) and *Possible Lines of a Polish–Soviet Settlement* (22 November 1943), in A. Polonsky, *The Great Powers and the Polish Question, 1941–45* (London, 1976), p. 160. • **50.** Jan M. Ciechanowski, *The Warsaw Rising of 1944* (Cambridge, 1974), p. 48. • **51.** Winston Churchill, *The Second World War* (London, 1948), vol. 1. • **52.** Telegram: Demel to Iranek-Osmecki, text in Zbigniew S. Siemaszko, *Łączność i Polityka* (London, 1992), p. 96. • **53.** Siemaszko, *Tatar*, op. cit., p. 39. • **54.** Ibid., pp. 23–4, 43–4. • **55.** HIA Poland, MSZ File, June 1944. Ambassador J. Ciechanowski (Washington)–Foreign Minister Romer. 11 June 1944. No. 3/SZ – tjn/29c. • **56.** Siemaszko, *Tatar*, op. cit., pp. 46–7. This conversation has been reconstructed from an account written by Tabor in 1981, shortly before his death. It may be compared with: L. Mitkiewicz, *W najwyższym sztabie zachodnich Aliantów, 1943–5* (London, 1971), p. 177. • **57.** Note by RSM Stefan Zamoyski, 13 June 1944, SPP 2–3-2–1-4. • **58.** S. Mikołajczyk, *The Rape of Poland* (New York, 1948), p. 60. • **59.** Jan Ciechanowski, *Defeat in Victory* (New York, 1947), passim. • **60.** Such was the considered opinion of a British insider. 'Gen. Tabor . . . saw both the British Chiefs of Staff and the Combined Chiefs of Staff, and all possible efforts were made . . . to secure . . . Allied assistance for a general rising. The efforts were not successful: no promises were given, indeed the difficulties were made very plain . . . But no attempt was made to control or to prohibit a general rising: this was explicitly left to the Poles to decide.' Mackenzie, op. cit., pp. 521–2. • **61.** *Notatka z uroczystości dekorowania gen. S. Tabora orderem Łaźni* / C.B. Military / w Londynie dnia

10.vii.1944r. SPP TP3 Teczka Gen S. Tatara. • **62.** The National Archives (TNA): PRO COPY HS 4/156, Polish General Staff VI Bureau no. 6131/Tjn/44 29 July 1944: quoted by E. D. R. Harrison, 'The British Special Operations Executive and Poland', *Historical Journal* 43.4 (Cambridge, 2000), p. 1084. • **63.** The National Archives (TNA): PRO COPY HS 4/156, Polish General Staff 1050/Ti/Sztab/44 1 August 1944: Harrison, ibid.

Chapter II: The German Occupation pp. 71–118

• **1.** See Norman Davies, 'One thousand years of Polish–German camaraderie' in Roger Bartlett and Karen Schönwälder (eds), *The German lands and Eastern Europe: essays on the history of their social, cultural and political relations* (London, 1999). • **2.** Władysław Studnicki-Gizbert (1867–1953). • **3.** Lucjan Blit, *The Eastern Pretender* (London, 1965), p. 17. • **4.** *Encyclopedia Judaica* (Jerusalem, 1970), vol. X, p. 339. • **5.** Julian Tuwim, 'My Żydzi Polscy', in A. Kunert (ed.), *Polacy – Żydzi: Wybór źródeł* (Warsaw, 2001), pp. 446–9, with German and English translations. • **6.** William J. Rose, *Poland* (Harmondsworth, 1939), pp. 161–3. • **7.** Ibid., p. 216. • **8.** Stefan Starzyński (1893–1943). See M. M. Drozdowski, *Stefan Starzyński, Prezydent Warszawy* (Warsaw, 1980). • **9.** Jan Lechoń, 'Pieśń o Stefanie Starzyńskim', *Poezja polska: antologia II*, passim. • **10.** Jan Lechoń, 'Piosenka', ibid., p. 179. • **11.** John Connelly, 'Nazis and Slavs: from racial theory to racist practice', *Central European History*, vol. 32, nr. 1, pp. 1–33. • **12.** 23 August 1939, from the notes of Admiral Canaris. Quoted by L. P. Lochner, *What about Germany?* (New York, 1942), p. 2: after Dr Mark Levene. • **13.** J. Fest, *Hitler* (Harmondsworth, 1982), p. 611. • **14.** Ibid. • **15.** Museum of Tolerance Multimedia Learning Center (Los Angeles) after Time-Life Books Inc. <http://motlc.wiesenthal.com/index.html>. • **16.** *The Goebbels Diaries, 1939–41*, trans. F. Taylor (Harmondsworth, 1984), p. 16. • **17.** E. Duraczyński, *Wojna: Okupacja, 1939–43* (Warsaw, 1974), pp. 34–6. • **18.** R. Lukas, *Did The Children Cry? Hitler's War Against Jewish and Polish Children, 1939–45* (New York, 1994), p. 5. • **19.** Ibid., p. 603. • **20.** Joachim Fest, 'Imitation of a Man of Violence', in *The Face of the Third Reich* (London, 1979), pp. 315–31. • **21.** Ibid., p. 325. • **22.** Hans Frank, *Das Diensttagebuch des deutschen Gouverneurs in Polen 1939–45* (Stuttgart, 1975), pp. 121–3, 418–24. • **23.** Max Weinrich, *Hitler's Professors* (London, 1999), p. 167. • **24.** T. Strzembosz, 'Hitlerowski Aparat Terroru', in *Akcje zbrojne podziemnej Warszawy, 1939–44* (Warsaw, 1978), pp. 44–53. • **25.** Maria Trzcińska, *Obóz Zagłady w Centrum Warszawy: Konzentrationslager Warschau* (Radom, 2002), p. 41. • **26.** Ibid., p. 40. • **27.** Strzembosz, op. cit., p. 365. • **28.** One should beware of contemporary representations in films like Lanzmann's *Shoah* and even Polański's *The Pianist*, which, to create a dramatic contrast between the Ghetto and the

Aryan Side, tend to depict the latter as a zone of milk and honey. • **29.** 2 October 1940: Bormann's notes as found in the *Führer*'s Bunker. Beria to Stalin 7 November 1945. GARF 9401/2/100, pp. 484–90. • **30.** R. Hilberg et al. (eds), *The Warsaw Diary of Adam Czerniaków: prelude to doom* (Chicago, 1999). • **31.** Jacek Leociak, 'Marszałkowska dzielnica zamknięta', *Rzeczpospolita*, 21–22 April 2001, being a review of his forthcoming book with Barbara Engelking-Boni, *Getto Warszawskie: Przewodnik po nieistniejącym mieście*. • **32.** Israel Shahak: meeting with the author, Jerusalem, January 1991. • **33.** Lukas, op. cit., chapters II, III. • **34.** Abraham Lewin, *A Cup of Tears: a Diary of the Warsaw Ghetto* (Oxford, 1988), passim. • **35.** E. T. Wood, S. M. Jankowski, *Karski: How one man tried to stop the Holocaust* (New York, 1994), passim. • **36.** Ibid. • **37.** J. M. Rymkiewicz, *Umschlagplatz*, Biblioteka Kultury, vol. 435 (Paris, 1988). • **38.** Calel Perechodnik, *Am I a murderer? Testament of a Jewish Ghetto policeman* (Boulder, Colorado, 1996). • **39.** Korczak. See Betty Lifton, *The King of Children: a biography of Janusz Korczak* (London, 1988). From Julian Tuwim, 'Lokomotywa' ('The Locomotive'). • **40.** Israel Shahak (Jerusalem), letter to the *New York Review of Books*, responding to Timothy Garton Ash's review of Claude Lanzmann's film *Shoah* (1985). • **41.** See Telegram no. II/5 Telegram no. 354, 25 September 1941. Rowecki-Sikorski, 'The overwhelming majority of the country has an anti-Semitic orientation', p. 198. • **42.** W. Broniewski, 'Żydom polskim' (1943), *Antologia*, op. cit., p. 304. • **43.** *The Goebbels Diaries*, op. cit., 10 October 1939, p. 16. • **44.** Joanna K. Hanson, *The Civilian Population and the Warsaw Rising of 1944* (Cambridge, 1982), pp. 22–3. • **45.** Jan T. Gross, *Polish Society under German Occupation* (Princeton, 1979), pp. 102–3. • **46.** Lukas, op. cit., passim. • **47.** Ibid., p. 93. • **48.** See M. Terles, *Ethnic Cleansing of Poles in Volhynia and Eastern Galicia* (Toronto, 1993); R. Torzecki, *Polacy i Ukraińcy: Sprawa Ukraińska w czasie II wojny światowej* (Warsaw, 1993); W. Poliszczuk, *Gorzka prawda* (Toronto, 1995). • **49.** *Encyclopedia Judaica* (1971), vol. XVI, under 'Warsaw'. • **50.** See Gunnar S. Paulsson, *Secret City, the hidden Jews of Warsaw, 1940–45* (New Haven, Connecticut, 2002). • **51.** See C. Madajczyk, *Generalna Gubernia w planach hitlerowskich* (Warsaw, 1961). • **52.** See Chapter IV, note 3. • **53.** 'W sprawie walk w getcie', *Wielka Polska*, 5 May 1943, in A. Kunert (ed.), *Polacy – Żydzi: Wybór źródeł* (Warsaw, 2001), II/29, pp. 253–5. • **54.** On Jedwabne, Jan T. Gross, *Neighbors* (New York, 2001); see also A. Polonsky and J. Michlic, *The Neighbours Respond* (Princeton, 2004). • **55.** Author's interview with Professor Jerzy Holzer, November 2001. • **56.** Tadeusz Żenczykowski, *Generał Grot: U kresu walki* (London, 1983). • **57.** Czesław Miłosz, *Native Realm: a Search for Self-definition* (London, 1988), p. 233. • **58.** Ibid., p. 239. • **59.** C. Klessmann, 'Die deutsche Kriegsführung im Osten und die Besatzungspolitik in Polen: Revisionsbestrebungen angesichts drohender Niederlagen', in Stanisława Lewandowska and Bernd Martin (eds), *Der Warschauer*

Aufstand (Warsaw, 1999), p. 74. • **60.** Quoted by N. Rich, *Hitler's War Aims* (London, 1974), vol. II, p. 96. • **61.** Fest, *Face of the Third Reich*, op. cit., p. 330. • **62.** Martin Broszat, *Nationalsozialistische Polenpolitik, 1939–45* (Stuttgart, 1961), p. 188. • **63.** Klessman, op. cit., p. 76. • **64.** H. Schwendemann, 'Der Kapitulation . . .' in Martin and Lewandowska, op. cit., pp. 234–53. • **65.** As reported to the British Foreign Office. • **66.** See Chapter VII, note 50. • **67.** Diary Entry of Heinrich Stechbarth, 30, July 1944, Karta Archive, Warsaw. • **68.** Stefan Korboński, *The Polish Underground State* (Boulder Colorado, 1978), p. 176. • **69.** *RW*, p. 1.

Chapter III: Eastern Approaches pp. 119–165

• **1.** Norman Davies, *White Eagle, Red Star: The Polish–Soviet War of 1919–20* (London, 1972): republished London, 2003. • **2.** Ibid., pp. 172–3. • **3.** Lord D'Abernon, *The Eighteenth Decisive Battle of World History* (London, 1931), pp. 8–9. • **4.** Gaston Pajewski: a Frenchman of Polish descent. De Gaulle's associate. • **5.** Karl Baedeker, *Russia, with Teheran, Port Arthur, and Peking: handbook for travellers* (Leipzig, 1914). • **6.** K. Rokossovsky, memoirs. See note o below. On the mores of Stalin's circle, see Simon Sebag-Montefiore, *Stalin: the Court of the Red Tsar* (London, 2003). • **7.** Wiesław Białkowski, *Rokossowski, na ile Polak?* (Warsaw, 1994), p. 50. • **8.** Gen. Konstantin F. Telegin. See Anthony Beevor, *Stalingrad* (London, 1998), pp. 388–9. Telegin reappears in Warsaw in September 1944. See Chapter V below. • **9.** Quoted in K. K. Rokossovsky, *Soldatskii dolg* (Moscow, 1968). • **10.** W. Anders, *An Army in Exile* (Nashville, 1981). • **11.** Antony Beevor, *Berlin: the Downfall* (London, 2002), p. 199. • **12.** See Allen Paul, *Katyń: the Untold Story of Stalin's Polish Massacre* (New York, 1991), pp. 132–4. • **13.** Anders, op. cit., pp. 57–8. • **14.** After Paul, op. cit., p. 260. US Congress, Selection Committee [on] the Facts, Evidence and Circumstances of the Katyń Forest Massacre, 1951–, *Hearings*, vol. VI, p. 1784. • **15.** Robert Conquest, *Harvest of Sorrow* (London, 1986). • **16.** See Chapter II, note 48. • **17.** Lewis (Bernstein) Namier (1888–1960), historian, author of numerous works on the eighteenth century and on Central Europe, such as *Diplomatic Prelude* (1948), *Conflicts* (1942), and *Facing East* (1947): biographies by J. Namier (1977) and Linda Colley (1989). On the Curzon Line episode, see Witold S. Sworakowski, *An Error regarding Eastern Galicia in Curzon's Note to the Soviet Government of July 11, 1920* (New York, 1944). • **18.** GARF, f3, op. 63, d237, pp. 52–93. Quoted by Sergei Kudryashov, 'Diplomatic Prelude: Stalin, the Allies and Poland', in A. Kemp-Welch (ed.), *Stalinism in Poland* (London, 1999), p. 38. • **19.** RGVA 36860/1/16: quoted by Beevor, *Berlin* op. cit., p. 168. • **20.** RGVA 38686/1/20: ibid., p. 168. • **21.** A. Solzhenitsyn, from *Prussian Nights: a narrative poem* (London, 1977), translated by Robert Conquest. (NB: this description was inspired by Solzhenitsyn's experiences on the Second Byelorussian Front in January 1945.) • **22.** TsAMo RF (Moscow) f233, op. 2307, d 108, pp. 1–2. Quoted by Kudryashov, op. cit., pp. 38–9. • **23.** GARF, f9401, op2, d64, L222–26. No. 202609, in T. Cariewskaya, et al., *Teczka Specjalna J. W. Stalina: Raporty NKWD z Polski, 1944–46* (Warsaw, 1998), pp. 26–31. • **24.** Mariola Kayser, 'The Polemic between Count Edward Raczyński and David Lloyd George on Anglo-Polish Relations at the outbreak of World War II', *Polish–Anglo-Saxon Studies* (Poznań), vol. 6–7, 1997, pp. 115–63. • **25.** Edward Hallet Carr (1892–1986), see M. Cox (ed.), *E. H. Carr: a critical appraisal* (Basingstoke, 2000). See his *The Soviet Impact on the Western World* (1946). Typically, despite its fourteen volumes, his *History of Soviet Russia* (1950–78) never reached Stalin. • **26.** See D. Caute, *The Fellow Travellers: intellectual friends of Communism* (New Haven, 1988). • **27.** Robert Conquest, *Stalin: Breaker of Nations* (London, 1993), p. 261. • **28.** Eric Hobsbawm, *Interesting Times: a twentieth century life* (London, 2002). • **29.** See F. Beckett, *Enemy Within: the rise and fall of the British Communist Party* (London, 1995). • **30.** Author's correspondence with Dr Robert Frost. • **31.** Martin Amis, *Koba the Dread* (London, 2002), p. 7. • **32.** Ibid., p. 8. • **33.** Christopher Hill (1912–2003), historian, author of numerous works on English seventeenth-century intellectual history: see also his *Lenin and the Russian Revolution* (1947). The extent of his involvement in the Communist movement during the war was only revealed after his death by Anthony Glees, who had withheld it from *The Secrets of the Service: British Intelligence and Communist Subversion* (London, 1987). • **34.** M. R. D. Foote at Polish Embassy, December 2001. • **35.** Andrew Rothstein (1898–c. 1980). His works during the period in question included *Workers in the Soviet Union* (1942), *Soviet policy during the Patriotic War* (1946), and *The teachings of Lenin and Stalin* (1948). He was dismissed from his post at London University by Dr G. Bolsover, who had been the British observer at the Moscow Trial of 1945. • **36.** Victor Rothwell, *Britain and the Cold War 1941–47* (London, 1982), pp. 93–4. • **37.** Quoted in ibid., p. 98. • **38.** Ibid. • **39.** Ibid. • **40.** Ibid., p. 92. • **41.** Ibid., p. 162. • **42.** D. Culbert (ed.), *Mission to Moscow* (Madison, 1980). • **43.** See Jan M. Ciechanowski, *The Warsaw Rising of 1944* (Cambridge, 1974), passim. The talks were inconclusive, but had been started as a form of reinsurance against a possible change of tack. • **44.** John Erickson, *The Road to Berlin* (London, 1983), pp. 281–2. • **45.** Alexander Werth, *Russia at War* (London, 1964), p. 867. • **46.** Ibid., p. 868. • **47.** Józef Garliński, *Poland in the Second World War, 1939–45* (London, 1985), p. 281. • **48.** *DWS*, pp. 8–9. • **49.** KR o Powstania W-im, *ZH* (1969), p. 137.

Chapter IV: Resistance pp. 167–240

• **1.** See Norman Davies, 'The Insurrectionary Tradition', *Heart of Europe: a short history of Poland* (Oxford, 1984, rev. ed. 2002), pp. 166–73. • **2.** Casimir Delavigne, 'La Varsovienne' (1830), in *Œuvres Complètes* (Paris, 1855), pp. 522–3. Translated into Polish by Karol Sienkiewicz, and set to music by Karol Karpiński. See Norman Davies, *God's Playground* (Oxford, 1981), vol. II, pp. 315–17. • **3.** M. Ney-Krwawicz, *The Polish Army, 1939–45* (London, 2001), p. 4. • **4.** See L. Bartelski, *Mokotów, 1944* (Warsaw, 1971) and J. Kłoczowski, 'Dowódca Baszty o swoim pułku', in *Państwo, Kościół, niepodległość* (Lublin, 1986), p. xi. • **5.** 'Hubal', the pseudonym of Maj. Henryk Dobrzański (1896–1940), who, with Bór-Komorowski, had been a member of the Polish equestrian team at the Berlin Olympics. • **6.** T. Strzembosz, *Rzeczpospolita podziemna* (Warsaw, 2000), p. 23. • **7.** Łódź was a city of mixed population – roughly 60% Polish, 30% Jewish and 10% German. Only the local Germans turned out to welcome the arriving Wehrmacht. • **8.** D. Levin, *The Lesser of Two Evils: Eastern European Jewry under Soviet rule, 1939–41* (Philadelphia/Jerusalem, 1995), p. 43. • **9.** Ibid. • **10.** 'Raport Jana Karskiego o sytuacji Żydów na okupowanych ziemiach polskich na początku 1940 r', *Dzieje najnowsze* (Warsaw, 1989), nr. 2, pp. 179–99. • **11.** Ibid., p. 194. • **12.** Carla Tonini, *Operazione Madagascar: la questione ebraica in Polonia, 1918–68* (Bologna, 1999), p. 165. • **13.** Stanisław Rosa, of the PPS, in Kraków. Jan Karski, *The Story of a Secret State* (Boston, 1944), p. 190. • **14.** 'Hymn Pierwszej Brigady' (1917–18), A. Hałasiński, T. Biernacki: in effect, the anthem of Pilsudski's Legions and subsequently of the inter-war Polish army: banned 1945–90. • **15.** P. Stachiewicz, *Geneza Oddziału 'Parasol'* (Warsaw, 1984), pp. 43–62. • **16.** Karski, *Secret State*, op. cit., p. 129. • **17.** Ibid., p. 132. • **18.** Ibid., passim. • **19.** Ibid., pp. 127–8. • **20.** Ibid., p. 258. • **21.** A. Borkiewicz, *Powstanie Warszawskie* (Warsaw, 1957), as reproduced in T. Strzembosz, op. cit., Table IX, pp. 159–60. • **22.** Dispositions as of 1 March 1944, after Kirchmayer (1957): extracted from T. Strzembosz, op. cit., Table XIII, p. 164. Numbers in brackets indicate skeleton platoons still in formation. • **23.** Jan Nowak-Jeziorański, as recorded in the TV film *Powstanie Warszawskie* (1994) and as interviewed on TV Polonia, January 2002. • **24.** After Karski, op. cit., p. 270. • **25.** Ibid., p. 267. • **26.** Czesław Miłosz, *Native Realm: a Search for Self-definition* (London, 1988), p. 247. • **27.** Krzysztof Kamil Baczyński, 'Historia', in *Ty jesteś moje imię . . .* ed. Małgorzata Baranowska (Warsaw, 1995), pp. 34–5. • **28.** An exploit of Prof. Jan Zachwatowicz. • **29.** Jan Stanisław Jankowski, 'Sable', Chief Delegate and Vice Premier, Kunert, *Sbkw*, I, pp. 88–90: later defendant at the Moscow Trial. • **30.** K. Leski, *Życie niewłaściwie urozmaicone* (Warsaw, 1989). • **31.** Jan Kozielewicz, 'Karski' (1914–93), *The Story of a Secret State* (London, 1944): see also

E. T. Wood, *Karski: how one man tried to stop the Holocaust* (London, 1994). • **32.** Zdzisław Jeziorański, 'Jan Nowak' (b. 1913): *Courier from Warsaw* (London, 1982): *Wojna w eterze: wspomnienia* (London, 1985). • **33.** J. Lerski, *Emisariusz JUR* (London, 1984). • **34.** J. Szatsznajder, *Cichociemni* (Wrocław, 1985), pp. 134–5. • **35.** Author's correspondence with Mr Andrzej Suchcitz. • **36.** Szatsznajder, op. cit., p. 61. • **37.** Bolesław Kontrym, 'Biały', 'Żmudzin', etc. (1898–1953): Kunert, *Sbkw*, II, pp. 93–95. A memorial tablet has been placed in the Holy Cross Church, Warsaw. • **38.** After Jerzy Lerski, op. cit., pp. 76–9. According to Lerski, Col. Perkins, who had lived in Bielsko Biała before the war, made a further comment about how pleased he was to learn that Soviet as well as German losses on the Eastern Front were 'swelling nicely'. After leaving Warsaw in January 1944, Lerski travelled by train to Paris on the false papers of a German engineer from Estonia, before walking across the Pyrenees to Gibraltar. He then worked as the private secretary to Tomasz Arciszewski, the Socialist Prime Minister of the Polish Government in London. • **39.** Order 84, 22 January 1943, quoted by Ney-Krwawicz, op. cit., p. 41. • **40.** T. Strzembosz, *Akcje zbrojne podziemnej Warszawy, 1939–44* (Warsaw, 1978), pp. 130–31. • **41.** Ibid., passim. • **42.** Ibid. • **43.** Ibid. • **44.** Ibid., pp. 130–31. • **45.** 8 November 1943. The Polish officer was Maj. Kontrym. Szatsznajder, op. cit., pp. 56–7. • **46.** On Zhegota, Teresa Prekerowa, *Konspiracyjna Rada Pomocy Żydom w Warszawie* (Warsaw, 1992); Irene Tomaszewski, *Żegota: the rescue of Jews in Wartime Poland* (Montreal, 1994); W. Bartoszewski, *Los Żydów Warszawy* (Warsaw, 1993). • **47.** Much of the clandestine Polish press was collected by the exiled Government in London, and is available in the Sikorski Museum. • **48.** The activities of the Polish–British Historical Commission, which was due to report in 2003, may be followed on <http://www.archiwa.gov.pl/kronika>. • **49.** Józef Garliński, *Hitler's Last Weapons: the Underground War against the V1 and the V2* (London, 1977). • **50.** 'Armed action? Yes – but limited', Bl 1 April 1943, quoted by Ney-Krwawicz, op. cit., pp. 164–5. • **51.** *The Stroop Report* (London, 1980). • **52.** Ibid., passim. • **53.** M. Edelman, *Getto walczy: udział Bundu w obronie getta warszawskiego* (Warsaw, 1945), also *The Ghetto Fights* (London, 1945): W. Bartoszewski, *The Warsaw Ghetto: a Christian's Testimony* (London, 1989). • **54.** Leon Uris, *Mila 18* (London, 1963). • **55.** Czesław Miłosz, 'Campo di Fiori', from *Collected Poems, 1931–87* (London, 1988). • **56.** M. Gilbert, *Auschwitz and the Allies* (London, 1981): The Abandonment of the Jews. • **57.** Israel Gutman, 'Emanuel Ringelblum: The Chronicles of the Warsaw Ghetto', *Polin*, vol. 3, 1988, pp. 5–16: see also E. Ringelblum, *Polish–Jewish Relations during the Second World War* (Jerusalem, 1974). • **58.** Stefan Korboński, *The Polish Underground State*, op. cit., p. 168. • **59.** Ney-Krwawicz, op. cit., pp. 27–31. • **60.** PSZ, vol. II, p. 332. • **61.** Note by Capt. Zamoyski of conversation between Col. Mitkiewicz and Gen. Macready, n.d. early

June 1943. (NB: Macready had opened by expressing his condolences for the recent death of Gen. Sikorski.) HIA, Poland, Sikorski Microfilm Collection, Reel 137. • **62.** See HIA, Col. L. Mitkiewicz Collection. Inter-Allied discussions 1943–44 on US and UK support by air for the Home Army. • **63.** Hull–Roosevelt, 23 November 1943. Roosevelt Library, Hyde Park. • **64.** Ney-Krwawicz, op. cit., pp. 32–3. • **65.** PSZ, vol. III, p. 209. • **66.** Ibid., p. 210. • **67.** Korboński, op. cit., p. 170. • **68.** Appendix to letter from Sosnkowski to President Raczkiewicz, 6 July 1944. SPP, Ldz Osob/GNW/tj/44. Quoted by Jan M. Ciechanowski, *The Warsaw Rising of 1944* (Cambridge, 1974), p. 285. • **69.** Ibid., p. 290. • **70.** SPP, Ldz 5480/44, JMC, p. 285. • **71.** W. Anders, *An Army in Exile* (Nashville, 1981), p. 201. • **72.** *AKD*, IV, nr. 714, 25 July 1944. • **73.** *AKD*, IV, nr. 715, 25 July 1944. • **74.** *AKD*, IV, nr. 725. • **75.** (Retinger's papers are in the Polish Library, London: BP-POSK, Rkps 1280.) 1280/Szu 3, nr37, p. 2 • **76.** 1280/Szu 1, passim. • **77.** Polyneuritis: correspondence with Prof. Orzechowska-Juzwenko of Wrocław. • **78.** J. Garliński, *Hitler's Last Weapons*, op. cit., pp. 162–4. • **79.** Ibid., note p. 165. • **80.** Author's interview with Lady Pamela Niven, formerly Pamela Leach, later Dyboska, 14 November 2002. • **81.** Precious little is known of Retinger's meeting with Premier Mikołajczyk. Whatever the former said about his stay in Poland, he would not have wished to deflect the Premier from his trip to Moscow. • **82.** Ciechanowski, op. cit., pp. 190ff. • **83.** GARF, f9401, d2, op65, pp. 378–82. Beria to Stalin, 16 July 1944. Published in Polish translation in *NKWD i Polskie Podziemie, 1944–45* (Kraków, 1998), nr. 1, pp. 37–41. • **84.** Ibid., passim. • **85.** 'Wilk', meaning 'wolf', was the pseudonym of Col. A. Krzyżanowski, and he had *not* been flown either from London or Warsaw. The NKVD probably confused him with his deputy chief of staff, Maj. Teodor Cetys, 'Viking', who was a *cichociemni* and had been flown in by SOE on 8/9 April 1942. • **86.** Raczyński: summary of meeting with Eden, 27 July 1944, sent to Foreign Minister Romer. HIA 'Poland – Ministerstwo Spraw Zagranicznych, 1944' various boxes, also to be found in GSHI – talks – MSZ, collection 33, quoted by Ciechanowski, op. cit., p. 67. • **87.** Ibid., passim. • **88.** Ibid., passim. • **89.** O. G. Sargent to Ambassador Raczyński, 28 July 1944, *AKD* IV, nr. 725, p. 18. • **90.** T. Bór-Komorowski, *Armia podziemna* (London, 1967), quoted by Bartoszewski, *DWS*, pp. 11–12. • **91.** Ibid., passim. • **92.** Jean-Paul Cointet, 'Paris: un enjeu de libération', *Paris, 40–44* (Paris, 2001), pp. 253–315. • **93.** Christine Levisse Touzé, *Paris libéré, Paris retrouvé* (Paris, 1944), p. 86. • **94.** Korboński, op. cit., p. 179. • **95.** Witold Sagajłło, *Man in the Middle: a Story of the Polish Resistance, 1940–45* (London, 1984), pp 131–2, 136–40. (See Capsule NKVD.) • **96.** F. Majorkiewicz, *Lata chmurne* (Warsaw, 1983), p. 209, quoted in *RW*, p. 4. • **97.** Kaz. Kumaniecki, quoted by Bartoszewski, *DWS*, passim. • **98.** Julian Biodrowski. Jan Szatsznajder, op. cit., pp. 12–14.

Chapter V: The Warsaw Rising pp. 243–430

• **Outbreak: 1.** *DWS*, pp. 13–14. • **2.** On Jacek Świtalski: Adam Czerniawski, *Scenes from a disturbed childhood* (London, 1991), p. 96. • **3.** Krystyna Krahelska, 'Danuta' (1914–44), see *Sbkw*, vol. II, pp. 96–7. • **4.** *DWS*, p. 19. • **5.** Ministerstwo Spraw Wewnętrznych, Wydział Społeczny, *Przegląd Prasy Krajowej w okresie Powstania Warszawskiego* (London, 1945), nr2/45. 'Odezwa', p. 1. • **6.** Stefan Kisielewski, *DWS*, pp. 14–15. • **7.** *DWS*, p. 17. • **8.** Himmler's speech at Jägerhöhe, 21 September 1944, quoted by Tadeusz Sawicki, *Rozkaz: zdławić powstanie* (Warsaw, 2001), p. 25. The *Reichsführer-SS* was recalling his conversation with Hitler seven weeks earlier. • **9.** Ibid. • **10.** Wolfgang Benz (ed.), 'Generalplan-Ost', in *Die Vertreibung der Deutschen aus dem Osten* (Frankfurt/Main, 1995), p. 54. • **11.** *DWS*, p. 37. • **12.** George Weigel, *Witness to Hope; the Biography of Pope John Paul II* (New York, 1999), pp. 71–2. • **13.** Protokół posiedzenie Rady Ministrów, 2/8/44. APISM, PRM K102/739. • **14.** *The Times*, 3 August 1944. • **15.** *AKD*, IV, nr. 754. • **16.** *AKD*, IV, p. 33. • **17.** *AKD*, IV, nr. 780. • **18.** Joanna Hanson, 'Prasa Brytyjska a Powstanie Warszawskie' in Z. Mankowski and J. Święch, *Powstanie Warszawskie w historiografii i literaturze, 1944–94* (Lublin, 1996), pp. 97–8. • **19.** M. Gilbert, *Winston S. Churchill* (London, 1986), vol. VII, *1941–45*, pp. 871–2. This speech was made one day before Churchill was officially informed of the outbreak of the Rising by the Polish President. See note 13 above. He clearly learned of the outbreak from another source, possibly SOE or Count Raczyński, but more probably, given the Muscovite tone of the sentiments, from the Foreign Office and hence from the British Embassy in Moscow. This last possibility begs the question of how and when Moscow received news of the outbreak. • **20.** *The Diaries of Sir Alexander Cadogan, 1938–45*, ed. D. Dilks (London, 1971), p. 653. • **21.** *RW*, p. 31. (English text in *Stalin's Corrrespondence with Churchill, Attlee, Roosevelt and Truman, 1941–45* (London, 1958), doc. 311, p. 248.) • **22.** *DWS*, p. 37. *RW*, p. 38 (English text in *Stalin's Correspondence*, op. cit., doc. 313, p. 249). • **23.** Leon Mitkiewicz, *W najwyższym sztabie zachodnich aliantów* (London, 1971), p. 195. • **24.** *AKD*, IV, p. 72. • **25.** Kunert, *RW*, p. 23. • **26.** *RW*, p. 23. Text, T. Żenczykowski, *Samotny bój Warszawy* (Paris, 1985), p. 58. • **27.** *RW*, p. 31. • **28.** T. Cariewskaya et al., *Teczka Specjalna J. W. Stalina: Raporty NKWD z Polski, 1944–46* (Warsaw, 1998), nr. 7. • **29.** Jan Karski, T. Cariewskaya et al., *The Great Powers and Poland, 1919–45* (Lanham, MD, 1985), p. 537. • **30.** *RW*, p. 23: A. Przygoński, *Stalin* (Warsaw, 1994), p. 101. • **31.** Col. Turner, 5 August 1944: Gen. Antonov to Comrade Stalin, 6 August 1944. Ośrodek Karta (Warsaw). 'Dokumenty Brytyjskiej Misji Wojskowej w ZSRR, Sierpień–Październik 1944' M/II/18 (Documents of the British Military Mission in the USSR August – October, 1944) being copies of documents from the ex-Soviet military archives supplied by Memorial. • **32.** Piotr Stachiewicz, *'Parasol': Dzieje Oddziału do Zadań Specjalnych 'Kedywu'* (Warsaw, 1984), pp. 467–98. • **33.** Reinefarth was complaining that he had more civilians to shoot than he had ammunition. See *RW*, 5 August 1944. **Impasse.** • **34.** Rokossovsky's Plan. See A. Ajnenkiel (ed.), *Na oczach Kremla: tragedia walczącej Warszawy w świetle dokumentów rosyjskich* (Warsaw, 1994). • **35.** *DWS*, pp. 156, 160. • **36.** Alexander Werth, *Russia at War, 1941–45* (London, 1964), p. 881. • **37.** 'Das satanische Spiel mit Warschau', reproduced in *RW*, illustration nr. 99. • **38.** J. Zawodny, *Nothing but Honour* (London, 1978), p. 68. • **39.** Michał Cichy, 'Czarne Karty Powstania', *Gazeta Wyborcza*, nr. 24, 29–30 January 1994: see also Leszek Zabrowski, 'Fabryka Bdzur o Powstaniu Warszawskim', *Gazeta Polska*, 13 July 1995. • **40.** AK Pluton 535, commanded by 2Lt. Miroslav Iringh, 'Stanko', fighting in 1 Company of the 'Tur' Battalion in the 'Kryśka' Grouping. A memorial to them now stands on Cherniakov Street. • **41.** Hanson, op. cit., p. 1. • **42.** J. Marszalec, *Ochrona porządku i bezpieczeństwa publicznego w Powstaniu Warszawskim* (Warsaw, 1999). • **43.** Zawodny, op. cit., p. 64. • **44.** Joanna K. Hanson, *The Civilian Population and the Warsaw Rising of 1944* (Cambridge, 1982), pp. 252–8. • **45.** Ibid., p. 257. • **46.** *AKD*, IV, 766808. • **47.** Witold Babiński, *Przyczyny Historyczne od okresu 1939–45* (London, 1967), esp. Appendix 74A, letter of 8 August from Gen. Sosnkowski to President Raczkiewicz: L.dz/770/GNW/Tj44. • **48.** For example, on 14 August 1944 the National Council failed to agree the wording of a resolution which sought to pay homage to the insurgents in Warsaw and to appeal 'to the civilized world' for assistance. Stenogram posiedzenia RN RP, 14 August 1944. APISM A5.4/140. • **49.** The *Manchester Guardian* had clearly obtained this material from the Polish Government. 'Radio Kościuszko' was referring to the underground operations of the People's Army. But the conclusions drawn were directed to armed resistance in general, and would have been understood as such both by listeners in Poland and by readers of the *Manchester Guardian*. • **50.** OK M/II/18, pp. 5–14. • **51.** Winston Churchill, *The Second World War* (London, 1952), vol. IV, p. 117. • **52.** The National Archives (TNA): PRO COPY HS/4/157, MP/CD/6199, MP to CD 17 August, quoted by E. D. R. Harrison, 'The British Special Operations Executive and Poland', *Historical Journal* 43.4 (Cambridge, 2000), p. 1989. • **53.** Ibid. • **54.** FDR Library, 12 August 1944, Stettinius to FDR, Map Room Box 19, Doc# red317. • **55.** FDR Library, 15 August 1944, US Joint Chiefs to General Eisenhower. Map Room, Box 33, Doc# WAR 80785. The message ends with the sentence: 'All such operations [to help Warsaw] must be tied with the Russians.' • **56.** Winston Churchill, *The Second World War* (London, 1952), vol. IV, p. 118. • **57.** Ibid., p. 119. • **58.** Ibid., pp. 123–4. • **59.** Ibid., p. 122. • **60.** Quoted in translation by Hanson, 'Prasa Brytyjska . . .', in Mańkowski and Święch, op. cit., p. 101. • **61.** Christine Levisse Touzé, *Paris libéré, Paris retrouvé*

(Paris, 1944), p. 74. • **62.** Ibid., p. 40. • **63.** *Biuletin Informacyjny*, 24 August 1944, quoted by *DWS*, p. 128. • **64.** Ibid. • **65.** J. Nowak, memoirs, quoted in ibid., p. 129. • **66.** Neil Orpen, *Airlift to Warsaw* (Cape Town, 1984), pp. 65–8. • **67.** Michael Peszke, *The Battle for Warsaw* (Boulder, Colorado, 1995). • **68.** *The Times*, 8 August 1941. • **69.** Glen B. Infield, *The Poltava Affair* (London, 1974), p. 110. • **70.** Churchill, op. cit., pp. 122–3. • **71.** Ibid. • **72.** Ibid., p. 123. • **73.** Karski, *Great Powers*, op. cit., p. 539. • **74.** HIA, Romer Microfilm Collection. London (General) File, 'Negotiations with Stalin and other Soviet leaders 1944'. • **75.** See note 34 above. • **76.** Order nr. 6, 13 August 1944, *Bijące serce Partii: Dzienniki Personalne Ministerstwa Publicznego* (Warsaw, 2001). • **77.** SPP. 3/19/2. 8 August 1944. • **78.** J. Harvey (ed.), *The War Diaries of Oliver Harvey* (London, 1978), pp. 349–50. Sir Oliver Harvey, later Lord Tasburgh (1893–1968), was Eden's private secretary for most of the war, later Ambassador to Paris. In a note to the entry for 13 August 1944, the editor adds that 'Berut' (sic) was really called Krasnodewski, a Communist Soviet agent imprisoned in Poland and exchanged in 1922. • **79.** Tadeusz Żenczykowski, *Generał Grot: U kresu walki* (London, 1983), p. 66. • **80.** TASS communiqué, 12 August as reported in *The Times*, 13 August 1944: *RW*, pp. 98–9. • **81.** George Kennan, *Memoirs, 1925–1950* (Boston, 1967), pp. 210–211. • **82.** There is some doubt concerning the date and scope of this order. The practice of arresting Home Army personnel had been in force since July. See Chapter IV above. • **83.** Werth, op. cit., pp. 876–8. • **84.** Capt. Witold Pilecki (1901–48), pseudonyms 'Roman Jezierski', 'Serafiński', 'Druh', 'Witold'; *Sbkw*, vol. II, pp. 151–2. • **85.** *RW*, p. 116. • **86.** M. Ney-Krwawicz, *The Polish Army, 1939–45* (London, 2001), p. 67. • **87.** St Marczak-Oborski, 'Do powstańca', *DWS*, p. 151. • **88.** *DWS*, p. 152. **Attrition.** • **89.** A. Silgailis, *Latvian Legion* (San José, Calif., 1986), pp. 245–50. • **90.** Hanson, op. cit., p. 157. • **91.** Quoted in J. Noakes and J. Pridham (eds), *Nazism 1919–45: A Documentary Reader* (Exeter, 1983–98), vol. III, p. 996. • **92.** Karski, op. cit., pp. 540–41. • **93.** Bór-Komorowski, dispatch to the Premier and the C.-in-C., 29 August 1944. GSHI, A XII. 3/88, quoted by Hanson op. cit. A full account of negotiations over the Premier's plan is in W. Pobóg-Malinowski, *Najnowsza Historia Polityczna Polska* (London, 1963), vol. II, pp. 752–9. • **94.** *AKD*, IV, nr. 975, pp. 251–4. English version: W. Anders, *An Army in Exile* (Nashville, 1981), pp. 220–1. • **95.** Geoffrey Barraclough (b. 1908), historian of medieval Germany. In 1944 he was writing his *Origins of Modern Germany* (Oxford, 1946). His views on Eastern Europe were embarrassingly dismissive and patronizing: i.e. rather medieval and Germanic. • **96.** George Orwell, *Tribune*, 1 September 1944: see Appendix 26. • **97.** Ambassador Harriman was considerably more level-headed than most of his counterparts in Washington. 'My recent meetings with Vyshinski and particularly with Molotov lead me to believe that these men are bloated with power and expect that they can force their will on us and all countries to accept their decisions without question'. Harriman to FDR, 17 August 1944. FDR Library, Doc. #GEM-675, PSF Box 48, file 'Poland-8/44'. • **98.** Winant to Hopkins, 1 September 1944: Hopkins to Winant, 4 September 1944. Harry Hopkins Papers, FDR Library, Box 10, 'Growing Crisis in Poland', Box 4. • **99.** Adm. Leahy to the President, 5 September 1944, Telegram Red 374, FDR Library, Map Room, Box 20. • **100.** Hull to Harriman, 12 September 1944, #63, FDR Library, Map Room, Box 20. • **101.** Anders, op. cit., pp. 191–2. • **102.** Ibid., p. 191. • **103.** Ibid., pp. 198–9. • **104.** In Anders's account, he had told Churchill 'there is no justice or honour in Russia, and not a single man whose word can be trusted. "Churchill pointed out how dangerous such language would be if spoken in public. No good, he said, could come from antagonising the Russians."' Ibid., p. 124. • **105.** Ibid., pp. 209–13. • **106.** Ibid., p. 214. • **107.** 31 August 1944. Gen. Anders to Lt.Col. Marian Dorotycz-Malewicz, 'Hańcza': in A. Suchcitz, 'Powstanie Warszawskie 1944 w archiwaliach polskich w Londynie', in *Rocznik*, PTNO vol. 40 (1996–7), pp. 71–2. • **108.** *Bijące Serce Partii*, op. cit., p. 329. See Appendix 24. **Junction.** • **109.** *DWS*, p. 138. • **110.** Ibid. • **111.** Ibid. • **112.** Bór-Komorowski to Rokossovsky, 17 September, *AKD*, IV, nr. 1091. • **113.** Zbigniew S. Siemaszko, 'Powstanie Warszawskie – kontakty z ZSSR i PKWN', *ZH*, nr. 16 (1969). • **114.** On the Czerniaków Bridgehead, see J. Margules, *Przyczółki warszawskie* (Warsaw, 1962): also H. Baczko, *Osiem dni na lewym brzegu* (Warsaw, 1946). • **115.** II, p. 51. • **116.** L. M. Bertelski, 'Życie Kulturalne Powstania Warszawskiego', in Mańkowski, Święch (eds), *Powstanie Warszawskie*, op. cit., pp. 137–44. • **117.** Jerzy Święch, 'Z dziejów poezji tyrtejskej', in ibid., pp. 145–65. • **118.** PPKOPW, III, p. 75. • **119.** Sawicki, op. cit., p. 113. • **120.** Ibid., p. 117. • **121.** 4 September 1944, W. Prag and W. Jakobmeyer, *Das Diensttagebuch des deutschen Generalgouverneurs in Polen, 1939–45* (Stuttgart, 1975), p. 906. • **122.** Hans Frank, *Diensttagebuch*, op. cit., 14 December 1943. • **123.** *AKD*, IV, nr. 1108, p. 353. • **124.** *AKD*, IV, Bór-Komorowski to Sosnkowski, nr. 1095, nr. 1113: Sosnkowski to Bór, 24 July 1944, nr. 1139. • **125.** Hanson, 'Prasa Brytyjska . . .' in Mańkowski, Święch, op. cit., pp. 101–2. • **126.** Anders, op. cit., p. 229. • **127.** The news was radioed to Warsaw and was published in the *Information Bulletin* of 18 September. • **128.** Churchill, op. cit., p. 181. • **129.** Ibid., p. 183. • **130.** Anders, op. cit., p. 231. • **131.** FDR Library, Memorandum, Bohlen (State Department) to Hopkins, 14 July 1944. Fiorello LaGuardia was President of the US Conference of Mayors. • **132.** FDR to Harriman, Telegram nr. 69, 22 September 1944. • **133.** Harriman to FDR, 23 September 1944. Doc. 232314Z, NCR 7551, FDR Library, Map Room, Box 35. • **134.** *RW*, 13 August 1944, pp. 113–14. • **135.** *AKD*, IV, nr. 1107. • **136.** Orpen, op. cit., pp. 151–2. • **137.** Ibid., p. 154. • **138.** See Zawodny, op. cit., p. 135: Orpen, op. cit., p. 160. • **139.** SACEUR to US War Department, message UX 68849, 3 October 1944, relaying the misinformation supplied by the Soviets two days earlier. FDR Library, PSF Box 48, file 'Poland 8/44'. • **140.** Zbigniew S. Siemaszko, 'Powstanie a Sowiety', op. cit., pp. 40–44. • **141.** L. Bartelski, *Praga: Warszawskie Termopile 1944* (Warsaw, 2000), p. 134. • **142.** Ibid., p. 138. • **143.** Ibid., p. 139. • **144.** Czesław Pieniak, 'Poppy', *Sbkw*, vol. III, pp. 133–4. • **145.** There is some doubt whether Kalugin was shot immediately or at a later date. • **146.** Due to wastage, the Communist People's Army (AL), Security Corps (KB), and the left-socialist Polish People's Army (PAL) had joined forces. According to recent estimates, the Communists may only have provided 400 insurgents to the struggle. See Jan Chodakiewicz et al. (eds), *Tajne oblicze GL-AL i PPR* (Warsaw, 1997), I, pp. 75–6, 79. This compares to an estimated 3,500 provided by the right-wing NSZ. See L. Żebrowski, *Narodowe Siły Zbrojne: dokumenty . . .* (Warsaw, 1994–96), 3 vols. • **147.** RGVA OK M/II/18 • **148.** Ibid. • **149.** See S. Jaczyński: 'Armia Czerwona nad Wisłą: polityczna czy militarna postawa wyczekująca?' in Stanisława Lewandowska and Bernd Martin (eds), *Powstanie Warszawskie 1944* (Warsaw, 1999), pp. 168–81. Also Cynthia Flohr, 'Pozorna zmiana stanowiska Stalina wobec Powstania warszawskiego we wrześniu 1944 roku', in ibid., pp. 182–204. • **150.** Kunert (ed.), *Bijące Serce Partii*, op. cit., vol. I, p. 352. • **151.** RGVA, OK M/II/18, pp. 60–99. • **152.** Ibid., passim. • **153.** 22 September 1944, ibid., p. 79. • **154.** Ibid. • **155.** Ibid., 25 September 1944, ibid., p. 90. • **156.** *RW*, 18 September 1944. • **157.** RGVA, OK M/II/18, passim. • **158.** See L. Ratajczyk, *Historia Wojskowości* (Warsaw, 1980), pp. 378–80. • **159.** Helena Martenowa: as interviewed in 1994 for the TV film *Powstanie Warszawskie.* • **160.** Z. Kliszko, *Powstanie Warzawskie* (Warsaw, 1967), p. 199. • **161.** Kazimierz Wierzyński, quoted by Bartoszewski, *DWS*, p. 319. • **162.** Mieczysław Ubisz, 'Wik', *Ostatni komunikat*, in 'Czas wirujący' (Warsaw, 1945). Wik worked during the Rising as an announcer for Radio 'Lightning'. Bartoszewski, *DWS*, pp. 302–3. **Finale.** • **163.** M. J. Kwiatkowski, *Powstanie* (Warsaw, 1990), p. 175. • **164.** After the relation of 'Sword' from the Czata 49 Battalion. Quoted by Bartoszewski, *DWS*, p. 85. • **165.** *RW*, pp. 225–6. • **166.** Ibid., p. 369. • **167.** Appendix 28 to T. Sawicki, op. cit., pp. 282–4. • **168.** *AKD*, IV, 1191. • **169.** Dziennik Polski (London), *Biuletyn Informacyjny* (Warsaw), 2 October 1944, quoted by Kunert, *RW*, p. 369. • **170.** *AKD*, IV, nr. 1180, pp. 409–10. • **171.** W. Jędrzejewicz (ed.), *Poland in the British Parliament, 1939–1945* (New York, 1962), vol. III, pp. 5–33. • **172.** After Churchill, op. cit., p. 127; the translator in Churchill's account of the broadcast does not seem to realize that the last line is a quotation from the Polish national anthem. • **173** SACEUR to US War Department, 3 October 1944, message UX 68849, FDR Library, PSF Box 48, file 'Poland 8/44'. • **174.** Georgii Zhukov, *The Memoirs of Marshal Zhukov* (London, 1971), pp. 551–2. • **175.** RGVA, OK M/II/18. • **176.** Jan Stanisław Jankowski, 28 September 1944, quoted in Bartoszewski, *DWS*, p. 306. • **177.** Jerzy Ścibor-Kamiński, quoted in *DWS*, p. 316. • **178.** *DWS*, p. 324. • **179.** Kazimierz Wierzyński, 'A więc stało się', quoted by Bartoszewski, *DWS*, p. 330.

Chapter VI: *Vae Victis* pp. 433–508

• **1.** J. Zawodny, *Nothing but Honour* (London, 1978), p. 193. • **2.** *RW*, p. 377. • **3.** Ibid. • **4.** *DWS*, p. 339: not confirmed in *RW*, p. 380. • **5.** RGVA, OK M/II/18, 5 October 1944. • **6.** Ibid., 6 October 1944. • **7.** Ibid., 10 October 1944. • **8.** *Bijące Serce Partii: Dzienniki Personalne Ministerstwa Publicznego* (Warsaw, 2001), p. 366. • **9.** Ibid., pp. 352–75. • **10.** *Tribune*, 6 October 1944. The *Observer* added its voice to those expressing sympathy. In a leader called 'Warsaw and the Allies', it commented: 'a proud and once flourishing capital will not be found on the map of Europe when the cease fire sounds . . . Should not the rebuilding of this tragic and heroic city be made a common Allied responsibility.' • **11.** M. Gilbert, *Winston S. Churchill* (London, 1986), vol. VII, *1941–45*, pp. 991–3. • **12.** Jan Karski, *The Great Powers and Poland* (Lanham, MD, 1985), pp. 545–56. • **13.** Ibid., p. 547. • **14.** T. Barman, *Diplomatic Correspondence* (London, 1968), pp. 175–6. • **15.** GARF, f9401, op2, d66, l395–97, Beria to Stalin, 15 October 1944. • **16.** Jeffrey Bines, *Operation Freston* (Saffron Walden, 1999), p. 18. • **17.** Ibid., p. 17. • **18.** Ibid., p. 61. • **19.** Ibid., pp. 67–8. • **20.** Ibid., pp. 73–4. • **21.** Ibid., p. 74. • **22.** P. Solly-Flood, 'Pilgrimage to Poland', *Blackwood's Magazine*, nr. 1657 (May, 1951), pp. 425–41. • **23.** Ibid., p. 441. Additional information derives from the author's interview with Messrs Pospieszalski, Zaremba, and Bines, Southgate, December 2002. • **24.** IWM Sound Archive, Lady Ryder of Warsaw, 1987, reel 2, quoted by E. D. R. Harrison, 'The British Special Operations Executive and Poland', *Historical Journal* 43.4 (Cambridge, 2000), p. 1090. • **25.** GARF, f9401, op2, d67, Beria to Stalin, 9 November 1944, and f9401, op2, d68, u93–9, Beria to Stalin, 8 December 1944. • **26.** Marek Ney-Krwawicz, *The Polish Home Army, 1939–45* (London, 2001), pp. 139–41. (*Biuletyn Informacyjny*, nr. 317, 19 January 1945. AKD. vol. V, pp. 239–40.) • **27.** Stanisław Supłatowicz, 'Kozak', Sat-Okh', *Biuletyn Informacyjny*, XIII, nr. 10 (162), October 2003, pp. 52–6. • **28.** GARF f9401, op2, d92, Serov to Beria, p. 145. • **29.** Moscow held the view that the Soviet Army liberated Warsaw in January 1945, and struck a medal to mark the occasion. See plate section 3, 'Images true and false'. • **30.** Radio Polskie, Warsaw, 18, 20, 25 March 1945. Translated transcript, The National Archives (TNA): PRO COPY FO371/47733A. • **31.** Stefan Korboński, *The Polish Underground State* (Boulder, Colorado), p. 216. • **32.** Ibid., pp. 218–19. • **33.** Anthony Beevor, *Berlin: the Downfall* (London, 2002). • **34.** The 'Special Files' for I. V. Stalin from the Secretariat of the NKVD – MVD of the USSR, 1944–53, V. A. Kozlov, S. V. Mironenko (eds), *Archive of Contemporary History*, vol. I

(Moscow, GARF), 1944. • **35.** USSR People's Commissariat of Justice, *Trial of the Organizers, Leaders and members of the Polish Diversionist Organizations . . . June 18–21, 1945* (Moscow, 1945): see also Z. Stypułkowski, *Invitation to Moscow* (New York, 1962). • **36.** No number is attached to this file, though it appears to belong to GARF, f9401, op2, d94, which, among other items, contains a batch of other files all dated April 1945 and all relating to the arrest and early interrogations of 'the Sixteen'. • **37.** Ibid., p. 2. • **38.** Ibid., p. 24. • **39.** Ibid., pp. 34–5. • **40.** The National Archives (TNA): PRO COPY HS4/256. • **41.** On the Moscow Trial of 1945, see, A. Chmielarz, A. Kunert, *Proces szesnastu: dokumenty NKWD* (Warsaw, 1995), translated as *The Moscow Trial* (Warsaw, 2000): also E. Duraczyński, *Generał Iwanow zaprasza* (Warsaw, 1989): as an example of Soviet propaganda, the National Council for American–Soviet Friendship, *The Case of the 16 Poles and the Plot for War on the USSR* (New York, 1945). • **42.** Dr G. Bolsover, 1947–77, Director of the School of Slavonic and East European Studies, University of London. • **43.** The National Archives (TNA): PRO COPY FO371 47621. Lord Dunglass, later Sir Alec Douglas-Home (1903–95), British Prime Minister, 1963–64. • **44.** Ibid., 'Memorandum on the Trial of General Okulicki and other Poles by the Military College of the Supreme Court of the USSR'. • **45.** The National Archives (TNA): PRO COPY FO N8715/35/55, 18 July 1945. • **46.** Ibid. • **47.** *Poland during the First Half of 1945* (London, 1945), p. 1. • **48.** Speech by Col. M. Dąbrowski in ibid., p. 53. • **49.** Ibid., p. 87. • **50.** The National Archives (TNA): PRO COPY FO N0917/35/55, 12 June 1945. • **51.** T. Cariewskaya et al., *Teczka Specjalna J. W. Stalina: Raporty NKWD z Polski, 1944–46* (Warsaw, 1998), nrs 6–11. • **52.** GARF, f9401, op2, d66 l141. *Teczka Specjalna*, op. cit., nr. 9. 23 August 1944. • **53.** GARF, f9401, op2, d66 l362. *Teczka Specjalna*, op. cit., nr. 11. 7 October 1944. • **54.** GARF, f9401, op2, d66 l288–90. • **55.** Ludwika Zacharasiewicz: see capsule GHOST TOWN (p. 492), with endnote. • **56.** Bolesław Taborski, 'Moja Wojna – początek i koniec' *ZH*, 1996, nr. 118, pp. 45–94. • **57.** Norman Davies and Roger Moorhouse, *Microcosm: A Portrait of a Central European City* (London, 2002), p. 389. • **58.** Ibid., passim. • **59.** Tadeusz Borowski (1922–51), see his *This way for the gas, ladies and gentlemen* (London, 1967). • **60.** Wacława Lutoborska (1901–45). Her name is recorded inaccurately on a memorial tablet at Belsen. Interview with Mr Lutoborski, Warsaw (2001). • **61.** Mauthausen Survivors Documentation Project is now in progress at the Boltzmann Institute, Vienna, with a Polish branch at the Karta Centre, Warsaw. • **62.** On Ravensbrück, see Denise Dufournier, *Ravensbruck: the women's camp of death* (London, 1948): also Wanda Połtawska, *And I am afraid of my dreams* (London, 1987). • **63.** Władysław Szpilman, *The Pianist: the Extraordinary True Story of One Man's Survival in Warsaw, 1939–45* (New York, 2000), pp. 171–2; *Pianista* (Kraków, 2000), pp. 161–2. • **64.** Ibid., pp. 176–8. • **65.** Cariewskaya et al.,

Teczka specjalna J. W. Stalina, op. cit., nr. 23, pp. 105–6. • **66.** L. Bartelski, *Praga: Warszawskie Termopile 1944* (Warsaw, 2000), pp. 142–3. • **67.** GARF, f9401, op2, d68, p. 3. • **68.** GARF, f9401, op2, d68, pp. 284–8. • **69.** On Piasecki, see L. Blit, *The Eastern Pretender* (London, 1965): also Antoni Dudek, Grzegorz Pytel, *Bolesław Piasecki: próba biografii politycznej* (London, 1990). • **70.** Blit, op. cit., p. 15. • **71.** Ferdynand Ossendowski (1878–1945): 'Pisarz i podróżnik z Milanówka', *Życie Warszawy*, 10 April 2001. • **72.** Maciej Kledzik, 'Robinsonowie', *Rzeczpospolita*, 18 January 2002: also Wacław Gluth-Nowowiejski, *Nie umieraj do jutra* (Warsaw, 1982). • **73.** Szpilman, op. cit., pp. 184–6. • **74.** Beevor, *Berlin*, op. cit. • **75.** Ibid., p. 16. • **76.** T. Bobrowski, 'Obóz w Rembertowie', in M. Fieldorf and L. Zachuta, *Generał 'Nil'* (Warsaw, 1993), pp. 162ff. • **77.** Ibid., 'W transporcie na Wschód', pp. 167–9. • **78.** Karta Pakiet Nr. 1 (1951). • **79.** Janina Fieldorf, 'O moim mężu' – a tape recording made in Gdańsk, 1977: published in *ZH* (Paris), nr. 101 (1992), pp. 91–114, and in *Zwoje* Internet journal, nr. 34. • **80.** Jan Rydel, *"Polska okupacja" w północno-zachodnich Niemczech, 1945–48: nieznany rozdział stosunków polsko-niemieckich* (Kraków, 2000). • **81.** Ibid. • **82.** See F. Bankowska, *Dziewczęta ze stalagu VIC Oberlangen: opracowanie i wybór tekstów* (Warsaw, 1998). • **83.** Sikorski Institute Archive. • **84.** Zbigniew S. Siemaszko, *Dziennik Polski*, London, 27 June 2002. • **85.** Hugh Dalton, 1940 Minister for SOE, 1945–47 Chancellor of the Exchequer, quoted by E. D. R. Harrison, op. cit., p. 1075.

Chapter VII: Stalinist Repression pp. 509–78

• **1.** S. Mikołajczyk, *The Rape of Poland* (New York, 1948); Bliss Lane, *I Saw Poland betrayed* (Oxford, 1981). • **2.** Norman Davies, *God's Playground* (Oxford, 1981), vol. II, p. 578. • **3.** (Stefan Starzewski), Teresa Torańska, *Them: Stalin's Polish puppets* (London, 1985), pp. 509–76. • **4.** Ibid. • **5.** From Adam Ważyk, *Poemat dla dorosłych* (Warsaw, 1956), see Davies, *God's Playground*, op. cit., vol. II, pp. 582–3. • **6.** From *Konrad Wallenrod* by Adam Mickiewicz. • **7.** G. Missalowa and J. Schoenbrenner, *Historia Polski* (Warsaw, 1951), vol. III, pp. 55–6. • **8.** Jerzy Borejsza. Stefan Arski. Arski, Foreword to *Targowica* and *Pasażerowie*; quoted by W. Bolecki, in 'Stosunek do Emigracji', *Słownik socrealizmu w Polsce* (Warsaw, to be published). • **9.** Lech Kaczyński, 'Jestem dzieckiem z gruzów', *Rzeczpospolita*, 1 August 2003. • **10.** Jerzy Andrzejewski. • **11.** Adam Borkiewicz. Jerzy Kirchmajer. • **12.** Kazimierz Brandys, *Człowiek nie umiera* (1951): see Z. Jarosiński, 'Powstanie Warszawskie w powojennej literaturze pięknej', in Z. Mańkowski and J. Święch (eds), *Powstanie Warszawskie w historigrafii i literaturze, 1944–94* (Lublin, 1996), pp. 200–1. • **13.** Bogdan Czeszko, *Pokolenie* (1951); in Jarosiński, ibid. • **14.** Ibid. • **15.** Maria Dąbrowska (1889–1965): see her *Dzienniki* (Warsaw, 1988). • **16.** Jan Józef Szczepański, 'W służbie Wielkiego Armatora', *Przed nieznanym trybunałem* (Warsaw, 1975), p. 13. Quoted by Jarosiński, op. cit. • **17.** 'Bór': TVP film (1994). • **18.** A Joint Anglo-Polish Commission was due to report on the fate of the missing Archive in 2003 (see Chapter IV, note 48). • **19.** Marcel Reich-Ranicki, *The Author of Himself* (London, 2001), pp. 198–9. • **20.** The secretive Bilderberg Group, which Retinger founded in 1953, came to be seen as the *bête noire* of the anti-capitalist and anti-globalization movement. Search 'Bilderberg' on the Internet and be surprised. • **21.** Keith Sword, Jan Ciechanowski and Norman Davies, *The formation of the Polish community in Great Britain: 1939–1950* (London, 1989). • **22.** The National Archives (TNA): PRO COPY WO309, FO1060/1229. • **23.** A. P. Scotland, *The London Cage* (London, 1957). • **24.** Zbigniew S. Siemaszko, *Działalność Generała Tatara*, (London, 1999). • **25.** Winston Churchill, *The Second World War*, vol. VI (London, 1954), pp. 127–8. • **26.** C. Wilmot, *Struggle for Europe* (London, 1952), p. 437. • **27.** Alexander Werth, *Russia at War* (London, 1964), pp. 882–3. • **28.** Peter Solly-Flood, 'Pilgrimage to Poland', *Blackwood's Magazine*, nr. 1627, Edinburgh, May 1951, p. 441. • **29.** T. Bór-Komorowski's memoirs, *Armia podziemna* (London, 1999), ran to four editions, most recently in 1979 by SPP, and were translated as *The Secret Army* (London, 1950). • **30.** S. Korboński, *The Polish Underground State* (Boulder, Colorado). • **31.** A. Bromke and T. Sypniewski, *Warsaw Rising: the First Conflict of the Cold War* (Montreal, 1954). • **32.** Stefan Korboński, 'Zieliński', was the organizer of the Directorate of Civilian Struggle, and during the Rising the director of a radio station: see his *W imieniu Rzeczypospolitej* (Paris, 1954). • **33.** 'Jan Nowak': Zdzisław Jeziorański, *Wojna w eterze: wspomnienia*, op. cit.: see also Jerzy 'George' Błażyński, *Mówi Józef Światło* (London, 1985): Józef Światło, *Za kulisami partii i bezpieki* (Warsaw, 1990). • **34.** See Norman Davies, 'Nuremberg', in *Europe: a history* (Oxford, 1996, New York, 1997), pp. 1048–58: see also Airey Neave, *Nuremberg: a personal record* (London, 1978). • **35.** H. W. Henderson, *The Glory and Shame of Warsaw* (Glasgow, 1945), p. 2. • **36.** Hans Frank under cross-examination at Nuremberg on 18 April 1946. See the Avalon Project, <http://www.yale.edu/lawweb/avalon/imt/proc/04-18-46.htm>. • **37.** Ann and John Tusa, *The Nuremberg Trial* (London, 1983), p. 171. • **38.** Ibid., p. 281. • **39.** Ibid., p. 484. • **40.** The National Archives (TNA): PRO COPY FO371/94780/NP1661/I, 3 April 1951. • **41.** K. Szwagrzyk, *Golgota Wrocławskie* (Wrocław, 2000). • **42.** Edward Buca, *Vorkuta* (London, 1976), pp. 46–50. • **43.** In order of mention: Stanisłas Radkiewicz; Roman Romkowski (Menashe Grynszpan); Mechislav Mietkowski (Mojżesz Bobrowicki); Jacek Różański (Goldberg); Julia Brystygier; Anatol Fejgin; 'Light': Józef Światło (Izaak Fleiszfarb). They all answered to the Party Secretary and Politburo member responsible for security affairs – Jakub Berman. • **44.** Anthony Beevor, *Berlin: the Downfall* (London, 2002), pp. 99–100. • **45.** Ibid., p. 420. • **46.** S. Staszewski, in

Torańska, *Them*, op. cit., passim. • **47.** K. Moczarski, *Conversations with an Executioner* (Englewood Cliffs, New Jersey, 1977), p. 3. • **48.** Ibid., p. 134. • **49.** Ibid., p. 220. • **50.** Ibid., p. 263. • **51.** T. Cariewskaya et al., *Teczka Specjalna J. W. Stalina: Raporty NKWD z Polski, 1944–46* (Warsaw, 1998), nr. 123, pp. 413–14. • **52.** GARF, f9401, op2, d173, July 1947: published in A. F. Noskowa (ed.), *NKWD i polskie podziemnie 1944–45* (Kraków, 1998), nr. 72, pp. 273–4. • **53.** Selivanovsky to Beria, August 1945, GARF f9401, op2, d98, *Osobaya Papka* 1–1, str 495. • **54.** Selivanovsky to Beria, 'Dokladnaya Zapiska o polozhenii Yevreiskogo naselenia v Pol'she', n.d. 1945, GARF, f9401, op2, d104, p. 1. • **55.** Ibid., p. 6. • **56.** Ibid. • **57.** Jerzy Zariański. Selivanovsky to Beria, received 8 August 1945, GARF, f9401. • **58.** Ibid. • **59.** *ZS*, p. 287, and Kunert. • **60.** M. R. D. Foot, *Six Faces of Courage* (London, 1980) contains a short biographical sketch of Pilecki (1901–48). • **61.** *Sbkw*, vol. II, pp. 93–5. • **62.** See Norman Davies and Roger Moorhouse, *Microcosm: A Portrait of a Central European City* (London, 2002). • **63.** Szwagrzyk, op. cit. • **64.** Jan Hryćkowiak. Czesław Łapiński. • **65.** Lucjan Załęski. • **66.** R. Kruszewski and W. Tycner, *Proces Kazimierza Pużaka, Prezydenta Podziemnego Państwa Polskiego* (Warsaw, 1992). • **67.** Quoted by Anne Applebaum, *Gulag* (London, 2003), p. 7. • **68.** A. Kaczyński, 'W Szponach Bezpieki', *Rzeczpospolita*, 1 March 2003. • **69.** *BSW*. • **70.** *Oni*, op. cit., p. 321. • **71.** Ibid., p. 319. • **72.** Ibid., p. 328. • **73.** Ibid., passim. • **74.** Siemaszko, op. cit., p. 274. • **75.** F. Majorkiewicz, *Lata chmurne, lata dumne* (Warsaw, 1983). • **76.** A. Przewoźnik and A. Strembosz, *Generał 'Nil': General 'Nil'* (in Polish and English) (Warsaw, 1999). • **77.** Helena Wolińska (Brus). • **78.** A. Przewoźnik and A. Strembosz, op. cit., p. 63. • **79.** Benjamin Wajsblech. Ibid. • **80.** Ibid., pp. 64–5. • **81.** Ibid., p. 65. • **82.** A. Przewoźnik and A. Strzembosz, op. cit., passim. • **83.** *Oni*, op. cit., p. 330. • **84.** Cardinal Stefan Wyszyński. • **85.** Marian P. Romaniuk, 'Ptaszyńska', *Donosy na Prymasa* (London, 1993), p. 172.

Chapter VIII: Echoes of the Rising pp. 579–617

• **1.** A. Przewoźnik and A. Strembosz, *General 'Nil': Generał 'Nil'* (in Polish and English) (Warsaw, 1999), p. 89. • **2.** K. Szwagrzyk, *Zbrodnie w majestacie prawa, 1944–55* (Warsaw, 2000), pp. 181–4. • **3.** Kazimierz Kąkol, see his *Spór o Powstanie Warszawskie: gorzka lekcja czy przepustka do historii* (Warsaw, 1985), also *Kardynał Wyszyński jakim go znałem* (Warsaw, 1985). • **4.** Jan Mazurkiewicz, 'Radosław'. • **5.** *Historia Polski* (PAN). • **6.** Eugeniusz Duraczyński, *Wojna i okupacja, wrzesień 1939 – kwiecień 1943* (Warsaw, 1974). • **7.** Zygmunt Mańkowski, 'Powstanie Warszawskie – w kręgu syntezy', in Z. Mańkowski and J. Swięch (eds), *Powstanie Warszawskie w historigrafi i literaturze, 1944–94* (Lublin, 1996), p. 48. • **8.** Ibid., p. 50. • **9.** Anna Klubówna, Jadwiga Stępieniowa, *W naszej ojczyźnie* (Warsaw, 1961), pp. 181–3, translated by the author. • **10.** M. Fieldorf and L. Zachuta, *Generał 'Nil'* (Warsaw, 1993), illustration nr. 109. • **11.** Jan Ciechanowski; Prof. Janusz Zawodny, author of *Nothing but Honour* (London, 1978), *Unconventional Warfare* (Philadelphia, 1962), and *Death in the Forest: the story of the Katyn Massacre* (Notre Dame, 1962). • **12.** Jan M. Ciechanowski, *The Warsaw Rising of 1944* (Cambridge, 1974), and J. K. Zawodny, *Nothing but Honour*, op. cit. • **13.** Ciechanowski, op. cit., p. 315. • **14.** T. Żenczykowski, *Samotny bój Warszawy* (Paris, 1985), p. 154. • **15.** Joseph G.: Józef Garliński. • **16.** J. Garliński, *Poland in the Second World War 1939–45* (London, 1985), pp. 276–99. • **17.** Interviewed for the TV film *Powstanie Warszawskie* (1994). • **18.** Scum beyond the Volga. • **19.** No other Poland. • **20.** 'Czekamy Ciebie' by Józef Szczepański. • **21.** Zbigniew Herbert. • **22.** Casimir W.: Kazimierz Wyka. K. K. Baczyński, *Utwory Zebrane* (Kraków, 1961); Kazimierz Wyka, *Krzysztof Baczyński, 1921–44* (Kraków, 1961); also Jerzy Zagórski, 'Śmierć Słowackiego' in *Tygodnik Powszechny*, 1947, nr. 14–15. • **23.** Stanisław Pigoń, quoted by Wyka, op. cit., p. 111. • **24.** Adam Mickiewicz. Baczyński. • **25.** Maria Dąbrowska, *Przygody człowieka myślącego* (Warsaw, 1972), p. 729. • **26.** Miron Białoszewski, *Pamiętnik z powstania warszawskiego* (1967), (Warsaw, 1988), pp. 92–3. • **27.** T. Strzyżewski (ed.), *Czarna księga PRL* (London, 1977), translated as *The Black Book of Polish Censorship* (New York, 1984). • **28.** Terence Prittie, *Willy Brandt* (London, 1974), pp. 175–6. • **29.** E. Berthoud, 'Mixed feelings on Ghetto tribute by Herr Brandt', *The Times*, 15 December 1970. • **30.** The National Archives (TNA): PRO COPY – FCO28/1443, p3/1, p2. • **31.** Kazimierz Moczarski. • **32.** Władysław Bartoszewski. • **33.** Jerzy Kłoczowski. • **34.** Lech Beynar, 'Paul'. J. Morawski, 'Pisarz pod nadzorem', *Rzeczpospolita*, 6–7 April 2002. • **35.** Aleksander Gieysztor. • **36.** Witold Lutosławski (1913–94): S. Stucky, *Lutosławski and his Music* (Cambridge, 1981); T. Kaczyński, *Conversations with Witold Lutosławski* (London, 1995). • **37.** Andrzej Panufnik, *Out of the City of Fear* (London, 1956). • **38.** Dr A. Bielawski (Warsaw) of Czata 49 and Prof. J. Bełza (Pebble Beach, Ca.), meeting with the author 1 August 2002. • **39.** Danuta Wiśniowiecka. • **40.** Wieńczysław Wagner. • **41.** Zbigniew Mróz. • **42.** Irena Findeisen, née Zieleniewska, now Bellert. • **43.** Jerzy Zubrzycki. • **44.** Maria Gatęska. • **45.** Letter to author, May 2002. • **46.** Wanda Lesiszowa, Cheadle, May 2002. • **47.** Tadeusz Tarnes, 20 May 2002. • **48.** Pope John Paul II, *Homilies* (Kraków, 1983), p. 31. • **49.** Ibid., p. 22. • **50.** Ibid., p. 20. • **51.** Antoni Nowosielski, *Powstanie Warszawskie* (Warsaw, 1981), pp. 20, 39, 45. • **52.** H. Krall. • **53.** Teresa Torańska, *Them: Stalin's Polish puppets* (London, 1985). • **54.** Norman Davies, *God's Playground: a short history of Poland* (Oxford, 1981). • **55.** R. Wapiński, *Historia dla 4 klasy liceum ogólnokształcącego oraz dla 3 klasy szkół technicznych* (Warsaw, 1982), p. 100. • **56.** Kevin Ruane, *Reasons of State: to kill a Polish priest* (London, 2002). • **57.** Ronald Reagan, 17 August 1984 <http://www.reagan.utexas.

edu/resource/speeches/1984/81784b.htm>. • **58.** Fieldorf and Zachuta, op. cit., nr. 27, p. 339. • **59.** 'Wielka Encyklopedia Powstania Warszawskiego Tom V: Na cenzurowanym', *Biuletyn Informacyjny*, XIII, nr. 5 (157) May 2003, pp. 35–7. • **60.** See, for instance, W. Roszkowski, *Historia Polski, 1914–94* (Warsaw, 1995), pp. 133–9. • **61.** In FDR Library, PSF Box 66, File Poland-Orlemanski-Lang [May to June 1944]. • **62.** G. Weinberg, *World at Arms: a global history of World War II* (Cambridge, 1994). • **63.** Stanisława Lewandowska and Bernd Martin (eds), *Powstanie Warszawskie, 1944* (Warsaw, 1999). • **64.** Letter from J. Nowak-Jeziorański, *Rzeczpospolita*, 29 March 2003. • **65.** TV film, *Powstanie Warszawskie* (Warsaw, 1994). • **66.** TV film, *Bór*. • **67.** L. Wałęsa, 1 May 1994. • **68.** R. Herzog, 1 August 1994. Warsaw. • **69.** Kapitan Wacław Micuta, 'Odsłonięcie Tablicy Pamiątkowej w 50-tą Rocznicę Uwolnienia Więźniów Żydowskich z Obozu Zagłady na Gęsiówce'. Mr Micuta's letter to the author, 18 December 2002. • **70.** NBC miniseries 'Uprising': see Internet site. • **71.** Roman Polański, *The Pianist* (2002), based on the true life story of Władysław Szpilman and his book, *The Pianist: the Extraordinary True Story of One Man's Survival in Warsaw, 1939–45* (New York, 2000); *Pianista* (Kraków, 2000). • **72.** *Nash Sovryemennik*, June 2002. • **73.** Adam Basak, 'Niemiecki Pomnik Powstania Warszawskiego' in *Odra* (Wrocław), nr. 7–8 (2001), pp. 126–7. • **74.** Władysław Bartoszewski, 'Postąpiłbym tak samo', *Rzeczpospolita*, 1 August 2003. • **75.** 'The Warsaw Rising: Its Course and Consequences'. Address at the Sorbonne, 9 October 2000, in *Above Divisions: Selected Speeches* . . . (Warsaw, 2001), p. 125. • **76.** Monument in Park Morskie Oko, Warsaw. • **77.** 'Traveller! Lower your head . . .', Inscription on the Monument to the Victims of Stalinist terror, Służewiec, Warsaw: translated by Norman Davies. • **78.** 'Diariusz Sejmu RP': <www.senat.gov.pl/k4/dok/diar/68/6807.htm>.

Interim Report pp. 619–637

• **1.** D. Reynolds (ed.), *Origins of the Cold War in Europe: international perspectives* (Yale, 1994): also Vojtěch Mastný, *Russia's Road to the Cold War, 1941–45* (New York, 1979); Victor Rothwell, *Britain and the Cold War 1941–47* (London, 1982). • **2.** Jan Nowak Jeziorański, 'Syndrom Powstania', *Tygodnik Powszechny* (Krakow), nr. 31, 4 August 2002. • **3.** General Marian Kukiel, quoted by Jan M. Ciechanowski, *The Warsaw Rising of 1944* (Cambridge, 1974), pp. 283ff. Oddly enough, in 1943 Gen. Kukiel had proposed a rising in Warsaw. Ibid., p. 284. • **4.** Jan M. Ciechanowski, 'Polityczne i Militarne Przyczyny Powstania', in Z. Mańkowski and J. Święch (eds), *Powstanie Warsawskie w historiografi i literaturze, 1944–94* (Lublin, 1996), p. 25. • **5.** Jan Karski, *The Great Powers and Poland, 1919–45* (Lanham, MD, 1945), p. 531. • **6.** Sir William Deakin, 'Churchill and Europe in 1944', the Crosby Kemper

Lecture, Westminster College, Fulton, MO, 19 March 1984: 'I have often wondered why, in the personal talks and correspondence between Roosevelt and Churchill, scant attention was given to the momentous problem of how to deal with Russians . . . The first test of our future relatons with the Soviet Union was to be the fate of Poland'. P5. http://www.westminster-mo.edu/cm/scholar/europe/europe1.asp>. • **7.** Stefan Korboński, *The Polish Underground State* (Boulder, Colorado, 1978), p. 172. • **8.** See Rothwell, op. cit. • **9.** Clark Kerr's tirade could only have taken place in the absence of clear instructions from London for the Premier to be given positive assistance. It is a prime example of the way in which Stalin's hard line was allowed to pass by default. See Chapter V, above. • **10.** Deakin, op. cit., p. 6. • **11.** Sir John Slessor, *The Central Blue: Recollections and Reflections* (London, 1956), p. 612: R. E. Sherwood, *Roosevelt and Hopkins: an intimate history* (New York, 1948). • **12.** See the testimony of Capt. Alan McIntosh (RAAF) in NAVIGATOR capsule, p. 308. Similar experiences were reported by American pilots on the Frantic run to Poltava. • **13.** E. D. R. Harrison, 'The British Special Operations Executive and Poland', *Historical Journal* 43.4 (Cambridge, 2000). • **14.** Ibid., p. 1078. • **15.** Peter Wilkinson, *Foreign Fields: the story of an SOE operative* (London, 1997), p. 124, quoted by Harrison. • **16.** Ibid.

Notes to Capsules

NKVD (p. 222) • **1.** After Witold Sagajłło, *Man in the Middle: a Story of the Polish Resistance* (London, 1984), pp. 131–2, 136–40. **RECRUIT** (p. 228) • **1.** 'Rysiek': Stanisław Aronson (Tel Aviv), *War Recollections: Poland, 1939–45*, (1988) typescript, pp. 1–7, 24–25: correspondence with the author. **MELECH** (p. 231) • **1.** The Personal Notes and Diary of Eugeniusz Melech, Part 2. <www.polbox.com/L/Lpgideon>. • **2.** Ibid., 'The Insurrection', 30 July, 1 August 1944. **IRKA I** (p. 234) • **1.** From the memoirs of Irena Findeisen, née Zieleniewska, now Bellert, written at the author's request (2002). • **2.** Miron Białoszewski, *Pamiętnik Powstania Warszawskiego* (Warsaw, 1988), p. 5. **PROSPECTS** (p. 238) • **1.** Stanislas Likiernik, *By Devil's Luck: A Tale of Resistance in Wartime Warsaw* (Edinburgh, 2001), p. 111. • **2.** Bartoszewski, *DWS*, p. 12. • **3.** Likiernik, op. cit., p. 11–12. • **4.** Zbigniew Mróz, 'Ed', Memoir dated August 1980, letter to the author, 8 January 2003. **BAPTISM OF FIRE** (p. 246) • **1.** Aronson, op. cit., pp. 26–30. **L-HOUR** (p. 250) • **1.** S. Likiernik, op. cit., pp. 112–15. • **2.** *SS Ustuf.* Gustaw Schielke. The conversation took place in a Warsaw prison in 1949. See K. Moczarski, *Conversations with an Executioner* (Eaglewood Cliffs, New Jersey, 1977), p. 262. **TRAPPED** (p. 255) • **1.** After C. Miłosz, *Native Realm: a Search for Self-Definition* (London, 1988), pp. 248–50. • **2.** Krzysztof Zanussi:. letter to the author, 2002. • **3.** J. Damski (source, 'Trader', see below). **MASSACRE** (p. 258) • **1.** From M. M. Drozdowski, *Kościół a Powstanie Warszawskie: wybór i opracowanie* (Warsaw, 1994). **GOOSE FARM** (p. 261) • **1.** W. Micuta, 'Wspomnienia z pierwszych dni Powstania Warszawskiego': Geneva, 1994. Typescript: meeting with the author, August 2002. **PROFESSOR** (p. 266) • **1.** From the memoir of Professor Hans Thieme, Captain in the 203rd Division: B. Lewandowska and S. Martin (eds), *Der Warschauer Aufstand* (Warsaw, 1999), pp. 269–74. **SEWER I** (p. 269) • **1.** Dr J. Rossman, ps. 'Marten': quoted in Bartoszewski, *DWS*, pp. 328–9. • **2.** Elżbieta Ostrowska, ps. 'Ela': Bartoszewski, ibid., pp. 39–40. • **3.** Jan Józef Lipski, ps. 'Rake', ibid., pp. 299–300. **BARRICADE** (p. 276) • **1.** Anna Świrczyńska, ps. 'Świt', *Budowałam barykadę* (1974), (Cracow, 1984). **PANTHER** (p. 281) • **1.** 'Dyon 1806'; cryptonym of the 1st Regiment of Dragoons. Letter from Andrzej Nowakowski of Rawdon (Quebec), 4 December 2002, based on notes written by Wojciech Kasznica shortly after the Rising. Mr Nowakowski is the son-in-law of Gen. Anders. **NIGHT PATROL** (p. 285) • **1.** 'Jan Nowak' (Zdzisław Jeziorański), quoted by Bartoszewski, *DWS*, pp. 164–5. Lt. 'Janusz' died of wounds received in following his orders. **MAGYAR** (p. 289) • **1.** Tadeusz Sarnicki (Jerzy Korwin), *Warszawa heroiczna. Pamiętnik z Powstania Warszawskiego*, Biblioteka Narodowa, MS BN II.7944 Mf 58194. • **2.** Bartoszewski, *DWS*, p. 105. **REFLECTIONS** (p. 292) • **1.** The first comments derive from various dates in 1942–43, only and the relation of 11 August 1944 is from the time of the Warsaw Rising. Quoted by Władisław Szpilman, *The Pianist: the Extraordinary True Story of One Man's Survival in Warsaw, 1939–45* (New York, 2000), pp. 193–208. **TRADER** (p. 295) • **1.** Interview, Los Angeles, 14 May 1988, as a contribution to a Holocaust educational project: <www.humboldt.edu/~rescuers/book/johndstory1.html>. **SAVAGERY** (p. 299) • **1.** Kamila Merwartowa, *Upiorne lata. Wspomnienia z lat 1939–45*. Rps Ossolineum, Wroclaw 15667/II; Mf 88475. **PAST** (p. 303) • **1.** From the Diary of Eugeniusz Melech, op. cit. The German author of the original notes, Kurt Heller, was from Munich, F.P.N.L. no. 49,773. **NAVIGATOR** (p. 308) • **1.** Dennis Richards, *Royal Air Force 1939–1945, The Balkans and the Middle East*, papers. • **2.** Personal recollection written in 2002 by Mr Alan McIntosh, Downer, Australia: to the author, 23 June 2003. **'1586'** (p. 312) • **1.** 'Destiny Can Wait': <www.geocities.com/skrzydla/301/Glebocki_ Chmiel_1586.html>. **REFUGEE** (p. 317) • **1.** 'Vlasovians': not Vlassovites, but members of Kaminski's RONA Brigade. Miłosz, op. cit., pp. 250–2. **WARD** (p. 324) • **1.** The National Archives (TNA): PRO COPY Prem3/352/12. 'The Allies gave full credit to Polish sources of information only after they had been endorsed by a Britisher. If we ourselves reported these incidents, the Allies . . . would think it was exaggerated Polish propoganda.' Quoted by L. Olson, S. Cloud, *For Your Freedom and Ours . . .* (London, 2003), p. 331. **BATTLE** (p. 329) • **1.** Quoted by

Bartoszewski, *DWS*, pp. 148–9. • **2.** Ibid., pp. 157–8. **HOSPITAL** (p. 333) • **1.** Jan Józef Lipski, quoted by Bartoszewski, *DSW*, pp. 154–5. Hospital of the Sisters of St Elizabeth, 29 August 1944. **FATHER** (p. 339) • **1.** Jerzy Lando, *Saved by my Face* (Edinburgh, 2002), pp. 201–2. Lando, born in 1922 in Łódź, was Jewish and fought with the nationalist Stronnictwo Narodowe. **CHILDHOOD** (p. 343) • **1.** Letter from Mr Zanussi to the author, 1 January 2002. **PRAYER** (p. 349) • **1.** (Rev.) Andrzej Janicki, *Na rozkaz: wspomnienia, 1937–47* (Henley-on-Thames, 1995), 'Drugi Front', pp. 108–9. **BRIEFE** (p. 352) • **1.** Peter Stolten (1924–45), of Berlin, killed 24 January 1945 in East Prussia near Allenstein. His letters, which are in the possession of his sister, were published in Lewandowska and Martin (eds), op. cit., pp. 265–8. **KATYN** (p. 356) • **1.** Roman Sulimir, 'Halina Sulimir, z domu Rudzka', in R. Spanily (ed.), *Pisane miłością: losy wdów katyńskich* (Gdynia, 2002), vol. II, pp. 679–85. Thanks to information supplied in 1990 by President Gorbachev, the family learned that their father had been killed in 1940 by the NKVD and that he had been buried in a mass grave near Charkov, in Ukraine. This site, analogous to Katyn, was one of three locations where the Soviet authorities murdered Polish POWs captured in 1939. **FRAGMENTS** (p. 360) • **1.** Jacek Fedorowicz: extracts from a memoir written at the author's request (May, 2002). **FELDWEBEL** (p. 364) • **1.** After Stanislas Likiernik, *By Devil's Luck*, op. cit., pp. 142–4. **GRAVES** (p. 369) • **1.** After Janicki, *Na rozkaz*, op. cit., pp. 107, 104. **SAXONS** (p. 373) • **1.** Herr Hasso Krappe, as recounted to the seminar at Karvica, 1996. Lewandowska and Martin (eds), op. cit., pp. 261–4. **AIRDROP** (p. 378) • **1.** Quoted by Bartoszewski, *DWS*, pp. 255–6. • **2.** H. Stechbarth, soldier in a transport company, Diary entry for 18 September 1944. Translated by Roger Moorhouse. **SISTERS** (p. 382) • **1.** Halina Dudzikówna, ps. 'Sławka', of the Miotła Battalion, 4 August 1944, Bartoszewski, *DWS*, pp. 29–30. • **2.** Siostra 'Teresa', Jadwiga Ledóchowska (an Ursuline), quoted by Bartoszewski, ibid., pp. 145–6. **ANGER** (p. 386) • **1.** Anonymous, *Warszawa heroiczna*, Rps BN II.79k l Mf 58193. • **2.** T. Sarnecki, *Warszawa heroiczna*, ibid., op. cit., Rps BN II.7944 Mf 58194. **AMAZON** (p. 390) • **1.** Halina Andrzejewska, quoted by Bartoszewski, *DWS*, pp. 248–9. **FOREST** (p. 394) • **1.** Ryszard Kapuściński, *Busz po polsku* (Warsaw, 1988), pp. 10–13. The field hospital belonged to Berling's 1st (Polish) Army: the casualties were coming from the fighting in Praga and on the Cherniakov Bridgehead. **SEWER II** (p. 399) • **1.** Kazimierz Pużak, 25–26 August. Bartoszewski, *DWS*, p. 139. • **2.** Memoir of Mrs Danuta Wiśniowiecka-Wardle of Bromley (Kent). Letter to the author, 21 June 2002. **CRUCIFIX** (p. 403) • **1.** Drozdowski, op. cit., pp. 230–1. **VANDALS** (p. 407) • **1.** Professor Bohdan Korzeniewski, after the war a well-known theatre director, quoted by Bartoszewski, *DWS*, op. cit., pp. 215–16. **WITNESS** (p. 410) • **1.** Efraim Krasucki, *Wspomnienia*, ŻIH, sygn. 301/1539.

• 2. Henryk Bursztyn, *Zeznanie o zamordowaniu swej rodziny przez AK w czasie powstania warszawskiego*, ŻIH, sygn. 301/1106. **• 3.** Stanisław Stefański, *Zeznanie*, sygn. 301/2972. All from the Jewish Historical Institute (ŻIH), Warsaw. **SWIMMER** (p. 413) **• 1.** Stanisław Krupa, ps. 'Nita', Maciek Company, Zoshka Battalion: quoted by Bartoszewski, *DWS*, pp. 274–5. **LOGISTICS** (p. 419) **• 1.** Aleksander Gieysztor: quoted by Bartoszewski, *DWS*, pp. 307–9. **CEASEFIRE** (p. 424) **• 1.** Zbigniew Czajkowski-Dąbczyński, *Dziennik Powstańca* (Warsaw, 2000), pp. 165–7. **• 2.** From Janicki, op. cit., passim. **VERSES** (p. 428) **• 1.** Bolesław Taborski, from *Poezja powstańczej Warszawy*, ed. I. Klemenska (Warsaw 1994), vol II. **• 2.** Zbigniew Jasiński, 'Żądamy amunicji' (August 1944). The BBC Polish Service had chosen an old hymn, 'Boże coś Polskę', as its theme tune. **• 3.** Marian Cuchnowski, 'Warszawo', **• 4.** Zbigniew Kabała 'Bobo', 'Armia Krajowa' (1964) **• 5.** Zofia Ilińska, 'Kobietom Warszawy . . . pędzonym przed czołgami'. **• 6.** Bolesław Taborski, 'Uwertura tragiczna' (1954) **• 7.** Bolesław Taborski, 'Do tysięcznej potęgi', from 'Czasy mijania', 1955. **IRKA II** (p. 473) **• 1.** From the memoirs of Irena Findeisen (née Zieleniewska), now Bellert (2002), op. cit. **EXODUS** (p. 476) **• 1.** T. Sarnecki, *Pamiętnik* . . ., op. cit. Manuscript. BN II 7944; Mf 58194. **• 2.** Anon, Manuscript BN II 7941; Mf 58193. **• 3.** Letter from Mr Zanussi to the author, 1 January 2002. **• 4.** Janicki, op. cit. **ADMIRATION** (p. 481) **• 1.** Peter Stolten (see BRIEFE I). 'Bandit' remained the standard German term for the insurgents, as it did in Soviet vocabulary. **POW** (p. 486) **• 1.** Janicki, *Na rozkaz*, op. cit. **• 2.** Lando, pp. 206–8. **GHOST TOWN** (p. 492) **• 1.** Ludwika Zachariasiewicz (b. 1922), *Wspomnienia*, Ośrodek Karta (from the archives of the Biblioteka Narodowa: Pakiet Opisowy, nr. 1, no file number). Zachariasiewicz remained in the security service until 1956. **SIBERIA** (p. 495) **• 1.** Letter to the author from Maria Getka (Melbourne, Australia), 2003. **FIRESTORM** (p. 499) **• 1.** Lech Hałko, 'Drezno, miasto kwiatów, operetek i nieposkromionej nienawiści', in *Kotwica Herbem Wybranym* (Warsaw, 1999), pp. 235–6. **FUGITIVE** (p. 505) **• 1.** Hałko, *Kotwica Herbem Wybranym*, op. cit., pp. 256–6. **BRITAIN** (p. 538) **• 1.** Janicki, op. cit., pp. 148–57. **USA** (p. 541) **• 1.** 'Wojciech Rostafiński: Notatka Biograficzna': letter from Mary Rostafińska to the author, 22 October 2002. **CANADA** (p. 546) **• 1.** Nelli Turzańska-Szymborska, letter to the author, Toronto, 3 October 2002. **AUSTRALIA** (p. 551) **• 1.** T. J. Torpiński (Sydney). **• 2.** Jerzy Fielder (Templestowe). **• 3.** Stanisław Kaczmarek. **• 4.** S. Szymkiewicz, correspondence with the author. **CAVIAHUE** (p. 557) **• 1.** Krystyna Junosza Woysław, 'Dowódca Baonu "Zośka" – Ryszard Białous (died 1992), Kapitan "Jerzy" w Argentynie', *Biuletyn Informacyjny*, Warsaw (March 2003), xiii, nr. 3(155), pp. 43–6. **MEXICO** (p. 561) **• 1.** Jerzy Skoryna, 'Echo powstania', *Gwiazda Polarna*, No. 16, 11 August 2001. **IRKA III** (p. 564) **• 1.** From the memoirs of Irena

Findeisen, op. cit. Letter to the author, 18 February 2002. **IRKA IV** (p. 569) • **1.** Irena Findeisen, ibid. **'BOOR'** (p. 574) • **1.** Adam Komorowski, after a memoir sent to Norman Davies, 15 July 2003.

Notes to Appendices

APPENDIX 16 (p. 659) • **1.** Studium Polski Podziemnej, *Armia Krajowa w dokumentach* (London, 1977), vol. IV, nr. 725, pp. 18–19: heading translated from the Polish. **APPENDIX 24** (p. 670) • **1.** Text published in the *Dziennik Ustaw* (Calendar of Statutes), Lublin, 31 August 1944. See A. Kunert (ed.) *Bijące Serce Partii: Dzienniki Personalne Ministerstwa Publicznego* (Warsaw, 2001), vol. 1, p. 328. • **2.** Ibid. p. 329. • **3.** Ibid. p. 327. **APPENDIX 29** (p. 678) • **1.** *Polskie Siły Zbrojne w drugiej wojnie światowej*, vol. III (London, 1950), pp. 870–73.

Index

NOTES: Appendix 35 gives a guide to the modified names used in the text. In the Index, Polish names and pseudonyms appear in their original forms.. Therefore those seeking references, who have the modified form of the name, should in the first instance refer to the Appendix to discover the original Polish form before consulting the Index.
Page numbers in *italic* refer to Capsules.